The Interpre

I and II Epistles of Peter, the three Epistles of John, and the Epistle of Jude

R. C. H. LENSKI

Augsburg Fortress
Minneapolis

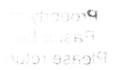

THE INTERPRETATION OF I AND II EPISTLES OF PETER,
THE THREE EPISTLES OF JOHN, AND THE EPISTLE OF JUDE
Commentary on the New Testament series

First paperback edition 2008

Richard C. H. Lenski's commentaries on the New Testament were published in the 1940s after the author's death. This volume was published
in 1945 by the Wartburg Press and assigned in 1961 to the Augsburg
Publishing House.

ISBN 978-0-8066-9011-7

The paper used in this publication meets the minimum requirements of
American National Standard for Information Sciences—Permanence of
Paper for Printed Library Materials, ANSI Z329.48-1984.

Manufactured in the U.S.A.

ABBREVIATIONS

R. = A Grammar of the Greek New Testament in the Light of Historical Research, by A. T. Robertson, fourth edition.

B.-D. = Friedrich Blass' Grammatik des neutestamentlichen Griechisch, vierte, voellig neu-gearbeitete Auflage besorgt von Albert Debrunner.

C.-K. = Biblisch-theologisches, Woerterbuch der Neutestamentlichen Graezitaet von Dr. Hermann Cremer, zehnte, etc., Auflage, herausgegeben von D. Dr. Julius Koegel.

B.-P. = Griechisch-Deutsches Woerterbuch zu den Schriften des Neuen Testaments, etc., von D. Walter Bauer, zweite, etc., Auflage zu Erwin Preuschens Vollstaendigem Griechisch-Deutschem Handwoerterbuch, etc.

M.-M. = The Vocabulary of the Greek Testament, Illustrated from the Papyri and other Nonliterary Sources, by James Hope Moulton and George Milligan.

G. K. = Theologisches Woerterbuch zum Neuen Testament, herausgegeben von Gerhard Kittel.

The First Epistle
of St. Peter

INTRODUCTION

The first Epistle of St. Peter was written by the apostle Peter while he was in Rome not long before his death under Nero in the year 64, while Paul was absent in Spain, and was addressed to all the Christians in the territories named, most of whom were Gentiles. We put these main facts into one statement at the head of our remarks instead of scattering them throughout a long, elaborate discussion.

When we say that the apostle Peter is the writer we deny that the epistle is a forgery, likewise that Silvanus is the writer who was authorized by Peter to do the writing in his name because Peter himself was unable to express himself properly in Greek.

If this epistle is a forgery, no matter when it was written, whether in the years after the destruction of Jerusalem or in the second century, it does not belong in the New Testament. Then there is also no need to write commentaries on it. The only task that remains is to show that the church of all the ages has been badly deceived by an unknown forger, and that it should have been more wide-awake. A rank forgery deserves no serious consideration on the part of Christian men. Pious intent on the part of the forger does not alter this conclusion; nor does the method of forgery. It makes no difference whether one man or two men perpetrated the forgery, i. e., whether one man forged the entire letter, or whether one man wrote the body of the letter and a second man attached the caption. (1:1, 2) and the conclusion (5:12-14).

Why a forger should use the name of Peter in a letter that is addressed to congregations that were for the most part founded by Paul is beyond comprehen-

sion. Why a forger should think of associating Peter
with Silvanus and Mark, two of Paul's assistants, is
another incomprehensible proceeding. Finally, that
the whole church should be deceived by a late forgery,
including all of the churches in the five provinces addressed in the forgery, is incredible. All the churches
in these five territories, who had never received a line
from Peter, suddenly read in this forgery that they
had received a whole letter from him and then smiled
and accepted the lie! Every church that did receive a
letter from an apostle kept it in its archives as a most
precious treasure, and other churches sought and obtained certified copies. Here there would be scores of
churches who never had received a letter that Paul
had addressed and sent to them, and suddenly this letter comes, from God knows where, and they all with
one consent say: "Yes, this is the letter Peter sent us;
we have had it for decades!" Inventing one liar is a
sorry business; what shall we say of inventing thousands, and all of these — good Christians?

Does 5:12 mean that Silvanus composed this epistle
in Peter's name? Was Peter unable to express himself
sufficiently well in Greek? Regarding διά in 5:12 see
the passage itself. Peter hailed from Galilee as did
John, James, Jude, and Matthew; Mark's home was
Jerusalem. We have the Greek which these men wrote.
That of Matthew is better than Mark's although we
know that Mark spent some years in the Diaspora. As
for James, he never left Palestine as far as we know,
yet the Greek he wrote certainly speaks for itself.
Galilee was bilingual. All the New Testament writers
that came from Galilee could speak and write Greek.
This must also be said about Jesus who certainly spoke
Greek and not Aramaic to Pilate, to mention only this
instance.   •

When Peter entered the Diaspora he cultivated the
Greek more intensively. His letter was written during

the last year of his life. Peter should know how to write the Greek with perfect ease, more so even than James. As for Silvanus, he was a Jew just as Peter was. The claim that he was more proficient in Greek than Peter is assumption — the more so since we do not possess a single line that he has written. He had no more advantages, as far as the Greek language is concerned, than Peter enjoyed.

Paul associates Silvanus and Timothy with himself when he writes to the Thessalonians. If Peter had desired to allot a share in the thought or in the formulation of his letter to Silvanus he should have done so in the greeting as Paul does in a number of instances even when his co-workers have but a slight share in the writing and Paul alone does the dictating. We must conclude that Silvanus was not the mouthpiece of Peter. Nor did Peter write in Aramaic and use Silvanus as a translator. This letter does not make the impression of being a translation.

But did Mark not serve as Peter's translator when Peter preached to Gentiles? Papias says: "Mark, who was (or who became) an interpreter of Peter, ἡρμενευτὴς Πέτρου, wrote down accurately all that he remembered of what the Lord had said or done though this was not set down in order." Mark was Peter's interpreter in the sense that when Mark wrote his Gospel he reproduced what he had heard Peter tell again and again about the words and the deeds of Jesus. "The idea that Mark performed the office of an interpreter, translating Peter's Aramaic discourses into Greek, or what is still more impossible, his Greek sermons into Latin, cannot be held by anyone having any knowledge at all of language conditions in the apostolic age." Zahn, *Introduction*, II, 443. In other words, when Peter travelled abroad he did not address audiences through an interpreter. Jerome is the first to voice this erroneous idea. As far as Peter's ability in Greek is concerned, it is enough to add that his short letter contains over sixty hapaxlegomena and resembles James in this respect.

*   *   *

The question as to how Peter came to write to these readers must be connected with the other questions as to where and when he wrote.

. Was he in Babylon, in the distant east? Is the phrase used in 5:13, "in Babylon," literal or figurative? We need not dwell long on this point. There is no hint in tradition that Peter was ever in the distant east. The city of Babylon no longer existed. Peter might, indeed, have gone to Babylon — tradition is full of silences. It is not, however, a question about Peter alone but also about Silvanus and about Mark (5:12, 13). All three would have had to have been in Babylon. The idea has even been advanced that the συνεκλεκτή (5:13) was Peter's wife! To place all these persons in Babylon is to claim too much. Egypt, too, had a small place called Babylon, but we need not discuss this hypothesis.

How would Peter, far off in Babylon, learn about the situation and the needs of the churches in Pontus, Galatia, etc., so as to be moved to write to them? If Peter had founded some of these churches he might have retained contact with them although he was now so far away from them. Yet when Paul, who had founded the most important of them, was in Spain, *his* contact with them ceased for the time being.

But the most disturbing feature is the fact that one apostle should write to another apostle's churches and do this from such a distance and at a time when the other was able himself to write, for if Peter wrote from Babylon he wrote before Paul went to Spain; yet before this time, even when he was in prison, Paul kept in contact with his churches.

"Babylon" is a figurative or symbolical designation for Rome. There Peter had with him Paul's two assistants, Silvanus and Mark, whom Paul had left behind on going to Spain. Tradition reports that Peter came to Rome, assigns his martyrdom to Rome, and says that it occurred at the very time when Paul was in Spain. We have traced Paul's movements after his release from the first imprisonment in Rome in the introduction to *The Interpretation of St. Paul's Epistles to Timothy and Titus*. We have shown that he went to Crete, to Ephesus and Colossæ, to Philippi, and then wintered in Nicopolis, and in the spring of 64 proceeded on his long-cherished tour to Spain. In all probability he went via Rome.

Peter was in Rome at that time. We conclude that the two apostles met — a most memorable meeting! They spoke of their past labors and success. Paul must have told that he had put Timothy in charge of the work in the province of Asia and of the progress in this section of the empire. Peter intended to remain in Rome while Paul now hastened on to Spain. Is it supposing too much to think that, since Paul would soon be so far away, he asked Peter to keep an eye on his great fields in Asia? News from these fields would come to Rome as the great center of the world. Paul did not know how long he would be away.

We piece together the following: Peter and Paul are together in Rome in the spring of 64; Mark and Silvanus remain with Peter; in July Rome is burned; in October Nero blames the Christians, and many are made martyrs. Peter himself is crucified. During this entire time Paul is in Spain. The conflagration brought about a terrifying change in the attitude of Nero and of the imperial government toward the Christians, a change that would extend to the far borders of the empire. At some time during these months, before the worst began to happen, Peter wrote this epistle to the churches in the five distant provinces.

We can outline only these few probabilities. Why was nothing written to the churches in the other provinces? That question remains open; still others might be asked.

What brought Peter to Rome, where he had been working for about a year when this epistle was written, and other questions of this nature we are unable to answer. The old Catholic claim that he was the first bishop of Rome and held this office for twenty or twenty-five years has long ago been exposed as fiction. In exposing and opposing the Roman Catholic claims some go to the opposite extreme of rejecting the tradition that Peter suffered martyrdom in Rome and deny that Peter ever visited Rome. Zahn, *Introduction*, II, 163-173, presents the data of the ancient tradition. Peter was in Rome for about one year. He was not there when Paul wrote his letters from prison, for it is incredible that Paul should not have included greetings from Peter in his letter if Peter had been in Rome at this time. The same holds true with regard to the Epistle to the Romans. If Peter was in Rome when Paul wrote this epistle from Corinth, Paul would have sent greetings also to him. On the other hand, if Paul was in Rome when Peter wrote his epistle, Peter would have sent Paul's greetings to the congregations addressed.

More may be said on this subject, but these points will suffice. Peter came to Rome after Paul's first imprisonment and wrote while Paul was absent from Rome. No apostle ever functioned as an elder or bishop of a single congregation. Not even John did this during his long sojourn in Ephesus. We must not reduce the apostleship of Peter to a Roman pastorate. James, who resided in Jerusalem, was not an apostle.

*   *   *

The congregations to which Peter writes were Gentile congregations that had a minority of Jews in their membership. We are ·acquainted with the congregations in Galatia and in the province of Asia, especially that in Ephesus, from the record in Acts and from several of Paul's letters. Paul and his assistants had founded them. The gospel had, however, spread with rapidity to many towns and localities that are not named in these records. In Acts 19:26 Demetrius charges that Paul's preaching was turning many people away from the pagan gods "almost throughout all Asia" (meaning the Roman province). How far the gospel had spread by the time Peter wrote his letter the greeting shows: it had advanced to the Black Sea on the north and into Cappadocia west of Galatia. We have no detailed account of the spread "almost throughout all Asia" to which Demetrius refers, and we also have no record to tell us how the gospel invaded still more distant territories.

We have a few indications. The congregation at Rome was founded by believers who came to the capital — that was one way in which churches were begun. One man, Epaphras, who was not even an assistant of Paul's, founded the church at Colossæ — which is another way in which new churches were started. When after his first imprisonment Paul assigned the work in Ephesus to Timothy, this was done because the church was growing by leaps and bounds in the whole province and needed a competent supervisor; Titus was similarly. for a more limited time assigned to a smaller field, the island of Crete. We are not surprised to read that at the beginning of the next century Pliny, the Roman governor of Bithynia, writes to the emperor Trajan about the suppression of the Christians in his province. The facts are beyond dispute: Christianity spread with great rapidity, missionary zeal was most active.

The order in which Peter names the five provinces has given cause for some remarks: Pontus — Galatia — Cappodocia — Asia — Bithynia (look at the map). He starts with the province in the far north, Pontus, goes to the adjoining Galatia, next to the adjoining Cappadocia on the east, then to the adjoining Asia on the west, and then back to the far north, Bithynia, thus following a sort of circle. By starting and ending at the far north he seems to emphasize the fact that churches had already spread that far. If the order of importance had been intended, Peter would have named the province of Asia first, which was nearest to Rome. Referring to the order in which Peter names the provinces as an argument for locating Peter in Babylon near the Euphrates is not very convincing.

The omission of Lycia and Pamphylia in the south is easily explained since these were not organized as provinces until the year 74. Mysia is omitted for the same reason. Peter does not pass beyond the Taurus range of mountains and probably combines Cilicia with Syria and its center Antioch. He regards the great territory he names as a vast unit. The point in naming Pontus first and its adjoining Bithynia last is not that of separating these two as widely as possible but that of starting at the most distant point and returning to one that is equally distant.

Pontus was made a province under Nero (Smith, *Bible Dictionary*, and others). Its western part was joined to Bithynia in 65 B. C. Its eastern part, Pontus Polemiacus, was joined to Galatia in 63 A. D. (Zahn, II, 154). In what sense Peter understood "Pontus" is thus problematical, especially since he names it separately from Bithynia.

Aquila and Priscilla hailed from Pontus (Acts 18: 2). The fact that Jews were located here, as they were in many other territories, is gleaned from Acts 2:9, 10. This brings us to the assumption of Origen and of other ancients that Peter wrote this epistle to Jewish congregations and not to Gentile congregations that had a few Jewish converts in their membership. We are told that these purely Jewish congregations were started before Paul and Barnabas undertook their first missionary tour through Galatia, that some of the converts made at Pentecost returned to their distant homes and founded these congregations, and that at a very early date Peter wrote this epistle to them. This assumption cannot be accepted. The converts made at Pentecost hailed from all the distant lands mentioned in Acts 2:9-11, but they had come to Jerusalem to remain in that city permanently. According to the record of Acts, Paul and Barnabas were the first to bring the gospel to Galatia, and they founded predominantly Gentile congregations. Ephesus had no church until Paul founded one there.

As to Acts 16:6, 7, these two verses must be considered together. Just as at that time the Spirit kept Paul out of Asia (Ephesus), so he kept him out of Bithynia and directed him to Europe. The great work in Asia had to wait until the events recorded in Acts 19:1, etc., transpired; the work near the Black Sea was not undertaken until a later time. In due time God's Spirit brought Paul to Asia (Ephesus), where he was allowed to labor for a long time, for more than two years; Paul himself never got to Bithynia and these northern regions, the Spirit provided other, later gospel-bearers. It is an unwarranted conclusion to assert that the Spirit prevented Paul from entering Bithynia because the gospel had already been planted there although only among the Jews, and that these Jewish converts and their churches were under Peter's guidance. What about Asia? If some of the converts made at Pentecost started Jewish churches in Pontus, did none return to Asia and start churches in Ephesus and in other great costal towns? Why consider only

Bithynia mentioned in Acts 16:7 and ignore Asia mentioned in v. 6? We shall consider this question further in the interpretation of the text.

*   *   *

To think that at the time when he wrote this letter Peter still had the faults that are noted in the four Gospels is to do a great injustice to this apostle. The Acts show him as the rock, the dependable leader of the Twelve. Paul and he stand out at the Jerusalem Conference, Acts 15. John and he were close friends according to the record of the Gospels and also according to that in the Acts. When Paul wrote Gal. 2:9, they were still together.

Minute comparison has been made between this short letter of Peter's and that of James and all of Paul's, and some have found in them a Pauline, a Petrine, and then also a Johannine type of theology. And the two former are thought to have been competing for the mastery in the early church. The supposed conflict and competition, together with all the deductions drawn therefrom, are illusory.

So also is the opposite opinion which thinks that Peter had no independent mind but that he appropriated thoughts and expressions from Paul's letters, especially from Romans and Ephesians and likewise from the letter of James. Peter's letter reads as if it were composed *wie aus einem Gusse*, as Stoeckhardt states it. There is no reason to assume that he was not acquainted with the letter of James and with nearly all those of Paul that had been written before the year 64. It has yet to be shown that he borrows from any of them. To be sure, he uses words and sometimes expressions that were used by the others, but he does so in the same free way which these others themselves employed, who also did not always coin every expression.

Men whose lives were occupied with the same thoughts and interests are likely to use the same or similar terms. When they touch upon the same doctrine they may phrase it in much the same way. The fact that Paul and Peter mention the foreknowledge of God when they refer to God's election is natural. It is as gratuitous to make Peter a borrower as to make James an antagonist of Paul's in view of the way in which these two discuss faith and works. Much more interesting is it to note the way in which James and also Peter allude to what the Gospels contain; both show that the Lord's language is familiar to them.

The independence of Peter is revealed in his use of unusual words, over sixty hapaxlegomena occurring in his first and twenty-four in his second letter although both epistles are brief. Von Hofmann is right: Peter "speaks his own language, born of Holy Scripture, molded by the New Testament saving facts, and formed in expression according to the purpose he has in mind." It has also been well said that the different types of doctrine, "Pauline," "Petrine," and "Johannine," exist only in the minds of the expositors concerned.

Outstanding in Peter's epistle is the use he makes of the main saving facts, the suffering, death, resurrection of Jesus, and his descent into hell when he is exhorting and fortifying his readers. He also stresses the significance of these facts, present grace and salvation, the consummation and eternal glory. He emphasizes all that the Spirit has done and still does in the readers and the faith and constancy that should result. Peter deals with the means of grace, the Word and baptism, with regeneration, faith, its preservation, sanctification. The power of his admonitions is based on the great primary fundamentals. The central parts of the Apostolic Creed appear in this short epistle; Luther's explanation of the Second Article of the Creed is taken in part from 1:18, etc. Wiesinger deserves renewed quotation when he sums up: "Did we not know who wrote this letter we should be forced to say: 'This is a rocklike man who writes thus, whose soul rests on a rock foundation, and who with his mighty testimony undertakes to fortify the souls of others against the pressure of the storms of suffering advancing upon them and to establish them upon the true rock basis.' " Shortly after Peter had written this letter he suffered martyrdom.

CHAPTER I

The Greeting, v. 1, 2

1) The greetings found in both of Peter's epistles are distinct. The regular three members of a greeting appear, but in the third member Peter has the optative of wish, an effective aorist passive, which is unusual and also places the first two members, the nominative "Peter," etc., and the dative "foreigners," etc., into an independent construction. Peter's method of greeting offers no particular difficulty; we may say that the nominative and the dative are used *ad sensum*.

In regard to the absence of the articles the usual explanation, that this construction stresses the qualitative force of the nouns, should be amplified: "in sentences which bear the nature of captions" the article tends to drop out (Hort, cited by Moulton, *Einleitung*, 131). Many phrases, many nouns with genitives, many personal designations do not have the article in the Greek. All of this applies here whether or not we may be able to indicate it in the translation. Many little niceties are lost when one translates.

Peter, Jesus Christ's apostle, to (such as are) **elect foreigners of** (the) **Diaspora of Pontus, Galatia, Cappadocia, Asia, and Bithynia in accord with God** (the) **Father's foreknowledge in connection with** (the) **Spirit's sanctification for obedience and sprinkling of Jesus Christ's blood: grace to you and peace be multiplied!**

Jesus himself gave Simon Bar-Jona the name "Peter" (Πέτρος, to be distinguished from πέτρα, feminine; see Matt. 16:17, 18). This came to be the apostle's regular name. Its use at this late period of his life when he writes to so many Gentile readers needs no comment. The brief apposition: "apostle of Jesus Christ," or as we may render: "Jesus Christ's apostle," states in what capacity Peter writes, namely as one commissioned by Jesus Christ. The motive for writing as well as the purpose of writing are combined. The readers will be most ready to hear and to heed what Christ's apostle feels impelled to say to them. "*An* apostle" in our versions makes the impression that Peter is only one of a number, which is not the point here. The genitive is possessive yet implies an agency. As an "apostle" Peter *belongs* to Jesus Christ because Jesus *appointed* him to his office. Peter now acts in that office. He is responsible to his Head, under his authority, and speaking by his authority. This suffices.

The readers are designated more elaborately. Much is gained when we read all that follows as a compact unit: "to (such as are) elect foreigners of (the) Diaspora of Pontus, Galatia, Cappadocia, Asia, and Bithynia in accord with God (the) Father's foreknowledge in connection with (the) Spirit's sanctification for obedience and sprinkling of Jesus Christ's blood." We resist the temptation to insert commas. This whole characterization states what Peter regards the readers to be, and what they are to consider themselves to be while Peter speaks to them. As such people he addresses them. Peter will use still other characterizations as he does in 2:9. The entire letter is intended for people who are* thus elaborately described; the whole of it is shaped to fit them. This long designation reflects to a high degree all that follows in the epistle. Even Paul has no dative that might be compared with this one in any of his epistolary greetings. While we must dwell on each item in this long designation of the readers we must ever keep its unity in mind.

The absence of the article expresses quality: "to such as are elect foreigners, etc." All the readers are such people. Ἐκλεκτοί, the verbal adjective, is found also in Matt. 22:14, but in the parable of Jesus the word is used as a noun while Peter uses it as an adjective: "to elect foreigners," etc. The A. V. is more correct in its translation of this word as an adjective than the R. V. which makes the word a noun: "to the elect who are sojourners" and even adds the article, which removes the qualitative sense. The verbal adjective has the force of a past passive participle: foreigners "elected by God" and thus made his own. The whole eternal elective act of God is suggested by this verbal. All that the Scriptures say about this act of God and about the persons involved in it may be thought of in this connection. Peter had all of it in mind. Note *"elect* race" in 2:9; also "a living stone with God *elect"* in 2:4.

Παρεπίδημοι are persons who belong to some other land and people, who are temporarily residing with a people to whom they do not belong. They are for the time being aliens, foreigners, strangers and not natives. They never expect to become the latter. They do not want to be considered or treated as natives by the δῆμος or people among whom they happen to be living; in fact, they know that they may even be expelled as Claudius once expelled the Jews from Rome.

Aliens are often held in contempt by the natives among whom they dwell. To this day they may be placed under severe restrictions in times of war; they may be interned or even repatriated. Yet, despite this estimate of the natives, by calling his readers *"elect* foreigners" Peter exalts his readers far above the natives among whom they live: they are God's chosen people while the people among whom they are scattered are nothing of the kind. In fact, God's election has made the Christians "foreigners" to the rest. At one time these Christians were common natives and lived on the same low level as the rest; now they are such no longer. They would not and, of course, should not descend to their former state from which God has raised them by his grace.

They live in the world but are no longer of the world. They no longer belong. They have become like Abraham, they are merely sojourners in a land that is now strange to them. They look for a city which has foundations, whose designer and maker is God; heaven is their home and fatherland. They confess that they are ξένοι and παρεπίδημοι on the earth; their desire is for a better country, that is, a heavenly one, the city God has prepared for them (Heb. 11:9-16). Peter uses παρεπίδημοι in 2:11 and there combines it with the synonymous πάροικοι as the two words are used in the LXX of Gen. 23:4 and Ps. 39:13.

While these are Old Testament terms, the combination "elect foreigners of (the) Dispersion of Pontus," etc., is decidedly Peter's own. The five provinces he names limit the Dispersion to the territory they cover. He might have written: "to such as are elect foreigners in Pontus," etc. By inserting the genitive διασπορᾶς Peter brings out the thought that his readers are scattered far and wide in these provinces; they are found in little groups here and there as Zahn states it; they are not like the Mormons who live close together in Utah but are like small oases in the desert or like islands in the sea. This emphasizes still more their situation as foreigners: they are small, scattered minorities surrounded by great, pagan majorities.

Peter uses the word Diaspora as it is employed in James 1:1. The Diaspora or Dispersion is a Jewish term to designate all those Jews who dwelt outside of the Holy Land in Gentile countries (John 7:35); it implied that the real home of all these Jews was their Holy Land, which alone they could love as such, to which their hearts were ever drawn. When this word is applied to Christians, "Dispersion" implies that heaven is their true home, that the earth and the world are to them a foreign land which they would at any time gladly leave for their home above.

It is good Greek to add the names of the provinces by means of genitives; in English we should say *"in* Pontus," etc. Regarding these five provinces and the order in which Peter lists them see the introduction. Some say that the readers are Christian Jews. They understand "Diaspora" literally and concretely: "Jews in Gentile lands," and they make the genitive case partitive: a part of these Jews, namely that part of them whose divine election has made them foreigners to the nonelect and unbelieving Jews. The answer to this interpretation is the fact that no Jews ever lived in these provinces (see the introduction). The genitive is qualitative, an abstract and not a concrete noun, it is therefore also used without the article: the readers were "Diaspora foreigners," their election had made them such. "Of Diaspora" places them in contrast, not merely with nonbelieving Jews, but also with all who are unbelieving and nonelect, most of whom were pagans. In fact, it is impossible to say that one kind of Jews constitutes "a Diaspora" among other Jews.

Did the readers understand this description of themselves? They surely understood what their election meant and how it made them foreigners to the world of other men. Moreover, their scattered condition was rather self-evident. The Old Testament allusion (Gen. 23:4; Ps. 39:13), coupled with the Jewish term "Diaspora," although this was a new designation for Christians, were as clear to Peter's readers as was Paul's designation in Eph. 2:19: "You are no more strangers and foreign dwellers, ξένοι and πάροικοι, but you are fellow citizens with the saints." Besides, Peter's entire epistle elucidates what he means by this designation. The opinion that Peter had visited these

Christians, say on his journey to Rome, is only an opinion without a hint in this epistle or elsewhere to support it.

2) The three phrases beginning with κατά, ἐν, and εἰς cannot be attached to ἀπόστολος, which is not only too far removed from them but is also found in the first member of the greeting. The phrases are usually construed with ἐκλεκτοῖς because this is a verbal and thus may have adverbial modifiers. The A. V. even puts the adjective into v. 2: "elect according to the foreknowledge," etc. It is correctly objected that Peter would then have written ἐκλεκτοῖς κατὰ πρόγνωσιν. Too much material intervenes between the adjective and the phrases. The phrases modify the entire dative: "to such as are elect foreigners of (the) Dispersion of Pontus," etc. They are such "in accord with God (the) Father's foreknowledge in connection with (the) Spirit's sanctification for obedience," etc. There is no need to supply τοῖς before the phrases, nor is it necessary to insert commas between them. Rom. 8:28: "those whom he foreknew he also predestinated" is not an exact duplicate although the same foreknowledge is referred to. Peter includes the condition of the Christians in the localities named in the Father's foreknowledge, i. e., also their being foreigners, their being a scattered Diaspora in these provinces. They are entirely what they are in accord with God the Father's foreknowledge.

The noun "foreknowledge" occurs only once again, in Acts 2:23, but it does not differ in meaning from the verb "to foreknow." The noun merely designates the act. The preposition πρό does not alter the act, it only dates the act. The kind of γνῶσις referred to is in no way in doubt in view of passages such as Ps. 1:6: "The Lord knoweth the way of the righteous"; Amos 3:2: "You only have I known of all the families of the earth"; negative with regard to the wicked Matt.

7:23: "I never knew you"; John 10:14: "I know my
sheep, and am known of mine"; II Tim. 2:19: "The
Lord knoweth them that are his." This has been defined as *noscere cum affectu et effectu,* "to know (foreknow) with affection and with a resultant effect." No
better definition has been offered. The dating in "foreknowing" or "foreknowledge" is only with reference
to us who are bound to time and not with reference to
God who is superior to time. To subject God to limitations of time or to stop his foreknowing at any point
of time is to make a serious mistake.

Some change the act of knowing into an act of the
will as when Calvin makes "foreknowledge" = "adop-
tion," or when others make it *Vorbeschluss, Zuvorer-
kueren.* It is a little more difficult to define the noun in
this way than the verb. Luther has the odd term *Ver-
sehung,* which substitutes the idea of seeing for that of
knowing and the perfective *ver-* for the temporal *vor-
her-,* neither of which is correct. See Rom. 8:29 for a
further treatment of this subject.

As the κατά phrase modifies the whole dative with
its genitives, so the ἐν phrase modifies this whole dative
plus the κατά phrase; and, we add, the εἰς phrase also
modifies all that precedes. Ἐν does not="by," German
durch, Latin *per* (διά), and is not instrumental. Nor
does this phrase modify ἐκλεκτοῖς and state "the historic
execution of the eternal election." Ἐν = "in connection
with," and to the entire preceding description of the
readers the phrase adds the further fact of their connection with the Holy Spirit's work of sanctification.

Ἁγιασμός, like the following ῥαντισμός, is a word that
expresses an action. It is not *Heiligkeit,* ἁγιωσύνη, the
state, but *Heiligung,* the Spirit's work of setting apart
for God (G. K., 114, etc.). To restrict this activity to
baptism is to make its force entirely too narrow. As
God's elect foreigners who are scattered throughout
many lands true Christians are what they are "in ac-

cord with the foreknowledge," which is a great comfort to them; and they are all that they are in such comforting accord "in connection with the sanctifying work of the Spirit" who keeps them ever separate as foreigners to the world by making them more and more separate and holy.

Πνεῦμα is used as a proper name and thus, like Θεὸς Πατήρ and Ἰησοῦς Χριστός, appears without the article. Peter intends to name the three persons of the Godhead in these three phrases and to connect what his readers are in the world with the Holy Trinity: elect foreigners dispersed in these provinces, as such graciously and lovingly foreknown of *God the Father* — as such in connection with the *Holy Spirit's* sanctifying work — as such, to carry the matter still farther, intended for obedience and sprinkling by the blood of *Jesus Christ*. A few commentators think of the "spirit," namely "in connection with sanctification of our spirit" (objective genitive); but the majority notes the trinitarian reference and the subjective genitive.

The order of the three phrases cannot be changed. Εἰς in the third points to intention and to result: "for obedience and sprinkling of Jesus Christ's blood." The phrase recalls Exod. 24:7, 8: when the people heard what Moses read they said: "All that the Lord hath said we will do and be obedient," and then Moses sprinkled them with the blood. This explains why "obedience" precedes "sprinkling." On the latter compare also Heb. 10:22 and 12:24.

Ὑπακοή is not found in secular Greek; it is here without modification and denotes the obedience of faith, which should not be converted into a mere moral obedience. Peter uses the word again in v. 14 and 22. The sanctifying work of the Spirit leads to obedience. If πίστις were used here, this would bring out the thought of confidence and trust; by using ὑπακοή Peter obtains the connotation of submission as it appears also in Exod. 24:7.

This last phrase has two objects, the second being "sprinkling of Jesus Christ's blood." "Of blood" is the objective genitive. We do not make it a compound: "Jesus Christ's blood-sprinkling," for "Jesus Christ's" is the possessive genitive with "blood" and not the subjective genitive with "sprinkling" (so also in the preceding phrase Πνεύματος is the subjective genitive). Who sprinkles us is not stated; we take it that he who sanctifies us is this one, for it is this sprinkling that sanctifies. We should not reduce either the sanctifying or the sprinkling to the one act of our baptism. Since it is placed last, we should include all that follows baptism, namely the constant cleansing from sin. "Blood" has the connotation of expiation. It is the blood shed for us on Calvary. "Sprinkling" = the application of this sacrificial blood; unless it is applied to the sinner, he remains in his sins. Living in obedience and constantly being cleansed with Christ's blood, we are what God intends us to be: total strangers to the world of men around us, wherever we may live.

To state that Gentile Christians would not understand Peter's expression, that only Jewish Christians would be able to do so, is to assume that the Old Testament was not used when Gentile converts were taught, but see v. 10-12. All Paul's letters to Gentile churches establish the contrary. By saying of himself only that he is writing as an apostle but designating his readers so fully Peter shows that their interests and needs prompt him to write.

The third member of the greeting: "grace to you and peace be multiplied," is, unlike Paul's greetings, the optative of wish; we find it again in Second Peter and in Jude. On "grace to you and peace" see Rom. 1:7; I Cor. 1:3; II Cor. 1:2, and several other epistles of Paul. The aorist passive optative is effective, and the verb, which is derived from πλῆθος, "mass or multitude," means "may grace and peace be made yours in a multitude of ways."

The Great Doxology, v. 3-12

3) Peter's great doxology resembles that which Paul wrote in Eph. 1:3-14. Yet each is decidedly distinct and original. In Paul's the Trinity indicates the division into three sections; in Peter's we also have the Trinity, but only in the second part (v. 5-9), since in the third part (v. 10-12) of the doxology only the second and the third persons are introduced. Paul's reaches from eternity to eternity; Peter's from our regeneration to heaven and to the Parousia. Paul wrote his doxology when he contemplated the whole *Una Sancta* and the whole soteriological work of the Trinity; Peter when he contemplates his readers and himself in their present state amid afflictions in the world. Paul introduces the divine election in the doxology; Peter has it already in the greeting. Paul speaks of the quickening from death in a separate section (Eph. 2:1, etc.); Peter speaks of the regeneration in the doxology itself. The purpose of Paul's doxology leads him to the summation of all things under Christ; Peter's purpose restricts him to the distress of his readers as foreigners (v. 1) in this world, whose hope and faith he inspires. Peter's doxology has little in common with that which Paul wrote in II Cor. 1:3, etc., the key word of which is consolation, but a consolation that was prompted by the consolation which Paul himself had just experienced.

It is exceptional to begin with a doxology, especially with one as grand as that of Peter. When Paul strikes such a note in Ephesians, this is but natural; he has the great *Una Sancta* before his eyes. When Peter breaks forth into a doxology when he is writing to Christians as foreigners in the world, that is a dif-

ferent matter; he sings the praise of God because of
the hope which God has given us, because of the end
of our faith at the revelation of Jesus Christ, because
of the fulfilled prophecies that are now preached to
us, things into which even angels desire to look. To
be sure, we are foreigners in this world, little groups
scattered here and there, but we are not inferior to
those who treat us as being inferior.

As already the adjective "elect" shows, and more
fully the three phrases which set forth the connection
of Father, Spirit, and Christ with our state in this
world, we as foreigners in this world are made strange
and alien to it by the wondrously high position which
God has bestowed upon us. We are a royal aristocracy,
natives of a heavenly kingdom, and thus foreigners to
this poor, wretched world. Instead of merely telling
the readers this in a calm, prosy way Peter expresses
his joy in an exalted praise in order to sweep the hearts
of his readers upward to the same joy and praise.
Note that the whole of v. 3-12 is one grand unit.

**Blessed the God and Father of our Lord Jesus
Christ! the One who according to his great mercy
begot us again unto living hope by means of Jesus
Christ's resurrection from the dead, unto an inheritance incorruptible and unstained and unfading,
safeguarded in (the) heavens for you, the ones being protected in connection with God's power by
means of faith for salvation ready to be revealed in
connection with the last season; in which, etc.**

Εὐλογητός is regular in doxologies; its use in these
great Christian doxological outbursts is not to be compared with the Jewish formulas which are introduced
at the mention of the holy name, exclamations such as
"blessed be he." These great Christian doxologies have
their antecedents in the great Old Testament psalms,
such as Psalm 103. This is no mere adoration of the
name; this is adoration of God for all that he has

done for us. The grammarians debate as to whether
to supply ἐστί, εἴη, or ἔστω; we supply nothing, this is
an exclamation: "Blessed the God and Father!" The
verbal means "well-spoken." We speak well of God
when we truly say what he is and does in his attributes
and his works. No task should give us greater delight.

There is too little contemplation of God, too little
praise of him in our hearts, especially in our earthly
distress. The Scriptures constantly show us the better
way. They teach no immersion in God, no sinking
away of the mind and the emotions in God as these
are cultivated by the mystics, even the best of whom
are morbid, the rest, like those of India, pagan. Peter
sings the true glory of God when he is contemplating
his great soteriological acts and blessings.

Like Paul, he uses the full liturgical name: "the
God and Father of our Lord Jesus Christ," he in whom
our whole salvation is bound up. This name is really
a concentrated confession. All that the Scriptures reveal of our Savior God is crowded into this name. The
discussions of the commentators as to whether Peter
intends to say that God is only the Father of our Lord
Jesus Christ or also his God, generally overlook the
great point just stated.

In v. 2 Θεὸς Πατήρ needs neither the article nor καί;
in v. 3 both are in place, but in the usual Greek man-
ner the one article makes one person of the two nouns.
For Jesus according to his human nature God is his
God, and for Jesus in his deity God is his Father; his
God since the incarnation, his Father from all eternity.
See the discussion in connection with II Cor. 1:3. In
Eph. 1:17 we have *the God* of our Lord Jesus Christ."
We note also Matt. 27:46, and John 20:17. But note
"our Lord" which connects us with Christ and through
him with God. "Lord" is wholly soteriological: he
who purchased and won us, to whom we belong as our
Savior King.

We take issue with those who seek to eliminate everything "metaphysical," in particular the *generatio aeterna* which the church has always found in the designation "Father of Jesus Christ." For this we are offered the substitute that "God" refers to the omnipotence and "Father" to the love displayed for "our Lord Jesus Christ" in the work of salvation. Yet, unless our Lord is "true God, born of the Father from eternity" and thus also "true man, born of the Virgin Mary," no salvation remains for which to glorify God.

'Ο ἀναγεννήσας is an apposition: "the One who begot us again." This verb, which is used here and in v. 23, is peculiar to Peter: "to beget spiritually, to a new spiritual life." This is the new birth referred to in John 3:3, the quickening mentioned in Eph. 2:5, 6 and Col. 2:13, the new creation spoken of in Eph. 2:10 and Gal. 6:15. We are begotten again when the life from God is implanted into our souls. This is the same as the implanting of faith in Christ which fills the heart with new powers, new motives, thoughts, volitions, etc., so that a new creature appears. The aorist participle is historical and states a past fact.

This act of God's took place "in accord with his great mercy," it harmonized with his mercy. Ἔλεος is the proper word, for its connotation is the pitiful condition in which we lay and from which God raised us to an entirely different state. One begets children whom he then loves, on whom he showers fatherly gifts, who are his heirs. All these great connotations are suggested by the apposition and appear in hundreds of Scripture passages.

The greatness of God's mercy appears when we see what we were at one time by virtue of our natural birth and what we now are by virtue of our spiritual rebirth. It was, indeed, an evidence of great mercy for God to stoop down to such wretched creatures as we were. Great also is the evidence of mercy when we note to what God begot us: "to living hope," the opposite of an empty, false, deceptive hope. This hope is not "lively" (A. V.) or "living" because it is bright, strong, active in us but because God guarantees and produces its fulfillment. All men have some sort of hope, but while so many deceive themselves with the dead hopes of their own making, we, whom God himself begot, have a living hope that rests on God's promises and power. When the hopes of others go to pieces in the last flood, our hope will sail triumphantly into the harbor of eternal fulfillment.

Note how Peter combines the beginning of our spiritual life with its consummation. So much lies between these two extremes; but when we as strangers are called to suffer in this world which is now so alien and often so hostile to us, our hearts praise the great mercy of him who begot us as his own and who will presently usher us into heaven and his own glorious presence. We might say a great deal more about hope; take a concordance and note the references yourself (v. 21; 3:15; and especially those mentioned in the New Testament).

Shall we translate: "living by means of Jesus Christ's resurrection from the dead" ("hope living by means of" is the same)? We do not think that "living" requires such a modifier, the meaning of which would be obscure. Nor do we insert a comma and thus have two parallel phrases, both equally modifying ἀναγεννήσας. We construe as Peter wrote: "he who begot us to living hope by means of Jesus Christ's resurrection from the dead." "Us" does not refer only to the apostles who saw the risen Lord but to Peter and to his readers. The resurrection of Jesus Christ is the crowning point of his redemptive work which showed that he is, indeed, the Son of God and the Savior of the world, and that his dying sacrifice is sufficient to cancel the sins of the world and to satisfy the righteousness of God. Peter has already mentioned "Jesus Christ's blood." Christ's resurrection is the heart of the gospel and thus ever constitutes the means for begetting us to a living hope. No man has spiritual life and hope save by the resurrection of Christ. He is the resurrection and the life; we live because he lives.

For the fourth time Peter names "Jesus Christ." He loves the very sound of the words. Ἀνάστασις is active, and "Jesus Christ" is the subjective genitive. The phrase ἐκ νεκρῶν is discussed fully in connection with Matt. 17:10; Mark 9:9; Luke 9:7; John 2:22; Acts 3:16. Modernistic and former rationalistic denials of Christ's resurrection destroy the heart of his saving work, here in particular also our regeneration and our living hope. Note the effective correspondence of the terms employed: ἀναγεννήσας . . . ζῶσαν . . . δι' ἀναστάσεως, "the One who begot — living — by resurrection."

4) The subjective hope is followed by the objective thing hoped for; the second εἰς phrase is thus appositional to the first. We were begotten, writes Peter, "unto an inheritance," etc. Our inheritance is the heavenly kingdom in all its glory. It is already ours now, for we are the born heirs; as such heirs we shall presently enter upon full possession and enjoyment of it. Being such heirs and waiting in hope for our heavenly inheritance makes us the "elect foreigners" that we are in this world (v. 1). The children of this world have no inheritance awaiting them at the end of their existence.

Wonderful, certain, and not far off is this our inheritance. Three beautiful adjectives describe it: ἄφθαρτον, ἀμίαντον, καὶ ἀμάραντον, all three have a *privativum*. "Incorruptible" = which neither moth, rust, thieves, nor any other destructive force can in any way

injure as they do the inheritances of the earth. Even
if any man obtains these, they are subject to corrupt-
ing forces, are transient, unenduring.

"Unstained" = without the least stain or defilement of sin, so pure and lofty that we can let our hope
and desire go out to this inheritance without reserve,
something that we can say of no earthly inheritance.

"Unfading" = "amaranthine," imperishable, never
withering, disappointing, becoming old and worn. The
delight of it will never lessen or grow stale. Huss, who
was martyred at Constance, combines the three attributes: Our inheritance will never lose anything
through age or sickness on our part or through any
damage to itself; it will never be marred by impurity;
and it will never lessen in delight because it has been
enjoyed so long.

We note that the three terms are negative. Even
Peter could not alter that fact. The glory of our heavenly inheritance is so far beyond direct human conception that the Scriptures must often resort to figures of
speech instead of to literal terms or to weak compar-
isons with earth and thus to such negatives, which tell
us what will *not* be in heaven. The realities themselves
transcend human language.

The certainty of our inheritance is expressed by
a participle and a relative clause: the inheritance itself is safeguarded for us, the heirs, and we, the heirs,
are likewise guarded and protected so that we shall
not lose the inheritance. The perfect participle has
present and continuous implication: "having ever been
and thus ever continuing to be safeguarded in the heavens for you." The passive makes God the one who
guards and keeps our inheritance for us. He keeps it
safe. Many an earthly heir has never obtained his inheritance; false, faithless, weak guardians lost it for
him. Εἰς ὑμᾶς = a dative as it does in modern Greek,
R. 535. From "us" Peter turns to "you" as Paul often

does and applies what he says to his readers in the most direct way.

5) An apposition to "you" states the other side, namely that the readers, too, are under a protecting guard. Φρουρεῖν is a military term and this harmonizes with δύναμις, "power." We are amid foes who are bent on robbing us of our inheritance; but the keeper of Israel sleeps not nor slumbers. "The angel of the Lord encampeth round about them that fear him and delivereth them," Ps. 34:7. "We pray that God would so guard and keep us that the devil, the world, and our flesh may not deceive us nor entice us into misbelief and other great shame and vice; and though we be assailed by them, we may finally prevail and obtain the victory." Luther. Δύναμις is omnipotence. While it is doctrinally safe to think of the gracious power of the Holy Spirit, the connection with φρουρεῖν excludes this; ἐν is not "by," nor is it instrumental, it means "in connection with" God's omnipotent power, the connection being apparent from the context.

It is a serious misunderstanding to think of God's omnipotence as filling our faith with power and making it able to overcome all our foes. It is still more serious to suppose that omnipotence produces faith in us and to base this supposition on Eph. 1:19, see the discussion of this passage. Nowhere do the Scriptures confuse grace and omnipotence. Faith is kindled and is preserved and made strong by grace alone. Grace alone reaches into the heart and the soul and works spiritual effects; and this grace always uses the Word and the sacraments as its means. Omnipotence has a different function; it does not operate in or upon our faith but above, over, around us, upon our enemies. It kept Daniel in the lions' den, the three men in the fiery furnace, set bounds for Satan in afflicting Job, freed Peter from Herod's prison, preserved Paul amid dangers, hardships, persecutions, etc. Great and wonderful is this protection of omnipotence, without which we should soon be overwhelmed.

That is why the military verb φρουρεῖν is used: in connection with his omnipotence God posts sentinels and guards for our protection. We may well think of his holy angels (Heb. 1:14). The A. V.'s translation is inexact in placing the three phrases together after the participle; the R. V. places the phrases as Peter does: "who by the power of God are guarded through faith unto salvation." Despite Peter's care in the order of the words some think that God's omnipotence uses our faith as its means, the omnipotence making our faith its weapon. These ideas are foreign to Scripture. Διὰ πίστεως means that faith trusts the guarding and protecting power of God's almighty power. In every danger our faith turns to God, prays to him that he may use his power to shield us, make a way of escape for us (I Cor. 10:13). When, like Peter on one occasion, we are foolhardy and depend on our own strength we fall as Peter on that occasion denied Christ.

The aim of this protection is "salvation," the inheritance incorruptible, etc., mentioned in v. 4, safely kept for us in heaven and "ready to be revealed in connection with the last period or season." Everything is ready and complete for its glorious unveiling. The last καιρός is now here, has been here ever since Christ finished his redemption and ascended on high. Chiliasts think of a period of a 1,000 years yet to come when Christ will do still more work in the millennium. We are now living in the last time; in a little while the great curtain shall be drawn aside, our entire salvation shall be revealed. Peter is speaking of the immense things that are impending in the mighty power of God and thus does not deal with the death of individual Christians before Christ's Parousia, when their souls enter heaven while their bodies still wait in the dust of the earth.

6)   First, certainty; next, joy. First, living hope, an inheritance safely kept for us in heaven, and we ourselves kept for this inheritance; next, while we wait, joy despite trials, these trials only refining us like gold. The grand doxology simply moves forward with a relative clause. This is Greek, which loves connectives, tying though to thought; in English we should place a period and begin a main clause. Peter thus proceeds: **in which you continue to exult though now for a little while, if it is necessary, put to grief in manifold trials in order that the testing out of your faith,** (a testing out) **more precious than of gold that perishes though tested out by means of fire, may be found unto praise and glory and honor at Jesus Christ's revelation, whom, etc.**

The ἐν καιρῷ ἐσχάτῳ is not to be regarded as a date for the 'revelation of our salvation. The word καιρός should obviate this thought. Peter does not say "at the last *day*" or mean "*at* the last period" (a *kairos* of a 1,000 years) but says "in connection with the last period." The revelation of our salvation is connected with the present period of time in which we are living. The connection is the thought that the revelation may occur at any moment in this period. This was not the case during any previous period. Those who think of a future date make the present tense a future: "you will exult," and then labor to prove this correct. Or they make "in which" a neuter: in which things we exult, namely in our inheritance and in the coming revelation of our salvation. Yet ἀγαλλιάομαι is never construed with ἐν but with ἐπί to state the object "over" which one exults. "In which" is purely temporal, it equals "in this period" in connection with which our salvation is ready, is to be revealed at any moment.

"We continue to exult" is the durative indicative; there is nothing in this relative clause to indicate that this verb form is an imperative. This form of this verb is not found in the secular Greek; it generally occurs in the middle voice: *jubelndes und danksagendes Lob-preisen* (G. K., 18). Its meaning is much stronger than "rejoice," yet we see no reason for making it a cultus term or for restricting the exultation to eschatology. Peter says that in this whole period we ever and ever exult, jubilate, celebrate, and do this in spite of the fact that we are subject to grief in manifold trials. The participle is concessive: "though now for a little while (accusative to indicate duration), if it is necessary, put to grief in manifold trials." Compare James 1:2: "Consider it all joy when you fall into all kinds of trials," where the same word πειρασμός is used, which means "trial" and not "temptation." James regards the trials themselves as occasions for joy; Peter admits that they produce grief, but that our exulting is not lessened thereby.

Two points are touched upon in connection with this grief: it is only for a little while, it will soon cease; it occurs only when God finds it necessary. Robertson regards δέον ἐστί as a periphrastic present tense; the neuter participle is but an adjective in the Greek, and there is no reason for a periphrastic present, which would overstress the duration and would conflict with "a little while." In this wicked world, where we live as foreigners (v. 1), our trials are "manifold," being now of one kind, now of another. They often hurt severely, yet we keep on jubilating and celebrating.

7) This sounds paradoxical. Like James (1:3), Peter solves the paradox. We see God's purpose in these trials: "in order that the testing out of your faith, (a testing out) more precious than of gold that perishes though tested out by means of fire, may be found (aorist, definitely found) unto praise," etc. We continue to exult; so little is the short grief of our trials able to stop us from exulting that, seeing God's

purpose in these trials, we exult the more. Gold is
nothing but a perishing metal (descriptive present
participle) ; it will not outlast this earth although it is
now tested out by fire to prove that it is gold and not
brass or something else. Paul loves the words δόκιμος,
δοκιμάζω, the figure of testing out metals, coins, etc. The
form δόκιμος is now recognized as an adjective on the
basis of the papyri; both Peter and James (1:3) substantivize it and add the same genitive: "the testing
out of your faith," i. e., the genuineness of our faith
established by test. This testing is more precious than
that of gold even when (δέ) it is tested out and proved
genuine by means of fire.

If gold, perishable though it is, being only of
earthly, temporal value, is tested out and proved genuine, how much more should faith with its eternal value
for us not also be tested and proved genuine? By men-
tioning fire as the means for proving gold genuine
Peter alludes to our trials which often seem to be fiery.
"In the fiery oven the straw burns, but the gold is
purified." Augustine. "The fire does not lessen the
gold but makes it pure and bright, removing any ad-
mixture. So God lays the cross upon all Christians in
order to purify and cleanse them well that their faith
may remain pure even as the Word is pure, and that
we may cling to the Word alone and trust in nothing
else. For we all need such a purifying and cross greatly
because of our old, gross Adam." Luther. These fathers add a thought: that of removing dross from the
gold, that of purifying our faith. Peter speaks only
of proving the gold to be gold, the faith to be faith —
τὸ δοκίμιον, *die Echtheit*, the genuineness (B.-P. 316).

We are not merely put to grief but are put to grief
for this great purpose of God: "to be found unto praise
and glory and honor at the revelation of Jesus Christ."
We should not suppose that the genuineness of our faith
will not be discovered by God (passive, not the middle)

until the last day when Christ is revealed at the Parousia. "At the revelation of Jesus Christ" is not attached to "may be found" but belongs where Peter has it: "praise and glory and honor at (or in connection with, ἐν) the revelation," etc. God finds the testing out, the genuineness, now whenever a successful test is made; and thus at Christ's revelation he will bestow upon us "praise," namely his commendation, "glory," like the glory of Christ, and "honor," high distinction. What God now finds (actually finds, aorist) is what pertains to the reward of grace which he will bestow upon us at the last day.

The claim that τὸ δοκίμιον means *Pruefungsmittel* has Peter say that the means for testing us, namely the trials, are by God to be found more precious than fire which tests gold as though the comparative value of the means of testing us and of fire is to be determined. Peter speaks of the tested genuineness of our faith which God intends to find so as to reward it at the last day and states that such genuineness is more valuable than any tested genuineness of gold although men do test out gold even by fire in order to make sure that it is genuine gold. Peter does not say that faith is like gold, trials like fire, but that the genuineness of the one is like that of the other, save that that of faith is the more valuable.

In v. 5 our "salvation *is to be revealed*"; now Peter uses the noun and says "at Jesus Christ's *revelation*." Now we appear only as foreigners in the world (v. 1), all the praise, glory, and honor are still unseen; so Christ, too, is hidden and veiled, and men do not see him. I John 3:2. A complete revelation shall take place at the last day. When Christ shall be revealed to the whole earthly universe, our heavenly salvation shall also be revealed. This double revelation is one that shall take place before the universe, no less. No wonder Christians jubilate and exult.

8) Peter continues with relative clauses: **whom not having seen you continue to love, in whom, now not seeing yet believing, you continue to exult with joy inexpressible and glorified, bringing away the end of your faith, salvation of souls.**

We usually love one whom we have seen and have in this way come to prize, we also continue to love him after he is gone. But Peter's readers had never seen Jesus and therefore could not love him in this way. Although they had never looked upon him with their natural eyes they continue to love him (ἀγαπᾶν) with the high love of intelligence and corresponding purpose. A contrast with Peter himself is implied, for Peter had seen Jesus both before and after his resurrection (John 21:15, etc.: "Lovest thou me?" asked first with ἀγαπᾶν and then with even φιλεῖν). Peter silently places himself below his readers. It is more praiseworthy to love as they do than to love as Peter does.

Peter mentions love first and faith second, the fruit and then the tree; he could, of course, have reversed this order. We note, too, that he uses two finite verbs to express the loving and the exultation, for he intends to coordinate these two feelings. Faith is expressed by a participle, but only in order to make it the source of the exultation: "in whom, now not seeing yet believing, you continue to exult," etc. Εἰς ὅν is to be construed with πιστεύοντες, their trust goes out to him. This is the same conception of faith that we find in Heb. 11:1, "conviction in regard to things not seen." Peter must have had in mind the words of Jesus: "Blessed are they that have not seen, and yet have believed!" John 20:29. Thomas demanded to see before he would believe; it was no credit to him. Peter's readers were doing far better than that.

Οὐ with a participle is exceptional, μή is the common negation with participles. When the former is used, there is always a reason for such a construction; that is especially the case in this sentence where both οὐ and μή appear. To speak of objective and subjective negation is a distinction that was formerly made; likewise to speak of fact and of condition or to deny that there is a distinction. "Here οὐ harmonizes with the tense of ἰδόντες as an actual experience while μή with ὁρῶντες is in accord with the concessive idea in contrast with πιστεύοντες." R. 1138. You did not (οὐ) see him states the clear-cut fact as such a fact; you do not (μή) see him simply states the present fact in the ordinary Greek way.

Peter repeats "you continue to exult" from v. 6. The tense is the same although some texts have the active form instead of the middle of the second verb. It is again stated that this present tense must have a future meaning: "you shall exult." We are told that exulting with inexpressible and glorified joy can refer only to the exultation at the last day, and that not seeing Jesus *now* implies that we *shall* see him at the last day, and that this gives a future meaning to "you exult." But these efforts to secure a future meaning for the verb are misdirected. We have three verbs in the present tense: "you continue to exult (v. 6) — you continue to love — you continue to exult," the third verb even repeating the first. This third present verb is modified by two present participles, "believing while not seeing" (actions that certainly take place now) and "bringing away the end of your faith," an action that also takes place now as one after the other of the readers dies and thus brings away the end of his faith, eternal salvation. In the face of this it is impossible to put a future meaning into this plain present indicative "you are exulting."

But is our exulting now a jubilation "with joy inexpressible and glorified" (perfect participle: one that has been and thus is now glorified)? The answer is

found in 4:14: "If you are reproached for the name
of Christ, blessed (are you)! because the Spirit of the
(divine) glory and of God is resting upon you." This
beatitude has us exult *now* with a joy which is beyond
poor human utterance (ἀνεκλάλητος) and glorified by
the Spirit of glory. We are not yet glorified, but our
joy is, for we have tasted of the powers of the eons to
come (Heb. 6:5) and cannot utter what this taste
really is because it is filled with glory. Peter puts
"glorified" in the second place, because he would state
why our joy cannot be put into utterance. Those who
call this extravagant language have not caught the
spirit of Peter.

It is sometimes assumed that the construction of
ἀγαλλιᾶσθε is loose or irregular; Peter is carried away by
his thought. It is expected that with εἰς ὅν, κτλ., Peter
should state *in whom* the readers exult just as he states
whom we love. Since Peter does not do this, an irregularity is assumed. But let us note what Peter
writes: "whom not having seen you continue to love;
believing in whom you do not now see, you continue
to exult," etc. The second verb needs no object; as it
needs and has none in v. 6, so again it needs none in
v. 8. In v. 6 Peter writes: "we continue to exult though
having been grieved," etc.; in v. 8 he writes in the
same way but now uses two participles: "believing, we
continue to exult, bringing away the end of our faith,"
etc. All is as regular as one could wish it.

9) Κομιζόμενοι is used as it is in Heb. 10:36; 11:13,
19, 39 and means, "carrying or bringing away for yourselves" so as to have and ever after to enjoy. The
present participle is iterative: one by one carries away
the τέλος, "the end or goal" of his faith, which Peter
himself defines as "salvation of souls," namely the final
rescue when the soul enters heaven. Ψυχή is not in contrast with "body" as though only the soul is finally
saved; the word designates the person, the real being

that is saved, and not merely a part of it. When the soul is saved, the body, too, is saved and will in due time join the soul.

10) First, certainty; next exultation; and now as the third part of the great doxology, the divine means for bestowing both on the readers, the gospel of the prophets that was preached by the preachers who were sent by the Holy Spirit. As it did in v. 6, the doxology continues with a relative, the antecedent of which is incorporated: **concerning which salvation there earnestly sought and searched prophets, they who prophesied concerning this grace regarding you, searching in regard to what or what kind of period the Spirit of Christ in them was indicating when testifying in advance about the sufferings regarding Christ and the glories after them; to whom, etc.** "For verily I say unto you, that many prophets and righteous men have desired to see those things which ye see, and have not seen them; and to hear those things which ye hear, and have not heard them," Matt. 13:17.

What the prophets sought to find out concerned the salvation which Peter has just mentioned; the question they sought to answer shows that it concerned this salvation and thus why Peter speaks of their search, their question, and its answer in his doxology. The verb is repeated for the sake of emphasis, and both verbs are compounded with intensifying ἐκ: "they earnestly sought and earnestly searched." The former is more general, the latter more specific, applying, as it does, also to documents (the simplex is used in John 5:39: "Search the Scriptures"). The second verb is even repeated with a participle: "searching" (v. 11), which drops ἐκ as is usual in such repetitions (R. 563).

"Prophets" did this, i. e., men who were prophets. The apposition does not restrict this word to a certain number as though not all of them searched thus; it describes all of them as "the men who prophesied concerning this grace regarding you" (εἰς occurs several times in this sense). The repetition "prophets — they who prophesied" emphasizes the character and the function of these men: men who were chosen by God as his mouthpiece. "As he spake by the mouth of his holy prophets, which have been since the world began," Luke 1:70. "Ought not Christ to have suffered these things and to enter into his glory? And beginning at Moses and all the prophets, he expounded unto them in all the Scriptures the things concerning himself," Luke 24:26, 27. Note also: "the Lord God of the holy prophets," Rev. 22:6. The apposition is Peter's own; it is he who says that they prophesied "concerning this grace regarding you"; the fulfillment of their prophecies had become reality when Peter wrote.

.The article used with χάριτος and the attributive phrase mean "this grace regarding you." "Grace" has the same force it had in v. 2: all the unmerited *favor Dei* which Peter's readers were receiving. The ancient prophets had told all about it throughout all of the past ages. We should not omit David (Acts 2:30), nor Moses (John 5:46; Acts 26:22; Deut. 18:15, 18). Peter's reference to the prophets does not make all his readers former Jews. Not only did the whole Gentile church have the Old Testament as its Bible; from beginning to end this Bible told of the grace of God regarding also the Gentiles.

11) The question which all of the prophets sought to answer from their own prophecies was "in regard to what (period) or what kind of period the Spirit in them was indicating when testifying in advance about the sufferings regarding Christ and the glories after them." The question is alternative, and "or" is not disjunctive (as if two contrasted questions are referred to) but conjunctive (one question that could be stated either way): "What or what kind of period is this?"

In regard to this the prophets kept making search. The idea is not that they were learned theologians who were pursuing scholarly investigations; they were men who were filled with a great desire for the arrival of this great "period" of grace, who longed for nothing more than themselves to see this period. "Was indicating" is the imperfect and describes how the Holy Spirit kept making such indication.

It is noteworthy that Peter writes "the Spirit of Christ" just as in other passages the Scriptures use the expression "the Spirit of God." The deity and the pre-existence of Christ are involved: Christ's Spirit testified in advance about Christ's sufferings and glories, i. e., when as the incarnate Logos he would suffer in his humiliation and after that be crowned with glories in his exaltation. We usually note the singular "glory" in such connections; here the plural "glories" matches the plural "sufferings" and is used on this account. Both "sufferings" and "glories" pertain to Christ's human nature. The two εἰς = "regarding," "in regard to"; they are like the εἰς used in v. 10.

Two great thoughts are stated: 1) the Holy Spirit was in the prophets when he testified as he did; 2) these prophets studied their own utterances and writings in order to discover what they contained. This comprises the entire doctrine of the Inspiration of the Scriptures. The Spirit spoke through the prophets; much that he said the prophets themselves did not at once grasp but studied to discover it somewhat as a messenger may study some message he is ordered to transmit. "For not by man's will has prophecy ever come, but, being borne along by the Holy Spirit, men made utterance from God," II Pet. 2:21.

It is asked: "Where do the prophets say that they are ever searching in regard to what period or what kind of period the Spirit indicates in the prophecies about Christ?" One may reply by asking: "Where does the Old Testament say that many prophets and kings desired to see and to hear what the Twelve saw and heard?" (Matt. 13:17). The longing for the days of the Messiah runs through the entire Old Testament. It begins with Eve (Gen. 4:1). On the strength of such a question to make these prophets New Testament prophets, and to state that these are not the apostles but other prophets, is to invite the counterquestion: "Where does the New Testament say that *these* prophets made such inquiries?" Therefore this view cannot be successfully sustained.

12) The two aorists occurring in v. 10: "prophets earnestly sought and earnestly searched," already imply that they obtained an answer to their question. This is now stated: **to whom it was revealed that not for themselves but for you they were min-istering the things which now have been announced to you by means of those preaching the gospel to you by the Holy Spirit commissioned from heaven, into which things (even) angels desire to look.**

The answer came to the prophets by means of revelation, through the same Spirit who testified to them about the suffering and the glorified Savior. There is no need to regard this as a special, separate revelation, apart from and different from the revelations which the prophets received otherwise. We know of no such peculiar difference. Matt. 13:17 extends the longing beyond the prophets themselves; it includes many righteous. "Watchman, what of the night? Watchman, what of the night?" was the cry of many (Isa. 22:11); and the prophet foretells that Israel's "watchman shall lift up the voice" when the beautiful feet of messengers bring the tidings of salvation (Isa. 52:7, 8).

In the meantime the revelation granted to the prophets was to the effect that not for themselves but for the readers of Peter's letter were they ministering in regard to the things which the gospel messengers had now announced to Peter's readers. The imperfect "were ministering" is descriptive, it does not, however, imply that their ministry had nothing to do with themselves and with the generations of their time but that the great events which the Spirit was testifying to in advance, the sufferings pertaining to Christ and his glories, were to occur in the future, were to be announced or proclaimed (second aorist passive) as having occurred to future generations and thus to Peter's present readers.

It is stated that this was not a satisfactory answer to the question of the prophets. It was a most pertinent answer. Like so many of the answers that Jesus gave to questions that were put to him, this answer which was revealed to the prophets stated the main thought, namely that, following Christ's humiliation and exaltation, there would come the world-wide announcement of the saving gospel. The Spirit thus shed a flood of light on all the Messianic prophecies that reached beyond the Jewish nation, thus on Gen. 22:17, 18, Abraham's children that are to be as numerous as the stars, his seed blessing "all the nations of the earth"; on Isa. 2:2-5, all nations flowing unto the exalted house of the Lord. These are but a few samples. We have the corresponding thought of the New Testament: Jesus picturing many coming from the east and the west to feast with Abraham, Isaac, and Jacob in the kingdom (Matt. 8:11); the writer of Hebrews (11: 40) saying that the Old Testament believers are to reach the goal "not without us" of the New Testament. These are again but a few samples.

Instead of stating the thought abstractly, namely that the prophets were ministering to future generations in many nations, Peter states it concretely and personally: "ministering *to you*," and even adds: "these things which have been announced (aorist in the Greek which cares to state only the past fact) *to you* by means of those gospelizing you," etc. Αὐτὰ ἅ belong together; it is incorrect to say that the relative clause introduces a new line of thought. It is likewise incorrect to assert that "the ones who preached the gospel to you" (ὑμᾶς, this verb is construed with the dative or with the accusative) does not include the apostles, in this case Paul who labored in Galatia and in the province of Asia. We know what these things were which the gospel preachers published, which Peter's readers had heard and believed, the very things which the Spirit had testified in advance, the sufferings and glories of Christ, now no longer to be awaited, now realities that had come to pass. All these preachers used the old prophecies in all of their preaching; the old prophets were, indeed, ministering to Peter's readers.

The whole New Testament gospel rests on the Spirit's Old Testament testimony that was made through the Old Testament prophets. Cancel that testimony, and you remove the basis of the gospel of Christ. It was revealed to the prophets that their ministry was to be far grander than a ministry merely for themselves and for their time; it was a ministry for all of the future ages, for Peter's readers as well as for us to this day. The doxology of Peter is thus justified also in view of the means which God employed for our salvation and faith, namely the prophetic Word of the Old Testament followed by the New Testament preaching.

It makes little difference whether we have a simple dative Πνεύματι Ἁγίῳ or ἐν with this dative: "by the Holy Spirit" or "in connection with the Holy Spirit." The addition "sent or commissioned from heaven" undoubtedly refers to the outpouring of the Spirit on Pentecost. The Spirit moved these gospel preachers. If we could limit "those gospelizing you" to the apostles we should be willing to make this reference to the Spirit refer to inspiration; but we see no way of estab-

lishing this limitation. Not even historically. Was
Barnabas inspired every time he preached in Galatia?
Were the other assistants of Paul always inspired when
they preached in Asia? We do not know who the
preachers were that evangelized Pontus, Bithynia, and
Cappadocia but we hesitate to claim inspiration for
them. In fact, Gal. 2:11, etc., teaches us that even
Peter was not always inspired.

The ἃ clause is paralleled by the εἰς ἃ clause, and both
depend on αὐτά. So great and blessed are the things
pertaining to Christ that the Spirit who inspired the
prophets testified them in advance; that the Spirit enabled the gospel preachers to announce them where-
ever they went; and that even "angels desire to look
into them." We may recall Exod. 25:20, 21, the cheru-
bim on the mercy seat in the Tabernacle; the seraphim
in Isa. 6:2-8; the angels in connection with the giving
of the law, Acts 7:53; the angels in connection with the
birth and in connection with the resurrection of Christ,
and many other instances; their ministering to the
heirs of salvation; and then Eph. 3:10, the manifold
wisdom of God, hidden from the beginning in God,
made known to the angels by means of (διά) the New
Testament *Una Sancta*. The anarthrous ἄγγελοι emphasizes the fact that these beings are "angels." The
aorist infinitive means "to look into" effectively so as
to understand. The verb itself does not mean a mere
glance, "to peep covertly into," but simply "to look";
it conveys the thought that even when they do look
such heavenly beings cannot fully understand all that
these great things pertaining to Christ and to our
salvation contain.

Peter has the climax: prophets — gospel preachers
— angels, all concerned with Christ and our salvation,
the Holy Spirit being back of them all. Add this third
part of the doxology to the other two parts with all
that they touch upon and it will become evident that

this doxology is in grandeur second only to the one Paul wrote in Eph. 1:3-14.

Hortations
Due to the Relation to God, 1:13-2:10

Be Holy in All Your Conduct, v. 13-16

13) With διό Peter bases his hortation on the entire preceding doxology in which he expects his readers to join. Realizing all that his doxology says of them in their blessed relation to God, the readers will be ready to respond to the admonitions that are then justified. The first of these is that their whole manner of life should be holy even as the God whose praise they sing is holy.

Wherefore, having girded up the loins of your mind, as being sober, set your hope completely on the grace being brought to you in connection with Jesus Christ's revelation, as children of obedience not fashioning yourselves to the former lusts in the (old) ignorance, on the contrary, in accord with the Holy One who called you be you also on your part holy in all conduct!

Girding up the loins refers to the long, loose robes worn by Orientals, which were drawn up and belted at the waist when one wanted to walk or work with energy. This expression is used figuratively with reference to the mind, which includes thinking as well as the resultant willing, and the thought is: "Make up your minds decisively!" hence the aorist is used. Instead of letting their thoughts, purposes, decisions hang loose while they move leisurely along in life as impulse and occasion may move them, the readers are to gird up their minds like people who are energetically set on going somewhere. To gird up the loins means business, decision, action, not idling, not drifting after this and that momentary attraction.

The first participle is a decisive aorist, the second a present tense that describes a state: "as being sober," as having this quality. Our versions translate it with an imperative, but they do so only in order to make their English smoother. Both participles, the one denoting an act, the other a state, are subsidiary to the main verb "set your hope upon"; in order to do this one must make up his mind (aorist) and must be in a state of soberness (present). *Sobrietas spiritualis* is referred to, which is so frequently inculcated in Scripture: 4:7; 5:8; I Thess. 5:6, 8; Titus 2:4, 6; etc. Soberness is the opposite of infatuation with the things of this world, a calm, steady state of mind which weighs and estimates things aright and thus enables us to make the right decision. Not only the world with its allurements but also the various forms of religious error and delusion intoxicate the mind. The tenses determine the order: in a sober state of mind the readers are to make up their mind.

Thus they are to set their hope completely, with finality, on the grace being brought to them in connection with Jesus Christ's revelation. We cannot agree with Hort and M.-M. 629, who construe the adverb with the participle, even when the combination is understood to mean: "being sober with perfect sobriety." Τελείως does not mean "perfectly"; it conveys the idea of τέλος and thus = "with finality," in a way that ends matters. One is not sober in this way, but one may set his hope on something in this way. The English translation "to be perfectly sober" should not mislead the reader in regard to this Greek adverb. The aorist imperative goes well with the adverb: "set your hope with finality on the grace being brought to you," i. e., do not set your hope on this grace only tentatively or in a halfhearted way. This aorist is not constative as combining all of the hoping in the readers' lives; it denotes one decisive act.

Peter reverts to v. 3, to the living hope to which
the God and Father of our Lord Jesus Christ begot
the readers. Hope is a key word of this epistle. It expects something in the future. Peter has already said
that this is an inheritance incorruptible, unstained, unfading, kept for us in the heavens. He is not repeating
this sure object of our hope but tells his readers on
what they are to rest their hope for the heavenly inheritance, namely on God's grace (v. 2 and 10), "the
grace now being brought to us in connection with Jesus
Christ's revelation." Some again misunderstand ἐν
when they translate (as do our versions) "*at* Jesus
Christ's revelation." In the first place, as was the case
in v. 7, "Jesus Christ's revelation" undoubtedly is his
Parousia (compare, 4:13; I Cor. 1:7; II Thess. 1:7;
Rev. 1:1) and not some other revelation (the incarnation or the resurrection). Are we to set our hope on a
future grace at the end of the world so that the present
participle "being brought" really means "will be
brought"? These misunderstandings are cleared up
when ἐν is properly understood. The grace on which we
are to set our hope is the same as that mentioned in
v. 2 and 10, which is brought to us *now* in Word and
sacrament (constantly brought, present participle),
and this grace is connected with (ἐν, in connection
with) Christ's coming revelation, with his Parousia;
for all the grace which we constantly receive points
us to the glory and the inheritance of the last day. That
is why we are to set our *hope* on this grace, it will
carry us safely to the last day.

14) Hope and holiness are closely associated in
the Scriptures and must not be separated in life; compare, I John 3:3: "And everyone that hath this hope
set on him purifieth himself, even as he is pure." So
Peter writes: "as children of obedience not fashioning
yourselves to the former lusts in the (old) ignorance "
etc. "Children of obedience" takes us back to v. 3

God "begot us again to a living hope"; also to v. 2: "in sanctification unto obedience." Childhood and obedience go together. Luther and the A. V. translate: "as obedient children"; but the genitive is stronger than that. It describes the constitution and the character of these children, which is impressed upon them from their very birth, belongs to their very nature. In the same way they are termed "children of light," Eph. 5:8; the ungodly are "the sons of the disobedience," Eph. 2:2, and in v. 3, "children of wrath," in II Pet. 2:14, "children of curse."

The obedience here referred to is obedience to God's saving will or to the gospel and not a mere legal obedience or a moral life apart from the gospel. It consists in believing in Christ and in following him in love. "This is the work of God, that ye believe on him whom he hath sent," John 6:29.

What we are by virtue of our new spiritual nature must be manifested in our life and actions. Thus negatively: "not fashioning yourselves to the former lusts in the (old) ignorance." Συσχηματίζεσθαι = to adopt a certain σχῆμα for oneself, and here σχῆμα (our "scheme") is a certain form, fashion, or design of life, a *habitus*. Instead of referring to the wrong fashion of others as Paul does in Rom. 12:2: "Be not fashioned according to this world," Peter points to the wrong fashion of life which his readers themselves formerly had: not fashioning yourselves "to the lusts formerly in your ignorance." "Formerly" = before God begot you again (v. 3). "Formerly in the ignorance" is attributive, being placed between ταῖς and ἐπιθυμίαις, and thus describes the lusts referred to, *Begierden*, which is really a *vox media*, "desires," but is seldom used in a good sense. It would be monstrous for children of obedience to go back and to fashion and fit themselves again to those lusts of a former time "in the ignorance" in which they then lived. What have children of obedience to do with those old castoff lusts? The involuntary response must be: "Nothing whatever!"

"The ignorance" means pagan ignorance as it does in Acts 17:30 and Eph. 4:18. An issue is made of the use of this word in the present connection; it is said that the word shows that the readers were former Jews. Now ignorance is predicated also of the Jews in Acts 3:17; Rom. 10:3 (Luke 23:34; John 8:19); I Tim. 1:13. But there was this difference: the Jews knew God and his Word, the pagans did not. The Jews were zealous about God, "but not according to knowledge," Rom. 10:2; the pagans ran after idols. The Jews ignorantly tried to set up their own righteousness, Rom. 10:3, etc.; the pagans were ignorant of even the false Jewish righteousness. The Jews, too, lived "in the lusts of their flesh," Eph. 2:3, but not because of ignorance; they made the law an outward, formal thing, but the very Word they had contradicted them. Pagan ignorance was a mark of the lusts of pagans. One cannot prove that Peter's readers were former Jews by means of these lusts formerly "in ignorance." Some were former Jews, most of them were former pagans.

15) From the negative side Peter turns to the positive with the strong adversative ἀλλά; he does not, however, continue the participial construction but changes to a strong imperative: "on the contrary, in accord with the Holy One who called you be you also on your part holy in all conduct!" R. 127 calls the way in which Peter places modifiers between the article and the noun Thucididean; thus τὸν καλέσαντα ὑμᾶς ἅγιον. God is called "the Holy One" as our Caller in order to show that we, too, must be holy.

To the ideas of Father, children, being begotten again, Peter adds that of being called. The call brings us to him; and since he is holy, all those who are called must also be holy. God is holy in that he loves all that is pure and good and hates, abominates, and punishes all that is sinful. God is absolutely and *per se* immutably holy from all eternity, and he has without deviation revealed himself to men as being holy. But this revelation was given for the purpose of lifting us, who had fallen into sin, back unto holiness, for God is the source of holiness for men. Peter writes that the Holy One has called us to communion with himself, out of the darkness of ignorance to his own marvelous light (2:9), out of evil unto blessing (3:9), out of shame to eternal glory in Christ (5:10).

The aorist participle "called you" is historical and states the fact. The tense also implies that the call was effective, it brought the readers to faith and fellowship with the Holy One. The call is always issued by means of the gospel, which comes through "those preaching the gospel" (v. 12) and is filled with the saving power of grace. Αὐτοί is emphatic: "you also on your part," and the aorist imperative γενήθητε, which matches the aorist ἐλπίσατε, is simply a substitute for the aorist of εἶναι, which is not used. The passive form is only a form. The Koine loves and even coins such passives. The meaning is not "become!" but "be!" i. e., be decisively, settle it once for all that you be holy. When πᾶς has the article following it, it denotes a whole; when it is used without the article, as it is here, it summarizes a multiplicity: all or every manner of conduct, whether in business or pleasure, labor or rest, joy or sorrow, easy or difficult situations.

To be holy is our obligation, but not in the sense of an outward, legal requirement that is laid upon us, for which we must furnish the ability and the power, but as the result of God's call which furnishes the power and the ability. The gospel call to holiness always includes the bestowal of this spiritual power. The hand that points us to holiness is the hand that extends its grace to us to make us holy; by pointing us upward it lifts us upward. Thus the plea is cut off: "I am not able to be holy." The call to be holy implies that we still lack complete holiness, but also that we are able to overcome this lack by grace. This call spurs us on to use God's grace to the fullest extent in every part of our conduct so as to make it pleasing to the Holy One.

16) An Old Testament statement is cited to fortify Peter's injunction: **wherefore it has been written** and thus stands on record to this day (perfect tense): **Holy shall you be because I myself am holy,** Lev. 11:44; 19:2; 20:26. The future tense is imperatival. The requirement of holiness is fundamental for God's children in both Testaments. What God asked of Israel when he made that people his own he now asks and must ask of us whom he has called by Jesus Christ. God does not connive at sin and unholy living since forgiveness has come through Christ. Let no one think that he can remain among the children of obedience while he still fashions his conduct according to the old lusts. Only the pure in heart shall see God, and without holiness it is impossible to see him. Christ died, not to save us *in* our sins, but *from* our sins.

Conduct Yourselves in Fear, v. 17-21

17) When Peter calls God "the Holy One," who himself emphasizes the fact that he is holy, he indicates that men are to fear God, especially when they approach him. For that reason this second hortation follows the first, that the Holy One's children must themselves be holy. As the Holy One, God is the incorruptible Judge whom even we, his children, must face. Rabbinical Judaism preserved the conception of the *rex tremendae majestatis* who is approached only in fear. In the Jewish prayer *Shemone-Esre* he is addressed as the "great, mighty, and terrible God," and again: "Holy art thou, and terrible is thy name." G.

K. 98. With our great hope in God we must combine holy fear in all our earthly conduct.

Thus Peter continues: **And if you call as Father upon him who without respect to persons judges according to each one's work, conduct yourselves in fear for the time of your being transients, knowing that not with corruptible things, with silver or gold, were you ransomed out of your vain conduct handed down by your fathers but with precious blood as of a lamb blemishless and spotless, (namely that) of Christ, foreknown, on the one hand, before the world's foundation, made manifest, on the other hand, at the end of the times because of you, the believers through him in God, the One who raised him from the dead and gave him glory so that your faith and hope is with respect to God.**

Καί connects this section directly with the previous hortation; the third hortation, v. 22, has no connective. "As children of obedience" of the One who begot us (v. 3) and is holy we, too, must be holy (v. 16). As his children we will call upon him as "Father," we will draw near to the Holy One in prayer, and we must, therefore, conduct ourselves for the time that we are aliens in this world with holy fear lest at any time we lift up to the Holy One hands that are not holy (I Tim. 2:8) but stained with sin. The condition "if you call upon" is one of reality and takes it for granted that the readers do so, the present tense is iterative. To keep calling upon God "as Father" is to assume the position and to perform the acts of "obedient children" (v. 14) and to ask for this Father's gifts and blessings. Our calling upon him as Father is our answer to his having called us to be his own (v. 15).

But note well that when we call upon God "as Father," it is God, "the Holy One," he who in his holiness "without respect to persons judges each one's work." Obedient children will be the last to approach

God with presumption and to imagine that all they need to do is to call him "Father" in order to be acknowledged as his children. This the scribes and Pharisees once did (John 8:3), whom Jesus told that they knew neither him nor the Father (v. 19) and by their deeds proved to them that God was not their Father, that their father was the devil (v. 42-44), for he that is of God heareth God's words, which they did not do because they were not of God, they were not his children, he was not their Father (v. 47). Peter has in mind the Lord's Prayer: "Our Father who art in heaven," but also all that he had heard Jesus say to the scribes and Pharisees, all that Jesus said in the Sermon on the Mount about the Father seeing in secret (Matt. 6:4, 6), as well as many another word about God's Fatherhood and our childhood and sonship.

So many still think only of the word "Father" and forget that he is "the Holy One who without respect to persons judges each one according to his works." They convert him into an indulgent grandfather God who shuts an eye to the sins of his children, who, like Eli of old, takes no stern measures with them when they disobey. Not in vain do the apostles constantly repeat that God is no respecter of persons, that as such he accepts both Jewish and Gentile believers as children (Acts 10:34) but also judges all with absolute impartiality (Rom. 2:11; Eph. 6:9; Col. 3:25; James 2:1).

This compound of πρόσωπον, "face, countenance," and λαμβάνειν, "to take or accept," means that a judge shows favoritism to the person at the bar in disregard of the evidence and the facts of the case. God judges every man without favoritism or partiality of any kind "in accord with that man's work." Πατέρα is the predicate object, τὸν κρίνοντα the direct object, the substantivized present participle being qualitative: "him who judges" now or at any time.

The plural "works" is usually used, and this spreads them out; the singular "work" summarizes. We should not think that God selects only one work or a few that are either fair or faulty; he takes the real sum and substance of each man's life, which is either a doing of his gospel will or a rejection of that will. There is no discrepancy between judging according to work and judging according to faith: the work is the evidence of the presence or of the absence of faith. God sees and knows both the faith and its work as also the unbelief and its work; but in his public judgment he refers to the work because this is the public evidence which all men and all angels can see, all thus corroborate God's just and impartial judgments. No Christian is exempt from judgment. In fact, every Christian is happy to be judged, for his faith itself is the truest obedience, and all its fruit of work is evidence of that obedience and itself also true obedience.

On this ground Peter rests his hortation "conduct yourselves (second passive in the middle sense, intransitive) for the time of your παροικία (your being transients or πάροικοι, 2:11) in fear." The verb resumes ἀναστροφή which was used in v. 16; the aorist imperative is peremptory and is in line with the imperatives used in v. 13 and 15. This is not the "fear" of slaves which casts out love (I John 4:18), nor the awe of the infinite Creator in which the creature must stand, but the fear which is opposed to security, lightness, and indifference of mind in regard to God and his saving will and Word. "Fear God" (2:17). "Let us cleanse ourselves from all defilement of flesh and spirit, perfecting holiness in the fear of God," II Cor. 7:1. We call the impartial Judge our Father and ask his fatherly gifts and blessings; instead of destroying this relation our fear conserves it. Knowing that this impartial Judge is our Father, our fear will keep us from compelling him to disown and disinherit us.

As long as we are in this our παροικία, living as outsiders in this sinful world ("foreigners," in v. 1), beset with temptations and assailed even by our own flesh, this true and proper fear should never leave our hearts. Barnabas, one of the postapostolic fathers, wrote: "Let us be careful lest we yield to slothful rest and go to sleep in our sins after we have already been called so that the evil one may not get us into his power and exclude us from the kingdom of God." Quenstedt adds: "The apostle does not mean, lest we be not in God's grace but lest we fall from grace. Fear is the opposite of [false] security, not of joyful faith; and we do not reject the fear of vigilance and caution which is afraid of insulting God and falling into the danger of forsaking him, but we reject the fear that is due to doubt."

When men demand a God whom they need not fear, they demand an idol that does not exist. To decry the holy fear of God as an unethical motive is to pervert it. To be sure, those who are not obedient children of this Father and holy Judge cannot have the right conception of this motive; what awaits them is the terror of the Lord whom they defy. The truer the child of God, the more this child will dread to offend, even to ignore God and his just judgment. A prevalent opinion thinks that only the Old Testament preaches fear, the New Testament nothing but love. Jesus and the entire New Testament bid us fear God.

18) What prompts this fear and must ever be its source is the preciousness of the ransom paid for us. The participle is causal: "conduct yourselves in fear because you know" (the participle is an aorist like the imperative). Called of God, the Holy One, who is the absolutely impartial Judge, and by that call made holy and obedient children who may approach and call upon God as their Father, the readers certainly know the great cost of their ransom from the old con-

duct which they inherited from their pagan forefathers. This immense price should keep them in holy fear lest it have been paid in vain for them, and the impartial Judge should be compelled to render a verdict against them who, after being called, after being his children, regarded that price as nothing and went back to their old conduct. What verdict this impartial Judge would have to pronounce upon them is apparent. Matt. 11:20-24; 12:41-45.

'Ελυτρώθητε has its full native meaning, "you were ransomed," set free by the payment of a λύτρον, a ransom price. This ransom is named together with the slavery and bondage from which it set the readers free. "The Son of man came . . . to give his life a ransom for many," λύτρον ἀντὶ πολλῶν. See also Rom. 3:24; Col. 1:14; I Tim. 2:6; Titus 2:14; I Cor. 6:20. "You were bought with a price." Peter emphasizes the greatness of the ransom price: "not with corruptible things," and then names "silver or gold" as samples; compare v. 7, "gold that perishes." The most precious earthly metals are corruptible and perishable because they have value only among men, only for time. They are here fitly singled out since earthly captives are ransomed by the payment of a money price.

"Out of your vain conduct handed down from your fathers" states the bondage from which no gold or silver and no price that men could pay was able to ransom them. All the treasure of the world could not ransom a single pagan and save him from his pagan life. No corrupt ransom can save from a corrupt life. 'Αναστροφή repeats the noun that was used in v. 15 and the verb that was used in v. 17. Peter calls this conduct ματαία, "vain," in the sense that it fails to lead to the proper end. It was not κενή, "empty," because it was filled with godlessness, lusts, and countless sins; but it led to no good end, it carried the readers farther and farther from God, and they became men who were hopelessly lost. This conduct the readers had "given over to them from their fathers," it was the tradition they inherited; their fathers and former generations had nothing better to pass on to their descendants. Peter does not mention original sin directly but implies its existence. Save for God and the ransom he provided, the readers would have remained in their frightful bondage.

Peter speaks only of ransoming from former conduct and not from the bondage of guilt. The reason is apparent, namely his admonition to holy conduct. In his explanation of the Second Article of the Creed Luther also states this purpose of the ransoming: "purchased and won me . . . not with silver or gold but with his holy, precious blood, and with his innocent suffering and death, that I may be his own, and live under him in his kingdom and serve him," etc., with a totally new conduct. The ransoming out of vain conduct and out of guilt always go together. The old, unregenerate conduct is full of guilt and curse; to be placed in the new, regenerate conduct means to be freed from the old conduct and from its guilt.

"Handed down by your fathers" has been regarded as a reference to the Jews in an attempt to prove that Peter's readers were former Jews, for were they not strong traditionalists who clung to the teachings of their fathers? But the real fathers of the Jews were the patriarchs, prophets, etc. Peter's adjective refers to the entire conduct and not to a matter such as the traditions of the Pharisees who were but a Jewish sect. Peter has in mind the whole round of pagan life; he is writing to Christians who, for the most part, have come out of paganism and its dreadful bondage.

19) Great was the ransom price that was paid, it was "precious blood." The word τίμιος is already significant, for animal blood would scarcely be called "precious." Precious fits the idea of ransom, for ran-

som prices are high, a cheap ransom is out of the question, even silver and gold do not suffice. The fact that precious "blood" was paid as the ransom price for the readers at once suggests that someone died in their stead. Peter surely has in mind Matt. 20:28: δοῦναι τὴν ψυχὴν αὐτοῦ λύτρον ἀντὶ πολλῶν, "to give his life a ransom for many"; also John 10:15 (and 17): τὴν ψυχήν μου τίθημι ὑπὲρ τῶν προβάτων, "my life I lay down in behalf of the sheep." When Peter says "with precious blood" he undoubtedly means sacrificial blood shed in a sacrificial, expiatory death. That is why he does not say "death," for a death might occur in many ways and not necessarily by the shedding of blood. The connotation of sacrifice and substitution in "blood" has been denied; but all that one needs to do is to review the passages which deal with Christ's blood and his bloody death to see that this denial must itself be denied.

We construe together: "with precious blood as of a lamb blemishless and spotless." This combination brings out completely the thought that sacrificial, expiatory, substitutional blood is referred to. The very word "lamb" = one slain in sacrifice. Peter undoubtedly has in mind John 1:29, the words of the Baptist, whose disciple Peter had once been: "Behold the Lamb of God, which taketh away the sin of the world," plus v. 34: "This is the Son of God," whose blood is "precious" indeed.

It is generally assumed that Peter is thinking of Isa. 53, but it is debated whether he has in mind also the other sacrifices of lambs, in particular the Paschal lamb. Of what did the Baptist think when he called Jesus "the Lamb of God"? In our opinion this debate is misleading. It is settled when we note that Peter does not use ὡς as a comparative, in the sense of "like of a lamb," i. e., like some lamb in the Jewish sacrifices, but in the sense of reality, "as of a lamb." Heb. 12:7

is another instance: ὡς υἱοῖς ὑμῖν προσφέρεται ὁ Θεός: "as with sons, who are actually sons and not only like sons, God is dealing with you." The Old Testament and the Baptist do no more than to furnish the term "lamb" to Peter, by which he means Christ himself in his sacrifice, he being the one and only Lamb.

This clears up several other points. First of all the two adjectives: ἀμώμου καὶ ἀσπίλου, "of a lamb blemishless and spotless." The second adjective is not used in the Old Testament with reference to the lambs to be sacrificed. Peter is thinking of Christ himself, of the antitype which exceeds the type, and thus designates him as "a lamb." The point is that Christ is the great original, the types are only imperfect copies. This must not be reversed in our thinking so that Christ is made the copy. While ἄσπιλος may be used with reference to an animal, this is not done when blood and sacrifice are the context. Compare Eph. 5:27, "not having spot," also II Pet. 3:14, both refer to persons.

The observation is correct that the second adjective determines the force of the first and not vice versa. In other words, the person of Christ himself is in the mind of the writer and not an animal (lamb) and its physical condition. The absence of the article which makes "of a lamb" qualitative, is like Rev. 5:6: ἀρνίον ὡς ἐσφαγμένον, "a Lamb as having been slain," the noun is qualitative, ὡς again denotes actuality and is not to be taken in the sense of "like." The meaning is not: "some lamb" belonging to a class of lambs, all of which are blemishless and spotless; but Christ alone as such a lamb, there being no other.

Secondly, this explains why the apposition "as of a lamb," etc., is placed before "of Christ." To state that this relation must be reversed, that "of Christ" is the apposition, implies that one does not understand "the refined accuracy" (Bigg, page 4) with which Peter uses ὡς, an accuracy that is found in "the masters' style"; Bigg furnishes examples from Plato, Josephus, and the skillful writer of Hebrews (12:7) : "This subtilty was a stumbling block in later Greek." In 2:12 Peter has the other order, the apposition being placed second: καταλαλοῦσιν ὑμῶν ὡς κακοποιῶν.

20) Μέν and δέ balance the two participial modifiers, which bring out the thought that our ransom was certainly not paid with cheap, perishable values; it consists of precious blood of an incomparable lamb, namely of Christ, "foreknown, on the one hand (μέν), before the foundation of the world, made manifest, on the other hand (δέ), at the end of the times on your account," etc. First a perfect passive participle to denote the entire extent of the foreknowing; next an aorist passive participle to indicate the one historical act of making manifest or publishing; both have God as the agent. Here, as in v. 1, efforts have been made to change God's foreknowing into an act of the will, a decree, a foreordination or predestination. Peter might have said that Christ was predestinated, foreordained, elected, but he does not use such a term.

Other coordinate activities are necessarily connected with God's foreknowledge, especially decisions of his will. These may precede or may follow his foreknowledge; but however closely related to it they may be, these acts are not the foreknowledge itself. When we say this we must ever remember that God is not subject to time, that for him there is no "before" and no "after"; to speak of a sequence in connection with God is to use poor human language because we cannot even think in other, more adequate terms. So we say that in regard to Christ and to his precious blood the foreknowledge of God rested on his gracious decision to send him as our Ransomer; because God so decided he foreknew, the verb implies, not a bare previous knowledge, but one in which God was most deeply concerned *cum affectu et effectu*. The two activities are clearly distinct as Peter himself shows in Acts 2:23, where he speaks of Christ's deliverance into his sacrificial death "by the determinate counsel and (resting on this βουλή) foreknowledge of God." In the same way God's foreordination and counsel in regard to Christ are mentioned in Acts 4:28, but his foreknowledge is not referred to. For God, Christ was "the Lamb slain from the foundation of the world," Rev. 13:8.

Brenz writes thus: "The eye of God sees history in an entirely different way from the eye of flesh. God's eye sees everything in an instant. If in the eyes of God, Christ had not already existed as the One incarnate, dead, and glorified in the time of Adam and of Abraham, the patriarchs could never have obtained forgiveness of sins and justification." Besser's statement is still better; he says that Christ's sacrifice was seen by God as eternally present. "Before the foundation of the world" is an apostolic phrase, it = before time existed, thus in eternity, timelessly, God foreknew.

But all such references to eternity, as well as all connection between time and eternity, are beyond human comprehension. The foreknowledge in regard to Christ is connected with the foreknowledge concerning all who in the course of time come to believe in him, although in regard to them the foreordination follows the foreknowledge while in regard to Christ it precedes — as we remind ourselves anew in the poor human way of thinking to which we are bound, to which also Scripture condescends.

All that was foreknown by God before time and the world existed "was made manifest (or public) at the end of the times," of those between Adam and the days of Christ on earth. This publication was made when our Ransomer finally appeared and shed his blood, and when the gospel news of his ransoming was announced to all the world. The question is asked as to whether Peter includes Christ's pre-existence. It seems an idle

question since Christ is the Son of God. The adjective
ἔσχατον is used as a noun; compare "in the last days,"
Acts 2:17, and ἐπ᾽ ἐσχάτου τῶν ἡμερῶν τούτων, "at the end of
these days," Heb. 1:1.

The blood of him who was thus foreknown by God
eternally and manifested in the fulness of time has a
preciousness which utterly outranks any ransom that
consists of corruptible things. This blood is able to
ransom our souls. We who know and consider this
properly are bound to prize our ransoming so as to
walk in fear in order that at the end God, the impartial
Judge, may not pronounce upon us the awful verdict
we should deserve if we disregarded or scorned this
ransom.

21)   Peter makes all that he says about Christ's
precious blood most personal when he says that Christ
was foreknown and made manifest "because of you,
the believers in God, who raised him from the dead
and gave him glory." The publication was intended for
all men. When Peter says: δι᾽ ὑμᾶς, "because, on account
of you" or "for your sakes" he singles out his readers
because God's saving acts were accomplishing their
blessed purpose in them. Hence the apposition: you,
"the believers through him in God," etc.; πιστοί, like
πιστεύω, is construed with εἰς. What Peter says may be
addressed to us believers today. Christ and his ransoming blood are conceived as the medium or means that
produce faith in the readers; and thus they are described as "the believers in God, the One who raised
him from the dead and gave him glory," etc. By means
of these acts God declared that Christ's blood was
efficient as a ransom.

God raised up him who shed his blood and laid
down his life for us and then exalted him in glory.
Both statements refer to Christ's human nature; on the
glory compare John 17:1, 4, 5; on both acts Heb. 2:9,
10; 13:20. In both acts all the grace of God toward us

is manifested mightily, which justifies our faith in him completely and sets before us foreigners in this world the most glorious hope. But we should remember that this God is our holy and impartial Judge who will most certainly judge us whom he ransomed for himself at so great a price.

"Of the sixty-two instances of ὥστε with the infinitive in the New Testament nearly all are consecutive, not final nor even subfinal," R. 1000; hence: "so that your faith and hope is with respect to (or toward) God" and not "might be" (our versions). The emphasis is on εἰς Θεόν; he is the great surety for both our faith or confidence and our hope. The latter is added with reference to Peter's readers because they are addressed as "foreigners" in this world who have been begotten of God to a "living hope" (v. 1 and 3) and are to set their hope on God's grace (v. 13). With their faith and their hope so solidly anchored, the readers are to watch their conduct so that it may ever be that of "obedient children" who are passing the time of their position as aliens in this foreign world in fear.

It is rather fanciful to find a *parallelismus membrorum* in this statement: faith directed to God as the One who raised up Christ, hope directed to him as to One who gave Christ glory. Both faith and hope are directed to God, both are supported by God's raising up and glorifying Christ. Just as our faith looks to these two acts of God, so also does our hope. Nor should we say that "our faith is also hope toward God." To say that ὑμῶν applies only to faith, and that "hope" is thus a predicate, is to misunderstand the Greek; "our" is to be construed with both nouns and need not be repeated. Hope is added to faith because "living hope" was mentioned in v. 3 and because of our setting our hope on God's grace (v. 13). To place all the emphasis on "hope" is to do more than Peter himself does. Faith is never called "also hope." To live as "foreigners" in this world is possible only when we have both faith and hope, both of them looking to God and to what he has done in Christ, our ransom, who freed us from the old bondage.

Love Each Other from the Heart, v. 22-25

22)   God's call makes us his obedient children (v. 14), and by putting us into this relation to him (faith, hope, fear) it also places us into relation with each other. Thus love to each other follows the fear of God. We may say that when all "foreigners" (v. 1) in a foreign land are of the same nation they will surely stick together and aid each other; much more will this be the case if they are brothers and sisters who have the same Father (v. 17, also v. 3). The two admonitions: ἐλπίσατε (v. 13) and ἀναστράφητε (v. 17) are closely connected and are, therefore, connected with καί; this third admonition: ἀγαπήσατε, a decisive aorist like the other two and thus belonging to them, is without a coordinating καί, it is thus left to stand more independently.

Having purified your souls in the obedience to the truth for unhypocritical brotherly affection, love each other from the heart strenuously as having been begotten again, not from corruptible seed, but from incorruptible by means of God's living and abiding Word.

The two perfect participles, the one standing before, the other after the imperative, denote states that began in the past and are continuing: ἡγνικότες — ἀναγεγεννημένοι, the purified state, the regenerate state that began at the time of the conversion of the readers is still their state. The second participle is passive, they were begotten (in v. 3 we have the simple aorist active to denote the past fact: "the One who begot"). If these two perfects were aorists, they would simply register the past facts; if they were present tenses they would

den'ote only the present condition, the perfects say
more. "Having purified" goes back only to the result
of "having been begotten," and hence the latter is
added: the former is the proximate, the latter the
ultimate reason; the one states what we were able to
do, the other what God did regarding us.

'Αγνίζω is used with reference to ritual purifying,
but in the present connection it is moral: "having purified your souls in the obedience to the truth" (τῆς
ἀληθείας, an objective genitive). This recalls the "obedience" mentioned in v.. 2 as well as the "children of
obedience" mentioned in v. 14. "To the obedience"
with its article is specific to denote the obedience which
the truth requires and embraces the whole of it, the
acceptance of the truth in faith and the submission to
it in life. This truth is the whole gospel reality (ἀλήθεια,
"reality"). Yet Peter refers only to that feature of the
obedience which is especially required here: "for unhypocritical (unfeigned, sincere, honest) brotherly affection," φιλαδελφία, a compound of φιλία affection, not
ἀγάπη, which is reserved for the imperative. Brethren
should have brotherly affection for each other (see the
two verbs ἀγαπᾶν and φιλεῖν in John 21:15-17). The adjective = not wearing a mask such as ancient actors
wore on the stage to represent some fictitious character. There is always danger that we pretend like an
actor instead of having actual affection.

To have purified our souls for sincere, brotherly
affection is to have removed all evil thoughts and feelings from our hearts regarding our brethren; love has
free room to exert itself. Purity and truth match.
Truth itself is pure and produces purity; all impurity
conflicts with the gospel truth. Truth and "unhypocritical" also match. Truth is honest, lies pretend and
hide behind masks and shams. The A. V. follows the
ill-attested variant which adds "through the Spirit,"
which is correct enough but is not a part of the text.

With such purified souls Peter tells his readers to love each other from the heart strenuously. Again he writes an effective, strong aorist imperative (as he did in v. 13, 17). Ἐκ καρδίας (no article is needed with such phrases) recalls I John 3:18: "My little children, let us not love in word, neither with the tongue, but in deed and truth." "From the heart" marks the depth while the adverb ἐκτενῶς marks the intensity, "strenuously" as one stretches out and extends his effort to the limit. It is a mark of Peter's style to have one modifier preceding, another following, each being placed with discrimination.

Our loving efforts are not always appreciated, are sometimes received with coldness or even rebuffs. Often, too, brethren are not very lovable, and while we ourselves have love in our heart we do not always manifest it fully. Many a child has loved father or mother, but when death calls one or the other away, it has regretted too late that it has not shown its love more fully while the parent was still alive. Peter is unlocking the floodgates so that the full stream may gush forth.

Ἀγαπᾶν = the love of full intelligence and understanding coupled with corresponding purpose. This verb is often faultily defined even in the dictionaries although it is found throughout Scripture. In the LXX it may still be used to denote the lower forms of love; in the New Testament the definition we here give is the one that applies throughout even when publicans love publicans.

23) "Having been born again" (compare v. 3) brings out the thought that Peter's readers are, indeed, brethren, and are that in a far higher than the common, physical sense: "not from corruptible seed (σπορά, *Aussaat*, sown seed) but from incorruptible." We have the same word which was used in v. 18: "not with corruptible things were you ransomed." Cor-

ruptible seed brings forth flesh unto death; the incorruptible seed of the Word brings forth life everlasting. In v. 3 the One who begot us and to what he begot us are made prominent; now the divine seed or sowing by which we have been begotten as children of God is emphasized. "Out off" ἐκ, states the source of spiritual life and names the seed; διά adds the thought that this seed is the means for our being begotten and adds the idea of what this seed really is: "by means of God's living and abiding Word," v. 25: "And this is the utterance, the one proclaimed as good news to us," i. e., the gospel.

"Living" recalls v. 3, "unto a living hope." We construe both participles with λόγου and not with Θεοῦ. God is, indeed, often called "living," but not "abiding." With the expression "living and abiding Word" Peter simply states the main point of the quotation from Isa. 40:6-8; hence the R. V. margin should be canceled. Heb. 4:12 calls the Word "living and active"; Jesus says: "Heaven and earth shall pass away, but my Word shall not pass away," Matt. 24:35. The point is to show the exalted nature of the life that is in us believers, the life that makes us brethren in the divine sense: we all have been begotten of incorruptible seed by means of God's living and abiding Word. This life in us constitutes us "foreigners" to all unregenerate men, "elect," and far above them (v. 1), a family and a brotherhood whose true fatherland is heaven, "the city that has the foundations, whose architect and maker is God," Heb. 11:10. While we are, indeed, to love all men, yet as brethren we are able to love only those who are equally regenerated with us. "Love the brotherhood" (2:17). "Let us do good unto all men, especially unto them who are of the household of faith," Gal. 6:10.

24) Διότι introduces a quotation, yet not as a proof but only as a statement of the ancient prophet that says

exactly what Peter himself says about the nature of the Word. It is so much to the point because it compares the corruptible and the incorruptible (flesh and the Word) : **for** (to use the words of another, namely Isa. 40:6-8)

**All flesh (is) as grass,
and all its glory as bloom of grass.
Withered the grass, fallen the bloom!
But the utterance of the Lord abides for the
    eon.
And this is the utterance, the one proclaimed as good
news for you.**

"All flesh" = all men in their natural state as they exist in their bodily, natural life, as they are born to their earthly parents. All flesh is "as grass," χόρτος, herbage that grows in meadow and in field, mostly grass. The second line heightens the simile: "and all its glory as bloom of grass." The Hebrew has "goodliness," all that is fair, attractive, grand about "flesh." It is like "bloom of grass," its tasselled flower. The simile is true: all that man is proud of in his earthly existence, beauty, strength, wealth, honor, art, education, learning, virtue, achievement, greatness, is but the bloom of the grass and no more. ·

Stunning is the third line which has the verbs placed forward: "Withered the grass, fallen the bloom!" two gnomic aorists to denote what always happens. The tenses are timeless. In the hot Orient the sun blasts grass and herbage even more rapidly than in our temperate climate. Ξηραίνω = "to dry up"; ἐκπίπτω, "to fall off." Transient, indeed!

25) But the ῥῆμα, the spoken Word, of the Lord (Yahweh) remains for the eon, εἰς τὸν αἰῶνα, forever. From this μένει Peter has taken his μένοντος; as that of Isaiah is construed with ῥῆμα Κυρίου, so that of Peter is construed with λόγου Θεοῦ. Δέ adds the explanatory

statement: "Now this is the utterance that is gospeled (or was gospeled) for you," for the gospel, too, is God's own utterance. Preached as glad tidings to you, it entered your hearts and regenerated you, imparted its eternal life to you, overcame what is corruptible and perishing by replacing it with what is incorruptible and remains forever. It is for us, then, to rejoice in our ransoming and regeneration, in our faith and our hope, and ever to remember the price of the former and the power of the latter so that, living in fear and exercising our new life in love, we may reach the end of our faith, "salvation of souls" (v. 9).

CHAPTER II

Long for the Guileless Milk of the Word,
v. 1-3

1) The great doxology (1:3-12) begins with praise to God, who is the One who begot us again. All hortations that follow grow out of this our relation to God: 1) since he who begot us is holy, we, too, must be holy (1:13-16); 2) since he is our Judge and has ransomed us at so great a price, we must conduct ourselves with fear (1:17-21); 3) since we are begotten of the incorruptible seed of the Word we are brethren, and thus our relation to each other must be one of love, of children of the one Father (1:22-25). So Peter now proceeds to the next hortation: 4) since we have been begotten by means of the eternal Word we should long for the milk of the Word as our true and proper nourishment. We thus see how Peter's hortations advance step by step in proper order.

Accordingly, having put away from yourselves all baseness and all guile and hypocrisies and envies and all defamations, as newborn babes long for the milk native to the Word, without guile, in order that in connection with it you may be made to grow unto salvation, if you did taste that the Lord is benignant. Oὖν adds this admonition as being one that accords with what has just been said in 1:23-25 about our having been begotten again by means of God's living and abiding Word. Born anew of the Word, we must be nourished to growth by the Word.

Our having been begotten again means that we have once for all broken with our past life and have started anew in a spiritual life: "having put away from yourselves (aorist: definitely, effectively, as

being reborn by the Word) all baseness," etc. This
must be emphasized, for without this decisive break
with the past it would be useless for Peter to urge
his readers to nourish themselves with the Word. The
vices that must be put away are those that pertain
to our relation with men. The idea is not that sins
that are committed directly against God do not matter,
but that our treatment of men is the evidence and the
result of our new relation to God. We note that this
truth is expressed in I John 4:20. It is an easy matter
to apply this test in any case, and it is the more proper
here where the admonition to the love of the brethren
has just preceded. In Matt. 5:23 Jesus, too, bids his
hearers to get into the right relation with a fellow man
before they try to draw nigh to God.

We should distinguish between κακία, "baseness,"
and πονηρία, "wickedness," and hence not translate as
the R. V. does. Nor does this word mean "malice"
(A. V., R. V. margin) ; the word means "baseness,"
meanness, all good-for-nothingness, and connotes dis-
gracefulness. It includes all the sins against the second
table of the law. The rest of the vices are specifications
of "all baseness." "All guile" = craft, cunning, which
intends to deceive and to mislead others to their own
hurt and to our own supposed advantage, the original
meaning of δόλος being a bait for fish. We should group
together "all guile and hypocrisies and envies," for the
three "all" introduce three separate groups. One form
of guile is hypocrisy toward others (compare the explanation of "unhypocritical" in 1:22). Back of this
guile and hypocrisy there is often envy, the ill-will
that is stirred up at sight of the good fortune of others.
The two plurals indicate the different forms of these
sins, which are types of "all baseness."

The third group, "all defamations" = all speaking
against others that runs them down. This is also plural
because Peter has begun to use plurals. Like Jesus in

Matt. 5:22, Peters stops with the misuse of the tongue and does not add base deeds. It is sufficient to stop with this because defamations are the first outward evidence, and where this is absent, base deeds will not follow. First the tongue lashes out, then the hand or the fist follow.

2) "As just-now-born babes" matches the participles used in 1:3, 23; all three expressions refer to our regeneration and new birth. The ἄρτι, "now or just now," of this compound verbal is not to be understood in a literal sense: recent converts who are still in the condition of babes and sucklings, who are, therefore, to be fed only milk and not solid food. Peter does not introduce a contrast between milk and solid food such as that mentioned in I Cor. 3:2 and Heb. 5:13, 14.

An argument in regard to the length of time Peter's readers have been Christians that is based on this expression, is unsound. Paul's work in Galatia and in the province of Asia had been done many years ago, and Peter also includes all of these earliest converts. Peter wants all of his readers, whether they are beginners or veterans in the new life, to act as just-born babes in regard to their longing to be nourished with the Word. The point of the figurative language is this: as a babe longs for nothing but its mother's milk and will take nothing else, so every Christian should take no spiritual nourishment save the Word. The imagery is beautiful and expressive. Look at a babe at its mother's breast! In this way you should ever drink the milk of the Word. Peter understood the intent of Jesus' action which is recorded in Matt. 18:2, 3 and here carries the illustration which Jesus used still farther, down to babes that have just been born.

The rendering of the A. V.: "the sincere milk of the Word," is truer to the sense than that of the R. V.

The *crux interpretum* is found in the first adjective of the expression τὸ λογικὸν ἄδολον γάλα. We have no proper English word to render λογικόν, which is found only here and in Rom. 12:1. The opinion that Peter adds this world in order to indicate that "milk" is to be understood figuratively so that we may translate "the spiritual milk," is unwarranted since the figurative "just-born" babes precedes and needs no addition to convey the idea that it is not to be taken literally. Λογικός is used by secular writers in the sense of "reasonable," "logical" (see Liddell and Scott for samples); but whereas this might be considered as a meaning in Rom. 12:1, who would think of using it in connection with "milk," although the R. V. margin does so?

We note that ἄδολον, "guileless," resumes the idea of δόλος (v. 1); and thus it seems that λογικόν resumes the thought of διὰ λόγου in 1:23 and thus designates this milk as being that of the Word, derived from the Word, or — preferably — as being of the same nature as the Word, say "native to the Word." We note in support of this view that the first meaning of λογικός is "belonging to speech, capable of speech" (Liddell and Scott), thus here belonging to λόγος, the one mentioned in 1:23: "God's Word living and abiding." Word-milk is the meaning. The A. V.'s translation "the milk of the Word" thus approaches Peter's meaning, considering the fact that the English lacks an adjective such as the Greek has in λογικός, which is derived from λόγος. Compare also such words as ψυχικός (for which we have no English term), πνευματικός, etc.: belonging to and of the nature of ψυχή (the natural life); belonging to and of the nature of πνεῦμα or spirit, for which word we do have "spiritual."

By calling this milk λογικόν Peter would state its nature: the milk that belongs to the divine λόγος or

Word; by adding ἄδολον he brings out the thought that
this milk is unlike that found in any other λόγος: it is
without the least guile to mislead or to deceive. All
other (human) word (teaching, doctrine, spoken or
written) is not "guileless." This divine Word is;
"guileless" states the moral quality of this Word-milk.
It is perfectly safe for babes to take although they,
being just born, have no ability to be careful as to
what they drink. We do not think that ἄδολον means
"unadulterated." As far as the two adjectives are
concerned, why should we suppose that only the first
and not also the second indicates that "the milk" is
figurative, spiritual milk — if such an indication were
necessary, which it is not?

"Long for this milk!" Peter writes and uses the
decisive aorist imperative exactly as he did in 1:13,
17, 23. These aorists are used because they are
stronger than present imperatives would be. Call them
constative if you will. The implication is: long for
this milk and for none other. Even Christians often
hanker after the fleshpots of Egypt and grow tired of
the simple, wholesome, saving Word, which is manna
for the soul. To cease longing for the divine milk is
the most serious sign of spiritual decline, which soon
ends in spiritual death. A starved babe pales and dies.
Note Ps. 119:20: "My soul breaketh for the longing
that it hath unto thy judgments at all times."

"In order that in connection with it you may be
made to grow unto salvation" does not mean that
the readers cease to be newborn babes and grow up
to be men. Paul speaks of childhood and manhood in
this way by making full-grown manhood the ideal.
Not so Peter. As he states no contrast between milk
and solid food, so he has no advance from babes to
men. We are ever babes, ever long for this divine
milk, and so grow unto salvation, the end of our faith,

salvation of souls (1:9). Ἐν means "in connection with" this milk.

We should not extend the idea of the verb αὐξηθῆτε as though it indicates a growth from babyhood to old age. It is an aorist passive and deals only with babes, who grow in the sense of being alive and hearty and thus as babes attain eternal salvation. God makes them grow thus; while the aorist is constative it has its termination only in salvation and not in any stage of growth. Peter's thought is quite simple and should not be made complex.

3) When Peter attaches the condition of reality: "if you did taste that the Lord is benignant," he asks his readers to recall their experience with the Lord and counts on the fact that they have found the Lord χρηστός, kind or benignant, bestowing only what is wholesome and pleasant. There is no play on words between χρηστός and Χριστός, for Peter uses Κύριος, and the adjective that is derived from χράομαι has nothing to do with χρίω, "to anoint, the Anointed." He alludes to Ps. 34:9: "Oh, taste and see that the Lord is good!" Peter is not quoting; he simply appropriates the psalmist's statement to express his own thought. What is true of Yahweh is equally true of Christ.

Having tasted that the Lord is benignant does not make the Lord "the milk" as some suppose. They overlook the passive verb "be made to grow," which implies an agent, namely this beneficent Lord. It would be a strange conception to picture the Lord as milk. Nor does Peter say, nor does the psalmist say that we are to taste the Lord but that we are to taste "that he is good," beneficent in bestowing this precious milk of the Word upon us, in making us grow unto salvation. Do we know of anyone else who has such food for us? What we taste is his benignity, which we experience in his Word. "Taste" is a suitable word for both "milk" and benignity.

Living Stones in a Spiritual House
— Yea, a Holy and Royal Priesthood,
v. 4-10

4)   A new line of thought is begun: from the idea of babes who merely receive the beneficent care of the Lord, Peter advances, with imagery that is entirely different, to living stones in a spiritual house, yea, to holy, royal priests who render acceptable sacrifice. Yet by starting this new line of thought with a relative clause Peter indicates that this and the preceding paragraphs belong together, our experience of the Lord's care and what he makes of us. He retains the idea of life in the expression "living stones," the life to which we have been begotten (1:3, 23). He pictures us as "a spiritual house," namely the Lord's temple, and advances from that image to the figure of priests serving in this temple. This is, indeed, a distinguished priesthood, especially when we remember what we once were (v. 9b, 10).

The simplicity of the connection by means of a relative clause is admirable. The striking change of figure plus the advance from a house to priests in that house, is no less than grand. This is the great doctrine of the spiritual priesthood of all believers, and that a royal priesthood, one that was long forgotten in Catholicism but was brought fully to light again by Luther and the Reformation.

Four hortations have preceded, but this paragraph is not a hortation. Peter does not urge: "Be such stones, such a house, such a priesthood!" He declares that we *are* all of this. This means that he now sets forth the basis on which the preceding hortations rest. No wonder he bids us to be holy in all our conduct (1:13-16), to conduct ourselves in fear of God (v. 17-21), to be bound together in love (v. 22-25), to keep only to the Word (2:1-3) — all four hortations growing directly out of our connection with God as children who have been begotten by him. We only point out these things; they deserve our fullest, penetrating study.

Still more is to be said. We are "elect foreigners" in this world and are now fully shown what this means, and why at the beginning of this letter Peter breaks forth in exalted praise of God for what he has made of us who at one time were no people of his at all (v. 10). Our holy relation to God as his holy and royal priesthood makes us foreigners to the profane world. What if the unholy world visits manifold trials, hardships, persecutions upon us to cause us grief (1:6); what are these in comparison with our heavenly birth and our royal, priestly standing with God?

This section closes the first part of Peter's letter, closes it in the same grand way in which the doxology (1:3-12) began it; and it is now apparent how closely knit this whole first part is, also how perfectly it is adapted to the readers and meets their need as foreigners in this world.

Peter writes: **To whom coming, a living stone, by men, indeed, having been on test rejected, with God, however, elect, in honor, you yourselves also as living stones are built a spiritual house for a holy priesthood to offer up spiritual sacrifices acceptable to God through Jesus Christ.**

Is οἰκοδομεῖσθε an indicative passive: "you are being built," or an imperative passive or middle: "be built" or "build yourselves"? To point to the preceding imperatives as proof for the use of another imperative means to overlook the fact that the four preceding imperatives are aorists, which this fifth would not be. This cannot be accounted for by saying that durative action is now in place whereas such action is not in place in the other imperatives. Quite the contrary; "be setting your hope" (1:13), "be conducting yourselves" (1:17), "be loving" (1:22), "be longing for" (2:2) would be entirely in place if "be built, let yourselves be built, or build yourselves" were intended as a fifth imperative. The argument for another imperative overlooks the fact that we now have a relative clause, and that an imperative is not to be expected in a relative connection. Furthermore, to find an imperative idea in the participle "to whom coming" or in the infinitive "to offer up sacrifices" is unwarranted even if the main verb were imperative.

Then, too, a passive: "be built," would be incongruous. A command to build would apply only to the builder and order that *he* build and not to the stones which the builder uses. This is also true in the case of the permissive "let yourselves be built." *Stones* do not let themselves be built. "Build yourselves" (middle reflexive) cannot be the sense, for when the verb (or its compound "build up") is so used, the reflexive pronoun is added as the examples show. This whole paragraph states what God is doing for us and what we now are (note v. 9) in contrast with what we once were (v. 10). Therefore the connection is properly made by means of a relative clause, relative to our connection with Christ, not commanding anything but setting forth our connection with Christ the Lord (v. 3), which includes his Word, which serves as the basis for the four hortations occurring in 1:13-2:3. If we were not being built up as is here stated, if we were not what v. 9 states that we are, such hortations could not be addressed to us.

We may ask why Peter uses such a figure in support of his hortations: a temple and a priesthood which culminate in the grand designations used in v. 9. "*Elect*," here and in v. 9, "those once not a people but now God's people," (v. 10), "*living* stones," and all that is said of Christ and of our connection with him, should lead us to see the pertinency of Peter's figure and of the Scripture that supports it. We are *"elect strangers"* in the world (1:1), ours is a *"living* hope" (1:3); thus we are God's holy temple and a priesthood in the world and thus foreigners to the world. Looked down upon by the world and subjected to many trials as foreigners, we are in reality foreigners because God has elected and made us far superior to the world (John 15:19-21). It has no use for such a holy temple and such a priesthood, for the world is low and utterly profane. The Christ that is our all the world rejects; to the world he is a stone of stumbling (v. 8). If we follow out these connections, the thought of Peter will rise before us in all its power.

"To whom coming" is merely descriptive without special reference to time; hence the verb is not an aorist, "having come," which would be historical. Peter needs only to say "to whom *coming"* since in 1:15 he has mentioned "the One who *called* you" and has described his readers as "the *believers* through Christ in God," 1:21. There is no need of taking the present tense to refer to a constant coming to Christ; it is enough to think of our contact with him, which is also indicated by repetition of the πρός of the participle instead of the usual dative, πρός being the face-to-face preposition as Robertson calls it. God's gracious call brings us to Christ and makes us believers; and thus "coming to Christ" we are built up, etc.

Λίθον ζῶντα is an apposition to the relative ὅν and describes Christ to whom the readers come. When we translate "*a* living stone," this is due only to the helplessness of the English. The absence of the Greek article intends only to stress the qualitative force of the noun "stone," which the added modifiers make entirely definite so that we may also translate "*the* living stone," etc. Peter himself cites the Old Testament passages which describe Christ as "the living stone." Stones are dead; we even say "stone-dead." This fact makes the paradox of the *living* stone all the greater.

There is in reality a double figure in "stone." There is first a reference to other stones as they are used for a building, and there is secondly a reference to stumbling over a stone (v. 8), which Jesus himself greatly intensifies in Matt. 21:44 by picturing this stone as also falling on the unbeliever and crushing him to powder. "Living" describes this stone as one that is full of life and has all the power of life, for this stone is the person of our Lord. Λίθος, too, is the proper word because a stone that is used for building is referred to. Peter does not use πέτρος, "a rock" or "boulder," nor πέτρα, embedded rock, which would be fitting only in the case of stumbling (v. 8), compare Rom. 9:33.

Peter quotes Ps. 118:22 (Matt. 21:42), the very passage which he, like Jesus, once used against the Sanhedrin, Acts 4:11: "by men, indeed, (μέν) having been on test rejected, with God, however (δέ), elect, in honor." There is a contrast between men and God. Peter amplifies: those who first rejected this stone were "the builders" (v. 7), the leaders of Israel, the Sanhedrin; all others who still reject him merely repeat that act of the Jews, hence Peter says rejected "by men." The perfect participle ἀποδεδοκιμασμένον contains these thoughts: men tested this stone, in their judgment this stone did not meet the test, thus they rejected this stone, and it now remains in this condition, namely tested by them and rejected.

"On the other hand (δέ), with God elect, in honor" does not add the counterpart: "tested by God and approved as genuine" as though God needed to test Christ; no, this stone ever was "with God elect, in honor" (v. 6; Isa. 28:16). God chose this stone in the first place because he knew it was what it was; he prized and honored it accordingly, and there was never a question that it would fulfill its great purpose. By the very tests which these men who reject this stone apply they show that they want only a poor, earthly stone; by their tests and their findings they place themselves most violently in opposition to God.

5) Peter borrows the words "stone," "rejected," "elect, in honor" from the Old Testament; but Peter himself adds the paradoxical conception that this wonderful stone is living. This stunning paradox he extends so as to include his readers who, by coming to the living stone, are also no less than "living stones." Christ himself declares that he is the life (John 14:6; 11:25; compare 1:4); he has life in himself just as the Father has (John 5:25). The truth that those who through God's call come to ˘Christ as believers are partakers of Christ's life is likewise frequently declared (John 3:15, 16). The fact that Peter combines this life with the imagery of stones is the striking and significant feature in this connection. Peter uses ὡς as he used it in 1:19. He would not say that his readers are *like* living stones — for nature has no such stones — but desires to say that they *are* such stones, strange as this may sound. Yet, after having called Christ "the living stone" to say that the readers καὶ αὐτοί are such living stones takes away some of the newness of the conception, especially when the great predicate is at once added.

When he is speaking of Christ, Peter does not use ὡς but the direct apposition λίθον ζῶντα; when he is speaking of his readers he says ὡς λίθοι ζῶντες. The fact that they are "as living stones" is due to their connection with Christ, "the living stone." The terms "Christ" and "Christian" show the same similarity of expression. Both of Peter's expressions become clear and pertinent when we consider the predication "you yourselves are built a spiritual house for a holy priesthood to offer up spiritual sacrifices," etc. These living stones do not lie about loosely, they constitute a "spiritual house for a holy priesthood," etc. We have been prepared for this predicate by the preceding participle "coming to the Lord" (Christ). Peter does not go beyond this coming to him; all his readers are joined to Christ and thus are this house; the circumstance that this fact also joins all the readers to each other need not be added.

The agent back of οἰκοδομεῖσθε is God. The present tense, like that of the participle προσερχόμενοι, is merely descriptive. Some regard the tense as a progressive present to indicate God's continuous work in the readers; we deem it better not to understand it as referring to an unfinished house because no priesthood could function in such a temple. At any period of its history the *Una Sancta* is a completed temple in which God dwells and accepts the sacrifices offered to him. This fact explains why the aorist "were built" would be inappropriate, for that tense would refer only to the historical past as though a certain date when the house was finished were in the mind of the writer; but we could not name such a date.

When these living stones are combined, the result is "a spiritual house," "the church of the living God," I Tim. 3:15. "Spiritual" is the opposite of material. This word helps us to understand what kind of life is referred to by the participle "living" as we now look at the result of this our coming to Christ. Israel had a material temple, a type and a symbol of the spiritual house that Israel itself was to be yet failed to be. The New Testament church is this true spiritual house of God. Peter does not write ἱερόν, "temple," because that word would also include the courts and the additional buildings about the sanctuary proper. So he also does not write ναός, "sanctuary," because that would imply auxiliary structures since a sanctuary was never without these. Οἶκος, "house," avoids both of these connotations which are not wanted here.

We read the entire predication as a unit: "are built a spiritual house for a holy priesthood to offer up spiritual sacrifices," etc. We insert no comma. The house and its purpose belong together. In this passage οἶκος does not mean a dwelling for a family; all priests do not dwell in one residence, and still less do they offer up sacrifices in their residences. The reference to "priesthood" and to "sacrifices" makes this house a temple or sanctuary in which God dwells and receives these sacrifices.

The A. V.'s translation omits εἰς on insufficient textual authority. Its omission causes the incongruity of making "priesthood" an apposition to "house" and thus states that both are built of living stones. A spiritual house "for" a holy priesthood is conceivable; stones built into a priesthood are not. As Paul does in a number of figures, Peter, too, lets the reality dominate the figure and not, as we are often inclined to do, the figure the reality. Thus he does not let the living stones (his readers) be a mere house in which others (who would they be?) offer sacrifices to God; Peter's readers are "a spiritual house for a holy priesthood to offer up sacrifices," etc., i. e., they are both this house and this priesthood; the house and its priesthood are never separated. Hence this is a spiritual house. Ἱεράτευμα is not "priesthood" (abstract) in the sense of priestly office, although this idea would simplify the thought, but the whole body of priests (concrete).

The distinction between high priest and common priests no longer exists since one is our High Priest forever, who, after offering up himself once for all, has passed into the heavens. So all believers now constitute the priesthood on earth. No longer are some persons priests while many more are the people for whom such priests function. All of the material, bloody sacrifices have been abolished; all believers have the same right of direct priestly access to God, all of their sacrifices are now purely "spiritual." Credit Luther with bringing this great Scriptural fact to light once more and let no self-constituted priesthood ever insert itself between us believers and God! "Holy priesthood" = separated unto God. We are constantly called ἅγιοι, "holy ones" (saints), in Holy Writ (1:15, 16) ; this is sometimes changed to ἡγιασμένοι, "they who have been made holy," have been cleansed and sanctified by the truth (John 17:17-19) in justification and in a new life.

The main task of the Old Testament priests was the offering of material, animal sacrifices, all of which pointed to Christ's great sacrifice to come. These are no longer needed since Christ offered his all-sufficient sacrifice once for all. Now there remain for God's holy priesthood only the sacrifices of praise and thanksgiving, seeing that all the treasures of God's grace are now poured out upon us through Christ. Thus Peter writes regarding all his readers: "to offer up spiritual sacrifices acceptable to God through Jesus Christ," ἀνενέγκαι, aorist, derived from ἀναφέρειν, to carry or bring up on the altar of their hearts. The aorist infinitive is effective: actually to bring. "Spiritual sacrifices" matches "spiritual house," the adjectives are placed chiastically, the repetition emphasizes the fact that everything in the relation of the readers to God through Christ is now altogether spiritual.

Regarding these sacrifices note Heb. 13:15: "Through him, therefore, let us keep offering up sacrifice of praise constantly to God, that is, fruit of lips confessing his name; moreover, the doing of good and fellowship do not be forgetting, for with such sacrifices God is well pleased." Rom. 12:1: "To present your bodies a living sacrifice well pleasing to God." Paul uses "living" much as Peter does. Phil. 4:18: "An odor of a sweet smell, a sacrifice acceptable, well pleasing to God." Rev. 8:3: "The prayers of all the saints upon the golden altar before the throne." The public preaching of the Word is not included among these sacrifices of the universal priesthood of believers because, although this work is also to be rendered as a sacrifice to God, a special call to perform this duty is necessary, and it is allotted only to those who are thus specifically called.

These sacrifices are "acceptable to God through Jesus Christ" because they are rendered in his name and for his honor as evidences and fruits of the life he has begotten in us (1:3, 23). "Through Jesus Christ" = their acceptance is mediated wholly through him (διά to express mediation). We approach God only through Christ, on the strength of his sacrifice for us; and he and his sacrifice cover up all imperfections that still cling to our sacrifices. It should be generally known that Masonry uses this passage from Peter in its ritual; but it significantly omits this last phrase "through Jesus Christ" and thus certifies to its own anti-Christian character.

Peter's words suggest an implied contrast with the Old Testament people of God: they had a house of God, but we ourselves are now the house; their temple was built of dead stones, we are living stones; they approached God through a priesthood, we ourselves are the priesthood; they offered up material sacrifices, ours are purely spiritual. Rome insists that we must still approach God through a specific priesthood, the papal hierarchy; others have similar ideas about the office of the ministry being an intermediary between the believers and God. Regarding these errors compare *C. Tr.* 523, 63-69.

6) What Peter has just said is contained already in the Old Testament prophecies which speak of Christ

as a wonderful stone. God would lay this stone, and the prophecies state what this stone and God's laying of it mean for those who believe as well as for those who reject this stone and are disobedient in unbelief. These quotations are not to be regarded as a proof for what Peter says in vs. 4, 5. We see at a glance that they contain nothing about the priesthood and the sacrifices of believers. All of the citations deal with Christ as the great stone elect and honored by God, our blessed relation to this stone, and this stone's effect on those who reject it. We may thus say that Peter proves from Scripture that Christ is, indeed, the living stone (v. 4). But this is too narrow a view, for these Old Testament passages elucidate and add to what Peter himself says about this stone. Peter lets the Old Testament Scriptures speak for him instead of himself saying what they contain. Verses 4, 5 are expository of v. 6-8, the latter also being expository of the former. This is the object of the quotations; vs. 4-8 are a unit.

After we understand the purpose of these quotations, their form of citation will also become clear to us. Peter takes three passages which have the figure of the stone or rock. Since he is concerned about the substance of the thought, verbatim accuracy would be pedantic, interpretative rendering is what Peter offers just as we to this day adapt the wording of a quotation for the purpose we may have in hand save in regard to those words which are essential for our purpose. The formula διότι περιέχει ἐν γραφῇ thus states no more than that the quotations are found somewhere in the Scripture. The verb is impersonal, the connective indicates that Scripture warrants the way in which Peter speaks of Christ in v. 4, 5.

Wherefore it is contained in Scripture:

Behold, I place in Zion a stone as corner-head, elect, in honor;

**And the one believing on him shall not be
ashamed** (Isa. 28:16) ;
for you, accordingly, is the honor as the ones believing, but for such as disbelieve
**The stone which those building did on test
reject,**
This One became corner-head (Ps. 118:22) ;
and :
**A stone of stumbling and a rock of entrap-
ment** (Isa. 8:14),
who stumble against the Word by being disobedient,
for which they also were appointed.

The Hebrew reads: "Behold, I lay in Zion for a
foundation a stone, a tried stone, a precious cornerstone, a sure foundation; he that believes shall not
make haste." The LXX renders *ad sensum* and inter-
pretatively: "Behold I lay for the foundations of Zion
a stone of great value, elect, corner-head, precious, for
her foundations; and he who believes on me shall not
be ashamed." Peter cites only what he needs for his
purpose: "stone" and "elect, precious," which he uses
in v. 4; then the elucidating adjective ἀκρογωνιαῖον, "as
corner-head," plus the clause about the one believing
(in v. 4: "to whom coming," i. e., in faith). Peter
does not make use of the two references to "the foundations" (LXX, τὰ θεμέλια). He does not follow Eph.
2:20; only after a fashion does he follow I Cor. 3:11,
12 where Paul makes Christ the entire foundation without reference to a cornerstone. Peter speaks of his
readers as being built up, as living stones, as forming
a spiritual house. Thus he retains from Isaiah the
adjective which speaks of the cornerstone and indicates
that the prophecy contains the same conception, which
is sufficient for Peter. His interest lies in the purpose
of this house or building which is intended "for a holy
priesthood" (v. 5), to which he reverts in vs. 9, 10.

We thus see the pertinency of the way in which he uses Isa. 28:16.

Astounding, indeed, is the fact that God should place such a stone, hence the exclamation "lo" or "behold." The tense is the prophetic present. The value of the stone is expressed by ἐκλεκτόν, ἔντιμον, the purpose it serves by ἀκρογωνιαῖον.

This figure is often misunderstood; it is thought that the cornerstone merely joins two walls, Jewish and Gentile Christians, as if these were the foundation whereas Christians are the house, Zion (a name for the church). Or it is thought that the whole house is carried or is held together by the cornerstone. Or that the cornerstone is the first one to be laid at the bottom of the excavation, or the one last laid to complete the foundation. The cornerstone is the significant stone of the entire structure. Hence it is idealized, and we still lay it with a special ceremony as we lay no other stone. It governs all the angles and all the lines of both the foundation and the building and is thus placed at the head of the corner, i. e., to form the projecting (not the inner) angle.

Peter retains the LXX's translation of the second line: "the one believing shall not be ashamed," which is interpretative of the Hebrew "shall not make haste or flee," for the one who must hurry away in flight does so because he is ashamed, his misplaced faith ends in bitter disappointment, and he thus hastens to get away and to hide. The negation is a litotes: the one who rests his faith and confidence on Christ (ἐπί is the proper preposition) shall stand solid and safe forever.

7) At this point Peter himself interprets: "for you, accordingly, is the honor as the ones believing." Both ὑμῖν at the beginning and τοῖς πιστεύουσιν at the end have the emphasis, the latter thus also being juxtaposed

in sharp contract with ἀπιστοῦσι. Despised as the readers
are in the world as merely tolerated foreigners (1:1),
all this honor with which God honors Christ devolves
also on them as the ones believing on Christ. Joined
as living stones to Christ, the living stone, his honor
is also theirs. They need never be ashamed; everywhere in the world they are the spiritual house for
God's priesthood to offer up spiritual sacrifices to God.
Honor, indeed! But all of it comes through Christ
alone.

In sharp contrast to these believers Paul sets "such
as disbelieve." He omits the article in order to stress
the quality more. But he now weaves the quotations
into his own statement "but to such as disbelieve 'the
stone which those building did on test reject, this one
became corner-head' (Ps. 118:22), and 'A stone of
stumbling and a rock entrapment' (Isa. 8:14), who
stumble," etc. This wondrous stone means everything
also to any and to all who refuse to believe: their rejection is fatal to them. In the first place, God nullifies
their rejection and makes this stone the corner-head;
in the second place, this stone destroys them.

The first passage reads like a brief parable. There
was a certain stone, and there were builders busily at
work. For the kind of building they were planning
they took many stones, but this particular stone they
considered totally unfit, *ma'am*, "to reject," LXX,
ἀποδοκιμάζειν, "to reject after a test," the same verb that
was used in v. 4. Yet, strange to say, this stone "became corner-head." We know how it became this; the
psalmist adds that it is Yahweh's doing, marvelous in
our eyes. It was done in spite of the builders. Delitzsch
states that *ro'sh phinnah* cannot be translated "cornerstone," but Eduard Koenig in his excellent *Woerterbuch* defines "head of the corner = cornerstone" exactly as the LXX). So we do not accept such definitions

as the stone at the top of the gable, the keystone of the arch, the capstone of a pillar at the eaves where the gable starts, also those listed in connection with v. 6.

. The prophecy of the psalm has in mind the Jewish Sanhedrin when it speaks of "those building." And, for what *they* wanted to make of Israel Jesus was, indeed, wholly unfit. They wanted a political house in which they could continue their secular domination of Israel and extend their power over the Gentiles. The Jewish nation followed them in disbelief. Peter applies the prophecy of the psalm to all who still repeat this disbelief and this rejection. The two verbs ἀπεδοκίμασαν and ἐγενήθη, "did reject," "did become," are prophetic aorists, both speak of the coming fact as being already history. Note what Jesus adds to the prophecy in Matt. 21:44 and in Luke 20:18.

8) With a simple "and" Peter borrows a double designation of Christ for such as disbelieve from Isa. 8:14: "A stone of stumbling and a rock of entrapment." Peter wants only these two designations; λίθος, "stone," is again mentioned but is now elucidated by πέτρα, "a rocky mass or cliff." Both terms reveal the destructive effect of Christ; the genitives are qualitative. Πρόσκομμα is not a word that expresses an action, "stumbling," but a term that indicates a result as the suffix -μα (R. 151) shows: the smash or crash accomplished. Since the two designations are synonymous, this stone is not one against which the disbelievers strike merely a foot and are thrown down and rise up more or less hurt, but one against which they strike with the entire body in a dreadful crash which knocks out their brains. This stone (λίθος, a dressed stone to be placed in the foundation) is of vast size; it is the cornerstone of the whole *Una Sancta*. Its character for unbelievers is marked by this frightful effect. Look at Israel (Rom. 9:33); it is shattered, broken, demolished completely as Isaiah foretold.

In πέτρα the idea of a stone for the purpose of building is dropped, and only the idea of size is retained; it is a great rocky cliff, and the genitive σκανδάλου, "entrapment," brings out fully the thought of the deadliness of this rocky mass for all disbelievers. A *skandalon* is the crooked stick of a trap, to which the bait is affixed, by which the trap is sprung that kills the victim. If we translate metaphorically "offense," it is offense with a deadly effect, from which recovery is impossible. The idea of luring or enticing into the deadly trap with bait is included. In Isa. 8:14 the figures of the gin and the snare are added; both are also deadly to the victim. To state that a rocky cliff does not act as a deadly trap is to forget the fact that the reality governs the figure and not the figure the reality. Strange, indeed! Men cannot let this rock alone by simply walking past it, by wholly ignoring it; unbelievers are drawn to it as to a deadly trap, they are lured to run against this towering rock and kill themselves.

Continuing with his own words, Peter adds the relative clause: "they who stumble against the Word by being disobedient, for which they also were appointed," and thus further describes "such as disbelieve" which was stated in v. 7. Peter uses only the thought that is expressed in πρόσκομμα but would also include that suggested by σκάνδαλον. All who disbelieve "smash against (*anprallen*, B.-P. 1149) the Word by being disobedient."

Some German commentators and the R. V. margin construe τῷ λόγῳ with the participle: "to the Word being disobedient." They do this because they think that after "stone of stumbling" "the Word" cannot be named as that against which these disobedient ones stumble unless Peter intends to identify "stone" and "the Word." They overlook the fact that Peter's relative clause advances the thought. How do these people come into hostile contact with Jesus as "a stone of stumbling," etc.? By means of "the Word." They stumble against Christ when they run foul of the Word, stumble against that. Stone and Word are not identified in Peter's explanatory clause, yet τῷ λόγῳ is to be construed with οἱ προσκόπτουσι.

"By being disobedient" is thus properly added as showing how they run against the Word: they refuse to obey that Word which brings Christ to them. They refuse to cling to the Rock of Ages. Although disbelieving and disobeying are different concepts, the second elucidates the first. Eve disbelieved the plain Word of God by disobeying it. The worst type of disobedience is disbelief. The will of God is that we believe on him whom he has sent for our salvation (John 6:40); his will is found in the Word. To believe is, first of all, to obey.

It is startling to read: "for which they also were placed (set, appointed)." Calvinists explain this as an eternal decree of reprobation, all Scripture to the contrary notwithstanding. They place the action of the verb in the *voluntas antecedens* whereas it belongs in the *voluntas consequens*. The former does not take into account man's reaction to Christ and to the Word; the latter does as Mark 16:16 plainly states. God cannot and will not change either Christ or his Word. He will certainly not remove this great stone and rock, his Son, our Savior, to please wicked men; that would entail to abandon all men to damnation. So when, after God's grace is brought to men to save them by faith, they reject this grace and God's Savior they are to be crushed and destroyed. This Christ is "set for the fall of many, a sign which shall be spoken against" in disobedient unbelief, Luke 2:34. He that believeth not shall be damned.

9) After having thus fully described the "living stone" with which Peter begins in v. 4 he proceeds

to the "holy priesthood" which he mentioned in v. 5 by developing this as it is to be applied to his readers: **You, however, (are) a race elect, a royal priesthood, a nation holy, a people for possession in order that you may announce abroad the fame of the One who called you out of darkness into his wonderful light — those once no people, now, however, God's people — those not having been granted mercy, now, however, granted mercy.** From a wide range of Old Testament passages the apostle selects these illustrious designations and applies them to his readers. They are, indeed, "foreigners" to the world (1:1; 2:11), but, lo, what "elect foreigners" (1:1)! Let the world treat them as outsiders, theirs is the most sacred aristocracy.

"A race elect" recalls such passages as Deut. 7:6, 7; Isa. 43:10, 20; 44:1, 2, "elect" is applied also to Christ, the cornerstone, in 2:6. As God chose Abraham and the Abrahamitic nation, so the readers are now "a race elect." Israel was chosen on the condition that it should abide in God's covenant, and when it hardened itself in unbelief, God rejected this race and expelled it out of Canaan as a standing sign for all time. In Peter's readers his grace prevails as believing ones (v. 7), and so they are "a race elect" among all the races of the world. Peter refers to their present state. With the terms "race, priesthood, nation, people," Peter considers his readers as one body, as belonging to the great *Una Sancta* on earth. Natural descent and all other differences are obliterated, swallowed up by the spiritual condition and status of the readers. How happy they should be to read what the apostle calls them!

"A royal priesthood" as well as "a holy nation" and "a people for possession" allude to Exod. 19:5, 6, where we read, "a kingdom of priests," "a holy nation," "a peculiar treasure unto me above all people." With the words "royal priesthood" Peter resumes the "holy priesthood to offer up spiritual sacrifices acceptable to God through Jesus Christ" (v. 5). "*Elect* race," elected to be no less than a *priesthood,* which is already high, yea, a "*royal,*" "kingly" priesthood. As was already stated in v. 5, priests have the right and the authority to approach God directly, no one is to speak to God *for* them, or come *between* them and God.

The fact that these priests (Peter's readers) are priests in the true sense of the word, men who offer sacrifices, v. 6 has already shown. Without the work of offering up sacrifices no one is a priest. This basic conception is not elaborated here; another idea is added and even emphasized, namely that we occupy so high a position that no man can be higher in this life: as a "priesthood," a body that is made up entirely of priests, no man stands *between* us and God, and as a body of "royal" priests no man stands *over* us in our relation to God. The adjective as well as the noun reveal in a double way the *exaltation* of our position and our function, the constant *direct, immediate* contact with God.

While Exodus 19 describes Israel, too, as being "a kingdom of priests," Israel still had its Levitical priesthood with its many ceremonial sacrifices, who functioned *between* Israel and God and were placed *over* the people in their contact with God. This priesthood was, however, only temporary, provisional, represented and typified the eternal priesthood of the royal Priest, Christ. Although Israel was "a kingdom of priests," etc., (Exodus 19), it was not yet such a body of priests in the fullest sense of the word; the complete "royal priesthood" in the fullest sense of this designation could not appear until our "great High Priest's" (Heb. 4:14) work had been done. Then the provisional Levitical priesthood came to an end.

The expression used in Exodus 19, "a kingdom of priests," and Peter's wording, "a royal priesthood," emphasize a feature that is far above all that we find in the Levitical and Aaronitic priesthood of Israel. This priesthood was not royal, kingly. None of those who functioned in it were kings. When it was established at Sinai, and the Tabernacle was built, Israel had no kings; centuries elapsed before Israel received its first king, Saul. "A royal priesthood" takes us back to Melchizedek (Heb. 7:1, etc.) who was both king and priest, whom Abraham himself honored accordingly, who typified Christ who was King and Priest in one, who was not from the tribe of Levi but of Judah as Hebrews explains all of this. "A royal priesthood" thus connects us directly via Melchizedek with the King-priest, our Lord Jesus Christ, through whom we offer up our sacrifices accepted of God (v. 5). He has made us "a kingdom," "priests" (Rev. 1:6; 5:10). Our royalty and our priestliness are derived from our relation to him alone.

Both the adjective and the noun denote our objective standing with God through Christ. This we are to realize fully. All too few do so. Learn to think of yourself as highly as Peter and as John do. The fact that our character and our conduct should be according is self-evident, but there is an application we should make. The basic concept is found in the noun "priesthood," the addition is the adjective "royal"; hence the thought is not: "a kingdom consisting entirely of priests"; but: "priests who are royal" like Melchizedek and thus like Christ. But the noun and the adjective are a unified concept like the other designations used in this verse, "race elect" and "a nation holy"; there is no man *between* us and God, no being *over* us save God. See the author's little volume, *Kings and Priests*, where much more is added from Scripture.

"A holy nation" is one that is wholly separated from the unholy and dedicated to God (1:15, 16; Exod. 19:6). Ἔθνος is the regular word for "nation" which is also used when speaking of the Jews as a national body. It aptly describes Peter's readers. Although they have come from many earthly nations, spiritually they now formed a distinct, "holy," superior, and exalted nation, and thus were "foreigners" among the common, earthly nations (1:1 and 2:11). By way of application we may say that we should completely give up the desire "to be like other people," for this would cause us to lose our standing with God. Our holiness is obtained by imputation and, resting on this, by acquisition (Eph. 5:26, 27).

The fourth term: λαὸς εἰς περιποίησιν, "a people for possession," also harks back to Exod. 19:5: "a peculiar treasure unto me above all people"; Deut. 7:6: "a special people unto himself, above all people that are upon the face of the earth"; Mal. 3:17: "They shall be mine, saith the Lord of hosts, in that day when I make up my jewels (margin: special treasure)." Similarly Paul writes λαὸς περιούσιος in Titus 2:14, "a people select." Περιποίησις = the act of possessing as one's own. We are bought with a price (I Cor. 6:20; 7:23) and thus are in God's possession. Λαός is the proper word; it is often used in a sort of sacred sense with reference to the people of Israel. All four nouns: "race, priesthood, nation, people," are collectives, each has its own connotation, all of them include the whole *Una Sancta*, the communion of saints.

It would be a mistake to suppose that we can be all that Peter states and at the same time sit down quietly and contemplate our honor and our excellence. These are not static but dynamic terms; they include what Peter puts into the purpose clause, in which we may read an undertone of admonition: "in order that you may announce abroad (announce effectively, aorist) the fame of the one who called you out of darkness into his wonderful light." This is what v. 5 means when it states: "To offer up spiritual sacrifices acceptable to God through Jesus Christ." A commoner way of stating this same truth is that used by Jesus: to confess him or his name before men. Peter uses the thought of Isa. 43:21 (compare 42:12) : "This people have I formed for myself, that they show forth my praise."

On the meaning of ἀρετή (the singular occurs in II Pet. 1:3; the plural here) in secular and in Scriptural usage we refer the student to G. K. 457, etc.; B.-P., 166. Suffice it to say that here, where Peter repeats Isa. 43:21: "they shall show forth my praise," the rendering "praises" (A. V.) is to the point (not "virtues," A. V. margin), not "excellencies" (R. V.), but the plural of the German *Ruhm,* "fame," which we do not pluralize although we may say "all the fame." The genitive indicates what fame and praise are referred to: "of the One who called us," etc., (1:15). Because of what we are it is our great function that by word and by deed, by our confession and by our conduct we at all times and under all circumstances publish in our own midst and to all men about us him who called us out of darkness, etc. Ἐκ in the verb gives it the meaning announce "out" or "abroad." True believers cannot keep still, they simply must speak out with lip and with life. Thus they function as a royal priesthood and ever offer up sacrifices of praise and thanksgiving. This is the confessional and the missionary spirit and activity of God's people; for the sake of this God lets us remain in the world.

"Darkness" is the terrible state of the world under the prince of darkness, the state of blindness, lifelessness, death, in which the world still lies. God's call, operating through the gospel, brought us out of this state "into his marvelous light," the light of truth, life, blessedness which are found in his kingdom of grace. Instead of hiding the fact that we are foreigners in this world we proclaim it and tell with delight who has made us what we are and how he has done what he did. Is this divine purpose being carried out by you? Supply the applicatory thoughts yourself.

10) Peter closes with a double, most effective apposition: "those once no people, now, however, God's people; those not having been mercied, now, however, mercied." Peter adapts expressions found in Hosea 2:23 to his own use, compare Deut. 32:21. We see what God has done for the readers: "once a non-people" (οὐ negates λαός), not a people in any sense, nothing but sheep without a shepherd; "now God's people," the extreme opposite. All who are far from God and Christ are a non-people spiritually; only those who come to Christ (v. 4) are a real people, God's people, he being their King, Savior, Protector, Provider, Benefactor.

The inwardness of this thought is brought out by the second apposition. "Those not having been mercied," with the perfect passive participle, are those who during the past were left in their sad condition for a long time. Peter again (1:3) uses the thought of "mercy" and not that of "grace" because he thinks of the wretched consequences which sin produces. Those who believe that the readers of this epistle were former Jews and not former Gentiles encounter a difficulty here; Peter could not say of Jews that they have not been granted mercy. In Rom. 9:25 Paul, too, applies Hosea's phrases to former Gentiles. The aorist in the expression "now, however, mercied" may simply indicate the past historical fact or may be ingressive: "got mercy bestowed on them."

This closes the first main part of the epistle (1:13-2:10).

Hortations Due to the Relations to Men, 2:11-3:12

Summary, v. 11, 12

11)   All of these hortations deal with our relations to men and thus naturally follow those that emanate from our relation to God. Peter begins with a brief summary admonition, a preamble to the specific relations that follow.

Beloved, I urge that as outsiders and foreigners you hold yourselves aloof from fleshly lusts which are of a kind that campaign against the soul, having your conduct among the Gentiles excellent in order that in what they speak against you as doers of baseness, due to your excellent works, when they look upon (them), they may glorify God in the day of visitation.

Peter urges his readers to keep away from all fleshly lusts for the sake of their own souls and so to conduct themselves in their pagan surroundings that the very thing for which they are slandered may make these slanderers glorify God when he visits them with his grace. We readily see that Peter turns to a different set of admonitions, and that this first admonition is preliminary and comprehensive.

Here and in 4:12 he employs the address ἀγαπητοί, "beloved." He draws his readers closely to his heart with intelligent, purposeful love, a love that will call forth a corresponding love and a readiness to obey. Παρακαλῶ = I urge, admonish, exhort, comfort, according to the context; here the first meaning is the best; "beseech" is not correct. In 1:3 Peter has used the term παρεπίδημοι, "foreigners"; he now doubles this by adding πάροικοι, "outsiders." In Heb. 11:9 we have the verb: Abraham "lived as an outsider" in Canaan, the land that God had willed to him in his testament.

A *paroikos* is one who dwells beside the native citizens, who is allowed to do so under restricted rights which are less than those granted the citizens. We have seen how Christians have become such outsiders and foreigners to the people among whom they have always dwelt and together with whom they are actually citizens of the land in which they dwell: their new relation to God has made them aliens, and the doubling of the nouns emphasizes this fact.

Peter, therefore, urges them "to hold themselves aloof from fleshly lusts." The Gentiles among whom they live are natives of the world and thus follow the promptings of the flesh and its many lusts; σαρκικός = κατὰ σάρκα, what accords with flesh, "fleshly"; σάρκινος = σὰρξ ὤν, what is flesh, "fleshy." Right here we see how Christians appear as outsiders and aliens to their Gentile neighbors: they hold themselves aloof from these neighbors in regard to all such lusts, they are spiritual in their nature and their conduct, no longer fleshly. There is a gulf between them and their neighbors.

Αἵτινες is both qualitative and causal (R. 728) : these lusts are of such a kind and for that reason campaign against the soul like a στράτευμα or army. The verb used is not πολεμεῖν, "to war," but στρατεύεσθαι, "to engage in a campaign," and personifies these fleshly lusts which intend to capture the soul in order to enslave and to destroy it. The appeal of this relative clause is one of spiritual self-interest.

12)   Since Peter has a participle follow the infinitive, we see that ἀπέχεσθαι and the danger to our souls are the supreme thought, and that ἔχοντες, which stresses the interest of the other people whom we may be able to influence for good, is dependent on the safety of our own souls. Peter has already admonished his readers in regard to "conduct" in their relation to God and has used the same word that is here employed,

ἀναστροφή (1:15, 18) ; here he stresses the fact that their conduct "among the Gentiles" must ever be καλή, morally excellent, noble, the adjective conveying the thought that it is even admirable in the eyes of those pagans who have any moral sense left. The word ἔθνη does not make Peter's readers former Jews. Peter says nothing about conduct toward unconverted Jews. "Gentiles" is used in the religious sense of pagans, "a non-people" as far as God is concerned, such as Peter's readers themselves were before they got to be mercied of God (v. 10) and became Christians.

The purpose of such noble conduct is this, that these pagans "in what they speak against you as doers of baseness may (in this very thing), due to the noble works, when they look upon them, glorify God in the day of visitation." The relative phrase "in which thing" is to be construed with both verbs: the thing in connection with which they at first speak against you, in connection with that very thing they may eventually glorify God when the day of their visitation arrives, i. e., when God looks in on them with his mercy and brings them to conversion. The relative is neuter and singular and thus does not resume the feminine "conduct," nor is it the same as "the noble works," which is plural. The relative refers to this thing, that Peter's readers have become outsiders and foreigners to their pagan neighbors, have deserted the pagan gods for the true God, have become all that v. 9 records of them. This arouses the hostility of the pagan community; in connection with it (ἐν) they speak against you as κακοποιοί, "bad actors," which does not mean "criminals" but persons who do what is bad, base, good-for-nothing.

There is no need to extend the meaning of the word nor to specify the charges that were brought against the readers. In any case, when a number of people in a pagan city cut markedly loose from the rest and adopt a religion that condemns the old religion of the rest as radically as the Christian faith condemns paganism, this minority will certainly hear themselves called bad actors in the whole matter. At the time when Peter writes this hostility was being intensified since Nero himself and the capital of the empire were beginning no longer to regard Christianity as a part of Judaism, which was tolerated and privileged, but as a *religio illicita* (see the introduction). The provinces would follow the attitude of Rome and of Nero. Christians were thus bound to be "spoken against as bad actors" more than ever.

Yet, ἐκ τῶν καλῶν ἔργων, as the result or outcome of the excellent works of the readers when they conduct themselves among their pagan neighbors in a morally excellent way, when these pagans look upon these excellent works (the participle needs no object in the Greek), they will in many cases be so impressed as themselves to be drawn to Christianity, become converted as Peter's readers were converted, and will thus actually (aorist) glorify God when this day of grace arrives for them. The good works of true believers have a strong missionary power. Deeds that are done by consistent conduct speak louder than words. Deeds that re-enforce doctrine, the gospel in both Word and life, draw men to God through Jesus Christ. Worldly Christians hinder home missionary work. Note that καλός is repeated; it is once found in the comprehensive singular "excellent conduct" and then in the multiplied plural "excellent works."

The addition ἐν ἡμέρᾳ ἐπισκοπῆς excludes the thought that these pagans glorify God only by praising the noble works of the Christians while they remain pagans. The expression "glorify τὸν Θεόν, the true God," is too strong for that thought; still stronger is the phrase "in the day of visitation," which recalls Luke 19:44: "because thou knewest not the time of thy visitation." Isa. 10:3 has the phrase, Jeremiah has much to say about God's visitation, others, too, mention it. God visits also with punishment, but here, as in Luke 19, the visitation takes place when God looks upon a person with grace and mercy (v. 10b). To think of the last day is not in the line of the thought; likewise to compromise: glorify God at the last day as people whom God has converted during their day of life on earth. Peter is restating the word of Jesus spoken in Matt. 5:16: "that they may see your excellent works and may glorify your Father, the One in the heavens."

This brief but comprehensive summary heads the following admonitions, all of which deal with our relations to men while the relation to God (1:13-2:10) is ever kept in mind. In these relations our own soul's interest is vital, and it is this for the sake of the glory of God and the salvation of other men.

Government, 13-17

13) We do not think that Peter follows an abstract outline and thus starts with obedience to the government. Peter's readers were, of course, under a pagan government, and the question was always asked in how far and on what principle *God's* people should obey *pagan* rulers. The question became acute when Christians were spoken against as κακοποιοί, "bad actors," and were treated as such by the government when some of them were accused and indicted before the authorities. There was more danger of this at the time when Peter writes, and it is thus that he takes up this subject.

Be subject to every human institution for the Lord's sake, whether to a king as supreme or to governors as having been sent through him for vengeance on doers of baseness and praise on doers of good.

The aorist imperative is as decisive and as strong as the aorists used in 1:13, 17, 22; 2:2; the passive of ὑποτάσσω is used in the middle sense. Κτίσις = creation, here "every human creation" in the sense of "every human institution" created by man. Some stress the point that government is here said to be human as though this were a view that is different from Paul's: "there is no authority except from God." Peter is said to be a republican, Paul a monarchist, so that Peter would represent the modern view of government as emanating from the people and not the view of rule by divine right. But this supposed difference is specious. Paul says that the ἐξουσία in all government, whatever its human form may be, is of divine origin, a statement that Peter would not think of contradicting. Peter is not speaking of the source of the ἐξουσία or "authority" in government but of its form, which is, indeed, "a human creation," that has a king as supreme and governors who are sent through him and govern in his name.

No special form of government is advocated by the New Testament. Peter deals with the human form as it was then existing in the Roman empire, Nero being the Caesar who is included under βασιλεύς ὡς ὑπερέχων: "whether a king as supreme." It also includes his "governors," no matter whether they were *legati Augusti*, proconsuls, procurators, or had some other title. While the citizens of Rome refused to call the emperor *rex*, the Greek-speaking people of the empire commonly called him "king."

14) We need not hesitate to connect the εἰς phrase only with "governors." They were sent by the king "for vengeance on doers of baseness and praise on doers of good" (Rom. 13:3, 4). They were to act as the king's representatives in this double function, and thus the phrase need not modify "king" who certainly, by appointing these governors, himself aimed to punish

evil men and to praise good men. The absence of the
article makes all the nouns qualitative. Peter uses
κακοποιοί, the same word that was used in v. 12; the
context differs; in v. 12 the Christians are vilified as
bad actors, in v. 14 the bad actors are proven to be
such in court. Ancient rulers, too, had praise for good
men and often honored them in a public way as governments in all lands still do.

Peter speaks of the rulers in their normal functions
as Paul does in Rom. 13. What Peter has to say when
rulers become tyrannous his early record shows, Acts
4:19; 5:29. The way in which Peter speaks of the
functions of rulers has been used to prove that his
readers were in no danger at the present time, and
that no danger from the government was threatening
in the near future. But v. 12 sounds a different note.

Nor is the present paragraph on government merely
abstract and theoretical. Christians need admonition
regarding government when government is likely to
turn against them; they are then to be admonished that
their course of conduct is not to be rebellion but submission. To extend this submission to the point of
denying the faith on a ruler's demand is obviously
wrong even if we did not have Acts 4:19 and 5:29.
The submission is to be the normal one, always διὰ τὸν
Κύριον, "because of, for the sake of the Lord," which we
regard as meaning more than that the Lord's name
may not be vilified; Paul says "for conscience's sake,"
a conscience bound by the Lord (i. e., Christ).

15) Ὅτι states the reason for this submission:
**because so is the will of God that by doing good you
muzzle the ignorance of foolish men, as free and not
as having this freedom as a veil for baseness but as
slaves of God.**

Peter does not say: "Submit because your submission is God's will." That fact has already been said in
a much finer way; it has not been given by a legal

command but by an appeal to a gospel motive: "for
the Lord's sake." What Peter makes prominènt is one
particular reason for submission for the Lord's sake,
namely that what God has willed (θέλημα, a term expressing a result) is οὕτως "so" or "thus," as follows,
namely "that by doing good you keep muzzling the
ignorance of foolish men," such as try to speak against
you as doers of baseness (v. 12). Οὕτως is not τοῦτο,
"this"; the adverb cannot refer backward: "thus by
submitting yourselves," because God never considered
the alternative that his people would not be subject
to human institutions such as government, and because
ὅτι already points forward to the reason for submission, namely the form of what God willed.

The infinitive is not in apposition to οὕτως (R. 1078)
or to θέλημα but to both, to "so is the will of God that,"
etc. God wants us to do good irrespective of foolish
men, for the highest kind of reasons in regard to himself as well as also to ourselves; it is only incidental,
secondary, that his will is as it is, that by our doing
good we muzzle the ignorance of foolish men who seek
to find something base in our deeds and in their ignorance do not see that all baseness is lacking. Τοῦτο
would change the sense and leave the impression that
this muzzling is a main reason for our doing good.

The infinitive means "to muzzle" and only metaphorically "to silence." The original meaning is in
place, for these ignoramuses want to bite us like dogs.
Our constant doing good acts like a constant muzzling.
"Ignorance" implies that they ought to have more
sense; moreover, it is a mild judgment and recalls the
not knowing voiced in Luke 23:34, the ignorance mentioned in Acts 3:17; I Tim. 1:13. The durative "keep
muzzling" appears to imply a constant tendency to
bark and to bite.

16) The addition "as free," etc., is still subordinate. The nominative is not a change of construc-

tion, for this continues the subject of ὑποτάγητε and not the implied accusative subject of φιμοῦν; nor is μή due to the imperative, it is the common negative with participles. We subject ourselves to government for the Lord's sake as being perfectly free and in no way as slaves to men; how free Acts 4:19 and 5:29 indicate. Καί is important. It is not δέ, "but," for our very freedom is this, that we do not have this our freedom "as a veil for baseness," practice some sort of baseness behind this veil in secret. See Gal. 5:1, 13. The word is not "cloak" but veil, and κακία is the same word that was used in the compounds found in v. 12 and 14; it is not "maliciousness" (A. V.), "malice," "wickedness" (R. V. and margin), but "baseness" as already explained. "Free," indeed, "but as slaves of God," whom he has bought for his own (I Cor. 6:20; 7:23), who have no will of their own but obey only the will of their master, God. This slavery to God is the truest and most complete human freedom; all other so-called freedom is fiction.

17) Some commentators are puzzled because Peter concludes this hortation with an aorist imperative plus three present imperatives, only the last of which deals with government. This is not a sudden broadening beyond government that returns to the main point in the last imperative; this is not saying that loving the brethren and fearing God are not in conflict with honoring the king and the government. Peter specifies how we are to do good so as to shut the mouths of ignorant men. **Honor all!** This is the decisive aorist which we have in 1:13, 17, 22; 2:2, 13. Peter separates and puts the next three imperatives into a group by themselves and makes them durative presents.

Keep loving the brotherhood! This is the same injunction that is found in 1:22 save for the tense, "love" is to be taken in the same sense, compare

Heb. 13:1. The limitation is the same as that found in Gal. 6:10: to those who are one with us we are able to show manifestations of love which we cannot show to others; the same is true also with regard to God and his children. "Brotherhood" conceives all the brethren as one body. **Keep fearing God!** — "in fear" (1:17), avoiding all sin and disobedience to him. **Keep honoring the king!** i. e., as a king, as one in this office. It is mentioned in the singular because we honor one in this office in a distinct way and not as we honor all men in general.

What can even ignorant men say against us if we follow these injunctions? What charge can they bring against us before any magistrate if we live thus: honoring all men, in particular loving our brethren, fearing God in holy reverence, honoring the king?

Slaves, v. 18-25

18) In Paul's admonitions to different classes of members slaves have the last place; Peter speaks of them first because, as his readers were under pagan rulers, so Christian slaves were under pagan masters. Peter does not call them δοῦλοι or slaves as Paul does but οἰκέται, "houseslaves," who belong to the οἶκος or *familia*; this term is like the Latin *famulus* or our "domestic." There were many slaves throughout the empire, and when Christianity was preached to them, many slaves were converted to it. The subject of slavery is a large subject, both as to the nature of slavery in the empire and as to the attitude of Christianity toward slavery. See *The Interpretation of St. Paul's Epistle to Philemon*.

The houseslaves, continuing in subjection in all fear to the masters, not only to the good and gentle but also to the perverse! In this way they are to conduct themselves as Christians in their station of life. The sentence has no finite verb, the nominative participle is not intended as a verb, nor is ἐστέ or εἰσί to be supplied, for the participle merely continues the idea of ὑποτάγητε expressed in v. 13.

We have the same construction in 3:1 regarding "wives," and in 3:7, 8 it is also extended to other participles that no longer continue the idea of subjection. This is good Greek, the desire being to make all of these admonitions a continued chain by means of participles. Subjection to the masters is the part of Christian slaves, not a subjection like that of pagan slaves, which is due to mere human compulsion, but one that is due to submission to God's will. In v. 13 we have: "to every human institution," one that is only "human" and not a divine arrangement. God did not institute slavery, men did that, but Christian slaves bow submissively to this human bondage.

"In all fear" does not mean in fear of the masters, in dread of punishment from them. The dative τοῖς δεσπόταις depends on the participle and is not equal to a genitive: "in all fear *of* the masters." Roman law gave great power to owners of slaves, but Christian slaves conduct themselves "in all fear of God" (1:17), they dread to transgress his will and to sin against him. "The houseslaves" and "the masters" name these classes objectively. The former is a nominative and not a vocative although vocatives often have the article. Our versions have translated this nominative as a vocative.

It was comparatively easy to live under good and gentle masters, yet Christian slaves were to be just as ready to serve and to obey "the perverse," τοῖς σκολιοῖς, "crooked," those who order one thing now and just about the opposite then. "Froward" (our versions) makes the impression that these masters were contrary, obstinate. Peter refers to masters that were hard to please because they order a thing done in one way, and when it is done that way, scold because they wanted it done another way and thus keep the poor slaves in constant uncertainty because of their whims.

'Επιεικής is a beautiful word; it is a companion to πραΰς. The latter is found in the heart, the former is manifested toward others and is always the kindliness of a superior toward an inferior. Trench: "The greatly forgiven servant in the parable (Matt. 18:23) had known the ἐπιείκεια of his lord and king; the same was therefore justly expected of him." We may translate this word "gentle" or "kindly." Whether their masters made it easy or hard for them, Christian slaves were to be submissive: not presumptuous in the one case, not grumbling and surly in the other.

19) **For this is grace, if because of conscious-ness of God one bears up under griefs, suffering wrongfully. For what sort of reputation** (is it) **if sinning and getting cuffed you shall stand it? But if doing good and suffering you shall stand it, this** (is) **favor with God.**

The motive that should prompt slaves to be subject to even perverse masters is shown by pointing to what this means for them in regard to God, which also com-forts and cheers them in their trying position. The "if" clause is in apposition to "this," and χάρις = "favor" (not "thankworthy" or "thank," A. V. and margin; not "acceptable," R. V.). The action described in the "if" clause assures the Christian slave of God's favor.

The first meaning of συνείδησις is "consciousness," "co-knowledge": "The word would seem to have been 'baptized' by Paul into a new and deeper connotation, and to have been used by him as equivalent to τὸ συνειδός — 'conscience' " (M.-M. 604). Since it is here con-strued with the objective genitive, we render "because of consciousness of God" in preference to our versions' rendering of the genitive: "for conscience toward God." "Conscience" alone is not sufficient, for even pagans have a conscience; Peter has in mind an enlightened conscience, one that judges a person's acts in connection with God.

If, for the sake of such a conscience, a slave "bears griefs, suffering wrongfully," this is favor with God. Arbitrary pagan masters may abuse the slave and often do this because he has become a Christian. All such "griefs," which are inflicted to make the poor, helpless slave suffer, are in reality "grace or favor" that comes to him from God if he, indeed, bears up under (ὑποφέρει) them because he is conscious of God who sees all and will reward him.

20) Peter adds the negative side and then repeats the positive. "For what kind of reputation (κλέος, *Ruf*, *Ruhm*, fame) is it if sinning and cuffed you shall stand it?" Suppose this Christian slave, whose master keeps abusing him, should become resentful and, instead of keeping conscious of God (obeying his conscience), should sin against it and cease to do his best for his master and thus get cuffed, slapped, fisticuffed since this is his lot under his mean master anyway — what kind of a reputation would that be for him as far as God is concerned? Our versions have κλέος = "glory" because they could perhaps find no better word; the word = "report, rumor," which, when it is spread = "fame." Could God look with favor on such action?

The two "if" clauses are placed chiastically. We should also note that in v. 19 the emphasis rests on the phrase that mentions the conscience and thus in the case of the other two "if" clauses on sinning (against conscience) and on doing good and not on the two secondary participles "being cuffed and suffering"; for, as v. 19 shows, this abuse is the poor slave's lot under his ugly master in any case. His choice lies between resentment ("sinning" against what his Christian conscience tells him) and suffering in that way and losing God's favor or doing good to his master (as his conscience tells him) and suffering in this way and thus continuing in God's favor. The choice should not be difficult to make. His master will not show him favor but only abuse. God will show him favor if this slave keeps true to his Christian conscience; he himself forfeits this divine favor if he resents his master's treatment and thus sins against God. The two ὑπομενεῖτε do not mean "shall take it patiently" but simply "shall endure or stand it." From "anyone," which he used in v. 19, Peter advances to the personal plural "you"; the future "shall stand it" is future to the participle when the cuffing and the suffering come.

Verses 19 and 20 are closely connected and are worded with concise precision, especially in regard to the emphatic placement of the διά phrase and of the participles. Suffering runs through the three statements: this slave and any of the readers who are under such masters will have to suffer and be cuffed and knocked about in any case. That, too, is why πάσχοντες in v. 20 reverts to πάσχων in v. 19 with κολαφιζόμενοι intervening. When this feature of Peter's style is noticed, his meaning will become clear.

21) **For for this you were called because also Christ suffered in your behalf, leaving behind for you a writing-copy in order that you may follow his tracks — he the One who did not do sin, neither was guile found in his mouth; he the One who, being reviled, kept not reviling in turn; suffering, kept not threatening but kept committing (himself) to the One judging righteously; he the One who his own self carried up our sins in his body on the wood in order that, having ceased to exist for the sins, we may live for righteousness; he the One with whose stripes you were healed!**

Τοῦτο has the same force as the two τοῦτο in verses 19 and 20, "for this," namely not merely to suffer, not merely to do good to others, but to do good and to suffer

for and while doing it. We see how well this applies
to slaves who were maltreated by their masters, often
only because they had become Christian and in spite
of the good, conscientious service which they rendered.
Such poor slaves Peter points to the example of Jesus,
whom they were called to follow by the gospel.

While Peter points to Jesus' example for these
slaves in their distressful condition in order to keep
them true to their saving call, this blessed example has
value for all of his readers and also for all of us to
this day. For this all of us are called to suffer and to
be abused while we as followers of Christ conscienti-
ously do good to others. By thus holding up the example of Jesus, Peter by no means makes him only an
example as rationalists and modernists do. From start
to finish Peter presents Jesus, our example, as our
Savior, who, by becoming our example, also enables us
to follow his example by ridding us of our sins by bearing them for us and thus placing us into a new life.

Ὅτι = "because"; it is not declarative "that." The
reason these slaves are called "for this," namely to suffer while doing good, is due to the fact that they are
called to follow a Savior who, in order to save us and
to do us the highest good, suffered infinitely more for
our sins. There is, of course, a great difference. It is
not merely the fact that his example is perfect in every
way while our following is always imperfect, but the
fact that his suffering for our good was expiatory while
ours, however severe it may be, cannot be that, need
not be that. His expiation is complete.

"Also Christ suffered in our behalf" is to be understood in the sense of 3:18: "because also Christ suffered once for sins, One righteous instead of unrighteous ones," etc. We see that ὑπέρ, "in behalf of," means
no less than "instead of." We reserve the fuller exposition for 3:18. By all this suffering of his the
Christ who suffered thus leaves us a ὑπογραμμόν (found

only here in the Scriptures), a writing or a drawing that is to be placed under another sheet and to be retraced on that upper sheet by the pupil, "writing to be used as a perfect model for copy." The ἵνα clause explains by using another figure: "in order that we may follow his tracks," ἴχνος, the German *Spur*, footprints left in the soil. The aorist means "actually follow." We must go the way the Master went. When he was doing the highest good for others he suffered; this is the reason that our call obligates us to suffer in our humble way when we do good to others for conscience's sake.

22) Four relatives follow. All four are not mere relatives but have demonstrative force, a use of the relative that is quite regular, and one that is the more assured here because of the emphatic repetition. So we do not translate with a common "who" but with "he, the One who." "He did not do sin," sin of any kind; the aorist states the great fact as such; he was absolutely sinless.

"Neither was guile found in his mouth," not even this trace of sin. Peter uses Isa. 53:9: "because lawlessness (ἀνομίαν, LXX) he did not do, nor guile in his mouth"; yet Peter does not quote, he only restates. He has already described Christ as "a lamb blemishless and spotless" in 1:19. Note the reference to "all guile" in 2:1 and "not speaking guile" in 3:10. The thought agrees with James 3:2, that sin of any kind will show itself first of all by means of the tongue. Peter's use of Isaiah 53 is so pertinent because he has used ἁμαρτάνοντες in v. 20, and because maltreated slaves would be tempted to use "guile" to deceive their masters in order to escape being cuffed. These slaves, like all of us, must ever look at Christ who was without sin and guile.

The Gospel records substantiate what Peter says. Jesus stands forth as the sinless One. In all his clashes with his cunning enemies no trace of evasion, guile, deceit, trickery is found, nothing but the pure, holy truth; with that alone he discomfited them. Some think that "was found" refers to his trial before the San- hedrin when all the false witnesses failed to fasten any- thing adverse upon him and when, with his life at stake, he made oath to the truth that he was the Mes- siah, the Son of God. On Christ's sinlessness compare Luke 23:41; John 8:46; II Cor. 5:21; Heb. 4:15.

23) The second demonstrative relative selects two points of the sinless conduct of Jesus, which may refer to Isa. 53:7, a lamb not opening his mouth: reviled, Jesus did not retort with reviling; suffering, he did not reply by threatening; instead of this he was silent and committed himself to God, the One who judges righteously. Here we have three descriptive imperfects which stand out amid the simple aorists of fact. They, too, state facts but present them as on a moving film, the present participles letting us picture the scenes of reviling and suffering, the imperfect verbs letting us dwell on the silent victim as no reviling, no threaten- ing reply issues from his lips. Peter has in mind the scenes of the great passion in which the provocation to retaliate was extreme. We think especially of the mockery and the abuse of the Sanhedrin, of the scourg- ing and the mockery of the soldiers, and of the mockery and the reviling under the cross. Some think of the patience of Jesus, but Peter says nothing about this although Jesus suffered in perfect patience.

Παρεδίδου has no object and is not reflexive but ac- tive. The Germans can help themselves by translating *stellte es heim* and leave "it" undefined. Since a per- sonal object is used in juridical connections, our ver- sions appear to be correct when they supply this object in their English translations: "he committed himself," which is better than "his cause" (margins). The ap- plication of this example of Jesus to maltreated slaves lies on the surface: let them ever commit themselves to him who judges righteously and keep their hearts and their lips from muttering reviling and threatening replies.

24) The third demonstrative relative states that all this sinless suffering of Christ, which is such an example for those who are called to Christ and must suffer, was a suffering *for them,* to rid them of their sins, to give them a new life in which they may live for righteousness. The point is not the fact that there were wicked men on earth when Christ lived here, and that he suffered terribly at their hands, and that there are still wicked men, and that some of us, like these helpless slaves, also suffer much from them; but that what Christ suffered was suffered in our behalf (ὑπὲρ ὑμῶν, v. 21), was inflicted upon him by *our* sins, from which to save us he died on the cross. The example of Christ will be of no avail unless we note his expiation of our sins, get free of them through him, get into the new life, and so live in the true righteousness and patiently endure, like Christ, what men inflict upon us. Peter is not a moralist, he preaches the full gospel of expiation, substitution, and regeneration: "he the One who his own self carried up our sins in his body up on the wood in order that," etc.

'Αναφέρω is a ritual term. We see it so used in Lev. 14:20 (LXX, ἀνοίσει ἐπί, shall bring up upon the altar) and in James 2:21, ἀνενέγκας ἐπί, "having brought Isaac, his son, up upon the altar." The verb thus tells us that Christ made a sacrifice. The object is placed forward for the sake of emphasis, and ἡμῶν and αὐτός are juxtaposed: "the sins that are *ours he himself* carried up in his body," etc. Peter speaks as his old teacher, the Baptist, did in John 1:29, 36. Himself sinless, Jesus carried up our sins and acted as our substitute. Yahweh laid on him the inquity of us all, Isa. 53:6, made his soul (life) an offering for sin (v. 10), to bear their iniquities, pouring out his soul (life) unto death (v.

11, 12). Peter is exact: Christ carried up our sins "in his body" (Heb. 10:5: "a body didst thou fit for me"). We see Christ on his way to Golgotha, his body loaded with all our sins, bruised, broken, suffering, to die the bloody death on the cross.

Αὐτός, "he himself" (emphatic) carried up our sins — voluntarily. For this he had become incarnate. Ἐπὶ τὸ ξύλον, "upon the wood" ("tree," our versions), is highly significant (Acts 5:30; 10:39), for Gal. 3:13 points out the fact that to be hung on wood (a post or gibbet) means no less than to become accursed according to Deut. 21:23: "Accursed everyone that hangs on wood." He took the curse of our sins on his own body and by his sacrificial death on the wood expiated the curse in our stead. What is the suffering which we now endure compared to that? Since Christ's suffering is expiatory and sacrificial it is not only far greater but also entirely different from our poor sufferings. *Our* sins, guilt, curse he bore, they brought him to the wood; shall we, then, not quietly bear our suffering and follow in his tracks?

This he did "in order that we, having ceased to exist for the sins, may live for the (true) righteousness." Ἀπογίνομαι is rare and is used as the opposite of γίνομαι which explains the dative ταῖς ἁμαρτίαις: "having ceased to exist for the sins." To cease to exist is thus taken to mean "to die" (our versions); but this is inexact, for then Peter, like Paul, would have used the verb "to die"; "to cease existing" for something is stronger and more to the point. To state that "to die" is a correct translation because "may live" follows (these two being opposites) is only to say that Peter should have used the verb "to die," but he does not use it even with reference to Christ. The aorist means actually ceasing to exist even as the aorist ζήσωμεν, means actually to live (not "might live," R. V., which is too potential). Peter intends to state that he and his readers have actually ceased to exist for the sins and are thus actually to live for the righteousness, the one that is such in God's judgment.

This cessation occurred by repentance and faith, and thus this new life for righteousness began. It is specious to argue that the sins for which we ceased to exist are past sins because they are the ones which Christ carried up upon the wood. Christ atoned for *all* our sins, and we should not date them.

Shall we regard also the fourth relative as a demonstrative? This is usually not done even as the other three are not so regarded. Yet this last relative is stronger when it is regarded as a demonstrative: "he with whose stripes you were healed" (using Isa. 53:5). This fourth pronoun, a genitive, rounds out the great statement about Christ. The dative of means τῷ μώλωπι is collective so that we translate it with the plural "stripes." This reference to "stripes" is so appropriate because slaves, too, were whipped and scourged, and this paragraph is intended especially for maltreated slaves. The expression is highly paradoxical because stripes, which make bloody welts and lay even the flesh bare, are said to have wrought healing. It is solved by remembering that they were administered on Christ's body and thus healed us.

It has been well said that here we again have the doctrine of Christ's vicarious, substitutionary suffering. We see no reason for inserting the idea "healed of our disease," Isaiah mentions griefs and sorrows but not disease. Peter's thought concerns the wounds that sins inflict on us; these were healed by means of Christ's wounds. The healing stripes of Christ save us from eternal death (Luke 12:48, πληγαί) ; any Christian slave may then well bear the blows which his ugly master inflicts on him.

We cannot approve the interpretation: "Christ has borne our sins, thus others' sins, and therewith intended to bring about our conversion. Thus also Christian slaves and Christians in general should bear and suffer others' sins, the wrong done them by the adversaries of their faith, and do this also with the intent, if possible, of converting them." Our suffering from other men's sins is never expiatory. Christ's bearing *fremde Suende* is never a true parallel to our bearing *fremde Suende*. It is dangerous to say so. Peter does not hint that abused slaves are to bear their abuse with missionary intent; "doing good" in v. 20 means rendering sincere, beneficial service as slaves and cannot be taken to mean more than this.

25) "For" is explanatory of not merely the last relative clause but of all four of these clauses: **For you were as sheep wandering astray but turned yourselves now to the Shepherd and Overseer of your souls.** Peter appropriates still more of Isa. 53, in this first clause a part of v. 6. It is argued that because "sheep" is used, Peter's readers cannot be Gentiles but must be Jewish Christians who were in the fold as sheep and then wandered away and have now returned. John 10:16: "Other sheep have I, which are not of this fold; them also must I bring," is brushed aside with the remark that Peter lived entirely in the Old Testament. These were Gentile Christians who were at one time pagan, who wandered astray like sheep without a shepherd. The tense is not periphrastic; πλανώμενοι is only a descriptive participle that is derived from πλανάω, "to make wander away," thus the passive (used in the middle sense) means "to wander astray."

The passive of ἐπιστρέφω is also used in the middle sense although the passive "were turned" would be fitting here; the form is the second passive. The aorist simply states the past fact to express which the English uses the perfect: "did turn yourselves now" means "now" since Christ has borne your sins. The use of but one article makes both nouns a unified designation:

"the Shepherd and Overseer of your souls." Now these slaves who are being addressed by Peter, like all other readers, are under Christ who is their Shepherd. We need not quote all the passages which call Christ our "Shepherd" and state all that we thus have in him. By doubling the term and adding "Overseer" Peter makes the thought more emphatic. Wandering sheep have no one to look after them and are thus doomed to perish; Christ looks after his sheep. The rendering "bishop" is inadequate because it suggests the much later ecclesiastical use of this word.

Πρεσβύτερος, "elder," and also ἐπίσκοπος are used in the New Testament with reference to the pastors of the church; Peter's use of the latter word with reference to Christ has nothing in particular to do with this congregational office. Peter has in mind only the general figure of sheep who once went astray and had no one to guard them and then came to Christ who cares for their needs. The thought that the slaves who are compelled to suffer at the hands of their masters have Jesus as their Shepherd and Overseer is one of great comfort to them. His gentle hand keeps them, and he is not unmindful of their hard condition. To be sure, ἐπίσκοπος denotes one who is placed over us; but, compared with πρεσβύτερος, it is a term that denotes service; the thought of dignity is far more prominent in the latter term.

CHAPTER III

Wives, v. 1-6

1) The entire series of admonitions from 2:13 to 3:12 is conceived as a unit, and this is indicated by the construction: the finite ὑποτάγητε at the beginning in 2:13, followed in 2:18 by the participle ὑποτασσόμενοι, in 3:1 by ὑποτασσόμεναι, in 3:7 by another participle, and in 3:8 by adjectives. This is the structural framework; all else, however it may be construed, whether as independent sentences or not, is conceived as being subordinate. When this structure is understood, we shall not connect the participle in 2:18 or the one in 3:1 with any of the imperatives in 2:17, or make imperatives and finite verbs of the participles.

Likewise, wives continuing in subjection to their own husbands in order that, even if some are disobedient to the Word, by means of the conduct of the wives without word they may be gained, having looked upon your conduct pure in fear.

"Likewise" means that for "wives" there are also requirements that are due to their station and relation, namely in relation to their husbands. By leaving out the article and by simply using "wives," Peter stresses the qualitative force of this noun. This is not a vocative (our versions) any more than are "the houseslaves" in 2:18, "the husbands" in 3:7, and "all" in 3:8; vocatives would call for finite verbs. "Continuing to be subject" is again the Christian obligation just as it was in the case of slaves, but, as the qualitative (anarthrous) "wives" indicates, in this case a subjection of a quality befitting wives; those now addressed are not slaves but wives. Eph. 5:22; Col. 3:18 are close parallels.

All Scripture, in particular also the New Testament, asks Christian wives to be subject to their husbands, and what is asked of the husbands should certainly make any wife's subjection a delight instead of an infliction. Paul enters upon a fuller discussion of this whole subject, not only as it pertains to wives alone, but also as it pertains to the whole Christian status of women as this goes back to creation itself. Peter is content with the simple participial statement: "continuing in subjection to their own husbands," "their own" emphasizing the close relation of wives to husbands. Peter has the third person and not "your" (our versions) and thus no vocative.

The purpose clause applies only to Christian women whose husbands are still unbelievers. The fact that such wives will also be subject to their pagan husbands is taken for granted. These wives have a special goal in view which they greatly desire to have realized, namely that their husbands "may be gained" for Christ. In the Koine the future indicative may follow ἵνα, R. 984. Peter indicates the most effective means for attaining this purpose and places the phrases forward for the sake of emphasis: "by means of the conduct of the wives without word"; they are to let their Christian conduct do the speaking, are not to argue about religion with their husbands. "Without word" cannot mean "without the Word," for no man is converted without the Word, and the simple λόγος, here given the second place after ὁ λόγος, cannot have the same meaning as the articulated noun. Overanxious wives attempt to talk their husbands into conversion, which is generally a great mistake. "Without word" (argument) does not mean that they are never to speak about religion, but that they are not to resort to constant argument and persuasive or nagging discussion.

2) True wisdom is shown by living so that the husbands may be gained "on having looked upon your conduct pure in fear." By constantly having a true Christian wife before his eyes, by having seen the blessed change produced in her by the gospel, many a husband will also be gained. It is excellent Greek to place the modifiers between the article and the noun: τὴν ἐν φόβῳ ἁγνὴν ἀναστροφὴν ὑμῶν; the adjective means morally "pure" in the whole of life and not just sexually "chaste" (our versions). "Conduct" is the same word that was used in 1:16, 17 (verb), 18. "In fear" is to be understood in the same sense as it was in 1:17 and 2:18, namely the holy fear of God.

3) With ὑμῶν, "your conduct," Peter turns to the second person, but with ὧν he drops back into the third: **whose let be, not the outward adornment of plaiting of hair and of placing around gold things or of putting on robes but the hidden man of the heart in connection with the incorruption of the meek and quiet spirit, which in the sight of God is of great price.**

In ὧν ἔστω we have the common Greek idiom of the genitive with εἶναι, here with the genitive of a relative pronoun; we should say "theirs let be" or "to whom let belong, not the outward adorning . . . but the hidden man," etc. We need not supply another word. Ὁ κόσμος and its modifiers and ὁ ἄνθρωπος, etc., are the subjects; the one is not to belong to Christian wives, the other is to belong to them. Οὐ and not μή is used, not because of the sharp contrast in ἀλλά (R. 1161), but quite regularly as negating a single concept: "not the adorning," etc.; κόσμος is to be understood in its original sense: *Schmuck, Putz,* orderly arrangement or ornament. The fact that the word has come to be used in the meaning "cosmos," "world," has no effect on its meaning here; nor should we say that it suggests the thought of "worldly adornment."

We may call the genitives appositional (R. 498):
the outward adornment which these women are not
to have consists in plaiting of hair (an idiomatic plural
in the Greek), putting around the neck, fingers, wrists,
and ankles χρυσία, gold objects (chains, rings, bracelets,
not "jewels of gold," R. V.), or of putting on of robes.
It is interesting to compare Isa. 3:18-23. James 2:2
presents a finely dressed gentleman. Like Peter, Paul
also writes about woman's finery: braids, gold, pearls,
costly apparel (I Tim. 2:9). The idea both express
is not that women should dress in Quaker drab, but
that they should be beyond the vanity of display in
order to attract attention to themselves. Both Peter
and Paul mention the hair because the style of that day
preferred elaborate and startling coiffures. R. 127 and
others call attention to the fact that all the modifica-
tions are placed between the article and the noun; they
call this stylistic arrangement Thucydidean. Some,
however, doubt that Peter could have written in this
manner because in their estimation he was a rather
unlearned Jew.

4) Objection is raised because "the outward
adornment," etc., and "the hidden man," etc., are not
true contrasts. They are not; ordinary writers would
contrast "the outward adornment" with "the inward
adornment." In the positive member of the contrast
Peter advances beyond mere ornament and names "the
hidden man of the heart" as the inward personality
which is to shine with spiritual beauty. This exceeds
mere rhetorical style; this is no less than mastery of
thought. Peter may well have remembered Ps. 45:13.
He writes as Paul does in Rom. 2:28, 29, and in Rom.
7:22 and II Cor. 4:16 Paul has only "the inner man."

Yet "the hidden man of the heart" is not a designation of the regenerate or spiritual man. Only the

body can wear *outward* ornamentation, the man of the heart is "hidden" as is the heart (the seat of the real personality). We regard the genitive as appositional: the hidden man is the heart. Since it is *hidden,* the real being of a person must have something better than silk and satin, gold trinkets, and skillfully dressed-up hair. The heart must be "in connection with the incorruption of the meek and quiet spirit" which is produced by regeneration. Only a few commentators note that Peter uses τὸ ἄφθαρτον as an abstract substantive (the A. V. does); most of them, like the R. V., think that this is an adjective and supply κόσμῳ: "in the incorruptible ornament of a meek and quiet spirit" (R. V.: "in the incorruptible apparel"). Peter substantivizes the adjective in a truly classic and elegant manner; some, we may suppose, would again place such a stylistic nicety beyond him.

We do not place a comma before ἐν but read the whole as a unit just as also ὁ . . . κόσμος is a unit. Without the incorruption of a meek and quiet spirit the hidden man of the heart would be filled with a vain, proud, self-assertive spirit, the mark of an unregenerate heart. Πνεῦμα is to be understood in the ethical sense of temperament or character. Peter does not name the virtues when he uses the nouns "meekness" and "quietness" because he does *not* want to parallel them with the outward ornamentation of the body. These Christian virtues are far more than adornments which are put on for a while so that men may see and admire them and are then taken off again. Peter avoids such a parallel. The incorruption is permanently connected with the hidden man of the heart, and it is the meek and quiet spirit (appositional genitive) which constitutes this thing that is incorruptible. In 1:7 Peter says of gold that it is "perishing"; in 1:18 gold and silver are termed "corruptible things." This indicates why he now uses "incorruption." The meek and quiet spirit in the heart is imperishable; it is the true beauty, not one that is put on, but one that is inherent; it is not an earthly, bodily, outward thing but is inherent in the soul.

The two adjectives "meek and quiet" match the participle "continuing in subjection" and bring out the true Christian character of the wife's submissiveness. Although it is inward, these adjectives state that this spirit at the same time manifests itself outwardly by the entire conduct. Paganism knew meekness as a human virtue only to a slight degree, only in the sense of an equitable mind; the Scriptures elevate meekness and regard it as a spiritual virtue that is pleasing to God. Paganism despised the person who was not masterful, who did not assert his own will and make others bow to it; Christianity elevated lowliness and did not regard it as a form of weakness but as a mark of inner, spiritual strength. See what Jesus says about the meek in Matt. 5:5; so meekness is ever extolled. It springs from our relation to God, from the consciousness of our sinfulness and thus extends also to men and suggests a willing bearing of what their sins inflict upon us (see Trench). All this was beyond the pagan conception because it belongs to our regenerate spirit or character, to our life in the kingdom.

"Meek and quiet" go together, the doubling intensifies the virtue. This meekness is always quiet; loudness, intemperate, irate speech and action are foreign to it. A steady, balanced strength keeps it on an even keel. Such a Christian wife is a treasure for any husband. When a heathen husband sees that by conversion his wife is changed from vanity, love of display, and other feminine vices to the true beauty of a new spirit, he must surely be drawn to a religion that is able to produce such wonders of grace. Paul notes cases of the opposite kind, where the unbelieving spouse may even depart and thus break up the marriage (I Cor. 7:15) ; Peter passes these cases by, they are not pertinent to his simple admonitory purpose.

"Which in the sight of God is of great price" with its neuter ὅ refers to the entire preceding clause; we should not say that the antecedent of "which" is doubtful. God regards such virtue and conduct as πολυτελές, as valuable indeed. In order to produce this inner, spiritual excellence and beauty in every wife and woman he sends us his Word and Spirt.

5) "For" explains by introducing examples; it is often used for this purpose. **For thus at one time also the holy wives, those hoping in God, kept adorning themselves, continuing in subjection to their own husbands as Sarah obeyed Abraham, calling him lord, whose children you became, continuing doing good and fearing no terrifying.**

While the word γυναῖκες may mean either women or wives, we prefer the latter meaning in this connection because of the following "their own husbands" (ἄνδρες may also mean either men or husbands, here, as in v. 1, it has the latter meaning). This does not prevent us from making applications to unmarried women. In what sense these wives of old are called "holy" is indicated by the participle "those hoping in God," which does not pertain only to some of these holy women but to all of them; their holiness consisted in their hoping in God, in their expecting all their glory from him when he should call them to himself, hence they cared nothing for corruptible, earthly vanities. "Thus," as just stated in v. 4, "they kept adorning themselves" (imperfect) ; the verb resumes ὁ κόσμος, the idea of "adornment" spoken of in v. 3, but is now to be understood in the true spiritual sense. The hidden man of the heart made them spiritually beautiful, and for this beauty they constantly strove.

The feature of their holiness which especially interests Peter he adds by means of the participle "continuing in subjection to their own husbands" (compare v. 11). This, in particular, made them lovely. When some wives today imagine that such subjection is a loss to them they are sadly mistaken. These holy women still shine from the sacred page; but look at the other kind.

6) Sarah is singled out. We are given the reason. The fact that she obeyed Abraham and called him "lord" (Gen. 18:12) is only the mark of her character, her being subject to her own husband. The real reason for singling her out lies in the relative clause "whose children you became" when you were converted by the gospel. Of none of the other holy women could Peter appropriately say that the wives whom he addresses became their children. Abraham is the father of believers, and thus Abraham's wife Sarah is after a fashion placed on the same level; all believing wives are also called her children. This certainly exalts Sarah, yet does so only because she was obedient to Abraham and called him her lord.

Peter does not enter more fully into the history of Sarah. Gen. 18:12 is not merely one historical incident in her life but one· that reveals her constant attitude toward her husband: as she then called him "my lord" so she ever called and trusted him. This is the force of the present, durative participle καλοῦσα, which modifies the constative aorist ὑπήκουσε. This would also be the sense of the inferior variant which has the imperfect ὑπήκουε in conformity with the imperfect ἐκόσμουν.

Mistaken conceptions regarding the gnomic aorist cause the A. V. to render ἐγενήθητε whose children "you are,": the R. V. even translates "ye now are." This rendering is also due to the two following present participles. But the gnomic aorist is not used in personal relative clauses. This aorist is historical: the wives addressed as "you" are Christian wives, and they "became" such by their conversion. Peter states the past fact as such a fact, for only because they are Christian wives can he admonish them as he does in this whole paragraph.

But what about the two present participles "doing good," etc.? They are not causal. In order to be causal they should be aorists. Then, however, the resultant sense would be misleading, for how much good would a wife have to do, or how long would she have to do good and not fear before she became a child of Sarah *by* these actions? We now see why our versions render the aorist as a present tense; this enables them to translate "as long as ye do well," etc., (A. V.), "if you do well," etc., (R. V.). To be sure, if they stopped doing well, etc., they would not be Sarah's children; but, true as this is, these tenses do not say this. These durative present participles are *subsequent* to the aorist "you became." These wives "became" Sarah's children and are thus doing good, etc. A past, definite fact is followed by continuous actions. There are a number of examples in the New Testament where present participles have this force.

The objection that these participles are admonitory is not warranted, not even when it is urged that, if these wives are *now* doing good, etc., this whole admonition would be unnecessary. Are we to be admonished only when we do wrong? Do all the Biblical admonitions imply that we are *not* doing what they bid us do? This is an unwarranted assumption. These objections are answered by the first present participle found in v. 1: ὑποτασσόμεναι, "continuing to be in subjection," which implies that these wives are now doing what Peter asks. The same is true with regard to the same participle which is addressed to the slaves in

2:18; likewise with regard to the participle that is addressed to the husbands in 3:7.

All of these participles are compliments to these persons, Peter's acknowledgment that they are doing what they ought to do. He admonishes them to continue in this way. The very best of us ever need such admonitions. Thank God, the Scriptures constantly tell us to continue. Yet, while the present participle in v. 1 is *admonitory*, this is not the case with regard to these two closing participles. The admonition. has been given; these two participles are pure *acknowlededgment* on the part of Peter. They are full of encouragement to these wives, something that they and we all need in addition to admonition.

"Doing good" means as wives to their husbands just as "doing good" in 2:20 means as slaves to their masters; we extend neither to signify saving good in particular. When Peter means this he states it with all clearness as he does regarding wives and their unbelieving husbands. Here Sarah and Abraham are mentioned. Abraham was certainly saved without Sarah's doing good to him in order to effect his salvation.

Μὴ φοβούμεναι μηδεμίαν πτόησιν alludes to Prov. 3:25: οὐ φοβηθήσῃ πτόησιν ἐπελθοῦσαν: "fear not terror that has come up nor coming desolation of ungodly ones." In the expression "fearing terror" we have what R. 479 calls an analogous accusative; it is not a cognate accusative, which would be φόβον. The sense is that these Christian women are to let nothing terrifying frighten them from their course. Pagan women may disdain and insult them because they have adopted a nobler wifehood, they yet remain unafraid. Pagan husbands may resent their Christianity; this, too, does not frighten them. While πτόησις is a word that expresses an action it is here used in the objective sense: "not a single frightening."

Husbands, v. 7

7) **The husbands, likewise, continuing to dwell according to knowledge as with a weaker vessel, the wifely one, continuing to render honor as also joint heirs of life's grace, so that your prayers may not be hindered.**

Both the nominative and the participle have been explained in 2:18 and in 3:1; we have neither a vocative nor an imperative. As was the case in 2:18 and 3:1, the participle is descriptive, and because it is appended to the imperative used in 2:13, it has a gentle hortative force: Peter wants to see all the husbands continuing to dwell, etc. As it did in v. 1, "likewise" applies to all that is said. Something pertains to wives especially as something pertains to houseslaves; what pertains to wives naturally concerns itself with "their own husbands," and v. 1-6 tell us what it is. So it is with regard to "the husbands." Peter "likewise" has something to say to them as a class; it naturally concerns itself with their wives, and we hear what it is.

To refer "likewise" to all of the imperatives occurring in 2:17 or to any one of them is contrary to the sense. This adverb is to be construed with the whole statement: as something pertaining to the station and the relation of others, so also something pertaining to the station and the relation of this class, "the husbands," is here set down.

The first participle governs the first ὡς, the second participle the second ὡς. We correct the inversion found in both of our versions, which combines the two ὡς with the second participle. Was there any danger that the Christian husbands would not continue to dwell with their wives so that Peter had to tell them that this was expected of them? We supply nothing after the participle. These husbands are living with their Christian wives and are not in danger of running away. What is expected of them is their "continuing to dwell according to knowledge as with a weaker utensil, (namely) the wifely one, continuing (thus) to render honor," etc. These husbands are doing this; what is indicated is their continuance to do so.

Peter merely points out the main things, not as though these were new, but simply in order to call them to mind. One of these things is that they follow knowledge, which means Scripture knowledge, over against pagan ignorance regarding the relation of husband and wife. The other is that in accord with such knowledge the Christian husbands dwell "as with a weaker vessel, (namely) the wifely one." Peter uses σκεῦος as Paul does in I Thess. 4:4. Paul states how a Christian man acquires a wife in a sanctified and honorable way, Peter how a Christian husband lives with a wife.

The expression "a weaker vessel" implies that the husband, too, is a vessel. Neither the participle nor "vessel" has a special sexual meaning. The fact that a sexual union is referred to the word "husbands" and the word "wives" in v. 1 indicate. The reason our versions supply "them" (A. V.) and "your wives" (R. V.) after the participle is due to the fact that the subject, "the husbands," is plural while the dative object, "with a weaker vessel," is singular; but Peter must write the singular "as with a weaker vessel," for a plural might easily be understood as admitting the possession of several "weaker vessels." This would be polygamy.

"As with a weaker vessel" is made clear by the addition of the articulated adjective "the wifely one." When it is thus added it is a sort of apposition (as all such adjectives are, R. 776) and avoids what the R. V. margin takes the Greek to mean: "the female vessel as weaker." "As" is to be construed with "a weaker vessel," and "the wifely (one)" states the one referred to. Nor does γυναικεῖον mean "female" (for which concept the Greek has a different word) but

either "wifely" or "womanly." Since "the husbands"
are mentioned, "wifely" is evidently the better translation. The thought that this neuter adjective (neuter
only because of σκεῦος) is here substantivized and made
a noun is unwarranted, for if Peter had wanted a noun
for the word "wife" he could have written γυνή, "wife."
Pardon these explanations; they are offered only because such interpretations have been given to these
words of Peter.

The wife *is* the weaker vessel. Paganism always
tends to abuse her on this account. Her rights are reduced, often greatly. Her status is lowered, often
shamefully. Heavy loads are put upon her. She is
made man's plaything or man's slave. The fact that
she is weaker is always exploited. That is why Peter
inserts the phrase regarding "knowledge." Christian
knowledge will accord the wife all the consideration
and the thoughtfulness which God intends for her "as
a weaker vessel" in her "wifely" relation. Peter himself had a wife (I Cor. 9:5). Whether she was still
alive at this time and was with Peter at this writing
we do not know.

As the first participle is followed by ὡς, so is the
second one. Neither ὡς = "like," both point to facts;
nor is the second causal: "because also fellow heirs."
Both participles introduce considerations which the
Christian husbands' "knowledge" provides for their
conduct toward their Christian wives. This second
participle is subordinate to the first: "continuing to
render honor as also joint heirs of life's grace." Καί
should not be transposed: "and as" (A. V.); Peter
writes "as also." While she is "a weaker vessel," every
Christian wife is "also" an heir of God's grace, and
there is no difference in this respect between her and
her Christian husband (Gal. 3:28).

This participle also denotes continuance and asks
the husbands to do what they have been doing. We

may indicate the relation of the two participles thus: "continuing to dwell, etc., while continuing to render honor," etc. The honor here referred to is different from the honor which Christians accord to "all" or to the king (2:17). To be fellow heirs of the eternal kingdom is the highest position to which poor mortals may rise, and it is this spiritual height which prompts mutual honoring.

Peter properly uses the plural "joint heirs"; we have indicated why the singular "weaker vessel" is necessary. The nominative "as also (being) joint heirs" is by no means improved by the few copyists who changed it into a dative; "as also *to* joint heirs." The preceding dative does not call for another dative, for the dative "as with a weaker vessel" is due to σύν in the first participle. "As also joint heirs" simply states the fact and implies that, as the Christian husbands are heirs, so their Christian wives are heirs with them. As far as the case, the nominative or the dative, is concerned, this makes no change in the fact that the wives are "joint heirs," and neither case makes the husbands "joint heirs" except as all heirs are joint heirs.

The insertion "of *manifold grace* of life" is another supposed improvement, "manifold" being taken from 4:10. Our mutual inheritance is "grace," here as always God's unmerited favor toward sinners which pardons them and takes them into his kingdom of grace. It is Peter's combination when he writes "life's grace" (both nouns are qualitative) or "grace of life." This is the spiritual life we now possess. We have no warrant to think only of the life to come. We are heirs who have already inherited so much and live in the enjoyment of this our inheritance. The genitive "of life" is objective (not appositional): grace for life or grace producing spiritual life.

The question is raised as to whether Peter speaks only of Christian wives or includes also such as are not Christian. All argument for including also the latter is unconvincing. To point to v. 1 where the Christian conduct of the wife is to win her pagan hushand to the faith and to claim that Peter ought now to say the same thing regarding the husband's conduct producing the same effect, does not make *two* classes of "joint heirs," one actual, the other prospective as we have this second class in v. 1: "even if *some* are disobedient." Peter presupposes intelligent readers who will themselves make the application to unbelieving wives on the basis of what is said in v. 1 about unbelieving husbands. That is why he is so brief when he speaks about "the husbands." Moreover, in v. 2-6 and especially in vs. 5, 6 the reference to unbelieving spouses is dropped, it has already been attended to (v. 1). This applies also to v. 7.

Εἰς τό does *not* always express pure purpose; here it indicates contemplated result. These husbands have been treating their Christian wives as they should. Peter takes it for granted that they will continue to do so and thus names the contemplated result: "so that your prayers may not be hindered." How could they engage in prayers or expect God to hear them if they persist in, or fall back into, the old pagan ignorance in the treatment of their wives?

Ἐγκόπτεσθαι, to have an obstacle thrown in the way, does not restrict the thought to preventing the prayers from reaching their destination at God's throne of grace. The thought includes all manner of hindering. A husband who treats his wife in the wrong way will himself be unfit to pray, will scarcely pray at all. There will be no family altar, no life of prayer. His worship in the congregation will be equally affected.

Peter's word to "the husbands" is brief but contains a great deal. In fact, it covers their whole Christian obligation.

All, v. 8-12

8) From the specific relation to government (2: 13-17) and from the three special groups and relations of the members (2:18-3:7, slaves, wives, husbands), Peter turns to the obligations resting on all the members as they live in this world in contact with each other and with their Gentile neighbors and thus harks back to 2:11, 12 and closes this part of his letter as he began it. The underlying thought is throughout that genuine Christian conduct not only hushes up vilification of Christians but also wins many non-Christians. Even aside from this fact God's calling lays these obligations upon us.

Now, finally, all, same-minded, sympathetic, fraternally friendly, compassionate, lowly-minded, not giving back a base thing for a base thing or reviling for reviling but contrariwise, continuing to bless, because for this you were called that you inherit blessing.

"All" is a nominative as is explained in 2:18; 3:1; 3:7, which have similar nominatives. Instead of using predicative participles Peter now uses adjectives which simply describe (like the participles occurring in 2:18; 3:1; 3:7) and have a mild hortatory note. R. 945 thinks that the imperative ἔστε is to be supplied; we think that nothing is to be supplied.

All the readers are expected to continue to be "same-minded," all intent on the same thing. Sentiment, aim, purpose are to be identical; there is to be no division even inwardly. Peter rightly puts "same-minded" first, for nothing will so impress the world about us nor be so good for our own selves. To be contrary-minded is to harm oneself and others. Peter does not need to say that this "same" mind is the one that was in Christ (Phil. 2:5).

"Sympathetic," like "same-minded," is a hapax-legomenon: sharing the feelings of others whether these are joyful or painful. The adjective "fraternally friendly" or "affectionate" occurs twice in Maccabees; Peter has the noun in 1:22. "Same-minded, sharing feelings, fraternally affectionate" apply to all Christians in their relation with each other. "Compassionate" applies also to non-Christians, to any who may be in distress. Some texts have φιλόφρονες, "friendly-minded," but the support for this reading is too weak. "Lowly-minded," the opposite of haughty or high-minded, is the virtue of which Paul says so much in Phil. 2.

9) Peter returns to a use of participles and now adds specifications: "not giving back a base or mean thing for a base or mean thing," retaliating, tit for tat, taking vengeance (Rom. 12:17) in this manner. "Or" adds a more specific wrong: "reviling for reviling" (2:23, Christ's example: "he reviled not again"); ἀντί is explained by R. 573 as denoting exchange. "But the very contrary" is the Christian's conduct, namely "blessing" (Matt. 5:44; Rom. 12:14), calling down good on those who revile us.

The supposition that ἵνα always denotes purpose cannot be valid here; here ἵνα introduces a clause that is appositional to τοῦτο, and τοῦτο cannot refer to anything that precedes. "For this were you called (by him who called you, 1:15) that you inherit a blessing," effective aorist subjunctive: actually inherit. God called us to inherit his infinite blessing; this impels us to bless others. The exposition appears in Matt. 18:21-35. The interpretation that we inherit the blessing which we bestow on others breaks down on the word "inherit"; no one inherits what he bestows. We are called to bless because we ourselves were blessed by God through his call.

10) With a simple "for" Peter introduces Ps. 34:12-16a, not as proof, but as elucidation: we are called to inherit a blessing, God's own everlasting blessing. Let us, then, not lose it as the unmerciful retainer lost his as recorded in Matt. 18:32-34. Peter quotes the LXX which renders the Hebrew well and changes only to the third person to fit the present connection and thus also makes the opening question the subject of the imperatives. **For,**

> **He who wants to love life**
> **And to see good days,**
> **Let him stop the tongue from any base thing**
> **And lips from uttering guile;**
> **Moreover, let him incline away from base-**
> **ness and do good;**
> **Let him seek peace and pursue it.**
> **Because the Lord's eyes (are) upon righteous**
> **ones**
> **And his ears for their begging;**
> **But the Lord's countenance (is) against such**
> **as are doing things base.**

"To love life" means to love it with intelligence and corresponding purpose. Such love includes the γνῶσις referred to in v. 7; the word Peter employs is not merely φιλεῖν, "to like" life. The thought is wanting a life here on earth that is worth while, that one can love with full intelligence and purpose. The parallel line expounds: "and to see good days" (Hebrew: "days that he may see good"; LXX: "loves to see good days"), i. e., days that are really beneficial and not vain and empty. David and Peter are not thinking of easy, pleasant, sunshiny days but of a life and of days that are full of rich fruit.

The negative prescription for such a life is: "Let him stop the tongue from any base thing"; read what James 3:6, etc., says about the tongue, which amply shows how the tongue ruins so many lives. The word κακόν means "what is base or mean" morally. The parallel line repeats and adds the illuminating word "guile": "and lips from uttering guile" (no guile was found in Christ's mouth, 2:22). In 2:1 baseness and guile are to be put away, see δόλος there. It goes without saying that only a heart that is free from anything base and from guile is able to control the tongue and the utterance. In the ablative (R. 1061) τοῦ μὴ λαλῆσαι, the μή is redundant (R. 1171) and thus not translated.

11) Δέ, "moreover," introduces the positive side of the prescription with its negative and its positive features: leaning away from anything base and doing what is good and truly beneficial; which the parallel line expounds: "Let him seek peace and pursue it" in order to capture it. As we take ἀγαθόν in its fullest sense, so we also regard εἰρήνη: first, good for the soul, next, *shalom*, peace for the soul, well-being, when God is our friend. Combine Rom. 14:19 and Heb. 12:14, plus Rom. 12:18.

12) The fact that this is the meaning the great final reason for this prescription makes plain: "Because the Lord's eyes (are) upon such as are righteous" (no article, qualitative), ever watching them to bless them, "and his ears (are) for their begging," to answer them with help, comfort, support. He finds them "righteous ones" in his judgment and never fails them.

But "such as are doing things base" have another experience: the Lord's countenance is against them. Ἐπί has both meanings: "over" and "against"; the context determines which is to be selected. Although base men may seem to prosper, Ps. 73 shows what it means to have Yahweh set his face against them.

With these significant lines from Holy Writ itself Peter closes his series of hortations regarding the Christian's life in general among men, brethren and outsiders.

Hortations Due to Sufferings and Trials, 3:13-5:11

How to Suffer for Doing Good, v. 13-17

13) Divide the epistle as one may, the subject of suffering and trials begins at this point; the naming of certain classes (2:18; 3:1; 3:7) and then of "all" (3:8) has reached its end. The simple connective καί and the fact that Peter still speaks of doing good lead some to attach these verses to the preceding ones; but the new note is introduced in the very first clause, namely someone's treating the readers basely. This is the subject of the last grand part of the letter. It rests on all that Peter has thus far written, and καί is thus proper. The real purpose of Peter has now been reached, namely to enlighten, comfort, and strengthen the readers in suffering and trial. They have had some taste of it in their previous experience; now there is the prospect that these sufferings will become far more severe. We have pointed out the change that was taking place at Rome, Nero's hostility to Christianity, which was bound to have its effect also in the provinces of the empire (see the introduction); Peter writes mainly for this reason, in order to fortify the readers in advance.

And who is he that will treat you basely if you get to be zealots for the good? The rhetorical question implies that no one will do this. It is mighty hard for anybody to mistreat people who are zealots for goodness, i. e., for doing what is beneficial to others. Peter substantivizes the future participle (rarely used) by writing ὁ κακώσων, which agrees with the ἐάν clause, the apodosis of which has a future tense. Ἐάν introduces an expectancy, and γένησθε is ingressive: "if, as I expect (ἐάν), you get to the point of not merely doing good but of being actual zealots for the good," people whose one great passion is "the good" (the classic use of the adjective as a noun).

Peter's meaning is not that his readers will thus escape all base treatment and persecution, for this is the very subject with which he proposes to deal. Despite all the good which Christians may do, the world does not really like them and is on occasion bound to vent its hatred. What Peter says is that zealousness for the good robs opponents of any real reason for mean treatment of the readers; as in the case of Jesus, who constantly went about dispensing good, some other reason for mean treatment will have to be trumped up.

14) Nevertheless, if also you should be suffering for righteousness' sake, blessed (are you)! While nobody can in reality make zealousness for good a reason for base treatment, Christians may have to suffer "for righteousness' sake." The unrighteous world cannot tolerate righteousness. The very presence of true righteousness irritates it, for this righteousness silently condemns its own unrighteousness. Thus Christians may often have to suffer in various ways. Peter now deals with such sufferings; in 4:12 he speaks of trials. Some commentators confuse εἰ καί and καὶ εἰ; the latter hints at improbability: "even if," the former means "if also" and treats the protasis as a matter of indifference: "If there is a conflict, it makes no real difficulty. There is sometimes a tone of contempt in εἰ καί. The matter is belittled," R. 1026. That is the case here.

We see why. Because to suffer thus, as already Jesus said in Matt. 5:10, assures to you the verdict: "Blessed!" Jesus expresses the same beatitude. We regard it as being exclamatory. Μακάριοι is the *'ashre* of the psalms (e. g., Ps. 1:1). It is a judgment with reference to those to whom it is addressed, a divine judgment which declares that theirs is true spiritual soul blessedness for which they must be called fortunate in the highest sense; the opposite is οὐαί, "Woe!"

We have εἰ with the optative (present, durative or iterative), a very rare construction in the Koine; it is a condition of potentiality: "might have to be suffering." Peter states it thus in the hope that the readers may, after all, despite the threatening clouds that are arising in Rome, escape special suffering. To say that he indicates an improbability is not exact. What he has in mind is not a balancing of probability and improbability. When he looks at the future he expresses his own desire that the readers may be spared; yet, if this should not be the case, it is really of no moment since any suffering that might come would be only blessedness. One always speaks subjectively when using conditional clauses. In this connection Peter wants his readers to think of suffering only as something that *might* come. Even when one is rather certain that something will come he may yet wish to speak of it in this way.

With δέ Peter adds the other, namely the negative, side and alludes to the wording of Isa. 8:12: **And do not fear their fear, neither be disturbed (shaken, upset), but sanctify the Lord, Christ, in your hearts, ready always for defense to everyone asking you reason concerning the hope in you, but with meekness and fear, keeping a good conscience in order that in what they continue to speak against you they may be put to shame who abuse your good conduct in connection with Christ.**

If Peter had in mind improbability or only remote possibility, these strong imperatives, three decisive aorists, would be out of place. Then the strong words about fear and being shaken would also not have been written.

"Do not fear their fear!" is a strong expression because it has the cognate accusative. The sense of the translation of the LXX is: "Do not fear with the fear the people have!" Peter is not quoting but only alluding to Isaiah and thus says "their fear," the fear they would inspire in you (the subjective genitive is to be understood in this sense). The sense is: "Do not let them scare you!" Αὐτῶν needs no formal antecedent. "Neither be disturbed!" means both in your minds and your conduct.

15) In the face of suffering the readers must sanctify the Lord, Christ, in their hearts; that will keep out all fear of men. The A. V. follows the very inferior variant "the Lord God," which is only an alteration that was made in agreement with the LXX's "the Lord of hosts" (God). The R. V. translates "Christ as Lord" because it regards Κύριον as a predicative apposition since it lacks the article and τὸν Χριστόν as the object since it has the article. This construction might pass if it were not for the allusion to Isa. 8:13. Κύριον is a proper name and thus has no article. Because it is a name for God in Isa. 8:13, Peter must add τὸν Χριστόν since he refers "the Lord" to Christ. The article must be used to indicate that Χριστόν is a second name and thus an apposition, for Κύριον Χριστόν would be a unit designation, "Lord Christ." Because Peter has only an allusion, the Christological import of his use of Κύριος to designate Christ is so strong. As the word refers to God's deity in Isa. 8:13, it here refers to the deity of Christ. We are to sanctify Christ in our hearts as the prophet demands this same sanctifying of the Lord of hosts by Israel in their hearts.

To sanctify Christ in our hearts is ever to keep him in our hearts as "the Holy One." In order to do this properly we ourselves must be "holy," ἅγιοι, sanctified. He is ours, and we are his; we separate him for our hearts and are separated for him. This sanctifying of him means that we keep ourselves from sin and give the world no cause for slandering either him or ourselves. And it further means that we fear him alone lest we sin against him by fearing men instead of him and by letting their threats prevent us from bowing to him alone. The objection that "in our hearts" is not found in Isa. 8:13; that a reference not to hearts but to conduct would be in place here if "sanctify" is to be modified; that, therefore, the phrase is to be construed with what follows, forgets the fact that this is allusion and not quotation, that sanctifying starts in the heart, and that "conduct" duly follows in v. 16.

With hearts that are ever sanctifying Christ the readers face their opponents, "ready always for defense to everyone asking you reason concerning the hope in you." This is the "living hope" mentioned in 1:3 to which we have been begotten again by God, the hope in God (1:21; 3:5), and it comprises all that we expect from God on the basis of Christ. Ἀπολογία is the regular term for the defense which a defendant makes before a judge (Acts 22:1; 25:16). He must first be heard (John 7:51). Peter is not thinking only of court trials, for he lets "everyone" ask λόγον, "account," *Rechenschaft* (which is not only a classical term but also a juridical term).

Let whoever will constitute himself a judge, the Christian is never to evade or to put him off, he is to be ready to present his case, his defense, to render account as to what his hope embraces, and as to why he holds it in his heart. We may say that he is to be ready always to testify, to correct ignorance about Christ, to spread the gospel light, to win others for Christ, to justify his own hope, and as Peter adds here (v. 16), to silence evil speakers with his good conduct which certainly speaks for itself and puts slander to shame.

But this defense is ever to be made "in company with (μετά) meekness and fear." On "meekness" see "the meek spirit" referred to in 3:4. "When you are asked about your hope you are not to answer with haughty words and carry things off with audacity and force as though you meant to tear up trees, but with fear and humility as though you stood before God's judgment and were making answer. For if it should now come to pass that you were to be called before kings and nobles and had equipped yourself a good while with statements and thoughts: Just wait, I will answer them right! it may well come about that the devil takes the sword out of your hand, and before you are aware gives you a thrust so that you stand disgraced and have equipped yourself in vain, might also snatch out of your heart the statements which you fixed best so that you would be left even if you had them well in mind, for he has noted your thoughts in advance. Now God lets this happen to dampen your haughtiness and to humble you." Luther, who certainly had plenty of experience. "With fear" means the fear of Christ as it did in 1:17; 2:18; 3:2.

16) Hence Peter also writes: "having (keeping) a good conscience," yet not only before but also after making a defense. Do so with this purpose, that in the very thing in which accusers speak against you they may be put to shame who abuse your good conduct in connection with Christ (ἀναστροφή as in 1:15, the verb in 1:17). It is not correct to state that the verb ἐπηρεάζω is always intransitive and thus cannot have "conduct" as its object; see Luke 6:28. This does not mean that all who are thus put to shame will cease their slander; yet something will be accomplished as is noted also in 2:15, in fact, a good deal may be accomplished.

17) Peter concludes these directions with the motivating consideration: **For better** (it is) **while**

doing good, if the will of God should will, to suffer than while doing ill. The statement is entirely general and thus brings to a succinct, axiomatic expression what has been said already in 2:15, 19, 20: "So is the will of God that by doing good you muzzle the ignorance of foolish men"; "This is grace if because of consciousness of God one bears up under griefs, suffering wrongfully . . . if doing good and suffering you shall stand it, this is favor with God." Also 3:14: "Blessed if you suffer for righteousness' sake!" In 4:14 we have another such "blessed." Add 4:14-19. Peter explains himself.

Peter does not need to say that if we do ill, it might be God's will that we suffer. But many are surprised to be made to suffer when they are doing good. Yet that is precisely what God's will wills in some instances. We have the potential optative as in v. 14, and it is to be understood in much the same sense. When this happens, if it should so happen in some instance (as Peter states it), it is certainly "better," i. e., preferable in every way than to suffer when doing basely. The latter would be shame and disgrace (2:20a); the former is noble, in fact, is like the suffering of Christ. When a Christian growls and grumbles or accuses God of injustice for letting him suffer he, of course, spoils it all. He no longer has the glory of suffering innocently. This is gone, he should hang his head in shame.

The Exaltation of Christ an Assurance to Those Who Suffer, v. 18-22

18) The only reason we have for making a special paragraph of this section is the fact that this piece forms a *sedes doctrinae* and throughout deals with Christ. It belongs to v. 13-17 in reality as ὅτι καί, "because also Christ," plainly shows.

It is essential to understand this connective. In
2:21 we also have ὅτι καὶ Χριστὸς ἔπαθεν, "because also
Christ suffered," but there Peter at once adds
ὑπολιμπάνων ὑπογραμμόν, "leaving behind for you a *writing-copy* in order that you may *follow* his tracks."
Such an addition is not appended here. In 2:21 Peter
presents Christ's *sufferings* as an *example* which mis-
treated *slaves* are to follow. In the present connection
Peter does nothing of the kind. Here the sufferings of
Christ are combined with his *exaltation*; this exaltation
is presented at length and is made the main thought.
We have the picture of Christ being infinitely exalted
over the disobedient who are now in hell, who were
made to see his triumph. This goes far beyond 2:21-25,
far beyond the Sufferer, sinless, patient, never opening
his mouth to revile when he was reviled, to threaten
when suffering, committing himself to the righteous
Judge, carrying our sins up upon the wood to save us,
so that we have him as the Shepherd and Overseer of
our souls.

Here the great point is *assurance* for us when by
the will of God we suffer for righteousness' sake. Then
we are μακάριοι, "*blessed.*" Christ's mighty exaltation
after his suffering proves this. The proof and the assurance are tremendous. For Christ was not only glorified in his own person; he not only leads us to God as
the fruit of his suffering in our behalf; in his exaltation
he triumphed over the disobedient who were consigned
to prison in hell. Are we, then, not blessed indeed when
we suffer for his sake? Now the disobedient exalt
themselves and tread us under foot; but see the disobedient in hell! Noah and his family are saved; we,
too, are saved "by the resurrection of Christ," by this
exaltation of Christ at God's right hand.

It is a misunderstanding of this section to think
that Christ is presented as another example for us.
To point to ἀγαθοποιοῦντας, "doing good," to take this to

mean that by our suffering we should try to win our
persecutors for Christ (to interpret "doing good and
suffering" in 2:20 in the same way, the slaves thus
seeking to win their mean masters for Christ), is to
misunderstand all that follows. Some find the thought
in this section that the gospel is still being preached
in hell, that continued mission work is being carried on
in hades! Some even add the complete *apokatastasis*,
the conversion of the devils. The fact that Christ
descended to hell in *glory* while we are to do good in
order to save our persecutors by our *suffering*, is disregarded.

The idea of "doing good" in order to save those who
hurt us is found in v. 1. But Peter does not speak of
"doing good" when he addresses the wives of unbelieving husbands; he speaks of "being in subjection"
when he is addressing all wives, and in the case of
those who have pagan husbands he speaks of "your
pure conduct in fear (of God)." This missionary idea
of "doing good," which is extended into hell, is wanting
at its very source. In v. 17 (as in 2:20) suffering while
doing good refers to the whole good life of Christians
(and so also of slaves, 2:20) as "grace with God," as
our *own* sanctification whether *men* appreciate it or
not. As far as men are concerned, our being "zealots
for the good" (v. 13) robs them of all just reason for
treating us basely (v. 13); it puts them to shame when
they speak against us and abuse our good conduct connected with Christ (v. 16). That is what Peter says.

**Because also Christ suffered once for sins, One
Righteous in place of unrighteous ones, in order that
he may bring us to God, (he), on the one hand, put
to death by means of flesh, on the other hand, vivified by means of spirit; in connection with which,
etc.**

"Because also," etc., connects this section with the
whole of v. 13-17 and not only with v. 17. So also this

connective joins the whole of v. 18-22 and not only
v. 18 to the preceding. As it is impossible to separate
v. 17 from what precedes, so it is impossible to separate v. 18 from what follows. We who are saved
suffer and are blessed because Christ suffered and was
glorified as our Savior. His glorification is the cause
(ὅτι) of this our being "blessed," and since our blessedness still lies in the future to so large an extent (I John
3:2), this "because" is the guarantee or assurance
for us.

Here are the great facts: also Christ *suffered* once
for sins, One Righteous in place of unrighteous ones,
suffered to the extent that by means of his flesh he,
on the one hand (μέν), was actually *put to death*, but,
on the other hand (δέ), as the Righteous One who suffered and died in place of the unrighteous, *was vivified*
by means of his spirit and thus *did* what follows: assured us that we who suffer for righteousness' sake
are, indeed, μακάριοι (v. 14). The textual question as
to whether to read ἔπαθεν, "suffered," or ἀπέθανεν, "died,"
is a matter for the text critics to decide, seeing that
Codex *Aleph* changes "suffered" into "died" also in
2:21 and 4:1, and both A and C insert ὑπὲρ ἡμῶν (ὑμῶν)
before ἀπέθανεν in 3:18. "Christ suffered" resumes this
verb which was used in v. 13 and 17; the fact that this
was suffering which ended in death is made plain by
θανατωθείς, "put to death."

"Once" he suffered "concerning sins." Both the adverb and the phrase bring out the thought that Christ's
suffering was one of expiation, and both "once" and
the aorist "he did suffer" imply that the expiation was
effected; see this valuable "once" (ἅπαξ) in Heb. 9:26,
28. The thought is emphasized by the addition of the
apposition: "One Righteous in place of unrighteous
ones"; it was vicarious, substitutionary suffering. In
Acts 3:14 Peter calls Christ "the Holy and Righteous
One" (Ps. 16:10); Stephen calls him "the Righteous

One" in Acts 7:52; Ananias calls him this in Acts 22:14; compare Luke 23:47; Matt. 27:19, 24; I John 2:1. The terms are purposely juridical: "One Righteous — unrighteous ones," and refer to God's verdicts and are thus more significant than "One Sinless — sinners." God's verdicts regarding Jesus appear in Matt. 3:17; Luke 9:35; John 12:28, God's voice from heaven; and the fact of God's raising him from the dead and placing him at his right hand is especially such a verdict.

On ὑπέρ as denoting substitution in the meaning "instead of" in hundreds of connections in the papyri and in the decisive New Testament passages see the pertinent chapter in Robertson, *The Minister and his Greek New Testament*, 35, etc., also his *Grammar*, 630, etc. "It is futile to try to get rid of substitution on grammatical arguments about ὑπέρ." "The papyri forbid our emptying ὑπέρ of this wealth of meaning in the interest of any theological theory." Robertson refers to the theories that deny Christ's substitution and invent something else on the claim that Peter's and Paul's ὑπέρ cannot mean substitution and was used by them to deny this very thought. Ὑπέρ, "over," then "in behalf of," gets the meaning "in place of" in all connections in which "in behalf of" brings no benefit unless there is a substitution "instead of." This is plain both here and in 2:21. Here substitution is joined to expiation. One may reject both but one cannot deny that Peter states both here.

We do not think that προσάγω means what some find in it, namely that Christ brings *us* to God as a pure and holy sacrifice; the verb is used here as it is used in Lev. 3:12; 4:4; 8:14. Not as sacrificial victims are we brought to God. Others think that Christ enabled us to become priests (2:5, 9), brought us to draw nigh to God as priests. This thought is sometimes elaborated: we are to do priestly service for others and by our doing good to bring them to conversion, which is the idea noted above. Both sacrifice and priesthood are foreign to Peter's words. We are brought to God (aorist, effectively, actually) when we who are *unrighteous* are by faith in Christ's vicarious expiation justified and *declared righteous*. Beyond that Peter's words do not go. On our "priesthood" see 2:5, 9.

How Christ's having suffered concerning sins just once does, indeed, bring us to God is shown by his glorification. As a further apposition Peter adds two illuminating participles: "put to death by means of flesh, vivified by means of spirit," and balances them by μέν and δέ, which, however, do not mean *zwar*, "although" (concessive) and *aber*, "but" (adversative), but: "on the one hand — on the other hand" (balance, correlation). The two great facts are to be taken together and are to be construed with "Christ suffered once regarding sins, One Righteous in place of unrighteous ones," with saving effect upon us believers. All three, the verb and the participles, are aorists, mighty historical facts.

The participles are passive. They do not say that Christ died and became alive but that he was put to death, was made alive — "whom *you* crucified, *God* made both Lord and Christ" (Acts 2:36); "whom *you* crucified, whom *God* raised from the dead" (Acts 4: 10). Christ's suffering was of such a nature that he was put to death. That is not said in order to show its greatness or to make some kind of a comparison with our suffering; that is said because the suffering of Christ "concerning sins" was sacrificial, expiatory, "One Righteous in place of unrighteous ones," i. e., substitutionary so that the sacrificial victim must be put to death. "Vivified," brought back to life, is placed beside "put to death." The sacrifice "concerning sins" was all-sufficient, was attested as sufficient by the *vivi-*

fication. God accepted the sacrifice of Christ and attests the acceptance by his act of returning Christ to life. The Scriptures add that this includes the glorification; Peter himself adds it in what follows.

Other sacrificial victims remain dead; not so Christ. Whatever the efficacy of such deaths may be, of Christ alone as one who was "vivified" can it be said that "he leads us to God." All the Old Testament sacrifices could only point to Christ's sacrifice and become effective because of the efficacy of his sacrifice; for their value they all depended on him as one who was "put to death and vivified." It is true, "vivified" crowns "put to death"; but this lies in the fact itself and not in the use of μέν . . . δέ as some have thought. There is no thought of paralleling our suffering with Christ's, our resurrection with his vivification. Christ's resurrection is not mentioned until v. 21. What is here said about Christ's sacrificial suffering and being put to death and then being vivified is intended to be the basis for our being "blessed" when we must suffer "for righteousness' sake" in this hostile world, the basis of our assurance of being thus "blessed" (v. 13, 14).

One is a bit surprised to note that the dictionaries and the grammars have no reference to the two datives, and that commentators, too, hesitate to classify these datives. The R. V. has: *"in* the flesh — *in* the spirit"; the A. V.: *"in* the flesh — *by* the Spirit"; Luther has two *nach,* "according to." Yet Peter has written neither ἐν nor κατά. Few will attempt to construe the two datives differently as the A. V. does. The discussion centers on the significance of σάρξ and πνεῦμα, especially on the latter, and this is what seems to cause the reluctance in regard to classifying these datives.

They are datives of means. They indicate neither sphere nor norm. On Calvary we see how Christ was "put to death"; they nailed his body to the ξύλον or "wood"; in 2:24 "he carried up our sins in his body upon the wood"; compare as being pertinent Col. 1:22: "in the body of his flesh by means of the death." It was "by means of flesh," by having flesh, our human bodily nature, that men slew Christ; the absence of the article makes "flesh" qualitative. How did Christ die? Mark 15:37, 39 use ἐκπνέω; Luke 23:46 does likewise: "he breathed out," breathed his last, the breath left his body. Matt. 27:50 says more: ἀφῆκε τὸ πνεῦμα, "he let go the spirit"; John 19:30, παρέδωκε τὸ πνεῦμα, "he gave up the spirit," which recalls Luke's εἰς χειράς σου παρατίθεμαι τὸ πνεῦμά μου: "Father, into thy hands I deposit my spirit." All the Evangelists use choice terms when they describe Jesus' death.

Although in John 10:15, 17 Jesus himself says, τὴν ψυχήν μου τίθημι, "I lay down my life" (the ψυχή that animates my body), no Evangelist uses this word when he describes Jesus' death. To be sure, Jesus died when his ψυχή or "life" went out of him; but the ἐγώ, the real personality, has its seat in the πνεῦμα, in the human spirit. This spirit of his Jesus deposited into his Father's hands, this he let go or gave up in the instant of death. Death sundered its connection with his σῶμα or body (2:24), which connection was by way of his ψυχή. His spirit went to heaven, to Paradise, to his Father's hands; his body, his flesh was left dead on the cross. See further *The Interpretation of St. Matthew's Gospel*, 1103, etc.; or that of St. John, 1285, etc.

How was Christ vivified? The human spirit which went to heaven returned to the body that was lying in the tomb. Spirit and body, which had been separated in death, were reunited in the vivification. How else than "by means of spirit" (again qualitative) could Christ have been made alive again after having been put to death?

Simple as this is, the comments of some interpreters are rather confusing. Some look upon this as an act of the Holy Spirit (C.-K. 950) and, like the

A. V., regard one of these datives as a dative of the
agent. Some think that σαρκί means "according to his
human nature" and πνεύματι "according to his divine
nature," and others oppose this as being wrong. Rom.
1:4; I Tim. 3:16; Heb. 9:14 are referred to as proof
that "spirit" denotes Christ's divine nature.

The matter regarding the two natures of Christ is
simple. As true man Jesus has body, soul, and spirit;
but as true God the person and the nature of the eternal
Logos, the divine ἐγώ, takes the place of what in us is
a human, creature ἐγώ. Thus God became man (did not
join himself to *some* man). Ever since the incarnation
body, soul, spirit (all human) belong to the Logos, are
his forever in an indissoluble union. Death did not
affect this union, did not sunder this union. The life-
less body was still that of the Logos; the human spirit,
which had been torn from it by death, was in heaven.
On Easter morning body and spirit were reunited.
That is all. Whether the agent of the passive ζωοποιηθείς
is God or Christ himself makes no difference; all the
opera ad extra are *indivisa aut communa*.

Do the two aorist participles denote an action that
is *subsequent* to that of the aorist verb? The acts, of
course, occurred in this order: suffered — put to death
— vivified, about which there is no question, grammatical or otherwise. R. 1111, etc., finds no sub-
sequence in aorist participles, but one need not be
satisfied with Burton's view, which R. 1114 adopts,
that the two participles define the whole preceding
clause. They are added appositionally to the subject,
each having only its aoristic, punctiliar force. For not
merely the fact that Christ suffered enables him to lead
us to God; this Sufferer was actually put to death and
was vivified.

19)   Peter continues: **in connection with which
also to the spirits in prison, on having gone** (to
them), **he made herald proclamation,** (these spirits)

such as were disobedient at one time when the long-suffering of God kept waiting in Noah's days while the ark was being constructed, in which few, that is, eight souls, were brought safely through by means of water; etc.

We now see why Peter stops with the *vivificatio* in v. 18 and does not at once proceed to the *resurrectio* by saying "raised up." The latter term is regularly used so as to include both the vivification of Christ's dead body and its appearances to chosen witnesses. Peter must restrict his thought to the vivification because he intends to speak of what occurred *before* Jesus appeared to his disciples on earth. Until Easter morning Christ's body lay dead in the tomb while his spirit (in English we may also say his "soul" because we use "soul" much as we do "spirit"; to use ψυχή in the Greek would be wrong) was in heaven. Then Christ's spirit was suddenly reunited with his body. This is the *vivificatio*.

In that instant, after body and spirit had been united, Christ left the closed tomb. The linen wrappings were suddenly empty and lay flat, the body having miraculously gone out of them (John 20:5-8), mute, but eloquent, evidence of what had occurred. In that instant, but timelessly, Christ in his human body and spirit descended to hell and did what Peter relates. In the other world time and space as we know both here on earth do not exist. Our minds are chained to both in their thinking and in their language; hence we ask so many useless questions where acts that take place in eternity and in the other world are concerned. In the other world no act requires time for its execution. This is really inconceivable to our minds; we are compelled to speak as if time were involved and must thus ever tell ourselves that this is *not* in fact the case. In this way we are kept from deductions that are based on our concepts of time, knowing that such

deductions would be false. How long after the cloud
enveloped the ascending body of Jesus did it take that
body to reach heaven and the right hand of God in the
glory of heaven? This part of the ascension was *timeless.*

The translation "in which spirit" Christ went, etc.,
is misleading. Not in his human spirit alone did Christ
descend to hell. Not in his divine nature alone. This is
said to those who think that πνεῦμα in v. 18 refers to
the divine nature. Not "by the Holy Spirit" (A. V.;
also C.-K.; etc.) was the descent made. Because Christ
went to speak to πνεύματα, "spirits," it was not necessary
that he himself come to them as a πνεῦμα, "a spirit."
Jesus spoke to the devil and to the demons in the possessed without being a bodiless spirit. Peter uses ἐν
in its first and original sense: Christ descended into
hades "in connection with" the spirit by means of
which his body had been made alive in the tomb. The
descent followed the quickening which joined spirit
and body. The assumption that the body was left behind in the descent does not agree with what Peter says
in the plainest way.

This idea led Calvin and his followers to date the
descent, not at the time of the *vivificatio* of the body
on Easter morning, but at the time of the death on
Good Friday, and to make the descent the climax of
Christ's humiliation, Christ entered hell to suffer there
until Easter morning as though Peter had written:
θανατωθεὶς σαρκὶ πορευθείς, κτλ., and then ζωοποιηθεὶς πνεύματι,
"put to death by means of flesh he went" to hades and
after that "he was vivified." Peter states the opposite:
the vivification is the entrance of Jesus into the state
of glorification and exaltation, and his first act in that
state is his glorious descent into hell with body and
spirit united. The death pertained to Christ's human
nature; the vivification likewise; the descent *ad in-*

feros also; and, let us add, also the ascent to heaven and the *sessio* at God's right hand.

Peter has the data and the order of the Apostles' Creed: "*suffered* under Pontius Pilate, was crucified, *dead*, and buried; he *descended* into hell; the third day he *rose again* from the dead (v. 21) and *sitteth at the right hand of God*, etc." (v. 22). The return to judgment is mentioned in 5:4.

The participle πορευθείς is to be construed with the verb ἐκήρυξεν. In English we should coordinate: "he went and made herald proclamation" (as our versions do); the Greek is more exact and by using the participle marks the act of having gone as subsidiary to that of speaking as a herald. The dative states to whom Christ spoke: τοῖς ἐν φυλακῇ πνεύμασι, "to the spirits in prison"; and these words are placed before the verb because they are emphatic. The Scriptures know of only one φυλακή, "prison," that confines "spirits," namely hell, "hades," "the Gehenna of the fire" (Matt. 5:22; 18:9). To call this the *Totenreich*, the realm of the dead, is to give a strange meaning to the word φυλακή, "prison," for all the dead are supposed to go into this fictitious *Totenreich*, this place between heaven and hell, a recent Romanizing Protestant invention. Note II Pet. 2:9, 10, in fact, all of v. 4-10.

20) It is to be observed that ἀπειθήσασί ποτε, κτλ., is not added attributively by means of a repetition of the article τοῖς, but predicatively without the article (R. 778). This is speaking grammatically; but it brings out the thought that Peter intends to say that Christ did not make herald proclamation to those only who were disobedient at the time of the flood, which thought would require τοῖς ἀπειθήσασι (the article repeated), but to all the spirits in prison, all these being *such as* were disobedient (the participle is merely qualitative) when (to instance a notable case) the longsuffering of God

waited no less than 120 years, waited in vain, before sending the judgment.

Some suppose that this anarthrous participle means that Christ made herald proclamation *only* to the victims of the flood and thus raise the question: "Why just to these?" and supply such answers as the following: that Peter selects these because they perished by water and because he refers to baptism; that by selecting these Peter does not intend to exclude the rest of the damned in hell. This question is excluded by the anarthrous and qualitative character of the participle. Moreover, these people *perished* in the flood while baptism *saves*; the eight souls of Noah's family were *saved* but not the spirits in prison.

The ὅτε clause leads some to think that in hell Christ dealt only with the antediluvians who perished in the Flood, and they then seek for reasons that Christ singled these out. But ποτε ὅτε, "once when," is not intended as such a restriction or limitation of τοῖς πνεύμασι. This would be expressed by a second τοῖς before ἀπειθήσασι and by a third τοῖς with a participial clause in place of ὅτε, at least by the latter. "Once when" introduces only a sample of the unbelief of disobedience, which is illustrative of all the spirits of the damned in prison. All God's longsuffering could do nothing with these antediluvians as it could do nothing with all these spirits which God had to consign to hell. This sample is the more in point because the Flood is a standing type of the final judgment.

By means of "once when" Peter might have referred to Sodom and Gomorrah as Jesus does in Matt. 10:15, and Paul in Rom. 9:29, Jude in v. 7, and Peter himself in II Pet. 2:6 and made them "an example of those about to be ungodly," which is the same idea that is expressed in our passage. But this "example" would not be fitting. Lot was not saved *"by means of"* the fire which destroyed these cities, he was saved only *from* this fire. Noah was saved *"by means of* water," δι᾿ ὕδατος, as we, too, are now saved by means of the water of baptism. As in II Pet. 2:6 the ungodly of Sodom and Gomorrah are a ὑπόδειγμα or "example" of all future ungodliness, so the disobedience of the men who lived at the time of Noah and the flood is the mark and the quality of all the damned in hell. They "disobeyed" has the same meaning it had in 2:8, "disobedient to the Word," and in 4:17, "those disobeying the gospel of God." Peter has in mind the disobedience of unbelief which, to be sure, includes also moral wickedness, but only as the outgrowth of unbelief's disobedience.

God's longsuffering (his holding out long under heavy provocation) waited in the days of Noah, delayed the judgment, waited for repentance and faith 120 years — alas, in vain! During those 120 years the world had Noah "as a herald of righteousness" (II Pet. 2:5) who condemned the world because of its unbelief and its unrighteousness (Heb. 11:7; see the exegesis). Noah's preparation of the ark is especially mentioned, the participle in the genitive absolute being the same as the verb used in Heb. 11:7, for this building of the ark was itself a factual preaching of the impending judgment. Peter's brief reference recalls all that Gen. 6 states. Men remained fixed and hardened in their disobedience of unbelief "in the days of Noah." Even all this warning left them unmoved. Did they laugh at Noah for building a big boat on dry land? How would it ever reach water and float? When had the earth ever had a flood of such proportions as to drown all living things? This is the character and the quality of all "the spirits in prison"; this brought them to hell.

We may now look at ἐκήρυξεν in v. 19, about which there has been so much discussion. The verb means to make a herald proclamation, has always meant this.

He who κηρύσσει is a κῆρυξ, "herald"; what he proclaims
is a κήρυγμα, "a herald's announcement." The word has
ever been a *vox media*. Hence in scores of places, when
the announcement made is the gospel, the objects appended say so: to herald the Word (Mark 1:45), the
acceptable year of the Lord (Luke 4:19), the gospel
(Matt. 4:23 and often), Christ or Jesus (Acts 8:5 and
often). This verb is sometimes used together with
εὐαγγελίζεσθαι, "to proclaim good news." But it is also
used when the law is its object (Rom. 2:21, not to
steal), when circumcision (Gal. 5:11) is the object.
When it is without an object as we have it here, the
context should indicate what the κήρυγμα or heralded
proclamation may be.

It lies in the nature of the case that in the New
Testament κηρύσσειν is used to indicate the heralding of
the gospel, for this was to be publicly proclaimed in
all the world as if by heralds. With it went the proclamation of the law: "He that believeth not shall be
damned." In II Pet. 2:5 Noah is called a κῆρυξ or
"herald," and he certainly proclaimed the coming judgment of the flood. And we are told that because the
verb is so often used in the New Testament to indicate
gospel heralding it must have this meaning in our
passage: Christ preached the gospel to the spirits in
prison. It is claimed that when no object is added the
verb *must* have this sense. Any substantial difference
between κηρύσσειν and εὐαγγελίζεσθαι is thus erased. Even
some dictionaries agree with this interpretation. For-
tunately, they all register the fact that κηρύσσειν means
"to herald." When C.-K., 599, adds that the thing
demands *Nachachtung*, this may be understood correctly: those who hear are to pay attention; yet he,
perhaps, intends to say: those who hear are to obey
or savingly to believe. When we are further told that
κηρύσσειν is used here because of ἀπειθήσασι we feel that
this statement wants to leave the door open for such as

were disobedient to Christ but now at last "in prison"
obey, believe, and are saved.

Those who claim that Christ preached the gospel
in hell have a probation after death. Some elaborate
this thought. If Christ did this, it must *somehow* still
be done: missionary work will be carried on in hell.
Most of them, however, seek to tone down this idea.
This probation after death is intended for those who
disobeyed *ignorantly,* who *never* heard the gospel. They
point to the many babes that perished in the flood as
if Peter makes a restriction, as if "disobeyed" does
not mean actual disobedience of the Word which Noah
preached. As for the eternal fate of babes, this concern
is pointless since the question pertains to all babes
who die without means of grace, regarding which we
have no revelation save the hint in Matt. 18:14 (see
the exposition).

The Scriptures teach no probation after death, no
missionary work in hell, and none in a *Totenreich,* for
none exists. Mark 16:16; Heb. 9:27. In hell Dives says
to Abraham at the mention of Moses and the prophets:
"No, father Abraham!" — the same fixed disobedience of unbelief. We need not elaborate the subject.

Like the fire of Sodom, etc., the flood is recorded
in Scripture as a type of the final judgment. Neither
could be a type of this judgment if probation and being
saved were still possible after judgment. The time
of grace ends when the μακροθυμία or "longsuffering" of
God is exhausted as it was "in the days of Noah." When
Peter wants to speak about εὐαγγελίζεσθαι he uses this
word as witness 1:12 and 4:6; here and in II Pet. 2:5
(which also deals with Noah) heralding alone is the
thought; Noah is the herald of a judgment that is impending; Christ is the far greater Herald who has a
proclamation for those who are already judged.

Let us note that Peter's interest does not lie in the
contents of Christ's proclamation. The *fact* that Christ

went to hell and made it, went there in the instant of his vivification after his death and made a proclamation to *the damned* in hell — this is the point that Peter impresses. The fact that the proclamation was not evangelical but damnatory goes without saying. When one is answering the question as to why Peter says this about the descent into hell one should not think only of these damned spirits since Peter himself adds all that follows about those who were saved in the flood, what their saving typifies for his readers through the resurrection of Jesus Christ and his enthronement in heaven at God's right hand with all angels, authorities, and powers subject to him who died and was vivified in his human nature. The descent and the ascent with its eternal enthronement belong together. Our comment should not separate them.

The ὅτι in v. 18 fortifies the whole of v. 13-17 by the whole of v. 18-22. Even before we look at the details about the eight souls that were saved, our baptism, and the new life, about Christ's resurrection and heavenly enthronement, we see Peter's object in bringing all these facts regarding Christ (passion to final glorification) to the attention of his readers. Μακάριοι are they, "blessed" indeed when suffering for righteousness' sake in this wicked world. This fact is the cause and the assurance of their blessedness, that down to the disobedient in hell all enemies of Christ are under his feet while for the readers, from the time of their baptism onward, there is salvation through him who died and rose again and sits at God's right hand. With all this before them, the readers will count themselves "blessed," will not fear the fear of men or be shaken, will sanctify the Lord, Christ, in their hearts, will be ready to answer men at any time regarding their hope, always keep a good conscience, etc. (v. 14-16). This is the mighty way in which Peter fortifies his readers in the face of impending persecution.

"While the ark was being constructed" points back to the disobedience of unbelief which had this warning but scorned it. The thought is, of course, not that men, too, should have constructed arks to save them as Noah did but that, if they had repented in obedience to the warning, they would not have been destroyed by a flood (compare Nineveh). The relative clause εἰς ἥν (static εἰς, "wherein," our versions; not the old "into," which still appears in B.-D. 205) turns to the blessed side of Noah's deliverance and with this to the salvation of the readers. Only a few, namely eight souls, were saved.

This mention of "few," so very few at that time, is made for the comfort of the readers who are "a little flock" compared with the whole unbelieving world about them. Look at all unbelievers who perished in the flood, whose spirits are now with all the other damned in hell. How they cowered when Christ appeared to them in their eternal prison! Peter correctly writes "eight ψυχαί" and not πνεύματα; "souls" or "persons" or even "lives" is the correct rendering. Those in hell were disembodied "spirits," their bodies were still on earth.

We translate: these eight "were brought safely through by means of water." Διά in the phrase is not due to the διά in the verb as R. 560 supposes but simply states the means by which the eight were brought through with complete safety. It is not local with reference to the ark moving "through the water." Water was the means for destroying all the rest; that same water was the means for floating the ark with its eight souls. Water was a means of judgment in the case of those, a means of saving in the case of these. We may add that Christ also has the same effect upon men (Luke 2:34); the Christ whom the damned saw in terror in hell is the same Christ who is our hope in heaven.

21)   We have already stated why Peter selected the judgment by water instead of Sodom and the judgment by fire: it enables him to refer to baptism and its saving water: **which as a type saves also you now as baptism, not a putting away of filth of flesh but an offer of a good conscience toward God through Jesus Christ's resurrection, he who is at God's right** (hand)**, having gone into heaven, angels and authorities and powers having been placed in subjection to him.**

The subject is ὅ, its antecedent is "water." The preliminary apposition to ὅ is ἀντίτυπον: water "as a type" saves you now, namely as a type of the water "by means of which" Noah and his family were brought safely through the flood judgment. The final apposition βάπτισμα states which water has this saving effect, "baptism," the suffix -μα denoting a result, the accomplished baptism. Two further appositions follow, but these define what the inner effect of baptism is, i. e., show how it indeed "saves."

'Αντίτυπος ordinarily means *nachgebildet,* formed as a copy of an original. But this adjective is also, though less frequently, used without expressing this inner relation in which the copy is viewed as being inferior to the original. This is the case here, where we have only a correspondence or likeness: water in each case — also a saving effect of water. The fact that the second water, that of baptism, saves in a far higher way is apparent and is also stated by Peter at length. This excludes the idea that *antitupon* means that the water of the flood is a type-prophecy of baptism. As far as the eight souls and as far as Peter's readers are concerned, there is only an analogous saving effect of water. We may translate with an adverbial expression, "by way of a type," or, as we do, by substantivizing the adjective: "as a type."

This is one of the passages (Titus 3:5; Mark 16:16)
which says directly that baptism "saves," yea, that the
water of baptism saves, certainly not as mere water
but as the water of baptism, i. e., connected with the
Word (Eph. 5:26), with "the Name of the Father,"
etc., (Matt. 28:19). "Which (water) now saves.
also you."

Peter even explains what baptism is and justifies.
his statement that its water "saves." These appositions have the effect of explanatory clauses as if Peter
had written: "for it is not . . . but it is," etc. "Not
a putting away of filth of flesh" = not a bodily cleansing, an outward, bodily rite. The deductions that the
readers held this view, and that Peter corrects them,
are unwarranted. One of the commonest means of
emphasizing the positive is to place it in contrast with
the negative. There were, indeed, ceremonial lustra-
tions; the Jews had them, for instance the washing
which the high priest had to undergo before officiat-
ing. All such washings really cleansed only the body
and were symbolical; they did not "save" spiritually,
were never intended to do so. Peter denies that baptism is such a minor rite and thus gives an answer to
those who see in baptism only "an ordinance," a symbol, a sign of grace already obtained or yet to be obtained, or a mere mark of obedience.

Immersionists also find little support for their view
here. The only persons who were immersed were those
who were drowned by the flood waters. Their case is
like that of the Egyptians who were drowned by immersion in the Red Sea (Exod. 14:28, 29; compare I
Cor. 10:1, 2).

The sacrament "saves" because it is not a mere
outward rite but "an offer of a good conscience toward
God through Jesus Christ's resurrection," etc. The
A. V. selects the common meaning of ἐπερώτημα, "an answer," one made to God by us. The R. V. does less well

with its "interrogation," margin "inquiry," "appeal," addressed to God by us. This is taken to mean that we ask God for a good conscience in the act of baptism, or that by obeying the command to be baptized we have a good conscience because of this our act of obedience and the answer we thereby make to God in baptism. See Thayer in regard to the way in which this is understood; he interprets it as *the vow* to have a good conscience in regard to God.

This word is forensic; the whole expression is parallel to the negative "not a putting away of filth of flesh." C.-K., 455. Bengel approached this meaning but made the word subjective: the *rogatio qua nos deum compellamus cum bona conscientia, peccatis remissis et depositis*, the claim which a good conscience has upon God with sins remitted and abolished. Schlatter has the correct interpretation: this ἐπερώτημα is God's *Antrag* or *Anbietung*. "God puts the question before man as to whether he wants to have a good conscience and receives the answer in the believing 'yes' of the one accepting baptism." The forensic sense lies in God's formal proposition, which, when it is accepted, is *rechtskraeftig*, legally binding.

The genitive "of a good conscience" is objective, and εἰς Θεόν is to be construed with it (as our versions have it). The order of the words parallels the negative which has σαρκός before ἀπόθεσις and ῥύπου after, and thus "of a good conscience" is put before ἐπερώτημα and εἰς Θεόν after. This careful order puts the emphasis first on "flesh" and again first on "a good conscience" and thus places these two into opposition: flesh-cleansing amounts to nothing, a good conscience is everything. Secondly, also "filth" is emphatic, and, like it, "toward God": to get rid of bodily dirt is nothing, but to be right εἰς (toward or regarding) God is everything.

The point of all this is the fact that in baptism *God* bestows something on *us* which becomes ours by baptism. Peter calls this "a good conscience toward God," and a glance at v. 16 shows the reason: men speak against us, but we keep the good conscience bestowed on us by baptism, these evil men are able to revile only our 'good conduct. So baptism truly "saves," so we remain "blessed," when, if God wills, we suffer from the disobedient in the world. All of this is the direct opposite of the view that *we* bring something to *God* in baptism, say obedience to the "ordinance" of baptism, a good conscience, a request for one, the answer of one, or the vow to have one.

We construe: "God's ἐπερώτημα through Jesus Christ's resurrection, he who," etc. In baptism God extends the saving proffer of a good conscience toward him only "by means of Jesus Christ's resurrection"; διά = means or mediation. We have already stated the difference between the vivification and the resurrection and have pointed out that the latter also includes the glorious appearance of the living Savior to the disciples and to chosen witnesses (I Cor. 15:4-8). The vivification is sufficient for the descent to hell. Christ, again alive, descended gloriously in body and in soul. Now, however, all that is comprised in his resurrection for the baptized believers is the basis of their blessedness, the medium of the good conscience toward God that was bestowed on them in and by baptism.

One might construe the phrase with "saves": "saves also you . . . through Jesus Christ's resurrection." This is in substance the same as construing: God's "offer through," etc. Christ's suffering and death are crowned by his resurrection, his ascension, and his *sessio* at God's right hand. These glorious acts complete his work. The resurrection (here we have the active term, his rising up) is the factual evidence that his substitutionary expiation of our sins is all-sufficient and that it has been accepted as such by God.

Thus the risen Lord instituted baptism for all nations (Matt. 28:19) with the promise that it saves (Mark 16:16). Without his resurrection there is no baptism, no salvation, no conscience-cleansing to comfort us when we are persecuted for righteousness' sake, in fact, no righteousness at all. Redemption was finished on the cross (John 19:30); the resurrection is God's own attestation to this effect (Acts 2:36, with v. 38 on baptism; 5:30-32).

22) Ὅς is a demonstrative relative: "he who is at God's right (hand), having gone into heaven, angels," etc. The demonstrative force is felt when we note that this is not a genitive "of Jesus Christ, *of* whom," but a nominative "he who." Peter intends to say: "This is the One who arose from the dead, whose resurrection assures us all blessedness."

He went into heaven = his ascension. One should note that πορευθείς is the same participle that was used in v. 19 to denote the descent into hell. Both are predicated of Christ's human nature (body and soul) which is in union with the divine. No man saw the descent; the ascent was seen in its first stage but not after the cloud enveloped Christ, when it became timeless. Since it is expressed by means of a participle the ascent is made subsidiary even as it was a single act. The *sessio* at God's right hand is the supreme thought. Peter has the simple statement that he "is at God's right." For further explanation see the other passages which have fuller expressions, notably Heb. 1:3; 12:2.

The full exaltation of being at God's right hand in heaven is indicated by the genitive: "made subject to him angels and authorities and powers." One can only shake his head when these angels are identified with "the spirits in prison" (v. 19), which were human spirits. Nor can we accept the view that the three terms are to be regarded as indicating three ranks. These are good angels. As angels they are subservient to Christ and are his messengers (Heb. 1:14). All these angels have authority, they likewise have power and are thus designated according to the degree of authority and of power bestowed on each of them. The same is true in Rom. 8:38; I Cor. 15:24; Eph. 1:21. We do not divide perpendicularly but horizontally as is explained in the interpretation of these other passages. Christ in his human nature is at God's right hand. By virtue of the divine attributes bestowed on his human nature at his incarnation the man Christ Jesus now rules with divine glory and majesty over heaven, earth, and hell, all God's holy angels being his ministrants in this rule. Let the readers dismiss all fear of men (v. 14, 15).

Peter does not mention the demons, neither in v. 18 nor here. Only by deduction can we think of the demons, and it is immaterial whether from the descent into hell we deduce that the demons are powerless before Christ, or from his enthronement at God's right hand that they are under his feet.

What Peter does not introduce Paul treats in Col. 2:15. Both of these passages deal with the descent into hell. We refer the student to the exposition of Col. 2:15, which states that God, "having stripped the rulerships and authorities (i. e., the demons) put them to shame publicly by causing a triumph over them in connection with him" (literal translation). Paul writes in disdain of the Judaizers in Colossæ, who imagined that demons could hurt Christians through certain foods and earthly elements, of which up-to-date Christians had to beware; but all demons were abjectly crushed by Christ's descent into hell. The two *sedes doctrinae* supplement each other, and we may add Eph. 4:8 (Ps. 68:18).

We append the following in regard to v. 19. Augustine held the view that Christ preached to the antediluvians here on earth before the flood, preached to them *non in carne, quia nondum erat incarnatus, sed in spiritu, i. e., secundum divinitatem praedicavit.* Gerhard, von Hofmann, Besser, etc., have adopted his view. This interpretation cannot, however, be supported by the text of this passage.

Zezschwitz has the following. Peter adopts the fables of the Book of Enoch, the Book of Jubilees, and "Jewish tradition." In order to frustrate the plan of sending a Savior to be born of men the demons (Gen. 6:4) cohabited with women and begot a terrible progeny, half-devil, half-human, which was as little redeemable as were their fathers. In order that the whole human race might not become infected God wiped it out by the flood, save the family of Noah. The spirits of these half-devils were held in prison, namely apart in the lowest dungeons of hell, so that on the day of judgment they might not appear before God's tribunal together with the other sinners. Christ descended to them and pronounced their doom in advance of the final judgment. This is called the type. The antitype is the Antichrist, a spiritual son of Satan who by a *generatio spiritualis* seeks to corrupt the souls of men. This is the counterpart to the cohabitation of the demons mentioned in Gen. 6:4. This second effort Christ will destroy at his Parousia. Such an interpretation can scarcely be called exegesis.

CHAPTER IV

Suffering in the Light of Death and the Judgment, v. 1-6

1) **Christ, then, having suffered by means of flesh, do you also equip yourselves with the same idea.** Οὖν is only transitional. The genitive absolute states only the fact that Christ suffered by means of flesh. The dative is also a dative of means as are the two datives σαρκί and πνεύματι in 3:18. Christ became flesh (John 1:14), assumed our earthly human nature in order to live as man here on earth, and thus he suffered "by means of flesh." Peter has already mentioned the fact of Christ's suffering in 2:21 and 3:18, in the latter passage he added the detail that he suffered "once." The aorist participle refers to Christ's suffering as having been finished and completed. He suffered until he was put to death by means of flesh (3:18). "Suffered" is to be understood in this sense.

Some texts add "for us" in analogy with "for you," 2:21; but this brings in a thought that has already been treated in 2:21 and more fully in 3:18, a thought that would upset the present context; ὑπὲρ ἡμῶν must be canceled.

"Do you also equip yourselves with the same ἔννοιαν, idea." Paul's use of ὅπλα in Rom. 6:13 makes us hesitate to translate "do you also arm yourselves" (a military figure). A ὅπλον is any useful tool and a military weapon only where the context speaks of a soldier or of war, which is not the case here. The ἔννοια, *Einsicht* or thought, idea, is not for the purpose of fighting anybody but is a useful tool for us while we are still living this earthly life and are thus suffering by means

(177)

of flesh. "The same idea"= the one just expressed, namely that of suffering by means of flesh until death brings it to an end.

Peter does not say that Christ had this idea regarding himself, that he was so equipped, but that this idea is to be taken by us for our use from the fact that Christ suffered by means of flesh. When we now suffer, and much or little suffering brings us to our death, it is a useful thing to see how Christ suffered by means of flesh. The commentary is John 15:20; compare Matt. 10:24; Luke 6:40; John 13:16. If Christ was persecuted, we, his followers, shall also be; we cannot expect to be above our heavenly Master.

The fact that we suffer "for righteousness' sake," for doing good, is understood, having been stated already in 3:13-17. Peter is fortifying his readers in view of impending persecutions (see the introduction). The thought of this first sentence is complete.

Because the one who suffered by means of flesh has ceased from sin so as no longer to live the rest of the time in flesh for lusts of men but for God's will.

There is a discussion as to whether ὅτι is causal or declarative. Those who assert that it is the latter think that the clause states the contents of the ἔννοια: "the same idea, that the one who suffered has ceased from sin." But this would include Christ and would state that he, too, had ceased from sin by having suffered by means of flesh. Yet Christ never sinned and never ceased from sin. In answer to this reply we are told that, when his suffering was completed, Christ ceased from sin in the sense that he had nothing more to do with *our* sins, nothing more to suffer *for* them, while we cease from sinning when we ourselves *commit* no more sin. But this double meaning was scarcely Peter's intention. What is true of Christ in one peculiar, exceptional sense, and true of him alone, cannot be associated with what is true of us in a totally different sense and be called "the same idea." More may be said. The Scriptures nowhere express the thought that Christ ever wanted to get through with suffering for our sins and have no further contact with them.

Ὅτι is causal (our versions are correct). This clause does *not* refer to Christ; it refers only to us. We alone cease from sin, i. e., stop sinning. The tenses are important. The substantivized participle is an aorist, and ὁ παθὼν σαρκί expresses the same completed suffering by means of flesh as does the aorist παθόντος σαρκί which precedes. This means that the sufferer has reached death. This is not the present participle ὁ πάσχων, the one whose suffering is still in progress. It would not be true to say that a Christian who still suffers "has ceased from sin."

We are surprised to be told that even wicked men are stopped from sinning by suffering, and that suffering acts in the same way with regard to Christians. The wicked rage at their suffering when their sins find them out. Many a Christian grumbles and complains and even begins to question the justice of God. Read what Herod the Great did during his last suffering, or that other Herod mentioned in Acts 12:23 (compare the accounts of Josephus). True enough, suffering leads many a Christian to deeper repentance and thus, in the providence of God, has its wholesome uses; affliction sometimes also aids in inducing a sinner to repent. But even repentant sufferers must still pray the Lord's Prayer, must still confess their sins as John (I John 1:8, 9) and James (3:2) did.

Although Peter's statement is general, it applies only to Christians, and to each of them only when their suffering for Christ's sake is at an end, when they have died. And we do not include the wicked and say that death stops them from sinning. This is done by those who think that at death their spirits enter the so-called *Totenreich,* where they lead a shadowy existence, are inert, and are thus unable to sin. But Dives was in hell; he suffered torture in a flame; he cried with the old obduracy of unbelief: "No, father Abraham!" The supposition that one must have flesh or a body in order to be able to sin is unwarranted. Is the lack of a body the factor that stops a deceased Christian from sinning? It is the last repentance and divine cleansing; it is the glorification of his soul on entering heaven that does so.

The aorist participle is not gnomic, nor is the perfect πέπαυται. These tenses are in relation to each other: when the suffering is finished at death, the ceasing from sin sets in and then continues forever. When the soul of the Christian is with the Lord in heaven (Phil. 1:23), all sinning is forever at an end. The pertinency of this fact in the present connection is apparent. Because this goal awaits every Christian who suffers for righteousness' sake (3:14), he can, indeed, equip himself with the idea (ἔννοια) of suffering by means of flesh, drawing it from no less a source than Christ himself who suffered and was put to death by means of flesh but is now at God's right hand in glory.

2) Christians are to equip themselves for the reason or cause just stated, and the result is to be that they no longer live the remaining time in flesh (in their earthly, bodily existence) for lust of men (human lusts) but for God's will. Εἰς τό denotes result. The clause depends on ὁπλίσασθε but includes the reason for this equipment with the proper Christian idea. In fact, the result which Peter demands rests on all that precedes in this chapter. One should not confuse the tenses and have the result clause depend on the perfect πέπαυται and then argue that, because we are to spend the rest of our earthly lives aright, ceasing

from sin must also have occurred during our present earthly life. The cessation from sin sets in when the suffering by means of flesh has ended (ὁ παθών, aorist), which occurs when we have no further life to live in flesh.

It is the Christian's goal and hope to cease from sin forever. That is why after his conversion he wants to live the rest of his life here in flesh no longer for human lusts but for God's will. The two thoughts correspond. How can one who continues the old lusts and disregards what God wills (θέλημα) expect to enter the heavenly, sinless life at death? Every convert must regret the time in his unconverted state that he spent in living for man's (i. e., for human) lusts. Βιῶσαι = to live the earthly course of one's life; and the negated aorist infinitive = definitely, decisively no longer to live for lusts but for God; the two datives are *dativi commodi.* "Of men" and "of God" emphasize the opposition. We may observe that when Peter intends to say *"in* flesh" he writes an ἐν and does not use a simple dative, a fact which it is well to note with regard to the datives used in v. 1 and in 3:18.

3) "For" adds a pertinent remark: **For enough the time that has passed to have wrought out the counsel of the Gentiles, having proceeded in excesses, lusts, wine-swillings, carousals, drinking bouts, and unlawful idolatries; etc.**

"Enough" is mild and is the stronger for that reason. It was more than enough, the time, now happily passed and gone, for having worked out the counsel of the Gentiles. Βούλημα is what one intends, hence "counsel"; in v. 2 θέλημα is what one wills or has decided. Note the perfect tenses: time "that has passed," that has lasted a while but is now ended; "to have wrought" for a time but now no longer; "having proceeded" but now never again occurring. All of these tenses indicate a past continuance that has come to an end in the past. The last participle, πεπορευμένους, is in the accusative; it is regarded as modifying the implied accusative subject of the infinitive which Peter leaves indefinite by the same meiosis that he has used in connection with the adjective "enough."

All of the six items in the plural refer to public pagan sins and thus to the worst types of open sin. These are named because they make Peter's readers realize fully what "the counsel of the Gentiles" really is; they now blush at the reminder. But these public and open sins do not excuse or minimize the many others that might be listed here, private or secret. One sees most readily what a certain counsel is by noting its more glaring products.

'Ασέλγειαι = excesses, *Ausschweifungen*, when there is no check or rein, when men let themselves go; Second Peter uses this word several times. "Lasciviousness" is not exact. "Lusts" is equally comprehensive (note verse 2) and adds the inner vicious desires that drive to outward excesses. The next four are specific: οἰνοφλυγίαις (derived from wine and to bubble), "wine-swillings" will do; κῶμοι, *Gelage*, "carousings" (Gal. 5: 21); πότοι, "drinking bouts" (M.-M. 531). Finally, "unlawful idolatries." Peter is listing the pagan excesses that were connected with the practice of idolatry, the things commonly done at the celebrations in honor of heathen gods.

Because Peter says "the counsel of the *Gentiles*," and especially because he adds the adjective ἀθέμιτος to "idolatry," which means "unlawful" and not "abominable" (our versions), we are told that Peter is not writing to former Gentiles but to former Jews. We are referred to Rom. 2; but Rom. 2 deals with pagan moralists (in v. 1-16) and with Jewish moralists (in v. 17, etc.), see the author's *Interpretation.* We are pointed to Jews who adopted pagan ways; but unless

these Jews ceased to be Jews and became outright
pagans — which mighty few of them did — they would
not participate in orgies that honored idols. We are
told that Peter could not say "unlawful" from the
pagan standpoint; but he was writing to Christians
from the *Christian* standpoint. On the question regarding the readers see the introduction.

4) Peter continues: **in which connection they
deem strange your not continuing to run with** (them)
into the same outpouring of dissoluteness, (they)
**blaspheming — they the ones who shall give due
account in full to him who is ready to judge living
and dead.**

The plural verbs with the unnamed subject are
understandable as they are written. Peter refers to
the heathen communities in which his readers lived.
The relative "in which" is to be construed with "they
deem strange" and is properly singular: "in connection with this they deem it strange," the genitive absolute adds (almost like an object clause) what strikes
them as strange: "your not continuing to run with
them into the same outpouring of dissoluteness"
(ἀσωτία, *Liederlichkeit*, see Eph. 5:18; Titus 1:6), "the
same" as you ran into before. B.-P. 98 has *Strom der
Liederlichkeit*. This refusal to join them as you formerly did arouses the ire of the pagans so that they
blaspheme the Christians, their God, and their religion.
The Greek participle has case, number, and gender
and is thus far more flexible and intelligible than the
English participle; the plural nominative masculine
at once applies "blaspheming" to the subject "they."
There is no reason for toning down this word to the
meaning "speaking evil"; they cursed the Christians
and the whole religion which made people the opposite
of what they had once been.

5) Ἔχω with an adverb = to be; it is here substantivized: "he who is ready to judge." "Living and

dead" are qualitative, which is more strongly felt in the Greek than in English, where such points are generally ignored. This Judge is Christ; "living and dead" are all men, some of whom will be living here on earth when the Judge arrives. Peter says that the Judge stands ready and prepared to judge, he may proceed to judge at any moment. Then what about these blasphemers? Whether they are living or dead, they are the ones (οἱ with demonstrative force — "sudden vehement use" as it has been termed) who shall give due account ·in full for their blaspheming and their attacks upon the Christians; λόγον = "account," and ἀπό in the verb has the force of "due" and "in full," note the expression in Matt. 12:36; Luke 16:2; Acts 19:40; Heb. 13:17. Since it is here used with reference to blasphemers, "to render due account in full" has its full severity. This emphatic clause rings with doom for these blasphemers.

The fate that awaits them at the hands of him who is ready to judge living and dead is to fortify the readers for bearing the blasphemous attacks made on them and for forsaking all the pagan riotous and shameful ways. Unmoved, they are to meet the world's dread frown. The Master praises, what are men?

6) Γάρ adds a word of explanation. In so many instances the German commentators regard this connective as *begruendend* and thereby get into difficulties. Scores of γάρ are not illative but explanatory as R. 1190 points out; in fact, the illative use is not the primary one. This fact is of importance here. **For for this the gospel was proclaimed even to dead men in order that they be judged, on the one hand, according to men by means of flesh, on the other hand, that they live according to God my means of spirit.**

Εἰς τοῦτο is not "for this cause" (A. V.) but "unto this end" (R. V.) if "end" is understood in the sense of purpose, for the ἵνα clause is in apposition to τοῦτο and denotes aim or purpose. God's purpose in the preaching of the gospel is to have those who hear it to live forever. This was his purpose in having the gospel preached "even to such as are dead."

Peter says this in order to explain the threat uttered in v. 5, that all blasphemers of Christians shall give due account in full to the Judge of living and dead. They are not men who never heard the gospel; they came in full contact with it, saw its power exemplified in their own communities, in the Christians who forsook all heathen ways, who patiently bore the blasphemies heaped on them. Yet these blasphemers go on blaspheming; no wonder they have a terrible account to render to the Judge of the living and the dead. This is the more evident, as Peter explains (γάρ), when we note the blessed purpose of gospel preaching; this has always been that they may be judged and may live.

"For this even to dead men the gospel was proclaimed." The dative is placed forward for the sake of emphasis, καί aids the emphasis: "even to dead men." The absence of the article makes the noun qualitative just as ζῶντας καὶ νεκρούς are qualitative. The fact that the dative refers to physically dead men just as νεκρούς does in v. 5 is plain. Those who have the dative =spiritually dead men while they let the preceding accusative signify physically dead men cannot justify this shift from one meaning of νεκροί to another. The fact that the gospel always finds men spiritually dead when it is first preached to them is beyond question, for Peter himself says that the purpose of this preaching was that even the physically dead to whom it was preached should live.

The aorist passive εὐηγγελίσθη = even to dead men "it was gospeled" (impersonal), for which we say in English, "good tidings or the gospel was proclaimed." The tense is most important. It agrees with the dative.

It denotes the historical past. Peter does not say that the gospel *is* being preached even to the dead but was preached. When? When these physically dead were still among the living, when the purpose of such preaching could yet be attained. We have the same verb that was used in 1:12: "they who preached the gospel unto you," οἱ εὐαγγελισάμενοι; it is *not* κηρύσσειν, "to herald," as in 3:19. No *vox media* here but the *vox positiva*.

Yet there is an obvious difference between the two νεκροί mentioned in v. 5 and in v. 6. Christ stands ready to judge "living and dead," all who are still living when he comes to judgment, all who are dead when that day comes. Peter is thinking of the future as also the future tense shows: "they (the blasphemers) shall give due account"; whether they appear among the living or among the dead at that day, their reckoning shall be made. In v. 6 the tense is the aorist: "it was gospeled," *was* when Peter wrote; "to dead men," dead when Peter wrote. These are not all of the dead who shall face the Judge at the last day but those to whom the gospel was preached prior to Peter's writing, (by the gospel preachers mentioned in v. 1, 12), who at this writing were already dead. We say this at length, but it lies on the surface in Peter's words.

The purpose of this gospel preaching was (what it has always been, is, and will be): that they who heard it and have since then died *"be judged,* for one thing, or on the one hand, for another thing, or on the other hand, *go on living."* Μέν . . . δέ balance the two verbs. We cannot reproduce these neat and delicate particles; we can only indicate their balancing force by our cumbersome English. But μέν is not concessive over against δέ. Those German commentators are not correct who reproduce these particles by the neat German: *zwar . . . aber,* "while they be judged . . . yet may live." The purpose for which the gospel was

preached to these dead was a double purpose: that
they be judged — that they go on living. The particles
do no more than to fix attention on each verb separately,
μέν letting us expect δέ. "To be judged" is not the
whole purpose of gospel preaching, it is only one side
of it. We have already been told that Christ shall
judge dead men. The other side of this purpose of
gospel preaching was that they who heard it should
live. These two belong together, and μέν . . . . δέ
join them.

Because Peter has brought in the reference to
Christ's judging in connection with the blasphemers
he now connects the act of being judged with the
gospel that was preached to dead men. He uses the
same verb κρίνειν, "to judge," a *vox media*, even the
same tense, aorists, because the rendering and the
reception of a verdict are punctiliar acts. Only the
voice differs: Christ judges, men receive the judgment, are judged. In plain contrast with these is
the present tense ζῶσι: the purpose of gospel preaching for such as are now dead was that they live con-
tinuously, forever: "though he were dead, yet shall
he live" (John 11:25).

Both subjunctives have corresponding modifiers,
and it is because of their correspondence that μέν . . .
δέ balance the verbs: "for one thing, be judged according to men by means of flesh, for the other, go on
living according to God by means of spirit." The κατά
phrases and their anarthrous nouns are not at once as
clear in the English as they are in the Greek. The two
datives should be clear; but already when they were
interpreting 3:18 the commentators have not always
regarded them as datives of means, which applies also
to the one dative found in 4:1, 2. The sense is: in the
human way (κατά) by means of flesh (dative of means)
— in the divine way (κατά) by means of spirit (dative
of means).

It is not the purpose of gospel preaching to exempt the hearers of it from Christ's judgment but to make clear that we shall be judged as all men are judged. It is, in fact, the gospel's intent to prepare us for judgment, to meet Christ's judgment with παρρησία, confident assurance of acquittal. It is the gospel preaching's intent that those who hear it shall be judged κατὰ ἀνθρώπους σαρκί, the phrase and the dative belong together: "in the way of men by means of flesh." When they are thus judged, on the one hand, they are to be living "in the way of God by means of spirit," κατὰ Θεὸν πνεύματι, the phrase and the dative again belong together. Men have "flesh," body, bodily existence; thus flesh is the means for judging them.

In this connection one might refer to II Cor. 5:10: "that each one may receive the things (done) by means of the body," and all the many references to the body, the bodily members, the deeds for which we employ them in this life. The reply that Peter writes "flesh" and not "body" is met by Col. 1:22: "in the body of his flesh by means of death." It is met again by the three σαρκί occurring in 3:18 and 4:1, 2: Christ suffered "by means of flesh"; the Christians suffered "by means of flesh." These three σαρκί place the meaning of the fourth, the one occurring in our passage, beyond doubt. But we should leave these datives datives and not make them phrases by translating *"in* the flesh," or as the Germans say, *am Fleisch.*

This German translation would have Peter say that death is the judgment, i. e., that Christians are not spared the judgment of physical death. This idea occurs only to German commentators who have this preposition *an;* the English commentators have no exact equivalent for it and hence do not express this idea here or in 3:18 and 4:1, 2. Physical death is not the judgment for a blasphemer nor for a Christian. A secret judgment takes place at the moment of death, but that judgment is not the sundering of the body and the spirit, nor is it restricted to the body (flesh) ; it is a judgment on the whole man, body and spirit (or soul).

Peter does not speak of the preliminary, secret judgment; his two aorists κρῖναι and κριθῶσι speak of Christ's final judgment. This is quite evident in regard to the former; and the force of the latter is determined by the former. When we again look at II Cor. 5:10 and at all those passages that speak of the judgment we note that they make the final judgment turn on what man has done in the body.

This σαρκί alone answers the questions about gospel preaching to dead men in hades (usually called *Totenreich*) and that of any connection between our passage and 3:19, 20. No advocate of missionary work in hell has attempted to show that its purpose could be a judgment of the spirits in hell σαρκί. The departed leave the flesh or body in the grave. Let us suppose that they did believe the gospel in hell, then the resultant judgment could not be σαρκί. We must say that any act in hell would take place wholly apart from their dust in the grave here on earth.

Nor is it satisfactory to advance the restriction that the dead referred to are only those who never heard the gospel in this life. Then the aorist εὐηγγελίσθη should be changed to the present tense; and σαρκί would again offer difficulties. This idea of gospel preaching in hell has won adherents because it satisfies speculative minds in regard to a question which the Scriptures leave unanswered, namely, how will the Lord deal with those who never heard the gospel during this earthly life? The fact that Peter does not touch upon this question but speaks of blasphemers who scorned the gospel in this life, whose judgment is certain, is overlooked.

Μέν already points to the δέ even as the first half of the ἵνα clause is incomplete without the second half: "that they live according to God by means of spirit," ever live in the divine way, after the manner of God (no longer in a mere earthly existence), and do this, of course, by means of spirit. The A. V., which translated πνεύματι in 3:18 "by the Spirit," is not consistent and does not render this same dative "in the Spirit" in the present passage. Likewise, those who regard "spirit" in 3:19 as the divine nature shrink from doing so in 4:6 although the two datives are the same. This πνεῦμα is the human spirit. As to Christ, we need to say only that without it he could not have been true man; by the return of his spirit to his body that body was vivified in the tomb. The aim of gospel preaching is that those who hear it may live in the way of God in spirit. Since this is here said of those who are already dead and are awaiting the final judgment, the clause speaks of the life which they shall be living by means of spirit after judgment day.

All that Peter writes about the Christian hope is pertinent here. It centers in the judgment and in the eternal glorious life that follows. The fact that this involves the new life here on earth, a life that temporal death cannot touch, a life of which, by virtue of the resurrection, the body, too, shall partake, need not be mentioned in detail. See John 6:40, 44, 54; 11: 25, 26; even John 3:15, 16. "By means of spirit" these shall live, for the real seat of life eternal is man's spirit and not his ψυχή or his σῶμα. Already in our earthly existence we worship God ἐν πνεύματι (John 4:23), "in spirit." When our bodies are dust, our spirits live in glory. That life Christ's last judgment affirms forever. Yes, it is κατὰ Θεόν and not κατὰ ἀνθρώπους; it is like the glorious life of God. It is the ultimate feature of the aim of the gospel.

We may now revert to γάρ and to the context. What is said about the aim of gospel preaching has a double bearing. Christians who have died after bearing pagan blasphemies are safe indeed. The gospel that they heard brings them to the judgment of life. But what about the blasphemers who make Christians suffer during the time that they live in flesh? Whether they are dead or still alive, a terrible reckoning awaits them when they face the Judge. These are the facts that are to fortify Peter's admonition: "since Christ suffered by means of flesh, do you also equip yourselves with the same idea" (v. 1).

To state that Peter expounds Christ's right to judge the living and the dead, that Christ has this right only because the gospel is preached also to those in hell, and that Peter makes clear the absolute universality of the gospel by pointing to its saving promulgation even in hell, is to do an injustice to the holy Apostle Peter and to Christ himself.

What he says about the final judgment is not offered by Peter as an assurance against the misgiving or fear that the blasphemies of their pagan attackers might after all be true. Stoeckhardt seconds von Hofmann: "What a muddled Christian he would have to be whose anxiety worried him that the blasphemies against his upright life might remain uncontradicted and unrefuted and might thus deprive him of eternal salvation! It is, indeed, a comfort over against such blasphemies, or rather over against such blasphemies against Christianity, that our salvation does not depend on human judgment but on Christ's verdict, but not a comfort that quiets us regarding our salvation as though we might fare as we should deserve if our blasphemers were right, but a comfort that makes it easy to bear their blasphemies because there *lives* one who will not leave them unpunished."

*Exercising Christian Virtues in View
of the End, v. 7-11*

7) In v. 5 the Lord is ready to judge living and dead. In v. 7 the end is near. In v. 1-6 the negative side is prominent, the pagan sins we must avoid even at the price of suffering men's blasphemies for so doing; now in v. 7-11 all is positive. Moreover, these positive virtues are to appear in the contacts of Christians with each other. This paragraph ends with a doxology.

Now the end of all things has come near. Peter writes exactly as Paul does about the nearness of the end of all things, πάντα without the article (τὰ πάντα would be the existing things). Although it is here construed with "all things," τὸ τέλος, which is quite definite because of the article, has the same meaning that it has in v. 17 where the genitive denotes persons: "the end of the ungodly." B.-P. 1298 makes the first = *Aufhoeren*, cessation; the second *Ziel*, "goal." C.-K. 1044 is much better. The Greek never uses τέλος to denote a merely temporal end; τελευτή is the proper word for this idea. Even in temporal connections τέλος retains the idea of goal, not mere cessation but the conclusion, the *Erfolg*, the outcome or success. Thus πολέμου τέλος does not mean that war has just stopped, but that victory has been reached; τέλος ἀνδρός, that a man has come to maturity; the end of seed is its ripeness. Thus here and in v. 17 "the end" has the same meaning: *Ausgang, Abschluss*, the final goal. All things shall not cease (Rom. 8:19, etc.), shall not be annihilated; those who were disobedient to the gospel of God shall not cease to exist (v. 17). They shall reach their final goal.

The perfect ἤγγικε has its present connotation "has come near" and thus "is near" and may be translated "is near." Since Christ's first coming there is nothing more to expect except his second coming to judgment,

and this may occur at any time. The apostles had no
revelation as to the date of it. They were in the same
position in which we are at this date; they spoke as
we must now speak. None of us knows but what we
may live to see the end. We have the advantage of
knowing that it has been delayed for centuries, but
we know this, not from Scripture, but from the fact,
from history. To charge Paul or Peter with false
prophecy for saying 1900 years ago that the end is
near, is to treat them unfairly. They, as we, had to
live in constant expectation of Christ's sudden return.

**Accordingly, be of sound mind and be sober for
prayers!** Compare Titus 2:1-6 where Paul incul-
cates this soundness of mind, this balance in thought
and disposition, which is never flighty, unbalanced,
carried away by notions of our own or by attacks of
men. Peter adds: "Be sober for prayers." In II Tim.
4:5 Paul says, "Be thou sober in every way." Peter
has already said (1:13), "Having girded up the loins
of your mind as being sober." This is spiritual sobriety,
another term for soundness of mind; but it is here
connected with worship, "prayers"; the singular as
well as the plural of this word often refer to the whole
Christian worship (Acts 2:42).

Peter begins his positive exhortation with the mind
and disposition of his readers, with the inner steadiness
that should control them. Before he mentions what
they are to do for each other he reminds them of their
relation to God. They who pray aright to God, who
worship as they should, will gladly do all that is here
asked, will be aided and enabled in every way. The
aorist imperatives are like all of those that precede:
urgent, strong, decisive, and are used for this reason
alone.

8) **Before everything else having the love to
yourselves fully exerted because love hides a multitude of sins.** "Before all things" does not, of course,

mean before even your prayers and worship, but when you have turned from your worship, where you have strengthened your bond with God and with Christ, let your first concern be the fullest exercise of love to your own selves. This is ἀγάπη, the love of intelligence and true understanding coupled with corresponding purpose. The predicate adjective does not mean "fervent" (our versions) nor *nachhaltig*, constant, enduring, but "stretched out, put to full strain, exerted to the limit of its strength." The opposite is slight or ineffective effort. In ἐκτενής there lies the thought of exertion. There will be sins on the part of the brethren, which may tend to slacken our love for them; such sins make it hard to show them love. Although the strain may be great, love is to stand it. "For yourselves" is not quite the same as the reciprocal "for each other" but brings out the thought that all Christians are one body. The thought is that expressed in I Cor. 12:12, etc. Every Christian is one of ourselves, and thus we are to love all of them.

The participle ἔχοντες is not equal to an imperative (A. V., commentators, and grammars). It marks this "having" as being subordinate to the imperatives used in v. 1; an imperative would not do that. Peter wants to express this thought. It is fine, indeed, and most true. This love for ourselves blossoms when all of us engage in true worship as one body; it will grow limp and slack when such worship is omitted or is engaged in with only flighty, superficial minds.

We also note the reference to the pagans who blaspheme such worship since it separates Christians from their former idolatries (v. 5). Christians know what they are doing when they gather together for prayers by themselves; they are separate, a body of their own, and thus, connected with this fact (as the participle shows), they have this love for themselves. This is lost when the participle is not understood as a participle but it considered equal to an imperative.

The reason for having this love is the fact that it "hides a multitude of sins." Love hides them from its own sight and not from God's sight. Hate does the opposite; it pries about in order to discover some sin or some semblance of sin in a brother and then broadcasts it, even exaggerates it, gloats over. it. It is unjust to the apostle to say that he wants Christians to hush up and to hide criminality or vice that have occurred in their midst. Peter purposely says πλῆθος, "a multitude of sins," and thereby indicates the mass of daily sins of weakness which come to the attention of Christians because of their constant contact and association. It has been well said that we all pray daily for their forgiveness when we offer the Lord's Prayer. Only when Christians become mean and ugly do they favor the devil by dragging each other's failings out into public and smiting each other in the face.

Peter is not referring to sins that are committed against each other so that hiding means forgiving. What we are to do when a real offense has been committed in private Jesus tells us in Matt. 18:15, etc.; here, too, love handles the case and does all that it possibly can to remove the offense without publishing it, and when it must be made known to the church, this is also done in love and becomes a sad task. As far as mutual forgiving is concerned, Peter knew what Jesus had told him in Matt. 18:21, etc. How public offense is to be met by public rebuke Gal. 2:12-21 exhibits most clearly. We mention these things because many will think of them; Peter does not enter upon a discussion of them. Hundreds of sins of weakness, faults, mistakes, failings we ignore, dismiss. We bear with each other because we know our own failings. The fact that, when we deem it necessary, we warn, correct, strengthen each other need not be added in a compact admonition such as Peter here offers. Yet we may note that ἐκτενής and πλῆθος correspond. To cover a multitude calls for a greater strain than to cover a few.

9) Peter continues with a nominative plural adjective which is not equal to an imperative but, like the participle used in v. 8, is in a subordinate relation to v. 7: **hospitable to each other without murmuring.** The reciprocal ἀλλήλους is in place here. Much may be said about this ancient hospitality which provided lodging for a traveling Christian, gave him necessary information and help to become located, to transact his business, to find work, to expedite him on his journey. Some had to flee from their homes in other cities because of persecution and were often destitute. During their many extensive travels the apostles were guests at many Christian homes. Note Acts 16:15; Philemon 22. Hence all these references to hospitality in the apostolic letters. Also note Matt. 10:9-13. Even pagans remarked about how the Christians loved each other and received a wholly strange Christian as a brother.

While even the poorest would be ready to exercise such hospitality, those with means in any local church would open their doors first. The characteristic of this form of love is the fact that it is exercised "without grumbling." This is the sense of the phrase and not the implication that Peter's readers were grumblers and needed correction.

10) Peter continues with another participle: **according as each one received a charisma, ministering it for yourselves as excellent stewards of God's manifold grace.** Luther has the idea that natural charismata are excluded: "Gifts you have, which are not born with you, nor did you bring them as your own inheritance from your mother's body." Peter, however, says that "each one" did receive a charisma, and a glance at Rom. 12:6, etc., shows that many a

charisma is only some natural endowment or possession which is sanctified in the Christian by the Spirit.
Not all charismata were miraculous abilities such as
those mentioned in the list recorded in I Cor. 12:8-10.
Peter has the same idea that Paul had: not only does
every Christian have a χάρισμα, i. e., some endowment
that was graciously bestowed on him, but God intends
that such an endowment is to be used in διακονία, service
for the members of the church, a service to be ' rendered for the sake of service and benefit to others
with no thought of self save the joy of thus "ministering." The pronoun ἑαυτούς is again in place.

"As excellent stewards" explains what "received"
implies. An οἰκονόμος is one to whom certain property
is entrusted to be administered according to the own-
er's will and directions. In Luke 16:1 such an *oikono-
mos* is presented; but they were often slaves; they were
at times placed over great estates; they were often men
of high education and ability although they were slaves.
Peter mentions only the feature that God has entrusted
some charisma or other to each Christian. To be "an
excellent steward" he must administer it as the Be-
stower wants him to.

The objective genitive "of God's manifold grace"
brings out two points: 1) every charisma, whatever its
nature, is a gift of God's pure undeserved favor (χάρις),
which we should employ accordingly; 2) this grace is
"manifold," that is, while it is the same favor for all
it bestows all manner of charismata, not only in order
to employ "each one" of us, but also that we may minister "for yourselves,": i. e., for the whole body of
Christians so that it may lack nothing as a body. What
one cannot do, another will be able to do.

11) Peter omits the verbs in the two apodoses
and thus continues the construction and makes v.
7-11 a unit verbally as it is a unit in thought. We
are compelled to insert participles in English; this

is not necessary in the Greek, in fact, it would sound pedantic. A new sentence is not begun; we merely have two specifications: **if one speaks — as God's sayings; if one ministers — as out of strength which God supplies.** One may help with word or with deed. A reference to Acts 6:2, 4 is remote, for this passage suggests the office of preaching, about which Peter says nothing here. He refers to any Christian, man or woman. If such a one opens his mouth to speak (λαλεῖ), to impart something, it should be a speaking "as God's sayings," i. e., as offering God's own *logia*.

We should observe that Peter always uses ὡς to introduce realities, and thus "*logia* of God" are statements made by God, the word *logia* being used as it is in Rom. 3:2 and Heb. 5:12. We do not think that Peter uses λόγια in the sense of "oracles" (our versions; C.-K. 680), for that is a pagan conception; compare χρηματισμός. Peter wants a plural, and since λόγος Θεοῦ, "Word of God," is a concept that cannot be pluralized without misunderstanding, he uses the allied term *logia*, which is naturally a plural. The thought seems to be that in their talk Christians are to be governed by the pertinent things that God has said.

It is an extravagant idea to understand this to mean that "a Christian is to consider that the words flowing from his mouth are all charismatic, be they doctrine, prophecy, or speaking with tongues, produced by God, not originating with men." Were all Christians inspired? The idea that Peter is referring only to the services as Paul does in I Cor. 14:26, etc., is unwarranted. He refers to the common, daily talk of any and of all Christians, of women as well as of men; this is always to be helpful and is thus to be governed by what God has told us.

The same holds true with regard to deeds: "if anyone ministers." We have the same verb that was used in the participial form in verse 10, but it is now distinct from talk and is restricted to deeds. These, too, are to be truly helpful: "as out of strength which God supplies," ἰσχύς, "strength" as possessed, "ability," (A. V.); κράτος would mean strength in action. For both the tongue and the hand Christians are to use what God furnishes them and are thus to be good stewards of God. Ἧς is the attracted ἥν, and χορηγέω (originally, providing a grand donation for the expense of putting on a Greek chorus) is to be understood in the common sense of "provide" or "supply."

The aim of all of this is: **in order that in every way God through Jesus Christ may be glorified.** Every word and every deed are to glorify God through Christ, i. e., are to honor, praise, and magnify him. I Cor. 10:31 shows how far this extends. While God's glory is unchangeable, its recognition is to be increased. Thus we glorify him. Ἐν πᾶσι is neither "in all things" nor "in all men" but "in every respect" (B.-P. 1012).

Peter himself is moved to glorify God by a doxology (see the long one in 1:3-12): **to whom belongs the glory and the might for the eons of the eons! Amen.** The relative is emphatic: "he to whom," "he the One to whom." The dative with ἐστί is the common idiom for "belongs to him." There is some discussion as to whether the antecedent is "God" or "Jesus Christ." It is grammatically incorrect to construe: "to whom through Jesus Christ belongs the glory." In no other ascription is such a διά phrase placed before the relative; if it were intended to modify the relative clause, the διά phrase would have to follow the relative. It is asked why Peter did not write ὁ Θεός last if he intended to apply the ascription of glory to God and thus bring the antecedent and the relative together. To state it frankly, Peter knew his Greek too well. "God through Jesus Christ" is correct; "through Jesus Christ God" is strange.

We have no interest whatever in denying the ascription of divine glory to Christ; he is God, equal with the Father. The glory *is* ascribed to him in Heb. 13: 20, 21; II Pet. 3:18; Rev. 1:6, and elsewhere. Here, however, Peter has four decidedly emphatic placements of "God," which suffice to asure us that "to whom" == to God. In addition there is ἐστίν. This relative clause is thus not an exclamation as it is in all cases where the copula is omitted. This means that δοξάζηται and ἡ δόξα should be construed together: "in order that there *may be glorified* (constantly, present subjunctive) God through Jesus Christ — to whom belongs (indeed and of right) *the glory* and the might," etc. The relative clause states a fact; it does not express only Peter's feeling or voice his own glorification of God or of Christ. Like many relatives, this relative clause states the reason that all Christians should glorify God through Jesus Christ; it is because the glory *belongs* to him.

With it is associated the κράτος, which has already been explained. And these belong to him *in saecula saeculorum*, "for the eons of the eons," eons multiplied by eons, the plural with the genitive plural denoting a superlative in the highest degree: "forever and ever." Eternity is timelessness, a concept that is beyond human ability of comprehension; hence we must use terms that express time to designate what is not time. The phrase occurs twenty-one times; see further, for instance, Gal. 1:5; Phil. 4:20; I Tim. 1:17, where "Amen" also occurs. Far from being merely liturgical, C.-K. 143 rightly says, this Hebrew "amen" compels us to examine the reason in each instance of its use. It is not an expression of intellectual conviction but of an exalted, God-praising conviction of faith. Placed at the end and meaning "truth," "verity," this "amen" is solemn, confessional, in the nature of a seal.

Rejoice in Suffering that You May Rejoice
at the Revelation of Christ's Glory,
v. 12-19

12) The address "beloved" (see 2:11) does not indicate the beginning of a new section of the epistle after the "amen," for this amen only concludes the ascription of glory to God. The assurance of Peter's love for his readers by his once more calling them "beloved" is due to the subject matter that is now presented, the *severity* of the sufferings that may come upon some of his readers.

Beloved, be not deeming strange the fire-glow among you when occurring to you with a view of trial as something strange meeting you; but to the degree you are fellowshiping the sufferings of Christ be rejoicing in order that also at the revelation of his glory you may rejoice as exulting.

After áll the aorist imperatives occurring in the preceding hortation the present imperatives ξενίζεσθε and χαίρετε are notable. These imperatives, together with the present participles γινομένη and συμβαίνοντες and the present indicative κοινωνεῖτε of the subordinate clause, lead us to believe that Peter is no longer speaking of sufferings such as his readers had already experienced and of which there would naturally be a continuance but of impending sufferings that would be far more severe. None that they have thus far experienced have deserved to be called πύρωσις, "fire-glow," fiery ordeal; these, "when occurring to you," deserve this epithet.

They are on the way. The introduction explains how the situation has changed completely, and how this change prompts Peter to write to all these people in the provinces mentioned in 1:1. Nero and the imperial government in Rome are taking a hostile attitude toward Christianity, are treating it as a *religio illicita,*

so that the worst is to be expected. The Roman authorities in the provinces will soon adopt the same attitude.
When they do, the readers are not to be surprised but
are to rejoice that they are called upon to fellowship
the sufferings of Christ who was put to death by the
Jews (3:18).

Some of the commentators disregard these present
tenses and their significance. Some of them think that
Peter is now speaking of sufferings that are arising
in the midst of the readers themselves from renegades
in the churches. They place the major emphasis on the
attributive phrase ἐν ὑμῖν and regard this as the new
feature which Peter introduces at this point. Peter
writes: "be not surprised on account of the fiery ordeal
among you when it comes to you with a view of or
for the purpose of (πρός) trial." Ἐν ὑμῖν is merely attributive and intends to say that this fire and burning
will occur "among you," will not strike all of you but
only some of you. The dative is not the object of the
imperative but denotes cause (R. 532). The πρός phrase
at once adds the purpose of this coming fiery ordeal,
namely the fact that it is occurring or coming to you to
try you. Nobody translates πειρασμός "temptation," all
see that it means "trial," that it is not the same as
δόκιμον or δοκιμή (a test to prove something genuine) but
only a trial as to what one can endure.

While only some will be struck by the *Feuerglut*
as Peter's ἐν ὑμῖν plainly indicates, all the readers will
be affected by what is coming. It will try them all.
Peter says to all of them, "be not surprised because of
it," deem it not strange, "as a strange thing meeting
you" (συμβαίνω, walking with you).

13) It is not a ξένον, "a strange thing," at all,
to be deemed strange (ξενίζομαι); it is only "fellowshiping the sufferings of Christ." The use of κοινωνέω
after συμβαίνω is both beautiful and illuminating: when
this awful thing walks together with the readers (as-

sociative σύν in the participle), the readers are only
in fellowship with the sufferings of Christ. This is a
thought that is prominent and fully carried out by
Paul in Rom. 8:17; II Cor. 1:7; 4:10; Phil. 1:29; 3:10;
Col. 1:24. It goes back to Christ's word (John 15:
20, 21).

We fellowship Christ's sufferings when we suffer
for his name's sake, when the hatred that struck him
strikes us because of him. Never is there a thought
of fellowshiping in the expiation of Christ's suffering,
our suffering also being expiatory. In Matt. 5:12 persecution places us in the company of the persecuted
prophets (high exaltation indeed); here it places us
in the company of Christ himself, into an even greater
communion or κοινωνία. Is that "a strange thing" or to
be deemed strange? It is what we should deem proper,
natural, to be expected, yea, as Peter says (following
Matt. 5:12), a cause for joy.

Καθό = "to the degree" you so fellowship, be rejoicing. The degrees will vary even as Peter says that
the fiery ordeal will appear "among you," some will
be struck fully, fearfully, the rest will be affected more
or less. Thus καθό takes care of both classes. Those that
are struck the worst are not to lament; the fiercer the
ordeal, the more reason for their rejoicing, the closer
their fellowship with Christ's sufferings. Those involved to lesser degrees are not to be envied because
of their partial escape; they, too, fellowship, but not
so deeply. The thought is that Christ is drawing all
the readers into closer fellowship with his sufferings,
an honor, a distinction indeed, a cause for deepest rejoicing. This is the true view of what impends for the
readers; Peter calls on them to adopt it in advance.

In the ἵνα clause he carries the joy forward to the
last day: "in order that also at the revelation of his
glory you may rejoice as exulting." Joy now in the
ordeals as they come, but oh, what joy at that great

day! Peter has spoken about "the end" (v. 7), about
the judgment (v. 5), and he now keeps in line with
this; but he here uses "the revelation of Christ's
glory," the tremendous opposite of "the sufferings of
Christ" during the days of his humiliation. Peter has
in mind what Jesus says in Matt. 10:32; Luke 12:8
(8:38; 9:26); compare Paul, Rom. 8:17, 18; II Tim.
2:11, 12. Peter has already mentioned the ἀποκάλυψις,
"the revelation of Jesus Christ," in 1:7. It is the revelation occurring at his Parousia when all the angels
of God shall appear with him, when all the glory of
the deity shall shine forth in his human nature before
the whole universe of angels and of men.

Peter says "be rejoicing" now to the degree that
you share the sufferings of Christ "in order that you
may rejoice" then "as exulting." This last word is
properly an aorist (second aorist passive), rejoicing
with finality, with utter completeness. Ἀγαλλιώμενοι is
the same word that was used in 1:6, 8. Our versions
translate as though we had a cognate of "rejoice":
"may rejoice (be glad) with exceeding joy." This is
not such a cognate term but a participle which to rejoice adds the idea of exulting, jubilating, skipping
and bubbling over with shouts of delight. Although we
now rejoice to share Christ's sufferings (like the
Twelve in Acts 5:41), this is as nothing when compared with the joy at that great day. Peter just had
to add this participle to bring out this thought. Yes,
the worst persecution can be borne with joy when the
eye is fixed on the revelation of Christ's glory and the
unbounded joy that awaits the faithful.

14) **If you are being reproached in connection
with Christ's name, blessed** (are you)! **because the
Spirit of the glory and of God is resting upon you!**
The condition is one of present reality; Peter has in
mind such reproaches as are being heaped upon his
readers. These reproaches are in substance the same

as the blaspheming mentioned in v. 4. In v. 4, 5 the connection points to what the Judge will do with these blasphemers of the Christians; now the connection points to what the Holy Spirit does for the Christians who are so blasphemed and reproached. In v. 3, 4 the cause of the blasphemy is the fact that the Christians refuse to run with the pagan community in its riot of vices and idolatries, a negative side of their conduct; now Peter touches the positive side, the reproach "in connection with the name of Christ."

This phrase is often not correctly understood; neither the ἐν nor the ὄνομα. The German *bei* or *ueber* or *um willen* and the English "for," "the matter of," "by," are not satisfactory. So also is the supposition that Christ is the object of the reproaches and that the Christians are in Christ, which disregards ὄνομα. The phrase is not the same as "in Christ." His "name" is his revelation. By his name and revelation Christ draws near to us and is apprehended by us, by his name alone. We believe in his name or revelation, are baptized in his name, confess his name, etc. Ἐν = "in connection with." Christians are reproached "in connection with" this holy, blessed name or revelation of Christ, i. e., the gospel of Christ which they believe and follow in their lives. Our enemies hate this name (revelation) and us because we cling to it.

If we are thus reproached "in connection with" this name, "blessed" are we, μακάριοι. This same beatitude was written in 3:14 and was stated in the same exclamatory way, as a verdict on those so reproached. See 3:14. Every reproach causes our ears to hear a voice from heaven crying "Blessed, blessed!" upon us. The harsher the reproaches, the sweeter this heavenly verdict. Instead of shame, elation and joy should fill us on hearing such reproaches; instead of hanging our heads, we should lift them up to Christ with radiant faces.

In 3:14 "blessed" is followed by the negative: "Fear not their fear!" This is now amplified by the positive: "because the Spirit of the glory and of God is resting upon you." When Peter wrote 3:13, 14 he had in mind what he now writes, namely the positive reason for the great beatitude. The thought is that this reproach is so much strong evidence that God's Spirit rests upon us. The Spirit of God is mentioned because he brings us the name (revelation) of Christ; a helpful comment is found in John 16:13, 14 (be sure to read it). We have the entire Trinity: God — his Spirit — Christ, all are connected with us.

Peter says more than that the Spirit of God rests upon us; he calls him "the Spirit of glory." The genitives τῆς δόξης and τοῦ Θεοῦ are placed attributively between the article τό and its noun Πνεῦμα, and this article is repeated in order to make each of the genitives stand out separately. Another plain reason for repeating τό is the fact that Peter could not write: τὸ τῆς δόξης τοῦ Θεοῦ Πνεῦμα, for this would mean: "the Spirit of the glory of God"; nor could he write thus and insert καί: "the Spirit of the glory *and* of God," as if "the glory" and "God" were parallel and coordinate concepts, the two genitives being alike. They are not alike. The Spirit *bestows* the glory upon us and thus makes us blessed; the Spirit *belongs* to God and *is sent* by God. "Of the glory" is not qualitative, is not = "the glorious Spirit"; nor is "of God" qualitative = "the divine Spirit." The sense is not "the glorious, divine Spirit" nor "the glorious *and* divine Spirit."

From our enemies come *reproaches,* from the Spirit comes *the glory* that makes us blessed. Reproaches heap *shame* upon us ("let him not be ashamed," v. 16); the Spirit bestows *the glory* upon us. These two are made opposites. Peter achieves this by using one τό with this genitive, another τό with the second genitive which connects the Spirit with God. This is per-

fect Greek: not only the doubling of τό but also the
placing of each genitive between τό and Πνεῦμα. So also
is the wording "of *the* glory," τῆς δόξης, not *some* glory
(indefinite) but "*the* glory" (specific). This is "the
glory" which is connected with Christ, which the Spirit
bestows on us. Jesus says: "He shall glorify me; for
he shall receive of mine and shall show it unto you,"
John 16:15. "Show it" is the ὄνομα or revelation. Jesus
even adds: "All things that *the Father* has are mine;
therefore I said, that he shall take of mine, and shall
show it unto you." Just so Peter connects God — the
Spirit — Christ, and he connects these with what is
the Father's and thus Christ's and is taken by the
Spirit to show us and to give us the glory in the ὄνομα,
the name, the gospel revelation.

We thus decline to accept the views which make
two different concepts of the two τό. One is to read
τὸ (supply ὄνομα) τῆς δόξης, so that Peter would say "the
name of the glory and the Spirit of God rests upon
you." What "the name of the glory" means, and how it
is to be coordinated with God's Spirit, is difficult to
comprehend. Another view has τό substantivize τῆς
δόξης: "this *thing* that pertains to the glory." This is
a rather abstruse idea, and it is difficult to parallel it
with the Spirit of·God and to say that such a "thing"
rests upon us as does God's Spirit. No Greek reader
or hearer would do otherwise than to connect the two
τό (each having a genitive) with Πνεῦμα. Some seek for
Old Testament allusions for what Peter says and point
to Isa. 11:2 for the Spirit's resting upon a person; but
for "reproaching" Matt. 5:11 is by far best. The A. V.
follows a few inferior readings by adding two clauses
which the R. V. rightly cancels.

15) **For do not let anyone suffer as a murderer
or a thief or a bad actor or as an agitator.** Γάρ is
important for explaining how some Christian might
not only be reproached but might have to suffer for an

actual crime. Pagan enemies would connect his actions
with "the name of Christ" and blame the church and
Christ for his crime. Hence: "let no one ever be suffering (present imperative) as a man of this kind."
Peter names two crimes as samples: "as a murderer
or a thief." All the "or" are disjunctive and not conjunctive. The third term: "or a bad actor" (a doer
of what is base, κακόν) intends to cover any other crime.

We should note that ὡς is repeated with the fourth
item, which places this fourth term beside the three
that precede as denoting a crime of a separate and
different class. Ἀλλοτριοεπίσκοπος is found only here,
hence there is uncertainty as to its meaning. "A busybody in other men's matters" (A. V.), "a meddler."
etc. (R. V.), and other suppositions do not fit the context which not only calls for a crime but for one that
parallels all ordinary crimes. C.-K. 1002 follows Win-
dish: a man who tries to supervise what is the affair
of others, a political "agitator," *Aufruehrer,* whom
the authorities must squelch. Compare 2:13, etc., on
submission to the government. This meaning explains
the second ὡς and the fact that this crime is mentioned
last.

**16) But if as a Christian, let him not be
ashamed but let him glorify God in connection with
this name.** The implication is that if anyone of the
readers suffers as a murderer, etc., this is *not* suffering as a Christian. Such a reader would suffer as the
criminal that he really would be; see Luke 23:41:
"justly, for we receive the due reward of our deeds."
"But if as a Christian" repeats ὡς and puts "Christian"
in strong contrast with the four terms that were used
in v. 15 to designate criminals. A Christian suffers
"for righteousness' sake" (3:14). Again compare Luke
23:41: "but this man hath done nothing amiss." Peter
uses Χριστιανός (see Acts 11:26; 26:28) because of its

derivation from Χριστός; a Christian suffers innocently as Christ did.

We supply "suffers" in the protasis. Those who regard the "busybody" or "meddler" mentioned in v. 15 as a term that does not denote a crime think that the verb means no more than the verb "be reproached" in v. 14 does. But murderers and thieves are made to suffer the due reward of their crime by the government as all κακοποιοί (2:14), "doers of baseness" or "bad actors," are, and we have seen that the fourth term used in v. 15 means "agitators," whom the government also rightly punishes. When Peter now says: "but if (anyone suffers) as a Christian," he certainly means, "suffers for his Christianity as for a crime, suffers at the hands of the government" by being denounced to the authorities (2:12) as a κακοποιός, "a bad actor" (criminal). We have shown in the introduction that this had already been done in Rome. Christianity was being regarded by Nero as a *religio illicita*, a crime. Peter himself was soon to be executed as such a *kakopoios*; Paul was to follow. Peter thinks that the Roman governors in the provinces will be getting orders from Nero to prosecute all Christians as criminals, their crime being this illicit religion.

Peter says: "If anyone of you has to suffer as a Christian," as a criminal for being a true Christian, "let him not be ashamed but let him glorify God in connection with this name." Any church member who is untrue to his Christianity and commits some common crime or, still worse, becomes a political agitator under the profession of Christianity deserves all the shame which the governmental prosecution brings upon him by making him suffer the severity of the law even as he disgraces the name. Vastly different is the case of the church member who suffers imprisonment or even bloody martyrdom for the alleged crime of being a true Christian. "Let him not be ashamed" although all manner of shame be heaped upon him.

"Let him glorify God in connection with this name"; we have the same phrase with the same meaning that was used in v. 14. Let him confess "this name" to the glory of God. Let him die for it "if need be" (1:6), "if the will of God should will" (3:17). "Blessed is he (3:14; 4:14)!'"

The reading ἐν τῷ μέρει τούτῳ, which is adopted in the A. V.: "on this behalf" (Luther: *in solchem Fall*), is rightly discarded by the R. V. It seems to have been derived from II Cor. 3:10 (9:3). To think that Luther and the A. V. translate ἐν τῷ ὀνόματι τούτῳ by the phrases they employ is to overlook the fact that they follow the other reading in their *textus receptus*. The idea of adopting ἐν τῷ μέρει τούτῳ and making ὅτι the exposition of "this part" cannot save the inferior reading even if the thought were not sadly confused in this way as Keil has sufficiently shown. "In connection with this name" refers to the name (revelation) of "Christ." The connection is here so clearly apparent in the sufferer who suffers ·"as a Christian," who truly bears this designation which is derived from "Christ."

17) We regard ὅτι as *consecutivum* (explained in R. 1001): **seeing that** (it is) **the period for the verdict to start from the house of God.** In view of this period for the start (aorist infinitive) of the verdict from the house of God every Christian who suffers for being a Christian is not to be ashamed but is to glorify God in connection with the name of Christ. Κρῖμα is the verdict and not the act of judging. This is not the verdict that starts *with* or *on* the house of God (the German *am Hause* or *bei*, "with," our versions, "at," which this preposition never means) and then goes on to the rest of men. The very name "the house of God" (see I Tim. 3:15; Heb. 3:6: "whose house are we"; also οἰκεῖοι τοῦ Θεοῦ, "house-members of

God") makes it clear that Peter does not say that the first verdict of God shall strike his own house, the church, and after that a second verdict shall strike the wicked in the world. There is no thought that false Christians are to be exposed and the house of God is to be purified by removing them, or that the true Christians are by suffering to be purified from any sins that are still in them.

Peter is speaking about the verdict on the enemies of God's house. Ungodly men and sinners (v. 18) such as Nero in Rome are calling out this divine verdict on themselves by persecuting Christianity and Christians because they are Christians. The period in which Peter writes is the one when God's verdict on such men is to start, and its start is ἀπό, *from* the house of God, *from* the crimes these men are committing against God's house, his holy church. Every verdict starts from the object involved in the crime. The thought is the same as that expressed in v. 5 regarding blasphemers. Seeking Old Testament passages for judgments on the house of God is following an unsatisfactory trail.

Δέ is "moreover": **moreover, if first from us, what the end of those who are disobedient to the gospel of God?** Bad enough is this verdict when it starts first "from us," against whom these crimes are committed. "Us" = "the house of God" (Heb. 3:6: "whose house are we"). How serious this persecution of God's church is Paul lets us understand when he speaks of his own crime in this respect in Gal. 1:13; I Cor. 15:9; I Tim. 1:13. Paul escaped the verdict by finally not being disobedient to the gospel of God (Acts 26:19: "I was not disobedient," ἀπειθής).

But what about these persecutors? "What the end of those who are disobedient to the gospel of God?" Terrible enough to sin against *"the house of God"* — how terrible to end by disobeying *"the gospel of God"*! Terrible to have one's verdict "from us," "from God's house," from what one does to God's church. There is time to repent of that as we see in Paul's case.° But what if this "first" is followed by τὸ τέλος, "the end," namely that which belongs to those who constantly disobey (present participle) what is greater than God's house, namely God's own gospel?

The contrast lies between "the house of God" and "the gospel of God." It is frequently thought to lie between "us" and "those disobeying." The fact that the same preposition ἀπό makes "from us" merely say what "from the house of God" means is overlooked. A simple pronoun "us" cannot be the opposite of a characterizing, substantivized participle "those disobeying," otherwise Peter would have written "us obeying." This verdict is not for us, the house of God. It is only for those who deserve it, first because of their treatment of God's people, finally because of their treatment of God's gospel. What their end will be the godly readers may tell themselves. As far as testing out and purifying are concerned, Peter has completed the discussion of these in 1:7 (τὸ δοκίμιον ὑμῶν τῆς πίστεως ... διὰ πυρός, "the testing out of your faith . . . by means of fire"); he says nothing about them here. So we do not speak of *Laeuterung*, "purification." Our purification (or that of gold, 1:7) is never called "the verdict" or κρῖμα, nor could it be.

18) Not until he reaches this point does Peter compare the righteous and the ungodly: **And if the righteous is with difficulty saved, where will the ungodly and sinner appear?** Peter simply adopts the LXX's version of Prov. 11:31: Εἰ ὁ μὲν δίκαιος μόλις (μόγις) σώζεται, ὁ ἀσεβὴς καὶ ἁμαρτωλὸς ποῦ φανεῖται. The Hebrew reads: "Behold, the righteous shall be recompensed in the earth: much more the wicked and the sinner." Peter wants the thought as it is stated by the LXX. Μόλις (see B.-D. 33) = "with difficulty" and refers to the hard time that persecution causes the

Christian. Our versions have "scarcely," which leaves a wrong impression, as though only a few righteous ones are saved. "Scarcely, rarely," is only the second or derived meaning of the adverb — Thayer; Liddell and Scott define μόγις: "with toil and pain"; hence "hardly, scarcely."

"The ungodly and sinner (note, only one article), where will he appear?" expects the answer, "Nowhere." The preceding context lets us understand that "the ungodly and sinner" is the "disobedient" who persecutes the house of God and scorns the gospel of God.

19) Concluding the whole subject of the impending persecution of Christians because they are Christians, Peter says: **Wherefore also those suffering according to the will of God, let them deposit with a faithful Creator their souls in connection with well-doing.** This is the deduction (ὥστε) which those who suffer are to make and to act on. Καί is to be construed with "those suffering." Not all will have to suffer; "according to the will of God" implies the same thought. God's will determines this. This phrase excludes the idea that such suffering is a verdict on the house of God first and on the ungodly second, purifying the former, damning the latter; compare "thus is the will of God" in 2:15. Some will not need to suffer; they need no special admonition. Commentators tell us that martyrdom is not referred to, that "in welldoing" excludes it. This view is not acceptable. Persecution so easily leads to bloody death. Many in Rome were to suffer a horrible death. But this is true, that "those suffering" would suffer in various degrees, and only some would be put to death.

Παρατίθημι means "to deposit" just as παραθήκη = "deposit" (I Tim. 6:20; II Tim. 1:12, 14). The idea is that of depositing a treasure into safe and trustworthy hands. So all who suffer for their faith are to deposit τὰς ψυχάς, "their lives" or "their souls" (1:9), with their faithful Creator. He gave them their lives (souls); he allots suffering according to his good and gracious will. The reading "*as* with a faithful Creator" is too weakly attested; "with a faithful Creator" is stronger; there is no article in order to bring out the qualitative force of this noun. Even if we suffer death in persecution we need not fear (3:14) after we make this deposit. "Creator" indicates God's almighty power; he created heaven and earth. Κτίστης is a hapaxlegomenon. "Faithful" points to his promises which we trust, which he fulfills without fail. We are fortified for the suffering that persecution brings, fortified in every way.

The last phrase should not be understood to mean that the depositing is done *by* our well-doing. The acts mentioned here differ, the one is a depositing with the faithful Creator by trust and prayer, the other a doing to men by words and by deeds. Peter uses a rare word when he writes ἀγαθοποιΐα; it is found only here in the Bible. Ἐν is not *auf Grund von*; we again take it in its first meaning, "in connection with doing good." This doing good to others in and beyond the bounds of the church is one of the great marks of this epistle. Ever and ever, especially also when and where men make the Christian suffer, he does only what is good to others, what benefits them bodily, morally, spiritually even as Christ did when he, too, bore so much among men.

CHAPTER V

The Elders, Examples of the Flock,
v. 1-5a

1) When Peter admonishes the elders he does not at this late point in his epistle deal with them as a group that is comparable to the groups mentioned in 2:18 (houseslaves); in 3:1 (wives); in 3:7 (husbands); then "all" in 3:8. These elders do not constitute such a group, for they are over the entire flock, not because of their age, but because of their office. In the persecutions that are about to come their conduct and their care of the flock would be of the highest importance. That is why Peter now singles them out.

Elders, then, among you I urge, the fellow elder and witness of the sufferings of Christ, the partaker also of the glory about to be revealed: shepherd the flock of God in your care, overseeing it not constrainedly but voluntarily in accord with God, nor yet in a way out for shameful gain but eagerly, nor yet as lording it over the allotted charges but as being examples to the flock.

The absence of the article from the noun has it refer to "such as are elders" among the readers, and they are named πρεσβύτεροι, "elders," (presbyters) because of the dignity of their office whereas the word ἐπίσκοποι (I Tim. 3:1, 2; Titus 1:7, but "elders" in v. 5) would give them a title that is more in conformity with their work as "overseers." We have discussed this office in the passages cited; see also Acts 11:30. These were the pastors of the New Testament congregations, and each congregation had several who were chosen and called by the congregation; they were nearly always older, experienced men who, however, received no salary or pay. We may regard οὖν as transitional (B.-P. 945) ; the idea that it always deduces is unwarranted. Παρακαλῶ = to urge, to admonish or to exhort.

"I urge, the fellow elder and witness of the sufferings of Christ, the partaker also of the glory about to be revealed," adds two appositions (each with ὁ) to the "I" of the verb. Peter describes himself by means of these, and they show that what Peter urges upon elders he exemplifies in his own life and office. John, too, calls himself "the elder" (II John 1 ; III John 1) ; Papias, too, calls John "the elder" and speaks of the apostles as being elders. As apostolic elders they exercised oversight over many flocks; congregational elders exercised such oversight over the one flock that had called them. "Fellow elder" and John's simple "elder" state that the apostolic office was the same office as that held by the congregational elders. We are right in saying that when Jesus called the Twelve as apostles as recorded in Matthew 10 he instituted the office of the ministry.

Although these two offices are the same in substance, when he is identifying himself Peter adds the detail: "witness of the sufferings of Christ," not so much in order to indicate that there is a great difference between himself and the congregational elders, for he combines this noun and the other noun under one article, but in order in a direct way to connect him with the sufferings of Christ, which have been so repeatedly mentioned as our example in this epistle. Peter himself was an eyewitness of these sufferings. All Christians are to fellowship these sufferings (4:13, see this passage; 2:21). Peter himself saw them and is able to testify accordingly. To say that this means only that he is *preaching* these sufferings, that, if Peter intended to state more, he would have to write "the sufferings of *Jesus*" and not "of *Christ*," implies

stressing one word unduly and taking the force out of
another, the word μαρτύς, "witness." In 4:13, as in 1:11,
Peter has written "the sufferings of *Christ*," exactly
as he writes here. Christ suffered, 2:21; 4:1; in fact,
Peter always writes Jesus Christ or simply Christ and
never simply Jesus.

The second apposition: "the partaker also of the
glory about to be revealed," places the glory of Christ
beside his sufferings; it is not our sufferings and our
glory as in Rom. 8:18 but Christ's. As to Christ's
sufferings, in 4:13 Peter has already mentioned our
fellowshiping them (κοινωνεῖν) and thus adds κοινωνός,
one who fellowships Christ's glory. In 1:11 Christ's
sufferings and his glory are placed side by side just
as they are here. We see why Peter adds these appositions: they are to make all these elders most ready
to hear what Peter urges upon them. Now, they,
indeed, like Peter, may have to suffer much, but, like
Peter, they, too, are to be partakers of Christ's glory.
Peter knows how to touch upon the right motives just
as we see this done so vividly by Paul. Μέλλω with the
infinitive is a periphrastic future; here we have the
present infinitive to express durative future revelation.

2) The hortation follows: "shepherd the flock!"
do everything that shepherding requires. We have an
effective aorist imperative. Peter passes on to his
fellow shepherds the order which Jesus gave him in
John 21:16: ποίμαινε τὰ πρόβατά μου, "shepherd my sheep."
In John 21:15, 17 Jesus added βόσκε, "feed," which
some regard as having the same force as "shepherd." The
shepherding includes the feeding or pasturing (teaching the Word) but extends beyond that to the whole
care on the part of a shepherd. Shepherding should
not be reduced to preaching. In fine Greek style Peter
inserts ἐν ὑμῖν between the article and the noun, the
phrase means "the flock in your care." This is not
the case with regard to the ἐν ὑμῖν occurring in verse 1,

which is not placed between the article and the noun. The "you" referred to is the "you" implied in the imperative.

In John 10:14 and 21:15, etc., Christ calls the sheep "mine"; in Acts 20:28 Paul writes "the church of God." We meet such genitives quite regularly; in 4:17 we have "the house of God." "Flock" brings to mind all the shepherd imagery found in the Scriptures: the sheep gentle, defenseless, liable to stray, needing a shepherd, happy, peaceful under his care, pitiful when lost, scattered, etc. This is "God's flock" that was bought at a great price (Acts 20:28), that is exceedingly precious in his sight, a great trust placed into the hands of human shepherds who are to pattern after Yahweh, the Shepherd (Ps. 23:1), and Christ, the Archshepherd (v. 4). What shepherd could have the care of any part of *God's* flock and treat it carelessly! Peter's words are sparing but overflow with tender and serious meaning.

Some texts omit ἐπισκοποῦντες, but it is singularly appropriate, especially also for introducing all the following adverbial modifiers. This participle introduces the other designation for "elders," namely ἐπίσκοποι, "overseers" (Latin *episcopus,* our "bishop"). "Overseeing" is often taken to be an activity that is different from "shepherding" (ποιμάνατε) as if the latter were the preaching and the teaching and the overseeing the practical management. Some sheep (congregations) even want to do the latter themselves, the pastor is only to conduct the services. Strange sheep! Both terms have the same meaning, the figurative "shepherd the flock" is explained by the literal "overseeing." To oversee is to shepherd, and vice versa.

Thus the main point appears in the adverbial modifiers which are negative and positive. "Not constrainedly but voluntarily," not because they must but because they want to; not like drafted soldiers but like volunteers; not needing to be urged to every task but as running to put their hands to it, delighted to do it. Some texts, one of which is quite important, omit κατὰ Θεόν as do the A. V. and Luther. We are inclined to accept the phrase as being genuine, as casting light on "voluntarily," this being not a mere human eagerness but an eagerness "in accord with God" who by his Spirit has made the elders overseers of the church of God (Acts 20:28). Fleshly willingness will not do.

"Nor yet in a way out for shameful gain but eagerly" adds another point. We have the adjective αἰσχροκερδής in I Tim. 3:8 and Titus 1:7; the adverb occurs only here in Peter (G. K. 190). The idea is that any personal gain which is sought in a selfish way is shameful; the ministry is not intended for that purpose. The "for filthy lucre" of our versions is expressive, for filth is shameful. In our day shameful gain generally consists in eagerness to get a large salary and rich perquisites by prostituting the ministry to such low aims, but we should remember that in apostolic times elders were not salaried or paid. They could, however, abuse their office in a mercenary way, not necessarily by pilfering from eleemosynary funds, but by seeking and getting the trade of the church and in other ways. Προθύμως means "eagerly," with inner devotion.

3) The final contrast is not stated with adverbs but with participles used adverbially; like the preceding adverbs, it is dependent on ἐπισκοποῦντες: "nor yet as lording it over the allotted charges but (as) being examples to the flock" (objective genitive). The shepherds are not to be little popes or petty tyrants. Matt. 20:25; II Cor. 1:24. The use of κλῆροι as well as the fact that this is a plural have always caused some difficulty, and we thus have various suggestions as to the meaning. When it is stated that Peter might have said "nor as lording it over the flock but as

examples to it," this would be introducing a rather strange figure; it seems somewhat incongruous to speak of *lording* it over a *flock of sheep!* On the other hand, too much is put into this word when it is made to emphasize entrusted possession which is God's (C.-K. 604). Israel is called λαὸς ἔγκληρος τῷ Θεῷ, Deut. 4:20; κλῆρος τοῦ Θεοῦ, Deut. 9:29, and since Israel alone was this, there was no plural for these expressions. In Acts 17:4 we have προσεκληρώθησαν: some of them were persuaded and "were allotted" to Paul and Silas. So we deem it safe to make οἱ κλῆροι "the allotted charges." The elders of each congregation had received that congregation as their allotment. The participle and the object agree: one may deem it in his power to do as he pleases with what has been allotted to him. We still have preachers who act in this way.

The opposite is: "being τύποι to the flock," models for the flock to pattern after; as a die is struck, and its impress made by a blow, so the die makes the counterstamp and impress on the material.

Peter mentions three common sins of preachers: laziness, greed, popishness, all of which are especially objectionable in days of persecution. Peter demands voluntariness, unselfish devotion, models fit to be patterned after.

4) **And the Archshepherd having been manifested, you will bring away the unfading crown of the glory.** With a beautiful analogy Peter calls Christ "the Archshepherd," which recalls Jesus' own word about "the good Shepherd." He is the supreme Shepherd of the flock, all others are undershepherds, who must learn their shepherding from him. We may translate "having appeared" (not "shall appear") or "having been manifested," the aorist participle denotes a single act. His Parousia or epiphany at the last day is referred to. Then these true elders and shepherds "shall bring away for themselves (future middle) the

fadeless crown of the glory," fadeless or amaranthine as in 1:4, and στέφανον refers to a chaplet that encircles the head (on this word see James 1:12). The genitive "of the (heavenly) glory" is appositional like "of the life" in James 1:12. Here, where the context speaks of neither war nor kingship but of shepherd and flock, *stephanos*, like "the glory," denotes only the highest honor and distinction.

5a) **Likewise, younger men, be in subjection to elders!** This rounds out what Peter has to say regarding the elders during these troublous times. While elders are not to act as lords of the congregations, younger men are not to despise the elders and act as if they amount to nothing. Peter shields the standing and the authority of the elders. Younger men are to be in proper subjection to the elders of the church. The second aorist passive imperative is like the other aorist imperative, direct and to the point.

The view that Peter only bids the younger people to be subject to older people on the mere score of age is out of the line of the thought that precedes. "Likewise" connects with the foregoing. Peter "likewise" has a word for such as are not elders and pastors, whom he calls νεώτεροι, "younger." These are not deacons or younger church officers; there is nothing in the context that would suggest such a thought. The youths mentioned in Acts 5:6,. 10 are not deacons or officials but simply young men. .

The Final Exhortations to All Church Members,
v. 5b-11

5b) **Moreover, do you all with respect to each other apron yourselves with lowly-mindedness.** The dative ἀλλήλοις puzzles some interpreters. This cannot be translated as a reflexive, "gird yourselves" (R. V.). In order to construe this dative as a reciprocal pronoun one text and some versions (also A. V.) insert ὑποτασσόμενοι, and the same effect is secured by some editors and some commentators by placing a period after ἀλλήλοις. These procedures connect the words with the preceding: all are to be subject to one another. Hence the R. V. makes no break at this point but retains v. 1-11 as one paragraph. We feel, however, that the sense calls for a division at this point. With 5a Peter concludes what he has to say as pertaining to the elders. With πάντες he begins a new paragraph which pertains to "all." There is then no difficulty regarding the dative ἀλλήλοις. It is placed emphatically forward, exactly where it belongs after Peter has said something about the "elders." It is the dative of relation: "All of you in your relation to each other tie on the apron of lowly-mindedness!"

Some also have difficulty with ἐγκομβώσασθε. Does this word mean to tie on a girdle or to tie on an apron or to fasten on a stately robe? Some commentaries offer long discussions regarding this verb. When all is said, and especially when we note the object to be tied on, namely "lowly-mindedness," we think of a slave's apron that is tied on with its attached strings; and it may even be possible that Peter had in mind that act of Jesus' in the upper room when he tied on an apron and washed the disciples' feet and performed this slave's service to which none of them would stoop. Remember, too, how Peter behaved on that occasion. Then·he had an example of the lowly-mindedness which he now urges upon all.

The article used with ταπεινοφροσύνη = "the due lowly-mindedness." The word has the active sense of minding something, namely the superiority of others and our own unworthiness, minding this so that we act accordingly. M.-M. cannot list this noun; it does not appear in the Old Testament or in secular Greek, in Josephus and in Epictetus it is used only in the base sense which·the adjective ταπεινός has: "pusillanimity," which is a fault and not a virtue. The pagan and secular idea of manhood is strong self-assertion, imposing one's will on all others. When anyone bowed to others, it was done only· under compulsion and hence was ignominious. The pagan mind did not have the idea of ethical humility; it lacked the spiritual soil for ·such a concept. Christ and his ethics were required to make lowly-mindedness a great Christian virtue. Matt. 18:1-3; 20:25-28; the word occurs in Phil. 2:3; Col. 3:12.

When he states the reason for tying on due lowly-mindedness Peter adopts some words from Prov. 3: 34. We have already seen that Peter does not always quote but in some cases only alludes and in others just adopts. Here he follows the LXX and simply changes Κύριος into ὁ Θεός. James 4:6 quotes this passage from Proverbs and makes the same change. The Hebrew of this passage reads: "Surely, he scorneth the scorners, but he giveth grace unto the lowly." Peter writes: **because God resists haughty ones, but gives grace to lowly ones.**

The word ταπεινοί, "lowly ones," makes this passage match "lowly-mindedness." God's χάρις or "favor" with all the blessings that flow from it is intended for "lowly ones," is a glorious gift from God to them. Grace is always a gift, one that God loves to bestow. The lowly do not pretend to lowliness; they know all their sinfulness and weakness. Conscious of this, they are never "haughty." The fact that haughty ones are scorners (Hebrew) is only the manifestation of their overweaning pride. God must scorn or resist their wicked arrogance. See Luke 1:52; 18:14 where Jesus expresses the same thought in other words. The haughty would scorn grace and its gifts; the lowly alone are eager to accept grace.

6) Accordingly, be lowly under the mighty hand of God in order that he may exalt you in due season, etc. Ταπεινώθητε repeats the idea of ταπεινοῖς and of ταπεινοφροσύνην referred to in v. 5 and should be translated so as to make this evident: "be lowly," the effective aorist imperative. What folly to act haughtily "under the mighty hand of God," κραταιά, actively "mighty!" Shall this mighty hand be turned against us? The lowly it will "exalt" with its mighty power. See Matt. 23:12; Luke 14:11. That is the crowning grace that will be given to them. "In due season" implies that God will let the lowly remain in their lowly condition here on earth; the time for their exaltation is the last day, the day of the manifestation of Christ; then they shall receive the crown of the glory (v. 4). Who are we to be thus exalted and crowned? The very realization of what is here promised bows us under God's mighty hand in deepest lowliness.

7) But what about the time of our lowliness while we wait for our final exaltation? Must we just worry along under the oppression of the wicked world? Peter answers with a participial clause, participial because this is only a subordinate consideration: **all your worry casting upon him because he is caring for you,** literally: "there is care for him (impersonal verb) concerning you." Μέριμνα = worry or anxiety as when one does not know whether to do this or to do that, "distraction." We have the verb in Luke 10:41: Martha was distracted by all she wanted to do, not knowing to what to turn her hand and in desperation going to Jesus to have him order Mary to help her.

Everything of this kind we are to throw upon God because he is caring for us, attending to us and to all our needs. This is an allusion to Ps. 55:22: "Cast

thy burden upon the Lord, and he shall sustain thee."
Compare Ps. 37:5; also Luke 12:11, 12.

8) Two incisive aorist imperatives follow: **Be
sober!. Watch!** This is the same spiritual soberness
that was mentioned in 1:13 and 4:7 (II Tim. 4:5),
a balance in disposition, thought, and action, never
to be flighty, carried away by notions of our own or
of others. Next, "watch," be wide awake, not dull
and sleepy. The connotation of γρηγορεῖν is that of
being aroused to watch while ἀγρυπνεῖν connotes merely
the absence of sleep.

Without a connective Peter states what certainly
ought to keep every one of us sober and wide awake:
**Your opponent, (the) devil, as a lion roaring walks
around seeking to swallow someone.** Ἀντίδικος is the
word for an opponent in a court before a judge (Luke
18:3); but here, where we have the imagery of a
raging lion, it is used in the generalized sense of opponent or adversary. Because διάβολος has no article,
some think that it cannot be an apposition, and that
ἀντίδικος is an adjective. But the position of ὑμῶν obviates this; "devil" is minus the article because it is
regarded as a proper noun. This is a mere point of
grammar that does not affect the sense. "As" is not
"like" although "a lion roaring" is figurative; the devil
is such a lion.

A good deal is suggested by the term "roaring."
This lion is not silent, stealthily prowling around;
he is letting his frightful roar sound forth. At this
very time, under Nero, the roar of frightful persecution was being heard by the poor Christian victims.
In October of the year 64 the storm broke. Peter himself became a victim of it. See the introduction for
the dangerous situation that called forth this letter.
Not always does the devil roar thus although when
some preach on this text they often state this. Peter
does not say what James 4:7b states. Walking about,

roaring, "seeking to swallow someone," picture the danger.

Editors and grammarians are at variance with each other as to whether this is an indirect question with τίνα, which should have the subjunctive (possibly the (infinitive): *"whom* he may devour"; or the indefinite pronoun: "to devour *someone."* This, too, has no effect on the meaning. Καταπιεῖν = to drink down and not to eat up or "devour." The suggestion is that of drinking the victim's blood. Did Peter think of martyrs in the arena who were driven out from the dungeons to face actual lions? He must have thought at least of bloody death.

9) He continues: **whom stand against, firm as regards the faith, knowing that the same kinds of sufferings are being executed upon your brotherhood in the world.** Στερεοί = firm, hard, unbending, and the dative expresses relation: "as regards the faith"; it is not locative "in the faith" (R. 523). Τῇ πίστει is "the faith," objective faith; "firm as regards the faith," not denying the doctrine of Christianity for fear of a martyr's death. This is not the *fides qua creditur* but *quae creditur.* The subjective believing is expressed by the adjective "firm." This standing against the devil means refusal to deny Christ under threat of death. In James 4:7 standing against the devil is resisting his assaults when he comes with temptations; hence also when he is withstood he flees as one defeated. Peter is speaking of dying for the faith.

Therefore he points them to others who are meeting this same ordeal: "knowing that the same kinds of sufferings are being executed upon your brotherhood in the world." The fact that τὰ αὐτά has a genitive is exceptional. The sense is not: "the same sufferings" but "the same kinds of sufferings" (R. 505; 687), the same things in the way of sufferings. We regard the present infinitive as a passive: *sind der Bruederschaft auferlegt*, "are executed upon the brotherhood." Others prefer to regard it as the middle. The dative is due to ἐπί in the infinitive or is again a dative of relation. The abstract "brotherhood" is more exact than "brethren" would be. The whole body as such is affected although only some of its members suffer, and a certain number are martyred (I Cor. 12:26). "In the world" means here among men where suffering is our lot as it was that of Christ. Recall all that Peter has said regarding "the sufferings." He promises no cessation of these but only τὰ αὐτά, the same sort of things.

10) Δέ always adds something that is different; here a great promise is added to the admonition stated in v. 9. **Moreover, the God of all grace, the One who called you unto his eternal glory in connection with Christ after having suffered a little while, will himself equip, firm, strengthen (you). To him the might for the eons of the eons! Amen.** "The God of all grace," with its qualitative genitive, characterizes God as the source of all grace (compare χάρις in v. 5), all divine favor for us who do not deserve it. Compare II Cor. 1:3, "the God of all consolation." The apposition: "the One who called you unto his eternal glory in connection with Christ," points back to what the God of all grace has already done in grace, namely "called you" effectively. Εἰς states "to" what, and ἐν "in connection with" whom.

This is the gospel call; in the epistles καλεῖν always designates the successful gospel call. It assures us of God's eternal glory in heaven "after having suffered a little while." The aorist παθόντας is made clear by ὀλίγον; it is in contrast with αἰώνιον and is an accusative participle because of the accusative ὑμᾶς. We are called *unto* this glory as our final goal ("the crown of the glory," v. 4) ; it is not yet ours so that we suffer "a little while" preceding it. The aorist participle should not be construed with the following future tenses so that Peter would appear to say that *after* his readers have suffered the God of grace will equip, firm, strengthen them. To be so equipped, etc., is needed *now* and not *after* all suffering is over with. God's equipping will be done for this little while of suffering.

Only "a little while" (ὀλίγον, sc. χρόνον) endures the suffering, but the glory is "eternal." This is comfort. The future tenses are not optatives of wish, A. V., but indicate assurance. They are not merely futuristic: "shall equip," etc., but voluntative: "will equip." Αὐτός is emphatic: *he*, this God of grace, this One who has called you, etc., he will do this for you. A few texts insert θεμελιώσει, "will found," so that we have four verbs (A. V., "will settle you"). Καταρτίσει (perfective κατά plus ἀρτίζω, from which we have "artisan") means that God will equip, will outfit us with all that we need for this little while of suffering; στηρίξει (στερεοί in v. 9) that he will firm us, make us unyielding, so that we will hold to "the faith" even unto death; σθενώσει that he will give us strength. If we were alone we could not stand; with this help from God we can do so.

11) Peter closes this assurance with a brief doxology, compare 4:11. It is exclamatory and needs no copula. Peter does not use a relative "to whom" but αὐτῷ, which matches the preceding αὐτός, "to him." Since all the verbs denote acts of might, Peter names only κράτος, "might," and not also "glory" as he does in 4:11. Note the "mighty" hand of God in v. 6. He has "his eternal glory" in v. 10. "For the eons," etc., has the same force it had in 4:11. "To him the might" is confession and acknowledgment: it is, indeed, his. "Amen" is used as it was in 4:11.

Conclusion, v. 12-14

12) **By means of Silvanus, the faithful brother,
to you have I written, as I reckon, in brevity, urging
and testifying that this is God's genuine grace — in
which stand!** Διά indicates that Silvanus is the means
or the messenger for conveying this letter ὑμῖν, "to you."
But we may ask why ὑμῖν is placed next to this διά phrase
and given so prominent a position. The answer is that
Peter wants "through *Silvanus* to *you*" close together
in order in this way to indicate that Silvanus is the
bearer of the letter "to you." The combination of the
phrase and the dative "to you" is made even more
marked by the placing of the apposition τοῦ πιστοῦ ἀδελφοῦ
after ὑμῖν, embedding, as it were, the pronoun in the
genitives.

That this peculiar position of "to you" should
mean: "I have left the composition of this letter to
Silvanus and did not really write it myself," is an
assumption that stresses the preposition alone while
it ignores the dative. From the very beginning and
throughout the letter the readers are left under the
impression that Peter alone is the writer that is addressing them. Are they now at the very end of the
epistle suddenly to learn that that impression has been
false, that not Peter, "apostle of Jesus Christ" (1:1),
has been speaking but only Peter's mouthpiece Silvanus; that Peter himself felt incompetent to address
them at firsthand in words of his own composition?
That supposition is baseless, to say nothing of the
way in which it would be conveyed. The letter brings
no salutation from Silvanus while it does convey one
from Mark. How can that be done if this διά makes
Silvanus the composer instead of the bearer of this
letter? See still further in the introduction.

The fact that Peter calls Silvanus "the faithful
brother" differs in no way from Paul's fraternal praise
of his assistants, especially when he sends them on a

mission as Peter here sends Silvanus with this letter. It is not necessary to speculate as to why "the faithful brother" is added. Silvanus was a faithful brother; Peter would not have had him in his company if he were not.

The difference of opinion regarding this apposition becomes extreme when Peter is thought to say: "The faithful brother as I account him" (R. V.; the A. V. has a similar translation). But Peter would scarcely thus qualify and reduce the statement that Silvanus is a faithful brother. "I have written, as I reckon, in brevity" is to be construed together. Peter thinks that his letter is rather short. Ἔγραψα is the ordinary epistolary aorist (R. 846). Δι᾽ ὀλίγων uses the preposition διά in the sense of manner, which is an easy transition from the idea of means (R. 583); literally, "by means of few words" (supply λόγων) = "in brevity." The phrase is not an excuse as though the readers may think the words rather many; they state that Peter purposely intended to write but briefly as the readers may also see.

The participles add Peter's intent: "urging and testifying (ἐπί, on top of the urging) that this is God's genuine grace," all this that he does and will do for us (v. 10). Although it means suffering for a little while, God's grace supports us, and glory awaits us. Yes, this is genuine grace for us poor sinners. Peter urges this conviction and his own testimony to this fact upon his readers.

"In which stand!" This final imperative στῆτε is an effective aorist. There is no reason to regard it as unusual because it follows a relative, for in v. 9 Peter has the same construction. Some texts have the indicative ἑστήκατε (perfect in the present sense: "in which you stand"), apparently in order to have the more usual construction with the relative.

13) **There salutes you the one elect with you
in Babylon, also Mark, my son.** Ἡ συνεκλεκτή is feminine because it refers to ἐκκλησία, the church in Babylon, i. e., the entire church, which is jointly elect with
all the readers ˙of this letter. The word "elect" harks
back to 1:1: the readers are the elect foreigners in
five Roman provinces; the church from which Peter
writes and whose salutation he sends is "in Babylon."
Is this Babylon, the city on the Euphrates, or is "Babylon" an allegorical, symbolical designation for Rome,
the capital of the world? Zahn, *Introduction,* II, 158,
etc., 163, etc., traces the view that Rome is referred
to back to the second century; not until the Middle
Ages did some scholars think that Peter at one time
went to Babylon on the Euphrates, and they sought
to prove their opinion by a reference to our passage.
But Babylon had disappeared already at Peter's time;
this city no longer existed.

This is really not a question that concerns Peter
alone. We ask further: "Was there ever a time during the days of ˙the apostles when these *three* men,
Peter, Silvanus, and Mark, were together in the far
east, in what was once Babylon or in that territory?"
No commentator has succeeded in making this view
plausible. Some commentators place Peter there; but
what about the other two men?

Again, the question we have to face is this: "Shall
we abandon all the reliable data we possess and all
that the ancient tradition reports and operate with
a blank as far as the records and the traditions go and
have nothing to go on save this phrase in this epistle
and set up the hypothesis that Peter wrote this letter
from Babylon with Silvanus and Mark at his side?"
Add the supposition that these men must then have
heard in far-off Babylon about the Christians in Pontus, etc., (1:1) and about the imminence of persecution

for them, etc. Finally, how could *Peter* write to churches that belonged to *Paul's* field? When these questions are convincingly answered, we shall consider the literal Babylon, but not before that has been done.

It is objected that not until the time when John's Revelation was written is Rome ever termed "Babylon." She is given that name here by Peter. In Revelation Babylon does *not* refer to Rome but is used symbolically for the whole world's anti-Christian capital. But why did Peter not say outright "in Rome"? The figurative "Babylon" is used because of the personification "the one elect with you" and because of the figurative term "my son" as a designation for Mark. "Babylon" emphasizes the paganism of Rome, the great city of the world, all her pagan idolatry and corruption, and also — quite important — all her hostility to God's elect. Those living in this Babylon will be the first to suffer, in fact, it seems that their suffering had already begun when Peter writes. This salutation has the sound of: *Morituri salutamus!*

Since no salutation from Silvanus is added, this implies that he will deliver the letter. Since Mark is the only other person mentioned, we conclude that Peter had only Mark and Silvanus with him at this time. "My son" (υἱός) reminds us of Paul's τέκνον as a designation for Timothy, his "child." Mark, it would seem, had been converted by Peter as Timothy had been by Paul. As far as locating Mark in eastern Babylon is concerned, this is difficult to establish. There is a great gap also in his life, but who will synchronize a stay in Babylon with the known data of the life of either Mark or Silvanus?

14) **Salute one another with a kiss of love!** See at length on Rom. 16:16a. When this sentence is read to the congregation, each person addressed is to act as a proxy for Peter and is to bestow a kiss on another so that it would seem as though each received the

salutation of a kiss from Peter himself. In Rom. 16:
16; I Cor. 16:20; II Cor. 13:12; I Thess. 5:26, Paul
uses "holy kiss." Peter writes kiss "of love" even as
he has addressed his readers as "beloved." Peter's love
salutes every Christian who hears this letter read.

Peace to you .all that (are) **in connection with
Christ!** This is the same "peace" that was mentioned
in 1:2, the condition when all is well with us in our
relation to God, the peace that is established by grace.
The readers may suffer severely, but God's peace rests
upon them. Τοῖς ἐν Χριστῷ does not distinguish one group
from another group which is *not* "in connection with
Christ." The article with the phrase is an apposition
to ὑμῖν πᾶσι: "to you all, those in connection with
Christ." Faith connects all of them with Christ.

Soli Deo Gloria

The Second Epistle
of St. Peter

INTRODUCTION

Peter wrote this brief epistle, but just when, where, and to whom he wrote it can no longer be determined. A formerly held view is now being corrected: this epistle was not written *after* but *before* the one we call First Peter, and the two were *not* sent to the same readers.

The order in which the epistles appear in our New Testament has nothing to do with the date of their composition, for the longest are placed first, the shortest last. This is true with regard to Peter's two epistles, John's three epistles, and Paul's epistles. When Peter calls this "the second letter I write to you," we should not suppose that he is referring to First Peter as the first letter. This opinion was entertained for a long time but cannot be held now, for the two letters are not addressed to the same people.

First Peter is addressed to the Christians in Pontus, Galatia, Cappadocia, Asia, Bithynia, a part of Paul's great missionary field. It was written when Peter was in Rome and Paul had left for Spain, when in the year 64 under Nero the great change came for Christianity, when the imperial government began to regard it as a *religio illicita.* Thus First Peter deals at length with *the sufferings* which await the readers. Peter suffered martyrdom in the same year (64). Second Peter could not have been written to the same people a little later. Second Peter says nothing about impending sufferings; it warns against abominable *libertinists* who scoff at the Parousia of Christ. This letter recalls Paul's warnings as expressed in Acts 20: 29, 30, II Thess. 2:3; I Tim. 4:1, etc.; II Tim. 3:1-9; and John's in I John 2:18. These warnings are prophetic, and they begin as early as Acts 20. Peter's warning is of the same kind; compare the passages.

This warning of Peter's is the second which he issues to his readers. Such a warning is not found in First Peter. Both of Peter's warnings antedate First Peter. The only conclusion tenable is that the letter containing the first warning has been lost. It suffered the same fate as one of the letters which Paul wrote to the Corinthians (I Cor. 5:9). The word ἤδη which is used in 3:1 leads us to conclude that the interval occurring between Peter's first and second warnings was brief. Yet neither the address in 1:1 nor anything in the warning itself enable us at this late date to determine the location of the people to whom the two warnings were originally addressed. We likewise have no means of determining when Peter issued these warnings, i. e., how long before First Peter Second Peter was written. It may not have been a long time before, considering what Peter says in 1:13-15.

Peter was crucified in Rome. His stay there continued scarcely more than a year. It is hazardous to say that he wrote his two warnings while he was in Rome. In fact, this seems more than doubtful. For, if he wrote from Rome, it is difficult to determine how his first letter of warning became lost, and how his second letter of warning needed so long a period of time before it became generally known and accepted as coming from his pen. The probabilities are in favor of the assumption that these two letters were written long before Peter reached Rome, perhaps while he was on his journeys.

Who were the readers, and where were they living? Some have thought that they were Jewish Christians and base this supposition in part on the way in which Peter designates himself in 1:1: "Symeon (or Simon) Peter," in part also on his use of Old Testament illustrations and references. To this may be added the expression "your apostles" occurring in 3:2. The readers were thus thought to be Jewish Christians who were living in Palestine or near Palestine. But "Symeon" must be considered together with the ἰσότιμον used in 1:1: Peter designates himself as a Jewish Christian and acknowledges that his readers have obtained a faith "like precious." This recalls Acts 11:17: τὴν ἴσην δωρεὰν ἔδωκεν αὐτοῖς ὁ Θεός, "God gave to them (Gentiles) the *same* faith." Peter is writing to Gentile Christians whose faith is just as precious as his own faith and that of all Jewish Christians and must thus be guarded with the same care.

This conclusion is corroborated by 3:15, 16 where Peter says that his readers have received a letter from Paul and implies that they know about others of Paul's letters, all of which letters urge the readers to consider "the longsuffering of our Lord as salvation." It is most interesting to learn that Peter and Paul wrote letters to the same people. We know Paul's history so well that we can safely say that he never wrote to a group of Jewish Christians. Paul did not write Hebrews; see the introduction to Hebrews. Least of all can we suppose that Paul ever wrote to Jewish Christians who were brought to the faith by some of the other apostles, who are in 3:2 called "your apostles." So these are Gentile Christians to whom Peter sends · this letter.

When we thus have Gentile churches whom Peter and other apostles converted, to whom Paul wrote a letter, who also were acquainted with some of his other letters, we seem to have sufficient clews to identify the church or the churches addressed by Peter. But, scan, as we may, all of Paul's letters that are now found in the New Testament, we are after all unable to state with any degree of assurance to which churches Peter refers. Hence some think that the letter which Peter's readers have received from Paul is not included in our canon, is also one of the lost letters like Peter's first letter to these people and like Paul's first letter to the

Corinthians (I Cor. 5:9). This seems to multiply the lost letters of apostles; but, especially as far as Paul is concerned, this is not at all strange, for he must have written quite a number of letters that are not preserved, letters to certify the errands on which he sent his assistants from time to time, °letters to recommend Christian travellers, and thus also letters like the one to which he refers in I Cor. 5:9.

What Peter says in 3:15, 16 does not identify the group of Gentile Christians that is addressed by Peter. This passage merely dates Peter's letter at a time when some of Paul's letters were known to Peter's readers, and when they possessed one that had been sent to them by Paul. We can say no more than this.

Second Peter is as little a catholic epistle as is First Peter. "Catholic" means universal, including all the churches that existed in the world at that time. First Peter is addressed to five provinces and is thus *not* catholic. Second Peter is addressed to people who possess one of Paul's letters and are acquainted with several others and is thus also not catholic. The καθολική of the captions which were affixed to these letters at a later time is unwarranted. It is more appro-priate in the case of the letter of James, for when he wrote to the Jewish churches outside of Palestine, there were scarcely any other churches save the one in Jerusalem and those in Palestine.

The knowledge regarding Paul's letters, which is ascribed to Peter's readers, advances the time of composition say to somewhere in the neighborhood of the year 60 — precision is out of the question. One cannot surmise where Peter wrote it. When some think of Antioch they are offering an opinion. More important would be the location of the readers; but here, too, one supposition is no better than another — all are value-less.

*   *   *

It was late in the history of the church before Second Peter was generally acknowledged as Scripture. Bigg, pages 199-215, offers a finely arranged list of the *testimonia veterum*. The earliest and strongest is the use which Jude makes of Second Peter. The question as to why Second Peter was less favorably received by the early writers of the church than First Peter is not so easily answered. First Peter was written at Rome and was thus at once known there; it was sent to five great provinces as an encyclical and was thus at once multiplied. Second Peter seems to have had a far different career, so that when others obtained copies they did not promptly elevate it to the same level that First Peter occupied. Those who suppose that Second Peter was written after First Peter and was sent to the same churches as a second encyclical create an insoluble problem for themselves: why, then, was Second Peter not received everywhere on the same basis as First Peter?

Second Peter, like James, was sent to readers who are not definitely named in the greeting as to their location. When copies were circulated, their source could not be promptly traced. Nobody could go to the original place and verify the fact that Peter wrote this letter to that place. Peter's other letter (3:1) was actually lost. If search was made in Pontus, etc., on the supposition that Second Peter, like First Peter, had been sent to these same churches, none of them, of course, knew anything about Second Peter. That fact alone would be counted against this letter.

Likewise its subject matter. A letter like First Peter at once appealed to churches which had to suffer many persecutions, for its aim is to fortify against these very persecutions. Second Peter deals with the coming of libertinistic errorists and their judgment at Christ's Parousia. Three short chapters on this subject, even though the libertinists increased in number and in influence, could not have the same strong appeal as First Peter. The one letter could be used with strong personal effect, the other could not.

Take these things together — there may have been still others — and it will become clear to us why Second Peter was classed as one of the antilegomena by Eusebius. Add the fact that those are very likely right who think that Peter's remarks made in 1:13-15 induced forgers to write such works as the heterodox *Gospel of Peter*, the *Apocalypse of Peter*, which professes to add to our knowledge of the future life and draws on the imagery of the pagan poets, the *Praedicatio Petri*, which teaches communism, the Περίοδοι Πέτρου, which mentions Peter's wife and his daughter and describes the appearance of Peter and tells us that he was bald — just as the *Acts of Paul and Thecla* supply a portrait of Paul. These Petrine pseudepigrapha, which are more or less orthodox, could cast only a doubtful shadow on Second Peter in later times.

It has been well said that, despite these handicaps, and due to its own apostolic weight and authority, Second Peter was placed into the New Testament canon by the Synod of Laodicea about 370, whose verdict was reaffirmed by the Council of Hippo in 393. It has maintained its position in the canon ever since that date. The era of the Reformation brought the first challenge of its canonicity (Erasmus, Calvin, Grotius). New attacks were made by Semler in 1784. Able defenders have stepped into the breach, Zahn was one of the latest among German scholars.

*   *   *

Second Peter has been called a second-century forgery. Second Peter would be a senseless forgery. It would also be a forgery that was so well done that only Peter himself could have executed it. The very first verses refute the supposition of a forgery. "The church, which for more than fourteen centuries has received it, has either been imposed upon by what must in that case be regarded as a Satanic device, or derived from it spiritual instruction of the highest importance." Smith, *Bible Dictionary*, III, 2457.

Chapter two has been called an interpolation that was drawn from Jude. Someone who had Second Peter before him, which was composed of only chapters one, and three, took a part of Jude and out of that built a chapter which he interlarded into Second Peter but made a rather bad joint at 3:1-3. Why, pray, would any man want to do such a useless, senseless thing as that? An obvious question such as that is not answered. Do any ancient texts of Second Peter exist that have only two chapters? Such a question is disregarded by the theorist.

Jerome introduces the discussion regarding the linguistic differences between First and Second Peter by saying that many deny the latter to Peter *propter stili cum priore dissonantiam*; elsewhere he says of the two epistles *stilo inter se et charactere discrepant structuraque verborum*. Yet Bigg adds regarding Jerome that "his great authority practically laid the doubt about Second Peter to sleep in the Greek and Latin churches." R. 125, etc., presents most of the items that have been noted, including Deissmann's remark that the epistles of Peter and Jude have quite "unreal addresses" and that "letter-like touches are purely decorative" — things that no one before him observed when reading these epistles.

Robertson accepts the idea that Peter and John were ἀγράμματοι καὶ ἰδιῶται (Acts 4:13) in the sense that they were illiterate whereas the terms mean only that they had not been trained in the Jewish rabbinical schools, that they were laymen in this respect. In Acts 4:13 the Sanhedrists are astonished at Peter and at John and marvel at the fact that such laymen should speak with the παρρησία, freedom and readiness, that these two exhibited; and they took note that they had been with Jesus. The fact is that in Acts 4:13 the competency of Peter and of John astonish the Sanhedrists; they are impressed by it despite the fact that Peter and John had not had rabbinical training. In John 7:15 Jesus' own lack of such training is emphasized by the same Sanhedrists in order to discredit him with the people: "How does this fellow know letters, γράμματα, not having learned?" i. e., in the schools of our rabbis. But read Matt. 7:28, 29 regarding what the people thought about the ability of Jesus. Then turn to the powerful sermon of Peter recorded in Acts 2:14-36 (Pentecost) and to Peter's other addresses recorded in Acts for a true estimate of Peter's ability. Then also remember that Peter wrote his letters near the close of his life; he certainly had learned still more during all those years.

Robertson mentions still more along this line: "We know that Peter had interpreters (Mark, for instance), and Josephus such literary help, and Peter had amanuenses." Papias said that Mark was Peter's ἑρμηνευτής. On the basis of this remark Robertson makes the statement that Peter could preach only in Aramaic, that he, therefore, took an interpreter with him on his travels; that Peter spoke Aramaic to his Greek audiences, and that somebody then told those audiences in Greek what Peter had said and meant. Papias said that Mark was Peter's *hermeneutes* because Mark wrote the Gospel stories which he heard Peter tell over and over again. Mark's Gospel is in reality Peter's Gospel. Peter's missionary work would have amounted to little if Peter had been unable to speak in Greek. Compare the introduction to James regarding the linguistic ability of this man who never left Palestine as well as regarding the whole question of language in the Orient and in Palestine. On the remark about Papias compare the introduction to First Peter.

First Peter has 361 words that are not found in Second Peter, and Second Peter has 231 words that are not found in First Peter. First Peter also has sixty-three that are not found in the rest of the New Testament; Second Peter has fifty-seven (five of them doubtful), and only one (ἀπόθεσις) of these 120 occurs in both First and Second Peter. Yes, this seems "remarkable." The subject matter of the two epistles is totally different.

Secondly, Peter is an independent writer; he states his thoughts in his own way and not in Paul's way — remember that much of the New Testament is composed by Paul. Peter draws on the Old Testament and does also this in his own way. These facts lie on the surface.

As far as grammatical differences are concerned, what Jerome called difference in style, this has for a long time been recognized as an exaggeration and as altogether insufficient for assuming that different writers composed the two epistles. They present not only differences but also marked similarities. In both epistles there is a fondness for repeating a word that has just been used, a feature that is found also in James. Again, in both epistles there is a fondness for plural abstract nouns. In both epistles the main thought is not stated at once and then elaborated; the main thought is approached gradually, after due preparation. Thus Bigg writes: "So far we may agree with Weiss that no document in the New Testament is so like First Peter as Second Peter."

R. 127 agrees with a few notable men who have done a good deal for the proper interpretation of Second Peter, who, nevertheless, still think that Peter delegated the writing of First Peter to Silvanus while he wrote Second Peter himself or dictated it to a scribe or delegated its composition to Mark or to someone else. At least for one letter, and probably for both,

Peter furnished only the general ideas but not the language. We see how Robertson tries to make this idea plausible: Peter did not know *grammata*, etc. The cue for this idea of delegating the composition of the letter or the letters to some abler man is the phrase found in I Pet. 5:12 although one also meets this supposition in the case of a letter or two of Paul's. We have already examined I Pet. 5:12, 13; in regard to Second Peter we need to say even less, for some, who think that the composition of First Peter was delegated to another, still think that Second Peter was written by Peter himself.

This introduction has become too long; yet many longer ones have been offered to readers. We have tried to touch the more important issues raised in regard to this brief and trenchant epistle. Other points we leave to the interpretation proper.

CHAPTER I

THE GREETING

1) Symeon Peter, slave and apostle of Jesus Christ, to those having obtained faith of equal value with ours, in connection with righteousness from our God and Savior Jesus Christ: may grace to you and peace be multiplied in connection with knowledge from our God and Lord Jesus! This translation is in part already an interpretation.

The optative of wish is identical with that used in I Pet. 1:2, save for the added phrase. Jude 2 also has this optative but with three objects. Peter introduces himself as *"Symeon* Peter, *slave* and apostle of Jesus Christ"; in First Peter he calls himself only "Peter, apostle of Jesus Christ." A forger would never have added "Symeon" and would scarcely have added "slave" to "apostle." He would have copied the words used in First Peter. This greeting was written by Peter's own pen or was dictated by him. It is not a mere variation of I Pet. 1:1, 2, but every word is significant for his readers in regard to the contents of this letter.

"Symeon" is genuinely Semitic and has the stronger textual attestation; "Simon" is the Greek equivalent and is attested chiefly by Codex B. Peter intends to emphasize his Jewish origin. When he terms himself "slave of Jesus Christ," as Paul does at times, he does not refer to his office, for "apostle" does that. "Slave" places Peter on the same level with his readers as being one who, like all his readers, submits his will wholly to that of the divine Master who bought him and them to be his own (I Cor. 6:20; 7:23). The con-

notation of δοῦλος is not service or involuntary service
but unquestioning submission to Jesus Christ's will.

"Slave" would be out of the line of the thought
of the contents of First Peter. That letter comforts,
assures, fortifies Christians who are soon to suffer
severely. "Apostle" is sufficient for all that Peter has
to say by way of comfort and hortation in that letter.
The readers of Second Peter are to be fortified against
heretical libertinists, dogs turning to their own vomit,
sows that, after being washed, again wallow in the
mire, who mock at the Lord's glorious Parousia. Peter
and all his readers bow before that mighty Lord, they
are governed by his will alone and are horrified at
these fools who snap their fingers at this Lord's will
and the idea of his return. "Slave of Jesus Christ"
is eminently in place. Yet Peter is one of those slaves
to whom the Lord has given a great commission;
ἀπόστολος is derived from ἀποστέλλω, "to commission."
In this letter Peter, a fellow slave of his readers, is
carrying out a part of the great official commission
of his great Lord "Jesus Christ." He writes in this
double capacity.

When critics tell us that somebody living in the
second century impersonates Peter with no wrong intention but only in order to magnify Peter, and that
we should not speak of a forger since our present ideas
about such things differ entirely from the ideas of the
second century, these critics would be right provided
the impersonator of Peter indicated that he was only
impersonating with such harmless intent by at once
allowing his readers to know what he is doing. Compare the greeting found in First Peter, yea, those found
in all the New Testament letters; they are all alike,
intend to be alike. If the opening nominative in any
one of them is intended as a harmless impersonation
of the person named, that harmless fact is hidden,

completely hidden. The name for such an action is
forgery. The moral sense of all ages resents it as
forgery, and not merely as literary forgery but as a
forgery of the apostolic Word of God; Smith's *Bible
Dictionary* (see quotation in the introduction) calls it
"Satanic."

The dative designates the readers in regular letter
form: "to those having obtained faith of equal value
with ours," etc., ἰσότιμον ἡμῖν, literally, "of value equal
to us." We all wish that Peter might have added the
name of some place as he does in First Peter. This
dative reads as˙ though all who have such faith are
addressed; yet all students agree that Peter is writing
to the Christians of some one locality, perhaps to those
of only one city, one congregation. With this dative
he describes them as people who have obtained faith
that is just as valuable and precious as that ˙which
"we" have obtained. Peter wants his readers so to
regard themselves and their precious faith.

Who are the ἡμῖν? With whose faith is Peter com-
paring his readers' faith? This plural pronoun cannot
refer to Peter alone. Some think that it refers to
Peter and to the rest of the apostles, either the Twelve,
or these and Paul (because of 3:15), or only Peter,
John, and Paul. It would, however, be strange for Peter
to refer thus to the faith of the apostles alone, whether
of all or of only a few of them. Nowhere else is the
faith of ordinary Christians compared with that of
the apostles. Besides, Peter does not call himself only
an apostle. He first of all calls himself a slave of Jesus
Christ, and does this after naming himself "Symeon
Peter" and thus using his old Jewish name. We thus
conclude that Peter refers to himself and to all Jewish
Christians with ἡμῖν; that he is writing to certain Gentile Christians to whom also Paul has written a letter
(3:15). Peter says that their faith is just as valuable

and as precious as our faith, i. e., that of any and of all Jewish believers. That, of course, applies to all Gentile Christians everywhere. That is what Peter intends.

This does not force us to think that he is writing to all of them; that this is a grand encyclical to Gentiles. When he is writing to one particular group of Gentile Christians he very properly describes the whole class to which they belong: "to you Gentile believers, whose faith, like that of all Gentile believers, is of equal value with our faith, that of all Jewish believers." We have strong substantiation for this view; for in Acts 11:17 Peter says that "God gave.to them the *same* gift," ἴσην is like ἰσότιμον; compare also Acts 15: 7-9 where this equality is stated at length.

Why does Peter stress the fact that the faith of his Gentile readers is of equal value with that of the Jewish believers to whom he himself belongs? The answer is, first of all, that Jesus Christ, our God and Savior Jesus Christ, values *their* faith just as highly as he does the faith of Peter himself and of all Jewish Christians. The readers are to do the same. The rest of the answer is, as this entire letter shows, that.the faith of the readers must, therefore, be preserved and fortified. All that the word of prophecy makes so sure (verse 19), all this about "the eternal kingdom of our Lord and Savior Jesus Christ," all the Scriptural examples of judgment on the ungodly who would not believe (chapter 2), all this, finally, about the end of the world and "the promise of Christ's Parousia" (3:4), pertains to all Christians alike. None of these things are merely Jewish. Those who scoff at what the Word of prophecy says about them are condemned by that Word; and Peter's readers must not share their fate.

The statement that in the body of the letter no further reference is made to the distinction between Jewish and Gentile believers is only partially correct. There is no *distinction* in v. 1; there is *equality* of value.

Since this is settled at the very beginning, nothing further needs to be said. This Jewish apostle takes his Gentile readers into the Jewish Word of prophecy and fortifies them so that they may be prepared for their Lord's Parousia at the end of the world.

Λαγχάνω means "to obtain by lot" and then simply "to obtain," yet not without the connotation expressed in Acts 11:17, the fact that God *gave* them this valuable gift, their faith. A few commentators have difficulty with the added phrase ἐν δικαιοσύνῃ. The supposition that it means that God (or Christ) acted in a righteous manner by letting the Gentile believers obtain a faith that is equal in value to that of the Jewish believers, is untenable. Ἐν does not mean *auf Grund von*, "on the basis of," the word for which would would be ἐπί; nor "through," the word for this would be διά; nor is it "instrumental." We translate, "in connection with" righteousness. This involves the great genitive τοῦ Θεοῦ ἡμῶν καὶ Σωτῆρος Ἰησοῦ Χριστοῦ and thus the same genitive that is found in v. 2, which is likewise attached to an ἐν phrase, namely ἐν ἐπιγνώσει. We submit the claim that these two genitives are to be construed *alike* and not diversely. The one is not possessive: righteousness belonging to Christ, and the other objective: knowledge that knows Christ. In two successive ἐν phrases that have the same grand genitive such a difference is unlikely. These two great genitives denote origin or source: "in connection with righteousness *from* our God and Savior Jesus Christ" — "in connection with knowledge *from* our God and Lord Jesus."

Faith is always "in connection with righteousness," the quality which that one possesses whom Christ declares righteous. C.-K. 312 states: "Second Peter 1:1 refers, not to the future righteousness of God, but to the redemptive righteousness revealed in producing salvation through Christ." To this statement there

should be added the fact that this righteousness is the
quality that is bestowed by the verdict of *Christ*, the
righteous Judge, on all *faith* equally, the imputed righteousness. Whether ἐν includes also the subsequently
acquired righteousness is a minor question; if this is
included it, too, is *of* Christ in the sense of *from*. We
are sorry to see that C.-K. 253 regards the second great
genitive as being objective.

The position which ἡμῶν has with the genitives here,
in v. 2, and in v. 11, is immaterial (R. 785). It in no
way affects the question as to whether one or two persons are referred to. The use of the one article would
say that but *one* person is referred to, namely, "Jesus
Christ, our God and Savior," in v. 2 he is regarded
as "our God and Lord"; so also in 2:20; 3:2, 18; II
Thess. 1:12; Titus 2:13; Eph. 5:5; Jude 4 (accusative). R. 786. The effort to find a reference to two
persons, God and Christ, is nullified linguistically by
the use of but one article in the Greek. There is nothing more to say. The deity of Christ stands forth here
as a mountain that no false faith can plunge into
the sea.

Robertson quotes Moulton as "clear enough to close
the matter": "Familiarity with the everlasting apothe-
osis that flaunts itself in the papyri and inscriptions
of Ptolemaic and Imperial times lends strong support
to Wendland's contention that Christians, from the
latter part of i/A. D. onward, deliberately annexed
for their divine Master the phraseology that was
impiously arrogated to themselves by some of the worst
of men," meaning the Roman emperors. This applies
not only to ὁ Θεός but equally to Κύριος (used in paganism
for divine lord) and to Σωτήρ (a divine person that
saves). These two were regularly employed by pagans
as divine titles.

When in the face of all this in language and in
history anyone asserts that Jesus Christ is here not

called God, v. 9 states what is wrong with him: he
suffers from a dogmatism that, like the old Jewish
Sanhedrin, is determined to deny the deity of Christ
at every price.

These designations found in Second Peter, together
with Moulton's remarks, substantiate the fact that the
readers are Gentile Christians. Those who formerly
regarded them as Jewish lacked a good deal of the
material that is here offered.

Paul applies Σωτήρ to Christ as well as to God; see
the word of the angel in Luke 2:11. Peter does so also
in Acts 5:31. The very name "Jesus" = "Savior." All
that the Scriptures mean by σωτηρία, "salvation," lies in
the title "Savior." He is the Rescuer who rescues us
from sin and damnation and places us into complete,
eternal safety. The fact that he is very God is added
not only to indicate his power as Savior — which, of
course, it does — but also because of so much that follows in this letter, all of which rests on his deity. Need
we say that practically every word in verse one is
utterly beyond any second-century forger?

2) On the greeting proper see First Peter. The
added phrase: "in connection with knowledge from
our God and Lord Jesus," deserves fullest attention.
Peter does not have three subjects: "grace, peace, and
knowledge." As in verse 1 faith is "in connection with"
righteousness, so here grace and peace are "in connection with" knowledge; ἐν always indicates the connection that is natural to the context.

Ἐπίγνωσις is stronger than γνῶσις, it is *Erkenntnis* in
contrast with *Kenntnis*. There may be a false *gnosis,*
but never a false *epignosis*. The latter is a true, clear,
full knowledge that is personally embraced and has
the strongest effect on the personal religious life, C.-K.
253, also Trench. Its object is the Word. We thus see
how grace and peace are "in connection with" this
knowledge; unfortunately, we have no specific word

for *epignosis*. With Peter's prayerful wish regarding the *epignosis* compare Paul's prayer in Eph. 1:16, etc.

This is one of the key words of this letter (1:3, 8; 2:20), to which add *gnosis* occurring in 1:5, 6, and in 3:18. The aim of this letter is to increase this knowledge in the hearts of the readers so that, when grace and peace are multiplied, they may abound in all godliness and be fully fortified against all libertinists and all libertinism when this sort of thing arises to harass them. We have stated why we regard the genitive as a genitive of source. This true, full knowledge comes to the readers "from our God and Lord Jesus." So in verse 3 "all that pertains to life and godliness has been granted to us by means of the *epignosis*." Διά in verse 3 elucidates the ἐν found in verse 2.

The grand genitive magnifies the knowledge which Peter wants his readers to have. Peter substitutes Κύριος for Σωτήρ. "Lord" is, however, to be understood in the full soteriological sense of Savior-Lord. He is our Lord, we are his δοῦλοι (verse 1) who have been purchased and won by him to be his own forever. We know no authority save his; our will is his alone. Κύριος suggests his deity just as much as Θεός, a point that it is well to note also where the unmodified "Lord" occurs. We note that "Savior" is placed first, "Lord" second. Who would not follow the Lord who has rescued him as a Savior? There is no Lord like this Lord; no pleasure like serving this Lord as a δοῦλος or "slave." The two ἡμῶν are equally confessional although they have different places in the phrases. "Our" combines Peter and his readers, in fact, thereby includes all confessors of Jesus; and thus it differs from ἡμῖν in v. 1. "Jesus Christ," the full personal and official name used in verse 1, is reduced to "Jesus" as being a sufficient designation in connection with "our Lord."

Part One

**How the Entrance into the Kingdom of
our Lord and Savior Jesus Christ is
Richly Supplied, v. 3-21**

*Diligently Use What God Has Granted,
v. 3-7*

3) There is an unmistakable similarity between
the first grand sentence of First Peter, namely, 1:3-13,
and the one before us in II Peter 1:3-11. Just as I Pet.
1:3-9 is a unit and but one extended sentence, so is
II Pet. 1:3-9. The same mind conceived both sentences.
The connectives differ, but the comprehensive grasp
that links so much together, now in one way, now in
another, is plainly the same.

This similarity may be extended. In both of the
great opening sentences the vital thing in our hearts
is *faith*. In I Pet. 1:9 we are referred to the end of
this faith, "the salvation of souls"; in II Pet. 1:11
to "the entrance into the eternal kingdom of our Lord
Jesus Christ." In both instances the readers are referred to the prophets: in I Pet. 1:10-12; in II Pet. 1:
19-21. In both the ministry of the apostles and gospel
preachers is mentioned: in I Pet. 1:12 they are called
"those that proclaimed the good tidings to you"; in
II Pet. 1:16, "we made known to you the power and
Parousia of our Lord Jesus Christ." Here we have but
one mind, not two, not one that is genuine, and another
that is forging an imitation.

First Peter was written for those who are to meet
persecution and suffering, whose faith, faithfulness,
and *hope* are to be strengthened; Second Peter is written for those who are to meet false, libertinistic teachers, and whose faith, diligence in godliness, and *knowledge* are to be fortified. The readers are, therefore,
not the same. Hope is one thing, full knowledge is an-

other. Sufferers need steadfast hope; fighters against
loose errorists need true heart-knowledge. Yet in this
case, since the libertinists mock at the Lord's Parousia,
the true *knowledge* that withstands them is the certainty of the Lord's Parousia and thus the certainty
of the true Christian *hope*. The hope of First Peter
and the knowledge of Second Peter look to the same
glorious goal.

We do not divide v. 3-9, do not begin a new
sentence at verse 10. The whole of v. 3-11 is a unit.
Our versions connect ὡς with v. 2 as though v. 3, 4
were appended to the greeting, and as though v. 5
begins a new sentence. No greeting known to us has
such a peculiar extension. Ὡς is plainly causal and
is introductory to καὶ αὐτὸ τοῦτο δέ (v. 5). The main
verb is an imperative. **As his divine power has
granted all things to us regarding life and godliness
by means of the knowledge from the One who called
us with his own glory and praise, by means of which
(glory and praise) he has granted the to us precious
and greatest promises that by means of these we may
get to fellowship divine nature by having escaped
from the corruption in connection with lust in the
world: even with respect to this very fact, etc.**

Ὡς might be followed by οὕτω in verse 5: "as . . .
so"; but so much material is attached to the genitive
absolute introduced by "as" that the main clause is
ushered in by the similar but much stronger αὐτὸ τοῦτο,
"with respect to this very thing." "As" might introduce a finite verb; Peter uses a genitive absolute, the
more to show that what he says in this preamble (v.
3, 4) is subsidiary to the hortation expressed in verse
5, etc.

The verbal arrangement is masterly. Linking
clauses and participial modifiers, each in its own sub-
ordination, is characteristic of the Greek mind which
notes and indicates all these relations of thought and

thus rises above the English mind which is inclined
to ignore such important relations. Peter absorbed the
rich Greek method of thought and moved in it with
perfect ease; if the student of today wishes to follow
Peter's mind he will have to take all this into account.

"*His* divine power has granted," etc., refers to
Christ's power; "his *divine* power" as "our *God* and
Savior," as "our *God* and *Lord.*" "Divine power"
matches these two designations. The deity of Jesus
Christ is the foundation of this entire epistle; cancel
it, and a jumbled ruin is left. This divine power has
granted to us "all things, the ones regarding (πρός) life
and godliness." Τὰ πρός is an apposition to πάντα. Not
one thing has Christ's divine power withheld from us.
Eph. 1:3, "all spiritual blessing"; Rom. 8:32, "freely
give us all things," τὰ πάντα. The "life" referred to is
the one that is kindled in regeneration by the power of
the Spirit through the means of grace (Word and
Sacrament). All that pertains to this "life," all that
it needs to preserve, strengthen, and bring it to its
consummation, our God and Lord Jesus Christ's divine
power has presented to us.

To "life" Peter adds the comprehensive "godliness,"
which is the activity of this "life." Εὐσέβεια includes
our entire reverent, worshipful attitude and the actions
emanating from it. The opposite of "life and godliness" is "the corruption in connection with lust in the
world" (v. 4). Like the finite verb in v. 4, the perfect
participle "has granted" implies that the past act
of granting continues its effect to the present day and
is to continue thus. In δωρέομαι there lies the idea of
δώρημα: to make a present. That is exactly what Christ's
divine power has done.

When some read "divine power" they think of
divine omnipotence as if this alone is divine power.
But love, grace, mercy are also "divine power." In
the verb "has made us a present" there lies the very

thought of grace. For "life and godliness" we need the gifts that are bestowed by the power of grace. The presentation is "by means of the *epignosis* or knowledge," hence it comes by the gospel, "God's power for salvation to everyone believing" (Rom. 1:16), i. e., the power of grace. We regard both the perfect participle and the following perfect finite verb as middle and not as passive.

"Divine power" was required to give all these spiritual presents. They are priceless, their very source is divine. To prize them as such is certainly also to use them accordingly. More than this; by using them we certainly shall obtain "the entrance into the eternal kingdom of our Lord and Savior Jesus Christ" (v. 11; the end of our faith, salvation of souls, I Pet. 1:9). All these presents were given us for that purpose.

Christ's divine power has given these presents to us (to Peter and to his readers) "by means of the knowledge from him who called us with his own glory and praise." This repeats the key word *epignosis* used in v. 2. Peter, like James, loves such repetition. See the repetitions in v. 1, 2, also that of "granting." These are not mannerisms or indications of poverty of thought; they are purposeful, they emphasize, they link most closely.

Is this genitive objective, so that we are to know fully "him who called us" (God)? This is the generally accepted view which one might support with a reference to John 17:3. In v. 1, 2 we have two genitives of source: righteousness *from* our God, etc.; epignosis *from* our God, etc. So we here have: the epignosis *from* him who called us. We regard this as a genitive of source because τῆς ἐπιγνώσεως has the article of previous reference and thus refers back to the epignosis already mentioned in v. 2. It seems best to regard God as our Caller as was done in I Pet. 2:9. This makes Christ the source of the knowledge mentioned in v. 2, and

God the source of that referred to in v. 3. Those who regard these as objective genitives, of course, retain the same difference. There is really no difference in the thought. Christ is God, to know him is to know God, and vice versa; thus also to have knowledge from him is to have it from God, and vice versa.

Source is the point of emphasis: Christ's divine power presents all these things by means of the knowledge, the *source* of which is divine. Not cunningly devised fables (v. 16) ; Peter himself heard the divine voice from heaven (v. 18) ; holy men spoke, not by their own will, but by (ὑπό) the Holy Spirit from (ἀπό) God, v. 21. Peter himself thus stresses the *source* of our knowledge most elaborately. Our divine Caller is the source. This source makes this knowledge so firm and solid (βεβαιότερον, v. 19), hence so mighty for our "life and godliness," so mighty to resist the pseudo-prophets (2:1) and their rank liberalism. Add the fact that all that Christ taught had God as its source, and that Peter again and again had heard him stress this fact (John 7:16, 17; 8:28; 12:49; 14:10, 24; 17:8, 14). Our Caller (God) is the source of our epignosis.

In the epistles καλεῖν always denotes the 'successful call by means of the Word. Yet Peter does not say: called us "with his own Word." He says something far grander: called us "with his own glory and praise." When R. 533 says that this is "clearly instrumental, not dative," he means: "*with* his own glory" (means), and not "*to* glory," etc. (A. V.) God's glory and praise shine forth in the gospel-Word, in the precious and most magnificent promises that he has given us (v. 4). This glory and this praise of God, Peter says, were the means that drew and won us by God's call. Compare I Pet. 2:9, and see what this call made of us, especially that it means that we should now proclaim the ἀρεταί or praises of him who called us out of darkness into his marvelous light. Remember that all the glory and the praise of God are unfolded before our hearts in Christ, "as being his (God's) glory's effulgence and his being's impress," Heb. 1:3.

Feel the greatness of what Peter here says about Christ's gifts to him and to his readers. He writes with almost the same exaltation as he did in I Pet. 1:3, etc. His object is the same. How can his readers, who have this knowledge and this call, lend an ear to pseudo-prophets and by libertinism insult the glory and the praise that called them? Their course must ever be that sketched in v. 5-7, the end their entrance into the eternal kingdom of our Lord and Savior Jesus Christ (v. 11).

We need not enter the discussion regarding ἀρετή (C.-K. 160, etc.; G. K. 460; others). The plural used in I Pet. 2:9 = "praises"; "glory and praise" is perfectly to the point here, the two being synonymous with this difference that δόξα is the emanation of the divine attributes that reaches our eyes and our hearts, and "praise" (*Ruhm*, fame) that which reaches our ears from those who already know him. "Virtue" in our versions is objectionable; there is too much of the old pagan flavor left in this rendering. *Selbstbekundung, Selbsterweisung*, i. e., self-manifestation, in our opinion, omit the note of the effect produced on the beholders.

4) The plural relative "by means of which" is to be referred to "his own glory and praise." No other antecedent is pertinent. By means of these two the One who called us with them "has granted the to us precious and greatest promises," and the appositional ἵνα clause states their content: "that by means of these (our Caller's glory and praise) we may get to fellowship divine nature by escaping from the corruption," etc. Since ἡμῖν is placed where it is it = "the to us precious and greatest," etc., and is not the indirect object: "has granted to us." Here we have another

present: all these promises, which are truly "precious" or valuable and, when we see what they contain, the "greatest" that we can imagine. We do not reduce μέγιστα to mean only "exceeding great" as R. 670 does; there are none greater for us. Ἐπαγγέλματα == "promises" in the sense of "things promised" (a word expressing a result and not one that expresses an action).

We regard ἵνα as appositional and not as introducing a purpose clause; Peter cannot fail to say what these precious, greatest promises contain and say only what purpose they are to serve. The reason that so many commentators regard this as a ἵνα of purpose is due to the fact that they think that every ἵνα must introduce a purpose whereas in the Koine this particle often introduces result (both contemplated and actual) and often introduces a substantive clause as is the case here. This is not a purpose to be attained by means of the immense things promised, attained, as some think, at Christ's Parousia. This is what the things promised actually are; we are not left to surmise their contents. Here we have their contents and see that they are indeed "precious to us and the greatest." If we see this we shall also see that διὰ τούτων resumes δι' ὧν, the antecedent in both cases being "glory and praise." That is why we have the same preposition and also why we have "these" and not αὐτῶν, "them," i. e., "the promises."

Codex B has another διά in v. 3: διὰ δόξης καὶ ἀρετῆς, in place of the dative ἰδίᾳ δόξῃ, κτλ. Means — means — means. Peter is pointing them out: the knowledge by which all things that we need are granted to us — the glory and praise by which the greatest promises are granted — this very glory and praise by which we fellowship the divine nature. No wonder the preposition is repeated!

The adjective κοινωνοί which is derived from the noun for "fellowship" (we lack an equivalent English adjective) is inexactly rendered by "partakers"; we should keep the idea of fellowship lest, as Besser warns, we decorate ourselves "with a foreign feather." For this "divine nature" is not the *substantia* but the *qualitas;* it is more than the *imitatio*, it is rather the *imago Dei*. As a foreigner is naturalized, so we are fully transplanted into God's kingdom and are naturalized in it so that what is in that kingdom is properly ours. We are to be children and sons of God (John 1:12), begotten again, not of corruptible seed, but of incorruptible, through the Word of God which lives and abides forever (I Pet. 1:23). Ours is the restored divine image, righteousness and holiness (Eph. 4:24) plus knowledge (*epignosis*, Col. 3:10). The two former are divine attributes. When they are restored in us they do not deify us; yet they are derived from God and make us κοινωνοί of divine nature. Here belong all those passages that speak of the *unio mystica* such as Gal. 2:20: "Christ lives in me"; Phil. 1:21: "For me to live is Christ"; John 15:4, 5, "you in me, and I in you"; 14:23 and I John 2:24, also Rev. 3:20, which describe the *koinonia*.

The aorist means "actually be" in fellowship. When? The moment we "actually escape" (aorist) the corruption in the world. There is no intermediate state but only a sharp either — or. Yet this is true, not until the time of the Parousia will body and soul attain the consummation of this fellowship. The participle does not express a condition: *so ihr fliehet*, Luther. It is not the mere negative side of the fellowship. An action on our part (escape) is not correlative (negative) with a condition (positive) into which we are brought. This expression should be understood as the knowledge mentioned in v. 3 and as the reception of the promises are: as granting involves reception, so possession of the divine nature involves flight from the corruption and hence this flight is also expressed by a participle.

Θεία φύσις and φθορὰ ἐν τῷ κόσμῳ are direct opposites, as wide apart as the poles, as conflicting as fire and water, as exclusive of each other as life and death. What this "corruption" looks like we shall see in 2: 12-19. It is rottenness, its end is destruction and perdition. It is "in the world," the world of men is full of it, reeking to heaven, crying out to be swept into hell. The first ἐν is local, the second designates inner connection: the corruption "in connection with lust," "the lust of the flesh, and the lust of the eyes, and the pretension regarding the course of life, not of the Father, but of the world, and the world passes away, and the lust thereof," I John 2:16, 17. To escape suggests a terrible power that holds and enslaves; lust is corruption's snare. Note the fine way in which both Greek phrases are placed between the article and the main noun, an elegance of style that we have noted repeatedly in First Peter.

With these preliminary clauses Peter lays a perfect foundation for the hortation that follows. See what is granted us and by what divine means! We are in the fellowship of the divine nature, having escaped from the rotten, lusting world. Hence we must live as Peter now states, must reach the kingdom to which he points (v. 11).

5) Peter continues: **even with respect to this very fact, having brought along in all diligence, furnish in connection with your faith the** (corresponding) **praise, and in connection with the praise the** (corresponding) **knowledge, and in connection with the knowledge the** (corresponding) **self-control, and in connection with the self-control the** (corresponding) **perseverance, and in connection with the perseverance the** (corresponding) **godliness, and**

in connection with the godliness the (corresponding) fraternal friendliness, and in connection with the fraternal friendliness the (corresponding) love; for etc.

Here we have Peter's golden chain of Christian virtues. There are seven jewels, and all of them are fastened to faith.

Peter might have said: ὡς . . . καὶ οὕτω, "as . . . even thus"; he states it in a stronger way: ὡς . . . καὶ αὐτὸ τοῦτο δέ: "as . . . even with respect to this very thing," or we may say "for this very reason." Αὐτὸ τοῦτο is the adverbial accusative (R. 467, 686), which is common in Paul (R. 705). The δέ is not adversative. When it is used after καί, the δέ marks the fact that what follows is different from the preceding; by doing this it helps to emphasize the demonstrative. Our versions translate rather inaccurately: "And besides this" (A. V.); "Yea, and" (R. V.). Καί = "even" and does not begin a new sentence. Mark the progress indicated by the deictic demonstratives: v. 4, διὰ τούτων — v. 5, αὐτὸ τοῦτο — v. 8, ταῦτα — v. 9, again ταῦτα. "As regards this very thing" is properly the neuter singular, the antecedent being what v. 3, 4 state, in particular the double gift bestowed on us by Christ.

This very fact should prompt us to use the divine nature in which we have fellowship. The Greek marks the subsidiary action by the use of a participle; the English, which is less precise, would use two imperatives. By "bringing along in all diligence" the readers are to furnish or supply all that Peter states. The aorist participle, like the aorist imperative, is effective, decisive. Present tenses would be descriptive and milder. Peter wants a peremptory, strong command: "Bring along in" no less than "all diligence" and not only some! "Furnish!" with no "if" or "but" about it. The original sense of the latter verb (ἐπιχορηγέω) refers to the training and the staging of a grand chorus for some high civic or provincial celebration, the entire expense being provided by some rich patron; but the word became generalized and means "supply" or "furnish" and retains only the idea of furnishing completely, lavishly.

There are not eight items but only seven. The readers are not to furnish "faith." This they already have by virtue of their having been called (v. 3) : by his gospel call God gives us faith. Having this faith from God, it is not to remain "barren or unfruitful" (v. 8) but is to bring forth all its spiritual fruits. Thus Peter says: with all diligence "furnish in connection with your faith" this chain of golden fruit.

"As soon as the Holy Ghost, as has been said, through the Word and holy Sacraments has begun in us this his work of regeneration and renewal, it is certain that through the power of the Holy Ghost we can and should cooperate, although still in great weakness. But this does not occur from our carnal natural powers, but from the new powers and gifts which the Holy Ghost has begun in us in conversion, as St. Paul expressly and earnestly exhorts that 'as workers together with him we receive not the grace of God in vain,' II Cor. 6:1. But this is to be understood in no other way than that the converted man does good to such an extent and so long as God by his Holy Spirit rules, guides, and leads him, and that as soon as God would withdraw his gracious hand from him, he could not for a moment persevere in obedience to God. But if this were understood thus, that the converted man cooperates with the Holy Ghost in the manner as when two horses together draw a wagon, this could in no way be conceded without prejudice to the divine truth." *C. Tr.* 907, 65-66.

The divine nature in which we have fellowship (v. 4) is from God (thus "divine") and hence has power to produce what Peter says. Augustine is right: *Fides est mater et radix bonorum operum.* Faith is this, however, only as it constantly draws on God in this fellowship of the "divine nature" which we have from him. Thus all that by his grace we supply in living connection with our faith is. acceptable to God; if we supply anything in connection with our flesh, this is an abomination to him. Rom. 14:23.

Peter's seven nouns are often called virtues; yet knowledge is scarcely a virtue. In v. 8 "barren and un-fruitful" imply that Peter thinks of the seven as fruits of faith. While he connects each of the seven with ἐν, we see that all of them are to be traced to faith. Each time, when he adds the next, he repeats the one fruit, and this repetition emphasizes. He uses the article throughout. Abstract nouns may or may not have the article in the Greek, yet when. the article is used, the abstract noun is made specific. So it is here. Not any-thing that may be called ἀρετή, γνῶσις, etc., is to be sup-plied but *the* specific thing, *the* thing that corresponds to the preceding or, let us say, the true, Christian *aretē, gnosis,* etc.

The list of seven is arranged with reference to the pseudo-prophets (2:1) and to the way in which they live according to their pretended faith. For praise they supply disgrace; for knowledge, blindness; for self-control, libertinistic license; for perseverance in good, perseverance in evil; for godliness, ungodliness; for fraternal friendliness, dislike of God's children; for genuine love, its terrible absence.

In what sense is ἀρετή to be the first thing connected with faith? Many, like Luther and our versions, are satisfied with the term "virtue" although they often modify this: *strenuus animae tonus ac vigor,* Bengel; moral strength, manliness, manly activity. Regarding the pagan flavor of the word compare what we have said in v. 3 and in I Pet. 2:9. Peter uses it twice in succession, once with reference to God (v. 3), again

with reference to us, and both times it ought to be
taken in the same and not in a different sense. It
should not be *Tugend*, "virtue," when it is ascribed to
God. The plural found in I Pet. 2:9 means "praises"
(C.-K.; G. K.) ; the singular means "praise" in v. 3.
We submit that, when it is now used with reference
to us, the singular must again mean "praise," *Ruhm*,
fame.

The sense would then be as pertinent as it is in v. 3
and in I Pet. 2:9. Our faith is not to be hid like a lamp
under a bushel; it is to shine forth (Matt. 5:15, 16).
Its fame and its praise are to be known. That is why
ἀρετή is properly named first. The pseudo-prophets and
the libertinists have no faith and hence no praise or
fame with which to impress men and to glorify God.
Our faith puts us in fellowship with no less than "divine nature" (v. 4) ; thus as "praise" belongs to God,
and his own praise has drawn us to him in faith, so
this our faith should shine out and have its corresponding praise to impress, influence, and help draw men
to a like faith. God's praise (and glory) is like the
sun: it is immense. The praise connected with our
faith is only a reflection of his praise even as our faith
is wrought by his praise (and glory). Yet our faith
must have this its proper praise; its light must shine
out.   •

Connected with this praise must be the corresponding γνῶσις, "knowledge." Peter does not use the compound here as he does in v. 2 and 3. He keeps the
emphasis on "knowledge" as being vital to this entire
letter (note the remarks on v. 2 and 3) ; but with the
use of the simplex he pits the *gnosis* of his Christian
readers against the fake *gnosis* of the libertinists.
That, too, is why this knowledge is number two in the
list of seven, and why "in connection with the praise"
connected with our faith there must be· "the (corresponding) knowledge." Ignorance of the Word, false

conceptions of its teachings, would destroy the praise, would rob our faith of its proper praise; true knowledge of the Word enhances the praise. Read Col. 1:9, 10. "Wherefore be ye not foolish, but understand what the will of the Lord is," Eph. 5:17. The Jews had zeal, "but not according to knowledge," Rom. 10:2. Blind, ignorant faith is the scorn of men — rightly so. Let no Christian supply fuel for such scorn! Knowledge is a weapon that smites error, it wields the sword of the Spirit, which is the Word of God (Eph. 6:17). Do not invite derision by going into the fight with ignorance! Invite praise by wielding knowledge.

6) The next item is very properly ἐγκράτεια, "self-control," the very control that all libertinists lack. They give rein to their lusts; because of our knowledge we have the κράτος or active power to keep all appetites and desires under complete control. This proper self-control connected with knowledge of the Word is not a legalistic abstinence from what God permits; it is not of the style mentioned in Col. 2:21, 22. Nor is it the so-called temperance of prohibitionists or of Romish celibates. It, of course, controls all bodily appetites, but does so by controlling reason, emotions, and will through the knowledge of the Word and the will of God.

Next is ὑπομονή, literally, "remaining under," which Trench calls the *perseverantia*, the *brave* patience which lets nothing adverse force it to give up. This μακροθυμία, "longsuffering," is ascribed to God, it bears with evil *men*, but ὑπομονή is never predicated of God, for the Almighty is never affected by *things*. We, however, suffer from them, and ours must be steady, unwavering perseverance. "Patience" in our versions states only a part of what the word means. The libertinistic invasion foretold by Peter will distress his readers to no small degree; the steadfast "perseverance" that corresponds with and is connected with the true self-control will fortify, protect, and hold them true.

In connection with this true perseverance there should be "the (corresponding) godliness," godly attitude, conduct in general and true worship. The false prophets and their following will be ungodly (ἀσεβεῖν, 2:6) and distress the readers with "lawless works" as Lot was once distressed (2:7). Hence, connected with perseverance or endurance, there is to be this true godliness in Peter's readers.

7) Godliness in order to be true to God and to resist the ungodly and their lawless works, and then in connection therewith φιλαδελφία, "fraternal friendliness" toward all the brethren. We may say "brotherly affection." The godly must cling together like so many brothers (ἀδελφοί) of one family, like so many friends (φίλοι), in close friendship and friendliness (φιλία). There can be no *philadelphia* for the ungodly but only complete severance from them.

In connection with this "the (corresponding) ἀγάπη cr love." This noun and its corresponding verb are not always correctly defined. We have repeatedly defined this word for "love" as being the love of intelligence and full understanding which is always coupled with a strong, corresponding purpose. So God loved the foul world, knowing it fully and set on cleansing it; so we are to love even our enemies, understanding their enmity and set on freeing them from it. Φιλία is the love of affection; hence φίλημα = "kiss," the act of such affection. We cannot kiss our enemies; they would smite us in the face. Jesus warned and denounced his enemies, which was ἀγάπη; he did not "like" them, embrace them, call them his φίλοι (John 15:15), greet them with a kiss.

Only with this understanding may we say that this final item "love" is broader than "fraternal friendliness" and that it extends to all men as does the *agape* of God. As "faith" was the start and source, so "love" is mentioned last as being the complete crown. The false prophets and their following have no brotherly affection for true believers, in fact, their affection for each other, if we may call it so, is a base thing; and agape, this most precious fruit of faith, is wholly foreign to them.

When this section is used as a text for a sermon, the items are naturally generalized, i. e., the special reason for their selection by Peter is omitted. Indeed, apart from false prophets and libertinists our faith must diligently supply all that is here connected with it by Peter; there can be no question about that. We have other lists in the New Testament that are similar to this one, and the selection of items in the list is always governed by the main object of the epistle, by the situation of the readers. Lists of pagan virtues and of pagan vices are at times compared. We can see no profit in such a comparison. Paganism cannot shed light on the Christian life. Even when an identical term is used by pagans, one may be led astray unless care is exercised. There is a tendency today to be too *wissenschaftlich* by reading all New Testament words through pagan spectacles.

The Promise of the Entrance into the Eternal Kingdom of our Lord and Savior Jesus Christ, v. 8-11

8) "For" continues the grand sentence begun at v. 3 although, when we are translating it into English, we prefer to divide it. Peter supports his hortation by a positive (v. 8), then by a negative fact (v. 9), finally by a deduction (διό, v. 10) coupled with the supreme promise (v. 11).

Peter continues: **for these things, belonging to you and abounding, set** (you) **down as not barren or unfruitful with regard to the knowledge from**

our Lord Jesus Christ. Ὑπάρχω with the dative = *es steht zur Verfuegung*; here: "these things being at your disposal," i. e., "belonging to you." Peter adds: "and abounding," a word that Paul often uses to designate the abundance of spiritual gifts and works which he wants his readers to have. The participle is intransitive; it makes no difference whether we translate "abound" or "increase" since the things enumerated in v. 5-7 do not come about in a day, and in order to abound they must increase. "All diligence" (v. 5) will produce abundance; and the greater the abundance, the more evident it is that we are not "barren," etc.

Καθίστησιν = they set you down, they render or establish you; ὑμᾶς is understood, the two accusative adjectives are predicative: "as not barren (the same word that is used in James 2:20: faith without the works is barren) or unfruitful with regard (εἰς) to the *epignosis* (v. 2, 3) from our Lord Jesus Christ"; this genitive is a genitive of source as it was in v. 2, 3, which see. The sense is that these fruits of faith prove that the full, true knowledge which our Lord has bestowed upon us as the means (διὰ ἐπιγνώσεως in v. 3) for granting us "all things regarding life and godliness" has, indeed, produced what such knowledge should produce. This *epignosis* is a part of the "divine nature" in which we have fellowship; hence the point is again the *source* of this knowledge just as this is the point in v. 2, 3. The fact that this true knowledge also knows "our Lord Jesus Christ," its source, is self-evident. This genitive of source thus says more than an objective genitive would.

"Not barren nor fruitless for the knowledge" (εἰς = a dative, R. 594) is a litotes and here a meiosis, saying in a negative and a mild way what is intended to be positive and strong. *Epignosis* is again brought forward as the key word of this epistle; it is in contrast with the errorists who lack this soil and produce nothing but thorns and briars in their lives. Peter wants his readers to be fortified with this genuine knowledge in order to resist the invasion of error that is impending.

9) Another "for" substantiates in a negative way: **for he to whom are not present these things** (the same ταῦτα as in v. 8) **is blind, (he) being myopic, having received forgetfulness of the cleansing from his old sins.** There is not "but" (A. V.) but only an extension of the reasoning. Peter drops the personal "you" and changes to the third person singular "he to whom." He does not even think that his readers could lose their true knowledge; he only points to some errorist who has lost it. The grammars remark on the use of μή with the indicative in a relative clause; this is done because the relative is intended to be indefinite (R. 962; B.-D. 428, 4): any man who, etc.

Such a man is "blind," but he is so in a certain way, as "being myopic," μυωπάζων, being a μύωψ, a near-sighted person. This, too, is explained: λήθην λαβών, "having received lethe, amnesia, forgetfulness." The *epignosis* of real knowledge in his heart is lacking. Luther's *tappet mit der Hand* like a blind man is finely interpretative of the first participle; not so good is the A. V.'s "cannot see afar off," and the R. V.'s "seeing only what is near," margin, "closing his eyes." "Myopic" is exactly the proper word, for this is not a pagan who never heard the Word and is therefore blind; this is a person who knows about the Word but has only a useless glimmer left in his heart. "Having forgotten" is less exact than "having received forgetfulness"; this man let somebody give him amnesia. The one participle is present, μυωπάζων, to indicate this man's continuous condition; the other is aorist, λαβών, to indicate what produced this condition in the past.

Even the main thing is forgotten: "the cleansing from his old sins" when this man was baptized and justified, was rid of all the old sins of his past life, when a new life opened before him, one that accorded with the items mentioned in v. 5-7. The memory of that cleansing is not an utter blank; this amnesia is a blank in the heart: all the power, effect, blessing are blotted out. The deadness, the barrenness of "corruption" have returned (v. 4). Peter describes a complete case. Such cases are not always complete, nor are only such cases a warning. Spiritual myopia and amnesia progress. When the fruits begin to be wanting, the barrenness has begun to set in.

10) We need not make a break even at this point, for διό with μᾶλλον indicates a close connection in thought; it is unlike the διό occurring in v. 12. Peter repeats his admonition about diligence (v. 5) as a deduction from v. 8, 9 and now turns it so as to introduce the great promise at which the pseudo-prophets scoffed: **wherefore the more, brethren, be diligent in making sure for yourselves your calling and election, for by doing these things you will not stumble ever, for in this way there will be furnished for you richly the entrance into the eternal kingdom of our Lord and Savior Jesus Christ.**

The adverb μᾶλλον = "the more" and not "the rather" (A. V.) and recalls the *"all diligence"* mentioned in v. 5. This is the only place in both of his epistles where Peter uses the address "brethren," and this fact makes the appeal the stronger. With the term "brethren" he joins himself to his readers and separates himself and them from the gospel of loose living and from all its adherents.

When Peter urges more diligence he does not refer to mere outward works, in which alone some find diligence; for that reason Peter uses only abstract terms in v. 5-7 and begins with faith itself. It is on the basis of this first admonition, with all diligence to furnish the true sevenfold spiritual *evidences* of faith, that this further admonition now asks the readers to apply diligence to secure the great final *result*. The first result is subjective and immediate: "making sure for yourselves your calling and election"; the second is objective and occurs at the end of life: the entrance furnished us into the eternal kingdom.

We note that the infinitive is the middle voice, ποιεῖσθαι, and the present tense: *for themselves* the readers are to make sure, firm, secure their calling and election, and they are *to continue* doing this. It is equally important to note that Peter has one article with the two nouns and not two, that he regards τὴν κλῆσιν καὶ ἐκλογήν as a unit and does not even place ἡμῶν between the nouns. This making sure is to continue throughout life; it is to make us ourselves sure that we are, indeed, God's called and elect; our personal assurance and certainty are to pertain to our calling and election as being ever combined and not separate. This personal assurance is to rest on the true *evidence*, namely the evidence already described in v. 5-7, i. e., on the very evidence that Christ himself will hold up publicly to the entire universe at the last day (Matt. 25:34-40). It is never to rest only on our own claim and assertion that we are the called and elect.

Keil makes our election depend on our call: by our call we are segregated from the world. That is, of course, true. But this call takes place in time, the election in eternity. Others reverse this order and make our call depend on our election: we are called in time because we for some unknown reason have been elected in eternity. Just why *we* are elected is in their opinion a mystery. Calvin says that we are elected by an immutable, absolute decree of God, a decree of his absolute sovereignty. But Peter did not write "our election and call"; he wrote "our call and election."

The fact that κλῆσις always means the effective and successful gospel call is certain; follow the word (noun, verb, and verbal) through the epistles. The fact that the ἐκλογή is the eternal election is told us in so many words in Eph. 1:4, and in I Pet. 1:2: "elect according to God the Father's foreknowledge." The point is not *God's* relation to these acts of his. On that point we must ever remind ourselves that he is not subject to relations and limitations of time as we are; and it is this fact that causes us difficulty when we are dealing with eternity and with time. All that occurs in time from the first day to the last was present with God as already completed and done because he viewed it with his timeless, eternal mind.

Peter speaks of *our* certainty regarding these two acts of God, his calling and electing us. Our mind must combine these two in this order. In Rom. 8:29, 30 Paul combines them in the reverse order because he presents objectively the acts of God as our time-bound minds see them in their succession in God himself. Hence Paul writes: οὕς . . . τούτους, "those . . . whom," speaking objectively; not ἡμᾶς . . . οὕς "us . . . whom."

The Lutheran fathers have answered the rationalizing idea that what is eternally fixed and done cannot be made sure by us. Certainly, not as far as God is concerned. Peter is not dealing with God but with us, with our making our call and election sure for ourselves. Besser expounds admirably: "I know that the God of all mercy has called me to his eternal glory, unto which he chose me in Christ Jesus before the foundation of the world, and I am certain that he will keep me firm unto the end, unto the entrance into the eternal kingdom of our Lord Jesus Christ (v. 11). Whence comes this blessed firmness and certainty for me? From some special revelation concerning God's secret counsel? No; but from the common revelation of the divine will of grace in the gospel of Jesus Christ in whom I believe. Because I know in whom I believe, namely in the God who has saved me and called me with a holy calling according to his own purpose and grace, therefore I am persuaded that he is able to guard that which I have committed unto him against that day, II Tim. 2:9-12. When the God of all grace perfects, establishes, strengthens me in faith, I Pet. 5:10, then is my calling and election sure." John Gerhard states it briefly: "As certain as you are of your faith and perseverance, so certain are you of your election."

There is for us no certainty of our election apart from the certainty of our calling although the one took place in eternity, the other in time. This is not the *absolute* certainty of Calvin, which rests on an absolute decree for which Christ and his limited atonement and the means of grace and faith are only the mode of realization; but a *conditioned, ordinate* certainty, which is revealed in the Scriptures and is conditioned on Christ, the means of grace, the order of salvation. *"If you abide in my Word, then are you truly my disciples,"* John 8:32, i. e., ἐκλεκτοί. Even as we also confess: "That he will also strengthen, increase, and support to the end the good work which he has begun in them *if* they adhere to God's Word, pray diligently, abide in God's grace, and faithfully use the gifts received," Latin, *si modo*, German *wo sie* (*wenn sie*), *C. Tr.* 1069. To say that this is not certainty is to deny John 8:32 and our own confession.

Peter himself explains βεβαία ποιεῖσθαι, this continuous making sure and firm for ourselves, by using the same verb in the active participle: "for by doing these things you will not stumble ever," i. e., will never stumble. This is the same ταῦτα, "these things," that was used in v. 8, 9; it is placed forward in the same emphatic position and thus refers to the same things, namely to all those mentioned in v. 5-7. "These things" in v. 10 does not refer to the making firm our calling and election for ourselves for the reason that this "for" in the clause in v. 10 expounds *how* we make our calling, etc., sure. The transitive subjunctive is an aorist and thus denotes an act of stumbling that is final (as in Rom. 11:11): stumble so as to fall and lose salvation.

The Christian sins daily even when his calling and election are sure to him in the gospel manner. This reminds him of his danger. Such sins are not the fatal stumbling of which Peter speaks. When they hold fast the former cleansing (v. 9), this cleansing is renewed daily by daily forgiveness.

There is an implied warning: those who *fail* to do these things will, indeed, stumble decidedly (aorist) and fatally. Whether they will again be raised up to faith God alone knows. Many that stumble in this way are lost forever. The German theologians call them *die Zeitglaeubigen,* those who believe for a time and then fall away. By their own refusal to continue to do the things mentioned in v. 5-7 they furnish the evidence that God could not include them among the elect. Their final unbelief excludes them as completely as does the total unbelief of so many others.

• It makes no difference how we look at this sad fact with our finite minds that are bound to ideas of time, whether we view it from eternity (the timelessness of God) or from the time when these people live, believe for a while, fall, and then die, or from the day of judgment. The thought to hold fast is the fact that these distinctions, with which we labor and which are confusing to many when they try to apply them to God and to his eternal act of election, do not exist for *God.* Halt when the water becomes too deep, do not presume!

11) The "for" used in v. 10 points those who keep doing these things to the blessed certainty which

they have in this life; the parallel "for" occurring in
v. 11 points them to the end of their life and to the
last day. "There shall be furnished for you," with its
future tense, is a divine *promise*. Peter's hortation
is sealed with this promise. It is a divine seal also for
our own certainty of faith. Here is *the hope*, which
accompanies the faith and the love mentioned in v. 5-7.
While the word "hope" is not used in this epistle — in
First Peter it is the key word for assuring and comforting sufferers — the full substance of this hope is
repeatedly presented in our epistle, presented for the
knowledge (*gnosis, epignosis*) of the readers who must
face the scorners of this hope.

Οὕτω, "thus," "in this way," is emphatic and repeats
adverbially the three ταῦτα occurring in v. 8-10, "these
things," the continued doing of them. "Thus" has the
force of a result. Πλουσίως, "richly," is equally emphatic. It balances with the σπουδὴ πᾶσα, "all diligence,"
referred to in v. 5, to which also "thus" refers. The
richness of God's grace, which already in this life
grants us all things for spiritual life and godliness
(v. 3, 4), will at the end richly reward the diligence
with which we have used his gifts of grace. Some will
be saved "so as by fire" (I Cor. 3:15), like one who
barely escapes the fire. Peter wants his readers to be
saved "richly" at the end.

The verb and the subject are transposed and are
thus equally emphatic. Here we have the same verb
"to furnish" that was used in v. 5, and it has the same
connotation of sparing no expense. After God's grace
grants us everything for a godly life *we* are to furnish
the fruits (v. 5-8), and so *God* will richly furnish us
the grandest reward of grace at the end.

"The entrance into the kingdom" is not the objective road or portal as though this would be made
wide and grand for the diligent, and all the angels
would welcome them; the adverb is to be construed

with the verb. This is the subjective *Eintreten, Eingehen,* the act of entering. God supplies all that the act needs in a rich measure.' As for the way into heaven itself, this is Christ who is supplied by God already from the foundation of the world (Rev. 13:8). ·God "will furnish" makes grace glorious and rich to the very end.

"The eternal kingdom of our Lord and Savior Jesus Christ" is heaven into which the soul enters at death and the body at the Parousia. Here belong all those passages which describe heaven and the Parousia. "Kingdom" makes "our Lord and Savior" the eternal King. Consider together "our Lord and Savior Jesus Christ" and "our God and Savior Jesus Christ" (v. 1), "our God and Lord Jesus" (v. 2), and "our Lord Jesus Christ" (v. 8). He is God — Savior — Lord, and the possessive pronoun "our" confesses that he is such. Also consider together "righteousness from our God and Savior Jesus Christ" (v. 1), "knowledge from our God and Lord Jesus" (v. 2), "knowledge from our Lord Jesus Christ" (v. 8), and "the eternal kingdom of our Lord Jesus Christ" — righteousness — knowledge (*epignosis*) — the eternal kingdom.

Witz writes on the Christian life of faith: "It originates from heaven, it seeks heaven, it leads to heaven. It descends from the heavenly heights to prepare us for the eternal glory in the school of sanctification." Rooting and growing in faith are ever and ever the indispensable evidences of the Christian faith and state. Unfruitfulness, sloth, blindness, shortsightedness are the reverse. The diligent, "bearing precious seed, shall doubtless come again with rejoicing, bringing his sheaves with him" (Ps. 126:6) — "faring in with radiant display and with joy leaping into yonder life." Luther.

The promise made in v. 11, the climax of the whole admonition (v. 3-11), is intended as a bulwark against the pseudo-prophets and their following. Without obtruding his purpose, which will appear soon enough, Peter aims throughout this chapter to fortify his readers against the scoffers who will soon assail them. The pertinence of every line is thus evident; the titles and the wording of the greeting and of this promise in v. 11 are especially effective.

Peter's Personal Concern for His Readers, v. 12-15

12) To be told that Peter is personally concerned about his readers "in regard to these things" will make the readers the more attentive to them. **Wherefore** (because thus, as stated in v. 11, God furnishes the entrance into the eternal kingdom) **I shall be ready always to remind you concerning these things,** i. e., the same ταῦτα that was mentioned in v. 8-10 and referred to the seven things which the readers are to furnish in connection with their faith (v. 5-7) **although knowing** (them) **and having been strengthened in connection with the truth present** (with you).

The future μελλήσω is used as a finite verb and does not form a periphrastic future with the infinitive, for we should then have the present μέλλω. The R. V.'s translation is correct: "I shall be ready," *ich werde gedenken, beabsichtigen, im Sinne haben,* B.-P. 787. "It shall be my object always to remind you concerning these things" just as I am now doing this. The A. V. follows a very inferior reading that has a negative. "Always" is not to be reduced in force to "whenever I have a chance"; the adverb is to be construed with the infinitive and is emphatic. Such a constant reminding the readers have in this letter which they will keep and read again and again, by which they will "ever" be reminded of these things.

.Ὑμᾶς is modified by the two accusative participles:
you "though knowing (them) and having been
strengthened in connection with the truth present
(with you)." Peter acknowledges that his readers
"know" these things. The second perfect is used as
a present; but it is a form of οἶδα, to know by having
something present to the mind, and not of γινώσκω or
of ἐπιγινώσκω, to know with an effect and affect in the
heart (see *epignosis* in v. 2, 3, 8, and *gnosis* in v. 5,
6). The effect of this knowing is expressed by the
added participle "having been strengthened" and thus
now being in this strengthened condition (perfect
tense). Peter uses the verb that Jesus employed when
he told him: "Strengthen thy brethren!" Luke 22:32.

Because of ἐν our versions render "established in
the truth," which is smoother English. Yet Peter, like
Jesus, means "strengthen," to give a certain degree of
strength; and ἐν = "in connection with" the truth, the
connection being the fact that they know it, hence we
also have παρούσῃ; the truth "present with you." The
readers should have a constant reminding. In view of
what follows regarding the lying prophets who will
appear the readers will need all their strength. Their
defense and their safety will be in the truth which
they possess.

13) **Moreover, I consider it right as long as I
am in this tabernacle to keep stirring you in a reminder, knowing that the putting away of my tabernacle is swift even as also our Lord Jesus Christ
made plain to me.**

Δέ merely adds this as another consideration. Peter
deems it the right thing as long as (literally, "for so
much as") he is in this tent or tabernacle, i. e., his
earthly body which is only a temporary tent for this
life, to keep stirring them (present infinitive, durative) in reminding or in a reminder (not "remem-
brance," our versions). In John 6:18 the sea "was be-

ing stirred up" by the wind. The thought is that as long as Peter lives he deems it the right thing to make his readers keep on remembering by his reminding them (compare the infinitive in v. 12).

14) For he knows (εἰδώς as in v. 12) that the putting away of his tabernacle is swift as also our Lord Jesus Christ indicated to him. When his end comes, there will be no time for anything; it will be ταχινός, "swift," (the same adjective that is used in 2:1). There is some discussion as to whether this means "swift, sudden," or "soon." We prefer the former. If it were the latter, what about 2:1? We know nothing about when, how, and where the Lord made this indication to Peter about his dying soon. Then this letter must be dated shortly before Peter's end. John 13:36 and 21:18, etc., "indicate" a violent death by martyrdom, hence one that is swift. Peter was now an old man (John 21:18); the Lord said that when he became old, somebody would tie a rope around his body and hale him to his death; so executioners did with their victims. See the writer on that passage. Peter's end would be swift.

Peter again uses the full grand name for Jesus. He knows that what the Lord has indicated will surely occur, and his readers are to believe it with the same certainty. Peter has his own end before his eyes, which will be a swift end when it comes. He has just mentioned their entrance into the eternal kingdom (v. 11); he ever thinks of his own entrance there. They must be spiritually diligent; he certainly also aims to be. To put away a tent is not a mixing of figures. A tent is put away (ἀπό, not "off," our versions), is not to be used any more because its inhabitant is going to a permanent place (I Pet. 1:4). The Greek says "is swift" whereas we should mark the time and say "shall be swift."

15) In v. 13 Peter speaks about the time that
he still has to live; in v. 14 about his sudden and
swift death; now about the time when he will be
dead. His concern for his readers extends far beyond
his own decease. **Moreover, I shall use diligence for
you to be able also on any occasion after my own
decease to effect for yourselves the recollection of
these things.**

Δέ, "moreover," makes another point of this; καί
is to be construed with the adverb: "also on each (or
any) occasion" that may require it. Ἔχειν ὑμᾶς is to
be understood in the sense of *koennen*, "for you to be
able" (B.-P. 520), and is thus followed by the complementary infinitive ποιεῖσθαι (middle). The readers
are to be able also at any time after Peter's decease
to effect for themselves the recollection of these things.
Peter will be dead, unable again to write and to do
the reminding for them; they will be able to do it for
themselves whenever occasion arises.

It is interesting to note that Peter uses ἔξοδος just
as it is used with reference to Jesus and with reference
to his "decease" in the conversation that Moses and
Elijah had with him at the time of his Transfiguration
as recorded in Luke 9:31. It is the more interesting
because in v. 17, 18 Peter recalls the Transfiguration.
We also note that he uses the stronger possessive adjective ἐμήν: "my own decease," and not the weak enclitic pronoun μου, "my." "I shall use diligence" is the
same type of future as "I shall be ready" in v. 12.

There is a debate regarding what Peter means. Is
this a promise to do some more writing on "these
things" (the τούτων referred to in v. 12, which resumes
the ταῦτα occurring in v. 8-10)? Some have argued that
Peter promises more letters; others that this is a
reference to Mark's Gospel. Peter will see to it that
Mark shall write. These opinions stress the future

tense "I shall use diligence." Some think that Peter intended to write more letters, but that he was soon put to death and was prevented from carrying out his intention.

We ask ourselves why Peter should delay, why he did not write all that he had to say on "these things" right here in this letter since he knows that, when death comes to him, it will be swift and leave no time for writing. He proceeds to do that very thing in what follows; "I shall use diligence" need not refer to an indefinite future, it may well refer to the effort that Peter is about to make in the main body of this letter. Peruse it. Peter certainly proceeds to enable his readers at any future time to do their own reminding, namely to the effect that they must hold to "these things" mentioned in v. 5-7 as they are re-enforced by v. 8-11 on any and every occasion when libertinistic prophets and scoffers appear to mislead them. In other words, v. 15 is the preamble to all that follows. Peter does not put off what he has to say; that would not be right (δίκαιον, v. 13). His readers need only reread these chapters at any time and thus "effect for themselves the recollection of these things."

Not Myths but Divine Revelation,
v. 16-21

16) There is certainly reason for such diligence on Peter's part in view of the future which his readers will have to face. **For not by following out sophisticated myths did we make known to you the power and Parousia of our Lord Jesus Christ but as became eyewitnesses of his majesty, for instance, when receiving from God (the) Father honor and glory, a voice being brought to him, such a one by the majestically befitting glory: This is my Son, the beloved, in regard to whom I was well pleased! And this voice we on our part heard brought out of**

heaven, being together with him on the mount, the holy one.

In this epistle the issue is "the power and Parousia of our Lord Jesus Christ." The grand designations for Christ used in v. 1 and 2 plus "the eternal kingdom of our Lord and Savior Jesus Christ" in v. 11 reflect this issue which is fully revealed in 3:3-14: "the promise of his Parousia" (3:4), "not slack concerning his promise" (3:9), "the day of the Lord" (3:10). The pseudo-prophets, of whose coming Peter warns his readers, will charge that the true apostles followed out nothing but σεσοφισμένοι μῦθοι when they made known the Lord's Parousia, "sophisticated myths," of the nature of sophisms, "cunningly devised fables." In this way these lying prophets will seek to dispose of the apostolic teaching. The perfect participle conveys the thought that these myths have the abiding character of sophistication or spurious wisdom. In the aorist participle "by following out" there lies the sneer that what the apostles said about the Parousia was not even a "myth" but only a deduction from cunningly fabricated myths.

The double terms have but one article: "the power of our Lord Jesus Christ and Parousia," so that "power and Parousia" constitute one idea, "power" bringing out the thought of the omnipotent·might involved in the Lord's second coming (compare what is said in 3:10-13). The pagan use of the word "parousia" as a designation for the coming, presence, or visit of an emperor in some city, that city dating further events from such an imperial visit, sheds but little light on the Biblical use of this term. This word was used by the Twelve and by Jesus in Matt. 24:3, 27, 37, 39, and they had not borrowed it from paganism. The Twelve and Jesus also spoke Aramaic in Matthew 24 and used an Aramaic equivalent for this term.

Note that the aorist verbs and the participles occurring in v. 16-18 are strictly historical aorists that designate historical facts as facts and nothing more. Thus Peter speaks of the fact: we made known to you the Parousia. Again the fact: we did not follow out myths; on the contrary, the fact is that we were eyewitnesses of Christ's majesty. Paul, too, uses "myths" in I Tim. 1:4; 4:7 ("profane and old womanish myths"); II Tim. 4:4; Titus 1:14 (Jewish myths"); but these were silly inventions that were attached to Old Testament personages and were disseminated as most valuable wisdom. Here the apostles themselves will be charged with fabricating or using myths about Jesus with which they bolster up the notion of Christ's Parousia.

Precisely whom does Peter refer to when he says that we became "eyewitnesses of his majesty"? Only three men were eyewitnesses of Christ's Transfiguration, and only two of these three. were now living; Herod had killed James a long time ago (Acts 12:2). Some think that Peter's "we" refers only to John and to Peter, and that thus these two had brought the gospel to the people addressed in this letter. This idea is removed the moment the γάρ of v. 17 is understood. All the apostles were "eyewitnesses of his majesty." "We beheld his glory, glory of the Only-Begotten from the Father," beheld it when he tented among us, John 1:14. All of them also saw the risen Lord, saw his ascension. Nobody knows who of them brought the gospel to Peter's readers save that Peter was one of them. The "majesty" here referred to is divine: "our God and Savior" (v. 1), "our God and Lord" (v. 2); it is the majesty of the eternal King (v. 11).

17) When R. 1135 calls λαβών a violent anacoluthon he is evidently mistaken. This view is due to the fact that the meaning of γάρ is misunderstood. This

particle does not mean "for" in the sense that it introduces a finite verb which Peter omitted and thus causèd
an anacoluthon. All of the anacolutha, of which so
much is made especially in connection with Paul's epistles, are intentional, are used to convey what could not
be conveyed as well by other means. We hope that a
proper study of the anacoluthon as a legitimate form
of expression will soon be made.

The γάρ equals "for instance" as it does in other
cases where it introduces a specific instance after a
broader statement, here it introduces the fact that we
were eyewitnesses of his majesty. At the time of the
Transfiguration Peter, James, and John saw Christ in
his majesty — a notable instance, indeed. When Peter
writes: "This voice we on our part (ἡμεῖς) *heard*
brought out of heaven," it is quibbling to say that the
eyewitnesses are now suddenly converted into earwit-
nesses. When they were together with Jesus (asso-
ciative σύν and descriptive ὄντες) did they only hear
and not see? Does λαβών not say that Jesus "received
from God (the) Father honor and glory"? Do Peter's
readers not know the whole story of the Transfiguration?

In the Greek the participle has number, case, and
gender and is thus used in a manner that the English
participle cannot imitate. The form λαβών is a participle and not a finite verb because Peter intends to
have what he says about this instance regarded as
subsidiary; he could have reported still other instances
of the majesty. Although his statement is attached
to ἐκείνου and, back of that, to τοῦ Κυρίου, κτλ., which are
genitives, Peter does not continue with a genitive because he wants to follow with a succinct genitive absolute: φωνῆς, etc. He is perfectly free to use the nominative λαβών *ad sensum*, in fact, could do so even if
he had not chosen to use the following genitive ab-

solute. Every Greek reader or hearer understood the thought instantly and without effort especially since this is the nominative singular and a masculine.

The aorist λαβών denotes only the historical fact: "when receiving from God the Father honor and glory"; γάρ excludes any relation of time with something else. The nominative case itself prevents this. In the Greek "God Father" is considered as one name; "Father" is added here because "my Son" follows. The genitive absolute makes it clear that Christ's receiving honor and glory is the historical receiving at the time of the Transfiguration and not at some other time (resurrection, ascension). Since the genitive absolute: "a voice brought to him to this effect by majestic glory," etc., is simply placed beside λαβών, this is clear, for there is no dependence or relation of time in this genitive absolute. The aorist ἐνεχθείσης states no more than a fact. As *God* made Jesus "receive," so "a voice was brought" to him by *God*.

Instead of saying "God," Peter does more by saying "by the majestically befitting glory." This is the *glory* from which Jesus received honor and *glory*. Ὑπό is the regular preposition used to indicate the agent with a passive. So "the glory" is personified. Yet this is Peter's own expression for God (not a borrowed one). This is an exceptional adjective which is found in Deut. 33:26, and in II Macc. 8:15; 15:13; III Macc. 2:9, a compound of μέγας and πρέπει, "great" and "it befits." "Excellent" in our versions is an inadequate translation, for this μεγαλοπρεπής δόξα = the μεγαλειότης mentioned in v. 16, the one word meaning "greatness" in the sense of "majesty," the other "befittingly great," or, as we venture to indicate the correspondence, "majestically befitting" glory. We have here an instance of Peter's fondness for repeating: glory — glory; and the two terms compounded with "great." The correlative demonstratives such as τοιᾶσδε (here the feminine) have almost died out (R. 709) : "a voice, such a one, i. e., *so einzigartig* (B.-P. 1312), so phenomenal, by the majestically befitting glory."

Since Peter uses the accusative in v. 18: "this voice we heard," we see that "a voice . . . such a one" refers to *what* the voice said and not to the *kind* of voice that it was even as also the ὑπό phrase already indicates the *kind* of voice, the speaking was done "by the majestic glory." Thus Peter simply quotes what the glory said: "This is my Son, the beloved, in regard to whom I was well pleased!" It is the Father who says "my Son." The Father thus calls him the second person of the Godhead. "The beloved" is an apposition, and, like most verbals, this verbal adjective is passive: "beloved by the Father." The verb ἀγαπᾶν, from which ἀγαπητός is derived, denotes the highest type of love, that of fullest understanding and perfect corresponding purpose. The Son is truly worthy of this love of his Father.

We properly have such love indicated here and not that designated by φιλία or affection. The latter certainly also exists between the two divine persons, but here "the beloved" is the Son *ensarkos,* incarnate, whose human nature is transfigured in glory as it shall be forever when the redemption is complete. The fact that the Father loves the Son *asarkos* need not be announced. On three different occasions God proclaimed his approval of the incarnate Son and his work; at the time of his baptism, of his transfiguration, and shortly before his passion (John 12:28, etc.) Peter refers to the second of these three because of the glory in which the Son's human nature appeared.

Some regard ἀγαπητός as equivalent to μονογενής, "the only-begotten" and assert that this is the fixed meaning of this term. The evidence adduced, however, proves only this fact that an only son was at times also called "the beloved son" as, for instance, in Gen. 22:2, 12, 16, which is regarded as the chief proof passage.

We object to the sense that is attributed to μονογενής, namely that in John 1:14, 18; 3:16, 18; I John 4:9 the term refers only to the human birth of Jesus and not to the *generatio æterna* of the Son in his divine nature. The Son was "the only-begotten" from eternity and is called "the beloved" while he was in his human nature engaged in his redemptive work.

We have three accounts of the Transfiguration: Matt. 17:1, etc.; Mark 9:2, etc.; Luke 9:28, etc.; these three were not written by eyewitnesses. It is noteworthy that in place of "the beloved, in whom I was well pleased," Luke 9:36 has ὁ ἐκλελεγμένος, "the one who has been chosen or elected," although the variant reading "the beloved" also appears in important texts. It seems, however, that this reading was introduced only to make Luke to conform with Matthew and with Mark. The voice on the mount spoke in Aramaic, which the Evangelists and Peter translate. This means that Luke's translation is in substance the same as that of the others who write "in whom I was well pleased." This aorist is not gnomic. Our versions seem to have had this idea in mind when they translated it as a present tense: "In whom I *am* well pleased." This aorist is historical, and Luke's perfect tense "the one who has been elected or chosen" makes this clear.

The verb εὐδοκεῖν, "to be well pleased," often has an intensive meaning when it is used with reference to a person and is then equal to ἐκλέγεσθαι and αἱρετίζειν, the former of which was chosen by Luke: "to select or choose for oneself." The good pleasure expresses itself in the choice, Luke's perfect participle saying that, once so expressed, the choice stands; the aorist used by Peter and by the other two simply registers the past fact, which the Father's voice from heaven, however, states anew. The good pleasure of the Father's choice must be dated in eternity (Rev. 13:8). See C.-K. 353. Whereas Matthew and Mark have ἐν, Peter

has εἰς. This is either static εἰς: *"in* whom," or is to be
understood in the sense of "in regard to whom I was
pleased"; in English we should say "have been
pleased." The Father's good pleasure and choice refer
to the Son in his incarnation and his redemptive work
even as the Son's human nature was transfigured, and
the conversation with Moses and Elijah dealt with
"the decease (ἔξοδος) which the Son should accomplish
at Jerusalem" (Luke 9:31).

18) Peter says that this wondrous voice "was
brought or conveyed" to Jesus; how this was done he
does not presume to say. By adding the participle:
we "being together with him on the mount, the holy
one," he intends to say that he was one who was
present with others; they certainly were ἐπόπται, "eyewitnesses" in the fullest sense of the word (v. 16). By
adding the adjective "holy" with a second article Peter
lends it emphasis (R. 776).

Efforts to locate this mountain are futile. The tra-
ditional site, Mount Tabor, will not do at all since Jesus
had been in the north and had returned to Capernaum
and had as yet not gone as far south as Tabor. Peter
calls this mountain "the holy one" because of the fact
of the transfiguration; there is no trace of its having
been termed holy before this and for some prior reason.

Peter does not tell the whole story of the Transfiguration. He does not use the accounts of the Evangelists, for *he* helped to inform them, and not *they*
him. Thus all four accounts agree perfectly. The point
of importance for Peter is "this voice"; "we on our
part (the witnesses present) heard it conveyed to Jesus
out of heaven." Note that "voice" and "brought (conveyed)" are repeated. Peter has already noted the
phenomenal character of this voice: τοιᾶσδε marks what
it said and the kind of voice that it was, he again
emphasizes *"this* voice," and now stresses the fact that
"we on our part *heard* it." This is a direct revelation,

directly made by the Father himself, directly received
by the witnesses. Let those who will regard it as being merely a "myth." This revelation attests the glory
and the deity of the Son in his earthly life by a voice
and a revelation that were so *einzigartig*. This is he
whom Peter has truly named in v. 1, 2, 11, whose Parousia will come in spite of all scoffers, for whom
Peter's readers are to wait with unshakable assurance.

19) **And we have as more sure the prophetic
Word, to which you are doing well in giving heed
as to a lamp shining in a dismal place till day dawns
and a light-bearer arises in your hearts; etc.** "And"
adds in the sense of "and so" as when a resultant
fact is added. When Peter says "we have as more
certain," etc., he refers to himself and to all the apostles as those who made known the power and the Parousia of our Lord Jesus Christ. This "we" in the verb
does not refer to Peter and to his readers, for "you
do well" follows. Nor is it the emphatic "we" (ἡμεῖς)
used in v. 18 which = Peter, James, and John at the
time of the transfiguration. All the apostles became
eyewitnesses of Christ's majesty on many occasions,
namely from their first to their last contact with him
here on earth, and thus did not follow sophisticated
myths in what they made known about his Parousia.

Thus all the apostles "have as more sure the prophetic Word," namely "all prophecy of Scripture" (v.
20), the entire Old Testament which prophesied about
Christ, in particular also about his power and his Parousia (v. 16). When they became eyewitnesses of his
majesty, this their own experience with Christ made
the entire prophetic Word more sure to them, and so
they made it known to all to whom they preached.

Note that βεβαιότερον is predicative and thus emphatic: "we have as more sure (firm) the prophetic
Word." Luther misses this construction when he translates *wir haben ein festes prophetisches Wort* and

makes the comparative adjective attributive and not predicative and even loses the comparative idea. The A. V. does the same although it retains the comparative. The opinion that Peter compares the prophetic Word with the transfiguration and calls this Word "more sure" than the transfiguration (v. 17, 18) or than all the majesty which' the apostles came to see in Christ (v. 16-18) is untenable. No, after seeing Christ's majesty the Old Testament prophecies were surer than ever to the apostles; they based nothing of their preaching on "myths" of any kind. By its fulfillment the fulfilled prophecy is naturally made more sure than it was while it was still awaiting fulfillment.

Regarding this prophetic Word Peter says to his readers that "they are doing well in taking heed to it" (complementary participle, R. 1121). How well they are doing this the apposition states: "as to a lamp shining in a dismal place," etc. Αὐχμηρός is another of Peter's rare words, which our versions render "dark," and in which so many find the idea of darkness because Peter speaks of a lamp shining. They also find this "place" in the hearts of Peter's readers. But people who are doing well are not be likened to "a dismal place." The imagery does *not* refer to the outdoors and picture a traveller trying to pick his way amid a *strueppige Wildnis*, a *Wirrsal* of rocks, brambles, and jungle. This "place" is a house in which a "lamp" may afford some light until day breaks.

Peter indicates what kind of house this is; it is "dismal," indeed, with its "heresies of perdition" and denial of the Master (2:1), with heretics speaking evil of the truth, making merchandise of you (2:2, 3), and carrying on their libertinism, etc. In a house of this kind, that is dismal for any righteous soul (2:7), Peter's readers will be compelled to live their earthly lives. Their one hope and help is "the prophetic Word" which tells of Christ who also has come, and whose

majesty the apostles have actually seen, and foretells
the dawn of a better day at his Parousia. The room
that Peter has in mind is worse than dark; it is full
of dreadful dangers, and in order to see these and to
guard ourselves against them we need this divine and
brightly shining lamp.

The next clause is to be construed with the preceding one because it contains "your": you are doing well
in giving heed "till day dawn and a light-bearer arises
in *your* hearts." When day dawns, one no longer needs
"a lamp." Although he says only "day" (qualitative)
and not "*the* day," the great day of the Lord, Peter,
nevertheless, refers to that day; but its "dawning"
refers only to its breaking, to the great signs that
immediately usher it in for the whole world. This
dawning is described in 3:10-12.

The rest of the clause, and especially the phrase
"in your hearts," cause some perplexity. Φωσφόρος =
"light-bearer." One such "light-bearer" is the prophetic
Word which Peter says serves as a lamp during this
entire time until day breaks. It will be followed by
another "light-bearer," of which Peter says that it
will "arise," ἀνατέλλω; he uses a verb that refers to the
rising of the sun or of a star so that this "light-bearer"
is far greater than a stationary lamp with reference
to which such a verb cannot be used.

Some identify this "light-bearer" with the ὁ ἀστὴρ ὁ
πρωϊνός mentioned in Rev. 2:28, "the morning star," and
with ὁ ἀστὴρ ὁ λαμπρὸς ὁ πρωϊνός, "the star, the brilliant
one, the morning one," in Rev. 22:16, which Jesus says
"I am." Aside from this identification Peter's meaning is apprehended when our versions translate "daystar," i. e., not the sun itself but the bright morning
star, "Jupiter, Mars, Saturn, or Venus, when rising
shortly before the sun and forming a conspicuous object in the sky just before dawn" (*Standard Dic-*

tionary). Dawning day and this daystar's rising thus go together, the latter is the mark of the former.

Peter says that day will dawn and this harbinger of the day will arise "in your hearts." The best commentary is Luke 21:28: "When these things begin to come to pass, then look up, and lift up your head; for your redemption draweth nigh," and Matt. 24:32, "ye know that summer is nigh." Both the dawning day and its accompanying daystar's appearing above the horizon are objective. Yet "in your hearts" modifies both and is subjective. For these hearts will *apprehend* what is happening; the hearts of all other men will not apprehend. The approaching light of the eternal day will not merely come on the outside, it will fill the hearts of the believers. Peter states it beautifully and truly indeed.

As this dawn breaks more and more it will supersede the lamp of the prophetic Word just as fulfillment always supersedes prophecy. The readers will repeat the experience of the apostles: the more they became eyewitnesses of the majesty of Jesus, the more what they actually saw in Jesus took the place of what the old prophets had foretold about him (John 1:14). This will be true to the greatest degree when the dawn of the eternal day actually breaks (note the aorists in the "till" clause). It is quite correct to say that the believers who are living near the end of time will know what is taking place and will lift up their hearts in joyous expectation just as Jesus says in Luke 21:28. That this does not and cannot conflict with 3:10 and the figure of the thief coming in the night we shall see in the interpretation of 3:10.

We scarcely need to say that II Cor. 4:4, 6 are not parallel passages, for they deal with conversion, the conversion which the Corinthians had already experienced; moreover, II Cor. 4:6 uses the first creation of light by God recorded in Gen. 1:3 as its imagery. We also do not construe "in your hearts" with the statement made in verse 20. The phrase cannot be restricted to the daystar's arising but modifies the day's dawning as well.

20) The prophetic Word is surer than ever since the apostles saw the majesty of Jesus (foretold in this Word); three of them in particular witnessed also the transfiguration and heard that phenomenal voice from heaven. The readers certainly do well to heed this Word as their lamp till a still greater light-bearer finally arises: **realizing this, first of all, that no prophecy of Scripture occurs from one's own interpretation, for not by man's will was prophecy ever brought, but as borne along by the Holy Spirit from God men made utterance.**

The participle is not an anacoluthon as R. 1039 asserts but modifies the "you" in "you are doing well." In a fine Greek way the realizing of what is said about all of Scripture's prophecy is made subsidiary (hence the participle) to the heeding of this prophecy. Peter chose the proper word when he wrote γινώσκοντες, personal realizing and not merely intellectual knowing, which is never sufficient protection. Many things are to be realized, but the one mentioned here is the most important and thus πρῶτον, the very first.

It is not a Hebraism to place "not" with the verb: "all prophecy does not occur" is only the Greek idiom for the English "no prophecy occurs."

It is a prevalent conception that Peter intends to say: no person (some add: not even one of the prophets) is to interpret the Scripture's prophecies according to his own notion — which is, of course, true enough. Our versions translate in this way. Then, however, Peter does not say how we are to interpret these prophecies. The commentators add that we must let the Holy Spirit interpret the prophecies. Although

Peter does not say this, this, too, is true. Luther is a sample: "Thou art not to interpret thyself, the Holy Spirit himself is to interpret it, or it is to be left un-- interpreted." When we are told about the *darkness* and the obscurity of the Old Testament prophecies we dissent; such comment forgets that "the prophetic Word" is no less than "a shining *lamp.*" Its light is *clear* and not by any means dark according to Peter. He has especially shown that this is more than ever the case since Christ has come (v. 16-19).

The fact that ἐπιλύσεως means "interpretation" is beyond question. In Gen. 40:8 it is so used with refer-- ence to a dream; in Mark 4:34 the verb is used with reference to parables. The genitive is an ablative (R. 514). Ἰδίας does not refer to the prophecy of Scripture and does not convey the idea that this prophecy does not supply its *"own* interpretation." *Scriptura* un-- doubtedly *ex Scriptura explicanda est*; in this way the Spirit interprets Scripture. Οὐ γίνεται with its ablative = "does not occur from," come or originate from. It is not the interpretation of anyone that governs the prophecy, but the prophecy governs the interpretation. Peter reverts to v. 16. The apostles did not invent myths and then in order to square with such myths prophesy a Parousia of Christ; no prophecy of Scrip- ture was ever spoken in such a way: the prophet con-- ceiving the way in which he wanted his interpretation and then shaping the prophecy to suit. Then the scof-- fers would, indeed, be right in scoffing at all such prophecies and calling them "myths," yea, "sophisti- cated myths," whether they were invented by the apostles (v. 16) or by the Old Testament prophets.

The proposition here laid down is general, hence we have the present tense which is regularly used in such general statements and also the universal πᾶσα . . . οὐ: *"no* Scripture prophecy occurred," etc. To say that Peter should speak historically and use the aorist

is to tell him what he should write. What is wrong
with this general proposition?

To what lengths the opinion that Peter tells us how
Scripture must *not* be interpreted has led we see in
the case of the Council of Trent, Sessio IV: *ut nemo
suae prudentiae innixus in rebus fidei et morum ad
aedificationem doctrinae christianae pertinentium s.
Scripturam ad suos sensus contorquens contra eum
sensum, quem tenuit et tenet sancta Mater Ecclesia,
cuius est judicare de vero sensu et interpretatione
Scripturam sanctarum, aut etiam contra unanimem
consensum Patrum, ipsam scripturam sacram interpretari audeat.*

21)   Peter speaks of the origin of prophecy: "for
not by man's will was prophecy ever brought"; anything that any human being ever willed (θέλημα) had
absolutely nothing to do with divine prophecy. Only
false prophets utter prophecies that originate in what
they have willed. They want things to happen their
way and then so prophesy them; they fix up a certain
ἰδία ἐπίλυσις, a certain interpretation of their own, and
then fix up their prophecies so that men will find that
meaning in them. It is their standard procedure. They
cry: "Peace, peace!" just because they want peace
when peace is the last thing to expect, when God says
that there is none and is to be none. False prophets
foretold that Jerusalem would never fall, that it would
crush the Romans; that is what *they* wanted. They
fixed symbolical, allegorical, figurative language to bear
such an "interpretation," but Jerusalem was utterly
destroyed.

Ἀλλά states that true prophecy is the very opposite: "on the contrary, as borne along by the Holy
Spirit from God men made utterance." In v. 21 Peter
uses historical aorists. The present participle φερόμενοι
is descriptive: "borne along," ὑπό denotes the agent

with the passive: "by the Holy Spirit." The verb is
used with reference to ships that are borne along on
a certain course by the wind (Acts 27:15, 17).

Thus "men" ἐλάλησαν, "spoke," "made utterance"
(the opposite is to keep silence). The verb is not λέγω
as though these human beings contributed anything to
the substance of the thought. Peter's verb makes them
only mouthpieces of the Holy Spirit. In Matt. 1:22 the
angel expresses the same thought: "the thing spoken
by (ὑπό) the Lord by means of (διά) the prophet."
These significant prepositions appear often. The Lord
God "made utterance by the mouth (διὰ στόματος) of his
holy prophets," Luke 1:70. The Holy Spirit "spoke in
advance by means of (διά) David's mouth"; so also
Luke 3:18, 21; 4:25. Since ἐλάλησαν ἀπὸ Θεοῦ is placed
together, we translate, "spoke from God"; what they
spoke came wholly "from" him. The readers do well
to be heeding "the prophetic Word," "all Scripture
prophecy," as spoken in this way. Truly, it is the Word
of God (I Thess. 2:13), a shining lamp, indeed.

This is not a caution or a warning on the part of
Peter that his readers are not to misinterpret the
Scriptures. Peter does not say, "Be careful about using
this shining lamp!" He says, "*Use* it! It *is* a shining
lamp!"

There are men who interpret this passage and never
once use the word inspiration. This is one of the great
sedes for the fact of inspiration. Peter presents *the
fact,* not a theory, not a hypothesis. The fact is that
God and the Spirit are the real speakers, the *anthrōpoi*
are their mouthpieces. Our fathers, therefore, called
God the *causa efficiens* or *principalis,* the speakers
(writers) the *causae instrumentales.* The act itself
they called the *suggestio rerum et verborum,* meaning
by this what Peter calls φερόμενοι, "borne along by the
Spirit." Since both the Hebrew *ruach* and the Greek

πνεῦμα mean breath, wind, Peter's participle is most expressive to denote the act of inspiration, this word "inspire" (from the Latin) is equally perfect.

The result attests the divine act. As no man ever spoke like this man Jesus (John 7:46), so no book ever spoke like this Book. None was ever scrutinized down to its every particle like this one; none has had such intensive and extensive commentaries written about it, the last of which is not yet in sight. None has experienced such assaults and has after every surge of attack appeared only the more as "the impregnable rock of Holy Scripture" (Gladstone), a Gibraltar that only smiles at attack.

Our fathers used three illustrations for the two *causae*, efficient and instrumental: a man dictating to an amanuensis; a player blowing the flute; a plectrum striking the strings of a lyre; in all three the *tertium* is the fact that the *causa efficiens* produces its desired results by means of the *causae instrumentales*. The fathers offered these illustrations as illustrations of this point just as any man seeks to illumine some point by means of illustrations.

If a man's illustration is not adequate, show him a better one! Do so in the case of these three. But what has been done with our fathers' illustrations? Some have selected *one* of these illustrations and have charged the fathers with *"the dictation theory."* They never charge them with "the *flute* theory" or with "the *lyre* theory" but confine themselves to the one illustration. Since when is an illustration that I or any man uses "a *theory*"? An illustration should be distinguished from a theory. All similes limp, but only because they are only similes, for which reason those fathers also used no less than three. Compare the discussion of II Tim. 3:14-17, and of I Cor. 2:12, 13.

CHAPTER II

Part Two

How the Coming Pseudo-Teachers Look and Act, Chapter 2

Their Coming and Their Numerous Following Foretold, v. 1-3

1) Δέ is transitional and not adversative. Peter has emphasized ἐπίγνωσις, full and true heart-knowledge; all diligence in the whole round of Christian life; the absolute certainty of the prophetic Word of Scripture; the kingdom and the Parousia of our Lord Jesus Christ. Now he stresses the purpose of it all: the readers will soon have to face one of the worst types of false teachers whose life will be as rank as their teaching.

There occurred also pseudo-prophets among the people as also among you there will be pseudo-teachers, such as will bring in covertly heresies of perdition, denying even the absolute Master who bought them, bringing upon their own selves swift perdition.

The aorist "there occurred" states the historical fact. Καί, "also," reverts to 1:19-21; yet Peter does not say "pseudo-prophecy" in formal conformity with "prophecy" mentioned in 1:21 but names the false prophets, for what they offered was not "prophecy" but fiction, "myths" (v. 16). Such lying prophets appeared among the people, λαός refers to the people of Israel. They appeared beside God's true prophets and with their pretended prophecies tried to turn Israel from the true prophets and from the things they uttered by inspiration "from God" (1:21). Formally

"pseudo-prophets" matches the ἄνθρωποι mentioned in
1:21, "men who spoke from God borne along by the
Holy Spirit."

Ὡς καί is exact, "as also among you," etc. This is
misunderstood when it is taken to mean that Israel
had its false prophets in correspondence with the readers of this epistle; Peter says: Israel had false prophets
as the readers shall have false teachers. The two ἐν
indicate that "among Israel" as "among you" such
liars appeared and shall appear. Peter does not intend
to say that they had or shall have the whole field to
themselves but only that they try to invade it and to
wrest it from the true preachers.

We do not identify "pseudo-prophets" and "pseudo-
teachers." The former pretended to have received
direct revelations from God such as men like Elijah,
Isaiah, etc., received. They lied; they themselves made
up what they offered with the words, "Thus saith
Yahweh." Among Peter's readers such prophets would
not appear who claimed direct revelation and inspiration; they would be only "lying teachers," Peter even
adds: "such as will bring in covertly heresies of perdition." They will not pose as prophets or as apostles
of Christ; they will merely teach, namely lies that
pervert, falsify "the way of the truth."

Peter writes with clarity and with exactness. We
do not introduce I Cor. 14 and the charisma of "prophecy" which refers only to the gift of informing others
about the divine Word that had already been revealed.
Teachers did the same; they only expounded and explained the Word and did not merely state it. There
was but little difference between this kind of prophecy
and its teaching, and that has no pertinence here. The
false prophets that arose among Israel claimed to be
on the same high plane with such men as Elijah, etc.;
Peter's readers would have to face only lying teachers.

Peter's readers are now God's people as Israel once was. They must not be surprised to learn that something quite similar to what Israel experienced will also come to them. As Israel suffered from lying prophets, so Peter's readers will be troubled by lying teachers. The devil cannot let God's people alone; if he can no longer send lying prophets among them he will at least send lying teachers.

Οἵτινες is purely qualitative and intends to characterize and describe: "such as will bring in covertly heresies of perdition," etc. M.-M. 492 cite only two examples of the use of this verb and think that it means "to introduce." In the present connection the παρά of the verb has its full force: "to bring in privily" (our versions), sneakingly, covertly, so that unwary, simple people will not note what these teachers are bringing in; B.-P. 997 translates rightly *einschwaertzen,* which agrees with the subject "lying or false teachers" and with the object "heresies of perdition."

We also note a tendency to tone down the meaning of αἱρέσεις and to eliminate everything that is adverse from the word. It is reduced in force to *Sonderrichtungen,* to the opinions of differing philosophical "schools" of thought, where each school has as much right to its opinion as the other. We are likewise referred to the *hairesis* of the Pharisees and to that of the Sadducees, each being a Jewish party with its own tenets (Acts 5:17; 15:5). Derived from the middle of αἱρέω, the noun etymologically means a view, an opinion, a doctrine that one chooses for oneself and thereby separates oneself from the whole body, from others who choose a different view, etc., and thus form a party within the body.

A *hairesis* may be mild or grave in varying degrees. In postapostolic times the word came to have the sense in which we now use it: "heresy," a grave aberration and nothing less. We freely admit that this word had a varied meaning in apostolic times; but here Peter himself plainly refers to what were no less than the gravest kind of heresies; there were even many of them. The meaning of the word cannot be toned down in the present connection.

These are "heresies of perdition." Peter repeats "perdition"; these lying teachers bring upon their own selves "swift perdition," i. e., eternal damnation in hell. Ἀπώλεια means no less. The fact that they do it by means of their "heresies of perdition" is rather plain. To be sure, this is a characterizing genitive; the New Testament has many such. That it is Hebraistic, as is claimed, makes no difference. This genitive is far stronger than an adjective and should not be made an adjective: "damnable heresies" (A. V.), "destructive" (R. V.). All self-chosen views or doctrines that bear the stamp of perdition and bring "swift perdition" upon their advocates are *heresies* in the gravest sense of the word, no matter when they are held. Tone down the one word as much as one may, the other puts hell (perdition) into it nevertheless.

There is no reason to fault Peter for continuing with two descriptive, iterative present participles. Does καί not often mean "even"? These participles should *not* be finite verbs. As participles they subjoin, and this is exactly what Peter wants. Articles are *not* needed, for these would convert the participles into substantives and produce a sense that Peter does not want to express. The first participle: "denying," etc., makes evident the *crime* and the *guilt* of these lying teachers and shows that their heresies merit perdition beyond question; the second stresses the *result*. Being anarthrous, these participles are attached to and add to the main verb. Καί is to be construed with the object (R. V.) and not with the participle (A. V.).

"Denying even the absolute Master who bought them" implies that these heretics also deny and reject much else. As God is called δεσπότης, so Christ is called the same. Peter has twice called Christ God in the most significant way (1:1, 2). But Peter said: "our God and *Savior*," "our God and *Lord*"; and here he says: "the *Despotes* who *bought* them." Read Trench regarding the difference between δεσπότης and κύριος. A man is the former to his slaves, the latter to his wife (I Pet. 3:6, Sarah) and his children. From the former we have our word "despot," which is used in a rather evil sense. When it is applied to God and to Christ as God the term stresses their absolute, unrestricted power. But the addition "who bought them" conserves the fullest soteriological sense. Christ bought them at the tremendous price of his blood to be his own forever. Despite his absolute might and this act of purchase and ransoming these are men who "deny," disown, repudiate "even" him. They challenge his absolute power; they ungratefully scorn his buying them. Ingrate rebels!

Here we have an adequate answer to Calvin's limited atonement: the Sovereign, Christ, bought with his blood not only the elect but also those who go to perdition. Calvin does not accept this epistle as canonical; in his extensive commentary on the New Testament it is not treated. May this clause, perhaps, have been a reason for this omission?

"Bringing upon their own selves swift perdition" states their doom. "Swift" is the same adjective that was used in 1:14, which see. These teachers do this themselves. Arrogantly they run their course; then suddenly perdition strikes them down. "Swift" indicates what happens in the instant of death.

Peter prophesies, as Christ, as Paul do. All three of them foretell in no uncertain words. The prospect that they hold out is terrible. Pseudo-teachers did come;

their successors are still here. Their spiritual marks
are still the same. As teachers they want place and
position, authority and pay right in the church while
their teaching smells to heaven of the perdition that
awaits them at death.

2) Truthfully, though sorrowfully, Peter adds:
**And many shall follow their excesses, through whom
the way of the truth will be blasphemed.** Although
they are false in heart and in doctrine these teachers
will have a numerous following in their ἀσέλγειαι, *Ausschweifungen, Zuegellosigkeiten,* "excesses," when
there is no check or rein of divine truth, when they
run into all manner of extremes. "Pernicious ways"
(A. V.) is inexact; "lascivious doings" (R. V.) and
G. K. 488 leave the impression that this word refers
only to sexual aberrations. This is a general characterization, hence this abstract is pluralized; the
plural obviates a restriction to sex. All types and all
manner of excesses and extremes of immorality are
referred to.

When did pseudo-teachers ever lack a following?
The "many" referred to are not adherents that are
attracted from paganism but from the church, that
are attracted away from the diligence of true Christian activity (1:5, etc.) to the libertinism of these
teachers who put down the bars, who advocate full
freedom for the flesh. That is the bait that is still
effective in the case of many. The mediate effect is
the fact that "through these many followers the way
of the truth shall be blasphemed." This is the damage
that will be done to the church. The Hebrew *derek,*
the Greek ὁδός mean "way" (the plural is sometimes
used) in the sense that one puts a doctrine to practice.
The articulated genitive "of *the* truth" does not equal
an adjective: "the true way." "The truth" is the specific truth of the Word or gospel, the ἀλήθεια or "reality"

of which it consists, which we embrace and follow by faith and a godly life.

True Christianity is blasphemed, reviled, cursed, condemned by outsiders who see professed Christians running to all manner of excesses. "If that is Christianity," they will say, "curse it!" When many follow such excesses, outsiders are unable to distinguish and so blaspheme the whole "way." These false exponents seem true products of the way to them.

3) Peter adds another characterization. **And in covetousness with made-up words they will trade you in — they for whom the sentence this long while is not idle, and their perdition is not nodding in sleep!** Because "in covetousness" they are hungry for money they will use "manufactured arguments," πλαστοῖς λόγοις, "made-up words," to trade you in, to buy you as their followers so that you may help to pay them well. So many pseudo-teachers are out for what there is in it for them. Peter states this in a striking manner: "they will trade you in," but will do so with false coin, with λόγοι or "arguments" that are πλαστοί, "made up," manufactured, molded by themselves for this purpose, so that you may sell yourselves to them cheaply. They want you as so much goods that they have bought in order thereafter to mulct you. The world is full of examples. They offer no gold gospel coin of "the truth" but only "shinplasters" of false arguments; they have no concern for the sheep but only for shearing their wool.

With indignation and by means of a parallelism like that of the ancient prophets Peter once more adds the doom that is awaiting all such traders. The relative is demonstrative, almost exclamatory: *"they* for whom," etc. The κρῖμα is the "sentence" of the divine Judge. It has been handed down from his judgment seat "from of old," i. e., this long while, and is not inert or idle like the sentence of some earthly judge that is never executed. It is not sitting, twiddling its thumbs, too lazy to apprehend and to execute the miscreants.

"The sentence," τὸ κρῖμα, points to the Judge, "their perdition" (another of Peter's repetitions) points to the criminals and to the penalty decreed and is thus an advance in thought. "Does not nod in sleep," νυστάζει = does not forget what it is for. These liars may with their made-to-order arguments persuade themselves that this latter is the case. The double statement is an effective litotes, saying negatively what is true positively: this sentence has from of old been full of the deadliest energy to execute itself; this perdition has fixed its fiery eyes on these heretics who are keen to bring it on themselves. The supposition that Peter refers only to the final judgment at the Parousia contravenes v. 9.

This is prophecy. These are the facts as they will come to pass. This is the most powerful motive for true Christians to abhor all pseudo-teachers and their teaching. This is advance warning and fortification for Peter's readers. Nowhere do the Scriptures, least of all Jesus and his apostles, deal gently with false teachers of any kind as David wanted Joab, Abishai, and Ittai to deal with Absalom. Do you know of a crime that is more heinous than falsifying the Word?

*The Terrors of the Old Testament Judgments
and the Deliverance of the Righteous,
v. 4-10a*

4) These seven verses constitute one extended sentence: εἰ with the indicative is a long protasis of terrible reality (v. 4-8); v. 9 brings the double apodosis. The structure is skillful in detail, which is so noteworthy because the details that are included are so many. But the main feature is the unification,

which no breaking up into a number of sentences could
achieve. Up, up, up Peter builds the protasis until
in v. 9, 10 he caps it·all with the great apodosis. Peter
considers three great historical judgments in chronological order. Jude 5, etc., is different although in
v. 6, 7 Jude also refers to the angels and to Sodom and
Gomorrah.

Indeed, neither the sentence (κρῖμα) is idle, nor
the perdition asleep. Take a look into the past. **For
if God did not spare angels when sinning but, casting them with chains of blackness into Tartarus, delivered them as being kept unto judgment; and, etc.**
The "if" of reality leads the readers to say: "God certainly did!" Both the aorist participles and the main
verbs state historical facts. "Angels sinned"; the article would not be in place; Jude 6: "angels, those
who did not keep the principality belonging to themselves but left their own proper habitation." These
are the angels that fell before Adam's fall. What their
sin was neither Peter nor Jude state.

In their comments on this passage and on Jude 6
some interpreters advance the supposition that these
were angels who cohabited with women and begot a
wicked race which God had to destroy by means of the
flood. This is thought to be the meaning of Gen. 6:2,
4. At the end of I Pet. 3:22, last paragraph, we have
already referred to this interpretation. Verses 4 and
5 are thought to belong together in a special way and
recite what God did to these angels and to the race
of half-demons which they begot. We cannot take the
space to develop this subject here.

In his commentary on Genesis Delitzsch thoroughly refutes what he rightly calls "these fables of the
Jewish gnosticizing Haggadah." We note only that
Jesus himself says that angels are sexless, that they
cannot marry (Matt. 22:30). Genesis 6 says nothing
about angels; it speaks of "the sons of God" (the

descendants of Seth) marrying "the daughters of men",
(the descendants of Cain who could be called by no
higher name). In Genesis 5 the two lines, the gene-
alogies of Seth and of Cain, are given. The Book of
Enoch has added many late insertions. Now it makes
this, now that the sin of the wicked angels. Its oldest
parts speak of a fall and sin of the stars which did
not appear at their appointed time. The fiction about
evil angels begetting children occurs in the so-called
"Noah-Book," a late edition to the older parts of the
Book of Enoch.

God "did not spare" sinning angels although they
were angels but, "consigning them to Tartarus with
chains of darkness, delivered them as being kept for
judgment" — "has kept them for judgment of (the)
great day in eternal prison under blackness," Jude 6.

The aorist participle (one act) ταρταρώσας = "to cast
into Tartarus." The verb does not occur elsewhere in
the Bible; it is seldom found in other writings. The
noun "Tartarus" occurs three times in the LXX, but
there is no corresponding Hebrew term. The word is
of pagan origin, an evidence that Peter's readers are
converted pagans. It seems to be used because Peter
speaks of angels. Our versions' "cast them down to
hell" is entirely correct. Yet we meet the assertion
that "hades" is not referred to, nor "Gehenna," nor
"the realm of the dead" (a late fictional place).
"Hades" and "Gehenna" are hell, the place of all the
damned, which is "Tartarus," a term which any Greek
would understand in this sense.

Is the correct reading σειροῖς (σιροῖς), "pits" (such as
were used for storing grain or fruits), or σειραῖς,
"chains"? While textual evidence is in favor of the
former, everything else speaks in favor of the latter.
The very word "storage pits" is too odd a meaning to
be connected with hell; many, therefore, assume that
this is a scribe's mistake. Ζόφος is more than "dark-

ness" even as v. 17 has ὁ ζόφος τοῦ σκότους. These are "chains of blackness" such as only the infernal place knows. The dative is to be construed with the participle, next to which it is placed; those who construe it with "he delivered" violate the word order. So also we construe: "delivered unto judgment," the final participle "being kept" rounds out the whole thought.

This is the final public judgment κρίσις (not κρῖμα, "sentence," v. 3). It is interesting to compare I Cor. 6:3 in this connection. It is asked where Peter obtained these facts. One should then also ask where Paul obtained I Cor. 6:3. Some think that this information was obtained from the Old Testament (Isa. 24:21, 22 is one such passage), others that it was gleaned from Jewish nonbiblical sources (the *Book of Enoch*). The apostles had revelation as their source (John 16:13). Inquisitive minds may ask how the evil angels, after being cast into hell, are able to deceive men on the earth. The Scriptures do not say. They leave many questions about hell and the devils unanswered because we are bound for heaven and have no personal interest in hell and its occupants.

5) "And" joins the next terrible judgment to the first just as in v. 6 another "and" joins the third to the others. This means that v. 4 and 5 cannot be combined so as to refer to one judgment that strikes angels and men because of their sexual union. Peter writes: **and spared not an ancient world but guarded as eighth Noah, a herald of righteousness, when he brought a deluge upon a world of ungodly ones; and,** **etc.** Note the repetition: "he *spared not* an ancient world" although it was an entire world. Did men think that God's "sentence" (κρῖμα) had become idle, that their perdition was nodding in sleep (v. 3)?

Peter uses the ἀλλά clauses to introduce opposite thoughts: in verse 4 he uses it to introduce the judgment; now he uses it to introduce Noah's deliverance.

This is a most striking stylistic nuance that was most effective for Peter's readers. God "guarded" Noah when he brought a deluge upon "a (whole) world of ungodly ones."

The adjective is predicative: "as an eighth (person)," i. e., with seven others. The thought is not that he was number eight; he was number one but was the last to enter into the ark. It is asked how Peter knew that Noah was "*a herald* of righteousness" when the Old Testament calls him only "a righteous man." This seems to be a trivial question. Did Noah keep still during those 120 years? Did God leave the world in ignorance of the impending deluge? Did Peter write without revelation?

That delay of 120 years was an added season of grace. The preaching of Noah was to turn men to righteousness so that God might *not* be compelled to send the flood. God would have spared Sodom and Gomorrah if ten righteous had been found there, but there were not even ten (Gen. 18:32); in the whole world of Noah's time there were only eight. "Righteousness" is the objective genitive, it is not qualitative, not "a righteous herald." The word is to be understood in the full forensic sense. Noah proclaimed that quality which has God's judicial approval so that the ungodly might repent and thus be declared righteous by God. But they scorned his words, laughed at his ark, remained "a world of ungodly ones."

6) A third witness testifies: **and the cities of Sodom and Gomorrah, by turning them to ashes, he condemned with a catastrophe, setting an example for any in the future living ungodly and rescued righteous Lot, sore wearied by the conduct of the nefarious ones in excess, etc.**

Peter varies the wording in a skillful manner. Yet, as in v. 4, he has an aorist participle before the first main verb; κατέκρινεν matches the εἰς κρίσιν occurring in

v. 4, "righteous" repeats "righteousness," and "to act
ungodly" repeats "ungodly ones." Yet there is no
ἀλλά to place the condemnation and the rescue in opposition; καί simply places the two side by side. "Of
Sodom," etc., is the appositional genitive; "Sodom"
is a Greek plural.

Only three Greek words: "incinerated, condemned
with catastrophe." Now, however, a perfect participle
brings out the thought as to what this judgment signifies for all future time. While it is added only here,
Peter's readers see that also the other two tremendous
judgments have the same significance, in fact, any
other judgments that are prominent in history have
this significance. The perfect participle means that,
once being set as an example, the judgment remains so.

Μελλόντων ἀσεβεῖν, so apt a construction in the Greek,
cannot be duplicated in English. It is a genitive (objective) plural participle with a dependent present
infinitive and no article: "any about to be living ungodly," i. e., any that live so in the future. God has,
indeed, set such awful examples of the sudden judgment in the course of history so that all the world
may take warning as to what ungodliness must most
surely meet. The destruction of Jerusalem and of the
Jewish nation is most remarkable — lest it be regarded
as being merely a piece of ancient history. By a miracle of judgment God has for almost twenty centuries
kept the Jews, who are as hardened in obduracy as
ever, under the eyes and the noses of the whole world,
a ὑπόδειγμα indeed!

7) It is quibbling to fault Peter for calling Lot
"righteous"; Gen. 19:28-32 is plain. Peter describes
him as being "so wearied or worn down by the conduct
of the ἄθεσμοι in excess" (see ἀσέλγεια in verse 2).
Athesmoi (found only here) are *homines nefarii qui
nec jus nec fas curant* (a synonym is found in I Pet.
4:3), "nefarious ones" who care for neither law nor

conscience. Such were the Sodomites, and in this
nefariousness they went to unbridled excess, compare
Gen. 19:4-11. God rescued Lot.

8) The γάρ clause is not a parenthesis but naturally follows what precedes and elucidates what Lot
had to bear. It is perfectly plain why this is added:
Peter's readers are in much the same position as Lot;
they will be still more so when the pseudo-teachers
appear with their libertinistic excesses. Right here
is the proper place to add this clause, at the end of
the judgments: **for by sight and hearing the righteous one, dwelling among them, from day to day
kept torturing a righteous soul with lawless works.**

Robertson 126 calls βλέμμα an "apparent solecism";
but it is not, as Abbott claims, "baboo Greek," nor is
it like modern "pigeon English." Since the time of
Euripides (also Epictetus, Lucian, one papyrus, and
Philo) the word means *Anblicken, Sehen* (B.-P. 225),
which is exactly correct here beside ἀκοή.

It is difficult to understand why this clause should
be called *schwerfaellig*. Its word order is as exact as
it can be. Remember, the Greek word order indicates
careful emphasis. Here the emphasis rests on the first
datives and on the verb; these are placed in the emphatic positions. It was, indeed, just as Peter has
stated it: *"by sight and hearing . . .* Lot was doing no
less than *torturing* his soul." Since he is called "righteous Lot" in verse 7, "the righteous one" properly has
the article of previous reference; "a righteous soul"
also tellingly repeats "righteous" and by omitting the
article makes "a righteous soul" pointedly qualitative.
"Dwelling among them" is added in an unemphatic
position since this only explains that Lot had the
wickedness of the Sodomites constantly before his eyes
and his ears. There is no indication that Lot felt
twinges of conscience for "dwelling among them."

Unfortunately, Luther follows the Vulgate: *aspectu enim et auditu justus erat, habitans apud eos, qui diem de die animam justam iniquis operibus cruciebant*: *"denn dieweil er gerecht war und es sehen und hoeren musste, quaelten sie die gerechte Seele von Tag zu Tage mit ihren ungerechten Werken."* When the first two datives are regarded as modifying "the righteous one," and when the singular verb is changed into a plural, Peter is regarded as saying that Lot was constantly made to see and to hear with sneers that *he* was righteous, and that the *Sodomites* kept torturing his soul. In other words, why did he not get out of these cities? This interpretation calls for no refutation. It was *Lot* who kept torturing (not merely "vexing," our versions) a righteous soul (descriptive imperfect) "with lawless works" (no article, again qualitative), namely his own soul.

One reason that a few commentators complain about the awkwardness of this sentence is the fact that Peter has so many significant touches in this clause. They are plain enough in the Greek, but it is difficult to convey them into other languages in the same clear manner.

9) Now we have the apodosis, which truly matches the whole protasis (v. 4-8): **the Lord knows how to rescue godly ones out of temptation but to keep unrighteous ones for judgment day while being punished, especially those trailing along behind flesh in lust for defilement and despising lordship.**

It is overrefinement to say that Peter should write: "then this proves that." It is quibbling to demand that Peter should speak first of the unrighteous and secondly of the godly. It can readily be seen that Peter puts the unrighteous last because he has much more to say about them.

The subject and the verb are transposed, also the infinitive and the object are twice transposed, which

lends them an emphasis that is according. In verse 4
"God" is the proper term when referring to the Old
Testament judgments; that does not, however, make
"Lord" = "God" when Peter comes to speak about the
New Testament and has called Christ "God" in 1:1, 2,
and "God and Lord" in 1:2. He certainly knows how
to rescue (iterative present) godly ones (the opposite
of the "ungodly ones" referred to in v. 5) from temptation. Thus he rescued Noah and Lot.

Δέ, "on the other hand," he knows how to keep unrighteous ones (opposite of "righteous Lot," v. 7, "the
righteous one," and "a righteous soul," verse 8) for
judgment day while they are being punished. Τηρεῖν
markedly repeats the τηρουμένους used in v. 4 and refers
to keeping them in hell as the added participle shows:
"while being punished" ("under punishment," R. V.;
not final: "to be punished," A. V.). While the unrighteous are on earth, Christ still labors to save them;
but when all his labor is in vain, he holds them in hell
for the day of judgment at his Parousia.

10)   When Peter adds: "especially those trailing
along behind flesh," etc., we see that he refers to the
pseudo-teachers mentioned in v. 1, of whom he has
already said that they will bring in covertly heresies
of perdition, even denying the Master who bought
them. These are the worst, and they are thus named
"especially." The present participles describe them as
they are here on earth, hence we have the substan-
tivization "those trailing," etc. They are not leaders,
but travel or trail along "behind flesh," their leader.
Anarthrous "flesh" is strongly qualitative and is to be
understood in the ethical sense as being the opposite
of "spirit." The addition "in lust for defilement" makes
plain all the vileness that Peter has in mind. The genitive is objective: "lust for defilement." Men ought
to shrink from defilement; these men lust after it,
crave all its filth. With such lust "flesh" wants men

to tag behind it, and it will give that lust all the defilement that it wants.

The other characteristic is even worse: "despising
(thinking down on) lordship" (again anarthrous, qualitative). This carries forward the idea of "denying the
absolute Master" stated in verse 1. Vile flesh is their
leader, lordship that is lordship indeed they utterly
despise, repudiate entirely. Of course, Peter has
Christ's lordship in mind; here he speaks in general
terms and uses anarthrous nouns; the τούς marks the
great class here referred to, the worst of all, which
also enables Peter to proceed with smoothness to his
further denunciatory description.

Denunciation of the Heretical Leaders, *v. 10b-22*

10b) This section is poured out in one torrent.
It recalls Christ's denunciation of the Pharisees recorded in Matt. 23:13-39. Peter's is written in the
third person. The tenses vary. The explanation for
this is not the fact that some of these heretics were
already present when Peter wrote; he describes not
some but *all* of them. They are the ones of whom
Peter says in verse 1: "there *will be* pseudo-teachers."
All of them are still in the future. When he is de-
nouncing them Peter is not pedantically bound to
future tenses; he uses the present, the future, the
aorist as he needs them: these men *are* — shall be —
did; his readers understand perfectly that Peter refers
to the coming liars.

**Darers, self-pleasing, they do not tremble when
blaspheming glories, where angels, being greater in
strength and power, do not bring against them blasphemous judging before the Lord.** "Darers" is a
noun; "self-pleasing" is an adjective because the Greek
has no equivalent noun. The two nominative appositions that are thus placed forward are exclamatory.

Peter stands aghast before these "darers" who dare to do what he states; before these "self-pleasers" who let nothing, not even the divine lordship, stand in the way of their pleasure. They blaspheme "glories" without even a tremble. Can daring go farther, blasphemously mocking at the divine when this would interfere with their ἡδονή or pleasure?

Δόξαι, "glories," are the glorious attributes of Christ that are identical with "the glories" mentioned in I Pet. 1:11. In I Pet. 1:11 Peter says that the Spirit of Christ testified in advance to the Old Testament prophets the *sufferings* regarding Christ and the *glories* after these sufferings. Both the sufferings and the glories pertain to his human nature: the sufferings to his state of humiliation, the glories after the sufferings to his state of exaltation. As the sufferings are manifold (plural), so are also the glories (plural). The singular is more commonly used: "God *Father* of the glory" (Acts 7:2; Eph. 1:17); *"Jesus Christ* of the glory" (James 2:1), "the revelation of his glory" (I Pet. 4:13); "the Lord of the glory" (I Cor. 2:8); also "the *Spirit* of the glory and of God" (I Pet. 4:14). The singular always denotes the sum of the divine attributes shining forth; the plural, "the glories," which occurs in both epistles of Peter (and in Jude 8) spreads out this sum, each divine attribute of Christ (communicated to his human nature) being one of these great glories.

Any and all of them these false teachers blaspheme with brazen daring and do not even tremble. There is nothing more terrible that a man can do. Will Christ not instantly strike down him who mocks at his glories? When Peter's readers get to hear such blasphemy must they not be shocked? Such daring is more common than ever now. Whether it is done with a sneer or with polite words, the divine glories are denied to the man Christ Jesus by rationalists and modernists with horrible daring and with no tremor of fear.

Luther makes these *doxai* "majesties," our versions "dignities," leaving unsaid who is referred to. Some think of human magistrates, the majority thinks of angels, good angels, or devils, or both. God forbid that anyone should call the devils "glories"! Evil angels, devils, cannot be blasphemed, for God's own curse rests upon them. The good angels are called *doxai* nowhere in Scripture. To point to Eph. 1:21 and Col. 1:16 is unconvincing, δόξαι is the very term that is lacking in these passages. Peter uses it in I Pet. 1:11 with reference to *Christ*.

Peter is speaking of the greatest crime on the part of the coming heretical teachers. How can anyone believe that this climax of crime consists in blaspheming angels, yea, in blaspheming devils? Or in blaspheming *human* authorities? It consists in blasphemous attacks on the glories of our Lord and Savior Jesus Christ, the God-man. As the "lordship" in verse 10a is Christ's, so the "glories" are Christ's; the one is his whole "lordship," the other all the "glories" through which his divine attributes exercise their lordship. Despising the former in their minds, these men proceed openly to blaspheme also the latter in words.

11) The enormity of this their crime is made evident when Peter adds "where angels, being greater in strength and power (than these heretics who are mere men), do *not* bring against them (these men) blasphemous judging before the Lord" although they richly deserve it for blaspheming the Lord's own glories. The Greek word "blaspheme" and thus also the adjective have a wider application than they have in the English. They are applied not only to God and to things directly connected with him but also to men, when one denounces them in God's name.

When "angels" (qualitative, no article) is used without modifiers, the word always refers to good angels. They are, indeed, far greater than these blasphemous heretics. Yet when such angels hear these heretics blaspheme such things as the Lord's own "glories," in spite of all their burning indignation because of this horrible crime on the part of such worms of dust they do *not* come to their Lord and bring against these blasphemers a retaliatory act of judging (κρίσις, a word expressing an action) and in mockery hurl back on their own heads the blasphemy they have uttered.

Κατ᾽ αὐτῶν, "down on, against them," refers to these "darers, self-pleasing ones," these blasphemers who deserve "blasphemous judging." A strange exegesis regards "glories" as the antecedent, "glories" in the sense of devils! The good angels do not blaspheme even the devils! To justify such an exegesis we are told that one should consult Jude 9; yet Jude had not as yet written his epistle. We shall see later what Jude says. Jude, like Peter, would not call devils "glories."

12) After stating the supreme crime of the coming heretics Peter foretells their judgment. **But these as irrational animals, born** (only) **as physical for capture and perishing, blaspheming in connection with things they are ignorant of, in this their perishing shall even perish.**

We construe "as irrational animals"; this is modified by "born (only) as physical for capture and perishing" as animals generally are; the perfect participle "having been born as physical" states that they are still in this and in no higher state. The A. V. changes the word order and joins φυσικά, in the sense of "natural," to ζῶα: "as natural brute (ἄλογα) beasts." These men, Peter says, live as nothing but animals, they are born physically for the purpose that some other animal or man may sooner or later pounce upon them; they are thus born only for the purpose of perishing. A devastating description but one that is literally true. We can see men all about us living and finally perishing just as animals do, being just physical and nothing more.

This is the wider description that applies to any number of men who lead only an animal existence; hence Peter adds the narrower description with reference to these heretics: "blaspheming in connection with things they are ignorant of," being "irrational" to this frightful extent. The neuter plural ἐν οἷς incorporates its own antecedent. Among the "things" referred to are the "glories" mentioned in verse 10; but the neuter relative includes still more. Many holy things, of which these heretics in reality know nothing, are the objects of their blaspheming. Among men who are leading a mere animal existence these ignorant blasphemers are the most "irrational" and thus the worst. They could at least omit their blaspheming, the more so since they are so densely ignorant about the things at which they direct their blasphemy.

Peter is right: heretics cannot let sacred things alone. Everlastingly, as though the devil is riding them, they cast their slurs, their stabs, their ridicule, etc., at what they have never even learned to know.

These "in this their perishing shall even (shall indeed) perish"; we have ascensive, intensifying καί. The phrase "in this their perishing" has the article of previous reference. Both φθορά have the same meaning: physical perishing; but the verb "in this their (physical) perishing *shall indeed perish*" is intensified and equals "shall perish far worse than merely physically."

Peter's wording has been called rough in comparison with Jude 10. Rough? Why, Peter's language is concentrated, compact, and thus powerful, trenchant, devastating. Jude 10 is not its equal. Jude plainly repeats in a weaker way what Peter hurls as one blow. Three times blasphemy is used, three times perishing; and not only this, one of each three is not used in the same sense as are the other two; "blasphemous judging" is distinct, "shall indeed perish" is likewise. Jude does not have the equal of such telling expressions. Yes, Peter loves to repeat words (that is readily seen here), but one should also see *how* he does his repeating.

13) The long line of participles which follows makes a grand unit of v. 12-17. The whole section is woven as one great piece. The Greek is flexible, and Peter knows how to use its flexibility. He continues: **intending to bring away wages of unrighteousness, counting the revel in the daytime a pleasure; spots and blemishes, reveling in their deceits while feasting together with you; etc.**

The better reading is κομιούμενοι, which the A. V. follows. This is a future participle, and such future participles are rare in the New Testament and denote purpose. When they are anarthrous they are also volitive. Here the sense is "intending to bring away wages of unrighteousness" (not A. V.: "shall receive," i. e., bring away). This intent or purpose is very properly mentioned first in Peter's list, for this purpose and intent casts light on the entire description that follows. It heads the list; we do not connect it with verse 12.

The R. V. accepts the other reading: ἀδικούμενοι and then has difficulty with μισθὸν ἀδικίας and translates "suffering wrong *as* the hire of wrongdoing." The fact is that this reading causes difficulty for all those who prefer it, all renderings and explanations seem forced and labored. Mayor even asserts: "Another example of the author's love of farfetched and artificial expressions," i. e., an irresponsible use of words on Peter's part. This reading should be given up.

The intent of these libertinists is, in modern slang, "to get away with it." This explains the following.

They propose to bring away "wages of unrighteousness," what they can get out of unrighteousness (either genitive of origin, subjective, or qualitative genitive). What they will really get verse 12 has already stated.

Peter continues with descriptive present participles: "counting the revel in the daytime a pleasure," thinking it fun to devote not only the evening or the night but also the whole day to such reveling. The sense of τρυφή is put beyond question by the following ἐντρυφῶντες: revel in luxury (compare Luke 7:25). This is a part of what they intend to get out of unrighteousness. These convivialists begin early, Isa. 5:11.

Peter inserts two nominative nouns between the nominative participles; they are exclamatory as are those occurring in verse 10 and express Peter's disgust: "spots and blemishes!" or: "filthspots and scabs!" There is no need to combine them with the preceding or with the following participle.

"Reveling in their deceits while feasting together with you" — that is the worst of it. It is not a reveling in food, drink, and gaiety alone; it is reveling "in their deceits," in putting their lying, libertinistic teaching into practice by deceiving the true Christians. The entire damnableness of such conduct is thus made plain. "Feasting together with you" is added in order to round out the thought. You are to be caught by these deceits of theirs, by which they would persuade you Christians that you have all the right in the world to such revels in deceits. Libertinism catches many by its deceits.

The A. V. is again right in adopting the reading ἀπάταις and rejecting ἀγάπαις, the reading which is adopted by the R. V.: "in their love feasts." "*Their* love feasts" is not the same as Jude 12, "*your* love feasts." Somebody, it seems, altered Peter's statement by changing one letter; this was, perhaps, done in order to obtain the same word that Jude has; this, how-

ever, destroys the very point of Peter's clause, the
reveling "in deceits." There is no reason for ques-
tioning the reading ὑμῖν: "feasting with you," as though
"you" militates against the future coming of these
libertinists and speaks of them as being already present
among the readers. "You" will be the same congregations when these deceivers come.

14) Peter proceeds: **having eyes full of an
adulteress and unable to cease from sin;** this wording
is more graphic than "full of adultery" (abstract).
The vision of these eyes is filled only with the images
of an adulteress. These eyes are unable to cease from
sin (C.-K. 182 3, genitive of separation; R. 516,
ablative genitive). Peter thinks of Matt. 5:28.

With this goes **enticing** (baiting) **unstable** (i. e.,
weak) **souls:** luring women to commit adultery and
drawing men on to join these lewd fellows in adultery.

Sexual vice and covetousness go together in the
New Testament: **having a heart exercised** (like a
gymnast; the perfect to indicate the continuing condition) **in covetousness;** the genitive after γυμνάζω, a
construction that is also found in the classics. Theirs
is a heart that is fully trained and is ever training for
covetousness. Note how the two ἔχοντες make adultery
and covetousness parallels.

Again the exclamation: **children of curse!**
marked by a divine curse. Peter states what they are;
he does not curse them. "Darers, self-pleasing!" in
v. 10 is what they are for themselves; "spots and
blemishes!" in verse 13 is what they are in and for the
church; "children of curse!" is what they are for God.
These nominative exclamations could not be transposed.

15) The change from present participles to an
aorist finite verb with an aorist participle is made
with perfect smoothness. After looking at these
libertinists as they constantly act in this and in that

respect Peter now looks at them comprehensively in regard to everything that they will do when they come, looks at this prophetically as though it were already past and done: **having abandoned a right way, they went astray, following out the way of Balaam, the (son) of Bosor, who loved wages of unrighteousness but had rebuke for his own deviation from law, a dumb beast of burden by speaking in human voice hindered the prophet's deviation of mind.** The right or straight way is the one that is laid down for us by the Lord in his Word; the anarthrous noun is qualitative. This "way" they abandoned and wandered astray (the passive, it seems, is here used in the middle sense).

"Following out the way of Balaam" tells us what way they took; the aorist participle is merely prophetically historical to indicate the fact, and ἐκ indicates that they followed "out" this way to its end. It is the way that Balaam once chose and followed to its end, he being the one "who loved (simple historical aorist) wages of unrighteousness." Neither in verse 13 nor here are these wages restricted to money but include all that men hope to get out of unrighteousness by working for unrighteousness. Balaam was offered and sought to obtain much more than gold and silver. Ἠγάπησεν is the proper verb: he loved these wages intelligently and with corresponding purpose. He thought it all out, and his actions corresponded with his thought.

The readings for the name of Balaam's father vary: Bosor (correct) and Beor or Baior (used throughout in the LXX). Josephus and Philo do not have the name at all. The crux is how Peter comes to write "Bosor." Nobody knows.

16) Observe that the two statements go together: Balaam "loved wages of unrighteousness but had rebuke for his own deviation from law." These two facts

stand side by side. The wickedness of his love was made
plain to him by the rebuke. Did he give up his love?
The aorist implies that he did not, and the fact is that
he did not.

Peter adds the astounding phenomenon that was connected with the history of Balaam: "a voiceless beast
of burden (an ass, Matt. 21:5, voiceless or dumb, able
only to bray and not to speak) by speaking (φθέγγομαι,
a choice word) in human voice hindered the prophet's
deviation of mind," gave him his rebuke. Note that
παρανομία and παραφρονία correspond. In both words παρά
means "by the side of": Balaam's action was not on
the path of law but off to the side of this path; his
mind and thinking were of the same kind. The ass
hindered his thinking, but in spite of the rebuke he
had received Balaam eventually went to the end of his
unlawful way, to a miserable death.

Two points are here brought forward. 1) The perverse way of mind and conduct off to the side of the
straight way, the loving of and the clinging to this
deviation. 2) The rebuke, the hindrance put in the
way; having this and yet in spite of it following out the
perverse way to the end. Both apply to the libertinistic
teachers as we see them reflected in the history of the
prophet Balaam.

Not only does Numbers 22 to 24 give us the full
detailed story of Balaam, to which Num. 31:16 (Rev.
2:14) adds the final crime which he perpetrated by
advising the Midianites to corrupt the Israelites to
idolatry and to fornication (Num. 25:1-3 plus 31:16)
and his wretched death (Num. 31:8), but also the
entire Bible contains many references to Balaam: Deut.
23:4; Josh. 13:22; 24:9; Neh. 13:1, 2; Micah 6:5; our
passage; Jude 11; Rev. 2:14. These make this man
stand out as an example. We cannot consider all of
the details but recommend Keil's *Commentar* on Numbers. Balaam is a fearful example of a man who was

"a prophet," whom God told what not to do, whom God hindered in his wrongdoing by even letting a dumb ass speak to him, but who in spite of everything secretly clung to his love for what he thought he could get out of unrighteousness, and so perished.

He had to bless Israel and thus could not get the rich rewards which Balak promised him if he would curse Israel. Then, it seems, he went to the Israelites in order to reap reward there for having blessed and not cursed Israel at such loss to himself. Failing in getting such wages of unrighteousness from either Balak or from Israel, he gave his cunning advice to the Midianites to corrupt Israel and thus hoped for a high reward from them. These three attempts filled the measure of his wickedness. He was wretchedly slain.

The point which Peter would emphasize is not the fact that Balaam failed to get what he loved but that he so loved it that an ass had to give him a rebuke. Peter has called the coming libertinists "irrational animals"; for this reason he perhaps mentions the dumb ass of Balaam's story, the ass in this case being more rational than its master who, though he was a prophet, was blinded by his love for wages of unrighteousness.

17) The pseudo-teachers make a great pretense but disappoint utterly. **These are waterless springs, mists driven by whirlwind, for whom the blackness of the darkness has been kept.** Two poetic figures to express the same thought. In order to get their full force we should know the Orient where springs are so precious, and mists or fogs are valuable for refreshing all that grows by both moisture and shade (Sirach 43:24: "Against this," i. e., the sun that burns up what is green, "helps the thick fog, and the dew after the heat refreshes everything again"). These teachers are, however, "waterless springs"; those who expect living water from them will be disappointed. The second figure emphasizes the thought: ".mists driven by

whirlwind" (λαῖλαψ, Mark 4:37; Luke 8:23), not quietly blanketing the land with reviving moisture and
shade but being blown away with a rush.

Without a figure Peter adds: "for whom the blackness of the darkness (= the outer darkness, Matt. 22:
13) has been kept" (and is still being kept), i. e., reserved; ζόφος is found also in verse 4. This is the fate
that awaits them.

18) "For" elucidates. **For speaking grandiose
things of vainness, they entice in connection with
lusts by excesses of flesh those just escaping from
those conducting themselves in error, promising
them liberty, they themselves being slaves of the corruption.**

Peter repeats the choice word φθέγγομαι (verse 16)
and thereby aptly indicates how these wretched deceivers utter their ὑπέρογκα, grandiose things ("great
swelling words") of vainness. The genitive of the
noun derived from μάταιος does not equal empty (which
would be κενός). Their grandiose things have a certain content, are not hollow; "vainness" refers to the
quality of leading to nothing: all these grand things
are useless for any good purpose. When they are
speaking them these deceivers only entice (the participle is used in v. 14) by using these grandiose words
as bait to dazzle the minds of their poor victims.

But such grandiose words are not enough. These
deceivers put them "in connection with lusts" and do
their enticing "by excesses of flesh" (dative of means).
We note that "lusts" needs no qualifying genitive since
the word, especially in the plural and in evil contexts,
is itself used in the evil sense. So we combine σαρκὸς
ἀσελγείαις, "by excesses of flesh"; but see the note on
"excesses" in verse 2. Their appeal is made to lusts;
the language used by the deceivers is grandiose; the
means are excesses of flesh, i. e., taking the reins off
the flesh so that it can run wild.

The special victims of these vicious deceivers are the newly converted: "those just escaping from those conducting themselves in error," i. e., from the Gentiles living around them. The A. V. has translated with an aorist: "those that were clean escaped"; but the participle is a descriptive present: new converts just escaping. It makes no difference whether ὀλίγως is regarded as temporal or as local; the R. V.'s "just escaping" has reproduced the correct idea. These new converts are just getting away from the old pagan life of their neighbors and associates. On such converts that are still tender, are not yet mature, strong, trained to defend themselves, these monsters pounce and by words, swelling and extravagant, such as no true teacher would dream of using, allure and dazzle their victims by telling them that they can be true Christians, yea, the best kind of Christians and yet indulge their lusts by excesses of the flesh. Can you think of anything more damnable? Matt. 18:6. We note the masterly way in which Peter touches upon the enticing features and brings out the damnableness of the action.

19) The added participle is effective: "promising them liberty, they themselves (αὐτοί) being slaves of the corruption." Paul speaks of "the slavery of the corruption" in Rom. 8:21. Monstrous! Men, who are themselves slaves, in grandiose words promise escaping slaves liberty, a liberty that hurls them back into worse slavery! In 1:4 Peter has written: "having escaped from the corruption in connection with lust in the world"; in 2:12: "born for perishing." Although we are compelled to translate φθορά "corruption" and again "perishing," this is due only to the English, the Greek word has the same meaning throughout: *Vergehen, Untergang*. "*The* corruption" is specific for the worst kind of corruption.

In order to drive home the point about being "slaves" Peter explains: **for by what one has been**

worsted, by that he has also been made a slave, or
has been enslaved. This dictum is axiomatic. Note the
perfect tenses "has been worsted" so as to remain so;
"has been made a slave" so as ever to be one. The
agent is often stated by means of the dative; ἡττάομαι
often has ὑπό with the genitive to express the agent
but also has the dative and even the genitive without
a preposition (Liddell and Scott). Our versions have
translated "of whom," but no person is mentioned, and
"corruption" in the preceding clause is not personified.
One can be defeated and enslaved by something as well
as by somebody.

20) **For if such as escaped the defilements of
the world in connection with knowledge of our Lord
and Savior Jesus Christ are, nevertheless, by these
(defilements), on getting entangled again, worsted,
the last things have become worse for them than the
first,** i. e., their last state has become and remains
(perfect) worse than their first state was before their
escape from paganism.

We should note two points: 1) the anarthrous
ἀποφυγόντες, "such as did escape," is the subject of the
sentence; 2) τούτοις is the dative of the agent with the
passive ἡττῶνται; it is like the two preceding datives of the
agent, in particular like the ᾧ with ἥττηται. It should also
be recognized that the anarthrous "such as did escape,"
i. e., any of this kind whether they are new or old
converts, and the present tense "are worsted" make
the statement general; it is like the preceding statement: "by what one has been worsted, by that he has
been made a slave." The aorist participle "on getting
entangled again" is inserted in order to show only
when and how they are worsted; it happens when they
again get entangled with these defilements from which
they once escaped.

The discussion as to whether Peter is speaking of
the deceivers or of their victims, the new converts,

the ἀποφεύγοντες referred to in v. 18, is unnecessary. Peter first says: "Whatever defeats any person, that thing makes a slave of him." With γάρ he elucidates: "If such as did escape the defilements, etc., are nevertheless (δέ) defeated by their defilements they are in a slavery that is worse than the one in which they were before their escape." To whom does this apply? Peter himself says to such as once escaped and on getting entangled again are defeated. Peter is warning all his readers: entanglement leads to defeat, defeat to a state that is worse than the original paganism.

Peter's elucidation is entirely plain. In verse 19 he says, "by *what* one has been worsted"; now in verse 20, "by *these* (defilements) are worsted." One may also be worsted by something else; Peter wants his readers to think of these defilements in which false teachers will again seek to entangle them. The elucidation covers the enslavement. In verse 19: "by this thing has he been enslaved"; in verse 20: "the last state has become worse than the first" for such worsted ones. This seems to be plain enough.

The elucidation includes more. It is a pity to be worsted by the very things from which we have escaped. How is that possible? Peter explains: by getting entangled again (effective aorist). Πάλιν is to be construed with the participle where Peter places it. But τούτοις is *not* to be construed with the verb: "by these (defilements) are worsted." Entanglement causes defeat. Peter's meaning is: By all means keep from getting entangled again! He intends to address this warning to all his readers. The deceivers will work to get them entangled again. "Entangle" is the proper word; nets were used not only to catch animals but also in combat. We are familiar with gladiatorial combats in which one opponent used a net.

In verse 10 Peter has μιασμός, "defiling," (a word expressing action); now he has μιάσματα, "defilements,"

(a word expressing result), actual filth "of the world."
True, this is moral filth, but it should not be separated
from falseness and error in faith and in doctrine; the
deceivers are to be "pseudo-teachers" (verse 1). In
his elucidation Peter adds that "such as escaped" did
so "in connection with *epignosis* (full, true knowledge)
of our Lord and Savior Jesus Christ." This is the same
word that was used in 1:2, 3, 8, the key word of this
epistle; add *gnosis* used in 1:5, 6. In those other passages we had the genitive of source: knowledge "from"
our Lord; this genitive of source is also proper here:
by the great gift of true knowledge that our Lord and
Savior gives us we escaped. *He* enabled us to escape.
As our Savior he saved us by means of this escape.
All that we have already said in 1:1, 2, 3, 8, 16 on Jesus
Christ as "God," "Savior," "Lord" belongs also here.
Let us add that entanglement in the defilements of the
world and the resultant defeat take place only when
this *epignosis* or true heart-knowledge is sadly dark-
ened and lost, when we separate ourselves from him
who is its source, "our Lord and Savior Jesus Christ."

21) Why is the last state of such persons worse
than the first? **For it were better for them not to
have known the way of the righteousness than for
them, having gotten to know it, to turn away from
the holy commandment delivered to them.** Jesus
says that where only one devil dwelt at first, this devil
later returns with seven others, Matt. 12:45. Not
having known, they would eventually receive fewer
stripes; knowing and not doing, they have many stripes
awaiting them (Luke 12:47); compare also John 15:
22. Regarding ἦν and the imperfect to indicate matters
of the past (necessary, possible, proper) that the
present shows have not turned out as they should see
R. 886, etc. The English and the German have difficulty with the indicative because they look from the
present back to the past whereas the Greek begins in

the past (imperfect) and looks forward to the present. Therefore the English uses its subjunctive. This is not a conditional clause; no ἄν is used or implied, R. 920.

It were better for them not to have truly known (ἐπεγνωκέναι, to match ἐπίγνωσις used in v. 20) refers to the whole extent of this true knowing. Its object is now stated "the way of the (true) righteousness"; its source is our Lord and Savior, verse 20. This is not the way of the merely moral, righteous life; it includes faith. For without faith there is no righteousness (righteous state) or righteous life. It is "the way of the truth" (v. 2) to be both believed and obeyed; "a straight way" (v. 15), the opposite of "the way of Balaam." It is better not to have known this divine and blessed way and to have remained in pagan darkness "than for them, having gotten to know it (ἐπιγνοῦσιν, aorist participle to express the past fact, dative to agree with αὐτοῖς), to turn away (aorist: definitely to turn away) from the holy commandment delivered to them" by Christ. It is better to be a pagan, never to get out of pagan ignorance, than to become an apostate by sinking back into paganism.

"The holy commandment" is "the truth" (v. 2) and not only its moral features (the law). "Delivered to them" includes by human preachers, but the agent behind the passive is "our Lord and Savior Jesus Christ." To turn from his saving gospel commandment is to turn from salvation and from him, the Lord and Savior. That is what becoming entangled again and being worsted by the defilements of the world mean.

22) The filthiness of these "defilements" is presented in all its disgustingness: **There has come to them** (perfect: and so continues) **this thing** (content) **of the true proverb: Dog turned to his own vomit! and: Sow washed herself for a wallow of mire!** What the true proverb says has come to them. The proverb says it in two ways by using both the

dog and the sow as examples. What it says about the dog is taken from Prov. 26:11. What it says about the sow (feminine participle) is taken from secular sources; but Proverbs need not have originated the saying about the dog. This proverb regarding the sow is not otherwise preserved; yet other, and for the most part longer, wordings are found. An interesting one occurs in the history of Ahikar (Harris, in Moulton, *Einleitung*, 244) : "My son, you have acted like a swine which went with decent people to the bath and, when it came out, saw a stinking swamp and went and wallowed therein."

It is well to note that proverbs are not only naturally terse, but that some, as these two instances, are exclamations; hence we should not translate "*a* dog," "*a* sow." At the sight of a man who returns to filth of which he was rid people will point their finger at him and rightly exclaim: "Dog returned to his own vomit!" or: "Sow washed herself for wallow in mire!" In the latter we supply nothing, no second participle "turned" to wallow. The two participles are parallel in the exclamations. Yes, it takes a dog, a sow, to do this sort of thing; but the filthy pseudo-teachers will try to make such dogs and such sows of Peter's readers.

CHAPTER III

Part Three

Denial of the Parousia of the Lord, chapter 3

"Where Is the Promise of His Parousia?"
v. 1-7

1) First, the libertinism of the pseudo-teachers who shall come (chapter 2); secondly, their denial of Christ's Parousia (chapter 3). This denial supports their libertinism. The connection is obvious. Who could let himself go into immoral excess if he believed that the Lord is ready to return to judgment at any time? The climax of the "heresies" mentioned in 2:1 is the denial of Christ's Parousia. Peter crushes this denial and thereby destroys all the other lesser heresies that cluster around this main one.

The claim that the libertinists referred to in chapter 2 are not the same as the heretics mentioned in chapter 3 is untenable. All moral laxity must have and always has the necessary false doctrinal support. The claim that chapter 2 is a late interpolation is the extreme of the other claim that Peter opposes two sets of future false teachers.

Peter begins with a little preamble which resembles the longer one found in 1:12-15. **This already, beloved, I am writing to you as a second epistle, in which** (plural: both) **I am stirring your sincere mind in a reminder to remember the utterances spoken in advance by the holy prophets and the commandment of your apostles from the Lord and Savior.**

Peter makes a division at this point. For the fourth time he addresses his readers as "beloved"

(v. 8, 14, 17), lets his heart go out to them, and draws
their hearts to him. His loving heart is writing "this
already as a second epistle." Δευτέραν ἐπιστολήν is either
appositional or predicative to ταύτην.

The opinion that this other epistle is our First
Peter has been answered in the introduction. These
two epistles are not addressed to the same readers,
are not the same kind of a reminder of the prophecies
of the Parousia. Peter himself says that the two
letters addressed to his present readers have the same
subject and the same purpose. See the fuller details
in the introduction. Those are probably right who
hold that the first epistle that was written to the present readers has been lost. The two epistles here mentioned were written in rather close succession. Peter
says that in both of them "I am stirring your sincere
mind in a reminding or reminder," the epexegetical
infinitive (R. 1086) states the result (R. 127) that he
hopes to achieve by this reminding: "to remember" or
"that you remember" (aorist: effectively), etc. Reminding causes effective remembering in those who are
reminded. In 1:13 Peter has used the same expression:
διεγείρειν ἐν ὑπομνήσει, "to stir up in a reminding."

Instead of saying, as he does in 1:13, "stir *you* up,"
he says more, namely, "stir up your sincere mind."
Of course, the διάνοια, the thinking mind, receives the
reminding and does the remembering, but the adjective
is important. Peter's twofold reminding is directed
toward his readers' "sincere mind," εἰλικρινής, "pure"
as being free from wrong considerations (see Trench).
A mind like that of the false teachers mentioned in
chapter 2 would refuse to be stirred up, would scorn
any reminding that Peter could offer, would only the
more strenuously cling to its false ideas. Peter says
significantly "your sincere (pure) mind" and credits
his readers with having such a mind. His own pure
mind contacts their pure mind, his reminder thus

produces their effective remembering. All of the apostles were somehow masterful psychologists!

2) Peter wants effective remembering "of the utterances spoken in advance (the perfect to indicate permanence, the speaking still continues in Holy Writ) by the holy prophets" in the Old Testament; "holy," so that when the false teachers deny the truth of these prophetic utterances they become guilty of no less than blasphemy. Note what Peter has already said about the inspiration of the prophets (1:21). These Old Testament prophecies are the first things to remember effectively.

But Peter's readers have in addition "the commandment of your apostles from the Lord and Savior." Note how correctly Peter places the two genitives: "of your apostles" *between* τῆς and ἐντολῆς; "of the Lord," etc., *after,* because this is again a genitive of origin or source (as in 1:2, 8; 2:20). Some translators and some commentators seem to misunderstand these genitives. Chase would insert a διά: *"through* your apostles"; our versions "by." "Of the Lord," etc., is placed *outside* of the article, hence it is to be understood differently than the genitive that is *inside.* The Lord is the author of the ἐντολή of the apostles. He sent these apostles with this his commandment, which becomes theirs only in this way.

The holy prophets — the apostles — the Lord and Savior: mark this order. It will make clear that "apostles" is not to be understood in the wider sense so that apostolic assistants may be included. Peter says *"your* apostles." One may say that he refers to the Twelve including Paul (verse 15), for they had the identical "commandment," and the faith of all Christians had this apostolic foundation (Eph. 2:20). But "your apostles" must refer to the ones with whom the readers had come into personal contact. We know that they had such contact with Peter and with Paul (verse 15) ; this is sufficient to justify the wording "your apostles."

One may understand "the commandment" in the broader sense: "whatsoever I did command you" (Matt. 28:20), all of the Lord's teaching that we are commanded to believe and to follow; the entire context that follows, however, justifies us in understanding this expression in a narrower sense, namely as referring to the Lord's commandment to look for and to be ever ready for his Parousia. Of this the prophets made advance utterance, and this the apostles preached as coming "from the Lord and Savior" (the title is the same as that used in 1:11).

3)   Peter is stirring up the mind of his readers effectively to remember these things: **knowing this first that there shall come at the days' ends mockers in mockery, proceeding according to their own lusts and saying: Where is the promise of his Parousia? for since the fathers fell asleep all things remain on in this manner, from creation's beginning.**

Peter has written τοῦτο πρῶτον γινώσκοντες in 1:20; it is a turn of phrase which he probably used frequently when he was teaching and preaching. He did not feel that he should here use the accusative and not the nominative because an infinitive precedes, the implied subject of which is ὑμᾶς. To call this an anacoluthon as though it were an irregularity is unjustified. Peter proceeds *ad sensum*, and none of his readers would feel this as an irregularity.

Yes, the first thing they should know or realize is that "mockers shall come at the days' ends," meaning that the second thing to realize is the Parousia itself which shall come after these mockers have appeared. We have the same future tense as in 2:1: "there shall be pseudo-teachers, such as shall bring in covertly heresies of perdition." In 2:1 and 3:3 Peter is prophesying. First Peter 1:20 has the singular: "at the

times' *end*" (Jude 18: "at the time's end") ; Peter has
the plural: "at the days' *ends.*" We see that Peter
can vary his expressions. These ending days really
began after Pentecost, and they are called so because
nothing more is in prospect except the return of Christ
in his Parousia. Always, however, no date is assigned
for the Parousia.

There shall come "mockers in mockery" emphasizes the mocking by adding the cognate phrase, which
is good Greek and should not be termed Hebraistic.
By placing the verb first and the subject last Peter
makes both emphatic: *come they shall* . . . and
that *mockers* (no article, qualitative). They certainly
have come; we still hear their voices. Bigg calls
ἐμπαιγμονή "an impossible formation," but this statement
is on a par with the assertion that the whole verse is
not a part of the prophetic apostolic message. Although it has not yet been found elsewhere the word
is formed as a number of others are. Wohlenberg
offers four samples. Since they have been warned in
advance Peter's readers are not to be surprised when
such mockers appear; forewarned is forearmed.

When Peter adds the fact that such mockers will
proceed with their mockery "according to their own
lusts" he indicates that they are of the same nature
as the men described in chapter 2, and that he now
describes their worst crime, their blasphemous mockery. Mockery and lusts will go together. These are
their marks. The appearance of such men is a sign
of the days' ends.

4) Peter quotes their mockery. His revelation
is detailed, complete. His readers are to know all
about it before they hear it uttered. Peter shows them
the entire hollowness of this heretical mockery. His
readers are armed and made ready. This mockery is
concentrated in the question which the heretics will
fling at the readers: "Where is the promise of his

Parousia," i. e., where is its fulfillment? They mean:
"You say that Jesus promised a great Parousia; well,
show it to us, where is it?" Catch the sneer in this.
Catch also the folly. When the Parousia occurs, such
sneers will die in the mocking throats. Compare Isa.
5:19; Jer. 17:15; Matt. 24:38; Luke 17:26-30. On
"Parousia" see "the power of our Lord Jesus Christ
and Parousia" in 1:16.

These mockers will even present an argument:
"for since the fathers fell asleep all things remain
on in this way (οὕτως: so, as they are) from creation's
beginning"; ἀφ᾽ ἧς (ἡμέρας) = "since" (R. 978), really
ἀπ᾽ ἐκείνης ἡμέρας ἥ (dative, R. 719): "from that day
on which" the fathers fell asleep (aorist). These are
"the fathers" of the Christians who are living when
these mockers shall arrive; the fathers are formerly
living but now departed believers. Did all of these
not die without anything happening? Since they died,
"are not all things remaining in this manner (progressive present, R. 880), just as they are from the
very beginning of the creation onward?" "The
fathers" are not Old Testament people but any and
all Christians who are dead when the mockers point
derisively at them. Even now, they say, everything
moves on just as it did from creation's beginning
onward.

This type of argument is strong because it ignores
a good deal. So is many another argument. It upsets
those who fail to see what is ignorantly or purposely
ignored. The crushing answer to all such arguments
and thus also to this one is to show what they omit
or ignore. This is the logic involved. All conclusions
that are based on *some* facts but omit other, contrary
facts are false *in toto*. It is a fact that all things have
gone on in their accustomed way for ages and ages,
in particular since Jesus lived on earth. The time
since these arguments were used has now been extended

to almost 2,000 years. Ergo, quit talking about this Parousia of Jesus!

We note that denial of the Parousia involves very much more. In 2:1 we see that it signifies no less than denying the one who bought us. It denies his own Word and promise and that of all the apostles and the prophets. How many facts that are revealed by the Word may be thus denied Peter does not indicate. The present denials of the Parousia include the rejection of Christ's deity and of all the great saving facts. The longer the world stands as it is, the surer the mockers are that their fallacy is sound. Their predecessors operated with this hollow soundness from the start as Peter told his readers they would.

5, 6) Mockers shall come saying: "Where, etc.?" **For it escapes them in making this claim that there were heavens of old and an earth existing out of water and between water by the Word of God, by means of which things** (those presented in this whole situation) **the then world by being flooded perished; on the other hand** (it escapes them, that) **the present heavens and the earth by the same Word have been treasured up for fire, being kept for a day of judging and of perdition for the ungodly men.**

In this way Peter answers the assumption of the mockers and their reasoning that there will never be a Parousia of Christ. He simply states the two facts that escape these wise fellows. The one fact lies in the past, namely, the Flood; the other in the future. The Word of God that by its original creation put the world into such a condition that all living things on its surface perished "by water," that same Word is keeping the present heavens and earth "for fire" in order to send the ungodly to perdition, these mockers being among them.

Τοῦτο is to be construed with θέλοντας and means *bei dieser Behauptung* (B.-P. 554), "in making this claim," the one mentioned in v. 4; or *dies im Sinne habend*, "having this in their minds." Since these mockers have half-facts in their minds such as those advanced in v. 4, the facts mentioned in v. 5-7 escape them. The first forgotten fact is stated in v. 5, 6: there were heavens of old and an earth "existing out of water and between water by the Word of God," and by means of these things, i. e., these situations of the heavens and of the earth, the world of that time, i. e., the κόσμος of men, "inundated by water (κατακλυσθείς, see 2:5, κατακλυσμός) perished." Strange that this fact should escape the notice of anybody! But it does so to this day. All things have not been just so (οὕτως) as they are; at one time the whole cosmos of men perished (historical aorist; the passive participle is also an aorist).

Peter mentions the ancient heavens because they rained torrents. He describes the earth as existing (the second perfect feminine participle συνεστῶσα is to be understood in this sense, B.-P. 268) "out of water (having risen out of it) and between water" (that above in the clouds, that below in the fountains of the deep). Genesis 7:11: "The same day were all the fountains of the deep broken up, and the windows (literally, floodgates) of heaven were opened."

We translate δι᾽ ὕδατος "between water"; see R. 580 for the "between" idea of διά. Some commentators have difficulty with this phrase, some think that the solid earth "consists" of water. How did the heavens of old and the earth get to be thus? "By the Word of God." These mockers go back to the "beginning of creation"; so does Peter, but he goes back to the time when God by his Word made the heavens and the earth with water above, all around, and under the earth.

Δι᾽ ὧν puzzles some interpreters; they seek for the antecedent of this plural, and some of them change it into the singular: "by means of which λόγος." The

antecedent is not the two kinds of water; not the *logos*
(Word) and the water; and also not heavens and earth.
The antecedent ˙is the neuter plural: "by means of
which things," i. e., the existence of heavens from of
old and the existence of an earth with water in the
relation described. Without these things which were
so through God's own creative Word there could have
been no Flood. Three times Peter says, "water," for
he is writing about the Flood. Note that κόσμος is used
as it was in 2:5: "the world" of men; in v. 7 we have
"the ungodly men."

7) We have already noted in 2:5, etc., that the
Flood is a type of the last judgment, to which Peter
now turns with δέ, "on the other hand." He once more
points upward to "the present heavens," for in his
Parousia Christ will descend from them and to "the
earth." Will they, indeed, always remain "thus"
(οὕτως) as we now see them, as these mockers dream
and claim they will? "By the same Word" that made
both to be as described in v. 5 "they have been treasured up for fire." At one time *water* brought judgment; finally *fire* shall do so. At one time water
descended from the heavens upon the earth; finally
fire shall alter both the heavens and the earth completely. The periphrastic perfect "have been treasured
up" emphasizes the duration. To be thus treasured
up for fire = to have fire applied at last. Do not ask
me what kind of fire this will be. God has all the
varieties of fire that he needs for his purposes: the
fire to burn wood, the electric fire of the lightning bolt
that strikes in an instant in the sky, the fire that burns
in the sun, the fire to change the heavens and the earth
at the last day, and another most terrible unquenchable
fire for the devils and the damned in hell.

The durative present participle completes the
prophecy: "being kept for a day of judging and of
perdition (ἀπώλεια is found twice in 2:1) for ungodly

men" (objective genitive). This will be a day when Christ judges and sends all the ungodly to perdition. Critics ask where Peter got this information and then search for an answer in Jewish apocalyptic sources such as the Book of Enoch, also in Persian or in Egyptian sources or elsewhere. Peter had the Old Testament, the instruction of Jesus, the immediate revelation of the Spirit himself: "He shall show you things to come," John 16:13. "Treasured for fire" is further explained in v. 10-13.

"The Day of the Lord Will Come as a Thief,"
v. 8-13

8) **Moreover, let not this one thing escape you, beloved, that one day with the Lord** (is) **as a thousand years, and a thousand years as one day.**

Entirely too much escapes the mockers, hence their ignorant mocking (v. 5-7). This is a point that may escape even Peter's readers, which he, therefore, wants them to note well: "that one day with the Lord is as a thousand years, and a thousand years as one day." This is Peter's own statement which is based on Ps. 90:4: "A thousand years in thy sight are as yesterday when it is passed and as a watch in the night." God created time. "In the beginning," Genesis 1:1, is the first tick of the clock of time. It has ticked ever since that time, never faster, never slower. Thus we have the seconds, the minutes, the hours that to us are "a day" and finally a year and a thousand years. As time began, so it shall end (Rev. 10:6), time shall no longer exist, the last tick has been reached.

With the Lord time is evidently not what it is to us who live in time. He is above time. Peter does not say that the Lord is timeless, which he, of course, is, but that *his* relation to time must never be confused with *our* relation to time. A day seems short to us, a thousand years a very long period. With the Lord

a single day is "as a thousand years," and vice versa.
Let us not overlook the two ὡς, "as." Peter does not
say: "A single day *is* a thousand years, and a thousand
years *are* a single day." Peter does not use ὡς as being
equal to "like" or as a mere conception of the mind
but in the sense of "as in reality." Whether it be a
day or a thousand years as we count time, both are
really the same with the Lord; neither hampers nor
helps him. Those who apply this dictum to the word
"day" in Genesis 1 and make "day" in Genesis 1 = a
period that consists of millions of years find no support
in this passage. Nor does Peter refer to the thousand
years mentioned in Revelation 20.

9) Peter himself tells us what he means: **Not
slack** (or delaying) **is the Lord with his promise as
some consider slackness** (or delay), **but he is longsuffering in regard to you, not intending that some
perish, but that all have room for repentance.**

Τῆς ἐπαγγελίας is the genitive of separation: "the Lord
does not hold back *from* the promise, from fulfilling
it (B.-D. 180, 5), as some count holding back." These
"some" are not the mockers who claim that all this
talk about the Parousia is nothing, these are some
of the Christians who will be disturbed by these
mockers. Since the Parousia has not yet come, and
since time keeps going on, "some" who are unable to
account for this ever-increasing delay and who let what
verse 8 states escape them get uneasy and think that
the mockers are perhaps right in claiming that there is
nothing to this whole promise of Christ's return.

Peter furnishes the correct answer: God uses time
so as to serve his purposes of grace. For that purpose a single day is as a thousand years to him, a
thousand years as a single day. To him time, whether
it be brief or long, is an entirely minor matter just so
his gracious purpose is accomplished. Look at it in
this way. Then you will not think of delay, dilato-

riness, emptiness of the promise. Then you will see
that the Lord's waiting is his longsuffering toward you,
his holding out long with the blessed intention (βούλομαι
is often used in this sense, notably in I Tim. 2:8; 5:14;
Titus 3:8; etc.) that none are to perish (aorist), but
that all are to have room (i. e., fully have time and
opportunity, aorist) for μετάνοια, repentance, change of
mind and heart by contrition and faith. This longsuffering extends the time, puts off the Parousia.
What is a thousand years to the Lord if he can thereby
bring many to repentance?

The Lord alone knows how to extend his longsuffering. We now look back upon almost 2,000 years;
see how many have repented. Does that in any way
affect the certainty of the fulfillment of his promised
return? The mockers, who scorn repentance, scoff
at that promise because their wish is father to their
thought (θέλοντας, verse 5). Woe to them if that
promise is true!

10) Peter has settled the question of the Lord's
delay. He now tells his readers how the Lord's day
will come. The delay may be one of a thousand
years or of several thousands for that matter, all are
"as a single day" with the Lord; but when the time
of longsuffering is at an end, the Parousia and the
tremendous things that accompany it will not require
a thousand or several thousands of years; then one
day will be "as a thousand years." Suddenly, in-
stantaneously the end will come. The Lord will need
no time at all. **But there will come the Lord's day
as a thief, in which the heavens with a cracking
crash (M.-M. 564) shall pass away; moreover, elements, being heated, shall be dissolved, and earth
and the works in it shall be burned up.**

Peter purposely describes what shall occur on that
day of the Lord. There will be a sudden conflagration
of the universe. Since Peter puts this forward twice

(note verse 12) he leaves the impression that the mockers will not care to dwell on this feature. Peter, however, makes the application only to his readers. The verb is placed emphatically forward: "there shall come indeed." Although it is without the article, ἡμέρα is definite, is made so by the genitive. Jesus already used the comparison of a thief (Matt. 24:43; Luke 12:39). While it is briefer Peter's thought is the same; a thief comes and aims to come when no one expects him. The suddenness of the coming is meant in this sense — as far as we are concerned. So will the Lord's day come.

The description is the main feature. On that day the heavens, which at one time sent down torrents for the Flood (verse 5), will themselves pass away ῥοιζηδόν, with a sudden crackling, sizzling, sputtering roar, *mit sausendem Geraeusch, mit Gezisch, unter Geprassel, mit rauschender Schnelligkeit*, B.-P. 1182. Δέ, "on the other hand," the elements, being heated, shall be dissolved. Nearly every time the word occurs there is some discussion as to the meaning of στοιχεῖα. Because "earth" follows, some take the "elements" to be the stars. Peter makes no such restriction. Καυσούμενα means "heated" and explains "shall be dissolved."

Καί combines what is said about the elements and about the earth and the works in it, i. e., all that men have built on earth: earth and all these works shall be burned up. Jesus said: "The heaven and the earth shall pass away," Mark 13:31; Matt. 24:35. We consider the variant reading εὑρεθήσεται, "shall be found or discovered," out of the line of thought.

11) By repeating and thus emphasizing the things that shall occur Peter strikes the hortatory note already at this point. **All these things thus being dissolved, what kind of people ought you to be in holy conduct and godliness, expecting and**

eager for the Parousia of the day of God, on account
of which heavens, set on fire, shall be dissolved, and
elements, being heated, shall be melted!

The present tense of the genitive absolute is without a reference to time. Such a reference is not required in the Greek since the λυθήσεται occurring in
verse 10 has already taken care of it. So we do not
say that λυομένων aims to state that the dissolving is as
certain as if it were already taking place.

Ποταπούς is not used in indirect questions and thus
should be regarded as exclamatory with a note of
hortation: "What kind of persons ought you to be!"
The word δεῖ is used to express every kind of necessity
or obligation, the specific kind will be determined
according to the context. It is here indicated by the
"in holy conduct (a word that is used several times
in First Peter) and godliness." Peter uses a number
of abstract nouns in the plural. It would be awkward
to translate these into English, yet they are pertinent
here where each of the readers has his own conduct
and godliness. Peter makes the phrase weightier by
using two nouns: "in holy conduct and godliness."

12) He also uses two participles: "expecting and
being eager for the Parousia of the day of God." One
may expect and yet not be eager regarding what he
expects; also eagerness is to fill the hearts. We need
not labor the sense by taking σπεύδω in the sense of
"hasten," speed up the coming of the day of the Lord,
so that it will come sooner than it would otherwise
come. We question whether the holy conduct of Christians can hasten the day of judgment, whether this is
the teaching of the Bible. The decline of faith and
the coldness of love would have more of a tendency to
hurry the day along. This verb is widely used in the
sense of "to be eager" (see Liddell and Scott for illustrations), which fits perfectly here as an intensifying
synonym of "expecting."

In 1:16 we have "the power and Parousia of our Lord Jesus Christ"; in 3:4 "his Parousia"; now "the Parousia of the day of God." On παρουσία see 1:16. It fits both the Lord and the day since either can be present. Here "the Lord's day" precedes in verse 10, and so we have "the Parousia of the day"; but "of the day of God" — at which we pause since Peter twice uses "God" when he is naming Jesus Christ (see 1:1, 2). We regard *"Lord's* day" (verse 10) and now *"God's* day" as naming the same person: Jesus Christ.

In verse 10 Peter writes only "in which," now he says "on account or because of which" (day). That day shall bring to an end the whole present universe and thus shall be the cause that "heavens, set on fire, shall be dissolved, and elements, heated, shall be melted." Peter repeats verse 10 but now varies the wording. Both "heavens" and "elements" are qualitative because they are anarthrous. Although they are heavens they shall be "dissolved," for they, too, are "elements." "Set on fire" or "being fired" expounds the adverb "with a crackling crash" which was used in verse 10: they shall pass away, be dissolved in a roar of fire (Isa. 51:6, "like smoke"). The participle "being heated" is repeated with "elements," but in place of "shall be dissolved" we have the synonym "shall be melted" or rather the preferred reading "are melted" (present tense), which, like the genitive absolute, disregards the point of time. These variations between v. 10 and v. 12 are important for showing us how v. 7 is to be understood: "the present heavens and the earth treasured up for fire."

13) **But new heavens and an earth new according to his promise** (ἐπάγγελμα, a term that denotes result: the promise as it stands) **we are expecting, in which righteousness dwells.** The two "new" are placed chiastically and thus bring "heaven and earth" together. Καινός is new over against old. Heavens and

earth are to be new in this sense and not in the sense
of νέος, just called into existence. This is also the sense
of Rev. 21:1. We are expecting them according to
Christ's promise, at which the mockers may scoff all
they please (v. 4). Nor is the Lord slow and slack
with this promise (v. 9); he is only longsuffering. In
v. 11 Peter says "you"; with "we are expecting" he
now joins his readers in confessing his sure hope.

The old universe was spoiled by the fall. Sin per-
meated it with its effects. That includes all of nature,
animate and inanimate, the heavenly bodies, and the
heavens also. All shall become new. On that day fire
shall make them new so that in them "righteousness
dwells," even every trace of unrighteousness being
forever removed. We may call this a sort of personification of this quality (righteousness) on which
the approval of the Lord's eternal verdict rests. Read
Rev. 21:1-5.

The question is raised as to whether this universe
shall be annihilated, and a new heaven and earth shall
be created *ex nihilo*. In order to answer it one should
not stop with passages like Ps. 102:26; Isa. 51:6;
Jer. 34:4; Matt. 24:35; Mark 13:31; Heb. 1:11; Rev.
20:11. One should include also Rom. 8:19-22; I Cor.
7:31; Rev. 21:1-5. The heavens and the earth shall
be renovated, renewed, purified, made perfect. There
shall be no further separation between earth and the
abode of God; they shall be one at last. Besides Rev.
21:1-5 one should read the whole of Rev. 21:10-27 and
close with Heb. 11:10.

Look for These Things and Be Ready,
v. 14-18

14) **Wherefore, beloved, expecting these things,
be diligent to be found by him as spotless and unblemished in peace.** We once more have the loving
address, now in connection with Peter's final admoni-

tion. He repeats "expecting" from v. 12. The connection is causal: "since you expect these things, be diligent to be found." Αὐτῷ is the dative of the agent with the passive verb, R. 542 and A. V. It is strange that R. 537, B.-D. 192 ("dativus ethicus"), and the R. V. ("in his sight") should labor to make it a dative with the adjectives when the dative next to the passive infinitive is a dative of the agent. "Be found by him" undoubtedly refers to the judicial finding of Christ, the Judge, at the day of his Parousia.

Peter calls the libertinists and the mockers σπίλοι καὶ μῶμοι in 2:13, "spots and blemishes"; the readers are to be the opposite, ἄσπιλοι καὶ ἀμώμητοι, "spotless and unblemished." Both adjectives are predicative and are thus nominatives with the infinitive; they need not be accusatives. We are spotless and unblemished when we have daily forgiveness and live in obedience and expectation of the day of judgment. "In peace" is the same peace that Peter wants multiplied for his readers in 1:2. To be found "in peace" at the Parousia means in the peace which Christ has established, the condition when all is well between him and us. The best commentary is Matt. 25:34-40. "Be diligent" repeats the effective imperative from 1:10; and we may note Peter's own diligence in regard to his readers in 1:15.

15) In addition (καί) Peter urges: **And consider our Lord's longsuffering as salvation even as also our beloved brother Paul according to the wisdom given to him has written to you, as also in all (his) letters when speaking in them of these things; etc.** Peter reverts to verse 9 and now uses the noun "longsuffering" in place of the verb and also the same verb "consider." The delay in the Lord's return is "longsuffering" on his part; this silences the mockery (verse 4) which laughs at the Parousia as being something that will *never* come. Peter says: Consider the Lord's longsuffering in thus waiting "as salvation."

,Verse 9 has indicated how it is salvation: the Lord
does not intend that some should perish, but that all
have room for repentance. When the readers see this
longsuffering and see it as salvation for so many they
will be fortified against all mockers of the promise of
the Parousia.

What Peter adds is most interesting. First the
clause: "even as also our beloved brother Paul according to the wisdom given him wrote to you." To Peter
and to his readers Paul is "our beloved brother Paul,"
dearly loved and highly regarded. "According to the
wisdom given him" names and emphasizes Paul's
wisdom as being one that has been given to him by
the Lord; δοθεῖσαν is the very participle that Paul himself uses so often when he speaks of the grace "given
to me." This is true wisdom from on high. The letter
which Paul wrote to the people whom Peter addresses
was written *in toto* according to the wisdom which was
bestowed on Paul by the Lord. That is why Peter
appeals to it as seconding what he tells his readers
regarding how they should live in the expectation of
the Lord's Parousia.

Peter says "our beloved brother Paul"; he has already said "your apostles" in 3:2 when he had Paul
and himself in mind. Peter himself has written a
letter to these his readers (3:1); including the one
that Peter is now writing them they will have three,
all of them being to the same effect. Paul and Peter
agree perfectly. We scarcely need to say this, for all
the apostles agree perfectly since one and the same
Lord and Spirit bestow one and the same revelation and
inspiration upon them (John 16:13, 14). There is no
peculiar Pauline, Petrine, Johannine doctrine.

It is inconceivable that Paul should write to people
among whom only Peter and other apostles had worked
(Rom. 14:20), and equally inconceivable that such
people should have been Jewish and not Gentile Chris-

tians. The reason for Peter's writing First Peter to Christians that belonged to Paul's great field is clear (see the introduction to First Peter). A similar situation in which Paul could have written to people who lived in a field that belonged to Peter is hard to conceive. The very fact that we know Paul's history so well and Peter's only as far as Acts takes us leaves us at sea in regard to 2:1, 2, 15. To whom could these two men be "our apostles" who had worked among them, each of whom had written them a letter, to whom Peter is now writing another and referring to his own and to Paul's earlier one? No plausible answer to this question has ever been given.

The fact that v. 1 cannot refer to First Peter is plain. That letter has been lost. Have we this letter of Paul's to which Peter refers? Many say that we have, but when they try to identify it, there is complete disagreement. Romans, Ephesians, Galatians, Colossians, Thessalonians, Hebrews, even Laodiceans (Col. 4:16) have been mentioned. For ourselves we admit that the letter written by Paul, to which Peter refers, has been lost to us. We know of two other letters of Paul's that have been lost; he refers to the one in I Cor. 5:9, to the other in Col. 4:16. We confess that it seems strange that valuable apostolic letters should have become lost, at least two of Paul's and one of Peter's. But struggle as we may, all struggling is in vain. Arguing about *God*, and how *God* could permit such a thing is hypothetical human reasoning and is too thin to support any conclusion.

All this means — to our great regret — that we cannot identify the readers of Second Peter, to whom both Peter and Paul had already written a letter. Someone has said, although in another connection, that when we really do not know, the scientific — and let us add, the honest and the sensible — thing to do is to say so.

16)   Peter adds: "as also in all (his) letters when speaking concerning these things," the ones that Peter speaks of in this letter, i. e., coming heretics, libertinists, mockers, Christ's Parousia, the way in which Christians should expect it and be in constant readiness. Peter is acquainted with Paul's letters, and his readers are acquainted with them, at least with a good many of them. Ἐν πάσαις ἐπιστολαῖς, without ταῖς, is the correct reading (R. 773). If the article were used, the sense would be that of a fixed collection of all the Pauline letters; the assertion of B.-P. 275, 1, that the article dare not be absent is thus incorrect.

The assumption that Paul was already dead is unwarranted. Peter died in 64, Paul died after this date. The fact that churches to whom Paul had written a letter should have secured copies of other letters of his is easy to understand. What is so difficult to understand is the fact that two letters that were written directly to them by two such great apostles as Paul and Peter were should not have been copied and widely spread and thus have been preserved from becoming totally lost.

The participle λαλῶν is restrictive: "when speaking of these things." Paul's letters cover more territory; just now Peter's interest centers in "these things" about which he himself writes in this his own letter. *All* that Paul had written up to this time, and *all* that Peter now writes are in complete agreement. This is said so that Peter's readers may be certain and may stand firm when the heretics arrive.

Peter adds: **in which** (feminine: letters of Paul) **there are some things difficult to understand, which the ignorant and unstable wrest, as also the rest of the Scripture, to their own perdition.**

The reading ἐν αἷς is assured and not ἐν οἷς, "among which things." In Paul's various letters there are some things that are difficult to understand. To regard this

as a criticism of Paul on the part of· Peter is to misunderstand the words. Paul wrote a good deal; Peter
has already noted the divinely bestowed wisdom with
which he wrote. Such wisdom always penetrates to
the bottom of its subjects and does not skim over the
top as a shallow mind does. The effort to understand
some parts of such writings naturally taxes the νοῦς or
thinking faculty. That is what the mind is for. We
have but two brief letters of Peter, yet even in them
everything is not written in ABC fashion.

The point that Peter makes is the fact that some
people, namely the ignorant and unstable, wrest these
difficult things in Paul's letters, "torture" them, "put
them on the rack" (M.-M. 593), *sodass sich ein falscher Sinn ergibt* (B.-P. 1237), force them, like some
poor victim under torture, to say what their torturers
want them to say. These difficult things are chosen
for torture because the easier things cannot so readily
be forced and twisted.

These ignorant persons do not stop with certain
things in Paul's letters; they do the same with the rest
of the Scriptures; they would be compelled to because
all inspired writing speaks the same thing with the
same wisdom. But those who wrest such writings do
it "to their own perdition."

Peter is speaking of what is being already done
("wrest," present tense); he does not need to add
that the heretics, whose coming he has foretold, will
follow the same course. We know that they have
always done so, are now doing so. Because in 2:14
Peter uses "unstable souls" as a designation for the
future victims of false teachers is no reason for denying that such future false teachers will also themselves
not wrest the Scriptures.

To what writings does καὶ τὰς λοιπὰς γραφάς refer?
Zahn, *Introduction*, 277: to books in general, of course,
those of a religious character, such as would claim

recognition among Christian readers. This view is based on the use of λοιπός; if the Old Testament were referred to, it is said that ἄλλος or ἕτερος should have been used. The linguistic point has been labored by saying that if "the rest of the writings" referred to the Old Testament, this would make the whole Old Testament an appendix to Paul's letters, in fact, would say that the ignoramuses wrest *all* the Old Testament books and the *whole* of each book. So the Old Testament writings are ruled out or are only allowed a place by the side of other writings, chiefly, however, uninspired writings. Zahn's argument emphasizes the fact that an adjective such as "holy" is omitted.

But what about *"the* rest of the writings"? What about 1:19-21 with its reference to "every prophetic writing" and the assertion that these were truly inspired? Peter wrote 1:19-21 with a view to chapter 3. To say that the ignoramuses wrest not only some things in Peter's letters but do this as well with religious writings in general is merely saying that this is a sort of habit which they have. B.-P. 753 is not impressed by the argument derived from λοιπός, for he translates *die andern Schriften* just as our versions do. Mayor sums up: "The result of the whole discussion is practically to compel us to take τὰς λοιπὰς γραφάς in the obvious sense 'the rest of the Scriptures' [not just 'writings'], and we cannot escape the conclusion that the epistles of Paul are classed with these. The intention of the author of Second Peter seems to be to regard the Pauline epistles, or those of them that he knew, as γραφαί because they were read in the churches along with the lessons from the Old Testament."

We add John 16:13. Also Bigg's remark: "It does not necessarily follow that St. Peter placed his fellow apostles on the same level with Moses and the old prophets; but he may very well have placed them even higher." Let that settle the argument.

"For their own perdition" repeats the word ἀπώλεια that was used in 2:1, 3; 3:7. It is perversion of Scripture that insures "perdition." Be careful of Scripture!

17) Οὖν resumes the admonition. **You on your part, then, realizing (these things) in advance, keep on guarding yourselves lest by having been led off with the error of the nefarious ones you fall from your own stability!** Forewarned is forearmed. The middle means "keep guarding yourselves," and ἵνα μή = lest as it does with verbs of fear. The danger is that of being led away by the error of the nefarious ones (see 2:7) and thus falling from (out of) your own stability; note "unstable" in verse 16, "unstable souls" in 2:14, and "having been made stable in the present truth." The aorists mean actually being led off and actually falling from. This would be a calamity indeed.

18) **But keep growing in grace and knowledge from our Lord and Savior Jesus Christ!** This is the positive side. We again have the present imperative to denote continuance. One grows in grace and knowledge by assimilating more and more of the divine favor and of its gifts and of the divine truth. The key word "knowledge" again appears here at the very end of the epistle (1:5, 6; the compound in 1:2, 3; 2:20, 21).

The genitive is obviously to be construed with both "grace and knowledge"; it is obviously the same kind of a genitive with both. Some commentators note the latter and disagree with those who make "of our Lord and Savior Jesus Christ" a genitive of source with grace and an objective genitive with "knowledge." Yet they separate the genitive from "grace" and let "grace" stand alone. Why is it so difficult to see that "our Lord and Savior Jesus Christ" is the source and fountain of *both* "grace and knowledge"? Here we have additional evidence that also in 1:1 the genitive is that of source: "righteousness *from* our God and Savior

Jesus Christ"; "knowledge *from* our God and Lord
Jesus Christ"; so also in 2:20; 3:2, "commandment
from the Lord and Savior." On "our Lord" see 1:2;
"our Savior," 1:1.

Peter closes with a doxology: **To him the glory
both now and for eoh's day!** The "amen" is a late
addition. Peter's doxology fits his letter exactly and
is entirely unique. The uniqueness lies in "both now
and for eon's day." Only Sirach 18:8 has "in eon's
day," but he understands "day" in the sense of the
"eon" or eternity in which the longest earthly life is
as a drop in the ocean. Some understand Peter's
εἰς ἡμέραν αἰῶνος in the same way and make the genitive
an apposition. Better is the view that it is the qualitative genitive (C.-K. 94), but this is not satisfactory
enough. Still better is the view of G. K. 199, where,
however, the phrase is divided: εἰς ἡμέραν (sc. Κυρίου)
and εἰς τὸν αἰῶνα. We disregard the division but keep
the reference to the Lord, which undoubtedly = v. 10:
"there shall come ἡμέρα Κυρίου, the Lord's day." We
regard it as a possessive genitive: the last, great "day"
of the Lord which no longer belongs to "now" or to
time but to the "eon," eternity.

The burden of this epistle is that "day." We have
been told what shall occur then. Although that day
is called "day" it cannot be a day of twenty-four hours
or an earthly day. It belongs to eternity. All glory
belongs to our Lord and Savior Jesus Christ now and
specifically at the time of that wondrous day when he
shall return in eternal glory, when that day ushers in
eternity for the universe.

Soli Deo Gloria

The Interpretation of the
Epistles of St. John

The First Epistle
of St. John

THE USUAL ABBREVIATIONS ARE EMPLOYED

INTRODUCTION

The fact that the First Epistle of John was written by the Apostle John and by no one else is beyond serious question. This letter is an encyclical that is intended for the congregations that were under John's special care; it was occasioned by the antichristian teachings of Cerinthus and of his following. It is usually supposed that this letter was written only to the congregations in the province of Asia; but when Peter wrote in the year 64 he addressed all those in Pontus, Galatia, Cappadocia, Asia, and Bithynia, and we think that now, about twenty-five or thirty years later, John would address even a greater number in this extensive territory.

The same pen that wrote this letter wrote the Fourth Gospel. Before the year 66 John and other apostles were forced to leave Jerusalem because of the war that ended with the destruction of Jerusalem and the Jewish nation. John made Ephesus his headquarters and worked from this as a center until he died at an advanced age about the year 100. He was buried at Ephesus. He writes as an old man. He does not indicate that he is the founder of the congregations addressed in his letter but that he has been known to them for many years and that a tender bond of affection exists between him and all his many readers. Seven times he calls them τεκνία, "little children," twice he addresses them as παιδία, six times as "beloved." This is the voice of a father.

Cerinthus was active in Ephesus during this time. He taught that Jesus was the physical son of Joseph; that the "eon Christ" was united with Jesus at his baptism but left Jesus before his passion and his death. He rejected all the Gospels, all of Paul's letters, and

(363)

accepted only parts of Matthew and of Mark. He was
a former Jew from Egypt and combined Jewish ideas
with what we may call the beginnings of Gnosticism
and sought to produce a spiritualized Mosaism, which
was to be a universal religion. He retained circumcision and the Sabbath. The Jewish conception of the
millennium was attributed to him by the Alogi; hence
those church fathers who opposed chiliasm and thought
that Revelation taught this doctrine ascribed Revelation to Cerinthus and thus rejected this writing. This
heretic left no writings, but Irenæus (*Adv. Haer.* 1, 26;
3, 3, 4; etc.) and others supply a reliable account of
him and of his teaching.

According to Eusebius, Irenæus quotes Polycarp,
his teacher and a pupil of the Apostle John: "That
John, the disciple of the Lord, having gone to take a
bath in Ephesus and having seen Cerinthus inside, left
the baths, refusing to bathe, and said: 'Let us flee lest
also the baths fall in since Cerinthus is inside, the
enemy of the truth."

It is safe to date the composition of John's letter
at Ephesus some time after the year 80. It should not
be called "catholic," for it is not addressed to *all*
churches that were then in existence but only to all
those whom John can call "my little children."

This letter is plainly polemical. Dangerous heresy
called it forth. In this letter the writer emphasizes the
deity of Christ and pronounces a severe verdict on
those who deny the deity. Three times John uses the
frank word "liar." He also refers to "the blood of
Jesus Christ, the Son of God" (1:7; 5:5, 6), which is
directed at Cerinthus.

A second denunciation, resting on the first, deals
with the hatred against those who are born of God as
his sons and children, who are repeatedly urged to love
God. This thought is likewise stressed throughout the
letter and is directed at Cerinthus and his separatist

following. Other points of a similar nature are mentioned, these two stand out as supreme.

The question is discussed as to whether this letter was written before or after John's Gospel. It is immaterial what answer is given to this question. We think that the letter was written before the Gospel.

Since there were copies of this letter in so many churches late in the first century, the authorship and the authority of this letter were at the very beginning placed beyond question. Quotations and allusions to passages go back to the earliest times; tradition on this point is unanimously in favor of Johannine authorship. There is a direct line of evidence from John through his pupils Polycarp and Papias to Irenæus. Zahn, *Introduction*, III, 180, 184, 191. This letter was thus at once and without hesitation placed into the New Testament canon. Modern efforts to cast a doubt on its canonicity are unavailing.

A curious circumstance regarding the letter is the fact that it seems to have no divisions. Commentators divide it in one way or in another and state their reasons for such a division; but when one reads the letter, the proposed divisions do not satisfy. They are upset by the series of repetitions and reiterations that occur throughout the letter. That fact leads some interpreters to complain about the lack of logic; but this letter has no formal parts such as we commonly use and expect. It is constructed according to a different and a higher method.

Observe that "light" and "darkness" (1:5, 6) are repeated, also "truth" as light. Forgiveness of sin is mentioned several times. The truth that Jesus Christ is the Son of God is the golden thread of the entire pattern. Connected with him is his blood (1:7; 4:6), the propitiation for our sins and for the world's sins (2:4). "Liar" is used three times. "His commandments" (plural and singular) is found in 2:3-8; 3:23;

4:2, 3. Pivotal is. "love." As the letter moves along, new threads are woven into it, some that disappear, others that reappear. Yet the whole is but one pattern. The heretics are introduced at 2:18 'and reappear in 4:1, etc., and in 5:18, 19. Sons of God, children of God, being born of God begin at 2:29 and continue throughout the letter. Believing on the name of his Son Jesus Christ is introduced at 3:25 and is found also in 4:16; 5:1, 5, 13. Bearing witness appears toward the end (5:6-11). At the very end we have "idols," which seems strange to many. This inventory is not exhaustive.

What do these data mean? John rises above formal divisions and parts. This letter is built like an inverted pyramid or cone. The basic apex is laid down in 1:1-4; then the upward broadening begins. Starting with 1:5-10, the base rises and expands and continues in ever-widening circles as one new pertinent thought joins the preceding thought. One block is not laid beside the other so that joints are made. There are really no joints, not even where the new thoughts are introduced. The line of thought simply spirals in rising, widening circles until all is complete. Keeping. from idols (5:21) is only the brief, final touch.

This is an unusual structure in writing but for that very reason is superior to the common types of composition. There are others in Scripture that are equally unusual. One is Isa. 40 to 66 which is built of triads within greater triads, these again being within still greater triads, and each of the little triads is a block, a little individual poem by itself.

I have never found the like in all literature. No poetical composition approaches this in structure. Ecclesiastes and parts of Proverbs are also unique in structure. In the latter each little piece is a perfect verbal and thought gem by itself; it is like a diamond in which not one facet could be changed. Each gem, perfect in itself, can be admired by itself yet is set into a perfect pattern with a few others and with them forms a unit that is to be admired as such. Then these patterns are combined into still greater designs.

In the Biblical books there are grander buildings of thought than even our best secular writers have conceived. Inspiration has produced some marvelous, incomparable results. Let some competent student display them for us as they deserve to be displayed. John's First Epistle is built like this:

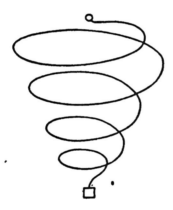

John's Pivotal Statement,
Centering on God's Son Jesus Christ,
1:1-4

1) When the structure of this epistle is unaerstood, as we attempt to sketch it in the last part of our introduction, we no longer expect the common ancient form of a letter which has the name of the writer, a designation of the readers, and a greeting. Such a beginning would be incongruous. We also do not say that the heading of the letter was lost, or that John wrote these four verses as a substitute for it. Preamble, exordium, preface, and the like are also terms that do not fit these four verses. They constitute no less than *John's basic, pivotal statement* on which he builds the thoughts of the epistle in ever-widening circles. Verses 1-4 are the first, the essential, the concentrated piece of the whole.

That which was from the beginning, that which we have heard, that which we have seen with our eyes, that which we did behold and our hands did handle concerning the Logos of the Life — and the Life was manifested, and we have seen and are bearing testimony and are declaring to you the Life, the eternal one, who as such was with the Father and was manifested to us — that which we have seen and have heard we are declaring also to you in order that you, too, may have fellowship with us, and this fellowship, moreover, of ours is with the Father and with his Son Jesus Christ; and these things we on our part are writing in order that our joy may be as having been filled full.

All this is thetical, positive: the deity of Jesus Christ, the Logos who was with the Father before time began, he being the Life who was manifested in time; him the apostles heard, saw, beheld, touched with their hands, they were the direct witnesses who testify, declare, write all this in order to have also John's present readers in the fellowship with them, this fellowship with the Father and his Son, to the joy of John and the other witnesses. Yet a cutting edge against a terrible negation underlies every word. Cerinthus and his supporters are not witnesses, have heard, seen, beheld, touched nothing; deny the deity of Jesus, the Life eternal; destroy the fellowship of the believers with the Father and his Son; contradict what the apostles testify, declare, write, and attempt to turn their joy into grief.

Read historically with the eyes of the first readers, the full significance of every line appears. Every repetition is freighted with power. All the clauses combine in a mighty basic unit that is impressive, convincing, uplifting, encouraging the readers to stand solid in the divine fellowship against any little antichrist who may have appeared (2:18).

The voice is that of John; it is the same voice that testifies in the Fourth Gospel. The simplest words convey the deepest, the loftiest thoughts. Καί is the great, simple connective. This prologue involuntarily recalls the greater one found in the Gospel.

Why the five neuters (the fifth occurs in v. 3): ὅ, "that which"? Besser has given the correct answer: *That which* was from the beginning was *He*, the Logos of the Life, God's Son Jesus Christ; *that which* we have heard, seen, beheld, handled was *He*. The neuter conveys more than the masculine would, namely in addition to the person all that this person was and is and ever will be for us. Throughout these neuter relative clauses speak of the person plus the grace, the power, the salvation, etc., that are conveyed to us by this person. Jesus Christ cannot be separated from what he was and is for us. Both belong together like the sun and its glorious light. The theme of this letter is the same as that of the Gospel: the eternal Son incarnate for our life and salvation to the confounding of all antichrists.

Like scores of such phrases in the Greek ἀπ' ἀρχῆς needs no article. This is the same "beginning" as that mentioned in Gen. 1:1 and John 1:1. In Gen. 1:1 "in the beginning" marks the moment when time began for the acts of creation that followed; in John 1:1 "in the beginning" marks the same moment but in order to tell us that already at that time the Logos *was*. "From the beginning" looks forward from that moment to all time that follows; but the verb ἦν (it is not "became," ἐγένετο, and not "has been") leaves all eternity open to "that which" already then "was." John looks forward from the beginning because he would call attention to the point that the Logos of the Life existed long, long before his manifestation in the fulness of time.

The four neuter relatives are identical: *"that which* was in the beginning" is *"that which* we have heard, *that which* we have seen with our eyes, *that which* we did behold and our hands handled."* All four are made plain by the added phrase περὶ τοῦ Λόγου τῆς Ζωῆς and the parenthetical, elucidative statement that follows. John does not use the simple accusative τὸν Λόγον τῆς Ζωῆς, for this could mean "the Word of life" or the gospel as preached and taught. He uses περὶ, "concerning," which excludes such a meaning, no one preaches. *concerning* the Scripture Word but preaches that Word itself. What the apostles heard, saw, beheld, handled was the personal Word, the person who is "the Logos of the Life." How they were able to do this verse 2 tells us twice: He was manifested, he was incarnated, the Logos became flesh and tented among us, and so we beheld his glory as of the

Only-begotten from the Father, full of grace and truth
(John 1:14).

Thus we object to the introduction of various objects: we have heard *the words of Christ;* we have
seen with our eyes *the miracles* of Christ; we have
beheld *the glory* of Christ; our hands handled *the
resurrection body* of Christ. John's verbs have one
object: "that which," and they do not divide this. This
object is made clear by the phrase "concerning the .
Logos of the Life." We do not reduce this to mean the
gospel or anything less than the Logos himself in his
whole manifestation.

The genitive in "the Logos of the Life" is appositional. "In him was life," John 1:4. "This is the true
God and eternal life," I John 5:20. "I am ... the life,"
John 14:6; "the resurrection and the life," 11:25. Absolutely and in himself he is "the Logos of the Life"
(John 5:26). This "Life" is not a mere idea, an abstraction such as we get by induction or deduction
when we study living creatures. It is the divine essence
itself in its personality and its activity. Yet "the Logos
became flesh" (John 1:14), "the life was manifested,"
in the fulness of time the Son was born of a woman
(Gal. 4:4, 5). The Logos of the Life became *"the Bread*
of life" so that those who receive him shall not hunger,
those who believe on him shall not thirst (John 6:35) ;
it likewise became *"the Light* of life," that whosoever
follows him shall not walk in darkness (John 8:12).
"Herein was the love of God manifested in us, that
God has sent his only-begotten Son into the world,
that *we may live* through him" (4:9). "The Life" is
repeated three times: Ὁ Λόγος τῆς Ζωῆς — ἡ Ζωή — τὴν Ζωὴν
τὴν Αἰώνιον, emphasizing the term, re-emphasizing it;
for he who is "the Life" eternal and in eternity was
manifested as the Bearer of life to us who were dead
in our sins.

John alone uses the term Logos; he uses it here, later in his Gospel, and in Rev. 19:13. This is the second person of the Godhead who is called "the Word" because he is the complete and final Revelator of the will and the thought of God. Rev. 19:11: "Faithful and true," v. 13: "and his name is called The Logos of God." He is the "Amen, the faithful and true Witness" in Rev. 3:14.

See further on John 1:1 and note that John did not borrow "Logos" from Philo, that the idea expressed by this name is found throughout the Old Testament. Like other titles of the Savior, the instructed church has always understood this one, for she is taught about the Savior.

The four asyndetic clauses with which John begins are most impressive. Four is the number of common rhetorical completeness. This is complete testimony; testimony that offers the completest assurance for the readers; testimony that stands for the truth and against any and all contradiction of that truth. The plurals "we" refer to the apostles; they are not editorial plurals that refer to John alone. The witness of one man is not accepted in court; there must be at least two, preferably three witnesses (Matt. 18:16; Deut. 17:6; 19:15; John 18:17, 18). Jesus himself follows this principle; in John 5:31-39 he appeals to two other witnesses besides himself. II Cor. 13:1; Heb. 10:28; Matt. 26:60. John here appeals to at least twelve witnesses. In I Cor. 15:5-8 Paul appeals to more than five hundred to establish the resurrection of Jesus. The facts are incontrovertible.

The four statements are cumulative, the evidence is piled up mountain-high. Each added verb says more than the one that precedes it; the four progress, form a climax. To see is more than to hear; to behold more than to see; to handle more than to behold. Four direct contacts constitute these witnesses as true and competent witnesses. Any one of these contacts would be sufficient to make one a witness; the four contacts are exhaustive. Ears, eyes, hands, all were employed.

John has two perfects and two aorists. The perfects convey the thought that what "we have heard," what "we have seen," has its continuous effect on us. John's Gospel uses a number of such significant perfects. Beside them John places two decisive aorists of fact: "we did actually behold," "we did actually handle." As the perfects stress the continuing effect, so the aorists stress the actuality. John wants both just as he uses four clauses.

The second and the fourth verb have additions. "We have seen with our eyes," i. e., with our *own* eyes; "our hands did handle," i. e., our *own* hands actually did so. These additions are placed chiastically. Seeing and beholding are not the same. What these witnesses saw they examined with all care at close range in order to see fully so that their eyes should in no way deceive them; thus they actually beheld. Their eyes were not enough, they used their hands to substantiate the experience of their ears and their eyes; they actually touched and handled. In John 1:14 all this is summed up: "we beheld his glory," etc. Among other passages that deserve notice are John 2:11; 6:68; 20:27, 29; Luke 24:39; Acts 10:41.

Can Cerinthus or can any of the antichrists (2:18) offer counterwitness? What have they heard, seen, beheld, handled? Nothing. They have absolutely nothing to offer but their own imaginations and delusions. That is true to this day with regard to all who deny the deity of Jesus, the efficacy of his blood for our sins, etc. The case is plain even for people who have only common sense and ordinary judgment: on the one side, competent witnesses in solid array — on the other, no witnesses at all, nothing but perverted men who with brazen boldness contradict the completest testimony. John gives them the right name in 2:22 as he does in 2:10 and 4:20.

2) John adds a parenthesis that is introduced by καί; he might have used a subordinate clause with γάρ: John chooses to coordinate, it is his method of expressing his thought, which is at once simple and direct. "And" makes the statement an independent statement, which is the more effective: "and the Life was manifested," the aorist states the past fact. "The Life" is "the Logos of the Life" who is now named more briefly as he is in John 1:4b and in 14:6. The verb includes the whole manifestation from the incarnation to the ascension but especially from the baptism until the ascension, the time when the apostles beheld his glory (John 1:14).

For the second time John says "and we have seen" and lets this one verb suffice; he uses the perfect to indicate the extent of their seeing the manifestation. But John now adds "and we are testifying and declaring to you the Life, the eternal one." The object is to be construed with all three "we" verbs. Not for themselves alone have they seen, but they have seen as witnesses who are ever to testify and to declare what they have seen. "You shall be my witnesses . . . to the end of the earth," Acts 1:8. We do not know whether any of the other apostles were still living when John wrote this letter; but like Abel, though dead, they still testify (Heb. 11:4); they do so to this day. In v. 4 John adds "we write these things" and shows in what form his readers have the apostolic testimony and declaration.

For the third time John names the Logos, and now he designates him as "the Life, the eternal one." It is true that elsewhere ζωὴ αἰώνιος means "the life eternal," either the life which we now have (John 3:15, 16, but minus the article) or the glorious life which we shall have (Mark 10:30; Luke 18:30). Here both "the Life" and "the Life, the eternal one," have the article of previous reference which refers back to "the Logos of the Life."

· Still more decisive is the relative clause "who as such was with the Father," ἥτις is qualitative. The feminine gender is only grammatical; the predication is that of a person, and hence we translate "who." John names the Son once more; he adds "eternal" because he wants us to understand that Christ the Life was a person whose distinctive quality it is that he was with the Father even in all eternity. We have πρὸς τὸν Πατέρα; in John 1:1 it is πρὸς τὸν Θεόν. Our English "with" conveys the idea of πρός rather inadequately. R. 623 calls it the "face-to-face" preposition and in 625 adds that it is employed for living relationship, intimate converse. We take this in the highest sense. It is not predicable of angels or of saints but of deity, of the Son alone.

In all eternity the Son *asarkos,* who was to be manifested and was manifested in the fulness of time *ensarkos,* was with his Father, was with God. In both the Epistle and the Gospel John puts this infinite fact into the simplest words. Only an inspired mind could do this. Speculative minds attempt to say more but fail and say less and thus what to that extent is not true.

John says once more: "And he was manifested to us," the apostles. But the full light now falls upon the simple statement: he who was with the Father, in interpersonal communion with the Father in all eternity, he "the Life," "the Life, the eternal one," was manifested to us, became flesh, tented among us, allowed us to behold his divine glory (John 1:14). John again has the simple καί, which indicates only the juxtaposition of the two statements, but for this reason they are clear as crystal. Like Cerinthus, all deniers of the full deity of Jesus will reject what John declares.

3) Fault should not be found with John's construction. The parenthetical statement (v. 2) is essential and is also lucid; John even continues as he began in .verse 1: "that which we have seen and have heard," the continuity being smooth and unbroken. But this relative clause is not a mere repetition of the clauses of verse 1 for the sake of emphasis. The repetition is now illuminated by all that verse 2 adds. All that verse 1 conveys is thus revealed in verse 3. Seeing is here placed before hearing because the two verbs "was made manifest" match seeing more directly than they do hearing; even such things do not escape John. Hearing is mentioned for the third time, for it refers to the words and the teachings of Jesus which are supreme in his entire manifestation.

John says once more, "We are declaring," but he now adds not merely "to you" but *"also to you."* This might mean that the apostles declare their entire testimony to many others and thus also to the many readers for whom this letter is intended, which fact is entirely true. Yet from the next clause: "in order that you, too, may have fellowship with *us*," we see that John is not thinking of his readers and of other Christians but of his readers in relation to the apostles. "Also to you" means that *you* may have what *we apostles* have.

"We are declaring" should be left as comprehensive as it is; it includes this letter as well as all oral preaching. This does not mean that all of the twelve apostles in person now or at any previous time preached the Logos of the Life to the readers of John's letter. "To declare," ἀπαγγέλλω = *melden* (G. K. 65) and in verse 2 is paired with witnessing. How the testimony of the apostles reached and reaches John's readers, whether by actually hearing one or more of them, by reading their written testimony, or by having it told them as apostolic testimony by other men, is entirely immaterial. It is unwarranted to say that the testimony was *one* although its form was now Pauline, now Petrine, now Johannine.

John does not say "in order that you, too, may know what we apostles know"; he advances at once to the blessed effect of the testimony: "in order that you may have fellowship with us" (John loves μετά). The present subjunctive "may have" is as comprehensive as is "we are declaring." Whenever and wherever the apostolic testimony is properly declared, its purpose is always fellowship with the apostles. This is also true with regard to all of John's readers.

John adds at once: "and this fellowship, moreover, of ours is with the Father and with his Son Jesus Christ"; καί adds this, δέ marks it as being another point. The article with "fellowship" is that of previous reference; its repetition with the possessive adjective makes it appositional and emphatic (R. 776), the adjective ἡμετέρα is stronger than a pronoun in the genitive would be: "this fellowship (of which I am speaking), the one that is our own," i. e., that of us apostles. John does not say that the fellowship of the apostles "may be" with the Father, etc., but that it *is*. Since the copula is omitted, the assertion is made more terse.

Why does John not say at once "that you, too, may be having fellowship with the Father and his Son"? Why does he insert the apostles and say with whom *their* fellowship is to be enjoyed? Because of the antichrists, Cerinthus and his separatist following. In the first advanced circle of thought (v. 5-10), in v. 6, 7 the true fellowship is set over against the false claim of fellowship with God. Cerinthus repudiated the testimony of the apostles regarding the Logos and the efficacy of his blood and thus scorned fellowship with John and with any of the apostles. Cerinthus claimed fellowship with God without the cleansing blood of Jesus, in his estimation only a man died on the cross. That is why John introduces the fellowship already here.

Our own fellowship as witnesses of the Logos incarnate is most emphatically "with the Father," that Father with whom the Life, the eternal one, was in all eternity, "and with his Son Jesus Christ," pointedly calling "Jesus Christ" the Father's Son, he being the one manifested here on earth to the apostle witnesses. The fellowship of the apostles is *not* with God alone but with *both* the Father and the Son. There is no other fellowship; all claim to the contrary is false. Apart from Jesus Christ no man is in fellowship with God. Thus only those who have fellowship with the apostles have fellowship with God and with his Son, and that Son is "Jesus Christ" in his *whole* manifestation, also on the cross, in his cleansing blood (v. 7), in his expiation for sins (2:2), in his coming in connection with blood (5:5).

Throughout the past centuries even as today those who reject the testimony of the apostles have no fellowship with them, have no fellowship with the Father and with his Son, who is none other than Jesus Christ. Although they may preach God and fellowship with God as much as they please they are antichrists (4:3) and deny the Father as well as the Son. "Everyone denying the Son, neither has the Father" (2:23), may he claim what he will. "Whoever confesses that Jesus is the Son of God, God remains in him, and he in God" (4:15), which alone is fellowship with God. All this is basic for the entire epistle and thus appears in John's basic statement (v. 1-4).

4) Καί adds the last thought: "and these things we on our part are writing in order that our joy may

be as having been filled full." Misunderstanding scribes
altered the text. They thought that John should say:
"These things we are writing *to you* in order that *your*
joy may be full" (A. V.). Grammars like B.-D. 280
and R. 406, 678 support this thought by asserting that
γράφομεν is the literary plural. This has "we are writing" = "I am writing" in 2:1. It has John speak of
what *he* is writing right now; some say that he has
in mind only these four verses. In one sentence there
are no less than *eleven* "we" verbs, to say nothing of
the "we" and "our" pronouns, and now *one* of these
"we" forms is to be regarded as editorial for "I."
This does not seem likely.

"These things we are writing," Zahn rightly says,
includes the entire New Testament literature, especially that which was written directly by the apostolic
witnesses but also that which is based on their witness,
the literature to which John is now contributing this
letter and will contribute his Gospel and his Revelation. "We are writing these things" expounds "we
are testifying and declaring to you"; for the readers
of John much of this testimony of the apostles is in
the form of writing. How many apostles they heard
orally is immaterial. It was the calling of the Twelve
"to disciple all nations," and that included also the
nations of all future ages. The promise made in Matt.
28:20 extends far, far beyond the lifetime of the
Twelve. They are discipling the nations now by these
writings. We who now believe their testimony and
their writings are in *their* fellowship, which is the
fellowship with God and with his Son Jesus Christ.

The purpose the apostles have in doing this writing is "that our joy may be as having been filled full."
The perfect passive participle is not a part of a periphrastic tense but the predicate of the copula (it is
used like an adjective). In the case of John this is
the same joy that he speaks about in III John 4:

"Greater joy I do not have than these things, that I keep hearing my own children walking in the truth." So Jesus said: "My food is that I do the will of him that did send me, and that I finish his work," John 4:34. Paul exclaims: "Woe is to me if I do not evangelize!" I Cor. 9:16. The writing of the apostles, like their oral speaking, could not be in vain. The cup of their joy is, indeed, "as having been filled full" to the brim, all antichristian opposition notwithstanding.

The First Circle of Facts,
Centering on the Fellowship with God,
1:5-2:2

5)   On the structure of John's letter see the introduction. From the basic statement (v. 1-4) John advances to the *fellowship* as his first expansion. The sum and substance of true religion is fellowship with God. Hence any number of men claim to have such fellowship, in particular the heretics who deny that Jesus Christ is the Son of God and that his blood alone places us into and maintains us in fellowship with God. That is true to this day. John's encyclical rightly lays the circle of facts centering on fellowship with God upon the great fact that Jesus Christ is the Logos of the Life, the Son of God, to which fact the apostles are witnesses.

The presentation is simple, clear as crystal, complete as a unit. John ranges the facts that are pertinent to fellowship with God together so that the readers may at once see that they are truly in this essential fellowship and may also note who is and who is not in it. The presentation of this group of facts is an assurance to the readers and at the same time strikes at the liars who deny the deity of Jesus and the power of his blood.

And this is the report which we have heard from him and are reporting back to you, that God is light, and in him there is not a single (bit) of darkness.

Jesus Christ, God's Son, revealed God to the apostles. Here belong John 1:18, and Heb. 1:1-3. In the Old Testament, God revealed himself through the prophets; but the fullest, completest revelation came through his own Son. The feature of this revelation that is pertinent to John's present purpose is the truth that God is light without even a trace of darkness. This is the great fact with reference to God which must be noted when fellowship between sinners like ourselves and God is considered. This fact regarding God is revealed already in the Old Testament, but it is revealed in its finality by God's own Son who "was with the Father" (v. 2), "who is in the bosom of the Father" (John 1:18).

The most terrible delusion results when this fact regarding God is in any way ignored when we consider our fellowship, our κοινωνία or communion with God. To think that we can remain in darkness and yet be in fellowship with him, in whom there is no darkness whatever, is the height of delusion, the saddest contradiction. It is elementary, axiomatic: "What communion has light with darkness?" II Cor. 6:14; John 3:19-21.

John connects this statement with the preceding one by means of a simple "and." We consider at the same time the two ἀπαγγέλλω used in v. 2, 3 and the ἀναγγέλλω and ἀγγελία occurring in this verse. The second verb occurs also in John 16:14, 15. Add ἄγγελος to this group. G. K. would also add εὐαγγέλιον, which is, however, a specific term for "*good* report or message." We may translate the noun "report" or "message." The first verb, which is compounded with ἀπό, indicates that the reporting comes "from" the reporters (who are witnesses, v. 2, 3); the verb that is compounded with ἀνά states that they report "back" to others what they have received (C.-K. 25). John uses the perfect "we have heard" for the third time, and the tense again indicates the lasting effect.

"From him" must mean from his Son Jesus Christ (v. 3). This would be in accordance with the verbs that are used in verse 1 and with the two other "we have heard." "From him" presents the final and the absolute source of all information. The present "we are reporting back to you" is identical with the present tenses used in v. 2, 3, plus "we are writing" in v. 4, and refers to all the reporting of all the apostles throughout their apostleship.

, "This is the report which," etc., emphasizes the specific fact mentioned in the appositional clause "that God is light, and darkness in him there is not one," i. e., not a single bit; the double negative is very strong in the Greek. The anarthrous predicate "light" is qualitative. Some reduce its meaning to "warmth, health, sight," or to the fact that God can be ·known; others call it ethical light. Light, life, love, etc., are attributes of God; and every attribute of God is only the very being and essence of God viewed from one angle because our finite minds cannot take in the whole of God with one mental grasp. The Scriptures condescend to our weak ability and speak now of one, now of another side of God's infinite being, yet they never divide him. Nevertheless, every attribute is infinite and incomprehensible to finite conception. Try as we may to understand even a single revelation of God's being, the reality towers above our comprehension. We can but bow in the dust, worship, and adore.

Aspiring minds strive to know more but do so vainly and with great danger to themselves. The very works of God such as creation and providence and the giving of his only-begotten Son are incomprehensible; how much more God himself! A God that is not infinitely above finite comprehension is *not* God. To reduce God to the range of finite thought is to produce a mental idol.

The very being of God is absolute light. This is one of God's transitive attributes like his omnipotence and his love, which ever reach out from God and do not merely rest quiescently in him. Neither "light" nor "darkness" are figurative; all physical light and dark-ness are trivial compared with what is here said about

God. John does not define "light" when he attributes it to God; nor can we furnish an adequate definition. Christ is called "the light of the world," which means the saving light that delivers us from the darkness. We are to be light and the children of light, to love and to walk in the light, to hate and to keep from the darkness. From these effects in us and from the terms which John uses with reference to us we may grope upward a little in order partially to understand what God is as light.

In v. 6 and 8 John uses "truth," ἀλήθεια, reality. Compare John 3:21. We have also the opposite word "liar" (v. 10). God is true, God is truth; and this helps us a little to grasp the thought that he is light. John says in v. 9 that God is "faithful and righteous." When he is speaking of us John uses "unrighteousness" in v. 9. Light in God, we thus venture to add, is righteousness, holiness in the absolute sense. The whole revelation of God in the Word, in particular all that his Son has revealed of him, show him as light in the sense of truth, righteousness (holiness).

The placing of the negative statement beside the positive always emphasizes. It does so here in the strongest way, especially by adding οὐδεμία in the emphatic position at the end; there is absolutely no darkness in God, not even one small shadow that might dim his truth, righteousness, and holiness.

6) Since this matter about the very being of God was revealed to the apostles by the Son of God himself, and since this was conveyed to us by these witnesses, it follows inevitably in regard to communion with God: **If we say that we are having fellowship with him and are walking in the darkness we are lying and are not doing the truth; but if we are walking in the light as he is in the light we do have fellowship with one another, and the blood of Jesus, his Son, cleanses us from all sin.**

John has six ἐάν clauses, three of them with the
aorist εἴπωμεν: "if we actually say." The "we" is now
broader than it was in v. 1-5 where there is a contrast
between the apostles and John's readers: "we — you."
In v. 6-10 "we" = John's readers plus himself or any
apostle; he no longer has a contrasting "you." John
might have said "if anyone," indefinite and general
(he does this in 2:1); by saying "we" he becomes
definite and general only as far as true Christians are
concerned; he would not include the antichristians
(2:18) in this "we."

If John had used εἰ with the indicative he would
have stated a reality and would have left a wrong
impression; by the use of ἐάν in both the negative and
the positive statements the conditional clauses are made
vivid. In the apodoses John uses present tenses and
not futures (as is done in common cases of expectancy). John is not speaking abstractly and theoreti-
cally when he says: "If we say that we are having
fellowship with him (who is absolute light) and are
walking in the darkness," for, although no apostle
and none of John's readers make such a preposterous,
self-contradictory claim, Cerinthus and his following
did claim this very thing. This is often regarded as a
reference to ethics, walking in all manner of sins,
but the apodosis says: then "we are lying and are not
doing *the truth.*"

"Are not doing the truth" is more than an emphasis
on "we are lying." Not to do the truth is not to have
it, for no one does it without having it in his heart;
and not doing it is evidence that the heart is without
the truth because of blank ignorance or because of
hostility such as that of Cerinthus and his followers.
Both "the darkness" and "the truth" are definite. In
v. 5 and again in 2:8-11 (five times) John has σκοτία;
we note that this is in opposition to "light" (v. 5, 8).
In v. 6 John uses σκότος as an opposition to "truth." We

may call this a slight difference, the point that remains
is the fact that τὸ σκότος is often used as though "the
darkness" is a power ("your hour and the power of
the darkness"), the devil's *power* of error, deceit, lie.
To walk in this darkness is to believe and to hold to
the lie, to reject and to fight the saving truth, to hate
this light (John 3:20), to make God, the light, a liar
(v. 10). The walk or conduct shows this clinging to
the lie just as does not doing the truth, i. e., what the
saving gospel truth tells us.

Ethics are included, but John has in mind first of
all doctrine and faith, here false doctrine as opposed
to the true. The whole claim to fellowship with God
is a lying. John minces no words. Our modern con-
siderateness toward heresies and heretics is unscrip-
tural and dangerous.

7) On the other hand (δέ), if we keep walking
in the light (believing and doing the gospel truth)
as he is in the light (God who is light in his very being)
then we do have fellowship with one another, namely
in our mutual fellowship with God. This is more than
the simple opposite of verse 6. This is no mere claim
to fellowship. This is more than a claim, this is fact:
"we *do have* fellowship." Those who have no fellowship with God are the ones who are most apt to set up
the claim to have it; those who have the divine fellowship need not make a claim to it. This is not: "We
do have fellowship *with him*," but more: "We do have
fellowship *with one another*." John adds the condition
"if we are walking in the light"; the notation "as he
(God) is in the light" thus places God and us in the
light, which is certainly the true fellowship ·with him.

John does not forget that in verse 3 he speaks of
the fellowship which his readers have with us, the
apostles, who are the chosen witnesses and proclaimers
of Jesus, the Son of the Father, and of all that he is.
He now adds to this: all who are walking in the light

as God is in the light (and are thus in fact having
fellowship with God) by that very fact have fellowship with one another; their fellowship with God
makes them one body, the *Una Sancta,* "the communion of saints" (Apostolic Creed). "In the light" is
the bond of union between God and us. To call this
merely ethical overlooks the fact that "the light" is
more; it is certainly "the truth." To walk in the light
is above all to believe the light, the truth, and then also
to obey it in word and in deed. What is in the soul
will become manifest in the conduct; this is not a mere
claim that contradicts open evidence.

When John says in verse 5: "God is light," and
now: "He is in the light," there is perfect harmony
between these two statements. For light shines forth.
Whoever *is* light is *eo ipso* in that light. The sun *is*
light and *is in* light. Jesus says of his disciples: "You
are the light of the world," Matt. 5:14. It is the same
light, the essence and the very attribute of God who
shined in our hearts for enlightenment of the knowledge of the glory of God in the face of Jesus Christ,
II Cor. 4:6.

Here we again have the strongest exclusion: none
who are in the darkness, who only lie by claiming fellowship with God, are in the fellowship with us; they
are without. John makes this so strong that he says
we ourselves would be outside, mere liars, if we did
not walk in the light. We observe that in the New
Testament the word κοινωνία is used only in a good or
sacred sense and is not used with reference to evil and
to those outside. John does not speak of a "communion" of those who walk in darkness, who lie and
do not the truth.

But are all of us not sinners; do our sins not
separate us from God? What about this fact with
reference to all that John says about our being in the
light and having fellowship or communion with God?

Here there lies the great gulf that separates us from all
these liars. "And the blood of Jesus, his Son, cleanses
us from all sin!" It is John's way of writing to state
this great truth with "and." This is the very truth
that those earliest Gnostics denied. In their speculation
the Logos did *not* become flesh; the Spirit or Logos
("the eon Christ" as they worded it) who descended
upon Jesus left him before his passion; the "Christ"
("the eon Christ") was *impassibilis,* could not suffer,
which was a sort of Docetism. This heresy claimed a
fellowship or communion *without* the sacrificial and
cleansing blood of "Jesus, his (God's) Son." This is
the claim of, all those who today scorn "the old blood
theology."

"The blood" is more specific than "the death" would
be, for "the blood" denotes sacrifice. It is always the
blood that is shed. The Lamb of God shed his blood
in expiation. He is the expiation for our sins, moreover not for ours only, but also for the whole world
(2:2). It is the blood "of Jesus, his Son," of Jesus as
a man who had the human nature and thus also blood
but who is "his Son" (v. 2, 3), the Logos of the Life
(v. 1), the second person of the Deity, who became
flesh (John 1:14), whose blood, when shed, has the
power to cleanse us from all sin.

It is said that καθαρίζειν does not have the same force
as ἀφιέναι which is used in verse 9, which is partially correct. The Son's blood "cleanses us from all sin" because all sin is *filth.* Rev. 1:5: he "washed us from
our sins in his blood"; compare Acts 15:9; Eph. 5:26;
Titus 2:14 on this cleansing. "To send away the sins"
(v. 9)· has reference to their *guilt,* to removing the
sins with all their guilt as far as the east is from the
west (Ps. 103:12; Isa. 43:25; 44:22; Micah 7:19).
Both acts are the same in substance. They denote the
sinner's justification; but "from all sin" ("all" and
"every" amount to the same thing with abstract nouns,

R. 772) indicates that constant justification is referred
to, including the fact that our sins are daily and richly
pardoned.

Some would make this cleansing the sanctifying
which prevents our sinning; others want this included.
If our fellowship with God must wait until we are no
longer sinners, then John himself was still outside of
the fellowship according to his own confession (v. 8).
· The blood of God's Son does sanctify us and counteract
our sinning, but it establishes and maintains our fellowship with the all-holy God of light by removing all
our *filthy*, abominable, damnable *guilt*.

The holy and precious blood of Christ.alone brings
us poor sinners into fellowship with God and keeps
us· there.   Here belong all those passages that speak
of "the blood," which deserve a fuller treatment by
some competent hand.

· 8)   To claim fellowship, saving connection, with
God without the cleansing of the blood of his Son is
possible only when sin is abolished and there is no
need of this blood of the Son. From what Irenæus
(I, 6, 20) says about Cerinthus and the early Gnostics
one may gather that by reason of a so-called "spiritual
sense" in them, a special superior "spiritual knowledge" (*gnosis*), they claimed to do as they pleased
without being contaminated by sin.   Some went so
far as to extol persons like Cain, Korah, and Judas
and to regard them as being gifted with superior freedom of thought and with intrepidity of action.   They
also claimed that, since the soul attains perfection only
by "knowledge" (*gnosis*), it was actually requisite to
do all manner of evil so as to attain perfection. ·

Since John's time sin has been abolished also in
various other ways.   The sinfulness of sin is denied.
It is regarded as a natural, transitional stage in human
development and is thus really not sin.   Or man is
really good, and what is called sin is a slight, negligible

thing in the sight of God. At most, sin needs no expiation, the wrath of God is called a fiction. The idea of sin is reduced to a mistake of the mortal mind, and it should be recognized as a mere mistake on our part. Finally, the perfectionists and holiness people lay aside the Lord's Prayer with its petition: "Forgive us our trespasses." They claim that they have no sins to be cleansed away.

Thus John adds this second statement as a parallel to v. 6: **If we say that we do not have sin we are deceiving ourselves, and the truth is not in us.** The force of the tenses is the same as it was in verse 6: the aorist denotes the actual claim, the present indicates what we are doing to ourselves and what is not in us. The claim is "that we do not have sin." We see little difference between this and verse 10: "that we have not been sinning." This latter statement reaches back from the present into the past and denotes the *sinning* while verse 8 speaks of *sin.* The claim that we do not have "sin" means "such a thing as sin," and not having such a thing means that nothing of the nature of sin clings to us to stain us as filth or to blacken us as guilt so that we need cleansing or removal. It is debated as to whether John includes original sin or speaks only of actual sin as though actual sins were ever committed by us except as outgrowths of the depravity that is inherent in us.

In verse 6 John says: "We are lying and are not doing the truth"; he now states it in stronger terms: "We are deceiving our own selves," i. e., are making our own selves the victims of our lying, are not only not *doing* the truth but are wholly devoid of it, "the truth *is not in us.*" This is the same ἀλήθεια that was mentioned in v. 6, the saving gospel truth or reality, the light that delivers from the darkness. When "the truth" is not in us, we are not by any means empty but are full of fictions, fables, myths, self-made fancies, notions that are *not so.* Already those early heretics called these things *gnosis,* already in First Corinthians Paul opposed such *gnosis* which paraded as "wisdom." No advance has been made, today the word that is used is merely a Latin instead of a Greek word: *"science," "scientific* religion." Professing to be wise, they became fools. The greatest fools are those who deceive their own selves.

Note that the "we" used in v. 8-10 includes John himself. This great apostle here confesses himself a sinner, says that his sins are remitted by God, cleansed away by the blood of Jesus, the Son of God. Perfectionism receives its mortal blow here. Paul delivers another blow in Phil. 3:12-14; James 3:1a does the . same.

9) **If we keep confessing our sins, faithful is he and righteous to remit to us the sins and to cleanse us from all unrighteousness.** This is what "doing the truth" when "the truth is in us" means: we shall ever confess our sins, admit, acknowledge them to God. Note the present, iterative subjunctive. John does not say how, when, where we do this confessing. To restrict it to private confession or, on the other hand, to public confession in the services of the congregation is unwarranted. John now uses the plural "our sins," which only spreads out the details that are included in the preceding singular. "Our sins" are not restricted to our conscious sins. Ps. 19:12; 90:8. True Christians want and obtain remission of all their sin and of all their sins.

"Faithful is he and righteous" refers to God. John has just mentioned *"his* Son" and the fellowship effected by the blood of his Son and the fact that the remission of our sins is fellowship with God. "Faithful" means true to his promise, and this is placed first; "and righteous" with its forensic sense as it is here

added to "faithful" and its connotation of promise
states that, when he acquits us according to his promise,
God, our Judge, is and remains "righteous." John
expresses the same truth that Paul writes about in
Rom. 3:26. The God who is light acts as a faithful and
righteous Judge when he acquits us and remits our
sins for the sake of Christ. Our acquittal is not an
act of partiality and favoritism for which God can be
charged with injustice. He is as righteous and just
when he is acquitting the confessing believer for the
sake of Christ's blood as when he is damning the nonconfessing rejector of Christ's blood. In every verdict
of God on men there is involved a verdict on God himself. How Catholics can make "faithful" refer to
peccata mortalia and "righteous" to *peccata venalia*
is difficult for us to understand.

The charge of injustice is frequently raised when
God damns some sinners and acquits other sinners.
The blood of Jesus Christ, his Son, (Rom. 3:24, 25,
the ransoming of Christ and our faith in Christ's
blood) nullifies this charge and makes it recoil upon
the heads of those who bring it. When they at last
face this Judge they and the entire universe will be
compelled to glorify all his acquittals as being absolutely righteous and just. John states this truth for
the sake of the fullest assurance of his readers against
all false argumentation of the liars who scorn the blood
of God's Son.

Our versions are more correct in translating the
ἵνα clause with a dependent infinitive than is R. 961,
998 who regards it as a clause of result. In the Koine
ἵνα crowded out many infinitives. We translate "faithful and righteous to remit to us the sins and to cleanse
us from all unrighteousness" by this remission. The
aorists indicate actuality; we may call them effective.
In verse 7 we have only "cleanses"; "righteous" adds

the idea of the Judge, and thus "to remit" is added to
the cleansing and explains that the remission effects
the cleansing.

We have already explained ἀφιέναι in connection
with "cleanses" in verse 7. This is the ἄφεσις which
shines forth so gloriously in all of Scripture. Our English "to forgive" and "forgiveness" are inadequate
translations. The sins "are sent away" as far as the
east is from the west — do you know where the ·one
begins and the other ends? To the depth of the sea —
there are still unmeasured depths. Sent away as a
·cloud is dissolved, never to appear again. When the
sinner thus has his sins sent away from him he is,
indeed, cleansed from all unrighteousness, from even
the least shadow of it. "All unrighteousness" is the
correct term, for the least "unrighteousness" would
compel the "righteous" God to pronounce the verdict
of damnation upon us. But forget not the blood of
Jesus, God's Son, nor the fact that we confess our sins,
trust in that blood, and in this trust lay all our sins
before the Judge.

To "all sin" (the mass) and "our sins" (the multitude) there is now added "all unrighteousness" as
characterizing sin and sins: anything contradicting
the divine norm of right; the abstract noun is not to
be restricted to actual sins. To be cleansed so completely of all unrighteousness is to be declared righteous by the righteous Judge, is to be admitted to fellowship with God who is light. No man who is not so .
cleansed is in this fellowship, may he claim what he will.

10)   As v. 9 amplifies v. 6, 7, so v. 10 amplifies
v. 8: **If we say that we have not been sinning, a liar
are we making him, and his Word is not in us.** The
claim "not to have sin" is the same as the claim "not
to have been sinning." The difference in the form of
the verbs is in accord with the difference between the
idea of mass in "sin" and the idea of multitude in "our

sins." The perfect ἡμαρτήκαμεν looks back over the past
life that continued up to the present moment and with
its negative forms the claim: "We have not been
sinning." It thus says in another way: "We do not
have sin" (verse 8).

The main point lies in the apodosis: "a liar are
we making him, and his Word is not in us." The
emphasis is on the predicative "a liar" which is placed
forward in the sentence. We are doing more than
just lying (v. 6), more than deceiving our own selves
by our lying (v. 8). These two statements are incomplete. The worst that we are doing by our false
claim is really blasphemous: we are making *God a
liar!* Some interpreters do not seem to feel the terrific
impact of this word. If you and I philosophize or
theologize our sins away and think that they do not
need the blood of Jesus, God's Son, we are making
God himself *a liar!* No less. Let us face this fact!
Let it frighten us away from such claims!

John continues with "and" although the clause
explains: "and his Word is not in us." This Word
is called "the truth" in v. 6 and 8 (John 17:17), "the
light" in v. 7. This truth and this light are the contents of "his Word," and they come to us in "his Word."
We do not reduce this word to a reference to the gospel,
to only the Old Testament, or to those parts of the
New Testament that John's readers had. The whole
Word of God declares that we are sinners. It says so
in a large number of places. From beginning to end it
deals with us as with sinners. Its history, its law, its
gospel present sinners, sinners: lost sinners, ransomed
sinners, saved sinners, damned sinners, glorified sinners.

To have God's Word "in us" is to have received
it in the heart, to hold it in faith, to be governed by
it and by all it says to us sinners. It is not in us when
we close our hearts to it and believe, hold, follow something else. This is making God a liar. There is a

formal acceptance of the Word, but this alone does not place his Word "in us," the truth "in us" (v. 8). What John says about God's Word as such applies to any part of it when this is rejected. To that degree it is not "in us," to that degree we make God a liar. God will be the Judge as to whether this is done in ignorance (vincible or invincible ignorance), from wrong motives (well or ill-meant motives), or wilfully, wickedly. Our generation condones a rejection of parts of the Word (the truth); it needs John to tell it what this really means so that none may deceive their own selves (verse 8) and others.

2:1) Because John has the address, "my little children," our versions and others think that a new line of thought begins at this point; the new line of thought begins with verse 3. **My little children, these things I am writing to you so that you may not sin.** The endearing address (only in this verse does it have the additional "my") seems natural when John tells his readers that he is writing these things about sin to them so that they may *not* sin. Jesus used τεκνία, "little children" (diminutive) in John 13:33; John uses it seven times, but it is an address that is befitting his great age and his long attachment to his readers, to whom he has ever been a kindly father. "These things" are not the ones that follow but those that precede as the purpose clause, "that you may not sin," shows. The fact that "I am writing" is *not* the same as the "we are writing" occurring in 1:4 we have explained in our interpretation of 1:4.

Two false deductions might be made from 1:8-10:1) since no Christian can ever say that he no longer sins he might think that there is no use to strive against sin (sloth, indifference, carelessness); 2) since remission is so easy, let God remit a few more sins to us (presumption, false security in sin). Either conclusion or both would be a sorry mistake. The readers must not disregard 1:5-7, the fact that we have fellowship with God who is light when we walk in the light even as he is in the light, and that then alone the blood of Jesus, God's Son, keeps cleansing us from sin, God ever remits these sins. All that John writes has as its purpose that we may *not* sin. The aorist is summary and effective. To find any type of perfectionism in the tense runs counter to all that John has already said in 1:7-10 as well as to what he now writes.

And if anyone sins (second aorist subjunctive, actually does sin), **we have a Paraclete with the Father, Jesus Christ, Righteous; and he is expiation**

regarding our sins; moreover, not regarding ours only, but also regarding the whole world. John does not say "if *we* sin," but "if *anyone* sins," for this act is done by the individual. Yet he continues with the plural: "a Paraclete have *we*," for "anyone" only individualizes. Anyone of us may sin, none is exempt, wholly immune, and whenever anyone does actually sin, there is ready for all of us this great Paraclete of ours who takes care of all of us in this respect.

. The best English word for "Paraclete" is probably "Advocate." This word has both a forensic and a common use. Demosthenes uses it to designate the friends of the accused who voluntarily step in and personally urge the judge to decide in his favor. That is the sense of this word here because "with the Father" as well as 1:9 refer to God as the Judge in the case. In John 14:16, 26; 15:26; 16:7, where the Holy Spirit is the Paraclete, we have a different case, for the term is there used in the nonforensic, the wider sense of one who comes to our aid. This term does not occur very often in literature; M.-M. 485 finds little in the papyri; Deissmann, *Light,* etc., 339, etc., finds only the meaning "advocate." Yet the term must have been frequently used in common speech, for the Jews had it in transliteration in both the Hebrew and the Aramaic; Jesus employed it in the latter language. Παράκλητος is a verbal adjective in form and is used as a noun: "one called to another's side in order to aid him." It is derived from the perfect passive παρακεκλῆσθαι and not from the present active παρακαλεῖν and thus does not = ὁ παρακαλῶν, C. K. 572, etc. In his translation of John's Gospel Luther has rendered this word *Troester,* which loses the passive sense and conveys only the general idea; here Luther has translated this word *Fuersprecher,* one who speaks in another's behalf, and it is again nonpassive.

On πρός compare 1:2. "Father" is used also there.
The case of any sinning Christian lies in the hands
of the Father who sent his Son Jesus Christ to save
us, and this same Jesus Christ is "face to face with,"
in the very presence of the Father when our sinning
is judged. Jesus spoke of the Spirit as being "another
Paraclete" and thereby called himself a paraclete, but
he was this in the general sense of the word. Now,
since he is with the Father, he acts in the Father's
court. It is "Jesus," he who at one time dwelt on earth
in lowliness, and "Christ" adds all his official work.
Δίκαιον is added qualitatively. See this designation of
Christ in Acts 3:14; 7:52; 22:14 and note that it is
· also predicated of the Father in 1:9. Both the Judge ·
and the Advocate are "righteous" and thus deal with
any sinning Christian's case.

"Righteous" or "Righteous One," as here applied
to "Jesus Christ," does not refer to his deity but to
Jesus as our Savior and Substitute: "a Righteous One
suffered in place of unrighteous ones" (I Pet. 3:18).
Not because he is merely in and for himself "a Righteous One" does Jesus act as our Advocate; then the
fact of God's own being righteous would certainly
suffice. Jesus is and can be our Advocate with the
righteous Father only because he is "the Righteous
One" who was slain for us (Acts 7:52; 3:14), because
he "became for us from God righteousness" (I Cor.
1:30).

· 2) For that reason John adds "and he is expiation
regarding our sins," etc., he as the "Righteous One"
in the sense just indicated, as having suffered for unrighteous ones. Note "from all unrighteousness" in
1:9. Ἱλασμός (found only here and in 4:10) means
Suehnung, Versuehnung, for which we prefer the
translation "expiation" to "propitiation." The abstract
is more significant than the concrete ἱλαστήρ, "expiator"

("propitiator"), would be, since, when it is applied
to a person, it combines the person with his act and
the effect of the act of expiating (C.-K. 521). We
prefer "expiation" because of 4:10: in his love God
commissioned his Son as expiation regarding our sins.
The thought is not that this expiation propitiated,
placated *God,* for he was full of infinite love when he
sent his Son; *we* needed expiation, needed it "regarding our sins," need it regarding them every day when
we still sin. The fact that this expiation was brought
about by "the blood of Jesus, God's Son," we know
from 1:7.

John says that it is effective, "not regarding our
sins only, but also regarding the whole world." Be-·
cause John does not say "regarding *the sins* of the
whole world," the grammarians say that he uses *oratio
variata* (R. 441). John advances the thought from
sins to the whole world of sinners. Christ made expiation for our sins and thereby for all sinners. We
understand κόσμος in the light of John 3:16 and think
that it includes all men, us among them, and not only
all unsaved men. John does not add this "but also"
as a matter of information for us regarding other
people but as assuring us that, because Christ is expiation (qualitative, without the article; like δίκαιον) "in
regard to the whole world," we are included.

Augustine and the Venerable Bede offer the interpretation that "the whole world" = *ecclesia electorum
per totum mundum dispersa,* which Calvin seconds: .
*sub "omnibus" reprobos non comprehendit, sed eos
designat, qui simul credituri erant et qui per varias
mundi plagas dispersi erant.* But see II Pet. 2:1: the
Lord bought even those who go to hell. "The whole
world" includes all men who ever lived or will live.

Christ's saving righteousness and expiation are the
basis for his action as our Advocate. We have him as
an Advocate (one called to our side). John does not say

that the whole world has him in this capacity. As our Advocate Christ, our expiation, acts for the remission of our sins (1:9). John does not use the word "intercede" or "intercession" (Rom. 8:34; Heb. 7:25). See these passages regarding the intercession.

The Second Circle of Facts,
Centering on the Commandment,
With Two Pertinent Samples,
2:3-17

3) We have explained the exceptional and superior structure of this letter in the introduction. On the basic section that centers in the Logos of the Life, God's Son (1:1-4), John lays the facts that pertain to our fellowship with God through the blood of the Son (1:5-2:2). On this he lays another tier of facts, all of them pertaining to the "commandment" as this is found in the Word (v. 3-8) and expands this by adding illustrative examples, love for the brother in the faith (v. 9-11) and avoidance of love for the world (v. 12-17). This letter is not arranged in blocks that are laid side by side but is built like an inverted cone. John's facts circle upward and outward in a natural inner sequence. Every new circular sweep has its plainly marked center so that every statement is closely integrated. The weave unfolds itself in a perfect pattern and design.

Six times "commandment" marks the new expansion in v. 3-9, it is twice used in the plural, to which "his Word" is added in v. 5. The "commandment" is not dismissed at the close of the circle; it is mentioned again in 3:23, 24; in 4:21; and in 5:2, 3. It is a help for understanding the structure to underscore the key words as they are repeated in each circle of facts.

From the true *fellowship with God*, which is mediated to us sinners by the blood of God's Son (1:7) and in spite of our still sinning is preserved to us by our Advocate Christ and his expiation for all our sins, John takes us into the *Word*, to the ἐντολή, "the behest" or *commandment* which governs our entire fellowship or communion with God and thus also our fellowship with each other (1:7), so that each loves his spiritual brother, and all of us no longer love the world. The light, the truth (1:6-8), which means "his Word" (1:10), must be "in us" (1:8, 10) so that we "do" it (1:6). All this is now expanded. "His commandment" is the new term that is added, but "his Word" which occurs in 2:5 repeats this term from 1:10 as "the light" in opposition to "the darkness" in 2:9-11 repeats this same opposition from 1:5-7. In moving on and up these repetitions tell us that we are only rising and broadening, and that we must remember all that has been presented.

And in connection with this we know that we have known him: if we are keeping his commandments. As in 1:5 καί introduces us into the first upward circle, so καί again introduces us to the next circle. Ἐν τούτῳ = "in connection with this"; ἐν is to be understood in its original sense. This is not instrumental ἐν (R. 591, etc.). This phrase is not resumptive as R. 700 thinks, does not resume what lies in the preceding; it signifies "in connection with this: if we are keeping," etc. John has this same construction in 5:3; compare also 5:2 which begins with ὅταν, "when" (B.-D. 394). The "if" clause is an epexegetical apposition. We do not have οἶδα, the verb that denotes mere intellectual knowing without effect and affect in the soul of him who thus knows, but γινώσκω which has this effect and affect. "We know that we have known him" (perfect tense: ever since the gospel revealed God to us and thus also now) is a beautiful, telling statement with its repetition of knowing: γινώσκομεν . . . ἐγνώκαμεν.

How can we be so certain that we do know God, have known him, are not deceiving our own selves (1:8), are not lying (1:6) when we say that we have

known (and do know) God? How do we *know* that
we *know*? Do .others not make the same claim (next
verse) with the same positiveness, the same assurance?
Have we a better certainty than they? To know God
(γινώσκω) is to have true fellowship with him (1:6, 7).
See this force of the verb as it is used by Jesus in John
10:14, 15; and the negation in Matt. 7:23; compare
John 17:7, 8 where the object is the ῥήματα or words
of Jesus and what these reveal about the Father and
about Jesus.   ·

John takes up the question that troubles the mind
of so many young people. Is our certainty better than
the certainty of men in other religions? Are we Christians merely because we are born into Christian families? If we had been born Jews or Mohammedans
would we not feel just as certain and be just as right
in feeling that we truly know God? Or is the certainty
of the skeptic not as good as the one we claim? Is the
whole of religion not a mere subjective matter, un-
proved, unprovable, especially to a real thinking, scientific mind?

Here is the answer. God has revealed himself, has
made himself known. *Those* have known and know
him, those *know* that they have known him, who are
keeping his commandments.

Read John 17:7, 8. Also Matt. 28:20: "to keep all
things whatsoever I did command you" to keep. Τηρεῖν
= to keep and to preserve inviolate in the heart so
that no one shall take away, alter, falsify, so that what
we keep governs us completely. The ἐντολαί are the
things that we are bidden to keep. Second Peter 2:21:
"to know (ἐπιγινώσκω) the Way of the righteousness."

Because John uses the word ἐντολαί, some think only
of moral commandments such as we have in the Mosaic
law. This view leads to uncertainty regarding fellowship with God (true religion). Men claim that without
a "blood theology" (1:7), without an expiation (ἱλασμός,

2:2) they know God, have fellowship with him. Jesus is only a noble example to them.

John quotes ἐντολαί and ἐντολή from Jesus' own lips (notably from John 14:15, 21, 23, 24; 15:10; Matt. 28:20); and just as Jesus does in John 14:23, 24, he identifies these "commandments" with τὸν λόγον μου, with τοὺς λόγους μου. In v. 5 John says "keep his Word" and in 1:10 "his Word in you." Those who do this, Jesus says, have him and the Father dwelling in them; John says that they have fellowship with God (1:6, 7) and here that they know God.

These "commandments" ("words") or the singular this "commandment" ("Word") are "the truth," "the light" mentioned in 1:6-8. See how in John 17:6-8 God's *giving*, Christ's *giving*, the disciples' *receiving*, their *knowing*, and their *keeping* "the Word" go together. The substance of this truth, light, Word, words, commandment, commandments consists of *all the divine verities* regarding God, and they produce actual fellowship with him in which we know him and know that we have known and know him. These verities, which are revealed and then received (John 17:8) by us and kept by us in heart and in life, give us the ultimate certainty so that we know that we have, indeed, known by the light. Only when we leave this light and go back into the darkness will doubt revive and self-deception and lying set in again.

The light, the truth, the Word, the commandment (singular or plural) are termed doctrine (II John 9, 10) and doctrines when we think of the divine *facts* revealed to us and are called ethical, moral when we think of the conduct and the life produced in us. They always go together, the one is never without the other; both produce a living certainty in us which grows as strong as our keeping and our clinging to these verities become.

All true certainty must have a *divine objective basis* which remains what it is whether any man subjectively rests upon it or not. This basis is what we have: the Word, the light, the truth (or eternal reality, ἀλήθεια), the commandments, etc. Those who lack this divine objective basis have, in whatever they substitute in place of it, only a sham basis, an illusion. Although they cling to it with all their powers, their certainty is also a mere illusion, a nut without a kernel. God brings the divine basis of certainty, his Word, etc., (use all the synonymous terms) to us, and its very nature as ἀλήθεια or reality produces the knowledge with effect and affect (γινώσκω, ἐπίγνωσις) which constitutes certainty and ever realizes itself as what it is. It is *subjective*, for it fills the heart, yet it is never to be confounded with other subjective certainties, for its basis is *objectively divine*, and it ever attests itself as no less, is realized as no less: thus "we know (γινώσκομεν) that we have known (ἐγνώκαμεν)."

4) Since John crushes the first beginnings of Gnosticism (Cerinthus and his following), of those who made a specialty of γνῶσις as men today in a different way boast of their "science," their knowing, he adds the issue regarding γινώσκειν, knowing. **The one saying: I have known him! and not keeping his commandments is a liar, and in this one the truth is not; but he whoever keeps his Word, truly in this one the love of God has been brought to its goal. In connection with this we know that we are in him.**

John varies his expressions. In 1:6, 8, 10 he has written "if we say" (aorist subjunctive) to designate false claims; in 2:1 "if anyone sins." To indicate another false claim he now uses the substantivized participles (present, descriptive): "the one saying and not keeping" (one article with both participles).

The man who claims: "I have known God!" (the action of the perfect continues to the present as it does in v. 3) and does not keep God's commandments is nothing but a plain liar, not merely because his claim and his conduct disagree and contradict each other, his conduct giving the lie to his claim, nor because he just fails to see this and is thus only a sadly *mistaken* liar — no, far worse, he is a *deliberate* liar: "in this one the truth is not." This does not mean that he lacks "truthfulness," which would be a mere tautology since every liar lacks truthfulness. The divine truth, light, Word, etc., are not "in this man"; he kept them out of his heart. This truth = God's "commandments," which we have explained in v. 3. He is keeping them in neither his heart nor his life. Through this truth alone we know God truly and thus have fellowship with God. This individual is an awful liar because he claims to know and to be in fellowship with God when his own repudiation of the commandments of God proclaims the fact that the divine truth and Word is not in him, the one and only means of truly knowing and having fellowship with God.

We do not reduce the force of this by referring it only to moral commandments, to the law of Moses. We apply what John states not only to those who reject the whole Word of God — Cerinthus accepted certain parts of it, so did the later heretics — but also to those who reject any part of its truth. To the extent of their rejection they are liars, to that extent the truth is not in them. In the words of 1:10: to that extent they make God a liar, and to that extent his Word is not in them. Those portions of the Word, of the truth, which they refuse to accept and to keep they call false, a lie, and thus lyingly they make God a liar. Is this language too severe for modern delicate ears? It is John's language which he learned from Jesus who had it from God.

5) On the other hand (δέ), he whoever keeps his Word, ὃς ἄν (a still different formulation), in this one

the love of God has truly been brought to its goal. How so? By his love God has brought him truly to know his God, truly to have fellowship with his God. The perfect tense is the same as that found in v. 3 and 4. The fact that John uses the word "whoever" does not imply that the perfect used in this verse is gnomic (R. 897). Τελειόω = to bring to a goal. We know what that goal is: knowledge of God, fellowship with God. C.-K. 1049 is inadequate: the love is completely in him, *es fehlt ihr nichts.* This perfect is a passive which has God as the agent: "the love of God has been brought to its goal by God"; it is scarcely a middle: "has attained its goal for itself."

Some think that "the love of God" has the objective genitive: our love *for* God has been brought to its goal. They find the same type of genitive in 2:15; 3:17; 4:12 (where the same verb is used); 5:3. But only in 5:3 does the context require the sense our love for God; in all the other passages (notably in 4:12) God's love for us is clearly referred to. This is not clear when the verb is misunderstood. Luther has translated it *ist vollendet;* our versions, "is — has been — perfected." The exponents of this view have difficulty with the thought that *our* love *for* God has attained or has been brought to perfection. They are not clear as to whether this love has been brought to a perfect stage or to some lesser stage. We are also told that John is speaking abstractly: if a man guards God's word perfectly, that man loves God perfectly.

From 1:5 onward the discussion has centered about fellowship and communion with God; it is advanced to the thought of truly knowing him and knowing that we know him and are in union with him. All of this has been developed over against the false Gnostic claims of knowing and of being in union with God. In these Gnostics God has not been able to accomplish contact by his love; he could not get his truth (1:8;

2:4), his Word (1:10) into their hearts nor reach his goal: fellowship with him by true knowledge of him. In our case, John says, God did, indeed, reach this goal: we have the fellowship (1:7), we have known him and know that we have.

John has told us where the fault lies: these heretics deny the Logos in Jesus, his deity, the efficacy of his blood (1:7), the expiation for our sins (2:2). Here is all the love of God, for God so loved the world, etc., John 3:16. The light, the truth, the Word, the commandments of God radiate this infinite love which reaches out to cleanse 'sinners and to embrace them in fellowship. But here are sinners who falsely say that they do not have sins and that they have not sinned (1:8, 10). Despite all that God says about sin in his Word, sin and sins are as nothing to them; although they are uncleansed and full of the darkness they claim that they have fellowship with the God of light (1:5, 6), claim to know him intimately, and set themselves up as the ones that have real *gnosis* (Gnostics).

These are the things that John is saying about God's love; he will speak about our love presently. On ἀγάπη see 4:7, 8.

In verse 3 John says: "In connection with this we *know* that we have known (and know) God." He now says again, but in an advanced manner: "In connection with this (that he has just said) we know that we are in him." The advance of thought lies in this that, instead of "we have known him," John writes "we are in him." As to be "in him" is "to know him," so both = "to have fellowship with him" (1:7). Each expression illuminates the other. God's love has brought us to this union with God, and we certainly know that it has attained this goal in us, know that we are in living connection ("fellowship") with God.

For a discussion of "in him" we refer the reader to Rom. 6:1. We are "in connection with" (ἐν) God when his light, his truth, his Word, his commandments are "in us." The Word is always the medium for this ἐν of the *unio mystica*; without this Word there is no connection with God despite all claims to the contrary. Only one divine means (the Word, etc.) reaches down from God to us sinners, cleanses us, and puts us in fellowship with God; there is no other means. To repudiate the means is to lose the result, the fellowship, the goal which God's love would attain. This *unio* is spiritual; it is not properly expressed to say that it is like that of living creatures "in" the air, of fish "in" the water, of plants "in" the earth; man living and breathing "in" the air, and the air also being "in" him. God does not resemble air, water, earth. He is a person.

6) John reverts to v. 1a, to the fact of his writing this in order that we may not sin, and now restates it in this form: **The one saying he is remaining in him is under obligation even as that One walked himself also to be walking.** This is the opposite of verse 4 where ὁ λέγων = the one making a false claim. John says that the one making the true claim of union with God ὀφείλει, is under obligation because of this claim, because of this abiding union with God, ever himself to walk just as "that One" did walk when he was here on earth.

John learned this word μένω from Jesus who uses it six times in John 15:4-7 when he is speaking of remaining in him, of not remaining in him, and of his words remaining in us. John uses it here when he is speaking of remaining (abiding) in God. Remaining in Christ is, of course, the same as remaining in God. The demonstrative ἐκεῖνος appears in 3:3, 5, 7, 16; 4:17, as a reference to Jesus; "that One" is at once recognized by what is predicated of him. The aorist "even as that One walked" is historical. The walk or conduct

of Jesus is the model for everyone who claims that he
is in union and fellowship with God. He will follow
in Jesus' steps. He has this obligation and recognizes,
obeys it. It is a spiritual obligation that is due to the
inward spiritual connection with God and his abiding
in this connection.

7) Fellowship with God is the essential. Heretics claim it, but their claim is a lie as John proves decisively. He and his readers have it; John proves that
statement and even shows how ·they know beyond a
doubt that they have it. But having fellowship with
God means also that John and his readers have fellowship "with one another." In 1 :7 this fact is stated without elaboration. The elaboration now follows. This
mutual fellowship is a second vital point for John and
for his readers. The heretics, Cerinthus and his followers, were seeking to break up this fellowship. They
were trying to make apostates of John's readers so
that they should hate the brethren whom they had
loved, hate the true fellowship in which they had been.
This is the historical background for v. 7-11.

Verses 7, 8 form the preamble to v. 9-11. We shall
see that v. 12-14 likewise form the preamble to v.
15-17. The substitution of a fictitious fellowship with
God always has as its correlate the sundering of fellowship with those who are in the true fellowship with
God, who hold to the blood of Jesus, God's Son (1:7),
to his expiation for constant cleansing from sins
(2:1); it always entails a separation from those who
hold to the Word, the truth, etc., and walk as Jesus
walked.

·**Beloved, not a new commandment am I writing
to you but an old commandment which you had from
the beginning. The commandment, this old one, is
the Word which you did hear. Again, a new commandment am I writing to you, the thing that is true**

in him and in you, because the darkness is passing away, and the light, the genuine one, is already shining.

John's love for his readers prompts the address "beloved"; and he now asks them to remain in the fellowship of mutual love. What he is writing is not a new commandment, καινή, that is to take the place of an old one which has directed them to this.time; no, it is an old one, the one they had had from the start, when they were first brought into fellowship with God and into fellowship with each other by means of the gospel, the blood of the Son, etc. The phrase ἀπ᾽ ἀρχῆς always gets its meaning from the context which is here not the same as it was in 1:1. Here the imperfect εἴχετε shows that the beginning referred to is that which began the having of the commandment on the part of John's readers.

We are pleased to note that John himself now defines just what he means by "the commandment"; it is the λόγος or Word which his readers did hear, which they heard in the beginning when by it they came into fellowship with God, etc. John has already so defined it in 1:10 where he calls the light and the truth God's Word. In 2:3, 4 he uses the plural "commandments," individual parts of the one Word; he now writes the singular "commandment" and looks at the parts as a unit. Jesus uses both λόγος and λόγοι, the Word and its parts, the words, in the same way.

It is important to note that by "commandment" John means "the Word which you heard," the Word that is "in you". by faith, that is not in those who contradict it and make God himself a liar (1:10): It is called a commandment or commandments because we are bidden to receive, to believe, to keep, to follow it. It is full of these blessed imperatives; note those mentioned in Acts 2:38 when the gospel won 3,000; in Acts 16:31; 17:30; and in many other passages.

Obeying the Word so often means believing it; disobeying it is unbelief. John is not speaking of a moral commandment, of the law that demands love, or of this law as it is used in the gospel.

8) Πάλιν = *wiederum* and means that, looking at it once more, what John is writing can, nevertheless, be called "a new commandment." We regard ὅ with its added causal clause as an apposition to ἐντολὴν καινήν: what John is writing, old as it is to his readers, is, nevertheless, a new commandment, new as being "the thing that is true (neuter) in him (Christ) and in you," true and thus new in connection with Christ and John's readers "because the darkness is passing away and the light, the genuine one, is already shining." At one time the darkness of paganism enshrouded the readers, now the genuine light is in them. Christ and the gospel have come into their hearts. More and more pagans are being brought from the darkness to the light; indeed, the darkness is thus passing away, the genuine light is shining (two progressive present tenses).

John is not assuring the readers that what he is writing is true and not empty fiction; he is telling them how this is a *new* commandment despite its oldness to the readers, *new* as being true (ἀληθές, real) in Christ and in them, real because of what happened before the Word came to them and they got to hear it. Compared with the long, unbroken night of paganism, this thing that is now so real in connection with Christ and in connection with themselves, this disappearing of the darkness, this shining of the light, the genuine one (ἀληθινόν, not sham), is certainly newness.

John says well: "The thing that is true *in him* and in you," and places "in him" first. His deity, his cleansing blood, his expiation, all that is connected with *him* are true, real. Let the heretics lie and call them untrue! All that is "in you," connected with you, your cleansing through the Son's blood, your remission of sins (1:9), your walking as he walked, are true things, are real. Let the heretics lie and call them untrue, unreal! Their supposed gnosis is self-delusion (1:8); the light they claim to have is not genuine, it leaves them in the old darkness. Any newness that they may claim is nothing of the kind. We read these verses in the light of their historical background and not abstractly.

Old — most certainly; it is the same Word, faith, life that Paul and Barnabas first brought; John is writing nothing different. Yet it is wondrously *new*, as new as when on their first missionary tour Paul and Barnabas made the darkness flee by letting the genuine light shine and shine. This little preamble lifts the hearts of the readers to praise God for this genuine light, to repudiate the heretics who seek to quench this light, to hold to the fellowship with the God who is light and in the light (1:5, 7), to go on walking in the light (1:7), to follow Jesus alone (2:6). Note that "the light" and "the darkness" are repeated from 1:5-7.

9) Precious, then, is our mutual fellowship in the light (1:7). John now develops this thought. **The one claiming he is in the light and hating his brother is in the darkness still. The one loving his brother remains in the light, and entrapment is not in him.**

Here we have one who makes a false claim such as those mentioned in 1:6, 8, 10, and in 2:4. One article governs both participles. John is thinking of a church member who has been deluded by the heretics. He has adopted their light which is not the genuine light (v. 8). His claim to be in the light is false, is evidenced as false by the fact of his hating his brother. This man is in the darkness ἕως ἄρτι, "up till now." The phrase suggests that John hopes that he will yet return to the genuine light and to the true love of the brethren and to fellowship with them.

10) Just what John means is shown by the opposite. The one loving his brother remains in the light and is free from the darkness, and his love is the clear evidence for this fact. The addition reveals John's meaning: "and entrapment is not in him."

We should understand σκάνδαλον correctly. It does not mean "occasion of stumbling" (our versions), it has but little connection with stumbling. One may stumble and yet remain on one's feet, may stumble and actually fall and yet arise again. A *skandalon* is the crooked trigger stick of a trap to which the bait is affixed and by which the trap is sprung. The verb σκανδαλίζειν means to catch in such a trap. The noun and the verb denote only the fatal, deadly entrapment of the victim. M.-M. 576; R. 174. When this word is used metaphorically it means bringing spiritual death.

The one who loves his brother and remains in the light has nothing in him that will be a trigger stick in a trap to kill any of his brethren spiritually. The other who is not in the light — what does he care for the spiritual life of any brother in the church? He hates, has no use for such brotherhood in the light, will set his traps of lying and deceit to catch and to kill Christians and to throw them into the darkness again.

John introduces terms that echo through this epistle: remain — love, and hate — brother, and what brother means, namely a child born of God. Read on and mark the terms as John expands them. This is much more than quarreling with a brother member of the church, more than the hatred that thus ensues; for by this hate the worst damage is done to the sinner himself and not to the church member sinned against.

11)   John uses singulars throughout, which generalize and yet make his statements concrete. "The light," "the darkness" (here σκοτία) are most definite. The former denotes the truth, the Word, the commandment as explained above, the other the opposite. **Now the one hating his brother is in the darkness and is walking in the darkness and does not know where he is going because the darkness did blind his eyes.**

Δέ is not "but" (adversative) ; it adds a fuller explanation. This is not the hating which is loveless "envy, suspicion, want of sympathy, harshness of judgment, pride" or such other manifestations of the old Adam in Christians. This individual is one of the haters who has turned heretic and hates the brethren that are true to the Word and refuse to give it up at his bidding. He is bent on being a *skandalon*, on dragging others into the night of spiritual death, into the same night in which he is, in which he walks, which has made his own eyes blind.

He is a missionary of the devil, of "the darkness," among the true Christians whom he hates because of the light that is in them. Their fellowship with each other he aims to destroy. There are many in our day who hate like this. Here belong Matt. 18:6, 7. These haters love to trap the little ones, to ruin the faith of children, of young people, of immature Christians. They double their damnation. They are the ones who claim that they have the light (v. 9), the gnosis, the science, and thus catch their pitiful prey. But they are in the darkness (in its fearful power), do nothing but walk in this darkness, do not see where (in the Greek as in common English ποῦ means "where" and not "whither") they are going (Luther: "to hell"). Although they boast that they alone see, the darkness has blinded their eyes. Jesus utters the same truth in John 12:35.

12) Once again, as in v. 7, 8, John has a preamble regarding his writing (v. 12-15), and it is preparatory to something else that would destroy fellowship with God and our spiritual fellowship with each other (1:7), namely the love of the world. So much of heresy is baited with the things that are in the world by offering its adherents liberal enjoyment of those things which the light tells them are freighted with dangers to them.

I am writing to you, little children, because there have been remitted for you the sins for the sake of his name. I am writing to you, fathers, because you have known him (who is) **from the beginning. I am writing to you, youths, because you have conquered the wicked one.**

Compare "I am writing — I am writing" in v. 7, 9. As in 2:1, 28; 3:7, 18; 4:4; 5:21, "little children" includes all the readers. It is an address that is befitting the aged apostle's fatherly concern. See verse 1. They will take to heart what their most venerable father is writing to them.

Ὅτι is causal. John states the reason that he is writing to them. The reason is a fact which makes them the "little children" that they are to John: "because there have been remitted for you (sent away from you) the sins for the sake of his name." The perfect (in form a Doric, Arcadian, Ionic perfect passive, R. 315, from ἀφίημι) means that from the time of their conversion onward to the present moment God has remitted their sins. On this remission see the exposition of 1:9. It is this remission that has placed them in fellowship with God and thus in fellowship with each other (1:7), this remission which the heretics would destroy for them by enticing them with the lusts of the world. This is the point of the "because" clause, this is the reason for John's writing.

In 1:7 John mentions "the blood of Jesus, God's Son," and in 2:1 his "expiation for our sins," the *causa meritoria* for this remission; he now names the *causa instrumentalis,* διὰ τὸ ὄνομα αὐτοῦ, "for the sake of his (Christ's) name." One should correlate and study the many phrases with ὄνομα, beginning with Matt. 28:19; Acts 2:38. The name is the revelation. By the name alone Christ comes to us with his blood and expiation; by his name alone can we approach him (faith). He and all saving power is in his name. Thus "because of, by reason of, for the sake of (διά with the accusative) his name God ever remits our sins."

13) John divides all of his readers into two classes: old and young, "fathers — youths," the masculines include the other sex. Some have thought that John speaks of three classes; but τεκνία is John's regular address for all the readers, and the order "little children — fathers — youths" would be abnormal, it should read "fathers — youths — little children" or the reverse. Nor would the causal clause be fitting if it referred only to little folks. John has the refrain "I am writing to you" and even repeats it with the aorist.

John's reason for writing to the fathers, the older church members, is a double one; the second one pertains to them in particular. Due to their age and their extended opportunity in life they "have known the One (who is) from the beginning," the article τόν substantivizes the phrase. This phrase is to be understood in the sense it has in 1:1 and not in the sense it has in 2:7. As this phrase is applied to Jesus, it designates him in his deity. Ever since the venerable members of the churches first heard the gospel they have known Jesus in his deity, have known that this makes him the Savior indeed (4:14). During all these years they have rested their faith in him because he is from the beginning. Now these heretics are denying the deity of Jesus, are claiming that he is the natural son of

Joseph, that his blood is not that of "the Son of God" (see 1:7; also 1:1, "the Logos of the Life," and 1:3, "his Son Jesus Christ"). "You have known" is to be understood in the same sense as it was in v. 3, to know with spiritual affect and effect.

All of the older members will thus know what is at stake far better than the youth. They are able to tell the youth what John means by writing as he does so that they, too, may see the full danger. Thus John states as his special reason for writing to the fathers: I am writing to you "because you have known the One from the beginning."

John cannot offer the same reason for writing to the youth. Νεανίσκοι are young persons, and the word refers to natural age. We should not spiritualize it and refer the word to immature Christians, whether these are old or young in years; the term for such Christians is νήπιοι, Matt. 11:25; Luke 10:21; Rom. 2:20; I Cor. 3:1; Heb. 5:13; etc. Yet John has the noblest kind of reason for writing this letter also to the young people: "because you have conquered the wicked one," ὁ πονηρός, the devil, Matt. 13:19, 38; John 17:15; Eph. 6:16; I John 3:12; 5:18, 19, the archenemy. The perfect "you have conquered" is to be understood in the same sense as the preceding perfects: a past victory that endures until the present. Πονηρός = actively, viciously wicked.

This is not a reference only to young men, to their strength, their delight for conflict, etc. John's letter is not addressed to the male membership alone, it is intended also for the venerable mothers and the young maidens. In the case of the older members John mentions their extended knowledge of the Eternal Son; in the case of the younger their victory over Satan. Their extensive knowledge is full of rich, garnered treasure; the victorious stand against the enemy is the beginning of the true Christian life, the first full consciousness of youthful hearts that they stand in the army of Christ with Satan overthrown, that it is theirs to retain the victory and the triumph under Christ and during all of their life to reap the glorious fruits.

14) John repeats: **I have written to you, lads, because you have known the Father. I have written to you, fathers, because you have known the One (who is) from the beginning. I have written to you, youths, because you are strong, and the Word of God remains in you, and you have conquered the wicked cne.**

We use the English perfect to translate John's three aorists "I did write." We ask why John writes these aorists after the three presents "I am writing." Various explanations are offered. The more important believe that John refers to his Gospel with these aorists. It is assumed that the readers have already received John's Gospel, or that this letter is sent to them together with the Gospel. Another explanation is to the effect that with "I am writing" John refers to the lines he is now penning and with "I did write" to the lines already written in this letter (up to 2:11). Few will accept this latter explanation.

The three ὅτι clauses exclude a reference to John's Gospel. The three reasons here stated cannot be regarded as the reasons that John wrote his Gospel. In · John 20:31 (cf., 19:35) John states the purpose for which he wrote his Gospel. He wrote the Gospel at the solicitation of the Ephesian elders. While it is a minor matter as to whether the Gospel antedates this epistle or not, we believe that the Gospel was written later than the epistle. The relative date of the two documents cannot be determined by the tenses used here.

These are epistolary aorists. The three γράφω, "I am writing," are plainly rhetorical repetition. When he doubled this repetition John could not use three more γράφω; but the Greek afforded him its epistolary aorist. R. 845 is right, John continues his rhetorical repetition. "One has merely to change his point of view and look back at the writer." This is a common idiom. When John says, "I am writing," he thinks of himself as now writing this letter; when he says, "I did write," he thinks of the time when his readers will peruse what he has written in this letter. The reasons stated by the six ὅτι clauses, as well as the sixfold use of the verb "to write," refer to this letter and not to two documents.

Παιδία is only a variant for τεκνία and designates all the readers. These neuter diminutives are endearing. Our versions translate both "little children" but do so only because the English has no other good word for the latter. We render "lads" (we might say "laddies") but do so only in order to show that a word that is different from *teknia* is used in the Greek. The reason for writing to all his dear ones, as stated in v. 12 and now in a different form, "because you have known the Father," is really one and the same. Only those know the Father whose sins have been remitted for the sake of Christ's name. He, the Father of the Son, (see 1:2, 3, 7; 2:1, where "the Father" and "his Son" have been used) has been their Father through Jesus Christ, his Son, ever since he remitted their sins.

John begins to touch the relation of childhood on which he intends to say much more. Our fellowship with God (1:7) is that of Father and children, no less. This we "know" in the way explained in 2:3; see 3:1. What the heretics claim to know about their fellowship with God without a reference to sins, to Christ, God's Son, and to his cleansing blood, is a lying claim (1:5-10). These men are trying to get their lying claim to take the place of the knowledge in the hearts of the readers. John writes because of the knowledge of his readers, to preserve and to fortify this knowledge.

Yet both τεκνία and παιδία denote only the relation of the readers to John, the venerable apostle, who loves them as his little ones, and the terms should not be extended beyond this.

As far as the fathers are concerned, John leaves the reason for writing to them unchanged. This is not a paucity of thought on John's part. The repetition emphasizes the knowledge of the deity of the Son. In predicating knowledge of the fathers in v. 13 and now again in v. 14 John amplifies by predicating knowledge of all his dear readers. "This is life eternal, that they know thee as the only real God, and him whom thou didst commission, Jesus as Christ," John 17:3.

Si Christum bene scis, satis est, si cetera nescis;
Si Christum nescis, nil est, si cetera discis.
                                   —Bugenhagen.

The reason for writing to the younger members is also the same as that stated in verse 13, but John now inserts two explanatory clauses. "You are strong" with true spiritual strength; with this strength "you have conquered the wicked one" and now stand as victors. This is, however, not strength of your own: "the Word of God remains in you" as the fountain of your strength, the source of all true knowledge and power. "Remain thou in the things which thou hast learned and hast been assured of, knowing of whom thou hast learned them; and that from a babe thou hast known the sacred writings which are able to make thee wise unto salvation through faith which is in Christ Jesus," II Tim. 3:14, 15. This strength which is drawn from the Word is to go on conquering all the allurements of the world which the devil will employ.

Fathers and mothers, pastors and teachers must make the young strong in the Word of God. There is no more blessed work. Then they will conquer and remain conquerors, and the devil will not capture them with love for the world.

15) Those who find three groups referred to in v. 12-24 apply the following only to the third group, namely to the young people. All that follows, as well as all that is written in this letter, is intended for all. John's preamble (v. 12-14) prefaces v. 15, etc. In v. 18 παιδία is used with the same force as it. is in v. 12. Many of the allurements of the world are especially captivating for youth, but let us not forget that John mentions also those that are especially captivating for older persons.

Do not love the world nor the things in the world! If anyone loves the world, there is not the love of the Father in him. It is useless to urge those who are still of the world not to love the world. We can never hope to pluck figs from thistles or grapes from thorns. Only when people have overcome the wicked one, know the Father, know the Son, have the remission of sins, can we admonish them as John does here.

John uses ἀγαπᾶν, the love that indicates direction of the will and intelligent, purposeful choice, and not φιλεῖν, which is used to denote natural, friendly affection. John might have used the latter. James 4:4 reads: "The friendship (φιλία, friendly affection) for the world is enmity against God; whoever then intends to be a friend (φίλος) of the world establishes himself an enemy of God." What James inserts by means of the "intends to be" lies in the verb that John uses, namely intention, purpose, choice, will.

Κόσμος (originally: ornament, order) has a variety of meanings in the New Testament: the universe, the earth, the whole human race, the ungodly that are far from God, finally, in the ethical sense, all that is opposed to Christ on earth. John refers to this last, not to the world as God made it but as the wicked one corrupted all that is in it so that it now lies in the wicked one (5:19), is ruled by him as the prince of the world, as a kingdom that is opposed to the Father and the kingdom in which Christ rules with grace. As children of God we have been delivered from the world in this sense, have conquered the wicked one; the world, in the sense of corrupt, ungodly men, hates us, knowing that we do not belong to their number, John 15:18, 19. Luther: "To be in the world, to see the world, to feel the world, is a different thing from loving the world; just as to have and to feel sin is a different thing from loving sin." John might have used the decisive aorist imperative which is used in so many New Testament admonitions. He uses the present imperative which forbids a course of action. This matches the idea of the verb, for loving is continuous.

"Nor the things of the world" points to the individual deceptive treasures, pleasures, honors of the world, its wealth, its power, its wisdom, etc. We are not forbidden to admire, appreciate, use aright the natural things of this earth such as relatives, friends, fatherland, the beauties and the grandeur of nature, home, occupation, and the thousands of useful, attractive, valuable things which God has put all around us. But whatever in its connection, tendency, and influence is hostile to God, to Christ, and to his kingdom, however alluring or attractive it may otherwise appear, is "a thing of the world," to which we must be hostile since we belong to God, to Christ, and to his kingdom.

Leo the Great: "Man, who cannot be without love, is either a lover of God or of the world." He can never be both. Besser: "Where the love of God has entered a heart it intends to be the sole queen." "Ye adulteresses, do you not know that the friendship for the world is enmity against God?" James 4:4. It is significant that John does not say only in a general way that we are not to love the world but also in particular that we are not to love "the things of the world," for we love the sinful world by loving some special sinful thing or some things of the world. Every sinful tie must be sundered so that we truly belong to God.

John cites a specific case: "If anyone loves the world, there is not the love of the Father in him." This is a simple, indisputable fact. This is often taken to mean that if a person loves the world he does not love the Father. This is, of course, true, but it does not go far enough. Already in verse 5 we have met this genitive "the love of God," and we found that genitive to be subjective because of the context. It is so here, the wording itself indicates as much: "there is not the Father's love in him." This says much more than the objective genitive would. In John 14:23 Jesus says: "If anyone loves me, my word will he guard; and *my Father will love him,* and we will come to him and will make abode with him for ourselves." John says now that anyone who loves the world prevents the Father from loving him and coming into that man's heart to make an abode there.

To be sure, this man does not love the Father, which is, however, only the reason that the Father's love for him can find no place in him. That place is already occupied, the Father's love is kept out.

16) The reason that the Father's love cannot be found in such a person's heart is **because everything that (is) in the world, the lust of the flesh, and the lust of the eyes, and the pretension regarding the course of life is not out of the Father but is out of the world; and the world is passing away, also its lust, but the one doing the will of God remains forever.** This is the reason the Father's love with all its gifts cannot enter into this person's heart; and not the reason this person does not love the Father.

We may translate either "all" or "everything" that is in the world; we prefer the latter because we have "the things in the world" and then specifications of these things, "the lust of the flesh," etc. This is the sinful desire springing from the flesh or depraved nature which seeks sinful gratification. When John adds "the lust of the eyes" he includes the lust that reaches out beyond what a person can actually get a hold of in his sinning. The lustful eyes rove afar for sinful pleasure. On the lusts of the flesh compare passages such as Phil. 3:19; I Cor. 15:32; 6:18, and all the lists of vices.

The world talks about "pleasant, merry companionships," "innocent amusements," "having a good time," etc., which are but euphonious phrases to hide vileness. The lust of the eyes recalls Matt. 5:28. The older exegetes think also of the glitter of gold. When the devil has properly trained the eye, what will it not see to keep the furnace of ungodly emotions and imaginations aglow? The world shouts "artistic," "beautifully realistic," freighted with "beautiful moral lessons," etc., and thus gilds vileness.

John might have added "the lust of the ears" since these also reach out far for vile gratification. Add this yourself; John only suggests.

'Αλαζονεία = hollow, vainglorious pretense. It is followed by the objective genitive τοῦ βίου, the *vita quam vivimus* as distinct from ζωή, the *vita qua vivimus*. This pretense does not ask regarding the Father's will but acts as though it had the sovereign direction of its course of life; see James 4:16, and G. K. 227. The translations "the pride of life" (A. V.), "the vainglory of life" (R. V.) convey a wrong idea; John has in mind that hollow arrogance which presumes that it can decide and direct the course of life without God, determine what it will do, gain, achieve, enjoy.

All that is "*in* the world" "is not *out* of the Father but is *out of* the world," εἶναι ἐκ expresses source. The Father is the source of light, life, blessing, holiness, salvation; the world is the source of sin, lust, ruin, death. How can a Christian give up union and fellowship (1:7) with God and go back to union and fellowship with the world? "What I love, to that my soul clings. What I love is what I live, what I delight in, and this becomes part of my unconscious life, of my meditation, my dreaming. What I love becomes more and more part of my very self. He who loves the world becomes worldly, a man filled with the world." Dryander.

17) If this is the source, what about the result? "And the world is passing away, also its lust." It is now in the act of passing away. It is its very nature not to last. Its doom is overtaking it. Its glory is fading, its flowers are withering, its promises are failing, its hopes are crumbling. Isa. 14:11. A thousand wrecks lie strewn along its path, and soon it shall be altogether wreck and ruin. This is also true regarding "the lust for it." What this implies for the lovers of the world John lets us conclude for ourselves. They will be left naked, wretched, shattered, doomed. All their treasures and pleasures will, like water, have slipped through their fingers, their castles will be in ashes, their crowns a curse. Luke 16:23. Their souls, burnt and blasted by the lusts for the world, will have nothing left but endless remorse and penalty.

Does the siren voice of the world tickle your ears? Hear the word of truth: "The world is passing away!" The bank is breaking, it was never solvent — will you deposit in it? The foundation is tottering, it was never solid but only sham — will you build on it? The mountain is rumbling, quaking, it was never anything but volcanic, ready to blow off its head at any time — will you build your city there?

With a sudden, striking contrast John adds: "but the one doing the will of God remains forever." What God wills (θέλημα, a term expressing a result) is contained in his Word (1:7, 10; 2:4, 5, 7, 10: the light, the truth, the Word, the commandment). This is his good and gracious will. To do it is to believe and to be saved (John 6:40). That is what it means "to remain for the eon," i. e., forever.

The Third Circle of Facts

The Antichrists,
Centering on the Word Remain
2:18-28

18)   Six times John writes μένειν, "to remain," in
v. 24-28 just as he six times writes "commandment"
in v. 3-8. These antichrists did not remain; they "went
out from us." The governing idea is thus still the
fellowship, the κοινωνία with God, which is also the *koinonia* we have with one another (1:6, 7). To remain is
salvation, to go out is damnation. The antichrists went
out and seek to induce us to go out. John's elaboration
circles on and up in a wider sweep. New pertinent
concepts and facts are woven in as he proceeds.

**Lads, it is final hour. And even as you heard that
Antichrist is coming, also now antichrists many have
come to be; whence we know that it is final hour.**
On παιδία see v. 13; John addresses all of his readers.
Ἐσχάτη ὥρα is not *"the* last hour." The linguistic remark
that the article is omitted in the predicate is incorrect,
for it is not omitted when the subject and the predicate
are identical and interchangeable (R. 768). Here, in
fact, "last hour" is the subject and can be called the
predicate only formally when ἐστί is considered impersonal. So also the remark is not applicable that
well-known concepts and concepts of which only one
specimen exists may appear without the article. "Last
hour" appears only here in this verse and is not used
otherwise.

The term is plainly qualitative. Moreover, the
Greek word "hour" is here used in the wider sense
as it is in John 4:21 where the whole New Testament
period is referred to, likewise in John 5:25. Compare

also John 16:2, 25, 26; in the latter verses hour and day have the same meaning. We may add Matt. 24:36, "that day and hour," i. e., that date (narrow) and general time (wide). In some of these passages "hour" is quite properly rendered "time" by our versions. So also B.-P. 1427 has *"letzte Zeit" in dieser Weltperiode* as a translation of our passage. The English does not seek to conserve the qualitative sense as the Greek does and does not say "it is last hour," "final hour," but inserts the article, which then loses the Greek qualitative idea.

"Final hour" does not include the whole New Testament era from the first coming of Christ to the second. Although this would not be far wrong, we should note that John states how we may know that what is final hour is setting in, namely by the appearing of antichrists. Their increase in number is the sign. So we say that "final hour" extends from the appearing of such antichrists until the Parousia; note the latter in verse 28. Nor need one go to the Old Testament 'for the meaning of "last hour." To be sure, the Old and the New Testaments agree. But John had both the added revelation of Jesus and the further revelation which Jesus promised the apostles (John 16:13).

The "last hour" should not be referred to the short period that immediately precedes the Parousia, and on the basis of this the charge be raised that John (Paul, too) was mistaken. Then these apostles were false prophets! None of the apostles knew the day or the hour of the Parousia (Matt. 24:36) or ever pretended to know this. It might, like a thief, arrive at any time. John is not determining the *duration* of the "final hour," he is pointing his readers to the sign which indicates its beginning, the appearance of many antichrists: "whence we know (γινώσκω, with concern to ourselves) that it is (indeed) final hour." John saw the first group of antichrists. He distinguishes

these from "Antichrist," of whom he does *not* say that
he has already come to be but only that "he is coming."
We of the present day see how the antichrists have
multiplied, how "Antichrist" himself is here (II Thess.
2), and thus how imminent is the Parousia. Yet even
we do not know the date of the Parousia.

"Even as you did hear that Antichrist is coming"
refers to the apostolic prophecies about "Antichrist,"
which especially Paul has left us in II Thess. 2. John
is writing to many churches that were founded by Paul
and by his assistants; their number had greatly increased by this time. In I Pet. 1:1 we catch a glimpse
of their increase from the beginning to the year 64;
by the time John writes this letter many more churches
had been added to this group.

From the beginning Paul had told his churches
about "Antichrist." In II Thess. 2:5 he says that he
did so when he first preached in Thessalonica. Paul
was not the sole possessor of this revelation; all the
apostles had it. All the churches were informed "that
Antichrist is coming." John says that "even as" his
readers had heard that prophecy, one that was not
yet fulfilled at the time when John writes this letter,
they see the fact that "also now antichrists many have
come to be" (perfect tense: and are now here). The
implication is that these many antichrists are forerunners of the coming Antichrist. "Even as — also
now" denotes a correspondence. "Antichrist" and
"antichrists many" does the same, it only elevates the
coming one above those that are already here.

John alone has this term: here, in v. 22, and in
II John 7. Paul furnishes the full description of the
coming Antichrist (II Thess. 2), but he does not use
this term. Those are certainly right who find John's
coming Antichrist in Paul's prophecy. In fact, Paul's
ὁ ἀντικείμενος (II Thess. 2:4), "the one opposing himself," and John's ἀντίχριστος are practically synonymous.

The student will find all that we have to say on "the great Antichrist" who is aptly so termed in distinction from the others, "the little antichrists," in our interpretation of II Thess. 2. The great Antichrist is the papacy.

John uses both "Antichrist" and "many antichrists" qualitatively, without the article. Neither term is individual so that "Antichrist" is a single man, "antichrists" a number of single men. Paul's description of the former is that of a single opposition that is headed by a succession, all opposing in the same way and continuing to the Parousia itself. On the other hand, the "many antichrists" are varied oppositions, each being started by one man and his following, perhaps having a succession of leaders and continuing for a longer or a shorter period as the case may be, each opposition and its leadership running its course. Thus Cerinthus started a Gnostic opposition. This developed, and other Gnostic leaders arose. This antichristian opposition ran its course and eventually died out.

The way in which John writes "antichrists many" appears to mean that other leaders of his type besides Cerinthus had already come to be. In the following ages new kinds of antichristian leaders arose. Church history describes them and the extent and the duration of the various movements. We are acquainted with those of recent times: Dowie, Russell, Mrs. Eddy, modernism, etc. As they have multiplied, many of the old antichristian falsehoods have been taken up anew, have been dressed up in new verbiage and have paraded as new discoveries. Thus Cerinthus made Jesus the son of Joseph, which is only the modernists' rejection of the Virgin birth. He denied that the blood of Jesus is the blood of the Son of God with power to cleanse from sin (1:7; 2:2), which the modernists likewise deny.

'Aντί in ἀντίχριστος denotes opposition: *Widerchrist,*
opponent of Christ; not substitution, not a man who
claims to be Christ, to be in the place of Jesus Christ.
C.-K. 1134; Trench, *Synonyms;* others. There have
been both kinds, and the latter ("false Christs," Matt.
24:24) are certainly also opponents of Christ. John's
"Antichrist" and "antichrists" convey only opposition.
We have John's own statement to this effect in v. 22,
23; compare II John 7.

**19) From us they went out; yea, they were not
of us. For if they were of us they would have remained with us; but that they may be** (definitely)
made manifest because not are these all of us. One
mark of the antichrists is the fact that they originate
in the church. In II Thess. 2:4 Paul makes this clear
regarding the great Antichrist who sits in the very
temple of God. However hostile to Christ and to Christianity paganism, Judaism, Mohammedanism, Masonry, and political powers and movements may be, none
of these is an "antichrist." "From us they went out"
these many antichrists of John's time. They broke the
koinonia, the fellowship with us (1:7). The conserva-
tion of this spiritual fellowship is John's basic concern
as we have already indicated.

"Went out from us" means inward and also outward separation. Hence John adds: "yea, they were
not of us," ἐξ ἡμῶν is now to be understood in the deeper
sense: in their hearts they were not of us, were not
really derived from us. We regard ἀλλά as confirmatory
and climacteric and not as adversative (R. 1185, etc.).
It is, indeed, no wonder that they left our churches
and set up opposition camps; they did not inwardly
belong to us. They were either false from the start or
became so and then left.

"For" explains: "if they were (inwardly) of us
they would have remained (outwardly) with us," μεθ'
ἡμῶν, "in our company." John begins to use the verb

"remain" which he repeats six times in v. 24-28; it is
the verb of fellowship (1:7). He has a condition
of unreality, the apodosis has the past perfect and
ἄν (the only New Testament instance), whereas the
aorist is usually employed (R. 906; 1015). Is the
protasis a present or is it, too, a past unreality? Is
ἦσαν, the imperfect, doing duty for itself (present unreality), or is it doing duty for the unusual aorist
(past unreality)? B.-D. 360, 3. Either is correct. "If
they *were still* of us they would have remained with
us." Such a mixed condition is often written. We think
that this is such a mixed condition. Others prefer: "If
they *had been* of us (as John has said that they were
not) they would have," etc.

"But that they might be manifest" is elliptical.
Some would supply nothing, but it is best to supply:
"but they went out from us in order that they might
(definitely, aorist) be made manifest as not being of
us." We regard ὅτι as equal to "because" (not "that").
We keep the Greek word order: "because not are these
all of us," i. e., all who are in our churches are not inwardly of us, some are false. This has become manifest in regard to the antichristians: we see that they
have actually left us. Others think that the sense is
that all the antichristians are not of us (R. V.), which
has, however, already been said. The A. V. makes the
impression that "not all" but that some of the antichristians were and are not of us. True, the Greek
often places οὐ with the verb whereas we place the
negative with the subject; but when "all" is used in
the sentence, one must watch the sense and see whether
οὐ is to be construed with "all": "not all" (only some),
or with the verb: "are not" (all of them).

20) Beside what John says about antichrists he
places what he says about his readers as true Christians (hence καί), yet he does not do this for the sake
of a strong contrast but as a preamble to what he

further says about antichrists. John's readers are fully
able to know what antichristianity is, John does not
need to teach them that at this late date.

**And you on your part have anointment from the
Holy One, and you all know. I did not write to you
because you do not know the truth but because you
know it, and because every lie is not of the truth.**

Χρίσμα, a term expressing result, is not the act of
anointing but the anointment received by such an act;
in v. 27 we have: "you received anointment from the
Holy One." To refer it to the oil itself is incongruous
in these two passages. Since it is without the article,
"anointment" is qualitative.

"You have it from the Holy One" indicates that
the anointment referred to is something that is of a
permanent nature. The Holy One = Christ (John 6:
69; Acts 3:14; 4:27; etc.). The readers received anointment in baptism: Χριστός, the Anointed, bestowed
as a gift from himself the χρίσμα, anointment, the Holy
Spirit, and thereby made them χριστοί, anointed ones,
χριστιανοί, Christians, who are now opposed by ἀντίχριστοι,
antichristians. John calls the bestowal of the Spirit a
χρίσμα because he speaks of the antichristians. These
derivatives come from χρίω, the sacred act of anointing,
and not from ἀλείφω, "to oil" in ordinary ways. Hence
we have the term for "Christ": "the Holy One." There
is no reference to the ecclesiastical ceremony of anointing with oil at baptism; this was a later custom that
was based on John's passages.

The thought involved is the fact that by the gift
of the Spirit in baptism the Holy One united these
anointed ones with himself (fellowship in 1:6, 7);
yet this is only involved as is separation from all antichristians. The next clause: "and you all know," states
what Christ's anointing bestows on true Christians,
namely the enlightenment of knowledge. John uses
οἶδα, "to know" with the mind and intellect. This is

Interpretation of First John

correct, for in v. 21-23 the object of this knowing is the mark of an antichrist, and how to recognize one. Mere recognition is expressed by this verb. Some texts have πάντα: "you know all things" (our versions). Interpreters say that "all things" is limited by "the truth." Even so, this says too much and says it unnecessarily. A Christian does not need to know everything in order to know who is an antichristian liar. Instruction in the catechism is enough. We prefer the well-attested reading πάντες: "you all know," i. e., all of you have knowledge enough for what I, John, am now writing about.

21) So John says: "I did not write to you because you do not know the truth," i. e., do not know enough of it to know who is an antichrist, "but because you know it, and because every lie is not of the truth" and thus is easily known as a lie by all who know the truth. The aorist "I did write" is epistolary like those used in v. 13, 14 and refers to this entire letter, the whole of which is directed against "antichrists." When the readers get this letter they are not to read it as though John wrote in order to teach them the ABC of Christianity; he wrote it, they are to tell themselves, in order to have them use all the knowledge of the truth that they already have in order to detect as a lie all that is not the truth but is of the devil. John 8:44.

22) John now puts the question: **Who is the liar if not the one denying that Jesus is not the Christ?** And he then adds emphatically: **This one is the antichrist, the one denying the Father and the Son! Everyone denying the Son neither has the Father; the one confessing the Son also has the Father.**

Both of our versions are correct: "Who is a liar?" (the English idiom) ; "Who is the liar?" (Greek) because the Greek article is generic. So again: "He is antichrist" — "He is the antichrist." Any Christian who is in possession of the Spirit and thus of the truth can easily tell that he is certainly a flagrant liar who denies that Jesus is the Christ; yea, this man is one of the antichrists whether he is a leader or a follower since by his denying Jesus to be the Christ he denies the Father as well as the Son.

The Jews declared that Jesus was not the Christ, not the Son of God, and Jesus proved to them that they neither knew the Father nor had him as their Father, John 8:42, etc., but were of the devil, the liar from the beginning, the father of lies. While John denounces the early Gnostics, Cerinthus and his following, his words certainly recall the words Jesus addressed to the Jews although the latter were not antichrists in the sense of having developed in the Christian Church.

Cerinthus dreamed of a heavenly Eon Χριστός, a fictional being whom he substituted for the Son who is of one essence with the Father; this Eon Christ was not Jesus who was merely Joseph's natural son. This Eon Christos descended upon Jesus at the time of his baptism but left Jesus before his passion so that only Joseph's physical son Jesus died on the cross. Thus this Gnosticism abolished the Son and the efficacy of the Son's blood (1:7). Without the Son there is no Father of the Son (compare 1:2, 3, "with the Father" — "the Father and his Son Jesus Christ"; 1:7, "Jesus, his Son"). What Cerinthus and all of his ilk had left has aptly been called an idol. Their great claim of fellowship with God was a lie (1:6); it was fellowship with the idol of their imagination. The modern types of such liars are Unitarians, modernists, anti-Trinitarian sects.

"Liar" harks back to 1:6, 10; compare 4:20. The οὐ in "Jesus is not the Christ" is not redundant (R. 1164); Demosthenes has it (B.-D. 429). Its use is due to the fact that the clause is conceived as indirect discourse. These liars said in so many words: "Jesus is not the Christ." John quotes them.

23) John's deduction is true: "Everyone denying the Son neither has the Father," i. e., fellowship with the Father. Not only is John 14:6b true, but those who have no Son of God *eo ipso* also have no Father however much they may use the term "Father" (in the Unitarian sense = Creator). For the third time John uses ὁ ἀρνούμενος, "the one denying," the denier.

Over against the denier he places the true confessor the more sharply because he does not use a δέ: "The one confessing the Son also has the Father" i. e., has fellowship with the Father through the Son's blood (1:7) and expiation (2:2). To confess is the opposite of to deny. Both are open, public statements. The confession voices faith and states what is in the heart; the denial voices unbelief, hostility, and reveals that these are in the heart. There is no avenue to the Father for any sinner save through the Son and through his expiating blood.

24) Verses 22 and 23 present the facts which the readers know and which they need not be taught. John states them in a brief, clean-cut way. These facts call for the admonition **You, what you heard from the beginning — let it continue to remain in you!**

We regard ὑμεῖς as a vocative: "You!" We disregard R. 437. B.-D. 466, 1 is better regarding both this "you" and the one used in v. 27; they find a *parallelismus membrorum* in both sentences:

"You, what you heard from the beginning,
Let it continue to remain in you."

"And you, the anointment you received from him, .
It continues to remain in you."

The verb is not enough; "in you" must be added so that ὑμεῖς is not a prolepsis of the subject. We accept this but add that "you" is an address, a vocative.

The verb "remain" is six times dinned into the hearts of the readers. This is not monotony; "to remain" is the essential thing. To receive in the beginning and not let what we received remain in us is fatal. John learned this verb from Jesus who used it six times in John 15:3, 4, 6, 7. John uses it again, note 2:6, 14, 17, 19; 3:9. "In you" and "not in you" imply remaining in you and not remaining in you — see the phrases as far back as 1:8, 10; and then in 2:4, 5, 8, 15, 16; etc. "To be in" is the correlate of "to remain in" and is likewise used by John again and again. These recurring expressions should be well noted in order to understand John's full meaning.

"What you heard from the beginning" = the "old commandment which you had from the beginning" (v. 7); the phrase "from the beginning" is identical. "You heard" states how they received what they are to let remain in them. This is the light, the truth, the Word, the commandment already named so often. The apostles report it to you, also write it to you (1:3, 4); it comes by way of teaching as John will add (v. 27). The great thing is: "Let it ever *remain in you!*"

If there remains (effectively, definitely, aorist) **in you what from the beginning you heard, you, too, in the Son and in the Father will continue to remain** (durative future tense). The light, truth, Word, commandment, teaching heard by the readers are the divine means for uniting them with the Father and the Son, and the continuance of this union depends on the fact that what they have heard ever continues to remain in them. In 1:3 John began by saying that the great purpose of the whole apostolic preaching is that you may have fellowship with the Father and with his Son Jesus Christ; not an empty claim of fellowship

like that of the heretics (1:5, etc.) but actual fellowship with our sins confessed, remitted, cleansed away
by the Son's blood. See how from the very first paragraph onward John widens the circle upward step by
step on this pivot of fellowship until he arrives where
he now is: our continuing to remain in the Son and
in the Father, in true union and communion with them.
In the following John circles on and up still higher,
and all of this is presented in an unbroken line.

True religion is this and this alone that we poor
sinners are again joined to God. False religion is to
imagine that we are joined to God (1:6). John has
unfolded the facts that are involved in the true union
and has shown how we may know that we are, indeed,
in this union; in addition to these facts John has shown
the lies by which men deceive themselves (1:8) in the
delusion that without the Son's blood, without the
truth and Word, by denying and ignoring their sins
they are in union with God. With crystal clarity we
are made to see all. Here we have the true revelation
in sentence after sentence that is inspired of God; this
is eternally true. This is religion! All that denies it
is false religion.

Note that John repeats "what from the beginning
you heard," and that the phrase is now placed emphatically forward. All that lying men have told you
since that time, are telling you now, by drawing you
away from what you heard aims to separate you from
the Father and the Son in the delusion that, like these
liars, you can be in union with God without a Son of
God, etc.

**25) And this is the promise which he himself
promised to us, the life, the eternal one.** "The promise" = "what you heard from the beginning." Christ
himself promised this to us. Its sum and substance is
"the life, the eternal one"; the adjective is added with
a second article and is like an apposition and has an

emphasis (R. 776). Hear how this promise is uttered again and again by Jesus. Begin with John 3:15, 16; 5:24; 8:51 — but it fills the entire Gospel. The mention of "life" reverts to "Life" and "the Life, the Eternal One" (Christ), occurring in 1:2; note also 5:11. The apostles were (and still are) Christ's intermediaries for conveying his promise.

To be in union with God and with his Son is to have "the life, the eternal one." Without the Son there is no life. John 17:3. It is true religion to have this life; it is false religion to imagine that one has it.

26) **These things I wrote to you in regard to those trying to deceive you.** "I wrote," epistolary aorist = you will see that I wrote when you get and read this letter. "These things" are all those that were especially written against the antichristian deceivers who are now busy among you. By designating them with a present participle John describes them in their activity; but this participle is also conative: "those trying to deceive you," "them that would lead you astray" (A. V.). John is writing his letter in order to aid the readers in meeting these attempts of deceivers who are even deceiving their own selves (1:8).

27) **And you, the anointment which you received from him, it remains in you; and you have no need for anyone to be teaching you. On the contrary, as his anointment continues to teach you concerning everything, it (what it teaches) is also true and is not a lie, and just as it did teach you, continue to remain in him!**

"And you!" is a vocative (see v. 24). "The anointment you have from the Holy One" (Christ), mentioned in v. 20, is now called "the anointment which you received from him." This, John says, "remains in you." By "the anointment" John refers to the Holy Spirit as he is bestowed upon us (see v. 20) by sacrament and by Word. Fanatics imagine that they can get possession of the Spirit in an immediate way without the Word (note that the Word is the power in the sacrament).

The anointment thus remains in you. It was not a transient experience. John is thinking of the Spirit's permanent indwelling by means of his enlightening Word, which appears from his thrice repeated "to teach." With the permanent possession which you have "you have no need for anyone to be teaching you" (note the durative present tense). You are not a group of ignoramuses that need to be taught over˙ and over again by apostles and by Christian teachers. This is not intended as praise for John's readers; it is the statement of a simple fact which is to be noted as such. When people were received into the church in John's time they were evidently first well taught, they received a real anointment with the Spirit by the Word and by baptism. Today many preachers and many churches receive people without this anointment. No wonder the results are according.

"On the contrary (ἀλλά), as his anointment continues to teach you concerning everything, it is true and is not a lie," i. e., what it teaches you. John uses the singular ἀληθές to match the other predicate "not a lie." Note that neither of these predicates could fit "his anointment." If the first were intended for "his anointment" it should be ἀληθινόν, "genuine" and not sham (see v. 8 for the distinction). Least of all can it be said that "the anointment is not a lie." Both predicates fit what is taught by the anointment. Yet note that this *continues* to teach (again the durative present tense). John's readers received continuous teaching after they had been brought into the church. This ought to be the case everywhere. All of this teaching is sound, "true" (John has repeatedly called it "the truth"), "not a lie" like that of the liars (1:6; 2:22) and deceivers in whom there is not the truth

(1:8). This is again the fact, and it is again to be noted as such.

Now the admonition: "and just as it (i. e., this anointment) taught you (by this past teaching down to the present), continue to remain in him!" In v. 24 we have the condition on which the readers "shall remain (μενεῖτε) in the Father and the Son," namely the effective remaining in them of what from the beginning they heard; now we have the admonition: "continue to remain in him" (Christ, the Son) just as his anointment did, in fact, teach you.

The construction and the meaning are simple. Both become involved and troublesome when they are translated as they are in our versions. John does not range subordinate clauses together in the way in which our versions seem to think that he does. Besides other points, ὡς cannot be continued by καὶ καθώς; the latter stands by itself: "and just as."

28) John repeats the imperative he has used in v. 27 (this form cannot well be the indicative): **And now, little children, continue to remain in him in order that, if he is made manifest, we may have boldness and may not be shamed away from him at his Parousia.** Continue to remain in living spiritual connection with him so that at his wondrous Parousia you may joyfully meet him and may not be driven away from him forever in shame. "Little children" is used as it was in verse 1, and "remain" is the important feature: now fellowship and then eternal glorious fellowship.

Ἐάν at times approaches ὅταν in force (B.-P. 327) so that the A. V. is not wrong when it translates "when" instead of "if he is made manifest." This manifestation is the glorious one that shall occur at the time of the Parousia (on Parousia see II Pet. 1:16). When it occurs (aorist, as it shall with suddenness), then to have (effective aorist) boldness to face him is the

essential thing for us. Here and in Hebrews παρρησία
= the undismayed confidence of faith, "the feeling of
freedom and joyfulness over against another person,
especially of a judge" (C.-K. 451) ; compare 4:17. The
opposite is "to be shamed away from him." This verb
is a passive, and ἀπ' αὐτοῦ fits it well; so we do not translate "be ashamed *before* him." Those who only claim
fellowship with God, who see in Jesus only a man, a
natural son of Joseph, who deny his deity, the blood
of Jesus, God's Son (1:7) — add all the other nega-
tions that John has introduced — will be covered with
shame and will shrink "away from him" when he
appears all-glorious, the final Judge, with a verdict
that damns them. Note Dan. 12:2; Mark 8:38. Remain
in Christ and escape such a fate.   .

The Fourth Circle of Facts,

Centering on Being Born of God as His · Children

2:29-3:24

The New Birth and Our Relation to God
2:29-3:10a

29) The symphony glides into a new variation of the great basic theme. Many of the notes that have been ringing in the chords continue on in richer harmony. All that has been written about fellowship with God and with Christ (1:3-6) with all that centers in this union, as it is unfolded down to v. 28, our remaining, remaining, remaining with boldness at the Parousia, means that we are children of God, born of him, and so all that has been said before unfolds still farther in a new harmony and a still greater richness. This is John's wonderful way of writing.

If you know that he is righteous you realize that also everyone doing the righteousness has been born from him.

John has called both God (1:9) and Jesus Christ (2:1) righteous. It is debated as to which of the two he refers to here. Inasmuch as to be born "from him" certainly means "from God" (3:1, 9; 4:7; 5:18), and inasmuch as the Scriptures never say that we are born from Christ, we refer both clauses to God although John has spoken about Christ in the preceding verses. When Christ is called "Righteous One" in 2:1, this refers to him in his soteriological work, and that passage should not be introduced here. John refers to 1:5, 6: God is light, we walk in the light even as he is in the light, which is evidence that we have fellowship with him. For "light" and "the light" John now substitutes "righteous" and "the righteousness"; for "walking in the light" he uses "doing the righteousness"; for "fellowship" he writes "have been born from him." All the other thoughts that are suggested by 1:5, etc., reappear in the advanced connection save that they are stated so as to match this connection: the taking away of our sins, our purifying ourselves, also our loving our brethren (compare 2:9-11).

"If you know" is the verb οἶδα which means to direct the mind to its object, here to the great fact that God is righteous. In the apodosis John writes γινώσκω: "you realize that everyone . . . has been born from him"; this verb means that the mind receives an affect and an effect from the object (C.-K. 388). One knows and admits that God is righteous; one knows and is profoundly affected by the deduction that everyone doing the righteousness has been born from God. There is no exception to this. Hence, if I do not the righteousness, it is evident that I am not born from God; but if I do it, there is evidence that I am so born.

There is no reason for making γινώσκετε an imperative. John's readers know and realize what he says; he does not need to admonish them to do the latter any more than to do the former. The fact that v. 28 has an imperative and 3:1 an exclamatory imperative is not a reason for the use of an imperative in the intervening conditional sentence. John impresses two facts, the second being dependent on the first, on the minds of his readers (εἰδῆτε) in order to show them all that lies in these facts as they affect themselves (γινώσκετε).

God is righteous; righteousness is one of his energetic attributes. He is righteous in all his ways: in his laws, his promises, his verdicts, or a single act of his. In their blindness men may call him unjust, but they will be compelled to see and will then have to say that he did justly, righteously. John could say that everyone that is born from him, every child of his, is also righteous; but he reverses this and says much more. Our *being* righteous proves that we are born from him, and our *doing* the righteousness is the *perceptible* evidence of our birth. By it we can judge in regard to the mysterious and the intangible fact that a spiritual birth has occurred in us. By this tangible, visible evidence we can to a safe degree judge also our fellow Christians and the non-Christians. "Everyone doing the righteousness has been born from God," and no one 'else.

Many acquit themselves and pronounce themselves "righteous." Jesus told the Pharisees: "You are the ones declaring yourselves righteous (acquitting yourselves) before men" (Luke 16:15) and imagine that your claim makes you what you claim. Among the 95 Theses which he drew up for the anniversary of the Reformation, Claus Harms has a thesis that says: people used to pay for the forgiveness of their sins, but they have now advanced — every sinner just forgives his own sins. Doing the righteousness necessarily includes having the righteousness, which is the same as being righteous. God *is* righteous; therefore all that he does is righteous. Only a fool expects to do righteousness (to have what he does pronounced righteous) while he is not righteous at all. Doing the righteousness is the same as "doing the truth," 1:6. Both are definite: "the truth" = what God's Word says; "the righteousness" = what God and his Word pronounce righteous. The words δίκαιος and δικαιοσύνη are always forensic.

This "doing," ever doing, is not what the world calls "living a moral life." A man can live such a life without having been born anew. Natural morality is not "the righteousness" which is declared such by God. John has already written 1:9 and 2:1-3. "Everyone

doing" means everyone whose sins God has remitted
and cleansed away, everyone who through the Advocate, Jesus Christ the Righteous One, has constant remission of sins, who thus heeds the admonition not to
sin (2:1), who keeps God's commandments, i. e., remains true to God's Word.

This is the man who has the plain, visible evidence
that he "has been born from God," (perfect tense: is
in that condition, continues in it). He is a new creature. He has been regenerated (John 3:3, 5). He has
been made a good tree, his good fruit being the decisive
evidence for this fact.

Socinus and the rationalists imagine that man gives
himself the new birth when he strives *Dei similem esse*,
tries to do good. Acts 10:35 is understood to mean that
even every earnest pagan, Jew, Mohammedan, ra-
tionalist, though he be without Christ and the Son's
blood (1:7), is accepted by God as his child. Others
imagine that by doing what is right we attain the new
birth, i. e., that the fruit produces the tree. Still others
in a pantheistic way see in the new birth a process by
which a person is absorbed into God or absorbs God in
himself.

John is elucidating the κοινωνία or fellowship with
God (1:3-7). This is produced by the new birth when
a new, spiritual life is kindled in us through Christ,
the Life, the Eternal One (1:2). This makes us the
children of God who is righteous, and the evidence of
our childhood is our doing the righteousness which his
judgment ever approves.

3:1) John begins to unfold what lies in the
astounding fact that we, who by nature are nothing
but poor sinners (1:8), have been born from God
who is righteous. In the first place, this makes us
"God's children." **See what great love the Father**

has given to us that we are called God's children!
And we are!

The aorist imperative is punctiliar: "Just take a
look at this love!" Ἴδετε is plural, and hence it is not
an interjection (A. V.) but governs an object clause.
Ποταπὴν ἀγάπην = "what manner of love" with the idea
of both quality and quantity: "what glorious, sublime
love," Luther. To see it aright is to sink down in adoration before it. It is beyond all comprehension.

Ἀγάπη is the love of comprehension and full understanding coupled with adequate purpose. As such it
knows and in this knowledge moves toward its purpose.
It is a pure gift; those are right who see that nothing
in us called forth this love. "Has given" matches the
perfect used in 2:29, "has been begotten"; this gift
remains. The subject and the verb are transposed in
order to emphasize both, the force of which is lost in
the English: "what love *has given* to us *the Father.*"
"To us" is not emphatic. "The Father" is the same
father that was mentioned in 1:2, 3; 2:1, the Father
of the Son but in Jesus Christ also our Father (Matt.
6:9). These two relations are kept distinct (John 20:
17) although they are joined.

The ἵνα clause is appositional and not final. It does
not mean "that we should be called" but expresses a
fact: "so that we are called," the aorist meaning "actually called," the passive indicating that this was done
by the Father himself. He, from whom we have been
born in infinite love, acknowledges us as his children;
all his love and all the gifts that it is able to bestow
upon us are ours. John adds emphatically: "And we
are" God's children. We cannot be called his children
by him without actually being his children.

Here we have a definition of fellowship with God
(1:6, 7); it is the fellowship of the Father and his
children. There are other fellowships. There are some
in which one gives as much as another gives, like friend

and friend, husband and wife. In this fellowship all
is one-sided: God gives, we only receive in gratitude.
Here the only true religion is defined; it is actual
fellowship with God and not merely fellowship claimed,
imagined (1:6) ; it is *a birth from God,* being actual
children of God. This is Christianity; all other religions are false. Only those who receive Christ by faith
are "God's children" (John 1:12).

**For this reason the world does not know us be-
cause it did not know him.** Διὰ τοῦτο makes the previous statement the reason that the world does not
know us, and ὅτι substantiates by pointing to something
additional that the world does not know. The verb
οἶδα could not be used here; γινώσκω is the proper
verb (John 1:10; 16:3; 17:25). The world sees that
we are here and thus knows us (οἶδα) ; but as "God's
children" we are utterly foreign to the world because
even our Father is utterly foreign to the world. The
world has no conception of what we are as those who
are born from God and thus God's actual children,
and the deepest reason for this ignorance is the fact
that it has no conception of our Father. I Cor. 2:14;
II Cor. 6:9a.

The world is proud of its knowledge, but the real
things worth knowing it does not know. The mystery
of regeneration is foolishness in its eyes; those who
are children of God in Christ it considers deluded. Its
own idea of a universal fatherhood of men without
redemption and regeneration it regards as the height
of wisdom. Let no true spiritual child of God count
on recognition from the world. It simply does not
know (γινώσκω). The names of God's greatest saints
are not engraved on the tablets of the world's temple
of fame. This cannot be otherwise; if it were, the
world would not be the world, and we should not be
God's children. Grieve not that the world does not know
you; this is one proof that you are God's child. If the

world knows you, you should grieve, for then there is proof that you are not God's child.

The aorist "did not know him" states the fact historically; since it never *knew* him it does not now *know* you. There is no need to modify the sense of the verb into "does not accept you as its own" or into "hates you"; to know in actual realization is enough. The world has only fictional, false conceptions regarding our Father and regarding us, his children. "The world" includes all unregenerate men; it is a collective and is not to be changed into an abstract such as "ungodliness."

2) The greatness of God's love in making us his children appears fully in view of the future that awaits us. **Beloved (see 2:7), now are we God's children, and not yet was it made manifest what we shall be. We know that, if it is made manifest, similar to him shall we be because we shall see him as he is.**

As one of God's children John addresses other such children in the love that binds them together as he now lifts their eyes to the glory that awaits them. "Now are we God's children" repeats this fact for the third time; but "now" fixes attention on the present time. We look very much like other people; the world does not comprehend that we are really anything higher and laughs at such an idea.

"And not yet was it made manifest (in the English idiom we use the perfect when we point backward; the Greek is content with its aorist) what we shall be"; not yet has God made a public display of the glory that belongs to his children, of the inheritance incorruptible, unstained, unfading, reserved for us in heaven (I Pet. 1:4). Not yet do we wear the white robes of heaven; not yet does the crown of glory sparkle on our brow. The robe of Christ's righteousness, our crown of hope, the diamond of faith, the pearls of love, are invisible to physical eyes. We still wrestle with the flesh; in a sinful world and with a mortal nature we plod on wearily. A child of God is here and now, indeed, like a diamond that is crystal white within but is still uncut and shows no brilliant flashes from reflecting facets.

This shall be changed completely. "We know (οἴδαμεν, know the fact) that, if it is made manifest (as it certainly will be), similar to him we shall be because we shall see him as he (actually) is." Here again (2:28) and with the same verb John uses ἐάν almost as though it were ὅταν, "when, whenever"; it is the "if" of strongest expectancy. One may hesitate as to whether ἐὰν φανερωθῇ has the same meaning here that it had in 2:18 and that ἐκεῖνος ἐφανερώθη has in 3:5, thus: "when *he* (Christ) shall be made manifest" (as in our versions). But here the impersonal "*it* was made manifest" precedes so closely that both surely have the same meaning. Thus: "when what we shall be is made manifest" we know "that similar to him (placed forward for the sake of emphasis) we shall be because we shall be even as he is."

The question arises as to whether John refers to the Father or to Christ with these pronouns. One cannot argue that God is invisible (I Tim. 6:16), for we shall, indeed, see God (Ps. 17:15; Matt. 5:8); this is the *visio Dei*. So we shall also be similar to God in the *imago Dei* of perfect righteousness and holiness (Eph. 4:25) including the *glorificatio*. Yet v. 5 speaks of Christ (although of his being made manifest in the flesh) as all agree; it is also best to refer v. 3 to Christ. So we do the same with the pronouns occurring in v. 2b. We have seen that in 2:28, 29 John turns from Christ to God; now from v. 1 and 2a he in 2b turns from God to Christ. The observation is thus correct that, as far as John is concerned, God and Christ need but a slight verbal distinction. When this is referred to Christ, we may cite passages such as Phil. 3:20, 21 which includes the glorification of also our body as made similar to Christ's glorious body, and all those passages which describe the visible φανέρωσις ("manifestation, appearance") of Christ at his Parousia (2: 28) such as Acts 1:11; I Thess. 4:16.

There is no stage of existence beyond being "children of God" to which we shall be raised by God at the time of Christ's coming. Ὅμοιος expresses similarity. *Non erimus idem, quod Deus, sed similes erimus Dei* (Luther, who interprets this as a similarity to God). *Non dantur gradus* υἱότητος (Calov) but only stages in our condition as children. Here on earth we are in a humiliation that is similar to that of Christ, eventually we shall be in a glory that is also similar to that of Christ. Hence the verb which is used, the passive of which at times has the sense of the middle: "to appear" (so in the A. V.). The aorist subjunctive "if it is made manifest" refers to the one great final manifestation. Ah, how all the children of the world will then look at us whom they now disregard, despise, and at times persecute!

☞ **3)** John now develops the "everyone doing the righteousness" which he wrote in 2:29. We are children of God and know that at the last God will make us glorious, similar to Christ. In John's simple way of writing the καί unfolds what this means regarding our conduct. We read the whole of v. 3-10a together as one continued series of incontrovertible facts and in the formulation note five successive πᾶς ὁ, four with the present, the fifth with the perfect participle, and two ὁ with present participles. This is continued in 10b where John specifies the essentials of brother love.

And everyone having this hope (set) on him continues to purify himself even as that One is pure. There is no exception. He who stops purifying himself has dropped this hope from his heart. The present tense is important. If this were perfectionism, an aorist would be required: "did purify himself." We have a plain mark by 'which to judge ourselves. To claim that we are God's children, who have been born of him, to claim the hope of heaven and glory and yet to stop self-purification is to be lying (1:6).

"Everyone having this hope" objectivizes the hope in the heart like having faith, having love, etc. 'Επ' αὐτῷ = set or resting "on him" as the One who will fulfill this hope for us. The world is full of men who have a certain kind of hope, but see on what it rests — not on Christ, on his blood and expiation (1:7; 2:2), on his promise (2:25). They invent their own foundation for the hope they have. It is sand, is swept away when the great flood comes (Matt. 7:24-27).

"Even as that One is pure," Christ in his whole earthly life. John does not say "even as that One was purifying, did purify himself." Jesus never had even a trace of sin. "Is pure" = purity is his inherent quality. "Is" does not equal "was," nor does "is" refer only to Christ's present state in heaven. It is like the "God is righteous" occurring in 2:29 as far as time is concerned: was — is — will be, this is immaterial. There is no incongruity between the clauses because our constant purifying is an *action* Christ's a *state* of purity. To keep striving after a perfect model is perfectly congruous.   .

The way in which the pronouns ἐν αὐτῷ and ἐκεῖνος are used in 2:6, the one referring to God, the other to Christ, leads some to regard .them in the same way here and thus also to refer the pronouns used in v. 2 to God. This is a real question. In trying to answer it one should not forget that ἐκεῖνος also refers to what immediately precedes and thus only resumes it even without emphasis (B.-P. 272, 1b). We have a plain case in v. 7, which it is well to consider since it follows so closely and is not remote as 2:6 is.

4) **Everyone doing the sin is also doing the lawlessness; and the sin is the lawlessness.** This is a fact, and there are no exceptions. "Everyone doing" is the same as it was in 2:29 where we have "doing the righteousness." Doing the righteousness — doing the sin — doing the lawlessness means being given to do; the participle and the verb are durative. The governing *habitus* is referred to as this is operative and apparent in action, in doing. The articulated nouns make the abstracts definite, which the ordinary English does not note. *The* righteousness, *the* sin, *the* lawlessness are not these manifestations in general but the righteousness that *God* declares to be such, the sin that misses the mark set by *God*, the lawlessness that violates *God's* law. We introduce no qualifiers such as mortal sin, willful, conscious transgressions of law, sin against conscience, or the limitation to deeds of sin.

We have the opposite of v. 3 and also of 2:29: the one keeps purifying himself, ever by the grace of God sweeping sin out of himself, ever giving himself to the righteousness (in thought, word, and deed) that has God's approval. The other gives himself over to the sin, the lawlessness despite God who abhors both. The one is a child of God; the other is a child of the devil (v. 10a).

It is John's habit to place simple facts side by side and to let them speak for themselves as they certainly do. We may express their relation to each other by logical particles, but when we do, the logic lies in the facts as facts even without the use of particles. So John says regarding the sin: "and the sin is the lawlessness." The two are identical, interchangeable, which is the force of the articulated predicate (R. 769, note his explanation on page 768). We often define by using interchangeable or even only synonymous terms; hence it should not be denied that this is that

type of a definition. It serves to bring out that side
of "the sin," namely "the lawlessness" (opposition to
and disregard of God's law), which makes "the sin"
the very opposite of "the righteousness." Both "the
righteousness" and "the lawlessness" are strong forensic terms: as the righteous Judge God declares
what is *righteous* (2:29) and what violates *his law*.

No one who is given to doing the lawlessness can
possibly have fellowship with the God of light (1:5, 6)
and of righteousness (2:29), be his child to enjoy his
fatherly love, to have the hope of glory.

5) Beside the two statements: Everyone with
the great hope purifying himself even as Christ is
pure, and: Everyone doing the sin, thereby also doing the lawlessness in direct opposition to God and
Christ — beside these John places the statement:
**And you know that that One was made manifest in
order to take away the sins, and sin in him there is
not.** The readers themselves know these facts as
well as John knows them, and they may now apply
them to the other facts that he has just stated in v. 3, 4.

The one is the fact that Jesus Christ was made
manifest (became flesh, lived, suffered, died, rose
again) in order to take away the sins. Compare "he
was made manifest to us" (the apostles). He who
existed from all eternity *asarkos* was made manifest
in time *ensarkos* as the Lamb of God that takes away
the sin of the world. John 1:14, 29. This was his great
mission, and he carried it out.

Αἴρειν has three meanings: to lift up from the
ground; to lift up in order to bear; to carry or take
away. The third meaning is to be preferred here. "The
evangelist thought of the expiatory power of the death
of Jesus so that we must translate (John 1:29): 'Behold, this is God's Lamb, the one taking away (by the
expiatory power of his blood, I John 1:7) the sin of
the world'" (G. K. 185). There is thus no reason in

connection with John 1:29 or our passage for being uncertain whether to translate "take away" or "bear" as the R. V. and its margin seem to be uncertain. Isa. 53:4-12. On αἴρειν, "to take away," in other connections see John 11:48; 17:15; 19:31, 38. Ἀφίημι and ἄφεσις, "to remit, send away," "remission," are regularly used with reference to the acts which God (Christ) performs in personal absolution (justification) and not to Christ's universal expiation. We should not confuse the two.

In John 1:29 we have "the sin of the world," here "the sins," which spreads them out in their multiplicity whereas in v. 4 "the sin" is the abstract made definite. Since Christ came for the very purpose of taking away the sins, it is plain that he who is given to do the sin, the lawlessness, scorns Christ's expiation or imagines that he can abuse it and thus demonstrates that he has prevented Christ's blood from putting him into fellowship with God (1:7) as a child of God and an heir of heaven (2:29-3:3).

"And sin in him there is not" is similar to v. 3: "even as that One is pure"; it also uses the present tense "is" in the same way. The anarthrous ἁμαρτία, anything of the nature of sin, is correct. As the absolutely Sinless One Christ was, indeed, able to be the sacrifice to take away the sins of others. John states the fact on this account, but also in connection with Christ's taking away the sins on account of his readers, who cannot be God's children through Christ's blood and expiation (1:7; 2:2) if they are still given to doing the sin. As Christ is pure, and sin is not in him, they must ever be purifying themselves, and when they find themselves sinning must flee to their Advocate with his expiation for such sins (2:1, 2).

6) Thus John advances to the facts: **Everyone remaining in him does not go on sinning; everyone sinning has not seen him, nor has he known him.**

Both facts are true without exception. John introduces "remaining," on which he rings the changes in
2:19, 24-28. Every person that is joined to Christ by
faith and by faith remains in Christ simply does not
go on sinning. These two facts exclude each other.
The durative present "does not go on sinning" is vital
for John's meaning; it has the same force that it had
in v. 4, "everyone doing the sin," given to doing it.
Not to go on sinning implies a decisive break with
sinning. Remaining in Christ, the expiator of sins, the
Sinless One, means faith in him and in his expiation
and thus a steady fight against sinning, a constant self-
purification by his grace and his help. It cannot mean
anything else.

Perfectionists misunderstood this statement and
think that it refers to total sanctification: has stopped
sinning altogether. They disregard the tense. They
ignore 1:8-10; 2:1, 2; 3:3. In 1:8, 9 John makes confession also of his own sins: "If we keep confessing
our sins." So in Rom. 7:14-25 Paul deplores the fact
of his still sinning, of the sin power trying to make
him its war captive (v. 23). Phil. 3:12, 13. Perfectionism takes John's statement out of its connection
and disregards the tense which John uses.

John states the opposite but again with an advance in thought: **Everyone continuing to sin** (going
on with sinning) **has not seen him, nor has he known
him.** If he says: "I have known him," he is a liar
(2:4). John uses "seeing him" as Jesus uses θεωρεῖν,
"behold," (in John 6:40) because he speaks positively:
"everyone beholding the Son and believing on him."
The true believer ever keeps his eyes on Jesus. John
says that the one going on in sinning "has not seen
Christ," has never as much as caught a glimpse of
him. The eyes of his understanding (Eph. 1:18) have
remained blinded by the darkness (2:11), have never
been opened or have become closed again.

The fact that this refers to spiritual seeing is made plain by the addition: "neither has he known him," which introduces the true, inward, spiritual knowing that was mentioned in 2:3-6. John regularly builds up his thought by interlocking and interweaving, by repeating and, when repeating, by adding new angles of view. Here γινώσκω is the fitting verb. This is not a mere intellectual comprehension but one that produces its spiritual affect and effect in him who knows. This sinner may talk about Christ, but his soul has not come to know him, has not made true contact with him. His *gnosis*, if he is a Gnostic, is false.

7) John turns to admonition. **Little children (see 2:1), let no one try to deceive you! The one doing the righteousness is righteous even as that One is righteous. The one doing the sin is from the devil because from the (very) beginning the devil keeps sinning. For this there was made manifest the Son of God, to destroy the works of the devil.**

The admonition shows why John is writing this. There are antichristian deceivers (2:18, 19) who were seeking to deceive or lead astray (πλανάω, 1:8) the readers. What they claimed about not having sin 1:8 indicates. Their entire doctrine on this subject has not been preserved. Yet from 1:6 plus 2:29 and now 3:7 we safely conclude that they thought that they were righteous without doing the righteousness. The aorist imperative would mean: "Let no one succeed in deceiving you!" The present: "Let no one engage in it, i. e., even try it!" *Obsta principiis!* It is a mistake to think that the fact of being a Christian is proof against cunning deceivers. The young, the inexperienced, the unfortified are not proof of this.

Here is the simple fact: "The one doing the righteousness (see 2:29) is righteous." Apply it to yourself, apply it to all around you. There is no appreciable difference between ὁ ποιῶν and the preceding πᾶς ὁ ποιῶν.

In neither case is an exception permitted; after twice using the latter John is now content with the former. John is, of course, speaking about conduct, but as conduct is the result of what a person *is*. What one is, his conduct shows, and vice versa. "Is righteous" and "is from the devil" are the opposites.

Δίκαιος is, as always, forensic. Yet ἐκ God (2:29), ἐκ the devil, and "having been born" (2:29; 3:9), and "God's children" let us think of regeneration. This does not, however, exclude justification. These two occur in the same instant. In the instant of the divine birth the divine verdict is ours; in the instant of its pronouncement we are reborn. Gal. 3:26-29. While John dwells on the birth and the new nature with its plain results that are evidenced in the conduct he does not ignore the righteous Judge (2:29) and his verdict on the δίκαιοι.

"Even as that One is righteous" refers to Christ (2:1; "pure" in 3:3). In 2:29 this refers to God, now it is referred to Christ. Here we have a plain case where αὐτός and ἐκεῖνος denote the same person, which must be considered when we are studying v. 3 and the preceding pronouns. God's verdict of approval ever rested upon Jesus. Only the righteous remain in him, in the Righteous One, and the fact that they are righteous is evidenced by their doing the righteousness. Jesus is our model, yet he is more than our model because of our union with him (1:3), our remaining in him, from which comes all that we are.

8) "The one doing the sin" betrays his origin, "he is from the devil." This man is described already in v. 4: "everyone doing the sin." John does not say "is or has been *born* from the devil." Such a verb would not be apt because "to be born" implies *life*, and all that comes from the devil is death. Yet the devil is the father of those doing the sin (John 8:44), they are "the children of the devil" (v. 10). This is not a

fatherhood of begetting like the high fatherhood of our Father but a fatherhood that is due to the derivation of our sins from the devil's sinning: "because from the (very) beginning the devil sins" (II Pet. 2:4), sins and sins (progressive present, gathering up the past and the present in one phrase, Moulton; R. 879, etc.). Those who follow him by steadily doing the sin are ἐκ, "from him," are his "children" in this way.

Let no one try to deceive you in regard to this! The gulf is as wide as that between heaven and hell. They are liars who tell you that they have bridged it. Either you are with God in righteousness, under his acquitting verdict, or you are in the devil's family. *Tertium non datur.*

Not only are those persons who are mentioned in v. 7, 8 so far apart, the one being with Christ, the other with the devil, but also another fact must be stated: "For this there was made manifest (see v. 5) the Son of God, that he destroy the works of the devil," aorist, actually destroy. Christ came to destroy effectively the works of the devil, the havoc which he wrought among men with his sinning. A pronoun will not do as a reference to Christ; John uses "the Son of God" (1:3, 7) and names him according to his deity. It is incorrect to say that his greatness, his power, and his majesty in contrast with those of the devil are not expressed. ▸ But he does not destroy the devil's works by means of his omnipotence: "he was made manifest," he came in his human nature in order by this to destroy the devil himself and his power of death, Heb. 3:11.

"The works of the devil" are all that he has wrought. Some restrict the thought to the sins that he has produced (v. 5), but John expands. Consider Luke 11:21. Why exclude the consequences of sin on the plea that these are the judgments of God? The effects accompany their cause, the Son destroys both

and even him who is the personal cause of them (Heb.
3:11). This destruction began decisively when the Son
came to earth; it goes forward inexorably now; it will
be consummated at the Son's Parousia. Woe to those
who are the devil's children! Εἰς τοῦτο makes the appositional accusative ἵνα clause (R. 699) emphatic.

9)   Linking back into 2:29 ("born from God")
and into 3:5 ("doing the sin"), John unfolds the
thought still farther: **Everyone that has been born
from God does not go on doing sin because his seed
remains in him; and he is not able to go on sinning
because he has been born from God.**

To this extent the Son of God has already destroyed
the devil's works in everyone that has been born of
God, that by regeneration has been born into a new
life, has become a child of God, has God as his Father.
Everyone who is so born "does not go on sinning."
The present durative ποιεῖ is as vital for John's meaning here as it was in v. 6. Οὐχ ἁμαρτάνει (v. 6) =
ἁμαρτίαν οὐ ποιεῖ: "does not go on sinning" — "does not
go on doing sin" (anarthrous: what is of the
nature of sin). He keeps purifying himself (v. 3), is
constantly busy sweeping out sin.

The cause of this great change lies in the fact of
his "having been born from God." John explains more
fully: "because his seed continues to remain in him,"
and once more he introduces this significant verb "remain." What is meant by this person's seed 'and this
seed's remaining in him, exerting such a power in him
that he does not, in fact, cannot go on in his old way,
sinning and sinning? The answer that this seed is
the Holy Spirit is accepted by some, but they feel that
calling the Holy Spirit "the seed" of the Christian will
not do. So they say that the *person* of the Spirit is not
referred to; but when they then state what *is* referred
to they offer abstractions such as *das Goettliche*, "a
gift from him and his nature."

This "seed" is the Word of God (1:10; 2:5, which he guards; 2:14), the light (1:6, 7), the truth (1:8; 2:4); the commandment (2:7, etc.). Here belong I Pet. 1:23 and James 1:18. It makes no difference whether we say that the word remains in us, or that we remain in the Word, the truth, etc. "Seed" is figurative, but the figure extends only to the fact that a seed has life in it. The Word of God is a living power (I Pet. 1:23). It is not necessary to extend this figure, to talk about vegetable seed and human seed, life germ, and to seek for analogies in natural life, seed growth, etc. Jesus and the holy writers dominate their figures and are not dominated by them. Does this interpretation of the "seed" as the Word lose the Holy Spirit? Indeed not! The great means by which the Spirit quickens, kindles life, keeps life alive, is the Word, in which he is, by which he works.

When he has the living Word in his reborn heart no one is able to go on sinning simply "because he has been born from God." The matter is axiomatic. All that can be done by way of explanation is to insert that the Word of God remains in the person and thus to shift the emphasis in the subject: "everyone *born* of God" does not, cannot go on sinning because of this *seed* in him, and to emphasize in the predicate that "*from* God this person is born." Note the position of ἐκ τοῦ Θεοῦ; it occurs first after the participle and then before the verb.

10) John closes the whole discussion: **In connection with this manifest are the children of God and the children of the devil,** so manifest that only the blind do not see who is who and the liars, the self-deceived, who make God a liar (1:6, 8, 10). On "children of God" see verse 1. Here we at last have "the children of the devil." There are none who are half and half; there is only an either-or. John has presented the manifest, plain, even visible difference. Every

cloud that the antichristians (2:18) may have raised for his readers is swept completely away.

The New Birth and Our Relation to the Brethren
10b-24

10b)   The division into verses and also the R. V.'s paragraphing seem to be faulty at this point. John now begins the development of the truth that those who have been born from God and are his children are by the fact of that birth brothers and love each other as brothers, and — what is most important in John's presentation — that through this love each brother furnishes evidence that he is a brother, a member of God's family. By its hatred of us the world shows that it does not belong to the divine family.

At this point John develops the thought expressed in 1:3: "you have fellowship *with us,*" the apostles, those who first gathered around Jesus, the Son, and were made his witnesses to all other men; in addition the thought expressed in 1:7: "we have fellowship *with each other*" as being cleansed by the blood of Jesus, God's Son. The first additional circle of thought, a small one, which shows that this means love between brother and brother appears in 2:9-11, where it is in strong opposition to hate, for the antichristians are not of us but went out from us (2:18, 19) and hate us who are in the light because they prefer the darkness. In this smaller circle John uses "the light" and "the darkness" and reverts to 1:5-7. John now advances this thought in accord with what he has added about our relation to God. We now see what "brother" really means. He is one of "the children of God," one born into God's family. We see how all such brothers naturally love, must love each other, how this love is the evidence of the fact of being a brother.

Into this wider circle (3:10b-24) John weaves in much more that he has already said: "remaining"

(2:24-28 and elsewhere), "the commandment" (2:3-8 and elsewhere), "knowing" (2:3-6 and elsewhere), "the world" (2:15), "boldness" (2:28); especially also Christ's sacrifice (1:7; 2:2; 3:16). Finally, John combines faith and love in verse 23. Then he reaches out still farther in his development (4:1, etc.) yet, as he has done before, retains all that he has said.

Unless this is clearly seen and appreciated we shall not understand the structure of John's letter and shall fail to note that it starts from its basic facts in 1:1-4 and spirals upward in gradually widening circles and retains all that precedes in every advance. The whole is one weave in one pattern with new colors introduced that reappear again and again. It is a perfectly designed, rich Oriental rug.

John begins as he did in 2:29b but now writes negatively: **Everyone not doing righteousness is not from God,** is *not* born of God, is *not* one of God's children (3:1), is, in fact, one of "the children of the devil" (v. 10a). All that is said in 2:29-3:10a is again brought to mind in this summary statement of fact. On what "doing righteousness" and "to be from God" means see 2:29.

And the one not loving his brother introduces the additional fact that is now to be unfolded, that our relation to God at once involves our relation to each other. It is introduced negatively because in 2:29b the positive has already been presented; the negative is its complement. At the same time, by saying that "the one *not* loving his brother" is *not* of God, John draws a decisive circle about "the children of God" and presents them as being separated from "the children of the devil." They are separated at the very source, their respective fathers; the one is the heavenly Father, God, the other the devil (John 8:44). This origin and source is itself secret and invisible, but the tangible, visible evidence is plain: love and the absence of love.

The reason John says "not loving his brother" instead of "not loving God" he will tell us in 4:20; his pattern will be completed in due time. Love for the brother is a part of "doing the righteousness." It is, we might say, a good example, and *exempla docent.* Yet this love and its absence mean more to John; they are so much evidence that is easily to be seen. Twice (v. 19 and 25) John says: "in connection with this we *know*" (γινώσκω). We know also in connection with other.facts and other evidence; read again 2:3, 5b, 13, 14. To know that we know (2:3), i. e., know with full effect upon ourselves, is essential. Hence true evidence that is fully understood by what it reveals is so important, and John points it out to his readers. The evidence furnished by love is both clear and unmistakable. John is as much the apostle of knowledge as of love; so is Paul who really wrote the grandest description of love (I Cor. 13).

11)   The negative fact just stated is at once proved by what John's readers have heard from the very beginning of their connection with God through Christ (ἀπ' ἀρχῆς as in 2:7). **Because this is the report** (ἀγγελία, repeated from 1:5) **which you heard from the beginning, that we keep loving one another.**

The ἵνα clause is in apposition with ἥν. This is not the Mosaic commandment of love to one's neighbor but what Jesus says in John 15:12, 17 to the effect that his disciples love one another. We love all men as our fellow creatures, but as spiritual brothers we can love only those who are such brothers. Because of love we do all manner of good to all men as opportunity offers, but especially to our spiritual brothers who are of the household (family) of faith, Gal. 5:10. This is true with reference to God himself. He is able to give gifts of love to his children which those who are not his children will not receive.

12) John inserts a pertinent negative illustration. **Not as Cain was from the wicked one** (the devil, verse 10a, a child of the devil) **and slew his brother.** This is not an anacoluthon, nor is anything to be supplied. No main clause is needed in order to express the sense, the subordinate clauses convey it completely. The main point is not the *fact* that Cain slew Abel but the *reason* that he did so. In χάριν τίνος (χάριν is placed before the interrogative) there lies neither the idea of purpose nor of *Grund*. ·

And why did he slay him? The answer shows that the point to be stressed is the fact that Cain's murder evidences that he "was of the wicked one." As one is ἐκ God and ἐκ the devil, so are one's works; and especially some of the outstanding works furnish plain, incontrovertible evidence concerning whence Cain's murder is such a work. Hence the answer. **Because his works were wicked while his brother's** (were) **righteous.** Cain was undoubtedly "from the *wicked* one," his deed of murder notoriously advertises the fact that his deeds were *wicked*, and that he was thus of the *wicked* one. "The devil" (verse 10) is here called "the wicked one" because of Cain's "wicked deeds."

It is not enough to regard "while his brother's were righteous" as saying only that Cain thus had no reason whatever for slaughtering, butchering his brother (this is the meaning of the verb which is significantly repeated). This addition regarding Abel's works brings out fully the point of the wickedness and its origin as this is noted also in Gen. 4:4 and Heb. 11:4 although not in Jude 11. The devil's children hate God's children just because the *righteous* works of these condemn their own works as the *wicked* works that they are. So they crown their other wicked works as Cain crowned his and thereby more than ever evidence the fact that they are "from the wicked one" who is the murderer from the beginning (John 8:44).

Note that δίκαια matches the δικαιοσύνην occurring in v. 10; both are forensic as always, see 2:29. Why such an extreme exemplification in this first murderer? The answer is found in v. 15 plus Matt. 5:21,22. We often fail to see what wickedness is in its first origin until after it produces its full-blown works.

13)   The new paragraph begins at 10b and not here (R. V.). **Be not marvelling, brethren, if the world keeps hating you.** This is a condition of reality. The world certainly continues to hate, the world being the world, not "having been born from God," not being "the children of God" (2:29-3:1) but "the children of the devil," "from the wicked one," their deeds being "wicked" (v. 10-12). Jesus has made this very plain in John 15:18-21 where he uses the same "if" clause. This hatred should never cause the least surprise. According to 2:19 John includes in "the world" all the antichristians who especially try to break up the fellowship of the true Christians with one another. It is for this reason also that John says so much about our relation to each other and our love for each other. "Brothers" or "brethren" is the proper form of address here and not "little children," for John is a brother and now speaks of brotherhood.

14)   **We on our part** (emphatic ἡμεῖς) **know** (the fact, οἴδαμεν) **that we have stepped over out of the death into the life** (we know it by this evidence) **because we are loving the brothers.** Ὅτι states the evidential reason; another and an important instance of this use of ὅτι is found in Luke 7:47. John expounds "having been born from God"; it means "that we have stepped over (βαίνω to take steps, μετά, over) out of the death into the life." God's grace, his Spirit, his Word led us out of the one into the other; being spiritually dead, we were made spiritually alive. This is the same

perfect tense that was used in 2:29 and 3:9, and it has full present connotation.

"The death," "the life" are as definite as "the truth," "the Word," "the commandment," "the righteousness," etc.; they are not simply "death" and "life" in general. It is well to note that both the physical life and the spiritual life are not seen directly but are apparent only from their evidence, their activity. The plainest activity of the spiritual life is that of loving those who are one with us, are our spiritual brothers. We are not merely being friends with them (φιλεῖν), but, understanding our spiritual relation to them, we act with a purpose that is according (ἀγαπᾶν).

The one not loving (thus) **remains in the death;** his not-loving being the plain evidence. John once more writes the verb "remains," which appears throughout this letter. The fact that love always shows itself, just as does the absence of love, John will add presently.

15) It startles us when John adds: **Everyone hating his brother is a man-murderer.** So the world hates us and thereby attests its Cainlike nature. Whether blood is actually shed or not makes no difference (Matt. 5:22). Ἀνθρωποκτόνος is the very word that Jesus used with reference to the devil in John 8:44; it applies to all the devil's children (v. 10b); included among these are the antichristians who have gone out from us (2:19). John has called the latter liars (1:6, 10; 2:22) and combines liar and man-murderer as Jesus does in John 8:44. Let the deniers of the deity and of the expiation of Jesus (1:7; 2:2) read this double verdict on them!

And you know — I need not tell you — **that every man-murderer does not have life eternal remaining in him.** John says "life eternal." It is a rather superficial interpretation to say that this refers to the fact that murderers are put to death by execution of the government. John speaks of the murderers

who murder by hating. This is not a crime in the eyes
of the world; it is what the world does the world over.
Worldly governments have killed even God's children;
many thought that they thereby did God a service. Not
to have life eternal is to be damned by God.

The view that by "has not remaining in him" John
means: once had life eternal but has lost it again,
stresses μένουσαν unduly and disregards ἔχει. Whether
such a murderer ever had life eternal and then became
apostate is immaterial and not the point. This certainly cannot be said of "the world" which hates us
and thereby commits this murder and thus together
with any apostates who have gone back to the world
"has not eternal life" so that this life could remain in
them at death.

So much for the hating that is murder in God's
judgment. It is the evidential mark of the world, of
all those who remain in death, who have not eternal
life as an abiding possession, and who, like Cain, hate
us who have stepped over out of their death into life
and want to rob us of this life and often, therefore,
persecute or even kill us physically. They thereby reveal the fact that the devil is their father who mur-
dered from the beginning, who has no life to give birth
to anyone but only the power of death, to hold men in
this death or to draw them back into it (Heb. 2:14).

16) Now "the love" which marks the children
of God. **In connection with this we have known** (with
the strongest affect and effect upon ourselves) **the love**
(articulated: the love that is love indeed) **that that
One in our behalf laid down his life.** It is important,
first of all, to realize just what love is. The Germans
have an advantage in that they can use *die Liebe* with
the article like the Greek: "the love" that is love and
not merely "love" in general. The same is true with
regard to love as with regard to life: neither is visible
to the eye, tangible to the hand; both are known as

being present only by their activity. So John names the evidence. We Christians have truly realized in our hearts (perfect: and do still realize) just what love is, namely "in connection with this that that One in our behalf laid down his life." No evidence of love can go beyond this. ῞Οτι is epexegetical and explains "this" (B.-D. 394) ; "because" in our versions is an inadequate rendering.

John uses ἐκεῖνος repeatedly as a reference to Christ. In Rom. 5:6-10 Paul states in so many words why this evidence of Christ's love is supreme. What person in all the world ever laid down his life for another except in the rare cases where the other was a good man? But Christ did this for "ungodly ones," for actual enemies. O love divine, all love excelling! John uses the expression τίθημι τὴν ψυχήν which he borrows from Jesus (John 10:11, 17, 18) ; it is not found in the papyri by M.-M. It means to go into death voluntarily. We know what this death meant for the Son of God.

Robertson 630, etc., *The Minister and his Greek New Testament,* 35, etc., has done much to answer the views that refused (and still refuse) to give ὑπέρ the resultant meaning "instead of"; but read this for yourself. On our passage he remarks: "Surely the very object of such death is to save life." Again: "Theological prejudice must be overruled." The secular linguistic evidence also overrules it.

Translate as you prefer: "on our behalf," "for us," "for our benefit," "instead of," substitution remains because without it Christ's death would be of no benefit to the ungodly. In 1:7 John says: "The blood of Jesus, his Son, cleanses us from all sin"; in 2:2: "He himself is the expiation (ἱλασμός) for our sins," etc. It is sacrificial, substitutionary blood that expiates. Such love "that One" put into action and evidence, and we have realized it, we have stepped over from the death into the life by means of his substitutionary death. Note that ἐκεῖνος and ὑπὲρ ἡμῶν are juxtaposed: "that One in our stead."

And we on our part (ἡμεῖς emphatic) **ought in behalf of the brothers to lay down the lives.** This evidence of our love ought not to be beyond us. Ἀδελφοί does not mean neighbors or men in general but "brothers" who are in the same family with us, begotten from God, God's children (2:29, etc.). Ὀφείλομεν means that the obligation rests upon us, i. e., when danger requires it, we willingly step in and lay down our lives to save the lives of our spiritual brethren. Ὑπέρ has the same force that it has in the statement about Christ.

The present tense is used in general statements. The love we have realized begets like love in us with a like visible evidence. John restricts the love of Christ and its evidence to us, to God's children; but he does so only because in our imitation of his love the supreme evidence we ought to be willing to furnish is restricted to our brothers in God's family. The fact that our dying for our brothers can do no more than to save them from physical death while Christ's dying gives us spiritual and eternal life (v. 14) is understood.

17) From the supreme evidence of love, namely giving up life itself for our fellow believers, John descends to the common evidence of giving bread to our needy fellow believers. Only rarely will the supreme sacrifice be asked of us by the Lord who died for us all; this lesser sacrifice will often be requested. **On the other hand, whoever has the life sustenance of the world and beholds his brother having need and locks his compassion away from him, how does the love for God remain in him?**

Δέ places this case beside the supreme one as being one that is different and one that deals with far less, only with earthly provisions for a needy brother. Yet because it deals with less — we may say with the least sort of evidence of love — it the more warrants the great conclusion: where this least evidence of love for one's brother does not appear, how can there be any love in the heart for God, the Father of us all?

Although it is now worded in the singular the statement is just as general as is the preceding one that has the plural. Βίος is used in its third meaning, *Lebensunterhalt*, one's "living," as it is in Mark 12:44, the poor widow's entire "living." We say: "I am making a living," enough to live on. The genitive "living of the world" helps to bring out the meaning. This is not in contrast with "life eternal," for the two are not comparable. Spiritual life is sustained by Word and sacrament; physical life in the world by provisions of the world.

John uses θεωρεῖν which does not mean merely to "see" (A. V.), which may be only a superficial look, but "to behold," to see fully the case of a brother who is to be truly loved as a brother, who has need, who lacks enough for a living. John uses three coordinate verbs (subjunctives) as is his habit: he has — he beholds — he locks or shuts, and subordinates none of the three by the use of a participle.

The Greek uses the plural τὰ σπλάγχνα, the nobler viscera, heart, lungs, liver (the seat of the emotions) to express these tender emotions themselves. We use "the heart" in the same manner. The A. V.'s translation "bowels" is inadequate, for it leads us to think of the intestines. We translate: "And locks his heart or his compassion away from" the needy brother, i. e., closes it up so that it does not go out to this poor brother. See how James 2:15, 16 pictures this heartlessness, this putting off the destitute brother with empty words.

John asks the readers themselves how "the love for God" remains in one who refuses to show this small evidence of love for a needy brother. The genitive is objective as 4:20 shows. Where such common evidence of love for a brother does not appear, there is evidently no love for the brother, and thus there "remains" (once more this important verb) also no love for God. The presence of love, as we have said, is assured only by its activity, its deeds, the evidence. John himself will consider this as he continues (4:7, etc.), for there is much more to be said. In 2:9-11 the subject is only begun; now we have only its first expansion. It is John's beautiful way to expand gradually.

18) **Little children** (2:1, tender address, so fitting here where love is urged), **let us not be loving** (John includes himself) **with word, neither with the tongue, but in connection with deed and with truth.** Let us not pretend love with sham, empty evidence, but let us furnish genuine evidence. The first two datives are datives of means. To use only "word" and "the tongue" is mere hypocritical pretense of loving. Anarthrous λόγῳ = "something that we say"; articulated τῇ γλώσσῃ = "the tongue" which each person has for saying something. James 2:15, 16 applies here still more.

For the positive thought John uses ἐν: "in connection with work (or deed) and with truth" (reality), both nouns are anarthrous, qualitative. Some mere word spoken by the tongue is no real evidence of love, which need not be stressed to mean that love never uses some word and the tongue for expressing itself. But love can never stop with this. It moves the hand to some corresponding deed of love, and that not for show (Acts 5:1, etc.) but combined with reality. Ἀλήθεια is properly added, for hypocrites may imitate love even by a deed. Our versions use "in" throughout and thus erase the difference. "In connection with" deed and truth joins these two to the activity of love and thus makes them the evidence of the presence of the love hidden in the heart; mere means, like some word spoken by the tongue, are not yet such evidence, no matter who seeks to palm them off as sufficient evidence.

19, 20) All that was said about love for the brother and the true evidence for such love is so vital because it reflects our relation to God. The question asked about our love for God in v. 17 reverts to this; but it does so because of what precedes, see v. 14 and recall the whole of 2:29-3:12. "The children of God" cannot be such children if they do not love also each other and show the evidence of such love. Hence John proceeds with our relation to God and offers the sweetest promise whereas without it, after what he said about our obligation to love the brethren, grave, disturbing doubt might assail us. **In connection with this we shall know that we are from the truth and shall persuade our hearts before him, if in regard to anything ($\ddot{o}$ $\tau\iota$) the heart condemns us, that God is greater than our heart and knows everything.**

We regard this as one sentence and not as two (A. V.); we do not punctuate with a semicolon (R. V.). We prefer the reading $\ddot{o}$ $\tau\iota$ $\dot{\epsilon}\dot{a}\nu$ (R. V.) and not $\ddot{o}\tau\iota$ (A. V., "for"). Also: "In connection with this . . . that God is greater than our heart," etc., and not: "because God is greater," etc. (R. V.). Those who prefer the reading that has two $\ddot{o}\tau\iota$ do not know what to do with the second except to make it a redundant repetition of the first which is to be omitted in translation (A. V.). No one has satisfactorily explained the insertion of this second $\ddot{o}\tau\iota$.

Think of what John has said in v. 16 about the real evidence of love! Many an honest Christian heart will question whether it is able to go that far. Even regarding v. 17, 18 many a heart will question whether it has always lived up to that as it should. Note that "we" includes John himself as it did in 1:10. This is what John means with "if in regard to anything the heart condemns us." The adverbial accusative ὅ τι is placed forward, and ἡμῶν is the genitive object of the verb. The English cannot duplicate the beautiful play on γινώσκω and καταγινώσκω, which is even repeated. The German can: *erkennen — gegen uns erkennen.* The second is forensic: a judge recognizes something as being valid against us, on which he must pronounce against us. The judge is in this instance our own heart which knows our inner motives (like conscience) and how often, at least inwardly, our love for a brother falls short of what it ought to be.

John does not deny the finding and the verdict of our heart or imply that our falling short escapes God or amounts to nothing in his sight. That would be lying, to use John's own expression. No; "in connection with *this* great fact shall we know that we are from the truth and shall persuade our hearts before him" when we come into his presence, for instance, when we pray (v. 22), namely the fact (epexegetical ὅτι) "that God is greater than our heart," so much greater that "he knows everything."

To be sure, he knows all our failures in love, all that our own heart finds against us; but he knows vastly more, namely all about our real spiritual state, that the measure of love we do have shows that we have stepped over from the death into the life (v. 14), that although we are as yet imperfect in love, and our own hearts penitently acknowledge it, we have been born from him and are his children (2:29, etc.).

Ἐκ τῆς ἀληθείας = ἐξ αὐτοῦ (2:29; 3:9 twice). "The truth" (1:8, etc.) = the light, the Word, as the source of our life. The anarthrous "truth" in v. 17 is not the same. The future tenses are certainly a blessed promise: "we shall know — shall persuade or assure our hearts," but they are also the regular tenses after protases with ἐάν. They are proper here: after we have tried to live up to v. 16-18, our hearts bring accusations against us, and then the question arises: "How shall we recognize that we are from the truth, persuade ourselves in God's presence?"

21) John has shown how the condemnation of our hearts is to be answered and silenced. We recall 1:9 and 2:1, 2 which cover all the sinning of believers. So he proceeds: **Beloved, if (thus) the heart does not condemn us, we** (indeed) **have boldness as regards God, and whatever we ask we receive from him because we are keeping his commandments and are doing the things pleasing in his sight.**

As was the case in v. 18, this assurance also deserves a loving address. This is not the case of a heart that fails to accuse us when it ought to, but of one that does so and yet does not do so because of v. 19, 20. Because John says only "if the heart does not condemn us," some interpret: if, in the first place, it never did this because it already knows what John says, and if, in the second place, it now does not after having heard what John says. John's own heart belongs in the former group. But John builds verse 21, etc., on what precedes. The cases are the same. The heart's condemnation always starts up anew; it would be a bad sign if it did not. John, you, and I will always be in the one class; the supposed first class does not exist.

The main point is the dealing of our heart with God, v. 19, ἔμπροσθεν αὐτοῦ, which is a juridical phrase that refers to an appearance before God as the Judge. So now, when we are sure of God's verdict despite our faults, "boldness have we πρός, face to face with God," παρρησία is to be understood as it was in 2:28 in the sense of assurance, confidence, joyful fearlessness. Robertson calls πρός the "face-to-face" preposition which is used to indicate intimate contact. In 2:28 it is boldness at the Parousia; now the boldness that we already have to step into God's presence.

22) "And" completes the thought. John is thinking of our being face to face with God when as his children we come to ask things of him in prayer. Asking something is the test, hence prayers of adoration, praise, thanksgiving are not referred to here. As he has done previously, John is speaking about *evidence*. We are children of God when we show the evidence of love in deed and in truth. We want as much of this evidence as possible, so valuable is it for us. Now on God's side we again need and want evidence that he, indeed, despite our shortcomings accepts us as his children in love. Besides what he himself declares about us in his Word there is a most convincing evidence, indeed, on his part, one that we can see every day: he treats us as his beloved children. "We constantly are receiving from him whatever we keep asking."

This clause: "because we (as his children) are keeping his commandments" (on which John has spoken at such length in 2:3-8) recalls all that he has said; he now weaves it in anew. To show what he means John adds "and are doing the things pleasing in his sight" and now adds the new phrase ἐνώπιον αὐτοῦ to ἔμπροσθεν αὐτοῦ and to πρὸς τὸν Θεόν. Our Father watches us and sees that we are doing the things that please him, of which he tells us in his Word, his commandments. Every answer to our petitions is thus the clearest factual evidence that he treats us as children. Blessed are we indeed (verse 1)!

"Whatever we ask we are receiving from him" is expounded still farther in 5:14, 15. John has no more restrictions and reservations than Jesus has in Matt. 7:8; Mark 11:24; John 14:13; 15:7; 16:23. Unfilial minds may think that these promises mean no matter what we ask; scoffers challenge us to ask this or that folly which they propose and feel sure that we shall *not* get what we ask; unbelief simply sets all such divine promises aside as being illusions of primitive minds. John addresses children of God. Will or can children of God ask from their Father anything that the children of the devil (verse 10) would like to have? We daily receive a thousand gifts and blessings from our Father beyond even what we know and ask; he even makes all things work together for our good, for us who love him. On God's side there are mountains of evidence for his love to us as his children (verse 1).

The only question for us is regarding the evidence on our side. Thank God, we do keep his commandments, we do do the things pleasing in his sight, and our Father accepts them. Not that he needs this our evidence, he knows all things (verse 20) before they make themselves evident. We are the ones who need our own evidence of love to assure our own hearts to the extent of such evidence and therefore ought to supply it in greatest abundance. It cannot equal the evidence that God furnishes us for his love. Where it falls short we supply the evidence of true repentance in the confession of sin and have the assurance given in 1:9 and 2:1, 2.

23) John speaks of gospel commandments in v. 22 and now sums them up for us. **And this is his commandment that we believe the name of his Son Jesus Christ and keep loving one another even as he gave us commandment.**

When we look at his gospel we see scores of places where he tells us what is pleasing in his sight; hence John uses the plural "commandments." Yet when we look at all of them, they coalesce into just one, the one that John names. These are not two commandments: to believe and to love. These two are one. You cannot believe without loving nor love without believing. The previous mention of "commandments" and "commandment" (2:3-8) is again taken up and elucidated; we have what the term actually means.

The ἵνα does not denote purpose; it introduces a subject clause in apposition with "this" and with "his commandment." The reading varies between the aorist πιστεύσωμεν and the present πιστεύωμεν. The latter means that we "ever continue believing" just as the next present tense says that we "ever continue loving." But it seems as though the aorist was changed to the present in order to make both verbs alike. The aorist is effective: definitely, effectively, once for all believe. It is not ingressive "come to believe," i. e., get to the point where we believe (R. 850). Nor does the aorist indicate that believing is basic as compared with loving. It is not the tense that conveys this idea; faith would be just as *grundlegend* if John had used the present tense. It is the nature of faith as compared with the nature of love that makes it basic whether we use the noun "faith" or the verb "to believe" in any of its tenses.

Some offer these distinctions in the meaning: πιστεύειν τινι is *assensus*, (so here); πιστεύειν τινα is *notitio*; πιστεύειν εἰς τινα is *fiducia*. These distinctions are specious. C.-K. 901, etc., discusses John's phraseology and in the case of our passage gives the meaning *anerkennen was jemand sagt, seinen Worten trauen*, acknowledge what one says, trust his words. The idea of trust and confidence lies in the verb itself and is never removed by the construction that follows: dative, accusative, a phrase, or a ὅτι clause. The idea that our heavenly Father wants only our assent and not our fullest confidence is palpably wrong.

The dative is in place because it is "the name of his Son Jesus Christ." John does not say "that we believe in or on his Son," or "in or on Jesus Christ, his Son." He says more. The ONOMA is the revelation. We regard the genitive as possessive. This name or revelation "of his Son" the Father sent us. The entire gospel reveals his Son Jesus Christ. It contains this revelation in prophecy and in fulfillment by the Son's own manifestation ("was made manifest," 1:2; 3:5, 8; 4:9). By his name alone is the Son brought to us; by his name alone we apprehend him in faith. We are baptized in connection with his name (revelation), Acts 2:38; we believe in his name, John 1:12; and that means "on the Lord Jesus Christ," Acts 16:31. All that John has said about the light, the truth, the Word = the name.

Once again he emphasizes the deity: *"his Son* Jesus Christ" (1:3, 7) over against the antichristians who deny the Father and the Son (2:22) — see the significance of this in these passages. Note, too, that "Jesus Christ" (1:3), in 1:7 simply "Jesus," points to the Son incarnate in Jesus and includes his blood by making it "the blood of his Son."

Our present-day modernists deny the ὄνομα as it is expressed in terms like "the Messiah," "the Logos," "the Son of God" by making these old, outworn categories or patterns of thought for which we must produce up-to-date, modern terms from which the deity is eliminated; coming generations will find also our modern terms outworn and will, of course, then produce their own as modernists do today. It seems that the old antichrists of John's day (2:18, 22) have not advanced much in their modern representatives. The denial is quite the same; the only new feature is the fact that the written testimony of the apostles must be nullified, which is done as indicated (outworn categories or patterns of thought).

John expands his elaboration by introducing the word "to believe." Follow this through from here onward in 4:1, 16; 5:1, 5, 10 (three times), 13. He weaves in this new, significant thread: love for our fellow children of God is the evidence of *faith.* We attach the last clause "even as he gave us commandment" to the whole ἵνα clause and not merely to the love as some do. The final word "commandment" cannot mean less than this word at the head of the sentence.

24) **And the one keeping his commandments remains in him, and he himself in him.**

John repeats anew all that he has said in 2:3-8 about God's commandments (now once more using the plural) together with all that he said in 2:19, 24-28; 3:6, 9, 17 about remaining. The exposition of these passages belongs also here. To remain in him = the fellowship mentioned in 1:3, 6, 7, with which the development starts. It is this that constitutes true religion.

Yet even here John advances when he adds God's remaining in us to our remaining in God (in true living connection with him). The two ever involve each other. This double remaining is repeated in 4:16. The Father's remaining in us rests on the statement of Jesus made in John 14:23.

The point has constantly been that of our knowing, γινώσκειν, with decisive effect upon ourselves, so decisive as not to be shaken by the lies of the antichristians. Pursue the word through 2:13, 14, 18, 29; 3:1, 6, 16, 19; and through the epistle. The light, the truth, the Word, the commandment enable us to know in this way. John now comes to the ultimate source of our thus knowing. **And in connection with this ye know that he remains in us: from the Spirit whom he gave us.** He names the Spirit as the ultimate source (ἐκ). He reserves this statement for this place where he reaches the ultimate object which we know, namely that God our Father remains in us. Thus, too, he now mentions "the Spirit" directly by name. In 2:20, 27 he does so indirectly in "the anointment" we received and have, which teaches us everything. This anointment consists in the abiding bestowal of the Holy Spirit in baptism.

All else that we know is subsidiary to this supreme fact and this supreme object of knowledge, namely "that God remains in us." True evidence for this is important, indeed, but much more important is the source of this knowledge. Its source is the Holy Spirit whom God himself gave us. John uses ἐν τούτῳ γινώσκομεν with different appositions for "this": "in connection with this . . . that," (3:16; 4:13) ; "in connection with this: every spirit confessing" (4:2) ; "in connection with this . . . when," etc. (5:2). John always has an apposition to "this," but each one is different: once it is a ὅτι clause, again a "when" clause, a clause without a particle, and here in 3:24 it is just the phrase ἐκ τοῦ Πνεύματος, "from the Spirit." There is no incongruity between ἐν and ἐκ because the ἐκ phrase is the apposition only to "this."

To say that God gave us the Spirit "immediately," and that from the Spirit so given we know in an "immediate" way that God remains in us, is to open the door to fanatical ideas, fancied revelations from the Spirit, morbid mysticism, etc. On Pentecost Christ sent the Spirit immediately, miraculously. He sent him to remain, to work in all the world. The Spirit was ever after given by Word and sacrament. Peter preached at Pentecost, the Twelve baptized 3,000. So God gave the Spirit to John's readers; so we have him as God's gift today. As he is given us by Word and sacrament, so he is now ours only by Word and sacrament. He speaks to us and in us, works in and through us, only by Word and sacrament. There we actually hear his voice, experience his power, and thus know fully with affect and effect (γινώσκομεν) that God remains in us. Those who attribute to him anything that is different from Word and sacrament do so without him. He is the source from whom by Word and sacrament we know, indeed, "that God remains in us."

The Fifth Circle of Facts,

Centering on Spirits,

4:1-6

1) The ultimate personal source through whom we know that God is in us, that we are, indeed, savingly connected with him (fellowship, 1:3-7) is God's own Spirit, who is given to us in Word and sacrament. From him comes this conviction, which in itself and because of this its source is true. This leads John to say still more since he is prompted by loving concern for his readers: **Beloved, be not believing every spirit but** (ever) **be testing out the spirits whether they are from God, because many pseudo-prophets have gone out into the world.**

Believe not every man but test out all men because many false men have gone out into the world as false teachers. John refers to the antichrists mentioned in 2:18 although he makes his statement broad so as to include more than Cerinthus and his antichristian following. Of the latter he says (2:19) that they went out from us because they were not from us. Now he says that they went out into the world, i. e., among men generally, to do their wicked work. He calls them ψευδοπροφῆται, "pseudo-prophets," because they pretend to have the Spirit of God, to be moved by him, to bring God's true Word to men, while they do nothing of the kind.

John's readers must not be credulous: "be not believing every spirit." John begins with "believing" in 3:23 and now develops this term as he continues. Here he again construes this verb with the dative: "Be not placing your confidence and trust in what every man, who calls himself a prophet of God, who claims to be bringing you God's Word, preaches and teaches and asks you to believe."

John says: "Do not be believing every spirit but (ever) be testing out the spirits." He does not use πνεῦμα and πνεύματα to designate the constituent part of a human being, which is the spirit that makes him a personal being and by the ψυχή animates his physical body, as Paul speaks of body, soul, and spirit; nor does John have in mind a supernatural spirit. "Spirit" is the person as such with his inner, spiritual character. There is no need to put more into this word.

Every person reveals what kind of a personality or spirit he is by his word and his action although he may try to hide what he really is. Proper testing will penetrate the deception, will show whether what is in his spirit or heart is "out of, i. e., derived from, God" or from some ungodly, antichristian source. This testing John wants all his readers to apply to all who come to them as prophets in order to teach them. It is vital to find out whether "the spirits," these prophets and their inner spiritual character, what is in their hearts, "are really from God." If the source (ἐκ), the spring, is divine and pure, one may drink; if the source is otherwise, it is poison.

Note well that all Christians are told to do this testing. It is not taken out of their hands and reserved for the clergy of the church. What John 7:48, 49 speaks about shall not occur. Papal authority in this matter is usurpation of the rights of Christians. Like unto it is the arrogant authority of some scientists, philosophers, educators, who claim to be sole possessors of the means for making genuine tests, who demand that young and old must without question accept their findings and insult those who propose to test for themselves not only these findings but "these spirits" themselves.

Christians will, of course, help each other in making the proper tests; some are more capable than others, have more experience than others; pastors are especially trained for this work. We accept all such aid; John is here offering it to his readers. Yet in the last analysis every Christian is personally responsible. Whom he believes or does not believe affects himself primarily. John wants himself to be tested by his readers.

Let us add that it is unscientific not to test and still more so to use false tests and not to test for the true source, i. e., whether teachers are ἐκ τοῦ Θεοῦ or not. This is the unscientific thing that all false teachers demand of us in regard to themselves. Woe to us when we refuse to bow to their demand! They then smite us with their anathema as does the papacy.

"Keep testing for the source, ever become more proficient in this work!" is John's behest. The world is full of counterfeit coin. It seems that all the apostles loved this word δοκιμάζειν. Paul uses it and its derivatives quite often. In their day metals and coins were constantly weighed and tested before they were accepted.

2) In connection with this know the Spirit of God: every spirit who confesses Jesus Christ as having come into flesh is from God; and every spirit who does not confess this Jesus is not from God. And this is the one of the Antichrist, in regard to whom you heard that he is coming, and he is now in the world already.

The durative (iterative) imperatives used in v. 1 are followed by another. "In connection with *this*" refers to this testing of "every spirit," etc., as explained in 3:24. John offers the touchstone for sound, sure testing, by the use of which the readers are to know (γινώσκω, with due effect upon themselves — follow this verb through the entire epistle!) "the Spirit of God,"

i. e., his actual presence as well as his absence in the case of any "spirit," of any man who comes to them, especially when he comes as a prophet, i. e., preacher or teacher. The matter to be found out, as already stated, is whether he and what is in him are "from God" as their source.

This is the test to apply: examine the man's confession. The Scriptures nowhere ask us to look into a man's heart. They know of no *Herzensrichterei*. God alone sees the heart; no man can see into another's heart. It is precarious to assert: "The man's heart is all right!" when the man's confession is wrong. The Lord has given us the one safe test, the confession. Beyond this our responsibility ceases. "What is the man's real confession?" is for us the only question. Since one confesses not only with his lips but also with his practice and his acts, we are to examine both; his heart we are to leave to the omniscient God.

Every spirit who (do not translate "which") confesses "Jesus Christ as having come in flesh" is from God; we have the same ἐξ αὐτοῦ that occurred in 2:29. There is no question that the inward, spiritual character of this true confessor is derived from God and the Holy Spirit as far as any judgment on our part is concerned. There is a difference in force between translating the participle as a participle and translating ἐληλυθότα as though it were the infinitive or equal to it. Our versions do the latter; one Greek text has the infinitive. But this would mean the confession of only a fact: "*that* Jesus Christ has come in flesh." The participle is attributive. This man confesses "*Jesus Christ*" himself "as having come in flesh," which means as his Lord and Savior. The fact that this can be truly done only by the Holy Spirit I Cor. 12:3 states. In 5:1 John says more.

"As having come in flesh" describes the vital point confessed about "Jesus Christ," namely his deity incarnate in flesh or human nature, once incarnate and remaining so (perfect participle). This person "Jesus (personal name: Savior) Christ" (the name which is derived from his office: Anointed to be our Prophet, High Priest, and King), who as God's Son (1:3, 7; 2:22, 23) existed from eternity, "has come" in the fulness of time "in flesh" (John 1:14). Cerinthus and his following denied the Son (2:22, 23) and thereby also the Father. These heretics made Jesus the physical son of Joseph upon whom "the Eon Christ" descended at his baptism but left Jesus again at his passion so that a mere man died on the cross. John says "every spirit who confesses" — to confess is the opposite of to deny — and "every spirit" includes all true confessors just as in v. 3 it includes all deniers, no matter whether they are adherents of Cerinthus or not.

It would be a serious mistake to think that John speaks of confessing only the one fact or doctrine of the Incarnation, of the Virgin Birth, of the two natures, so that it is of minor importance when other facts, doctrines, call them what you will, are either not confessed or are denied in some way. "Jesus Christ as having come in flesh" is not merely the center of the gospel but the whole of it. In Christ there inheres all that John has said and will yet say in this epistle, likewise all that John's Gospel, yea the whole New Testament and the Scripture contain. Like the seamless garment of Christ, Jesus Christ is one. He who clips off or alters any part never deals with what is immaterial although he may think so.

3) The negative is abbreviated in form: "and every spirit who does not confess this Jesus is not from God." The meiosis and litotes "does not confess" is stronger than "denies" and matches "is not from God." Τόν is the article of previous reference: "this Jesus" in the full sense of 2b.

"And this is the one of the Antichrist"; τό refers
to πνεῦμα, "the spirit of the Antichrist," the inwardness
of him. Some say that this is τό *proprium*, the action
of the Antichrist, i. e., the failure to confess this Jesus,
which is true enough. John is, however, dealing with
"the spirits" who are recognized as to what they are
by confession as by nonconfession. He repeats 2:18
where he says that his readers "heard" about the coming of the Antichrist. While in 2:18 he adds "and now
antichrists many have come to be," he now makes no
distinction, for the subject is now "the spirit of the
Antichrist," and of this he can say: "In regard to
whom you heard that he is coming (this spirit), and he
is now in the world already." A sample of such a
spirit is every person who does not confess as John
states. The negative μή appears in relative clauses but
not in a conditional or hypothetical sense, "if such
there be," but as not referring to some special person
(B.-D. 428, 4; R. 962) : "the spirit of the Antichrist"
appears in many persons already now.

4) According to the very canon here laid down
for testing the spirits, namely their confession or nonconfession, John certifies regarding his readers: **You
on your part are from God, little children.** He uses
the affectionate address that befits his age and his
fatherly position so well. Coming from him who teaches
them how to test out the spirits and is himself expert at
this, this finding of his means much for his readers.

These two kinds of spirits that are of opposite
origin never remain peacefully side by side. Those
who are not from God constantly attack those who
are from God. It is John's way of writing steadily to
advance in stating the facts. He does not stop with
telling his readers that they are from God but adds
and you have conquered them, have been and continue to be victorious over them (perfect tense). Their
efforts against you have left you firmer than ever.

According to John's own test anu finding this victory over them agrees with the origin of his readers as being "from God." In the Greek τὸ πνεῦμα and the plural are neuters, but this is only a grammatical feature; hence John uses the masculine αὐτούς, "them." From verse 1 onward he is speaking of persons.

No wonder John's readers are victorious: **because greater is the One in you,** namely God (reverting to 3:24), **than the one in the world,** the devil (3:10). John does not say "than the one in them" but again advances the thought by saying "in the world."

5) So he at once adds: **They are from the world,** the devil's domain. In the preceding John says only that these nonconfessing spirits are recognized by us (when we test them) as "not from God." Now he states their origin: "it is from the world," which matches with the fact that "the greater One," God, is not in them but only "the one in the world."

This explains still more: **For this reason they speak** (ever) **from the world,** for all their utterance they have no higher source, draw from no divine fountain, and no stream rises above its source. All these facts help us in our testing these spirits. So also does this, that **the world hears them,** genitive, listens to them as admired and authoritative spokesmen. It likes their speech; this their speech is the world's own language. It never rises any higher than that which the world considers wisdom. The world hears and nods full approval whenever they speak. This is true to this day. It generally also pays its speakers well. The accusative αὐτούς would refer more to *what* they speak.

6) **We on our part are from God.** John includes himself (compare verse 4). This, John says, is our origin. The implication is that, when *we* speak, *we* draw from a correspondingly high source, from God. We have the light, the truth, the Word, the command-

ment, etc., about which John has said so much. Some commentators refer this emphatic "we" to John alone or to him and the other apostles or to these and the other Christian teachers and tell us that John is contrasting only true and false prophets or teachers (v. 1). But the spirit of the Antichrist is to be found in the followers as well as in the leaders, and both certainly speak. John refers to himself and to his readers.

The one knowing God hears us; he who is not from God does not hear us. John once more writes the significant verb γινώσκω (see 2:3, 4 and follow the verb through the epistle). Cerinthus and his followers claimed "to know" God (Gnostics). The Christians alone *know* him, and *know* that they *know* him, and John adds the how and all the evidence. This is no mere intellectual knowing but a living apprehension with full effect on mind, heart, and life.

Note all the objects apprehended by this knowing as John has presented them. When *we* speak, John says, you and I — meaning on anything pertaining to our religion — "the one knowing God (characterizing present participle) hears us," again the genitive, really hears and heeds *us* as being the proper and true speakers. Luke 10:16; John 10:4, 5; 10:14. The genitive = the persons heard, the accusative would refer to *what* is heard. Some ignore the difference, but it holds throughout although not even to hear *the speakers* excludes hearing also *anything* they may speak.

Instead of saying "he who *does not know* God does not hear us," John substitutes "he who *is not from* God does not hear us." Only we who is from God, born from him and child of his (2:29-3:1, etc.), one of his family, has ears for us who speak from God, for God's Word, etc. The Pharisees did not even understand Jesus' language (John 8:43) but continually turned topsy-turvy what he said and mocked him in unbelief. I Cor. 2:14. In order to know and thus to hear with blessed results one must "be from God," born from him, must have "the eyes of your understanding enlightened," Eph. 1:18. Only thus are the speakers appreciated.

In the one clause John has ὁ with the participle: "the one knowing God"; in the other ὅς with a finite verb: "he who is not from God." John evidently wants to use expressions that are different in form. The one thus *knowing* God is in living relation with him as has been set forth at length and thus certainly hears when any of his fellow Christians speak on anything pertaining to God, his Son, etc. John properly uses the substantivized descriptive participle ὁ γινώσκων, "the one knowing God." The fact that he and we "*are from* God" the preceding clause states. To be from (origin, birth) and thus to know and to hear (effect, result) go together. In the opposite expression John names only the absence of the origin: "he who *is not from* God," and lays his finger on the ultimate difference and thus on the visible effect and result: "he does not hear us," the ones through whom God speaks. John's statements are most exact.

Now the conclusion: **From this** that the one hears us and that the other does not hear us, from **this plain and open evidence we know the spirit of the deceit,** we are able to distinguish the two without difficulty, not merely intellectually, but with inner effect upon ourselves so as to open our hearts to the one spirit and to close them to the other. John uses ἐκ τούτου, which is a little stronger than ἐν τούτῳ (3:16, 24; 4:2; 5:2). The ἐκ phrase = "from this fact."

One may regard the genitives as possessive genitives: the spirit that belongs to the truth — to the deceit; or as subjective genitives: the spirit that utters the truth — the deceit (the latter because speaking and hearing the speakers has just been mentioned). Because Jesus speaks of "the Spirit of the truth" in John

14:17; 15:26; 16:13 some conclude that John here refers to the Holy Spirit, and that thus "the spirit of the deceit" refers to the devil. But in verse 1 "be testing *the spirits* whether *they* are from God" cannot mean "be testing the Holy Spirit and the devil whether *they* are from God." John is stating how to test and to know the spiritual origin, nature, and quality of men, how to know who are pseudo-prophets and who belong to their following, how to know true teachers, apostles, believers who speak. You do not try to look into their hearts; you simply listen to what they *confess*, to what they *utter* (λαλεῖν, verse 5), to what they let you hear, and note *who* gives ear to the one speaker and *who* to the other speaker. That is how to tell *men* apart, the spirits of men.

We thus conclude that πνεῦμα is here used as it was in verse 1, to designate the inner, spiritual nature of a man, which belongs to the truth, confesses and speaks it, reveals it to your ears, or belongs to the deceit, fails to confess the truth (verse 3), speaks what pleases the world. The fact that the one confesses and speaks "from the Spirit whom God gave to us" has been noted in 3:24; the fact that the other has not the Holy Spirit and thus speaks as a child of the devil (3:10) has also been brought out. Here, however, not the Holy Spirit and the devil are to be tested by us but the character and the nature of the spirit of men.

John has spoken of "the truth" since 1:6 and as synonyms has used the light, the Word, the commandment. This is what he now means. We should not omit the definite article as our versions do. By ἡ πλάνη John means "the deceit" in accord with 1:8 where he has the verb and with 2:26 where he has the participle. "The error" is not exact. The very term "pseudo-prophets" denotes deceivers. The spirit of the deceit is ever active to deceive; it should not be restricted to its prophets, for it is active also in their followers.

The Sixth Circle of Facts,
Centering on Love
4:7-5:3

7) Just as verses 1-6 develop 2:18, etc., so all that has hitherto been said about love (1:9-11; 3:1, God's love; 3:13-18) is now fully developed. The basic fact is stated in 1:3, our fellowship with the Father and with his Son Jesus Christ. The elaboration spirals upward from this pivoted fact of fellowship. We are shown all that joins us to God, that we are in him, he in us ("remains in us," 3:24). All that creates this fellowship, the light, the truth, the Word, the Son's blood, remission of our sins, constant cleansing, plus all the evidence for our fellowship with God, all the assurance and effective knowledge of it — thread after thread — have been woven in; also the lying claims of fellowship with God (starting at 1:6), the deceivers and their deceits (antichrists 2:18; pseudo-prophets 4:1) have been presented.

Fellowship with God and with his Son involves fellowship with one another; this correlative fact is noted already in 1:7. It combines us in God, in the light, the truth, the confession, etc.; it joins us to each other in love; it separates us from the world and from all heretics who talk of fellowship with God and yet are not in the truth but in the darkness, who deny Christ's deity and his blood, etc.

All this is now carried still farther; it is centered on love but is enriched by the weaving in anew of other pertinent facts that also have been treated. More glorious light is shed on the whole and on every detail. The whole pattern, woven as a unit, nears completion, grows richer and more beautiful as so much of it is unrolled.

John simply links into 3:10, 11, 23 as a weaver repeats a color in his design. We belong together in love; we do not belong together with those who have the spirit of the deceit (v. 1-6). **Beloved, let us be loving one another because this love is from God. And everyone loving has been born from God and knows God; the one not loving did not know God because God is love.** John says: "Let us go on loving one another" as we have been doing all along. Such an admonition is well prefaced by "beloved" which voices John's own love for his readers. The main point, however, lies in the facts which support this admonition.

The first fact is that "this love is from God." Note the article. When our versions translate "love is of God," this is not exact. Strictly speaking, this means that love in general is from God as its one fountain and source. But is the love of the world for its own (John 15:19) from God; or the love of publican for publican (Matt. 5:46)? Are we not told not to love the world (2:15)? Only *"the* love," the one that John urges, the one of one Christian toward another, is from God. It is the love of our fellowship with one another (1:7) which results from our fellowship with God and with his Son Jesus Christ. It is for "one another"; it is returned as soon as it is bestowed.

There is no need to worry about our loving also our neighbor who is not a Christian. God loves all men and yet loves his children in a special way by bestowing all manner of loving gifts on them. He loves them in a way in which he cannot love the wicked. This is also true with regard to us. John speaks of this narrower range of love because this love exhibits so clearly our fellowship with God, yea, our origin from him.

Here it is: "And everyone loving has been born from God." "Has been born from God" links back into 2:29 (3:9). The exercise of this love for one another evidences our origin from God, our birth into God's family as his children (3:1), and proves that we are no longer "the children of the devil" (3:10). "Everyone loving" has no connection with the world's loving its own. Even our proper love for non-Christians is not considered, for our love for our fellow Christians exhibits our spiritual birth from God in the best way; it does this so clearly because the world does not love us.

John adds "and knows God" and weaves in this true heart knowledge which is always so effective; γινώσκει, as distinguished from οἶδα, has been explained repeatedly. We get the full force of this addition by noting 2:4. This lover of his fellow believers "knows God," but not as these incipient Gnostics who claim: "I have known God!" i. e., have the real knowledge of him. Thousands still make this false claim today.

8) "The one not loving did not know God." The one who lacks this love for true believers vitiates any claim on his part that he knows God. He never knew him, ἔγνω. The Greek often uses the simple aorist where we mark the relation of time and use the English perfect, "has not known God." Yet in 3:4 John, too, has the perfect. All that γινώσκω implies of affect and effect on the one who knows is again to be noted. This knowledge is the mark of true fellowship with God and with his Son. What Jesus will say to all those that are described here he states in Matt. 7:23: "never did I know you," ἔγνων; he uses even the same tense that is employed here.

The reason for the fact that the one not loving has not known God is as prominent as Mt. Everest: "because God is love." It would be wrong for more reasons than one to use the article with "love." Compare the other fact: "God is light" (1:5) and John's repetition: "God is love" (v. 16). It deserves to be preached, sung, and made known in all the world. Because John has the copula ἐστίν in these statements, light and love have been called the essential attributes of God, definitions of the essence of God. This is true, but it does not make God's other attributes something less. All of them are essential. Take away any one of them, say his omnipotence, and God ceases to be. God minus omnipotence is not God, is, in fact, unthinkable. All the references to attributes are condescensions on the part of Scriptural revelation to our finite minds which are unable to grasp the infinitude of God in one mental grasp. God is shown to us from various angles which we call his attributes. Even then each of them is infinite and only faintly apprehended. When we contemplate only one side of God we are overwhelmed and bow in the dust and worship.

The fact that love, infinite love, is one of God's attributes staggers us sinners most of all. No mind and no heart can fathom John 3:16 or what John reveals about God's love. Love is an energetic and not a quiescent attribute. God's love reveals itself in wondrous acts of love and reaches out to its object. John is not speaking of the love of the three persons of the Godhead for each other; in this connection it is enough to say that the one not loving has not known God because he has not known the manifestation of God's love in sending his own Son, etc., (v. 9, 10).

It is unwarranted to state that when we speak of God's love as an energetic attribute we reduce the force of what John says, change "God's Love-*essence*" into mere *manifestation* of love. Every attribute, whether it is quiescent like his eternity or his aseity, or energetic like his omnipotence or his love, is nothing but his indivisible essence, his entire being revealed and perceived in one respect. The revelation of the supreme manifestation of God's love (verse 9, "the love of God *was manifested*") is for us the revelation that God is love. Without this manifestation no sinner could know God, could know that God is love.   ·

Few will doubt that ὅτι is causal (not declarative in an object clause). This puts the facts in logical relation. The man *not loving* is not born from God and thus does not know God "because God is *love*," and this *love* of God was *manifested* by him. By not *loving* he is far from the *loving* God. The point of proof lies in what is evident: in the man no activity, in God the greatest activity. It is stated that, unless we include "the Essential Being of God" in the statement "God is love," the fallacy of an undistributed middle would result. This statement alters the term regarding the man. This does not merely say that he does not know God but that, *not loving*, he does not know God. The proof for this is not a fact about the essence of God (which, by the way, is beyond mortal knowing) but the fact of his *loving* as John says, the fact of his having manifested his love. The truth that all of God's acts, whether they are done by one or by another energetic attribute, are due to what in human language we term his being, essence, etc., is self-evident as we have already said.

"God is full of love," "the most benevolent of all beings, full of love to all his creatures," and similar statements drop far below what John has in mind when he says, "God is love." The rationalistic views that the God of love cannot punish, cannot damn to hell forever, cannot ask a blood sacrifice for sin, substitute a human conception of love for what God's love is, has done, and still does.   ·

The words ἀγάπη and ἀγαπᾶν are inadequately, sometimes wrongly defined. The noun is practically unknown to secular Greek; look at it in Liddell and Scott and in C.-K. The long essay in G. K. is disappointing. It places too much feeling into the word and finally arrives at the idea of electing. One looks in vain for something adequate regarding our passage. C.-K. offers us something better with his *Willensrichtung* (although this is inexact) to which *elegere* and *negligere* are added and finally also *Erbarmen*, and thus his definition for "love" in our passage is as follows: "God is all that he is, not for himself, but for us." We have followed the development of the word elsewhere. Warfield's essay in *Christian Doctrines* has much of value, but we cannot define "love" as being due to seeing something valuable in the object loved. The author is right when he includes "seeing."

'Aγάπη is defined as the love of intelligence, of *comprehension* and understanding. It always has that meaning in the New Testament, most completely so here where it speaks of God's love. Combined with this is *purpose*, a purpose that corresponds to the comprehension of the object, whether this is the Son, the Father, the child of God, the filthy world, the enemy, the things in the world (2:15). Saving ἀγάπη thus accompanies χάρις, ἔλεος, compassion, benevolence. "Love" is the widest term because of what it includes, the other terms have narrower connotations.

From the world's standpoint it is intelligent and correspondingly purposeful to love only its own; for publicans to love publicans. Our definition holds good. God loved the world = saw all its filthy, damnable state and put his purpose into action in order to cleanse and to save. We are to love our enemies, to see (comprehension) all that is wrong with them, to do all that we can to change them (corresponding purpose). So Christ even died for his enemies. We are not to love the world and the things of the world; only blinded intelligence, coupled with correspondingly blinded purpose, can do that. We might cite other examples. Φιλεῖν, φιλία indicate the love of affection; φίλος = friend, φίλημα = kiss, the act of affection, of friendship. Jesus did not like Caiaphas (φιλεῖν), he loved even this wicked fellow (ἀγαπᾶν). Peter was to be even a friend who was full of affection for Jesus (John 21:17; 15:14, 15, φίλοι, intimates). Only to friends does Jesus confide and trust everything.

9) **In this was made manifest the love of God in connection with us that God has sent his Son, the Only-begotten, into the world that we may live through him.**

God is love. Love as well as life reveals its presence by its acts. In 3:1 it is the Father's gift that makes us his children. What this gift involves is stated already in 1:7 and 2:2 and is now stated anew. Observe that John uses φανερόω, "to make manifest," in 1:2; 2:28; 3:2, 5, 8. The word is used here as it was in 1:2 but with reference to the love of God in connection with us. Ἐν ἡμῖν does not mean "toward us" (A. V.) although it was toward us; nor *an uns* (so the German commentators like B.-D. 220, 1); nor "among, with, or at us" (the English writers); nor "in us," i. e., in our hearts; nor "in our case" (R. V. margin). We, indeed, behold this manifestation, and it fills us with supreme joy; but the phrase ἐν ἡμῖν means that the manifestation was "in connection with us," it involved us as the recipients of God's love.

John 3:16 states that God's love includes the whole world, but the world must have its eyes opened to behold this love's manifestation, and the antichrists deny the manifestation that God made of his love (2:22). "Was made manifest in connection with us" thus names "us," the believers, as the ones who truly see what God has done in his infinite love. The historical aorist "was made manifest," like the aorist used in 1:2, does not speak of the time when our eyes and our hearts came to see what God had done (the time of our conversion); this aorist refers to the time when God sent his Son upon his saving mission. The agent of the passive is

God; we do not take the passive in the middle sense "became manifest" or "manifested itself."

Ὅτι is epexegetical of ἐν τούτῳ, the phrase emphasizes the clause: in no less than *this* did God manifest his love, *that,* etc. The object "his Son" is placed emphatically forward; the verb and the subject are reversed, and thus the subject is emphasized: *his Son* he has sent, *God* has sent. The English word order is too rigid to duplicate this twofold emphasis found in the Greek. John repeats "God" eleven times in v. 7-12: God — God — God, who is love. The adjective "the Only-begotten" is added with a second article, thus it is also emphasized and is like an apposition in climax (R. 776), in fact, we may call ὁ μονογενής a noun.

On "his Son" see 1:3, 7; 2:22. John alone calls him "the Only-begotten." We discuss this term at length in *The Interpretation of St. John's Gospel*, 75, etc., and together with it the efforts which would empty it of its meaning. Both "his Son" and "the Only-begotten" avow the deity of the Logos; the latter = the *aeterna Filii Dei generatio.* Both ὁ λόγος and ὁ μονογενής extend back into eternity. He was "the Logos," "the Son," "the Only-begotten" in eternity ἄσαρκος, before his incarnation, and is that still ἔνσαρκος, in his incarnation. "The Father" (1:3; 2:22, 23) is the correlative term for the first person. Let this suffice here.

Him God "has sent with a commission into the world." He arrived at the time of the incarnation (John 1:14); he executed that commission. Πέμπειν is also used: God *sent* the Son. Jesus regularly calls the Father "my Sender," ὁ πέμψας με. Ἀποστέλλειν means a little more: "to send with a commission to carry out," to send in this sense, to commission. The corresponding noun is "apostle," one sent on a commission, and is commonly used with reference to the Twelve and to Paul; in Heb. 3:1 even Christ himself is so called. The

perfect "has sent" adds the idea of the continuance of
the commission to the past fact.

The purpose of this sending and commission is
"that we may live through him"; διά indicates mediation, he is the personal Mediator, the execution of his
commission makes him the channel for bestowing spiritual, eternal life upon us. The aorist is effective:
actually live through him. With this verb John reverts
to 1:1, "the Logos of the life," and to 1:2, "the Life,
the eternal one." He is the fount of life for us. "We
may live" also links into 2:29; 3:9, our having been
born from God, thus being "the children of God,"
(3:1). Life goes together with being born. The mission of the Son, the Only-begotten, includes his entire
office, the part which he executed while he was here on
earth plus the part that he is still executing as our
Advocate (2:1), our eternal High Priest, and our
King.

To send the Son, the Only-begotten, on this mission
and for this purpose is, indeed, the supreme manifestation of God's love.

**10)   In this is the love, not that we on our part
did love God, but that he on his part did love us and
sent his Son as expiation regarding our sins.**

The point is that *God* is love, and that *God* is thus
the one source of love. *We* had no love for him; it was
he who had this supreme love for us so that he sent his
own Son as an expiation for our sins. When our versions translate: "Herein is love," and when commentators say that ἡ ἀγάπη means "love in the abstract,"
they forget the fact that the world loves its own like
publican loves publican, and that John does not include
this love. He writes the article which makes the abstract noun definite: "the love," the true love that alone
deserves the name love. We may also regard this as the
article of previous reference: "this love" of which he
is speaking. This love has its origin wholly in God who,

in fact, is love itself, not in any way in us who had nothing but our sins, the opposite of love for God. Aorists are in place here.

'Ιλασμόν is a predicate accusative: "as expiation in regard to our sins." This is a repetition of 2:2 where we offer the exposition. This does not cover the entire mission of the Son; "expiation" goes with "the blood of the Son" (1:7) and thus shows the fathomless greatness of this act of God's love in that he sacrificed his own Son for us sinners. This is, indeed, the climax of the manifestation of God's love. We sinners were never little fountains or little streams of the love that is love; we were the opposite. The love that is love has its source in God; this supreme manifestation of love for us on his part reveals and proves that blessed fact.

11) After having shed all this light on the real love John now reverts to the admonition with which he began. **Beloved, if thus God did love us, we, too, ought to be loving one another.** As was the case in verse 7, John's true love calls on his beloved ever to love and to show love to one another. The condition is one of reality. To put an uncertainty into it, to speak of difficulty in rendering it into English, to let this "if" mean "if it be true" (English subjunctive), is to misunderstand the Greek condition of reality. "If thus God did love us" means: God did thus love us, and I submit this fact to you who will not, like the Antichrist, for one moment deny that *thus* he loved us. The emphasis is on οὕτως, "*thus*," sending his Son, the Only-begotten, that we may live through him, in order that his Son might shed his blood in expiation for our sins so that, cleansed from them, we live indeed.

"Thus" is aimed at Cerinthus, at his following, and at all who are of a similar mind. To them Jesus was the son of Joseph; the Spirit, who was bestowed on Jesus at his baptism, left him before his passion and his death. The deity of Jesus, the expiating efficacy of his blood were thereby denied. What these people said about the love of God and about fellowship with God (1:6) was thus as false as what the deniers of Jesus' deity and his expiation by blood say today. We see why John emphasizes in this way: "in *this* was manifested the love of God — in *this* is the love, etc. — if *thus* God did love," etc. We must emphasize in this manner to this day. *This* is the love of God, not what those who do not know God (2:4) make of his love and of their sins (1:8).

But should John not say, "Then we, too, ought to love God who thus loved us"? He does, but in due time, in v. 19-21. John reaches our love to God through the evidence of this love, and this evidence is the fact that we who are in the family of God as "the children of God" (3:1) love one another. John leads us step by step, from fact to fact, until he brings us to the top. Many leap over these intervening steps and shout, "We love God!" They neither understand where alone this love is born (v. 7-10), nor what alone is the evidence of this love, namely that we who have spiritual life through the Son's expiation (v. 9, 10) love one another, love those born from God to this life, his children indeed (v. 29-3:1). It is thus that John begins with the admonition which he has voiced already in verse 7: "We, too, ought to be loving one another."

12) **God no one has ever beheld** (has seen, verse 20; John 1:18; I Tim. 6:16); he is invisible (Col. 1:15; I Tim. 1:17; Heb. 11:27). No human being has ever rested his eyes on God for any length of time (perfect tense). Yet: **If we continue to love one another,** we who are his children, born from him, **God remains in us,** God who is love, **and his love has been brought to its goal in us.** When we love our true brethren, although we have never beheld him, God who is love "remains in us" (3:24). John once

again returns to this verb which he has used so often. The fellowship of love with one another is the evidence of our fellowship with God; he uses this term which he has employed in 1:3, 6, 7.

John adds: "and his love has been brought to its goal in us," his love for us with all that is said about this love in the preceding. Its goal is reached in us when God and this his love enter our hearts in order to remain there. Save for the periphrastic perfect, this is the same statement that was made in 2:5; compare 4:17, 18 in a different connection.

We do not regard ἡ ἀγάπη αὐτοῦ as having an objective genitive: our love *for* God. This necessitates the meaning "has been completed" for the verb. It can never be said that our love for God has been completed in this life, nor would this agree with the present tense "if we continue to love one another." Our versions have translated "his love" (the subjective genitive: his love for us), but their rendering "is perfected in us" is not correct. God's love is ever perfect, is never subject to perfecting. His love aims at reaching a certain goal in us, the one we have indicated. When we keep loving one another, this goal has been reached by God's love; our loving one another is the evidence that God's goal has been attained in us. This is evidence that we can see; the stronger our love, the clearer and the stronger is the evidence.

The perfect "has been brought (by God) to its goal" means that this goal is being retained by God: he has entered into our hearts and remains there. Jesus speaks in the same manner in John 14:23. The periphrastic perfect emphasizes the continuance. One might take it in the sense of the middle: his love has attained its goal; we regard the passive as being preferable.

13) Our love for one another is evidence that God is remaining in us, that his love for us has not

been in vain but has been brought to this goal, namely God's union with us. Valuable as this evidence is, it must be taken together with what underlies it, namely God's gift of the Holy Spirit to us. It is this Spirit who produces the love of one to another in our hearts. All holy impulses and actions are his work, and so also is brotherly love with all its deeds of love. Hence John repeats from 3:24: **In connection with this we know that we remain in him, and he in us, that he has given to us from his Spirit.** On John's expression "in connection with this we know (truly realize)" see 3:24. "This" = "that he has given us," etc. This second ὅτι is epexegetical as it was in 3:16 and not causal.

A strange sense is the result when ἐν τούτῳ is referred to the preceding: "in connection with our perfected love" (verse 12 being understood in this manner). Then we could never realize that we remain in God and he in us, for who save a perfectionist dares to say that his love for God has been perfected? Even if a high degree of love gives you this knowledge, are you ready to claim such a degree of love? No; if this is the basis for our really knowing that we are united with God, we should have a slender basis, indeed, and should wrestle with constant doubt. "This" points forward to the second ὅτι, to God's gift of his Spirit.

In verse 13 John says: "God remains in us." We have seen how John advanced to this expression in 3:24 although he had before used only· "we remain in God." He now combines the two: "that we remain in him, and he in us"; the one is never without the other. To understand fully what John means follow γινώσκω, μένειν and "in him" through all that precedes. The force of these terms grows stronger as John proceeds. These and other terms of his are diamonds that have many facets, of which the spiritual eye never tires.

Some, like Robertson, say that ἐκ is partitive: "of his Spirit," part of the Spirit. But 3:24 says that God gave us the Spirit. Is John now saying that he has given us only a part of the Spirit? Since when is the Holy Spirit divided into parts? That very thought is strange. After saying that God gave to us the Spirit, John advances and says that God has also given to us *"from* his Spirit." Just as God does not come into our hearts without the greatest gift for us (his Spirit), so, when the Holy Spirit is given to us, he does not enter our hearts without gifts for us. God gave "the Spirit" to us (3:24) and thereby has given *"from* his Spirit" to us, has given us a number of gifts, all of which come "from" the Spirit as the source. Among them is this "fruit of the Spirit," which Paul names as the first in Gal. 5:22, "love," the love for one another of which John is speaking, which is so great a mark of our connection with God that Paul sings its praise in strains that go even beyond those of John (I Cor. 13). Ἐκ denotes source, it is not partitive. .

Our love for one another is evidence for our union with God, whose children we are; but when we look at the source of this love and see that it is a gift of God from his own Spirit, whom also he gave to us (3:24), we know by "this" that we remain in God, and he in us. We keep the coherence of John's facts as he builds ever higher and wider.

14) Καί adds a still greater assurance of knowledge. **And we ourselves have beheld and are testifying,** we, the apostles, I, John, being one of them. He repeats and links back into 1:2: "we have seen and are (ever) testifying" **that the Father sent the Son as Savior of the world.** He resumes v. 9, 10. All that we have said on 1:2 and on 4:9, 10 belongs also here. Yet John now substitutes for the predicate "as expiation regarding our sins," "as Savior of the world" — note "regarding the whole world" in 2:2. So great

is God's love. John is one who beheld this deed of God's, beheld it when he beheld the Savior himself and his glory full of grace and truth (John 1:14). All of this testimony John's readers have. This, too, God gave them from his Spirit who speaks through the apostles. The new term "Savior of the world" sheds still more light on what John has been saying.

15) Linking back into v. 13 but reversing the statements and thus linking back into all the expressions regarding remaining, John adds: **Whoever confesses** (actually, aorist) **that Jesus is the Son of God, God remains in him, and he in God.** In this way the connection with God is made, and in this way it continues. John links back into verses 2, 3. Confession is open evidence for the invisible inward union with God. Its substance is "Jesus Christ having come in flesh" (4:2), and this is proof that one is "from God," "born from him" (2:29), or in other words, "that Jesus is the Son of God." Here belongs all that we have said on "Son of God" (1:3, 7; 2:22, 23; 3:23; 4:9, 10), on the denials of his deity, on all that lies in the Sonship, namely the entire gospel with all its facts ("doctrines" when the facts are adequately and correctly worded). Regarding this confession and the Holy Spirit add I Cor. 12:3.

16) With what John says about the apostles and their testimony and about whoever confesses he connects the further statement: **And we on our part have known and have believed this love which God has in connection with us.** Because of the predicates the "we" used in verse 14 denotes the apostles; because of the predicates and because of ἐν ἡμῖν at the end this new "we" denotes John and his readers. John speaks with Peter as recorded in John 6:69: "We have believed and have known" but reverses the verbs: "we have known and still know, and have believed and still

believe" (perfect tenses). This, John implies, is back of our confession. As γινώσκω runs back through this epistle, so πιστεύω resumes 3:23. To know as John speaks of knowing is to believe, and vice versa. No inner realization can be without a corresponding confidence, no true confidence without such a realization.

The object of both verbs is "the love which God has in connection with us." This is the same ἐν ἡμῖν that was found in verse 9. It does not mean "to us" (A. V.), "in us" (R. V.), "in our case" (R. V. margin), the German *an uns*, etc.; but "in connection with us," ἐν being used in its original meaning, the connection being the one which the context indicates, here the fact that God's love succeeded in connecting itself with us. For that reason, too, John says "the love which God *has* in connection with us" while in the next breath he repeats from verse 8: "God *is* love." John's wording is always most exact.

God is love (see verse 8), and his love has succeeded in connecting itself with us through the Son's expiation (v. 9, 10); it has been brought to the goal in us, the goal indicated by John (v. 11, 12). So John is able to connect God himself, who is love, with all that he has been saying about "remaining," beginning with 2:24-28, then in 3:24, and last in 4:12, 15, and he is able to shed more light on this "remaining" by adding to "God is love": **and the one remaining in this love** which God has in connection with us, which has succeeded in connecting itself with us, **remains in God, and God remains in him.** He is in connection with us, he who is love, we are in connection with him. John again uses both expressions as he did in v. 15. The *unio mystica* is here described as being due to this love. Only by remaining in this love do we remain in God because God is love; only in this way do we remain in him.

Yet all that John has said about the manifestation of God's love and about the goal that it has attained in us (verse 9, etc.) must be retained. Without the Son's expiation as the Savior of the world, without our confession of the Son, which means that we know and believe this love of God, this double remaining is impossible. The heretics of John's time may talk as they please about God's love while they deny the deity and the expiation by means of the blood of Jesus, they do not remain in God, God does not remain in them. This is still true with regard to all who are like them today.

We see how all this unfolds the κοινωνία (fellowship) with the Father and with his Son Jesus Christ, with which John began in 1:3, with which he presented the first development in 1:5-10. True fellowship with God is his remaining in us and our remaining in him and not a mere claim of fellowship (1:6).

17) In verse 12 John says that God's love has been brought to its goal in us by God, this goal being that we continue to love one another. One goal of God's love is that love be kindled in our hearts, that we ever love all those that are in the family of God. This is, however, not the only or the whole goal which God's love attains in us. John is now able to say: **In this has this love been brought to its goal with us, that we have boldness in connection with the day of the judging because even as that One is, we on our part also are** (although still) **in this world.**

Ἐν τούτῳ = ἵνα, etc.; it is an epexegetical substantative clause and not a purpose clause. This, too, is the goal to which God's love has been brought μεθ' ἡμῶν, "in company with us," in its companionship with us, namely that with God's love as our companion we have boldness whenever we think of the day of judging (the day when God will judge) and have one great goal which God's love wants to reach in us.

In verse 12 John writes about the goal that is reached *"in* us"; he might again have used *"in* us." When he now uses μετά he makes God's love our companion, writes as though that love walks arm in arm with us and assures us in regard to the final judgment. John follows Jesus in combining God's love with the fact that we are not judged on the last day (John 3:16-18: "he that believeth on him is not judged"). On the day of judgment the believer merely comes to the light so that his deeds may be made manifest, that they have been wrought in connection with God (John 3:20). Κρίσις is a word that expresses an action: the day "of judging."

Ἡ ἀγάπη has the article of previous reference and thus refers to the same love that was mentioned in verse 16, God's love. Not only this, it is here said to be μεθ' ἡμῶν, our companion. This is not *our* love (whether for God, for our brethren, or for both), and the verb does not mean that *our* love "has been perfected" ("is made perfect," our versions), and the thought is not that only when *our* love gets to this stage, do we have boldness for the judgment day. Let us say that we should then be in a sad state, for we should never know whether our love is perfect enough. We must daily confess that our love falls short of the ideal (1:9). Our boldness for the judgment day rests on God's love, on v. 9, 10.

John writes: "we have boldness," have it now. The tense is perfectly plain when we translate ἐν τῇ ἡμέρᾳ τῆς κρίσεως "in connection with the day of judging." We are looking forward to that day and to the fact that on that day we shall stand with God. As we do so now we have no fear but only παρρησία, "boldness." This word at times has the sense of "confidence." When ἐν is taken to mean "in" in the sense of "on," "at," a clash in dates seems to result. John should then write: we shall have boldness on the day. John's present tense "we have" is correct when ἐν is properly understood.

Ὅτι is causal. God's love promptly reaches this goal, that we confidently face the final judgment; we face it with all our sins remitted, with our Advocate and his expiation, with his blood (1:7-2:2), to which add 4:9, 10. So John introduces ἐκεῖνος, "that One," namely Christ, whom he calls "expiation for our sins," "Savior of the world," in verses 10, 14. Yet John does not remain with these facts but advances by saying that we have boldness "because even as that One is, we on our part are (although still) in this world." The stress is on the subjects, hence ἐσμέν is not enough, but the emphatic ἡμεῖς is added.

"In this world" cannot be the predicate, for that One is in heaven, that One is no longer in this world as we are. His being in this world as we are in this world would also not be a cause for our confidence in regard to the final judgment. This means that the predicate for that One and for us is not expressed but is to be sought in the context. It means that "in this world" applies only to us, that it is added to us because, although we are still in this world, we are already filled with bold confidence at the thought of God's final judging.

In what respect are we already just as that One is so that this likeness between him and us fills us with such confidence? Many different answers are given. The context points to the love of God, the love that sent the Savior, love that saved us through him and thus attained in us the goal indicated. So we regard as John's thought: "because even as that One is, God's love in company with him, also we ourselves are, God's love in company also with us (μεθ' ἡμῶν) although we are still in this world." We think that also for this reason John uses μετά and not ἐν when he speaks

of God's love. If God's love walks arm in arm with us
(μετά) even as his love is ever with Jesus, the coming
judgment brings no fear to us.

John has already mentioned this boldness of ours
in 2:28 and in 3:21, and it is thus that he now weaves it
in anew in connection with God's love for us.

18) **There is no fear in connection with this
love; on the contrary, this goal-attaining love throws
out this fear because this fear has punishment; moreover, the one fearing has not been brought to the
goal in connection with this love.**

The Greek places the negative with the verb, the
English places it with the subject. "Fear" is the opposite of "boldness"; where the one is, the other is not.
John's statement is *not* axiomatic and general as some
regard it, as also our versions regard it. These overlook the fact that ἐν τῇ ἀγάπῃ has the article of previous
reference: "in connection with *the* love," i. e., with
this love of God for us of which John is speaking.
There is no place for fear on our part in connection
with this love of God for us. This love has removed
all our sins (1:9; 2:1, 2; 4:10); what is there left to
make us afraid?

"On the contrary (ἀλλά), this goal-attaining love
throws out this fear." Now also τὸν φόβον has the
article of previous reference. This love of God for
us throws out of our hearts this fear which John has
just mentioned and substitutes bold confidence (παρρησία,
verse 17) in its place. We have stated how God's love
does this. God does not let those who have been born
from him, the children of God (2:29-3:1), quake with
fear at the thought of the judgment day; his love pulls
this fear up by the very roots and throws it out as
though it were a poisonous weed. Whereas John first
says "in connection with this love" he now inserts the
adjective τελεία, which has the same meaning as the
verb he is using here and in verses 12, 17: τετελείωται,

"this goal-attaining love." Having this fear thrown out of our hearts and filling us with confidence instead is the very goal that this goal-attaining love of God promptly reaches in our hearts when God rids us of our sins through Christ.

Such fear (again the article of previous reference) cannot remain where God's love is brought to its goal in us; God cannot let it remain "because this fear has punishment," κόλασις, torturing punishment, the A. V. thus translating "torment." The verb "has" means "has to do with" (B.-P. 690). John states this in order to show why, in being brought to its goal, God's love necessarily throws out all such fear. This love would not reach its proper goal without that. This is stated with δέ: "moreover, the one fearing," living in such fear of punishment, "has not been brought to the goal (by God) in connection with this love" of God for us. If you still fear punishment from God you have prevented his love for you from remitting your sins and thus from planting sure confidence in your heart instead of this fear.

There is no danger of misunderstanding John's thought. All God's children are ever to fear God in true, childlike fear, are to shrink from offending him. This fear accompanies both God's love for us and our love for him. John is speaking of the fear which all the wicked, "the children of the devil" (3:10), must sooner or later suffer because of their unforgiven sins.

Our versions and some commentators refer John's words to *our* love for God: *our* love for him throws out fear of him, but it does so only when *our* love is perfect or has developed to a high degree. This is Catholic doctrine, according to which no one can be certain whether his love is perfect enough. In these verses John is speaking of what God's love does. He touches upon our love in verses 11, 12a and now returns to that.

19) **We on our part continue to love because he as first-one loved us.** We had no love at all (verse 10) ; God is πρῶτος, "the first one," who did the loving. The aorist repeats the ἠγάπησεν used in verse 10 and refers to the great manifestation of God's love there described. That astounding act of his love kindled love in our hearts so that we on our part continue to love. The objects of this our loving are not yet the point, so no objects are named. The emphatic ἡμεῖς is not in contrast with those who do not love. It places us and our loving beside God and his act of love, and ὅτι states that God's love is the cause of ours; ἡμεῖς balances αὐτός and not ὁ φοβούμενος.

20) John now mentions the objects of our love. **If someone says, I am loving God! and hates his brother he is a liar, for the one not loving his brother, whom he has seen, God, whom he has not seen, he cannot be loving.**

This elaborates the brief statement made in verse 12: "God no one has (ever) beheld," which was connected with our loving one another. The aorist "if someone says" considers the case of a single declaration by some person who asserts, "I am loving God." The essential thing in our loving is that we love *God*. This truth no one contradicts or questions so that John simply proceeds by taking this for granted. But this is true only in the Christian sense. Because God loved us *God* is the supreme object of our love.

There is a simple test by which we may verify both regarding ourselves and regarding others whether the claim: "I love God," is true or not. He who makes this claim "and hates his brother is a liar." This also means that he who makes this claim and loves his brother speaks the truth. Γάρ explains how this is to be understood. It is impossible for anyone to love God, whom he has not seen, when he does not love his brother, whom he has seen. To claim that this is possible, to say, "I am doing it," is to lie. Such supposed love for God is not love, it is a fiction. The God whom this person claims to love is also a figment of his mind, namely a self-made God who lets him hate his brother, which our God, who is love itself, cannot do.

The point· lies in the objects. It is sometimes thought to lie only in the relative clauses, namely in the verbs "has seen" — "has not seen," and the explanation is then given that it is *easier* to love one on whom our eyes have rested and can rest again and again than one upon whom our eyes have never rested nor rest; that he is a liar who claims to be doing the more difficult when he is not doing even the easier. This seems a somewhat weak thought for such strong language as "he is a liar" (cf. 1:6, 10; 2:22). Add to these verbs and these relatives their nouns *"his brother* whom he *sees"* — *"God* whom he does *not see."* These objects of love are even juxtaposed in order to give them a greater effect. John states only a part of the thought when he declares that it is impossible to love the latter while not loving the former; he states the rest in verse 21 and in 5:1-3, especially in 5:1, 2, for there we learn why this is impossible.

The explanation that loving the brother is loving God who is in the brother so that not loving the brother makes it impossible to love God, the brother being visible, God invisible, is on the right track but does not go far enough. John goes much farther.

21) In the first place he points to God's own commandment which was given us through Jesus (John 13:34; 15:12), which was noted already in 3:23, but which goes back to 1:7, to our having fellowship with one another. **And this commandment we have from him, that the one loving God love also his brother.** We do not go back to Matt. 22:37, 39, for there love to all men is referred to; John refers to the love which we are able to have only for him

who is our brother. The word "commandment" recalls
all that John says in 2:3-8 regarding our keeping God's
commandment (compare also Jesus' statements in
John 14:21, 23, 24; 15:10, 12, 14). This commandment
already shows that one who hates his brother cannot
love God, for love to God would most certainly keep
God's commandment.

5:1) Before giving the final explanation John
states who a child of God is, and who is thus a
brother of a child of God, and thereby takes us back
to 2:29-3:1, 9; 4:7, ("everyone having been *born
from God*," etc.), and at the same time back to 3:23,
"*believe* the name of his Son" (4:16, "believe").
Only the believer is the believer's brother; only the
reborn is brother to the reborn. **Everyone believing
that Jesus is the Christ has been born from God.**

The antichrists call each other "brother, brother";
so also do men in self-made brotherhoods. When such
brothers love one another, this is not evidence that
they love God. I must be born from God, be born
into God's family, to be a brother to those in this
family, to have them as my brothers ("the children
of God," 3:1), to love them as my brothers, and to
be loved as a brother by them. The love that John
speaks about in 4:20, 21 is the love that is possible only
between brother and brother. This is also necessary
because it at the same time means love for the Father
from whom all of us brothers have been born.

Only the believer is so born. John says that the
content of his faith is "that Jesus is the Christ," and
he says in 4:15 that this faith is confessed; so we can
easily know who is a believer and thus a brother born
from God. In 4:11 we have pointed out that John
there, too, strikes at the heresies of Cerinthus and of
his following. John does this from the very beginning

of this epistle as we have noted throughout. John, the apostle of love as he is often called, is not a sentimental pacifist but a very strong polemicist — "liar" (1:6, 10; 2:22; 4:20) is hurled like a bolt from his pen.

Since he uses the unmodified name "Jesus" (so also in 1:7) John has in mind the man Jesus, he who walked here on earth as a man. The heretics said "that is all that he was and that he is." To believe that the man Jesus is "the Christ," i. e., all that is contained in this term starting from 1:1-3; 1:7; 2:1, 2 on through to 4:9, 10, 14, means to believe the deity of Jesus, the expiation of his blood, the remission and the cleansing which this blood effects, in fact, the whole love of God that is expressed in the whole Saviorhood of Jesus, the whole gospel. John is not presenting the minimum content of faith but its full, normal, true content. After all that he has said his brief wording is sufficient.

The true believer "has been born from God," he alone. With this verb (which has the same tense it had in 2:29; 3:9) John refers to these passages. By this birth God made the true believer one of "the children of God" (3:1), a brother to all his other children. Thus John now advances to the statement: **And everyone loving the One who gave birth loves also the one who has been born from him.** John does not say, "He ought to love." The truth that the child of God loves the Father who begot him as his child and thus loves also his brother whom the Father has likewise begotten, is a simple fact. To imagine the opposite, namely that one who is so begotten should *not* love him who has likewise been begotten, is to imagine the impossible.

This is the basis for the "ought" used in 4:11. We have the full unfolding of what is implied in 1:3, the fellowship of the readers with us (the apostles); in 1:7, the fellowship with one another; and of all that lies in 2:9-11; 3:10-18; 4:11, 12, in loving one another, loving one's brother, not hating him. John goes to the root of it all. He weaves into one fabric all the threads of his epistle, all that he says about the Father, about Jesus, his Son, the Christ, and this Son's blood and mission, about our connection with the Father and the Son, about life (1:1, 2; 4:9), about passing from the death into the life, and about remaining in the death (3:14). In fact, a full exegesis of our verse would include the exegesis of all that precedes. This is John's wonderful way of writing: each brief, crystal-clear statement involves all that precedes.

Believing and love go together in 3:23, in 4:16 (God's love), and in this passage. The believing makes confession (4:15), loving shows itself in deeds (3:18). We thus have no difficulty in knowing whether we are in God, and he in us as his children, and who are our brothers who are likewise born from God with the same faith and the same love in their hearts. All this has at the same time its polemical side against those who went out from us because they were not of us (2:19), who are not in this family, who are not believers born of God and filled with this love, who lie when they claim fellowship with God (1:6) and declare, "I love God" (4:20), lie because they deny the Son and thus also the Father (2:22, 23) and prove it by not loving us, God's children, show their Cain-like nature, the fact that they are children of the devil not born from God (3:8-12).

2) John now weaves in our knowing, the γινώσκειν about which he has said so much. Trace the word back and note its full meaning, knowing with full affect and effect in ourselves. **In connection with this we know that we are loving the children of God,** those born from him (the plural now denoting all of them), **whenever we are loving God and are doing his commandments.** It is as simple as that.

Here are God's commandments. Review all that John says about "commandments," notably in 2:3-8, also in 3:22-24, finally in 4:21. By doing these commandments, gospel commandments which ask for both faith · and love (3:23), you are loving God; and by loving God you are loving the children of God. Just look at what you are *doing* with the commandments of God, who is love, then you cannot help *knowing*, i. e., realizing. The negative is, of course, equally true. Not to be doing God's commandments (3:23) leaves you with nothing but the lying claim that you are loving God (4:20) and have fellowship with him (1:6); and then any love for God's children, in fact, any claim that you are one of them and are born from God becomes fiction.

There are three boxes. The outer one is doing what God wants. Open that, and in it is loving God, the Father of all his children. Open that, and in it is loving his children. So you know. The apposition to ἐν τούτῳ is the ὅταν clause (compare the remarks on 3:24b; R. 700, and especially B.-D. 394: ὅτι to denote a fact, ἐάν or ὅταν to denote a supposition).

3) Γάρ adds the important explanation: **For this is the love for God, that we keep his commandments.** Just to make the claim: "I am loving God!" (4:20) amounts to nothing, is, in fact, lying (1:6). But remember 3:23 as well as 1:3, "fellowship with the Father and with his Son Jesus Christ." John weaves in τηρεῖν from 2:3, 4, the commandments have been given (3:22, 24) for the purpose of *keeping;* *doing* what each one says (5:2), actually loving not merely in word but in deed (3:18), when it comes to my brother, my fellow believer, is their chief aim.

Are these commandments burdensome, a heavy weight that is, if possible, to be avoided, to be complained about when it is shouldered? **And his commandments are not burdensome.** Is it a burden to

believe in the Son of God who died in expiation of our
sins (2:2; 3:23; 4:10)? There is no greater joy than
this confidence and trust. Is it a burden to be called
one of God's children (3:1), children of him who is
love (4:8, 16), and for the love of him who first loved
us (4:10) to love him and thus also his children even
as he loves us, and as they love us? Can there be any
greater joy than to stand in this circle of love, to have
this love poured out upon us, to be warmed into answering love by this love? No; his commandments are not
burdensome!

The Seventh Circle of Facts,

Centering on Testimony, Faith, Life

5:4-17

4) In 4:14 "we are testifying" recalls the beginning of the epistle: "we are testifying and are declaring to you" (1:2). John now weaves in the facts regarding this testimony. He does so at this point where he has connected believing with love. We have these two together in 3:23, and believing continues in the development in 4:1; 4:16; 5:1. John now joins testimony and believing. All testimony wants to be believed, it is offered for that purpose only. All true testimony ought to be believed; not to believe it is to make him who testifies a liar. John adds what this means for the liar.

John makes no formal division at this point. Hence one may add v. 4, 5 to the preceding. The only reason we divide here is the fact that John introduces the new terms "victory" and "winning victory" and connects these terms with "faith" and "believing," and thus passes on to "testimony" and "bearing testimony," which he now expands, which appear eight times and thus form the new center. The old division into chapters which is found in our versions lets the new circle begin at v. 1 although v. 1-3 still carries the key word "love," which is dropped in v. 4.

Because everyone who has been born from God (reaching back into 2:29; 3:9; 4:7; 5:1) **is victorious over the world; and this is the victory, the one that became victorious over the world, our faith.** John links the thought with 2:13, 14 where he says that the youths have achieved the victory over the wicked one and then tells all his readers not to love the world. The wicked one rules the world; to be victorious over him is to be a victor over the world and over all that is in it, which is not from the Father (2:16). If the youths have achieved this victory and stand in it (perfect tenses), this is certainly also true of all who are no longer youths. John now speaks of all of them and includes himself.

Ὅτι makes this victory the reason that our keeping God's commandments in love for God cannot be burdensome. How can victors find it hard to show their love for God by keeping his commandments which ask them to believe in the Son and to love one another (3:23)? They have been born from God, have been filled with strong, spiritual life, and are thus victorious over the world, over this power which would interfere with their keeping of God's commandments. It should certainly be easy for us victors to go on in our victory, to trample upon any interference from the world which is opposed to God, and to love God and to keep his commandments.

This becomes clearer when we see what this victory is, "the one that became victorious over the world," the aorist participle going back to the beginning of the victory. It is "our faith." When God, then, asks us to believe (4:23) he is asking us only to be victorious; when he asks us to love he is asking only for the fruit of faith which it naturally bears. Both faith and love show that we have been born from God (v. 1), that the power of a new life is in us, that in believing and in loving this power of the new life is showing its activity. It does so positively in regard to God and to God's children who are in the same victorious army with us and negatively in regard to the world, in keeping up our victory over it (present tense).

5) Here again, as in verse 1, John is not content with the words "believe" and "our faith" but adds the content of this faith. **Now who is the one that is victorious over the world but he who believes**

that Jesus is the Son of God? The question implies
that no one will think of a different answer. If our
victory is our faith, the victor is the believer. This
makes the abstract statement concrete. Yet everything
depends on *what* we believe. Believing some fiction,
some lie is not victory but defeat, surrender, victory
for the devil, the father of lies (John 8:44), for the
world, the devil's children (3:10) who cling to his lies
and his deceptions. Not a single lie is from the truth
(2:21). John has said much about the light, the truth,
the Word. He now states their substance: "that Jesus
is the Son of God"; in verse 1 it was: "that Jesus is
the Christ." This is *what* the believer believes, this is
what makes him a victor over the world.

John again links into all that he has said on the
deity of Jesus and on the power of his blood in 1:1-3, 7;
2:1, 2, 22, 23; 3:8, 23; 4:9, 10, 15; 5:1. Let us once
more add that the truth "that Jesus is the Son of God,"
"the Christ," the "expiation for our sins," the "Savior
of the world," is not *one* article of our faith but the
sum of *all* of them, not a piece of the gospel but the
whole gospel. It is necessary to say this and to cling
to it because so many imagine that "the truth" and "the
Word" can be cut into pieces, and that we can deny
this, that, and even many pieces and yet be true to the
Father and to the Son and to God's children.

6) **This One is the One who came by means of
water and blood; not in connection with water alone,
but in connection with the water and in connection
with the blood.**

The content of the faith of the victor over the world
is "that Jesus is the Son of God," a truth which
Cerinthus and his adherents denied outright by making
Jesus the natural son of Joseph and of Mary. That is
why this epistle from beginning to end holds up the
deity of Jesus, why it with such decisiveness stresses
the fact that he is "the Son of God." Deny this, and

you deny and have no Father (3:22, 23), and all talk of fellowship with God (1:6), i. e., all talk of true religion, is nothing but a lie.

But these antichristian heretics had more to say. This natural son of Joseph was joined to the eon Christ (the earliest Gnostic notion) at Jesus' baptism, but this Christ eon left the natural son of Joseph at the time of his passion so that Jesus died as a mere man who was never "the Son of God," was never the incarnate Logos, the second person of the Godhead, but had the Christ eon only for a time. This heresy deprived the death and "the blood of Jesus, the Son of God," of all efficacy as a ἱλασμός or "expiation" for the sins of the world (2:2; 4:10). In fact, these heretics denied that we have sins and also in this respect made God a liar (1:8-10). That is why John now says: "This One is the One," i. e., this Jesus who is the Son of God, "who came by means of water and of blood," and then adds specifically: "not in connection with the water alone" as Cerinthus claims, "but in connection with the water and in connection with the blood."

Οὗτος is the subject of ἐστί, and ὁ ἐλθών, κτλ., is the predicate: "this One" is "the One who came," etc. The aorist indicates the historical fact. "The One who *came* = 4:9, 10: "God *has sent* (commissioned) his Son, the Only-begotten, as expiation regarding our sins." This One came as the one thus sent and commissioned, this One being the Only-begotten, the Son of God.

Neither διά nor the two ἐν are local; nor does ἐν indicate manner (R. 583) or accompanying circumstance akin to μετά and σύν (R. 589). Jesus, the Son of God, did not come as one who walked *through* (local), or in the manner of water and of blood, or with water and blood accompanying him. The mission on which God sent his Son and in which he came as "Savior of the world" (4:14) made him use these two means (διά),

water and blood; when he came, it was not "in connection with" water alone (as the heretics claimed) but
"in connection with the water and in connection with
the blood." The ἐν is to be understood in its original
sense, the two articles are articles of previous reference
to "water" and to "blood."

The διά states what the connection indicated by ἐν
was: it was the connection of means. John is not referring to John 19:34 where blood is placed before water,
which also the heretics did not have in mind. The two
ἐν phrases also indicate two connections and not one
in which water and blood were combined. The first
is the baptism of Jesus, the Son of God, in and by
which he assumed his office as Savior of the world, for
which God had sent him. The second is his sacrificial
death on the cross where he shed his expiating blood;
compare what is said on "the blood of Jesus, his Son,"
in 1:7.

John utterly repudiates what the heretics made of
the baptism of Jesus. Read John 1:29-34: "the Lamb
of God which takes away the sin of the world," the
Lamb came to shed his blood for the sin and was "the
Son of God" as the voice of the Father declared from
heaven (Matt. 3:17; John 1:34). The heretics denied
what that voice said, denied "the blood of the Son of
God" (1:7), the expiation on the cross.

When the historical aorist ὁ ἐλθών is disregarded,
symbolical and figurative ideas are allowed play, and
when these are given free rein they go to extravagant
lengths. We list only the one that water and blood
denote the two sacraments, which is held by even
a man like Besser who in addition finds a reference to
John 19:34.

On whose testimony does this our victorious faith
in Jesus, the Son of God, and on this fact that he
came and thus carried out the mission on which God
had sent him (4:9, 10) rest? John reverts to 1:2:

"we are testifying," and to 4:14 where he writes the same words. **And the Spirit is the One giving testimony because the Spirit is the truth.** John no longer stresses the fact that he himself and the apostles are the ones testifying as he did in 1:2 and in 4:14, but he does not do this because their apostolic testifying is not sufficient for faith. John advances from the intermediate bearers of testimony to the ultimate One who testifies. As the epistle progresses it advances with every new addition. It does so here.

The ultimate One bearing testimony, from whom all the apostles also derive their testimony, on whom their own faith also rests, is the Holy Spirit, none less. The τὸ Πνεῦμα must refer to the third person of the Godhead. There is no need to mention what some, following their spiritualizing fancies, have found in this word. The Spirit is above all the One giving testimony, is thus the ultimate Testifier, "because the Spirit is the truth," the truth itself. Jesus calls him "the Spirit of the truth" (John 15:26; 16:13). Jesus adds: "*He* shall testify concerning me." To the apostles Jesus says: "And you, too, testify, because from the beginning you are with me" (John 15:27). All of this agrees with what John says in 1:2 and in 4:14 about the apostles' testifying and now about the Spirit as the One testifying. The relation of the apostles to the Spirit is plain: Jesus gave them the Spirit. They speak as being borne along by the Holy Spirit (II Pet. 1:21), the Spirit being the ultimate Testifier.

John says more than that the Spirit is "true"; he is "the truth" just as Jesus says this regarding himself (John 14:6), the embodiment of the saving truth, which he thus also imparts by his testimony in order to save us. We do not regard ὅτι as declarative: "*that* he is the truth" (Luther). This would be out of the line of thought. Τὸ μαρτυροῦν, "the One testifying," is the present tense because the Spirit has never ceased testifying. We hear his voice in the Scripture, notably in the New Testament. We should not translate this participle into English by means of a neuter word or speak of a neuter being "personified." The Greek Πνεῦμα is grammatically a neuter, but in the Greek it refers to the third person of the Godhead, and the predicate *"the One* testifying" is not *"something testifying."*

7, 8) But the law has ever required and requires to this day that two or three testify (Deut. 17:6; 19:15; Matt. 18:16; II Cor. 13:1); God himself adheres to this principle, (Heb. 10:28, 29); so does Jesus (Heb. 6:18; John 5:31-37). So John adds a second causal clause: **Because three are the ones giving testimony, the Spirit and the water and the blood, and the three are for one thing,** i. e., their testimony is one identical thing, the three agree without the least deviation in their one testimony in regard to Jesus and to his deity. ·The Spirit is the One testifying, he who is the truth itself because two others testify with him and substantiate even in a legal, formal way all that anyone can require in regard to testimony. The fact that these two others are not persons does not disqualify them. In Heb. 6:18 the second is not a second person; in John 5:36 Jesus names his "works" as testifying.

. The baptism of Jesus speaks volumes about his deity and about his entire mission. We have already pointed to John 1:29-34 and to the accounts of the baptism itself. The death of Jesus does the same; remember his words on the cross, in fact, his entire passion, the whole of which is the testimony of "the blood." The one supreme Testifier, the Spirit, has these two others to support him.

The R. V. is right in not even noting in the margin the interpolation found in the A. V. How completely spurious this insertion, often called *"Comma Joan-*

neum," really is Horn, *Introduction*, 7th ed., vol. IV, pp. 448-471, shows, offering even the facsimiles of the very late texts that contain the Comma and treating the whole subject exhaustively. Zahn, *Introduction*, III, 372, adds a few new items in his remarks on the subject.

9) **If we receive the testimony of men, the testimony of God is greater because this is the testimony of God,** (this) **that he has given testimony in regard to his Son.** We certainly receive the testimony of men in regard to all manner of things, many of them being most important. The testimony of God is infinitely greater because this is the testimony of God, this that (declarative ὅτι) he has been testifying, not about some small thing, but about the greatest of all, his own Son. What the Spirit, the water, and the blood say is God's own testimony; these three testifiers are furnished by him, by him because this testimony of his deals with his own Son. This constitutes its greatness. Once given, it stands now and ever — the perfect μεμαρτύρηκε. When the Father sends us three testifiers and through them in the most legal way testifies about his own Son, can we who daily receive the testimony of men refuse to accept this great testimony, which is great because it is given by God and is given about his Son?

10) John emphasizes this thought. He repeats the term "testimony" and the verb "testify" no less than eight times, "God" seven times, his "Son" six times. See the similar repetitions of "commandment" in 2:3-8; of the verb "to remain" in 2:24-28. **The one believing in the Son of God has this testimony in him** (in his heart, for believing so receives it); **the one not believing God has made him a liar because he has not believed in the testimony which God has testified concerning his Son.** The perfect tenses imply that he has done this from the moment when God

brought his testimony to his heart and this disbeliever
refused to believe God himself when he was testifying
concerning his own Son.

It is making God a liar when one refuses to believe
God's testimony regarding other matters; it is making
God a liar in the worst possible way when one refuses
to believe God's testimony about his own Son. Let the
disbelievers in the deity of Jesus note what they have
done. Compare 1:10 on making God a liar; and 2:22,
the fact that only liars do this. Yet they claim fellowship with God (1:6) as though God were a liar and
fellowships liars!   .

Note that believing is not a matter of the head and
the intellect alone but that it ever appeals to the heart.
Faith is the confidence of the heart, the *fiducia* that
holds "in him," in the believer, the objective testimony
of God and thus all that God's testimony contains as
John now makes plain.

**11, 12)   And this is the testimony, that God gave
to us life eternal, and this life is in connection with
his Son. The one having the Son has this life; the
one not having the Son of God does not have this life.**

Understand well what this testimony of God is,
which he has testified through his three testifiers, in
order that you may well understand what believing
this testimony is and what not believing it is. This
testimony about his Son is no less than "that God gave
to us life eternal"; with a simple καί John adds the
thought that "this life is in connection with his Son."
The articles used with ζωή (three times) are those of
previous reference: "this life." What connection life
eternal has with God's Son, John has stated in 4:9, 10
("that we may live through him"); in 3:14 ("we have
stepped over from the death into the life"); in 1:1, 2
(Jesus, "the Logos of the Life," "the Life that was
manifested," "the Life, the eternal one"), plus all the

passages on "having been begotten from God" (2:29; 3:9; 4:7; 5:1, 14, 18).

John binds everything together. God's testimony brings us his Son; eternal life is in his Son, is in him for us; it is given us in and by this testimony; to believe it is to have the Son, and to have him is to have this life; not to believe it is not to have the Son and this life. It is all as simple and as lucid as these brief statements make it.

John can say for himself and for his readers: "God gave to us life eternal," gave it to us when we believed his testimony and thereby received the Son into our possession with all that he is for us. Regarding the heretics he can now let the general statement suffice: "The one not having the Son does not have this life."

13) With a direct address to his readers John now combines the three terms into one succinct statement: the name of the Son of God — believing in his name — life eternal. The name comes to us through the "testimony." On ὄνομα and its use with "the Son of God" see 3:23. **These things I wrote to you in order that you may know that you have life eternal as those believing in the name of the Son of God.**

We think that it is fruitless to debate as to whether this epistolary aorist refers only to what immediately precedes or to the whole epistle; because of the way in which John writes, letting his thought spiral upward in ever-widening circles, what he just wrote is only a further advance on the rest. The whole of it, like the last sentences, is to bring to the mind of his readers the fact that they have life eternal as those who believe in the name (revelation) of the Son of God.

John uses οἶδα as he does also in the three following notable statements (verses 18-20) and not γινώσκω. His intention is not that he wants to exclude the knowing of the heart, which realizes with full effect upon the

readers (γινώσκω), but that he wants his readers to know
also intellectually, with a clear understanding of the
mind that they have life eternal only as believers in
the name of the Son of God over against all the heretics
who refuse to believe in this name and revelation and
deny the Son of God (2:22; 4:15). The readers must
know this with a clear mental perception in order to
meet and to refute these Gnostic heretics when they
come with the claim that they are the ones who know.
The aorist εἰδῆτε is effective: "that you may actually
know." This is the purpose of John's instructive, clear,
simple presentation. John has already said that he is
writing nothing new and strange (2:7, etc.), also that
his readers have for a long time realized and believed
(2:13, etc.; 4:16) ; John writes in order to fortify his
readers just as we must constantly be informed and
fortified anew.

14) The fact that John is thinking of the dangers that are besetting his readers becomes evident
in what he adds. **And this is the boldness which we
have regarding him that, if we ask anything in accord with his will, he hears us; and if we know that
he hears us, (hears) whatever we ask, we know
that we have the askings we have asked from him.**

John links back into 3:21, 22, which he now amplifies, but he states this as a preamble to the danger that
he has in mind, to what he expects his readers to do in
rescuing a brother from such danger. So he once more
reminds them of the great παρρησία, the boldness and
confidence that they have πρὸς αὐτόν, "face to face" with
God when they go to him in prayer (see 3:21 on this
preposition).

It is a fact that, if we ask anything according to
his will, he hears us. The fact that we as true believers
and God's children will never come face to face with
him and ask what is against his will is in a way self-
evident; hence it is not mentioned in so many of the

promises of Jesus regarding prayer nor in 3:21, 22.
That point is in place here because John speaks of
cases when God does not want us to ask. That is the
reason John does not now use the active of αἰτέω as he
did in 3:22 but twice writes the middle αἰτώμεθα and
then twice follows this with the simple active.

G. K. and others think that there is no difference
between these forms, at least, that none is intended.
But here and elsewhere, especially where the active
and the middle are used side by side, a difference is
apparent and certainly seems to be intended. It is
admitted that the middle is used in business dealings,
where one has the right to ask. Herod's oath gave
Salome a certain right to ask, a right of which she
made full use (Matt. 14:7). Why should the two middle
forms that are used here not include this right? Does
the phrase "according to his will" (θέλημα, what God
has willed and has made known as being willed by him)
not imply a certain right for our asking?

15) John repeats "he hears us" by saying "we
know that he hears us," we know it as a fact; Jesus
himself has told us so. The person one hears is stated
with the genitive, the thing one hears is stated in the
accusative: "he hears us" (genitive), hears "whatever
we ask" (accusative clause). "He hears" is to be
understood in its full sense: "we know that we have
the askings that we have asked from him." He hears
and grants. Αἰτήματα is the cognate object (R. 477).
It is a word that expresses a result like θέλημα: the
askings as made by our action of asking.

"We have asked" does not need to be the middle
here. R. 805 remarks that in these verses the difference
between the middle and the active may well be the
point; we think it is and do not follow B.-D. 316, 2
who says that the change in voice is "arbitrary" here
and in James 4:2, etc. Moulton, *Einleitung*, 253, etc.,
records several wrong opinions, objects to Blass's view

regarding "arbitrary," but seems to think that Mayor is right, who says that the active denotes that the asking is without the spirit of prayer, which is an untenable idea.

In ἐὰν οἴδαμεν we have the indicative; it is found once more in the New Testament in I Thess. 3:8; it occurs often in the papyri (R. 1010); in the modern Greek the indicative is used as frequently as the subjunctive.

16) Now there follows the application. **If one sees a brother sinning a sin not unto death he will ask, and he (God) will give to him** (that asks) **for those not sinning unto death. There is sin unto death. Not concerning that do I say that he make request.**

Here is a brother that is living in some sin (present, durative participle), and one of us (singular) sees it. Knowing what we all know about asking God and about God's hearing us, one of us asks God, and God gives this one life for this brother, "for those sinning"; the plural indicates that there will be others that sin from time to time. The future tenses are perfectly regular and are not intended as imperatives. This cannot be the case as far as δώσει is concerned.

The subject of the latter is God. This is indicated by the addition of αὐτῷ which must mean "to him" who does the asking. Some, like the R. V. margin, refer it to the sinning brother, but they must then make the plural τοῖς ἁμαρτάνουσι an apposition to the singular αὐτῷ, which, to say the least, is strange. In the R. V. "even" is added: "even to them that are sinning." If we supply anything we prefer to supply "God" with the verb. This leaves us the proper Scripture thought that God gives to him who asks. The idea that you and I give life to anyone is not Scriptural. Those who accept that idea say that this person gives life to his sinning brother when God, in answer to his prayers, enables him to do so. So, after all, the Giver is God, and the circumlocution has no advantage.

John says twice that in these cases the sinning is
"not unto death"; πρός is used as it was in v. 14 with
the meaning not facing death as the inevitable result.
Since ζωή is "life eternal" (v. 13), which, as we now
"have" it, is spiritual life, "death" must be its opposite,
namely the loss of spiritual life, which is spiritual
death. Once having been born from God (2:29; 3:9;
4:7; 5:4, 18) into the new life, "death" means that
this life has been lost. We are not to think of physical
death, either that which is inflicted by the government
(which is then conceived as punishment for a capital
crime) or that which results from the effects of the
sinning on the sinner's body. What God does when
he gives life for these sinners is to strengthen their
damaged, declining spiritual life, which they have not
as yet lost. Δώσει is used to match αἰτήσει: God *shall
give* to him who *shall ask*. He also gives not *to* but *for*
these sinners.

John says in elucidation: "There is (indeed) sin
unto death," and adds: "not concerning that do I say
that he (the petitioner) shall make request" (aorist,
to denote an actual request). This raises the question:
"What is sin unto death and sinning not unto death?"
When we answer this question we should not overlook
the "if one sees" (aorist, actually sees). A Christian
is able to see when another is not sinning unto death
and thus by implication when he is. This does not
mean that his sight is infallible, or that he may not
fear that his brother's sinning will bring him into
death. In certain cases, however, the death will be
so apparent that intercession is no longer in place "in
accord with God's will."

Those are right who say that the answer should not
be given abstractly but in the light of John's whole
epistle.

17) **Every wrong is sin,** all or every deviation
from God's norm of right, i. e., "all unrighteousness."

That is unquestioned by Christians. All ἀδικία, all ἁμαρτία must be guarded against by him who has been born from God (v. 18; 3:9). John writes these things so that his readers may not sin (2:1). All sin and all wrong are dangerous to our spiritual life. Who can tell what damage will result for him if he enters on a course of sinning? The wages of sin is death (Rom. 6:23). Thank God that all sins and all sinning are not unto death, that by confessing and fleeing to the intercession of our Advocate we may have our sins remitted and be cleansed (1:8-2:2)!

So we say that where the way for this is still open, the sinning is not unto death. Our intercession for each other is to the effect that God may help us to use this way. He has his means for driving us to the cross of Christ. John says ἁμαρτία οὐ πρὸς θάνατον because the phrase modifies the noun; in v. 16 he writes μή because it there modifies participles.

"Sin unto death," is that sinning which involves the closing of the door to the blood of Jesus Christ, his Son (1:7). It is the sin which itself denies the Son of God (2:22) and all the sinning that goes with this denial. John has added the main features. One is making God a liar (1:8, 10), claiming that one has no sin; another is stated in 1:6, lyingly claiming fellowship with God while repudiating his Word. Go through the epistle. Can one see this? Yes. Bengel thinks only of a state; the state is there, but John speaks throughout of more than a mere state, he speaks of all the acts that proclaim that state. He never counsels his readers to look into a man's heart. Clear evidence is the thing.

Confusion has resulted from making the distinction between "mortal" and "venial" sins and then listing certain gross sins as mortal. Romanists list seven: *superbia, avaritia, luxuria, ira, gula, invidia, acedia* (*Traegheit*, sloth), and then devise a penitential system that is to be applied by the church, in which the priests measure out the *satisfactio operis* in their sacrament of penance. The sin against the Holy Ghost has also been referred to; when it is wrongly defined it has not helped matters. See Matt. 12:31, etc.; Heb. 6:4, etc.; 10:25, etc.; also Acts 7:51.

The Final Summary,

Centering on "We Know"

5:18-21

18) John sums up; he has come to the end. He does it by means of three οἴδαμεν (compare v. 15 on the verb. "We know," these things are fixed for us, fixed as facts. Nothing can shake them in our minds.

The first is: **We know that everyone who has been born from God does not go on sinning; on the contrary, the one born from God keeps himself** (read ἑαυτόν). "Has been born from God" = 2:29; not sinning = 3:9. The perfect passive includes the resultant present state; the aorist passive is content to state the past fact (R. 1117). John has used τηρεῖν a number of times just as Jesus uses this word often; but only in this verse does John use it with the reflexive: "he keeps himself," namely by the strength of the spiritual life that is born in him.

This is, indeed, a fact. This is not the place to expand but to sum up. Hence John does not add the opposite negative, which has been done sufficiently in various ways. Yet here, too, the fact is to be used in order to draw a clear line between all the antichristian heretics and all who truly keep the commandments or the Word (2:3, 5).

This means safety: **and the wicked one does not fasten himself upon him,** ἅπτεται, middle voice. This is John's designation for the devil (2:13, 14; 3:12), he writes "the devil" in 3:8. The wicked one will try to fasten himself upon him but will not succeed. He and the sin unto death go together.

19) The second thing is this: **We know that we are from God, and the whole world lies in the wicked**

one. Ἐκ Θεοῦ goes back to 4:4 and restates what is said objectively in verse 18: "everyone who has been born from God." In "from" God (v. 18, 19) there lies the fact that all our spiritual life has its origin in God. How this origin shows itself John has just stated in v. 18, which sums up all that John has said to the same effect throughout the epistle.

● Parallel to the statement about the wicked one is this about the world: "and the whole world (as in 2:2) lies in the wicked one," lies prostrate in his power domain. Few will agree that τῷ πονηρῷ is now a neuter. "Evil one" in our versions is not as good as "wicked one," for πονηρός = actively, viciously wicked. In κεῖται there lies the idea of passivity which does not even struggle against the devil. He does not need to fasten himself on the world; he already has the whole of it completely in his power. This in no way contradicts 2:2, for John has also written 3:8.

20) What underlies the preceding two οἴδαμεν is now summed up in the third. **We know, moreover, that the Son of God is come, and he has given to us understanding so that we know the real One. And we are in connection with the real One, in connection with his Son Jesus Christ. This is the real God and life eternal.**

Δέ adds this final knowledge which is ours. "The Son of God has come," ἥκει is used as a present tense. This restates 3:8. This Son "has given to us" (with permanent effect, perfect tense) διάνοιαν, *Erkenntnis-vermoegen* (C.-K. 767, etc.), spiritual sense and ability to understand, "so that (ἵνα to express result, it is not epexegetical to διάνοιαν) we know the real One," namely God. John now writes the verb γινώσκω, "to realize with inner affect and effect." Ἵνα with the indicative appears three times in the New Testament (R. 984). The Koine permits the use of this indicative, and it is employed here to indicate a result clause.

'O ἀληθινός = "the real One" as opposed to spurious
gods, "idols" (verse 21). At the end of this epistle,
which has dealt with the antichrists who deny both
the Son and the Father and has not dealt with pagans
and with their idols or divinities, John writes "the real
One" as opposed to the fictional God of the heretics,
the God that they made for themselves in their unregenerate, lying *dianoia* as men still do today. No one
knows who God really is save the Son and he to whom
the Son reveals him (Matt. 11:27; John 1:18).

Just as it does in verses 18 and 19, καί now adds a
separate statement. This is best indicated in the
English by the use of a semicolon or by the construction
of a new sentence: "And we are in connection with
the real One." The Son of God has placed us in connection with the real God by giving us *dianoia* and
thus making us know God. There is nothing fictional
about either the God with whom we are connected
or about our being in him, about our fellowship and
connection with him. It is the Son of God himself
who made this real God known to us and joined us to
him. The heretics have no Son of God, have not the
Father, (2:22, 23), have only an illusion which they
call "God," so that their claim of having fellowship
with God is a lie (1:6). They do not have fellowship
with what *they* call "God" because their "God" does
not exist.

John's ἐν, "*in* the real One," in union and communion with him, in living spiritual connection with
him, summarizes all the similar "in" phrases that run
through this epistle, cf. 2:5, 6; 3:24, all the μένειν ἐν
statements, our "remaining in" God, this last "in"
taking us back to the κοινωνία, "the fellowship," mentioned in 1:3, 6, 7. They express the *unio mystica*
that is wrought for us by the Son through the light,
the truth, the Word, the gift of the Spirit, when we

were brought to faith, were born from God, were made "the children of God," were filled with God's love to us, with love to him and to all the other children of God, and were separated from the world, from the wicked one and from' his children (3:9, 10). Thus the entire epistle is summed up in this final ἐν phrase.

The ἐν τῷ ἀληθινῷ does not refer to a different person than does τὸν ἀληθινόν, namely "the real God." The article with the dative reads like an article of previous reference. Our versions translate otherwise: "And we are in him that is true (real), even in his Son Jesus Christ." This makes the second ἐν phrase appositional to the first so that "the real One" in the phrase = "his Son Jesus Christ." A comma is, therefore, placed between the ἐν phrases. If this were John's meaning, he would have omitted αὐτοῦ, would have written: "And we are in the real One, (namely) in the Son Jesus Christ." He wrote αὐτοῦ, the antecedent of which is τῷ ἀληθινῷ. We translate without the use of a comma: "And we are in the real One (God) in his Son Jesus Christ."

Only in this way are we in God. Apart from the Son no one is in God (John 14:6). He who denies the Son has not the Father (2:23). This is the burden of the entire epistle. This meaning cannot be eliminated at the climax. We are in the real One in Christ; no man is in God without Christ. But this Christ is not a mere man. The early Gnostics conceived him to be such, to them he was nothing more than the physical son of Joseph (see the introduction). That is why at the end of the epistle, in the summary, "the Son of God" is once more strongly emphasized: *"The Son of God* has come," etc. *He* made the real God known to us. We are in the real God only in and not apart from this real God's Son Jesus Christ; John now adds his name "Jesus Christ." The Gnostics dreamed

of an "eon Christ," which "eon" joined Jesus at his
baptism but left him before his passion so that only
a poor, helpless man died on the cross. But the blood
of Jesus is "the blood *of his* (God's) *Son*" (1:7), the
expiation for the world's sin (2:2; 4:10).

When this is seen, we shall fully understand this
summary statement: "And we are in the real One
(i. e., God) in his Son Jesus Christ."

Only in this verse in this epistle does John use ἐν
with Jesus Christ. He ordinarily uses this "in" only
with God. But note that at the beginning John has *two*
μετά: "and we have fellowship *with* the Father and
with his Son Jesus Christ" (1:3). The two "with"
are placed side by side and are connected by only a
καί. Now at the end both are advanced to "in," and
now the καί disappears and the two "in" are combined:
"in the real One in Christ." This is the ultimate fact.
It calls for an "in" (ἐν) also with reference to the Son.

This puts us in the clear for the clinching statement: "This One is the real God and life eternal."
Οὗτος, "the One" = "his Son Jesus Christ." Everything
depends on his deity, and his deity means no less than
this, that as the Father who is made known to us by
him is the only real God (I Thess. 1:9), so also his
Son Jesus Christ "is the real God" and eternal life.
If the Son is less, if he is not real God even as the
Father is the real God, then this entire epistle and all
that it declares about his blood, expiation, our fellowship with God, etc., are futile. That, too, is the reason
the predicate that refers to Jesus Christ is doubled:
"This One (his Son Jesus Christ) is the real God and
life eternal." "His Son Jesus Christ" takes us back
to 1:3; this Son is now defined as no less than what
he is: "the real God," God's "Son" in no inferior sense.
"And life eternal" takes us back to 1:2 and to the
double designation: "the Life was made manifest" —
"the Life, the eternal one, who was with (πρός, face to

face with) the Father" (see the exposition of 1:2).
John ends as he began.

This is the old exegesis. It played a great role
in the controversy with Arius who, because of his
denial of the eternal Sonship, was compelled to make
John say that "this One" (οὗτος) = God and not Jesus
Christ. This Arian exegesis became that of all later
anti-Trinitarians, of the old Socinians, of the English
deists, of the German rationalists, etc. Against them
stands the exegesis of the church as it was advanced
from the early days onward.

This exegesis of the church is now called a mistake
by a number of commentators who believe in the full
deity of Jesus as it is revealed in Scripture but feel
convinced that this οὗτος clause speaks of the Father
and not of his Son. The question is: "Of whom does
it speak?" There are weapons more than enough elsewhere in Scripture to smite all Arians without the use
of this clause. Is this also one of the weapons or not?
It is unfair when those who answer "no" intimate that
we who with the church answer "yes'" are swayed by
dogmatical interests. Whether we have one passage
more or one less in our tremendous arsenal against
Arius and his followers makes little difference to us.

In the first place, if οὗτος has as its antecedent
"the real God" (the Father), then the statement is
a tautology; John would say: "This *real* God is the
real God." He would say it after having twice said:
we know *the real God* and are in *the real God.* When
R. 707 thinks that the antecedent is αὐτοῦ, this makes
no difference, for the antecedent of the pronoun is
"the real One" (God). It is denied that, when this
clause is referred to God, it is a mere tautology. But
look and think for yourself. Remember, too, that not
a few think that Jesus is not called "God" outright in
other passages; to have Jesus here called "the real
God" seems even less probable to them.

Let us ignore the tautology. Where is the Father ever called "life eternal"? John 17:3 has been referred to. But Jesus says: "This is the eternal life (for them) that they know thee, the only real God, and him whom thou didst send, Jesus Christ." The Father is, indeed, called "the only real God" as John calls him in our passage, but neither the Father nor the Son is called "the eternal life" in John 17:3, for "the eternal life" is the life which *we* have (John 3:15, 16) and not a designation for God or for Christ himself. A complete exegesis must go back to ἡ ζωή and to τὴν ζωὴν τὴν αἰώνιον in 1:2, and must combine these designations of the Son of God with the predications made in 5:11-13; for when Jesus, too, calls himself "the Life" (John 14:6; 11:25; compare 1:4) he means that he in his *person* is the Life, the fountain of life for us.

It is this second predicate that is so decisive. When John 5:24, 26 is referred to, the designations of Jesus used in John 14:6; 11:25; I John 1:2 should not be overlooked. John 5:24, 26 contains no designation of either the Father or the Son as these other passages plus ours do; all of them are designations for what Jesus is as the eternal Son sent by the Father that we may live (4:9, 10). Instead of John 5:26 proving that in our passage the *Father* is called "life eternal," the fact is that John 5:26 proves why Jesus, the Son of God, truly calls *himself* "the Life" and is truly so called by John in various passages.

Here at the end John calls the Father, whom he has hitherto designated only by the terms "the Father" and "God," "the real One" (i. e., the genuine God), for John has now reached the end and the climax. He cites ἀληθινός from Jesus (John 17:3). So John has hitherto called Jesus "the Son of God" and "his (the Father's, God's) Son," and now, here at the end and the climax, John duplicates and calls also

Jesus Christ the real God's Son because he is the real God's only-begotten Son (4:9), yea, "the real God." As the Father is the real (genuine) God, so his Son is the real (genuine) God, and this Son places us in fellowship with the Father. Need we add the words that Jesus himself spoke in John 10:30; 12:45; 14:9?

21) John closes: **Little children, guard yourselves from the idols!** This final hortation may surprise us. Yet it is the final stone that rests upon and stands up from the great inverted pyramid that John has built in this epistle. When we understand the structure of this epistle we shall fully appreciate this its last word. It has been thought that this is the very last word that we have from John's pen. This assumes that all his other writings are the products of an earlier date, which is a rather hazardous assumption and not one on which to write a sermon: "The Last Words of the Last Apostle," as has been done.

On the affectionate address "little children" see 2:1. Like so many apostolic hortations, this, too, has the effective aorist imperative: "guard yourselves," let there be no question about it. The readers are to stand like armed guards, ready to conquer every attack (2:13, 14; 4:4; 5:4, 5, νικᾶν). We prefer the reading ἑαυτά, the neuter, to fit τεκνία, which some have changed to the masculine.

What John means by "the idols" from which his little children are to guard themselves is made plain by the context, in fact, by the entire epistle. John is not speaking of common pagan idols, which are then irrelevantly introduced at the very end of his epistle. These "idols" are the fictional conceptions of God that were held by Cerinthus and by his devotees. By calling these conceptions "the idols" John places them in the same class with all the pagan images and the imagined gods. This includes all the anti-Trinitarian conceptions of God, no matter by whom they are held.

John's epistle is intended for many churches and thus closes without a series of salutations as it also begins without the common epistolary greeting.

Soli Deo Gloria

The Second Epistle
of St. John

Introduction to the Second and to the Third Epistles of St. John

The apostle John in all probability wrote these two little letters in Ephesus on the same day, and they were to be sent to the same place. This place and the date of composition are unknown. Regarding the date we venture to say merely that the interval between the writing of these two letters and the composition of John's First Epistle cannot have been long.

John is sending out a few missionaries who expect to pass through the city in which the recipients of these two letters reside. John asks Gaius to provide lodging for these men and to help them on their way. Gaius has been aiding the gospel in this manner, and John strongly commends him for this. Gaius already knows the reason for sending these men. Diotrephes, the domineering spirit in the local congregation, is hostile to John and refuses to lodge and to help missionaries who come from John and also forbids the other members to do so under threat of expulsion from the congregation. So John asks Gaius to provide for the missionaries whom he is sending.

Had Diotrephes expelled Gaius for helping John's missionaries? This point is not entirely clear; perhaps he had. John informs Gaius that he is writing a letter to the congregation. This letter is our so-called Second Epistle of John. In both letters John announces his coming; John writes to Gaius that he hopes to come immediately.

A letter is sent to the congregation because Diotrephes cannot prevent its public reading. Many members of the congregation are still faithful to the gospel and faithful to its great surviving apostle. John writes ἐκ τῶν τέκνων σου and distinguishes these faithful ones from Diotrephes and the unfaithful. John wisely says nothing about his missionaries and the domination of Diotrephes. He announces his own coming. Then, as he tells Gaius, he will settle with this church boss. A letter is not the proper means for this task. The fact that missionaries are once again at the home of Gaius the congregation will see for itself and will know without being told why the congregation has not been asked to provide for them.

What John tells the members of the congregation is plain enough: admonition to hold to what they had from the beginning; warning against the many deceivers who have gone out into the world. Some of these evil missionaries will come also to them. John forbids them to receive such men; they are not even to greet them. These deceivers are the same as those referred to in the First Epistle of John: Gnostics, followers of Cerinthus who denied the deity of Jesus. One may well conclude that Diotrephes was favorable to these Gnostics and wanted their missionaries lodged and helped and not those that came from John. To what extent Diotrephes had already imbibed the Gnostic heresies is not indicated. John will bring matters to an issue when he presently arrives in person.

The story of the two letters is the best introduction to them. Read each letter in the light of the other.

*   *   *

Letters of this nature must have been put into the hands of many missionaries in apostolic times. As John tells Gaius, these men receive nothing from the Gentiles and are thus dependent on their own slender resources and on what help Christians may give them. All such letters have perished save these two. We are unable to say how these two came to be preserved.

The fact that both are written by the apostle John they proclaim in almost every line. The thought and the language are clearly those of the First Epistle as well as of the Fourth Gospel. The same heresy is also in the background of these epistles. The older contention that there was an "Elder John" in addition to the "Apostle John," and that the former wrote these letters, has at times been revived. This "Elder John" has been made the author of the Fourth Gospel also. In our *Interpretation of St. John's Gospel,* pages 15-18, we show that Dionysius and Eusebius invented this "Elder John" because they could not induce themselves to believe that the apostle John wrote the Apocalypse. They thought they had found him in a statement made by Papias (see the reference above). Then after attributing the Apocalypse to this "Elder John" and finding the term "the Elder" (ὁ πρεσβύτερος) in these two little letters, they more than ever felt sure that their assumption was a fact and pronounced also these two letters products of their "Elder." Their venture into higher criticism is seconded at this late day and is extended even to the Fourth Gospel.

For this reason Eusebius lists these two letters among the antilegomena, a rating that has persisted although it is quite valueless.

We say valueless because these two brief letters are the least important part of the New Testament canon. They are precious because the apostle John wrote them and because their contents, which are so in accord with all else that he wrote, supplement their authorship, and do it by adding the personal note: we love Gaius, we are distressed with Diotrephes, we hope that John remedied matters in that congregation as he promised to do.

* * *

The brevity and the personal, local nature of these letters explain why the writers of the early period of the church's history make little reference to them. We need not trace these references; others have done this for us. After examining the data which they supply we deem them quite sufficient for the purpose which they serve, namely to show us how early and how widely these short letters were known to prominent churchmen, and what they thought of them. Fausset, *Bible Cyclopedia,* offers a compact, useful survey.

Regarding the question of the "Elect Lady" see the interpretation itself. Those who think that each of these letters was sent to a different city at a different time, who also believe that a woman was the recipient of one, lose the most attractive part of both letters.

In these letters we catch a glimpse of John's activity in his old age. They present a little piece of church history. John has an unpleasant task and he performs it. Missionaries are still pressing farther and farther. Third John 5-8 is a rich missionary text; and verses 9-12 ought to interest every church official.

The Second Epistle of St. John

The Greeting, v. 1-3

1) The nominative to indicate the writer and the dative to mark the persons to whom he writes are duly used by John in both of these letters in which he follows the regular ancient method of letter writing. "Grace, mercy, peace from God (the) Father," etc., are also regularly found in Christian letter headings. But the future tense of the verb and the first person plural: "shall be with us," are unusual, are John's own wording. Like the greetings found in the other apostolic letters, also this one reflects what the body of the letter develops and thus contains a great deal.

The Elder to a mistress elect and to her children, whom I on my part love in connection with truth, and not I alone but also all who have known the truth for the sake of the truth remaining in us, and with us it shall remain forever: there shall be with us grace, mercy, peace from God (the) Father and from Jesus Christ, the Son of the Father, in connection with truth and love.

'Ο πρεσβύτερος, "the Elder," is the apostle John. This word was used to designate the pastors of congregations, each congregation had several "presbyters," "elders." It is not used in this sense by John, for John was not one of the pastors of the congregation at Ephesus. I Peter 5:1 has συμπρεσβύτερος, "fellow elder," which designates Peter in his apostolic office, in the capacity in which he wrote his First Epistle to all the Asian churches. John uses "the Presbyter" to designate himself in a sense that is still more distinct. He does not mean: one of the apostles who may be called an "elder" when, like Peter, he addresses elders.

of a church (pastors) ; John is not addressing such elders. He is *"the* Presbyter" in the sense that this title belongs only to him. On the theory regarding a Presbyter John who was not the apostle see the remarks in the introduction. If there had been such a person he could not have designated himself "the Presbyter" as is done here and in Third John.

John is "the Presbyter" because the churches gave him this title in an eminent sense as we speak of "the President," "the Governor," etc. When they titled John in this manner the churches intended to *honor* the *aged* apostle who *alone* had survived the other apostles. This honor was combined with the recognition of John's apostolic *authority* as being that of the one apostle who still remained to guide, teach, and direct the churches. Because he understood it in this sense John accepted the title. When one said "the Presbyter," all the members of the churches knew who was meant; when here and in Third John John himself writes "the Presbyter," the readers know who this is. The addition "John" is not only unnecessary but would also be misleading, for it would convey the thought that there were others like him, save that they had other names such as "the Presbyter this," "the Presbyter that," but all were equally eminent men. This was not true; there was only this one "the Presbyter," and there were no others who were to be ranked with him.

This is only the half of it. The other half is the fact that "the Presbyter" fits "a mistress elect and her children" and what is here communicated to them; compare Third John. John is not conveying the apostolic gospel message in these letters so that "the Apostle" or "Apostle of Jesus Christ" would be a proper designation of himself. The special slant of thought which such a title would convey is not the slant wanted in these letters, least of all in this one.

"A mistress" rules her family of "children," holds them to the Lord's "commandment." That is why she is κυρία. As "the Presbyter" John is the director of the many churches found in this entire Asian territory, where also all of them call him "the Presbyter" and acknowledge this his office and authority. As this Presbyter, John directs one of these churches to do what it ought to do as mistress of the family. As "the Presbyter," we may say as "the one general Pastor of all these churches," John looks after this one church in which there is trouble and also promises to come to it in person.

John has the same reason for using "the Presbyter" to designate himself that he has for addressing the church as "a mistress elect and her children." A mistress might refer to slaves. We should remember that in the Roman Empire as at one time in the south of our own country practically all people of means owned slaves. John eliminates such a connotation by at once adding "and her children" to "a mistress," thus making this congregation a mother of all its members. And yet when John says "a mistress" he indicates that she is not merely an indulgent mother who lets her children do as they please but one who properly controls her children and effectively corrects those who would get out of hand.

There was especially one man of this kind in the congregation, namely Diotrephes (III John 9). This man had gained some support. In verse 4 John is compelled to write the partitive ἐκ; he cannot say that he has rejoiced greatly because he has found *all* the children of this mother-mistress walking in what is truth. In Third John we shall see what Diotrephes is doing. We shall see in verse 5, etc., what John is compelled to ask this mistress to do. This congregation had not kept control over its members as a congregation should; it had allowed this Diotrephes to usurp a great deal of the control. One of the children was running things and not the congregation as the κυρία, the mistress.

This explains why John adds the adjective ἐκλεκτὴ κυρία, "a chosen mistress," "a mistress elect." The Lord himself chose this congregation and all its members (children) to be his own. That choice implies that the congregation shall be true to its divine Lord, and that as a real "mistress" it shall keep all its children in the truth, doing only the Lord's gospel command, and that it shall not, as Diotrephes did, fall in love with deceivers (verse 7) who were at that time becoming so numerous. To be "chosen" or "elect" means not only to receive and to delight in the Lord's favor; with this there goes the obligation to act as one who is elect.

Κύριος is our divine "Lord" Jesus Christ; but we do not transfer to the feminine κυρία, this congregation, all that lies in this title of Christ. The thought is not that as κυρία she stands beside our Κύριος as his wife or as his "bride" (νύμφη, Rev. 21:9; 22:17). This imagery refers to the whole *Una Sancta.* Pietistic language often extends it to individual souls in the most unwholesome manner. Κυρία pertains to τέκνα. The congregation is mistress of its children, is to manage its members aright. In pagan connections this word may be merely "a courteous form of address" as Deissmann, *Light,* etc., 154, concludes from a pagan letter; but it is not used in this way in these two Christian letters. In them κυρία implies business, serious business, that which the body of the letter presents.

Some have assumed that Second John has no connection with Third John. Thus John is thought to be addressing some woman who has a family of children and to be using *kyria* as a matter of courtesy (Deissmann is one of these). But why should he, then, call her "elect"? This leads to a discussion as to whether

her name was Eklektē or Kyria, Thayer writes the latter "Cyria." Kyria has been found as a woman's name; but if this term were a woman's name in our epistle, the adjective with the article should follow (Gaius is a sample in III John 1). Then her children would be only boys, for John proceeds with the masculine οὕς.

If her name was Eklektē, was her sister's name the same (v. 13)? In v. 4-6 John continues with the singular κυρία; how can he without further ado pass over into the plural in v. 7, etc.? He can do so if "mistress" is a collective and refers to the congregation. Besides all this, a family that has some children that are acting improperly would receive an admonition from the local elders or pastors and not from the apostle who is even coming to this family in person. The heads of our church bodies do not step in to correct this or that woman who has grown lax in managing her boys. This is the local pastor's work, which he alone can properly perform. · Regarding I Pet. 5:13 see verse 13 below.

Let us note all the words that are repeated from First John: to love — the truth — to know — to remain — Jesus Christ, the Son of the Father — the commandment — from the beginning — to walk — many deceivers went out into the world — to confess Jesus Christ coming in flesh — the Antichrist — to have the Father and the Son — to fellowship: overwhelming evidence that the same hand wrote both of these letters.

John says that he himself (emphatic ἐγώ) loves the members of this congregation, and not only he but also all who have known the truth, all true Christians. John indicates that this love impels him to write. This is that spiritual love which in First John is made one of the outstanding marks of all true Christians. The antichristian heretics and deceivers have no love for the members of the true church, they try

to tear it to pieces. We may, perhaps, here think of
I John 5:16, 17 (compare James 5:19, 20) ; John wants
to save Diotrephes from the error into which he
is lapsing.

Yet this love of John's is "in connection with truth"
(qualitative: with what is truth), namely the gospel
(compare I John 1:6). It is intelligent, purposeful
love that is never separated from the objective verity
of the gospel. It would not be the love that the Lord
wants and commands (verse 5) if in any way it disregarded the divine, saving truth.

All those who have known the truth (article of
previous reference) share with John this love for the
members of this congregation. John is writing in
behalf of all óf them. The whole church is concerned
about the spiritual soundness and welfare of every
single congregation. John does the writing because
he is "the Presbyter." John describes all these fellow
Christians as being those who have known the truth,
known it for a long time with its blessed effect upon
themselves (γινώσκω), of which also their love is clear
evidence. See how John keeps using γινώσκω in First
John, and how this weighty verb is to be kept distinct
from οἶδα.

2) It is "because of, for the sake of this truth
remaining in us" that John and all those who know
this truth love the members of this congregation and
do not want a single one of them to forsake this truth
and to fall a prey to the deceivers. "The truth" is "the
doctrine" (verses 9, 10), which includes all the words
in which the truth is adequately conveyed. The highest
concern of all who have come to realize the truth is and
ever must be the truth, for thus alone can there be
genuine concern for the souls of the members of the
church. To ask: "For which should the church be
concerned the more, for the truth, the doctrine or confession, or for the souls?" is to make a distinction that

may be misleading. The truth remains in us when we realize what it is and thus hold to it. It remains in us when we keep out the deceit.

John mentions the truth three times; he presently adds "the deceivers" and "the deceiver" (verse 7), which is highly significant in regard to Diotrephes and in regard to the body of this brief letter. Not by means of a second participle but with greater emphasis by means of a finite clause John adds that this truth "shall be with us forever." "Shall be" is not a mere wish; it is the certainty and the assurance of one who knows the truth. John varies the preposition from ἐν ἡμῖν to μεθ᾽ ἡμῶν; the truth remains "in us," in our hearts, as a possession, and it will be "with us," in our company, as our constant divine companion. John loves μετά; see it twice in I John 1:3. Both phrases are expressive, each in its own way. John includes his faithful readers in the "us."

3) In place of the usual exclamatory "grace to you and peace from God," etc., John uses a finite sentence and again writes "with us." This is not a greeting to the readers, it is another certitude and assurance for them, for himself, and for those who have known the truth. There shall, indeed, be in company with us, walking arm in arm with us, "grace, mercy, peace," and these three "in connection with truth and love," for the former three can never be separated from the latter two. Grace is God's undeserved favor toward us sinners; mercy is his pity for those who are in trouble and distress; peace is the well-being that results when grace and mercy are ours. Paul uses these three in the two epistles he wrote to Timothy. Παρά means that the three come to us from the side of God and of his Son.

But there is a point in the repetition of παρά and in the naming of the two Givers: "from God (the) Father and from Jesus Christ, the Son of the Father." These

two are equal (see the exposition of I John 5:20).
John purposely repeats "the Father" in order to convey fully what he means by Jesus Christ's being "the
Son" of the Father. The antichristian heresy of the
deceivers made Jesus the physical son of Joseph, denied
the efficacy of his blood, etc. See the introduction to
First John and the discussion in I John 1:7, "the
blood"; 2:2, "expiation"; 2:22, 23. Diotrephes was
becoming attached to the deceivers who promulgated
this heresy, was beginning to hate John, lodged and
entertained the missionaries of these heretics, and
closed the doors to missionaries that were sent out
by John.

John wants this letter to be read in public in the
congregation, a procedure that Diotrephes is not as yet
able to prevent. Every word is bound to go home.
Who is κύριος in this congregation? The congregation
is κυρία and not this church boss Diotrephes! What is
this truth that governs all the members of all the
churches, for the sake of which they love each other?
It is the truth that God is the Father of his Son Jesus
Christ and not the Gnostic fiction about God and a
mere man Jesus. Why does Diotrephes hate John and
John's missionaries and love the Gnostic proselytes?
Because he is giving up the truth. Get the full
historical background and let First John and Third
John aid you.

The Body of the Letter, v. 4-11

4) **I was rejoiced greatly because I have found
(some) of thy children walking in connection with
truth even as we received commandment from the
Father.**

Ἐχάρην is the second aorist passive: "I was rejoiced," and not the present active: "I rejoice," R. V.
John speaks of the past; verse 5 shows what he has to
say regarding the present. Ὅτι states what caused

his joy: "I have found some of thy children walking
in connection with truth," etc. The perfect tense must
be iterative, it would otherwise also be an aorist. John
does not say how he learned this fact. Some think of
a visit, others of reports that reached John. The latter
harmonizes with Third John: missionaries who came
through the city brought back a report to John about
the conditions obtaining in the local church.

John retains the figure of the congregation as a
mistress of her children by impressing the fact that all
the members are subject to the congregation as children are to their mother. Ἐκ τῶν τέκνων σου is partitive: "some of thy children." Alas, John cannot say
πάντα τὰ τέκνα σου, "all thy children." The partitive
does not, however, refer to only a few, for John would
then have said τινά, "some"; the partitive makes the
impression that only some were found who were not
walking in line with truth. "In truth" is qualitative
as it was in verse 1: "in what is properly called truth,"
and refers to the gospel truth. John's great joy was
caused by all those who were walking (acting, living)
according to the gospel as they should. The readers
can supply how the unfaithful ones affected John.

We have the parallel passage in III John 2, 3, where
John says that he was rejoiced because of what the
missionary brethren, on returning to John, testified
about Gaius' walking in connection with what is truth.
Περιπατοῦντας is, of course, masculine just like οὕς in
verse 1 although both refer to the neuter τέκνα. The
grammatical gender is properly ignored (R. 713) because "children" is figurative with reference to the
members of the church. When it is thought that John
is writing to a woman, these masculines are interpreted in various ways. In connection with verse 1 it
is thought that John had met only this lady's sons
when he paid a visit to the family. It is not stated
why he did not meet the daughters. Others tell us that

John met some of the sons in his travels elsewhere. It is said that the daughters had remained at home.

It is said also that ἐκ is *not* partitive. *All* of this lady's sons were faithful to the gospel. This family is regarded as a model family. But did John write to all such families? There were many thousands of them in John's churches. There were many even in the one congregation where this family had membership. Why a special letter from "the Presbyter" to only this one family? These questions must be answered by those who think that John wrote this letter to a woman.

According to the reports which John had received most of the members of this congregation walked in connection with gospel truth. John emphasizes the source of this truth; it is not necessary to do so in III John 3, 4. For the sake of Diotrephes and some others, and so they and the whole congregation may hear it, John adds: "even as we (including all those referred to by the "we" used in verse 3) received commandment from (again παρά) the Father." By "commandment" John means "the truth" as it tells us what to do: "And this is his commandment (this is what the whole gospel tells us to do) that we believe the name of his Son Jesus Christ and continue to love one another even as he gave us commandment," I John 3:23. These Gnostics with whom Diotrephes was flirting did not have even the Father, for they denied the deity of the Son (I John 2:23). No wonder that John cannot include Diotrephes and his clique in the congregation among those who have caused him joy. John has a point in every clause. For the third time he writes "Father," which is directed against the Gnostic delusion.

5) And now I am requesting thee, mistress, not as writing to thee a new commandment, but which we had from the beginning that we love one another. And this is this love, that we walk according to his

commandments. This is the commandment even as you heard it from the beginning, that in this we should walk.

"Now" is temporal; from the aorist John turns to the present. He is now coming to this congregation with a request which as "the Presbyter" he has a full right to make. It is here made to the congregation in a direct form: "I am requesting thee, mistress." In ἐρωτάω there lie dignity and due formality. You may imagine how this sounded when it was read before the whole congregation. That title κυρία has significance as it is now repeated. The congregation is the mistress, and no boss such as Diotrephes has the right to dictate to the members. Our versions fail to make a proper distinction when they translate both παρακαλῶ and ἐρωτῶ "beseech." Whereas the German *bitten* is correct as a translation of the latter (C.-K. 452), we agree with Trench to the extent that the word bears a certain gravity or dignity and thus fits the κυρία whom John addresses.

Thus also John inserts: "not as writing to thee a commandment (that is) new, καινήν (over against an old one that it is to supersede)"; no, only the one "which you had (all along) from the beginning" (see I John 2:7). This phrase is found also in I John 2:24; 3:11 and needs no article in the Greek. It is the commandment which the Father gave us through his Son Jesus Christ, which God himself made basic for all who know the truth (verse 1). It is not one that has been newly invented by John.

Ἵνα states what this commandment is. This clause is an accusative appositional clause (R. 992, 699): "that we love one another" (I John 3:11). John properly words this in the first person plural. It pertains to all of us, to John, to this congregation and all its members, and to all Christians everywhere. "That *you* love one another" is thus included; but to have

worded it in this form would not be nearly as effective
as to write "that *we* love." The clause does not depend
on ἐρωτῶ but is appositional to ἥν. John leaves "I am
requesting" without a formal grammatical object, yet
we see that what he requests is the observance of this
divine commandment of love. Observe the repetition
of "commandment," which recalls the repetitions found
in I John 2:3-8.

6) John defines "the love" that is referred to in
this commandment which his readers had had ever
since they became Christians; ἵνα is again appositional.
It is this, "that we walk according to his (the Father's)
commandments." Loving one another is not one doing
of one commandment among many others; it is doing
all God's commandments. But we should not think
of the Mosaic law but of the gospel and of what it asks
of us. We are walking in the whole gospel when we
love one another as brethren in Jesus Christ, God's
Son. Love itself is hidden in the heart, and thus John
writes "that we walk," this love displays itself in our
walk. in word and in deed. John repeats and thus
emphasizes this word.

This is "the love" referred to, and thus "this is the
commandment even as you heard from the beginning
(compare I John 3: 11) that in it (in this commandment) you walk (or should walk)"; ἵνα introduces a
nominative clause which is the predicate after "is." To
love is to walk; the commandment is to walk, to carry
out the commandment itself in word and in act. "Little
children, let us not be loving with word neither with the
tongue, but in deed and truth," I John 3:18.

John changes from the comprehensive "we" to the
specific "you." It is done by means of the verbal
ending without the use of the Greek pronouns, which
use would be emphatic and inject a contrast that is
wholly improper here where "you" are only a part
of "we," and we refers to all Christians everywhere,

you, the members of this one congregation, naturally being included in their number. The view that a single family, a mother and her children, is referred to again proves untenable in this passage.

A look at I John 3:23 answers the view that faith and doctrine are immaterial, that love apart from these is the whole of Christianity. Look at I John 4:9, 10 and see what the love of God is. This love of his is to fill our hearts, and our love is to be according, is with its roots to rest in all that God gave us in his love, in the whole gospel. Lose any of it, and you destroy some of the roots, take away their soil. The plant cannot flourish, it wilts. Love to one another is walking in all that God's love wants of us. Love to one another is the flower and the fruit that presuppose the whole plant down to its lowest roots, presuppose the whole soil in which these roots live.

How all this applies to Diotrephes and to his clique is plain. He hated John himself although John was an apostle; he closed the door of hospitality to John's missionaries, threatened the members who would receive them, and opened the door to Gnostic prose- lyters. In this way Diotrephes walked. What this indicated regarding his relation to the Father, to Jesus, his Son, about his faith and his doctrine, is certainly clear. John rightly treats this opposition according to the open evidence that it has furnished, which the entire congregation also sees and knows. From this he advances to the confession of faith and to the doctrine.

John does not name Diotrephes in this letter to the congregation. John is not settling with the opposi- tion by means of this letter; he is coming in person to do that (verse 12; III John 9, 10). In this short letter John lays down the basis on which he will attend to Diotrephes.

7) **Because many went out into the world, those
not confessing Jesus Christ as coming in flesh. This
is the deceiver and the Antichrist.** Ὅτι introduces an
independent sentence just as we, too, use "because."
It states the reason that John is writing all this. In
I John 4:1 he says: "Many pseudo-prophets have gone
out into the world"; here he calls them "deceivers"
and uses the simple aorist. Not content to be deceived
themselves, these men cannot rest until they have
deceived others, as many as possible. They do not
bother pagans; their prey are true Christians. "Into
the world" means far and wide in the world, wherever
they find Christians. They "went out" means from
their leader Cerinthus, from his headquarters; some
take it that they went out from the devil, the arch-
deceiver.

"Deceivers" is made definite: "those not confessing
Jesus Christ as coming in flesh." Compare I John
4:1, 2. John summarizes the deception of Cerinthus.
He denied the deity and the incarnation of Jesus Christ.
We have sketched this earliest form of Gnosticism in
the introduction to First John. Not to confess = to
deny (I John 2:23), and to deny is to lie. In I John
4:2 we have ἐν σαρκὶ ἐληλυθότα, the perfect participle, "as
having come in flesh" (incarnate, John 1:14); here
we have ἐρχόμενον ἐν σαρκί, "as coming in flesh," although
the participle is present in form it is really timeless.
Cerinthus did not deny that Jesus was a man; he
regarded Jesus as the physical son of Joseph and of
Mary. He denied the coming in flesh, the fact that in
Jesus Christ we have the eternal Son of God, born of
the Virgin, whose blood (I John 1:7) is the expiation
for the sins of the world (I John 2:2; 4:9, 10), and that
"this One is the real God and life eternal" (I John 5:20).

After saying "many deceivers" John adds: "This
is the deceiver and the Antichrist." This is scarcely a

distributive singular; it makes all these deceivers one awful deceiver who as "the deceiver" is also "the Antichrist," the great opponent and enemy of Christ. By this singular John does not refer to the devil although a connection with the devil is involved (I John 3:10). We read this in the light of I John 2:18, 19: "the Antichrist" is already present in these many deceivers, these many forerunners of the great Antichrist (II Thess. 2).

The greatness of the danger is thus made plain. Diotrephes is flirting with the great foe of Christ as he roamed about in the world at that time. This is the way in which he loves the brethren, this is what his hostile actions toward John and toward the gospel missionaries mean. John does not say this outright, he will do so when he comes in person in order to confront Diotrephes.

8) **Look to yourselves lest you destroy what you have wrought but that you may receive full reward.** The danger calls for a warning, the more so since Diotrephes has been giving hospitality to some of these deceivers. The two subjunctive aorists are effective: "may not actually destroy but may actually receive." We prefer the reading "what you have wrought." We use the perfect in English; the Greek is satisfied with its aorist (R. 842, etc.). John refers to the heavenly reward or pay, the word matches the idea of having worked. It is the reward of grace which is mentioned in Luke 19:17, 19. It will certainly be "full" to overflowing.

Diotrephes is destroying and tearing down what he and the congregation have accomplished by their spiritual upbuilding and by their missionary success. It is plain what the end of that would be. The eternal reward is at stake and no less.

9) John states the matter in a simple and a general form. **Everyone going ahead and not remaining**

in the doctrine of Christ has not God; the one remaining in the doctrine, this one has both the Father
and the Son. There is no exception either way. A
few texts that did not understand προάγων substitute
παραβαίνων, which the A. V. version adopts: "whosoever
transgresseth." Some of the interpretations show that
προάγων is still not understood. It is not ironical and
does not refer to an advance to higher knowledge as
the Gnostics claimed to have advanced. One article
is used with the two participles. "To go ahead" means
"not to remain"; when one remains he stays right
where he is. Leaping forward (πρό) from a safe place
to one that is wholly unsafe is folly. See how John
rings the changes on "remain" in I John 2:24-28.

Διδαχή = "doctrine" (A. V. is correct) ; "teaching"
(R. V.) would be διδασκαλία. "Of Christ" is the subjective genitive: the doctrine Christ taught and still
teaches through his apostles. John 1:18. This word
does not occur in First John, but its equivalents, "the
light, the truth, the Word," are found. "The doctrine,"
like "the Word," means that the truth is put into words
which we hear (verse 6), and so the truth comes to be
taught, realized and apprehended (γινώσκειν, verse 1),
which means "believed," trusted.

Much is being said about "doctrine." People say
that they do not want doctrine, and preachers try to
accommodate them. Do we not want the truth, the
great facts and realities about God, about Christ, and
about ourselves, to be put into the proper words so
that we may hear, realize, and believe them? Do we
want sophisticated myths (fables), II Pet. 1:16?

No matter in what direction one goes forward and
does not remain in the doctrine of Christ, "he has not
God" although he may shout ever so loudly, "I know
him!" (I John 2:4). This is the great delusion. I John
2:23. God, the real God (I John 5:20), is found only
in Christ (John 14:9, 11; 10:30), hence only in the

doctrine of Christ (John 1:18). John does not need
to add "and has not Christ" because he who forsakes
Christ's doctrine certainly also forsakes Christ.

The one remaining in the doctrine, this one (οὗτος),
this one alone, "has both the Father and the Son."
By having the one he has the other; a separation of the
two is impossible. To have them is to have salvation.
Not for nought does John say "has not *God*" and now
"has both the *Father* and the Son." These Gnostics
imagined that they had "God," but in their estimation
he was not "the Father" of "the Son"; to true believers
in Christ and in his doctrine God is "the Father" of
"his Son Jesus Christ" (I John 1:3).

10) In the light of v. 7-9 John writes: **If one
comes to you and does not bring this doctrine, do not
receive him into the house and do not say to him:
Greetings! For the one saying to him: Greetings!
fellowships his works, the wicked ones.**

John uses the condition of reality. These conditions
use οὐ as the negative. Hence no special force is to
be sought in the use of this negative. All conditions
exist only in the mind of the writer, who may conceive
them as really taking place or as likely to take place
(expectancy) or as not having taken place (past unreality) or as not taking place now (present unreality).
In view of III John 10 we feel entitled to say that
Diotrephes had been doing what John here forbids,
had been vilifying John, showing John's missionaries
the door, welcoming the itinerant proselyters of Cerinthus, lodging them himself or getting them lodgings
among the members. Speaking to the whole congregation, John forbids this very thing.

When one of these proselyters comes, one who is
a proselyter because he does not bring "this doctrine"
of Christ but a different doctrine, no matter what it
may be, brings it in order to spread it among the congregation and thus shows that he is a proselyter: do

you not take him into the house in order to supply him with a base for his operations, do not even greet him with χαίρειν: "Happiness to thee!" or: "Joy to thee!" wishing him well in his work. The present imperatives forbid this course of action.

11) John states why this is never to be done. The person who even as much as offers this greeting fellowships this proselyter's works. John adds the adjective with a second article: "the wicked ones," which is like an apposition and a climax (R. 776). Reason enough!

Χαίρειν was the common greeting on meeting or on parting. We have it in three letters, Acts 15:23; 23:26; James 1:1. Here the sense is: Do not even give the proselyter this greeting! Already this makes you a participant in the wicked works for which he has come. John does not refer only to the farewell greeting, when the proselyter leaves his host's house, but to a greeting of any nature.

Smith calls John's prohibition "unchristian counsel, contrary to the spirit and teaching of our Lord," and appeals to Mark 9:38, 39; Luke 9:51-56; Matt. 13: 28, 29 as though these passages permit us to furnish proselyters a home base for their operations in our midst and to wish them joy in what John calls their wicked works with the emphasis on wicked. Others speak of what was necessary in John's time, of the modern change of manners, of the greater tolerance of the present, and the like.

The feature that is overlooked is the fact that John is speaking of proselyters who seek entrance among Christians in order to do their proselyting among them. Where does the spirit of Christ bid or allow us to furnish them a home while they work at this wicked business and to wish them well when they come in order to do this work? Where does Christian ethics countenance anything of this kind? The doors of the homes of a Christian congregation cannot be barred too tightly against such spiritual poisoners; they cannot be met at the door with too stern a rebuff. Those who speak about the tolerance noted above would in a given case themselves bar out such nefarious proselyters just as John here tells his readers to do.

To what extent do John's words affect men who are not proselyters? To none. As occasion offers, we do any man a kindness. We do not even ask what he believes or whether he has a religious belief at all. I may take a Jew, a Mohammedan, a heathen, a tramp, a beggar under my roof; I may bid the time of day to any and to all men. But a notorious proselyting errorist? Do you as a true believer want even the least fellowship with *his* works? If he, because of your even kindly wishing him well, succeeds in snaring even one humble Christian, can you answer to God for your kindly wish? John's admonition: "Look to yourselves!" should make us wary. The state locks up murderers, thieves, criminals as a matter of protection. Is the church to aid and abet spiritual murderers and thieves? Not for one moment, all maudlin sentiment in the state and in the church to the contrary notwithstanding.

The Conclusion, v. 12, 13

12) Though having many things to write to you, I did not want to by means of paper and ink; but I am hoping to get to you and to speak mouth to mouth in order that your joy may be as having been filled.

Compare III John 13, 14a. This matter regarding Diotrephes is best handled face to face (III John·10). Since John is able to proceed to this congregation, and to do that immediately (III John 14), he has resolved not to settle matters in writing but gives notice of his coming. The fact that all these "many things" to

which John refers are not a lot of diverse things, but
that all revolve about the issue indicated in this letter,
on which III John 9-12 casts light, need not be argued.

John is not making an excuse but is giving information. We may regard ἠβουλήθην as an epistolary
aorist (R. 846). Χάρτης is a sheet of papyrus paper.
This word is found often in the papyri. The supposition that John is so old that he cannot write well
is unwarranted since he had amanuenses a plenty; he
could travel, which called for bodily strength in those
days. Homiletic reflections on how much better it is
to settle things mouth to mouth, how often things that
seemed amiss are thus found to be all right, are out of
place. John's coming to talk face to face refers to what
Diotrephes may expect according to III John 10. John
is coming to unhorse this congregational boss. That is
one thing; the other is the fact that no more proselyters
will be received by this or by any other man in the
congregation.

When John says that it is his purpose that "your
joy may be as having been filled" he speaks to the
general membership. The conduct of Diotrephes has
been lessening the joy which all the faithful members
found in their church life. Full joy must be theirs.
John will bring it. He will once more be able to send
gospel missionaries with recommendations to the entire
church, and no one will say them nay. The participle
is a predicate to the copula and is not a part of the
periphrastic tense. When John completes his mission
in the congregation he will leave enduring joy behind him.

13) **There salute thee the children of thy sister,
the elect one,** all the members of the church in whose
midst John is writing, which we take to be Ephesus.
By calling this church "thy sister" John means that
this church in Ephesus is also full mistress in her
domain. Although as "the Elder" he resides in this

congregation, and because of this fact, there is no boss there to lessen joy. By calling this Ephesian κυρία "the elect one" (note the emphasis conveyed by the second article) John stresses the high position and the obligation that belong to both congregations, each is equally "a mistress elect" of the Lord.

Soli Deo Gloria

The Third Epistle
of St. John

The Third Epistle of St. John

The Greeting, v. 1, 2

1) Although this letter is called John's third epistle because it is a trifle shorter than the second, the two letters were probably written on the same day and were sent to the same place, the second to the congregation, the third to one of the members. Each little letter was written on one sheet of papyrus, which accounts in part for their nearly equal length. **The Elder, to Gaius, the beloved, whom I on my part love in connection with truth.**

"The Elder" and the relative clause "whom I on my part love in connection with truth" are the same as those found in II John 1, which see. Note that John loves whomever he loves only in connection with what is truth (anarthrous). His love is governed by this truth even as his love is that of true comprehension and corresponding purpose. All that we know about the Gaius who is here addressed is contained in this letter. We can safely say that he is not one of those men of this name who are mentioned elsewhere in the New Testament.

2) We have seen in connection with Second John that John formulates his letter headings in his own way. He does so here, for he does not write χαίρειν as James does, nor "grace and peace" as Paul does, nor a greeting like the one found in Second John 3. Instead he addresses Gaius anew: **Beloved, in regard to everything I pray for thee to prosper and to be in health even as thy soul prospers.**

We need not wonder at this threefold mention of John's love for Gaius. Diotrephes hated Gaius because of what Gaius had been doing, namely lodging and helping John's missionaries on their journeys. John is asking Gaius to do this again with regard to the missionaries who bring him this letter, which we see is a letter of recommendation of them to Gaius. Diotrephes will then hate Gaius all the more. Here is compensation for Gaius; John sends him these repeated assurances of his love. To have this love of the great apostle, a love that is wholly in connection with truth, is better than to have the favor of a man like Diotrephes whose love is turning toward the Gnostic heresy and to the emissaries that are traveling as proselyters from city to city.

Εὔχομαι means to wish or to pray. Περὶ πάντων fits only the first infinitive. John prays that Gaius may be prosperous in all respects; then also that he may continue in good health. John is scarcely referring to a damage that was caused to Gaius in his business by the hatred of Diotrephes. This concern about the earthly prosperity of Gaius in all his affairs and about his good health refers to the ability of Gaius to take care of the missionaries whom John is sending from time to time. We must remember that these missionaries traveled on their own resources (verse 7), that Christian congregations gave them not only lodging when they passed through their city but also supplied them with whatever they needed as they went on to the next city. This required funds.

When a whole congregation contributed such funds, no one was really burdened even when such missionaries came rather frequently. It was another matter when, as in this city, the whole burden fell upon one man. It was asking not a little of him to do all of it. We shall see how Diotrephes prevented the congregation from doing its part. So John prays that the Lord will keep Gaius prosperous, and this includes the health of Gaius. John would not want to send his missionaries to a sick man's home and to burden a sick man with lodging them and outfitting them for the next stage of their journey. What John writes becomes clear as soon as we see its bearing.

As far as the spiritual prosperity of the soul of Gaius is concerned, John is fully assured of that and says so. His prayer is that the earthly prosperity of Gaius may be equal to his spiritual prosperity. John makes the well-being of the soul the governing concern; the material is to be "even as" (καθώς) the spiritual. The two cannot be reversed.

Some commentators refer to what they regard as illustrations like that about Flavia, who would be a miracle of piety if she were half as careful of her soul as she was of her body; or that of the gentleman who washed, dressed, and perfumed his body and spent hours doing this but was careless of his soul and spent not even as many minutes upon it. In what John says of Gaius this is wholly reversed; in the case of the Christian it must be. Εὐοδόω = to help on one's way; the passive means to prosper, to be prospered, to be successful. John wants prosperity and health for Gaius for spiritual ends. We cannot but think of Diotrephes, whose soul was in so sad a state that he had no love for John, that he tried to keep John's missionaries from any help which they might receive, and acted the tyrant toward those who wanted to help them.

The Body of the Epistle, v. 3-12

3) John explains what he says in v. 2. **For I was greatly rejoiced** (ἐχάρην λίαν, the same as in II John 4), **brethren coming and testifying to thy truth, even as thou on thy part dost walk in connection with truth.**

Brethren had returned to John from their missionary tours and had reported how Gaius had treated them despite the ugly hostility of Diotrephes. But John does not say that these brethren testified to the love of Gaius; they testified to Gaius' truth. Regarding

his own love John says that it is "in connection with
truth." To have the divine truth in the heart is the
essential thing. Then the love for all who have the
same truth in their hearts will flourish, especially also
if these others are missionaries, preachers of this truth
far and near. To have this truth means to have faith,
and this always brings forth love. Those who think
that they can have love while they let go of more or of
less of the truth are mistaken as to the nature of the
truth and as to the nature of the love.

By ἀλήθεια, which is used three times, John refers to
the same thing, the objective divine truth or reality
which forms the Word and gospel. This always remains objective whether we have it as ours or not,
whether we walk in it or in its opposite, the lie.
Having it in our hearts does not change it and make
it subjective; the subjectivity — if we *must* use the
word — is only our possession. All comments which
make either σου τῇ ἀληθείᾳ or ἐν ἀληθείᾳ or both subjective
are unwarranted. These brethren reported that Gaius
acted in harmony with the gospel truth and doctrine
(II John 9, 10), that thus this truth was his (σου), in
his heart. The conduct of Gaius was the open evidence
for what was in his heart. This rejoiced John greatly.
The conduct of Gaius was his expression of love.

The genitive σου is no more emphatic here than it
is in v. 2 and 6; there is a tendency to place these
genitive pronouns forward. When they are to be
emphatic they are made possessive adjectives as is done
in v. 4. But σύ is emphatic just as is ἐγώ in v. 1. John
could not say of Diotrephes that he, too, is walking
in what is truth. Ἐν ἀληθείᾳ lacks the article here and
in v. 1 only because of its qualitative force.

4) Regarding his own joy John adds: **Greater
joy than this I do not have that I hear that my own
children are walking in the truth,** i. e., in this truth
of which I am speaking (the article is in place here).

To receive reports such as this one about Gaius is John's greatest joy. We can judge how the report about Diotrephes affected John. John reveals the type of man that he was. Many do not have their joy rooted thus completely in the truth. Μειζότερος is a double comparative which B.-D. does not explain by calling it *vulgar;* B.-P. 781 does explain it: such comparatives were formed in the Koine when the feeling for the comparative force of the usual forms was fading and needed re-enforcement.

The plural τούτων means greater "than this," than these things that are comprised in such reports, and ἵνα states what they are. This clause is appositional, R. 699; yet not accusative (R. 992) in apposition with χαράν but a genitive apposition of τούτων. John is rejoiced to hear about anyone that walks in the gospel truth, but his greatest joy is to hear this about his own children; note that he writes the possessive adjective ἐμά and not the enclitic μου. His own children are those who have been under his personal spiritual care for a long time.

5) John comes to the burden of his letter, his request that Gaius may receive and help onward the missionaries whom John is now sending out, this letter serving as a credential and as a recommendation for them. **Beloved, a faithful thing thou art doing, whatever thou mayest (actually) perform for the brethren and at this strangers, who testified to thy love in the presence of the church; whom thou wilt do well in sending them forward in a manner worthy of God, for in behalf of the name they went out, taking nothing from the pagans.**

Without directly asking him John yet asks Gaius to take care of the missionaries once more. No greater compliment could be paid to Gaius than that John should take for granted that Gaius will do what is not even asked but is only implied. John does better

than to ask, he commends what Gaius will do for these
missionaries as though Gaius had already started upon
the doing. The apostles certainly knew how to call out
and how to acknowledge the best that is in a man.

Πιστόν is "a faithful thing," and it need not be
translated "a believing thing"; only a believer will
do a faithful thing. Ποιεῖς is an epistolary present;
note the future ποιήσεις in v. 6. What Gaius "will do"
for the missionaries whom John is sending "thou art
doing" describes from the standpoint of the time when
Gaius receives this letter. As John writes he places
himself beside Gaius as he is reading and acting on
this letter. When this present tense is understood, the
aorist ἐργάσῃ becomes clear: "whatever thou mayest
actually perform for the brethren" whom I am now
sending and whom I already see with thee when they
place this letter into thy hands. This aorist is constative. Moulton, *Einleitung*, 188, says that it summarizes in perspective all the trouble to which Gaius
will go for these brethren until he has expedited them
on their further journey. Ἐργάζεσθαι often expresses
the trouble or effort (*Muehe*) to which one goes.

John writes: "for the brethren and at that (τοῦτο,
adverbial accusative) strangers" (one article with the
two nouns). We may say "and this strangers." The
missionaries whom John is sending have, indeed, been
with Gaius before (v. 6), yet only on a previous
journey, so that Gaius knows them only superficially;
they are still only ξένοι to him, "strangers." This
enhances all that Gaius will do for them, and John does
not fail to note it and to credit Gaius in advance.

6) These brethren had previously enjoyed the
loving generosity of Gaius. In verse 3 John says that
he was rejoiced to hear their report about the truth
to which Gaius was holding; he now says that these
brethren also testified to the love of Gaius "in the
presence of the church," namely when they made their

public report about their previous missionary tour
to the church at Ephesus which had provided their
first supplies. The love and the generosity of Gaius
were appreciated not only by John but also by this
entire church. All of the Ephesians were happy to
know that Gaius joined them in enabling these missionaries to go out with the gospel. The whole congregation at the place where Gaius lived should have
done that; but since Diotrephes was bossing it, Gaius
bore the whole burden alone.

With the future tense, and no longer projecting
himself forward to the day when Gaius receives the
letter (as in v. 5), John says: "whom thou wilt do
well in sending forward in a manner worthy of God."
Gaius will lodge these missionaries, but this is the
least that he will do; he will also send them forward
on their journey, which does not mean with only a
friendly goodbye but with adequate supplies. Since
they traveled on foot and often covered considerable
distances until some other congregation or some friend
like Gaius gave them new supplies, this sending forward required money. The love of Gaius would not
be miserly. John knows that Gaius will send these
brethren forward "in a manner worthy of God," of
him in whose cause they are assuming no little hard-
ship even when they receive much help. Προπέμψας
is a sample of the complementary participle (which
is dying out in the Koine); it is aorist because it
denotes a single act.

7) Why will Gaius do so well by sending these
missionaries forward in such a manner? "For" explains. "In behalf of the name they went out" on
this tour, and they did this "receiving nothing from
the pagans," ἐθνικοί, the heathen to whom they went
out to preach "the name." See the weight that lies
in the brief phrase "in behalf of the name." This
means "Christ," but always the full revelation of

Christ; see further on I John 3:23. These mission--
aries not only could not expect to get anything from
the pagans whom they would win for the name; like
Paul, they would not take anything lest their converts
and others might think that this was what they were
after. The name dared not be compromised in any
way. So the missionaries went with their own means
and relied on the support of the older congregations.
Noble work they did, and noble (καλῶς) is the work
of helping them in every way. Diotrephes did not
think so.

8) **We on our part, therefore, ought to under-
take for such in order that we may be joint workers**
(with them) **for the truth.** This is the proper deduction from the fact that these missionaries go out in
behalf of the name and receive or take nothing. We
on our part, all the rest of us Christians, ought to join
hands with them in helping them. Ὑπολαμβάνειν cannot
here mean to receive under one's roof (R. 633), "to
welcome" (R. V.), to bestow hospitality, because the
ἵνα clause says that we thus become "joint workers"
with these missionaries. The word means "to assist."

There is a fine *paronomasia* between "*taking* nothing from the pagans" and "*undertaking* for such," i. e.,
providing for them. The R. V. misunderstands συνεργοί
and the dative as though the truth were a worker
and we its fellow workers; the A. V. has a better understanding of the Greek. We are joint workers with the
missionaries when we help support them; they and
we jointly work "*for* the truth" (gospel), τῇ ἀληθείᾳ,
a *dativus commodi*.

9) We now learn about the situation obtaining
in the local church in the city where Gaius lived. I
wrote something to the church. This is Second John.
After he had completed Second John, John took another
sheet of papyrus and wrote Third John. See the introduction. If Second John is addressed to some woman

and her family of children, then we know nothing about this letter to the church to which John refers. We are told that it has been lost. Some think of a letter that was written on a former occasion when John sent missionaries. We believe that John refers to Second John. All the similarities in phrasing substantiate this view. The situation seems to call for it. In both letters John says that he is coming; Second John 12 indicates why, and this letter to Gaius openly states why. Some manuscripts insert an ἄν, and then John says: "I would have written something to the church." But this makes the impression that John did not write.

Gaius will learn what John wrote to the church. John informs Gaius about this letter. In case Diotrephes tries to prevent its public reading, Diotrephes is not to succeed. To say that Second John cannot be this letter because of its contents is to misunderstand its contents and its language.

John is, of course, not sending his missionaries to the church in order to have the church care for them, he is sending them to Gaius, but certainly not without also saying something to the church. We have seen in Second John how what he writes to the church fits the situation exactly. In a way it says less than what John writes to Gaius, for it does not condescend to name Diotrephes; in a way it says more, for it openly names and describes the deceivers, it openly warns against them, even against taking them into the house or greeting them. The true missionaries alone are to be treated thus. Even to greet these deceivers is fellowship with their wicked works; to help the true missionaries of the name is to be joint workers with them for the truth. Every item in both letters corresponds.

Ἀλλά does not state why John must write but why this is all that there is left to be done at this moment before John himself comes and reckons with Dio-

trephes: **but Diotrephes, who loves to be the fore-
most of them, does not receive us.** We make the attributive adjective with its genitive a relative clause.
The sense is: "the ambitious Diotrephes." The adjective means that Diotrephes loves to be first, to be
considered the leader. He wants to be a boss, a dictator,
a lord of all the rest, instead of letting the congregation
be the κυρία or mistress who manages all her affairs as
ἐκλεκτή, chosen to do so by the Lord (see II John 1, κυρία).

From II John 7-11, in particular from verse 11,
we learn enough to know that Diotrephes barred out
John's missionaries in order to let the roaming Gnostic
emissaries in. To disregard Second John because the
love of Diotrephes for Gnosticism is not mentioned in
Third John is to overlook the fact that such repetition
is not necessary; Gaius will hear Second John read.
Third John is intended only for Gaius and thus points
out the viciousness of Diotrephes, his unholy love of
dominance.

"He is not receiving us" means: he is turning the
cold shoulder to me and to my missionaries and to all
that is connected with us. "Us" is not the editorial
plural since verbs that use "I" precede and follow. The
present tense indicates the entire attitude of Diotrephes.

10)   For this reason all that John can do at the
moment is to write something appropriate to the
congregation (Second John) and to postpone decisive action for the present. **Because of this, if I come,
I will remind** (them) **of his works which he is doing,
with wicked words prating against us; and not satisfied on this score, neither is he himself receiving the
brethren, and those wanting** (to do so) **he is forbidding and is throwing out of the church.**

In connection with First John we have noted that
ἐάν is used practically in the sense of "when"; it is used
so here: "when I come"; yet ἐάν leaves the matter in
God's hands, hence also in verse 14 as in II John 12

we have: "I hope." It is only a supposition to say that John was so old and feeble that he did not know whether he could come or not. He is still the mighty man with love for the truth, so mighty that he will crush this upstart Diotrephes with his evil words and deeds.

"I will remind" means that John will appear in the public assembly of the congregation and will there in public remind all the members what this man's works are. The members know, John needs only to remind them. What Diotrephes has been doing with his vicious tongue John puts into a subordinate participial modifier: "with wicked words prating against us" (me, my missionaries, etc.). Φλυαρῶ = to babble without sense, to spout or prate. Nothing is too wickedly vicious for Diotrephes to hurl at us. When John quotes all his language, and many witnesses testify as to its truth, these words will terrify this lordly boss.

John states the man's deeds with finite verbs, three of them. Not satisfied with words, the fellow proceeds to deeds. John uses "neither . . . and" as he did in John 4:11. Diotrephes himself is not receiving the brethren, the missionaries that John is sending out; he closes the door of his own house to the men who are bearing the name to the pagans. In this way he loves the truth, the holy name, "Jesus Christ, the Son of God," and what this name embodies. In order to catch the force of this one must know First John and what these earliest Gnostics made of Jesus. Then look at II John 7-11, noting verses 10, 11.

Still worse: those of the members who want to receive and to aid the missionary bearers of the name Diotrephes is forbidding to do anything of the kind and is shouting his wicked words against them. And to cap the climax, he is throwing out of the church those who do not take his orders. This first church boss was a thorough boss.

Was he one of the congregational elders? John does not say. Since in those days the elders were merely men who were chosen from the congregation itself, a man who was not an elder could, if he was of the mean and ambitious type, try to dominate both the' elders and the congregation. John's failure to mention any official position which Diotrephes occupied seems to me to agree best with this status of Diotrephes although I cannot venture to say more.

Had Diotrephes thrown Gaius out of the church? These present tenses say what Diotrephes is engaged in doing, they do not say that he accomplished his will in every case. He certainly kept his own house closed. Very likely, too, in most cases he succeeded in enforcing his demand that the rest also do so. He attained so much that John could send no missionaries to the congregation as such to be lodged with various members. We see this from the fact that John sends his missionaries directly to Gaius. Diotrephes would create so much trouble in the congregation that taking care of John's missionaries on the part of the congregation was practically at an end.

As to the throwing out, this, I think, was no more than a vicious attempt. Throwing out required a formal resolution on the part of the congregation. From the way in which Second John reads I doubt that Diotrephes had achieved the actual expulsions which he demanded. But his raging against the members who did not obey this boss may well have caused them to stay away from the church for the time being.

11) John adds the brief admonition: **Beloved, be not imitating the base but the good!** Τὸ κακόν = "the base," "the bad," anything that is spiritually and morally inferior; τὸ ἀγαθόν = anything that is spiritually and morally beneficial. The adjectives are neuter · singulars and are substantivized. They are used like abstract nouns yet are more concrete in force.

To imitate is to see the base or the good in someone else and then to copy it ourselves. So Paul urges: "Be imitators of me!" I Cor. 4:16; also 11:1; and in II Thess. 3:7, 9 he uses the verb: "you ought to imitate us" — "ourselves an example to you that you imitate us." John is, of course, thinking of Diotrephes and his base example but generalizes here: never copy anything that is base, copy only what is good.

Beside this brief injunction John places the axiomatic fact: **The one doing good is from God; the one doing the base has not seen God.** This is not intended as a deduction; one does not make deductions from an admonition, one fortifies an admonition. The logic is: Copy the good because doing this is evidence that one is from God, but shun the base because to do the base is evidence that one has not even gotten near enough to have as much as caught a glimpse of God.

In I John 2:29 we have the fuller expression "has been born from God" (also in 3:9; 4:7; 5:1, 18), which makes one "a child of God" (3:1, 2). In I John 5:19 John abbreviates to the simple phrase "we are from God" just as he has it here; ἐκ denotes spiritual *origin*. With this goes our being "in God" and remaining in God, and he "in us"; ἐν denotes the inner connection, the *unio mystica* (I John 3:24), the fellowship with God (1:3, 6, 7). "In" rests on "from" (out of).

The commentary on seeing God is John 1:18. No one has ever seen God with his actual eyes, yet his only-begotten Son has revealed God so that we do see him with the eyes of faith in his Word. John is speaking of the latter. He whose characteristic it is to do what is base has not seen God in his Word as all those see him who have been born from God and are thus from God, yea "in him," and "he in us." On this seeing God compare John 14:9; 10:30. All contact with God is made through Jesus, his Son, who is the

personal medium while the Word is the instrumental
medium. Not to have seen God is not to have been
brought into a saving contact with God despite Jesus
and the Word.

12) **To Demetrius testimony has been given by
all and by the truth itself; and, moreover, we ourselves give him testimony, and thou knowest that
our testimony is true.**

John is not holding this Demetrius up as an example
which Gaius should follow. The opinion that this
Demetrius lived in the city where Gaius resided and
was one of the noble members of the congregation, to
whom, therefore, the missionaries brought Second
John, who would certainly see to it that this letter
would be read to the congregation, is untenable. For
then Gaius would know Demetrius, would not need this
testimony in regard to his character. It does not help
matters to say that the testimony "by all" means "by
all the true members in the local congregation of
Gaius." Gaius would know this local testimony better
than John, who was living in Ephesus, could know it.
Of less value would be the testimony that "we ourselves" offer, namely John and the missionaries whom
he is sending; for how could men from Ephesus know
this man who lived in a distant city so well that their
testimony was weightier than even that of the good
members who resided in the city where this man lived?
Gaius himself would be one of these good members.

The only tenable view is that Demetrius was not
known or was only little known to Gaius; that he
was the leader of the missionaries who were sent by
John, whom Gaius was to lodge and to send forward.
This entire weighty endorsement of Demetrius, the
leader of the delegation that John is sending, is a part
of the recommendation and the certification that John
is sending along with and for his agents and thus goes
with verse 7. Endorsing the leader in a special way

in addition to endorsing the delegation as such (verse 7) is entirely in place because so much depends on the leader. Paul does the same in II Cor. 8:16-29 where he sends a delegation of two men, Titus being the leader, the other not being named. Paul recommends the latter but makes Titus chief (verse 23) and tells especially that Titus consented to come.

Everything is clear when we accept this view. All of the Ephesian Christians endorse Demetrius. "We ourselves" includes John and the other missionaries whom John is sending, and Gaius certainly knows that *their* testimony is true, that they would not endorse as a leader a man concerning whom they had the least doubt. When John inserts the statement that "the truth itself" has testified to the character of Demetrius he refers to the Word as an objective witness and thus places its testimony beside that of all the Ephesian Christians who subjectively compared the life of Demetrius with the Word.

These two witnesses "have testified," i. e., throughout the past and until now. "We ourselves" adds a third testimony even as two or three witnesses are always required (Matt. 18:16 and all the parallel passages, plus the example of Jesus himself). "We are testifying" means right now. Δέ adds this as the weightiest testimony, and thus John writes "thou knowest" that this testimony is beyond all question.

Yet one may ask why verse 7 is not sufficient, why John felt that he must endorse the leader of his delegation in so strong a manner. When a delegation arrives from afar in a place where there is serious trouble as there is here, when the leader of this delegation also bears a special letter to the congregation, which he will either read to the congregation or will place into the hands of one who certainly will read it, everything depends on this leader. John would make Gaius feel easy on this score. Gaius may trust Demetrius completely, he need not worry in the least, need not himself take any steps about the letter to the congregation. John has sent the right man.

Conclusion, v. 13-15

13, 14)   Many things I had to write to thee, but I do not want to write (them) to thee by means of ink and pen; moreover, I hope immediately to see thee, and we shall speak mouth to mouth.

John ends this letter so much similarly to Second John (verse 12) that, with all else corresponding closely, it becomes impossible for us to assume that these two letters were not written on the same day and to the same place. The variations are interesting.

John states the fact that he has many things to write to Gaius by means of an independent sentence and thus uses the imperfect: John had them but finally decides not to write them. The aorist infinitive means actually to write and thus to dispatch these many things. In Second John we have the aorist $ἠβουλήθην$, now we have the present $θέλω$, the former refers to a past decision, the latter to one that is being made as John writes. John had arrived at the decision not to write all he has to say to the congregation; regarding Gaius he arrives at such a decision when he writes this letter to Gaius. The present infinitive is in place here just as it is in Second John, for writing many things is thought of as taking some time. The aorist = to write and be done with; the present = to be writing and taking the time.

14)   In Second John John says: "I hope to get to you"; to Gaius he writes: "I hope immediately to see thee," hence I do not use "ink and pen" ($κάλαμος$, writing reed), in Second John it is "paper and ink." "Shortly" in our versions is not exact enough; $εὐθέως$ = "immediately."

We ask why John did not come at once with these missionaries, why he started immediately after they have left. John does not want these missionaries to become involved in the matter when he reckons with Diotrephes before the congregation. John also does not intend to come to the congregation unannounced (II John 12). He will follow on the heels of his missionaries; they will scarcely have left Gaius and have gone forward before John hopes to arrive and to attend to Diotrephes. When he is writing to the congregation John does not say "immediately," for he had sent no missionaries to the congregation, immediately after whom he intended to appear in person; he had sent them only to Gaius.

All of this is more than interesting. The congregation plus Diotrephes learn only that John is coming but not how soon he will arrive. Gaius is informed that John is coming *at once* and is timing his arrival so that he will appear a day or two after the missionaries have left. Thus John will suddenly appear on the scene, will have the congregation called together for a meeting, and will settle accounts with Diotrephes. This boss is not to have time to stir up and to marshal his forces.

I should like to have been present at this meeting to see and to hear how John dealt with Diotrephes and freed the congregation from his domination. The scene of that meeting must have been dramatic. John would, of course, appear with a few companions; the apostles seldom traveled alone. The fact that John and those coming with him would lodge with Gaius is implied in the statement made to Gaius: "We shall speak mouth to mouth." Gaius is thus informed when to look for John, and he will be glad to lodge him and his little party when they arrive.

John's "I hope" does not express an uncertainty. All of the apostles let the Lord control all of their movements. The aorist = "actually to see thee." In II John 12 the "face-to-face" preposition (R. 625) is significant. To Gaius, John writes "mouth to mouth" and "we shall speak," thou Gaius and I, as friends love to speak. Even these little expressions are exactly right.

15) **Peace to thee!** is exclamatory, God's and Christ's peace, which no Diotrephes shall disturb. **There salute thee the friends,** the many friends that Gaius has in Ephesus. **Salute the friends by name!** all the friends that John has in the place where Gaius lives. Each is to be greeted individually by name as Gaius meets them.

This letter is a jewel from the pen of John; it is like its companion, and thus these two letters have been cherished by the church.

Soli Deo Gloria

The Interpretation of the
Epistle of St. Jude

INTRODUCTION

Jude's epistle was written a few years after Second Peter. Both epistles were sent to the same people. Beyond the fact that they were Gentile Christians nothing of consequence can be said. This feature of the subject has been discussed in the introduction to Second Peter.

The fact that Jude uses Second Peter, or that Second Peter uses Jude, is obvious. The former is the case. Peter prophesies: "Also among you there *shall be* pseudo-teachers, such as," etc., (II Pet. 2:1), "there *shall come* mockers" (II Pet. 3:3). Jude 4 records the fulfillment of this prophecy: "there *did creep in covertly some men,* those who long ago have been written down in advance for this sentence." The kind of men, who, according to Peter, *shall* come, who, according to Jude, *did* actually come, Jude describes in terms that are taken from Peter, to which he adds expressions of his own. So Jude also repeats some of the divine judgments on the ungodly that were referred to by Peter and adds still others of the same kind. Jude rests on Second Peter.

Mayor answers this view and proves the opposite by just one sentence, namely that in his description Peter uses four present tenses (2:10, 17, 18; 3:5). Does this cancel the three future tenses: "there *shall* be pseudo-teachers," "they *shall* bring in covertly," "there *shall* come mockers"? Are these not prophecy? Peter has employed these future tenses in decisive places, the first and the second at the beginning of chapter 2, the third at the beginning of chapter 3. The first two prophetic futures begin the chapter in which the libertinism of these coming pseudo-teachers is set forth at length; the third prophetic future begins the chapter in which these mockers "in mockery" scoff at the Parousia of our Lord and Savior Jesus Christ.

After Peter has thus said that such men shall be and shall come among his readers he describes them fully and thus in a perfectly natural way says: "they do not tremble" (2:10); "they are waterless springs" (2:17); "they entice" (2:18); "it escapes them" (3:5). When he is painting their picture, these tenses are the proper ones; pseudo-teachers, mockers *shall* be, *shall* come, and then *are* this and that, *do* this and that. These subsequent descriptions do not cancel and annul Peter's three decisive future tenses and the prophecy which Peter utters.

Now look at Jude's aorist (v. 4): "There *did* creep in *covertly* some men," etc., the very ones with reference to whom Peter uses a future tense: "such as *shall* bring in *covertly* heresies of perdition," etc. (2:1). He uses a compound with παρά (on the side, covertly) and εἰς (in) exactly as Jude does. Peter has the prophetic future, Jude the aorist of fulfillment. Peter does not once use such an aorist with reference to these false teachers and mockers; they were yet to come. When Jude wrote, they had come, had *stolen* in; Peter said: they *shall steal* in their heresies. When some commentators consider the present tenses used by Peter they sometimes think that Peter means that the false teachers were already present, but this is evidently a misunderstanding. When they *shall* arrive, Peter says that his readers shall then find what these men *are* and *do*.

To crown it all Jude himself quotes Peter's future tenses: "But you on your part, beloved, remember the utterances, the ones spoken in advance (as prophecy) by the apostles of our Lord Jesus Christ, how they kept telling you: 'At the end of time there *shall be* mockers proceeding according to their own lusts of ungodliness.' " In v. 17, 18 Jude cites II Pet. 3:3. He cites "there shall be" from II Pet. 2:1 so that this prophetic future shall be noted. Jude has the same reference to the "apostles" that Peter has in 3:2: *"your* apostles" — Jude: "the apostles, how they kept telling *you*." We have seen that Peter refers to himself and to Paul when he speaks of "your apostles," which is also true in regard to Jude. Jude bids his readers to remember the prophecies of Peter and of Paul: "There *shall* be mockers."

If all this does not mean that Jude wrote *after* Peter, yea, wrote to the *same* people at a time when Peter's prophecy had been fulfilled, when the men who Peter said *shall* steal in heresies *did* themselves steal in — pray, what does it mean?

* * *

Jude is the brother of James; both men are "brothers of Jesus." What is to be said on this point the reader will find discussed at length in the introduction to the Epistle of James.

* * *

As to the probable date of Jude's letter little can be said. We obtain little by a study of the heretics who are referred to in this letter. Already as early as the time when he wrote Thessalonians Paul has to correct wrong ideas about the Parousia. In Corinth a jumble of "wisdom," libertinism, laxity, abuses, and denials of the resurrection of the body appears. Legalistic Judaizers invaded Galatia; then superstitious Judaizers appear in Colossæ; silly myths arise in Asia, and Timothy is to check them. Jesus prophesied regarding coming error (Matt. 7:15; 24:11); Paul did so already in Acts 20:29. We are not surprised to read in II Pet. 2 and 3 that this continued. Here, however, the heretics are distinct and are described in detail, and they arrived rather promptly. If we had a complete church history of the second half of the first century we could fix both the date and the locality of this letter. As it is, we cannot.

We attain little by computing when Jude might have been born and how long he might have lived. Bigg does this and strangely concludes that Second Peter and Jude were written at the same time but to readers who lived in different localities.

The way in which Jude writes about what the apostles "kept telling you" makes us think that Peter had already died, and that Jude wrote after the year 64. We feel less certain about Paul, who also had written to these people (II Pet. 3:15). He went to Spain and on his return was executed at Rome a few years after Peter's death. Jude's ἔλεγον ὑμῖν would apply to Paul during this sojourn in Spain as well as after his death.

Does this make Jude too old? Many men live to be eighty, some live even beyond this as Polycarp and John did. Who can say more? Jude felt that he must step in (verse 3), that no apostle was within reach who might act in the emergency that had arisen. Neither Peter nor Paul was at hand, John was beyond reach in Asia. Who is able at this time to say more?

A date that is fixed on the basis of Jude's use of the *Book of Enoch* or of the *Assumption of Moses* is questionable. One should read or at least know about this *Book of Enoch* in order to understand the perplexities which it causes. In what language was it written? It is acknowledged to be an accretion. What was the nucleus, what the date, and who the author of this nucleus? Who added the other sections, and when did he add them? After it had been known for a long time only from references found in early writers, some of whom valued this Book while others rejected it, Bruce in 1773 discovered three Ethiopic translations in Abyssinia, but these Ethiopic versions were not published until 1838. English translations by Laurence appeared in 1821, 1833, 1838. Zahn, *Einleitung*, II, 286, quotes from "the Greek text of the *Book of Enoch*, 1:9, edited first in 1892 by Bouriant" without, however, informing us about the origin of this Greek text. Zahn also quotes the English translation of the Ethiopic of 1:9 and the same sentence from an ancient Latin fragment.

Much information can be obtained from Smith, *Bible Dictionary*, I, 738, etc., and other good reference works. Smith does not mention Charles, *The Book of Enoch*, published in 1893.

It is taking a good deal for granted when we are told that Jude 14, 15 "quotes" the *Book of Enoch*, 1:9. Jude quotes only Enoch and does not say that he quotes any book or writing. But more will be said concerning Jude 14, 15 in the exegesis itself.

Nor is Jude 9 a quotation from the *Assumptio Mosis*. When this apocryphal work was written is not known. It exists only in fragmentary form, in Latin and in a translation from the Greek which was discovered by Ceriani in 1861. It had to be edited in order to be at all intelligible. It seems to be the composition of a patriotic Pharisee. The fragment presents Moses as appointing Joshua to be his successor, entrusting him with a writing that he is to preserve for the time of the end, and foretelling the future of Israel until the end of days and the entrance into the promised kingdom of God. Joshua is grieved at the irreparable loss of Moses and confesses his own inability to lead the people. Moses tells him to rely on God who, although he will chastise Israel, will keep his covenant. Here the fragment breaks off in the middle of a sentence.

It is thought that the lost portion contained an elaboration of Deut. 34:5, etc., namely the story that God used the angels for burying the body of Moses, that the devil claimed it, that Michael answered: "The

Lord rebuke thee!" The *Assumptio* is thought to have used Zech. 3:1, 2 as its model at this point. The ancients had the *Assumptio* intact, but when Zahn says that these older writers say that Jude *"quotes"* the *Assumptio* he fails to prove his point. He cites only the wording of Clement: *hic confirmat assumptionem Moysi,* "here he (Jude) confirms the Assumptio of Moses" — *confirms!* This is the reverse of saying that Jude *quotes.* When I quote I let another confirm me, I use him for confirming me. I confirm another when I *independently* say the same thing that he does. How Origen, Didymus, and Euthalius worded the matter Zahn (*Introduction,* II, 288) does not state; he lets Clement suffice. But Clement does not say that Jude *quotes;* he says that Jude *confirms* the *Asumptio.* Only an independent witness *confirms.* In *De Principiis,* III, 2, Origen has stated: "Which little work the Apostle Jude *meminit,* calls to mind, in his epistle." He, too, does not say that Jude quotes.

Something may be added. The *Assumptio* seems to have used the *Book of Enoch.* The latter was highly esteemed in the second century, and then, however, fell into disrepute. Just why this occurred is a matter of conjecture. Even if we could discover the why we should have no more than the individual opinions of a few ancients.

*   *   *

Regarding Jude as well as Second Peter, Bigg supplies the *testimonia veterum* which indicate that Jude's epistle was known as far back as the beginning of the second century. Small as this is and not of general interest, we certainly can expect no more. In his commentary on Matt. 13:55, Origen remarks: "Jude, the Lord's brother, wrote an epistle of few lines but full of the strong words of heavenly grace." Eusebius classes Jude among the antilegomena because it was not written by an apostle. The oldest manuscripts of the Syriac Peshito omit Jude. Jerome accepts it but remarks: *a plerisque rejicitur.* Jude is, however, in the canon of the Synod of Laodicea (363) and in that of Carthaginia (397) and has maintained its position ever since.

The men of the Reformation voiced doubts as to its canonical standing, and since then various commentators have for various reasons shared these doubts. The critics claim that Jude is a forgery like Second Peter. Why a second-century writer should select such a minor man as Jude to forge an epistle in his name is difficult to understand. Why one forger should utilize another forger is still more incredible; which is true whether the author of Second Peter or Jude is forger number one. And both of them were not detected until modern times.

JUDE

Jude's Greeting, v. 1, 2

1)   **Jude, Jesus Christ's slave, on the other hand, brother of James — to the called who have been loved in God** (the) **Father and have been kept for Jesus Christ — may mercy to you and peace and love be multiplied!**

Both Paul and Peter designate themselves "Jesus Christ's slave," i. e., one whose will is wholly that of his divine Lord. As such a slave Jude addresses his readers who will be glad to hear what such a man has to say. The word δοῦλος does not refer to an office. Peter can write in his second epistle "slave and apostle of Jesus Christ," not so Jude who, like his brother James, is not an apostle.

Δέ is in no sense adversative (German *aber*), and yet it is not καί, "and" (our versions). It adds, but adds something that is different. Jude's physical relation to James is different from his spiritual relation to Christ. The chiasm: "Jesus Christ's *slave — brother* of James" accords with this difference. On James, a "brother of the Lord," see the introduction to the Epistle of James.

It is sometimes said that Jude does not intend to identify himself by this reference to his brother. But he does certainly thereby identify himself; if it were not for this apposition, we could not know just which "Jude" is writing. It is all very well to say that Jude's first readers did not need such identification, but Jude did not seem to think so. The real question is: "Did 'brother, on the other hand, of James' intend to convey more?"

The opinion that this apposition is a roundabout way of calling himself "a brother of the Lord" since James was known as such a brother (Gal. 1:19), does not commend itself in view of Acts 1:14 and I Cor. 9:5 where the plural is used. Such indirectness is not in place. James 1:1 is satisfied with the use of "slave." But the idea commends itself that, when Jude wrote, his brother James was dead (had been killed in Jerusalem at Easter in 66). Jude is stepping in where his brother James might otherwise have done so.

Does this make the readers Jewish Christians? It is certain that they are the *same* congregation or the same congregations that are addressed by Second Peter. What Second Peter prophesies, Jude sees fulfilled (see the introduction). The two epistles contradict the opposite opinion. Then it is certain that the readers of these epistles were Gentile Christians (see the introduction to Second Peter), Christians to whom Peter and Paul were "your apostles" (II Pet. 3:2), to whom Paul, too, had written a letter (II Pet. 3:15), to whom both James and Jude were known. So much we can say with safety. But here we come to a dead halt. Where to locate these Gentile congregations or this congregation so as not to conflict with these findings is utterly beyond us. We cannot accept the various conjectures which ignore or set aside any of these items and arrive at a solution in this manner.

Jude uses the ordinary letter heading: first the nominative to name the writer, next the dative to indicate the person addressed: τοῖς κλητοῖς, with two modifying perfect participles between τοῖς and κλητοῖς. It is true: "the called who have been beloved," etc., is applicable to all Christians anywhere; yet this is not a "catholic" epistle that is addressed to the whole *Una Sancta*. Jude addresses only certain readers. These are most precious to God and have been kept safe but are now being assailed by ugly enemies and are in grave danger. This dative reflects the contents of the letter; the message fits the readers.

The dative is Jude's own. Although Paul often uses κλητοί to designate Christians who have been effectually called by God through the gospel, "the called" cannot be a distinctive Pauline term; for I Pet. 1:15 has "he that called you," and II Pet. 1:3 "he that called us." Jude's connotation is that God does not want to lose the people whom he has called to be his own. They are those "who have been loved in God (the) Father and have been kept for Jesus Christ." Like the other writers, Jude loves to repeat "Jesus Christ." They were so loved and kept in the past, and this continues to the present (perfect participles). "Having been kept for Jesus Christ," with the *dativus commodi*, is plain: God has been and is still keeping them for Christ. But the passive "having been loved" with the ἐν phrase "in God (the) Father" seems strange. The agent of both passives ought to be the same, namely God; not "loved by Jude and the other Christians" and "kept by God."

The way out of the difficulty is not, to say "loved by *Christ* in God" and "kept by *God* for Christ." In I Thess. 1:4; II Thess. 2:13; as well as in Col. 3:12 ἠγαπημένοι has God as the agent, and it has it here in Jude. C.-K. 13 is not clear. The solution seems to be this: although both participles are passives and *imply* God as the agent, Jude *omits* an indication of the agent and by the forward position of "in God (the) Father" and of "for Jesus Christ" emphasizes these modifiers instead of the agent of the passives: *"in God* you have been and are beloved, and *for Christ* you have been and are being kept." All this enduring love is yours in connection with *God,* and all this enduring care and keeping of you is for *Christ.* All this must now not be ruined by the false men who have stolen in among you.

2) Jude has the same aorist passive optative of
wish that Peter uses in I Pet. 1:2 and II Pet. 1:2. It
is so markedly different from all other New Testament
greetings that we must say that Jude follows Peter.
But whereas Peter twice has "grace to you and peace,"
Jude goes his own way: "mercy to you and peace and
love," etc. It is only a supposition that Jude intends
to form an extended chiasm, "mercy" matching "the
called," "peace" matching "having been guarded," and
"love" matching "having been loved." How "mercy"
and "those called" suggest each other is not apparent.
Ἔλεος, as distinct from χάρις, denotes the love that pities
the wretched, distressed, and suffering and comes to
their help. "Peace" is the condition when all is well
between God and us through Jesus Christ. "Love"
(ἀγάπη), that of full comprehension and corresponding
purpose, is the greatest of the three terms, on which
the other two rest.

The readers of Jude are suffering a terrible infliction and thus need "mercy" multiplied to them. Men
are trying to destroy their relation to God in Christ,
and thus they need "peace" multiplied, all that will
conserve their relation to God. And thus they will
need God's all-comprehending love with all its gifts.
"Multiplied to you" implies that they already have
these three, but that now, in the trying situation that
has developed, they more than ever need these three
gifts from God. Jude prays that they may have them.
We are unable to find a covert reference to the Trinity
as though "mercy" is the gift of Christ, "peace" that
of the Spirit, and "love" that of the Father. If anything, Christ is the Giver of "peace" (John 20:19, 21).

Jude's Reason for Writing, v. 3, 4

3) **Beloved, while exercising all diligence to
write to you concerning our common salvation, I was
compelled to write to you urging you to be contend-**

ing earnestly for the faith once delivered to the saints.

Jude says that in the midst of his plans for writing to his readers on a larger subject he all at once found himself compelled to write this letter in which he urges them to keep on contending earnestly for the faith delivered once for all to the saints. Ἔσχον is the epistolary aorist: the necessity that Jude feels *now* will lie in the past when this letter is read to his readers. This does not mean that Jude waited a while and then wrote. News had unexpectedly reached Jude that heretics had crept into the congregations; he finds that he must act at once, and he does so by means of this letter.

"I had necessity" implies two things: 1) there is a personal relation between Jude and these his readers as we see also from his purpose to write them "about our common salvation"; 2) there is no one else to step in and to do what is so necessary at this moment. We should like to know all about this relation, but that page is blank. Peter and Paul were in the same relation but could not step in now. In the introduction we show that both were dead at this time, or that Peter was dead, and that Paul was far off in Spain.

"Beloved" reaches out to the readers in love. In verses 1 and 2 the divine love is mentioned twice, Jude now voices his own love. Also Peter has this form of address, but it must have been often used by preachers. "All diligence" reminds us of II Pet. 1:5, 10, 15.

• Jude indicates only the general subject on which he was intending to write before the bad news arrived: "our common salvation," κοινή, which is alike for all of us. All that we can say is that this subject is broad and that no special necessity is involved in its choice. Only this much is evident, that Jude is closely connected with his readers. We venture to add that he is now quite old and wants to leave these people an instructive

and edifying writing for the future. The present
infinitive γράφειν, "to be writing," is correct (note the
aorist that follows). We take it that Jude had not
begun the actual composition but was making careful
preparation; he does not say "having *begun* to write."
Nobody knows whether Jude finally got to write on this
subject or not.

The aorist γράψαι = "actually to write" the present
letter, "urging you," etc. We inject no thought of
reluctance on Jude's part. The participle may mean
"urging, exhorting, admonishing, comforting" according to the context; "urging" will do here. Jude states
it in a positive form: "to keep earnestly contending
(ἐπί strengthens) for the faith," and not negatively:
"against the heresies or heretics." The negative is
implied, for one contends for something when there
are antagonists (verse 4). In Phil. 1:27 Paul has
written: "In one spirit, with one soul jointly contending for the faith of the gospel."

This is *fides quae creditur*. The statement of C.-K.
893 regarding πίστις: "To accept a significance of
doctrina fidei in the sense of a *fides quae creditur* is
everywhere superfluous," cannot be approved. "Faith"
often means *fides qua creditur*, the faith *by* which one
believes, the confidence in the heart (subjective); but
pistis is often undoubtedly the faith *which* one believes, the doctrine, teaching, creed, gospel, divine truth
(objective). It is so here in Jude, also in Phil. 1:27;
we need not labor the point. B.-P. 1063: *das, was
geglaubt wird, die Glaubenslehre;* C.-K. does not cite
Jude 3.

Nor can we agree with those who say that *pistis*
is here both subjective and objective. The fear of
losing the subjective idea is due to a failure to see
that the infinitive "to contend for earnestly" is actually
full of the subjective idea: only earnest believers contend for what they believe.

The objective sense of faith is placed beyond question by the attribute modifier "once delivered to the saints," the participle being an aorist passive: delivered to the saints by Christ. Some think that the apostles delivered the faith;' but they themselves are saints and had it delivered to them. "The saints" appears in Acts 9:13 and often after that as a current designation for Christians; but we cannot agree that the term means "the members of a cultus circle" (G. K. 108). The Christians are saints because they are separated from the world, set apart for God, cleansed by the blood of Christ, and thus living a holy life. By the faith in their hearts they hold to the faith delivered to them so that their sainthood may be defined also in this way.

Jude means that the faith was delivered to all the saints, to the whole *Una Sancta;* his readers belong to this number. What he urges them to do agrees with what they are and possess. "Once delivered (effective aorist) means "once for all" (the classical meaning) and not merely "on one occasion." Bengel is right: *Nulla alia fides dabitur,* there is no other faith. To offer doctrines that are other than this faith is to offer falsehood, poison. To subtract from or to add to this faith is to take away what Christ gave or to supply what he did not give. "Once" = for all time, "till the end of the world" (Matt. 28:20).

4) "For" explains what necessitates Jude's writing: **For there did creep in covertly some men, those who a while back have been written down in advance for this verdict, godless, changing the grace of our God into excess and denying our absolute Master and Lord, Jesus Christ.**

What Peter wrote in Second Peter to the very people to whom Jude now writes has come to pass. What Peter prophesied is now being fulfilled. Place II Pet. 2:1, etc., 3:3 beside Jude 4 and see how they

match. Peter prophesies: "there *shall* be among you
pseudo-teachers" — "there *shall* come mockers"; Jude:
"there *did* creep in covertly." Peter: "they *shall* bring
in *covertly*"; Jude: "they *did* creep in *covertly*."
Peter's future tense is a compound with παρά and εἰς;
so is Jude's aorist. Peter says: "they shall steal in
heresies"; Jude: "they stole in themselves."

More than this, decidedly more! Peter says: "denying the absolute Master"; Jude says: "denying our
absolute Master"; both have τὸν δεσπότην ἀρνούμενοι. Both
speak of ἀσέλγεια, Peter in 2:2, 18 in the plural, Jude
in the singular. Both speak of τὸ κρῖμα, Peter in verse 3,
Jude in verse 4. All the rest agrees although it is
couched in different words. Jude uses even some of
the examples of judgment that Peter employs.

Jude's readers still have Peter's letter. Jude points
them to Peter's own prophecy which had been made to
them a few years ago; what Peter prophesied has now
come to pass. The enemy has arrived, the readers
must earnestly contend.

The verb itself "there did creep in" (Liddell and
Scott: "insinuate themselves") is damning; the form
is the second aorist passive which is used in the middle
or intransitive sense. "Some men" = not many as yet.
Jude does not wait; the advance guard of these dangerous enemies must be thwarted. Where they came from
makes no difference. The substantivized perfect passive participle is an apposition: whoever they are and
whatever their number, they are "the ones who a while
back have been written down in advance for this
verdict." Peter made this advance record in his prophecy which is still in the hands of the readers. The
perfect tense says that Peter's advance writing still
stands; Jude implies that all that the readers need to
do is to read anew what Peter foretold.

The word πάλαι does not always mean "anciently,"
in the distant past, and, therefore, the document or

the documents here referred to are not necessarily
Old Testament writings. B.-P. 1129 speaks of the book
of the damned. In Mark 15:44 Pilate asks whether
Jesus died πάλαι, "a while ago," and this adverb reaches
back no farther than an hour. Few will still defend
the opinion that "written down in advance" means
"predestinated in eternity" to be heretics.

Κρῖμα (suffix -μα, a word expressing a result, R. 151)
= verdict, sentence; it is not κρίσις (suffix -ις, a word
indicating an action) which = judging. Each is a *vox
media* although the context often decides that the
verdict or the act of judging is adverse. Second Peter
2:3 also has τὸ κρῖμα: "they for whom *the verdict* (sentence) this long while is not idle, and their perdition
is not nodding in sleep."

When Jude writes: "they who a while back have
been written down in advance for *this* verdict (sentence)," some are puzzled as to what *"this* verdict"
means. The preceding words seem to contain no verdict, and the words that follow report the crimes of
these heretics and not a verdict on them. So some
think that Jude wrote in a hurry, carelessly; and Jude
is not here to defend himself. Jude's words are, however, quite plain: Peter wrote down the verdict of these
men in advance, and Jude says what it is, namely this:
"godless, changing the grace of our God into excess
and denying our absolute Master and Lord, Jesus
Christ." The supposition that a verdict names only
the penalty is unwarranted. In modern courts the
judge names the penalty, but the jury brings in the
verdict of guilt. When there is only a judge he does
both. Here the verdict states the guilt.

Peter wrote down in advance both the guilt and
the penalty, the latter as "perdition" in 2:1, 3 and as
"the blackness of the darkness" in 2:17. It does not
seem to be correct, then, to say that Jude is more severe
than Peter, for Jude stops with the guilt: Guilty as

"godless, as changing God's grace, etc., and as denying our Master, etc.!" A frightful κρίμα this indeed! To be sure, when Jude is *not* thought to write to the readers of Second Peter, or when Jude is thought to write *before* Second Peter, difficulty arises. But Jude uses a number of terms that are taken from Peter's much longer verdict and inserts the guilt with only three items.

"Godless!" is the first verdict. It is comprehensive, concise. Second Peter 2 furnishes the full details; Jude, too, will presently add many. What penalty goes with this is plain.

"Changing the grace of our God into excess!" is next in the verdict. Peter has ἀσέλγεια twice, even the plural in 2:2, 18. See the word in II Pet. 2:2; it does not mean "lasciviousness" (our versions, sexual only) but all kinds of "excess," hence also we have Peter's plural "excesses." Our God's unmerited favor toward us sinners these fellows turn into *Zuegellosigkeit*, into a charter that permits them to run wild in all types of moral excess. "They suppose that our God's grace" will close an eye to everything that they please to do.

"Denying our only absolute Master and Lord, Jesus Christ," completes the verdict — II Pet. 2:1: "denying the absolute Master who bought them." For "who bought them" Jude uses the soteriological equivalent "our Lord." From Peter we learn what this denial means, and why both he and Jude use δεσπότης (on which see the remarks under II Pet. 2:1). These men deny Christ's Parousia and the judgment to come. That is why both Peter and Jude cite the divine judgments which have been already executed, which stand as types of the final judgment at the Parousia of Christ, the absolute Master. They have to deny these; how can they otherwise riot in excess as they do?

Does τὸν μόνον δεσπότην καὶ Κύριον ἡμῶν Ἰησοῦν Χριστόν refer to one person or to two? To one. 1) In II Pet. 2:1 *Despotes* is unquestionably applied to Christ, and this usage answers the claim that it is always used only with reference to the first person and thus cannot be used with reference to the second. Jude undoubtedly quotes Peter's "denying the *Despotes*." 2) Ἡμῶν modifies both nouns as one person just as ἡμῶν modifies τοῦ Θεοῦ in the preceding clause, just as "Jesus Christ" is the apposition to both. 3) The addition of μόνον does not compel us to think that *Despotes* refers to the first person since "only" is elsewhere used with reference to this person; for whether it is used with reference to one or to the other person, "only" does not place that person in contrast to the others but in contrast to the false masters. 4) The one article makes one person of the two titles, and the name "Jesus Christ" is an apposition.

On page 786 Robertson says that, because Κύριος is often anarthrous like a proper noun, this "slightly weakens" the conclusion that Jude has in mind only one person. How else could Jude have referred to one person save by the standard Greek way of using one article? In order to get two persons one text and one version add Θεόν to δεσπότην as though this would insure two persons. In view of II Pet. 1:1, 2 we should still be entitled to translate: "our only absolute Master-God and Lord, Jesus Christ" — one person.

Jude Cites Three Examples of Judgment
and Applies Them,
v. 5-10

5) **Now to remind you is my intent, since you have come to know everything, that the Lord, after having saved a people once out of Egypt, the second time destroyed such as did not believe.** This is the first judgment which Jude cites.

Second Peter 2:4-8 mentions three such judgments, Jude does likewise. Each, as it were, offers three Scripture witnesses. Peter states his three in chronological order: the fallen angels — the Flood — Sodom and Gomorrah. Jude does not state his three according to the external order of time but according to a progressive inner order: 1) Israel, once *saved* out of Egypt, yet after that such as did not believe *destroyed;* 2) angels, created good and needing no saving yet falling away and for this kept for judging; 3) Sodom and the other cities, wicked in the first place, then going to extremes, and thus made an example for all time.

While Jude has three illustrations of judgment as Peter does and has two that are used by Peter, we see at once that Jude does his own thinking and does it well. To what Peter wrote a few years ago to the same readers he adds one striking, new example and an inner connection between the ones that are selected. The commentators, as a rule, do not stress this connection and thus do not point out why Jude uses Israel and properly places this illustration first. It is all very well to credit Peter with his chronological order; but why not be fair to Jude, why not accord him due credit?

The Greek text is confused. To bring order into it is not an easy task for the text critics. The text also causes considerable trouble to the exegetes. We do the best we can and ask the student to examine the variants for himself.

Δέ is merely transitional: "now" (R. V.) and not "therefore" (A. V.). Jude says: "to remind you (effective aorist) is my intent." Βούλομαι often means "I intend," notably in I Tim. 2:8; 5:14; 6:9; Titus 3:8. To remind them is all that Jude needs to do since his readers "have come to know everything," meaning all that the Old Testament histories contain. Jude's reminder is enough; he does not need to tell the whole history of the three cases of judgment which he presents.

Our versions make the participle concessive, which may pass. It is better to make it causal. But we object when Jude is charged with "a confused reminiscence" of II Pet. 1:12 and is faulted for not inserting the concessive καίπερ. A participle alone might be concessive; and Jude here states a reason. Regarding Jude's Greek R. 125 testifies: "The correctness of the Greek is quite consonant with the authorship of the brother of James, since Palestine was a bilingual country." Moulton agrees; Deissmann considers Jude a literary epistle in popular style and cosmopolite in tone with a certain degree of artistic expression. He includes Peter's epistles in this verdict. *Light,* etc., 242.

The first thing of which Jude reminds his readers is "that the Lord, after having saved a people once out of Egypt, the second time destroyed such as did not believe." Jude should not be charged with harshness. Nor should one say that Peter thinks of the saving of Noah and of Lot, Jude only of destruction. In this verse Jude says that only those who did not believe were destroyed. He places in direct opposition the fact that the Lord first *saved* λαόν, "a whole people" out of Egypt — the readers know in what a wonderful way he did this; and the fact that he then *destroyed,* not this whole people, but only such as did not believe. Note the qualitative force of the anarthrous λαόν. Note the crime: although they were thus *saved,* some did not *believe* after this.

We shall not discuss the variants: Κύριος with or without the article — Ἰησοῦς, "Jesus" or "Joshua" — ὁ Θεός. The position of ἅπαξ is textually uncertain. It does not fit "since you got to know"; it fits well "after having saved a people" and then balances with τὸ δεύτερον: *once* the Lord saved — *the second time* he destroyed. If we retain τούς we have: "those who did

not believe"; if we omit it we have: "such as did not
believe." The difference is immaterial.

After first saving the whole people out of Egypt
the Lord destroyed those who did not believe, destroyed
them by letting them perish in the desert. Joshua and
Caleb believed and were not destroyed. Also the
younger generation was not destroyed. Num. 14:20,
etc. The claim that Jude refers to a second saving of
the whole people, the one that was effected by Christ's
redemption, and a second destruction of the unbelieving
in the destruction of Jerusalem, cannot be considered.
The supposition that Jude wrote after the year 70 is
based on this view. Whether he wrote as late as that
or not makes little difference. What Jude says refers
to the terrible dying in the wilderness: saved *out of
Egypt* yet destroyed because of unbelief. When? The
answer is found in Num. 14:20, etc.

6) **Angels, too, those that did not keep the
principality belonging to themselves but abandoned
their own habitation he has kept with everlasting
bonds under blackness for a great day's judging.**

To say that "angels" should be named first means
not to see why they are placed second. No saving
preceded their fall. When he looks at its inwardness,
the case of Israel ranks first in the estimation of Jude
and in view of the application which he desires to make
to his readers: a whole people was *saved,* then so many
fell into unbelief and were *destroyed.* So the readers
were saved and were now God's people; they must not
fall into unbelief and be destroyed. The case of the
angels is different. From their creation onward they
had their own principality, their own glorious habitation with God. They did not keep the one, they left
the other; they are doomed. Their case is apt as a
second example of judgment.

Peter has the thought that, though they were
angels, God "did not spare them"; next that in the

Flood he "did not spare" the ancient world. Thus Peter properly places angels first, the ancient world second.

Jude says the same that Peter does in II Pet. 2:4; he has the same anarthrous ἄγγελοι; the same ζόφος, "blackness"; the same εἰς κρίσιν; the same verb τηρεῖν. Jude has Second Peter before him; yet Jude words his statement in his own way even as he places "angels" second.

The anarthrous and qualitative "angels" lets us feel how great they were, how high they stood. Τε = "too" and connects more closely than καί would. Israel and the angels belong together in a way that cannot include Sodom, etc. The apposition: "those that did not keep," etc., specifies which class of angels is referred to. Peter is content to say, "angels, such as did sin"; Jude amplifies: "angels, those that did not keep the principality belonging to themselves but abandoned their own habitation," both participles are historical aorists. We shall understand ἀρχή by examining passages such as Eph. 1:21 and noting that each angel has his ἀρχή ("rule, domain, principality") and corresponding to it his ἐξουσία ("authority"), his δύναμις ("power"), his κυριότης ("lordship"), his ὄνομα ("name, title").

Instead of keeping the high, glorious ἀρχή, rule and domain, assigned them by God (ἑαυτῶν, possessive genitive: "belonging to themselves") they were dissatisfied, wanted a still higher domain that did not belong to them, and left their own οἰκητήριον, "habitation" — we may say the capital from which they were by God designed to rule — as not being grand enough for them.

The church has always understood that their sin was pride, that they became rebels, that they arrogated to themselves what God had reserved for his own. Peter sums it up in "such as did sin." Add Gen. 3:5, Satan dangling before Eve the ambition of "being as gods"; also Matt. 4:9, demanding that Jesus worship

him. Beyond this we have no light on the sin and the
fall of the angels. We are not to know all about the
devils and their sin but are to be on our guard
against them.

How have some commentators interpreted this?
We have already stated this in connection with II Pet.
2:4, to which add the last paragraph under I Pet. 3:22.
We recall the Jewish fiction of the *Book of Enoch*,
which was derived from Gen. 6:4, to the effect that
these angels came to earth, married women or committed fornication with them, begot a race that was
half-devil and half-man, which was so wicked that God
sent the Flood lest all mankind be contaminated. This
is what II Pet. 2:4 and Jude 6 are said to mean. These
holy writers are regarded as drawing upon the *Book of
Enoch*. See the introduction; on Gen. 6 see II Pet. 2:4.
In the darkest days of witchcraft the belief prevailed
that a devil could act as an incubus and lie with a
woman and also as a succubus and lie with a man.
Some commentators state that the former happened
in Gen. 6. We need not repeat what we have said
regarding this in II Pet. 2:4.

God "has kept" the angels who fell "with everlasting bonds under blackness" — Second Peter: "with
chains of blackness" "being kept." Both Jude and
Peter have εἰς κρίσιν, Jude adds the genitive "a *great
day's* judging," meaning the great day of Christ's
Parousia (note I Cor. 6:3). Second Peter 2:9 has
"for a day of judging"; 3:7, "for a day of judging."
Joel 2:31 adds *"great"*: "till there comes the day of
the Lord, the *great* and shining one," Joel's passage
was quoted by Peter on Pentecost, Acts 2:20. Rev.
6:17: "there came the day, the *great* one"; 16:14:
"the battle of the *great* day." Where did Jude get
his expression? From what the *Book of Enoch* says
about its fictional angel Azazel, or from some other
place in this book?

Those who trace Jude and Peter back to the *Book of Enoch* do not trace back this book; it is a first and original source to them. We ask: "What is the source of this patchwork, the *Book of Enoch?*" This book is an accretion, and nobody is sure of the dates of its various parts or of the identity of any of the contributors, including the very first one; nobody can be sure that some of its expressions were not, perhaps, taken from Jude himself.

Paul has ἀΐδιος in Rom. 1:20; it is one of Philo's favorite words. We have translated δεσμά (δεσμοί) "bonds" but are not sure that this is correct. As far as we have followed this word, since the neuter and the masculine plural are alike in meaning, it appears to mean "confinement," it is often equal to "imprisonment" or even "prison" and not "chains" (II Pet. 2:4 has a different word) save as they may be a part of the confinement. Study the word yourself.

7) Continuing the same construction, Jude names the third illustration: To remind you I intend . . . **how Sodom and Gomorrah and the cities near them, in similar manner to these** (angels and destroyed Israelites), **because they committed exceeding fornication and went away after other flesh lie before** (the eyes) **as an indication of eternal fire in undergoing justice.**

Ὡς is not comparative: "even as" (our versions), but simply "how," it is like an indirect question (R. 1032). This is in place here instead of the ὅτι used in v. 5 (which governs both v. 5 and 6) because the cities referred to in v. 7 and what happened to them lie before the eyes of the readers even now. We should observe the tenses: in v. 5 an aorist, "the Lord destroyed," a simple past fact, those unbelieving Israelites are dead and gone; in v. 6 a perfect tense, "the Lord has kept" the fallen angels, is now keeping them under blackness. Neither of these two do we see. But Sodom, etc.: See *"how"* these πρόκεινται, "lie before" our very eyes in the region of the Dead Sea. At one time they were rich, verdant, a garden spot, now they are salt, blasted forever, a terrible place.

Lot chose Sodom because it was "as the garden of the Lord (like a paradise), like the land of Egypt (so rich and fertile), well watered everywhere before the Lord destroyed Sodom and Gomorrah," Gen. 13:10. But see how this region lies now! The writer was there in 1925. Not a thing grows; not a creature lives in the waters. They are so impregnated that the hand feels the clinging salt and the other chemicals; the body of a swimmer floats. It seems almost incredible that Gen. 13:10 could at one time have been true of this blasted land.

Two other cities besides Sodom and Gomorrah were destroyed, Admah and Zeboim (Deut. 29:23; Hos. 11:8). The fifth city, Zoar, was spared, but "all the plain" was destroyed (Gen. 19:21-25). Wisdom 10:6 speaks of "Pentapolis," the five-city region. Jude does not mention the other cities because he is "harsher than Peter" but because, when one looks at what lies before the eyes, "all the plain" and the Dead Sea (Gen. 19:25) are there and not only the place where Sodom and Gomorrah once stood. Jude is exact.

Verse 6 is closely connected with v. 5 by τε although the sin of the angels is very different from the sin of the unbelieving Israelites. In Jude's estimation the point to be noted is not similarity of sin but irrevocable and terrible judgment. So Jude connects v. 7 with v. 5 and 6 (not with v. 6 alone). This connection does not lie in ὡς; it lies in τὸν ὅμοιον τρόπον τούτοις, the adverbial accusative: "in similar manner to these," and "these" is masculine and refers to "angels, that kept not," etc., (v. 6) and to "those that did not believe" (Israelites, verse 5). The reference must be to both because τε connects these so closely. With this adverbial accusative Jude says that this third case is *similar* to *both* the other cases. The translation "like" for ὅμοιον is inexact (our versions). The similarity does not lie in the sins, for that of the Israelites is unbelief, that of the angels is not unbelief, nor is that of Sodom, etc. The similarity lies in the fact that all these *sinners*, unbelieving Israelites, rebel angels, fornicating Sodomites, *received a final, eternal penalty.*

Τούτοις does not refer to καὶ οὗτοι in verse 8, in fact, it cannot do so, for "also these" in verse 8 are the blasphemers who have appeared among Jude's readers. So also τούτοις does not refer to the people of Sodom and Gomorrah (people because the pronoun is masculine) as though Jude intends to say that the people of Admah and Zeboim were fornicators who were similar to those of Sodom and Gomorrah. Nor can the adverbial accusative be connected with the following participle, which is the construction of our versions and of some commentators. We place the adverbial between commas; the similarity is found in the *fate* of these cities and that of the "these," namely of the unbelievers mentioned in verse 5 and of the rebels referred to in verse 6.

The two participles are causal and are to be construed with "Sodom and Gomorrah and the cities near (περί is used in this sense) them": *"because* they committed exceeding fornication and went away after other flesh," both verbs are historical aorists. The sins differ: unbelief (v. 5); ambitious, dissatisfied rebellion (v. 6); frightful fornication (v. 7). The sinners differ: Israelites who had the Lord's promises; angels who had their glorious domain; pagans who had their lovely land. The three suffered similar, irrevocable punishment.

Ἐκ in the first participle intensifies: "committed exceeding fornication" that cried unto heaven. The second participle: "and went off after other flesh," is added for the sake of intensification. The idea is that expressed by the LXX's translation of Exod. 15:16: "went a whoring after other flesh," ἐκπορνεύσωσιν ὀπίσω; Lev. 17:7. Jude's wording is Scriptural; so is II Pet. 2:10: "those trailing along behind (ὀπίσω) flesh in lust for defilement." The most that can be placed into the ἐκ of the first participle and into ἕτερος is the thought that these fornicators were not satisfied with their own people and ran after every stranger that came within their reach. A sample is given in Gen. 19:4, etc.

We cannot accept the idea that Jude refers to intercourse with animals (Lev. 18:23). In all of the Biblical references to Sodom there is no hint to this effect. The same is true with respect to pederasty (Rom. 1:27).

C.-K. 983 is careful in regard to "after other flesh" and says only: *Objekt der Wollust.* Thayer, 569, etc., is sensible and correct: "used of those who are on the search for persons with whom they can gratify their lust." But B.-P. 1193 translates *hinter andersgeartetem Fleisch.* This suggests the view of those commentators who refer to Gen. 6:4 and to the fiction of the *Book of Enoch* that angels cohabited with human women and thus went after flesh that was of a *different kind* from their own. These commentators infer that the Sodomites did the same. But angels have no flesh of any kind. We have said enough about the angels in the preceding notes. But these human fornicators — what flesh of a different kind, nonhuman, did they go away after?

An appeal to Gen. 19:4, etc., will not answer this question, for this occurred when the cup of fornications was already full, when Jude's two aorist participles had already become facts, on the day before God's doom descended; nor did the Sodomites know that the two angels that came to Lot were not men.

These cities lie before (the eyes) as a δεῖγμα, "indication or sign" (not "example," our versions), that points like a finger to "eternal fire." The participle states how they lie before men's eyes to this day, namely "in undergoing justice" (δίκη). Our versions and others combine in the wrong way. The Cities of the Plain are not "suffering the punishment of eternal fire." What lies before us at the Dead Sea is "a *sign* of eternal fire." Fire and brimstone made the place what it is, a sign, indeed, of the eternal fire of hell, a warning for all time. So writes Jude.

8) **Yet in similar manner these, too, dreaming, for one thing, defile flesh; for the other, set at nought lordship; for still another, blaspheme glories.**

In spite of all these outstanding judgments of the Lord "these, too," namely the men mentioned in verse 4 who stole in among Jude's readers, "in a similar way" do the things for which fearful justice overtook those others. We have seen how Jude connects the three judgments in verses 5-7; we should, therefore, not think that with ὁμοίως and μέντοι he refers only to the Sodomites and leaves out the unbelieving Israelites and the rebel angels. Only this is true, that the three items now adduced do not parallel the three types of sins mentioned in v. 5-7; they are of a similar order and thus call down a similar justice.

Μέν is followed by two δέ, the three particles balance the three criminal acts by holding each item up beside the others. We cannot reproduce such neatness of expression in the English. The participle "dreaming" is predicatively attached to the subject and thereby pertains to all three verbs. In all that they do these libertinistic heretics act like dreamers, unreal images and pictures fill their minds. We speak in the same way when we tell a man who thinks that what is not true is nevertheless true: "You are dreaming!" There is no need to think that these men pretended

to have received revelations in dreams, B.-P. 419 thinks
that they had ecstatic dreams. Second Peter 2:1
foretold that they would be "false teachers" and not
"false prophets."

Jude says, for one thing, they defile flesh. This
is what Peter prophesied with his word "excesses"
(2:2, 18) ; with his description: "those trailing along
behind flesh in lust for defilement" (2:10) ; "irrational
animals" (verse 12) ; "defilements of the world"
(2:20) ; and other expressions. Jude says: "for
another thing, they set at nought lordship." This is
the fulfillment of Peter's prophecy "despising lordship"
(2:10). Both refer to the lordship of Christ of whom
Jude 4 says that they deny "our only absolute Master
and Lord, Jesus Christ"; his lordship means nothing
to them.

Jude says: "for still another thing, they blaspheme
glories." This is the fulfillment of Peter's prophecy
"they do not tremble when blaspheming glories"
(2:10), "as irrational animals . . . blaspheming
in connection with things they are ignorant of" (2:12),
namely of these glories. We refer the reader to II Pet.
2:10 for the exposition of δόξαι, "glories," and remark
only that these are Christ's glories, and that we are
surprised when some commentators tell us that Peter
and Jude have in mind devils when they use the word
"glories," or devils and good angels.

**9) But Michael, the archangel, when he, con-
tending with the devil, was exchanging words about
the body of Moses did not venture to bring against
him a judging of blasphemy but said: May the Lord
rebuke thee!**

Second Peter 2:11: "where angels, being greater
in strength and power, do not bring against them
(i. e., against these heretics who blaspheme Christ's
glories) blasphemous judging before the Lord." What
Peter says regarding angels in general, regarding their

not hurling the blasphemies of heretical mockers back upon their heads, Jude makes specific and refers to the great archangel Michael and his dealing with the devil at the time of the burial of Moses' body.

The Greek purposely places "the archangel" and "the devil" side by side: the archangel — the archfiend! If ever an enemy of Christ deserved "a judging of blasphemy" (Peter has "a blasphemous judging"), the devil did on the occasion of Moses' burial. Yet Michael's answer to him was not such a "judging" (κρίσις, a word expressing an action). The genitive "of blasphemy" is undoubtedly qualitative and is equal · to Peter's adjective. No angel, who was under provocation because of blaspheming men, yea, not even Michael, who was under provocation because of the devil himself and whom we should think to be fully justified in doing so, used blasphemous judging. How could their judging be "blasphemous" or "of blas-' phemy"? If one who is only an angel and a creature should arrogate to himself any of the glories, i. e., the attributes, that belong only to God and to Christ; if he should speak as though *he*, an angel, a creature, could damn with omnipotence, with justice, with omniscience. Not even faintly did Michael so express himself when the devil himself claimed the body of no less a person than Moses.

But these vile heretics among Jude's readers, as Peter said they would, blaspheme the glories of Christ in the most direct way, i. e., mock at his divine attributes, especially those that will shine forth in Christ's Parousia (of which Second Peter says so much). They must do this because, if Christ has these glories, what about these vile mockers and about all the shameful lusts in which they indulge? They must also deny Christ's Parousia and laugh at the idea of such a thing, for what will happen to them if Christ ever does return and judge the universe?

The logic is strong. Mockers, mere men, sinners — mighty angels, holy, heavenly, yea, Michael, the archangel. No provocation but only the mockers' own arrogant unbelief — the greatest provocation even by the devil himself. Outright, direct, wilful, insulting blasphemy of Christ's own glories — not even a word too much against even the devil.

When some commentators tell us that the devil is here called a δόξα, and that Michael respected him as "a glory" (we are sorry to note that our versions use the word "dignity"), they surprise us. In the Scriptures not even the good angels are called δόξαι (see II Pet. 2:10).

The middle διακρινόμενος is used in the sense of contending, it is here joined to διελέγετο (descriptive imperfect) ; the two διά in the compounds = "between" and denote a contending with words back and forth between Michael and Satan. In that altercation Michael said: "May the Lord rebuke thee!" the optative of wish (not the infinitive), R. 232. Michael honored the glories or attributes of the Lord by this word. Michael arrogated nothing to himself, archangel though he was, but turned the devil over to the Lord's judging. Woe to him whom the Lord rebukes in his infinite glories (omnipotence, justice, etc.) !

Whence did Jude (and we may include Peter with his generalizing statement in 2:11) obtain this information regarding Michael's contention with Satan about the body of Moses? This is generally regarded as the main question, but it is of only minor importance; the main question must be: "Is what Jude says true?"

Quite a number answers: Jude obtained it from the *Assumptio Mosis*; and some say that Jude "quotes" it. The fragment of the *Assumptio* that is extant breaks off in the middle of the sentence before Moses' death is reached. The ancients, who had the document intact, do not say that Jude *quotes* it; Clement: *hic confirmat assumptionem Moysi;* Origen: *cuijus libelli meminit in epistola sua apostolus Judas;* Didymus says far less, namely that objection is raised to Jude's epistle and to the *Assumptio propter eum locum, ubi significatur verbum archangeli de corpore Moyseos ad diabolum factum.*

These three church fathers are usually offered as proof that Jude *quotes* the *Assumption.* But one of them says that Jude *confirms* it as an independent witness confirms; the other that Jude *reminds* one of the little book; the third only that the archangel's word is found in both Jude and in the *Assumption.* We draw attention to this fact because even a good man like Plummer, on the strength of the statements made by Clement, Origen, and Didymus, says "that this (*Assumptio*) is the *source* of the illustration used by Jude." Not even one of these three says that. They do not say *where* Jude got the account. They leave the impression that he did not get it from the *Assumptio.* Didymus says only that both Jude and the little book contained the archangel's word to the devil.

Let us add that, when two ancient writings contain something that is similar or even identical, this does not prove that one writer drew from the other or quotes the other. In the present case the date of the *Assumptio* is still debated; no one can be sure that Jude ever saw the *Assumptio.* Scholars have drawn more than one hasty conclusion of this kind. Where did Paul obtain the names of the Egyptian sorcerers, Jannes and Jambres (II Tim. 3:8)?

The view that such information that is not recorded in the Old Testament was obtained by direct revelation, is not the correct answer. On the other hand, the view that such information is legendary, is equally incorrect. Legends are not facts. We do not believe them.

It is not always a safe procedure to point to another document and to be satisfied with that as the source.

It may be the source for that second writer; Jude had Peter's prophecy about the libertinistic mockers. In all historical matters the real question is where and how the first writer obtained his information. In a large number of cases we must confess that we do not know, for the writer does not tell us. Prophecy is given by direct revelation, much else also (Gal. 1:12); we do not know its extent and its boundary. The question about the original source is raised every now and then, but it becomes acute in cases like the present one where there were no human witnesses. This case of Michael and the devil is not by any means the only case. The honest answer is: "We do not know." We are compelled to give this answer in regard to the original source of even other and simpler things.

This is, however, not the whole answer. The holy writers were inspired. Jesus says that they would be "guided into all truth," kept in what is true, preserved from error, falsehood, legend, and the like. It is not the function of inspiration to supply facts; that is the function of revelation. Inspiration prevents error, assures us that what is written is true. No matter whence or how an inspired writer obtained his information, the Holy Spirit enabled him to sift out and adequately to present only what is genuine, true. That is the real point here.

Apply this as a test. Crude, wrong notions about natural phenomena prevailed, but not one of them got into the Old or the New Testament although we do not hesitate to say that the writers held such strange notions in their own minds. Ancient histories, documents, traditions contained some true things that were more or less admixed with fiction, legend, fancies. Take this *Assumption of Moses* or *the Book of Enoch* or ancient pagan histories. We always see that the inspired writer is protected, none of them adopts a single fiction.

So we say: "If Jude has recorded a legend and not a fact, his letter is *not* inspired, does *not* belong in the canon." The position that inspiration does not include discrimination between legend and fact; that Jude could know that what is said about Moses' body was a myth and yet use it; that if an inspired writer wrote today he might well use Dante's *Purgatory*, Shakespeare's *King Lear;* that inspiration did not preserve from "imperfections which have nothing to do with the truth that saves souls": this position makes the Bible only *partially inspired.* Who, then, knows what part is *not* inspired? Pursue the conclusions yourself. But do not fail to face "one jot or tittle" in Matt. 5:18 — "all truth," John 16:13 — "Thy Word is truth," John 17:17 — these from Jesus and many another certification to the same effect. To face these words and then to say, by an extension of the argument, that the Holy Spirit did not keep his writers from "imperfect grammar" is inconsistent. The grammar is adequate, is often wonderful in conveying the thought. This plea is like saying: "If the Spirit had put the diamonds of truth into a golden box, they would all be diamonds; if he used a wooden box, some are just paste diamonds!"

What happened to the body of Moses we know only from Deut. 34:6 and Jude 9. The Lord buried the body. The fact that he did this by the hand of angels, and that Michael was one of these, is not even strange. The fact that Satan interfered is not strange. Nor is Michael's rebuff strange. It was repeated on another occasion when Satan interfered (Zech. 3:2). On the latter passage Keil says: "May the Lord rebuke thee!" is a standing formula which points to God's judgment. On Deut. 34:6 he remarks that it may well be possible that Satan claimed the body of Moses for corruption and decay, and that the Lord's burying it by his own

angels seemed to indicate that Moses' body was to be
preserved from decay. It may be — who can say?

A few regard βλασφημίας as an objective genitive:
Michael did not bring a judging *"for* blasphemy,"
i. e., for the blasphemy the devil uttered. This is
untenable in view of II Pet. 2:10: "blasphemous judging"; untenable also because it breaks off the whole
point of the statement in which Michael (not Satan)
is compared with the mockers.

10) **But these blaspheme what all, on the one
hand, they do not know, what all, on the other hand,
physically, as the irrational animals, they do understand — in connection with these things they perish.**

Jude repeats II Pet. 2:12. Peter stresses φθορά in
his prophecy, but the fact that Jude does not do the
same is not a reason for saying that his sentence is
much smoother, or that it is weaker. The turn at the
end, "in these things they perish," comes with the same
impact as that achieved by Peter.

We do not weaken the force of the word by translating verses 8-10 "rail," "railing." These men blaspheme — no less — not only "glories," Christ's own
attributes, but these together with "what all they do
not know," what remains beyond their intelligence
(I Cor. 2:14). They are without spiritual sense, and
so spiritual things are beyond them, and when these
are brought to them they are treated with scoffing
and mocking, which is certainly blasphemy. Matt. 7:6.
The same thing is done to this day. The devil rides
many of these mockers ever to hurl their blasphemous
words about the holy things of God into our faces.
Μέν and δέ balance.

"What things, on the other hand, physically, as
the irrational animals (they are), they do understand"
are, of course, not spiritual things, those referred to
in the first clause, but what these unspiritual fellows
can grasp "physically," with their animal senses as

the irrational animals that they are. These they do
understand (ἐπίσταμαι), for it takes only natural and
not spiritual ability to do that. These things they
likewise blaspheme. Their profanity is so senseless.
Jude makes a striking·turn that is similar to that made
by Peter: "in connection with these things they
perish," i. e., go to ruin like the unbelieving Israelites,
like the rebel angels, like Sodom, etc.

Jude's Woe on the Heretics, v. 11-13

11) **Woe to them!** Οὐαί, like μακάριος, is an exclamation that arises from a strong emotion at the
sight of what stirs the soul. "Woe" is not a wish, not a
curse that calls down calamity, but a verdict that
repeats Christ's own judgment; see the "woes" pronounced by Jesus in Matt. 23:13, etc., the most terrible
statements he ever uttered.

Like the woes of Jesus, the judgment of Jude's
woe is supported by the fearful evidence: **because
they went on the way of Cain, and they poured themselves out for the error of Balaam at wages, and perished with the contradiction of Korah.**

We may note that Jude loves threes whereas Peter
loves to repeat important words. The beauty of this
statement lies in the three articulated datives, each
introducing a clause; yet each dative is construed in its
own way. Cain (mentioned also in Heb. 11:4; I John
3:11, 12) took the way of unrighteousness. Peter
says "the way of Balaam." Some would find more in
the case of Cain by adopting the statement of the
Jerusalem Targum on Gen. 4:7 which makes Cain the
first skeptic and sophist; some think of Cain as the
first murderer and speak of the heretics murdering
souls. It is enough to think of the way of Cain as
being the way of wickedness. Jude's readers had no
Targum, no Philo.

On the sin of Balaam see the exposition of II Pet. 2:15, 16. The passive is to be understood in the sense of the middle: "they poured themselves out," i. e., devoted themselves to. We construe as a *dativus commodi* "for the error of Balaam," for his love of gain. The added genitive μισθοῦ denotes price: "at wages" or "for pay" — Peter: "who loved wages." These heretics tried to get all that there was in it for themselves.

The third dative indicates means: "with the contradiction of Korah (Num. 16:1, etc.) they perished." Korah and his following rose up in contradiction of the office and the authority which God had invested in Moses and in Aaron, and the earth swallowed them up.

Jude has a climax: *taking* a bad way — *devoting oneself* to error for pay — *contradicting* God's Word and order. .The aorists are good Greek to indicate what has recently occurred whereas in the English we use the perfect: have gone, have poured out, have perished (R. 842, etc.). All of these actions have started recently. Those who think that in verse 8 δόξαι means "dignities" feel that they have support here where Korah contradicts the•dignitaries Moses and Aaron. But the "glories" mentioned in verse 8 refer to devils in their perversion.

12) Jude is still substantiating his woe: **These are the ones feasting along with you as filth-spots in your agapes, without fear shepherding themselves; clouds waterless, carried aside by winds; trees autumnal, fruitless, twice dead, plucked up by the roots; wild sea waves foaming out their own shames; stars wandering — they for whom the blackness of the darkness forever has been kept.**

Jude has five specifications. Οἱ substantivizes συνευωχούμενοι; σπιλάδες is predicative and is either a feminine noun or a feminine adjective used as a noun: "These are the ones feasting along with you as *filth-*

spots in your agapes." Wohlenberg criticizes the dictionaries of Grimm and of Preuschen for not saying a word on this meaning of σπιλάδες; the latter has been corrected in B.-P. 1223. The R. V. translates *"hidden rocks,"* i. e., in the sea, on which mariners are wrecked. This word never means *"hidden* rocks." Those who use it to designate "rocks" in the sea add other words; σπιλάς is a rock that is found anywhere. M.-M. cites the adjective σπιλάς in the sense of "dirty, foul," thus, "a dirty, foul wind," but adds that this wind produces a troubled and stormy effect on the water and then refers to Isa. 57:20. In this roundabout way he leads us to think of the sea and the hidden rocks that are not seen amid the tossing waves. Isa. 57:20 fits only verse 13: "wild sea waves foaming out their own shames."

Jude's σπιλάδες = "filth-spots" = Peter's σπίλοι, "spots" (2:13) and has as much right to be feminine as does νεφέλαι in this same verse. These fellows are a disgrace, actual eyesores at the agapes of Jude's readers. The agapes were congregational joint meals that ended with the celebration of the Lord's Supper. In I Cor. 11:20-34 Paul had to oppose grave abuses that occurred at these agapes. They were eventually dropped and were never revived; the Lord's Supper was celebrated at the public Sunday services without a meal preceding it. Jude indicates in what way these fellows acted as "filth-spots": all they want to do is to feast, "without fear shepherding themselves"; they are the only sheep that are provided for by themselves as the shepherds. *They* saw to it that they got the best with which to gorge themselves. Such action clashed with the very idea of the agape, a frugal joint meal in which love should see to it that *all* received alike, the poor slave who could bring nothing as well as the rich man who could bring plenty, the whole meal being a fit prelude to the holy Sacrament.

Jude puts "filth-spots in your agapes" first because the whole congregation could see at the very agapes what disgraceful fellows these were. The variant ἀπάταις was introduced from II Pet. 2:13 just as the ἀγάπαις used in Jude 12 was interpolated into II Pet. 2:13. The A. V.'s translation is correct in both passages; the R. V. thinks that Jude and Peter ought to use the *same* word. Jude does follow Peter in many points but constantly shows his independence, notably also in these verses.

The first point is that these fellows are disgracefully out for themselves only. The second is that they profit no one in any way. For this idea Jude has employed two figures: 1) "clouds waterless," that keep all the rain to themselves, "carried aside by winds," blown away, not shedding a drop. Second Peter 2:17 has "waterless springs, mists driven by whirlwind."

Our versions mistranslate the παρά of the participle, which means neither "carried about" (A. V.) nor "along" (R. V.) but "carried aside," leaving the expectant earth dry as far as they are concerned. 2) "Trees, autumnal," when they ought to be loaded with fruit and are "fruitless"; worse that that: "twice dead," once dead in themselves and thus fruitless, next "plucked up by the roots," literally, "having been uprooted," and thus without the possibility of yielding fruit for anyone. They are without the least spiritual life, the evidence being that they show not the least spiritual fruit to benefit anybody. "Autumnal" means that they have had the full season for producing fruit. Uprooted means that they are not in the Word of God. A dead tree, to say nothing of an uprooted one, cannot bring fruit in a thousand seasons.

13) The next figure presents what these men do produce: "wild sea waves foaming out their own shames," rolling upon the shore in surges and casting up on the land all manner of stuff that has to be cleaned

away. Here belongs Isa. 57:20. Jude does not follow Peter here.

Next is divine judgment: "stars wandering — they for whom the blackness of the darkness forever has been kept." Clouds — trees — wild sea waves — and now stars. All alike are figures that have been taken from *nature*. These "stars" should not be separated from "clouds," etc., and made the angels mentioned in the *Book of Enoch*, whose erring was the fact that they cohabited with women according to the interpretation of Gen. 6:4. But the word πλανήτης does not occur in the *Book of Enoch*. Like σπιλάδες, πλανῆται may be either a noun or an adjective; it is immaterial.

Jude's relative clause: "for whom the blackness of the darkness forever has been kept," is identical with Peter's clause which he wrote in 2:17, save that Jude adds εἰς αἰῶνα, "forever." In neither Peter nor in Jude does this clause modify the preceding figure, "mists" in Peter, "stars" in Jude; in both οἷς refers back to the persons, οὗτοι, the subjects described by the intervening figures: for these persons the blackness has been reserved, and that because "these persons" are what the figures record of them. It is thus incorrect to attach the relative to "stars" and to figure out how God has been keeping "the blackness of the darkness for stars." To speak of comets or of meteors is misleading. Ὁ ζόφος τοῦ σκότους doubles the idea of darkness by adding blackness and = τὸ σκότος τὸ ἐξώτερον (Jesus in Matt. 8:12; 22:13), "the darkness, the outer one," outside of this world, in hell.

Thus Jude's "stars, wanderers or wandering," is purely figurative like clouds, trees, waves, and what . is said of them. Unlike the north or polestar, planets have no fixed place in the sky, by which a mariner may constantly steer his course at night. Christ is the only guide (Heb. 13:8) ; errorists, libertinists are not; they constantly shift their positions. Πλανῆται

is commonly used as a designation for "planets." "The
blackness of the darkness forever" has been reserved
for these men. We construe the phrase with the nouns
and not with the verb: the eternal blackness of the
darkness; the A. V.'s translation is correct.

Jude Cites Enoch's Prophecy, v. 14-16

14) Jude cites the prophecy of Enoch regarding this judgment: **Moreover, there did prophesy
also for these, as seventh from Adam, Enoch, saying:
Lo, there came the Lord in connection with his holy
myriads to execute judging down on all and to convict all the ungodly concerning all their works of
ungodliness, which they ungodlywise did, and concerning all the hard things they said against him
as ungodly sinners.**

This is added testimony (δέ) regarding the judgment that will be visited upon these godless men among
Jude's readers. Καί is to be construed with τούτοις:
"also for these" as for the wicked generation of Enoch's
own time, which perished in the Flood. Enoch "prophesied," foretold the final judgment, and did so in no
uncertain terms. "Seventh from Adam" counts Adam
as the first. Gen. 5:4-20: Adam — Seth — Enos —
Cainan — Mahalaleel — Jared — Enoch. This apposition identifies Enoch, and it does not sound as though
all of Jude's readers had the *Book of Enoch* as they
had the LXX.

We confess that we do not understand how the
statement that Enoch was the seventh from Adam
conveys any special sacredness to him, or how it conveys the thought that he was a type for the seventh
world period and therefore prophesied for this period.
If Enoch was to be exalted, it would seem that a
reference to his translation to heaven would have been
in place (Gen. 5:24). Seventh from Adam identifies
Enoch, and that is all.

Enoch's prophecy is not recorded in the Old Testament because he was the seventh from Adam and thus lived long before the time when Moses wrote the Pentateuch. Jude aims to say that his readers need not look in the Old Testament for Enoch's words. We also note that Jude omits mention of the Flood in verses 5-7 while II Pet. 2:5 mentions it together with Noah. Jude thus amplifies Peter's statement by introducing Enoch who made this prophecy to the wicked generation that lived at the time of the Flood. They had Noah as a herald of righteousness (II Pet. 2:5), and, as Jude wants his readers to note, before Noah they had Enoch, the prophet. Thus, too, Jude properly places Enoch here and not with verses 5-7 and notes that Enoch's prophecy was intended "also for these." For Enoch prophesied the *final* judgment.

Enoch's "holy myriads," ten thousands of angels, are found throughout Scripture: Deut. 33:2; Dan. 7:10; Matt. 25:31; II Thess. 1:7.

15) The rest is so Biblical that comment is scarcely needed. The judging will include all men; the conviction will strike "all the ungodly" for "all their works of ungodliness which (the genitive is attracted from the accusative) they ungodlywise did" ($\dot{a}\sigma\epsilon\beta\epsilon\hat{\iota}\nu$ is transitive) and for "all the hard things they said against him as ungodly sinners." Peter and Jude characterize the libertinistic heretics as blasphemous mockers; Peter (3:4) states that they mocked at the Parousia of the great Judge and derided the very idea of his coming. Enoch's prophecy is tremendously to the point. The aorist $\check{\eta}\lambda\theta\epsilon$, "the Lord came," is prophetic.

The Ethiopic version of the *Book of Enoch* has this prophecy in two sections: "And, lo, he comes with ten thousand of his holy ones to execute judgment upon them, and he will destroy the ungodly, and will convict all flesh of all that the sinners and ungodly have wrought and ungodlywise committed

against him" (1:9) ; then in 5:4: "Ye have slander-
ously spoken proud and hard words with your impure
mouths against his greatness." Translation by Charles.

Wohlenberg and Zahn (*Introduction,* II, 286)
present the Greek fragment which has but one section:
ὅτι ἔρχεται σὺν ταῖς μυριάσιν αὐτοῦ καὶ τοῖς ἁγίοις αὐτοῦ ποιῆσαι
κρίσιν κατὰ πάντων καὶ ἀπόλεσει πάντας τοὺς ἀσεβεῖς καὶ ἐλέγξει
πᾶσαν σάρκα περὶ πάντων ἔργων τῆς ἀσεβείας αὐτῶν ὧν ἠσέβησαν
καὶ σκληρῶν ὧν ἐλάλησαν λόγων καὶ περὶ πάντων ὧν κατελάλησαν
κατ' αὐτοῦ ἁμαρτωλοὶ ἀσεβεῖς. There is also a late Latin
version which is of little moment.

Students of the *Book of Enoch* agree that the
original of at least the basic part of the *Book of Enoch,*
to which other men later made additions, was written
in Hebrew or in Aramaic, and that the Ethiopic, the
Greek, and the Latin are translations. All dates given
for all parts of the *Book of Enoch* are problematical;
opinions vary.

The question is not whether Jude had the *Book of
Enoch* or some part of it in the original or in some
version and quoted it, say from memory, but where
the writer of the *Book of Enoch* obtained Enoch's
words. This writer did not invent a prophecy of
Enoch's. If he obtained it somewhere, how can anyone
claim that the same source was not open also to Jude,
that Jude had only the *Book of Enoch* as *his* source?
Why grant the writer of the *Book of Enoch* an ancient
source and deny it to Jude? Consider the case of
"Jannes and Jambres" (II Tim. 3:8), where we cannot
point to a source that was similar to the *Book of
Enoch;* yet even if we could, that would not prove that
Paul obtained the names from such a book, for again
we ask: "Where did such a book obtain them?" So
much for the source.

This brings us to the question that is supreme for
us today, the *reliability* of the source. In connection
with verse 9 we pointed out that this is the supreme

question in that verse. Did Enoch prophesy in this manner? We may puzzle our heads to discover *how* things that are not recorded in the Old Testament were correctly handed down to later times. They evidently were. Stephen refers to a number of them in Acts 7. We even have the question as to where Moses and other prophets got this and that.

The *how* is of minor importance. We may or may not be able to establish that at this late date. The truthfulness, the trustworthiness, the reliability are the supreme points. Those who feel that Jude had only the *Book of Enoch* and say "apocryphal source," "legend," etc., at least imply: "Not trustworthy!" We who believe that Jude was inspired, that Paul was inspired, etc., know that the Holy Spirit guarded them against stating anything of any kind that was not true, not reliable.

See what Peter says regarding "sophisticated myths" (II Pet. 1:16) ; likewise Paul in I Tim. 1:4; 4:7; II Tim. 4:4; Titus 1:14. Look at the myths found in the *Book of Enoch*. What kept the Scriptures free from such things? There is only one answer: John 16:13. Reject that answer, and God alone knows what consequences will crowd themselves in.

Some of the early church fathers drew the extravagant conclusion that because, as they thought, Jude endorsed the *Book of Enoch*, it, too, must be regarded as being inspired; those of a later time drew the opposite conclusion: because Jude has what is found in the *Book of Enoch*, therefore Jude could not be inspired. Both of these mistakes, as well as the modern ascription of "apocryphal and legendary" sources to Jude, are avoided by a correct understanding of what inspiration did for the holy writers.

Jude quotes Enoch and not some book. How well or ill or in what manner the *Book of Enoch* reproduces Enoch's prophecy is a minor matter and does not affect

Jude. Jude quotes directly; whether the *Book of Enoch* quotes directly or indirectly — what difference does it make? Jude and the *Book of Enoch* say about the same thing; but that lends nothing to Jude, nor does it detract from him. Both Jude and the *Book of Enoch* have the marked repetitions of the word "ungodly" (noun, verb). Few will be bold enough to make the claim that Enoch did *not* utter this prophecy, that it is only a late *invention,* an invention by the first writer of the *Book of Enoch.*

16) **These are murmurers, complainers, proceeding according to their lusts, and their mouth speaks grandiose things, flattering for the sake of profit.**

Second Peter 3:3 (see also 2:10) has: "proceeding according to their own lusts"; 2:18: "speaking grandiose things of vainness." Jude evidently repeats Peter's prophecy as one that has been fulfilled; in both note the exceptional word ὑπέρογκα. Jude rounds out the thought with "ungodly sinners" in verse 15. "Murmurers, complainers" are to be understood in the widest sense; with the "proceeding according to their lusts" Jude has in mind men who cannot get enough to satisfy their lusts and thus complain.

With this goes grandiose talk (Peter puts this "in connection with lusts") to impress and entice people and at the same time the "flattering for the sake of profit." The expression θαυμάζω πρόσωπον is sometimes used in the good sense, but here it means admiring a person, flattering him to his face with the object of wheedling something out of him; χάριν is a preposition which is usually placed after its object.

The items are not contrasted but paint a portrait. Nor have we an anacoluthon (R. 439); the closing participle continues the predication, and the finite "their mouth speaks" is finite only in order to lift this point above the participles.

Jude Admonishes His Readers, v. 17-23

17) But you on your part, beloved, remember the words that have been spoken in advance by the apostles of our Lord Jesus Christ, how they were telling you: At the end of time there shall be mockers proceeding according to their own lusts for ungodliness.

Once more (verse 3) we have the loving address with emphatic "you on your part" in contrast to "these" (v. 10, 16; compare v. 19) and with the effective aorist imperative "remember." The perfect "having been spoken in advance" means that the words are still valid. In the weightiest way Jude calls the authors of them "the apostles of our Lord Jesus Christ." "How they were telling you" with its imperfect bids the readers dwell on what the apostles kept telling them.

Jude practically quotes II Pet. 3:3. We summarize what we say in the introductions to Jude and to Second Peter. Jude must step in. The apostles to whom he refers are Peter who is now dead, whose words Jude repeats, and Paul who is either dead or far away in Spain and entirely out of reach. Paul, too, had written these readers a letter (II Pet. 3:15). Peter's letter (3:2) calls on the readers "to remember the words spoken in advance by the holy prophets." Jude uses an identical wording save that he substitutes "apostles" for "holy prophets."

There is no need to generalize and to speak about all the apostles and all that they said orally and in writing. Jude uses Peter's prophecy; Paul's agreed with this according to Jude. The conception that Jude's epistle was written prior to Second Peter, and that Peter and Jude did not write to the same people, are views that we at least cannot square with what these epistles themselves say. If both wrote to the same people, Jude a few years after Peter, then every item is in line.

18) The verbal difference between this prophecy and II Pet. 3:3 is small. Like Peter, Jude does not copy another writer verbatim. Yet ἔσονται is used in II Pet. 2:1 so that Jude combines this and 3:3, both future tenses prophesy. "At the end of time" = Peter's "at the days' ends." Mockers proceeding according to their own lusts" is identical save for the possessive. Peter states the actual words of mockery; Jude does not reproduce them. The readers have Peter's letter, and Jude has mentioned the blaspheming of the mockers. See the exposition in II Pet. 3:3, 4. Jude adds as his own the genitive τῶν ἀσεβειῶν, which is either qualitative (our versions), subjective, or a genitive of source: produced *by* different kinds of ungodliness or, as we prefer, objective: their own lusts *for* different manifestations of ungodliness.

The opinion that Jude might consider himself as one of the apostles is answered already in verse 1.

19) The word "mockers" leads to the further characterization: **These are the ones making divisions, physical, not having spirit.** Their mocking remarks and sneers make an impression on some; II Pet. 2:2 foretold that many would follow the pseudo-teachers. Jude says that this is happening. The rare double compound is explained well by C.-K. 821, etc.: after listening to the mockers, some agree with them, and inner divisions are made in the congregations, the inner unity is destroyed. Luther's *Rotten machen* is quite correct. The few texts which add ἑαυτούς mistake the thought: these mockers do not divide "themselves" but the Christian membership, and thus these Christians no longer contend for the faith once for all delivered to the saints (verse 3).

Ψυχικοί adds to the thought. We have no good English equivalent for this Greek word. Our versions use "sensual." These men are governed only by the ψυχή which animates their bodies. In I Cor. 2:14; 15:44, 46 our versions use "natural" as a translation for ψυχικός. The opposite is being "spiritual" just as Jude also says, "not having spirit." In their divisive mockeries these men follow their natural, physical instincts, their lower nature, for they have no spiritual nature. We need not regard πνεῦμα as "the Holy Spirit" (our versions and others). Those who are devoid of "spirit" are so because the Holy Spirit does not dwell in them, has not regenerated them. To be sure, they have "spirit" as all human beings have, but, as is the case in all unregenerate men, the spirit is out of control, enslaved by sin, not released and enthroned as ruler by God's Spirit.

Jude is said to be Pauline in the use of these terms; but this use is apostolic psychology, yea, Biblical psychology, and it is not to be restricted to Paul although *psychikos* and *pneumatikos* do not occur in Peter's or in John's writings.

20) **But you on your part, beloved** (compare verse 17), **by building up yourselves by means of your most holy faith in connection with the Holy Spirit, while praying, keep yourselves in God's love, expecting the mercy of our Lord Jesus Christ for life eternal!**

The first participle and its modifiers state how the readers are to do this essential thing, to keep themselves in God's love, namely "by building up yourselves," etc. Our versions and others understand the dative as meaning "*on* your most holy faith" although we do not have ἐπί. This "faith" is objective as it was in verse 3 (which see), the truth or doctrine, *quae creditur*. We regard the dative as a dative of means and not as denoting a foundation: "by means of your most holy faith," by means of the most holy gospel doctrine. The superlative is not merely elative: "very holy," but a true superlative (R. 670). The fact that

the use of true superlatives has decreased in the Koine
is not reason for eliminating the ones that are still used.

Unlike our versions and others, we construe "building up yourselves by means of your most holy faith
in connection with the Holy Spirit," without whom no
one can use this faith or doctrine to build himself up.
If Jude means "praying in connection with the Holy
Spirit," this phrase should follow the participle. The
participle "praying" needs no modifier; it always refers
to true prayer or worship. Here it is a third modifier
of "building up yourselves." It states in what manner
and spirit the divine faith or truth is to be used so as
truly to build up the readers. Your most holy faith
is to be the one means; the Holy Spirit is to be the
great helper; praying is to be the devout attitude and
frame of mind and heart.

21) Thus, Jude's readers are told, "keep yourselves in God's love," effective aorist which is used in
all such hortations. This is the love of God for the
readers and not their love for God. To keep oneself
in God's love is to stay where God can love us as his
children and can shower upon us all the gifts of love
that he has for those who are his children. God, indeed, loves all men; but men are not urged "to keep
themselves" in this universal love since it already
extends to all of them without exception. God's love
cannot bestow the saving gifts upon those who spurn
his love; he can and does bestow them upon true
believers who as his children hunger for these gifts,
pray for them, use his Word and truth, let the Holy
Spirit lead and guide them in its proper use.

The final participle states what is to accompany
this keeping of themselves in God's love: "expecting
the mercy of our Lord Jesus Christ for life eternal,"
expecting it in unwavering hope. It is the mercy that
Christ will grant us at the last day, in the final judgment. It makes little difference whether we construe

"for life eternal" with "keep yourself in God's love" or with the participle; but since it is placed where it is, this phrase is to be construed with the latter. "Life eternal" = eternal blessedness. Jude properly says "mercy"; this word fits what Jesus will say to the blessed of his Father on judgment day, Matt. 25:34-40; compare Matt. 5:7. "God's love" and Christ's "mercy" resume these two terms from verse 2.

22) Jude tells his readers what to do about *themselves* over against the mockers (v. 20, 21); he now adds what they are to do in regard to any who are injured by the mockers. Note that he says nothing in regard to the mockers. He has in unmistakable terms described them as outcasts, and he does not need to say that the readers are to treat them as such.

The student must himself examine the textual variations; the expert text critics are themselves not certain. The main point is whether Jude names two classes or three; we think he lists three classes. Then the remaining textual variations scarcely affect the substance of the thought.

And some rebuke, such as dispute; some save by snatching them out of fire; some pity in fear, hating even the tunic that has become spotted from the flesh.

Οὓς μέν — οὓς δέ = "some — some" or "some — others." We accept the reading ἐλέγχετε and the accusative participle: "some rebuke, such as dispute." Being affected by the mockers, some Christians may start to dispute and to support claims put forth by the mockers. Such fellow members, Jude says, "refute," "convict," show and try to convince them that they are wrong. The present imperative means: at any time when such cases develop. In verse 9 Jude uses this participle in the sense of "disputing"; elsewhere it also has the meaning "doubting." The difference is immaterial since doubters dispute because of their doubts, and disputing is due to doubting.

The A. V. has followed a very inferior reading, the nominative participle διακρινόμενοι, and has this mean "making a difference." The difference is then found in the next two clauses: some save — some pity.

23) Doubting disputers are in danger, they need to be corrected and convinced. Another class is close to the fire: "some save (the same iterative present imperative) by snatching them out of the fire," by taking heroic measures as when one is snatched out of a burning house or, quoting Amos 4:11: "as a firebrand plucked out of the burning"; Zech. 3:2: "a brand plucked out of the burning." There is no need to say how this is to be done; we have such cases when erring Christians are saved from the very brink of hell by heroic measures. The A. V. follows the reading that makes only two groups, but this reading is now generally discarded.

Some get beyond help in spite of all effort. Jude says: "some pity in fear, hating even the tunic that has become spotted from the flesh." Nothing is left but to pity these. The verb ἐλεάω does not mean "to have mercy" in the sense of extending merciful help; it means only to pity. We take this group to be those that are beyond help and think that to pity them "in fear" is expounded by "hating even the tunic," etc., lest by our pity for them we ourselves become spotted. Others think that Jude refers to erring members who are received back into fellowship, and that the mercifully receiving them is to be done "in fear" by hating even their still spotted and stained tunic. This view understands the verb in the sense of actually bestowing mercy; but, surely, those that are still spotted with filth cannot be received back to be handled with fear, gingerly, at arm's length, lest we get this filth also on ourselves.

The participle is the perfect tense, which means that the spots and the stains of the past are still present. People of this kind, who are wearing such a tunic, surely cannot be taken back; they must first be thoroughly cleaned by repentance and amendment. Jude says χιτών, "tunic," a garment that is worn next to the skin by men and by women alike; not ἱμάτιον, the long, loose outer "robe" that was worn over the tunic. Tunic is the proper word when one is speaking of becoming spotted "from the flesh." The figure is expressive. Jude's readers are to avoid those that are so spotted. They may only pity them, yet even do this in fear, as hating the filthy tunic of their personal life, spotted and stained as it has become and still is.

Jude concludes his admonition: effective remembering (verse 17) — effective keeping in God's love — iterative convicting, saving, pitying for those caught in the danger.

Jude's Closing Doxology, v. 24, 25

24) Plummer prints as follows:

Now to the One able to guard you as non-stumbling,
And to place (you) in the presence of his glory as blemishless in exultation,
To (the) only God, our Savior
Through Jesus Christ, our Lord:
Glory, majesty, might, and authority
Before all the eon, and now, and for all the eons. Amen.

This arrangement brings out the beauty of the phrasing. Jude's doxology is decidedly his own. Very little of it appears in other doxologies. Jude's doxology fits his epistle as do the other doxologies that appear at the end of other epistles. It voices his own adoration, and all his readers are to second it with the same fervor.

"To the One able" to guard and place you does not mean that he will do this by means of his omnipotence but by means of his grace, mercy, Word, Spirit. He is able to guard you in this life despite all dangers, despite the mockers, "as non-stumbling," as not stumbling to a fatal fall. There is no lack in God; only by wilfully turning from his enabling grace can anyone be lost.

"And to place you in the presence of his glory as blemishless in exultation" means at the last great day when "the Son of man shall come in the glory of his Father" (Matt. 16:27). In Matt. 25:34, etc., Jesus describes how God will so place us. All blemishes are removed by justification. How we shall then jubilate! We do so already now (I Pet. 1:6, 8). The apposition names "the One able" to do all this: "the only God, our Savior." In verse 4 Jude has "only" with reference to Christ. In the absolute sense there is and can be no other. "Savior" is applied equally to the Father and to the Son. On the basis of little authority the A. V. inserts "wise," which some scribe inserted from Rom. 16:27.

25) "Through Jesus Christ, our Lord," is purposely placed next to God, our Savior, in order to have these two united. We construe "our Savior through Jesus Christ," etc. While one might say "through Jesus Christ glory," etc., to God, this does not seem to fit well with "before all the eon."

Jude has four terms: "glory," the sum of all the divine attributes in their radiant shining forth; "majesty" (Heb. 1:3; 8:1; ascribed to Christ in II Pet. 1:16) as King, Δεσπότης, absolute Ruler; "might" as in action; "authority," the right and the power to rule (these four items indicate a complete enumeration). We supply neither εἴη nor ἐστί; this is an exclamation, a grand exclamatory acknowledgment and confession (it should not be called a prayer). All true believers will join in it.

Jude alone has "before all the eon, and now, and for all the eons." "Before all the eon" means in all eternity, before the whole world eon of time began; "for all the eons" means for all eternity (which is conceived as eons upon eons). Between them is "now," time as it is now rolling on. This is poor human language which sectionalizes eternity, which is the opposite of time and cannot be divided even in thought. Scripture condescends to our mental limitation. "Amen," see Rom. 1:25.

Soli Deo Gloria

CPSIA information can be obtained at www.ICGtesting.com
Printed in the USA
LVOW011524231011

251710LV00005B/20/P

9 780806 690117